BASIC STATISTICS
FOR BUSINESS
AND ECONOMICS

BASIC STATISTICS FOR BUSINESS AND ECONOMICS

Leonard J. Kazmier

Arizona State University

McGraw-Hill Book Company

New York   St. Louis   San Francisco   Auckland   Bogotá   Düsseldorf
Johannesburg   London   Madrid   Mexico   Montreal   New Delhi
Panama   Paris   São Paulo   Singapore   Sydney   Tokyo   Toronto

This book was set in Press Roman by Hemisphere Publishing Corporation.
The editor was Charles E. Stewart; the cover was designed by Scott Chelius;
the production supervisor was Diane Renda.
Fairfield Graphics was printer and binder.

BASIC STATISTICS FOR BUSINESS AND ECONOMICS

2 3 4 5 6 7 8 9 0 F G R F G R 7 8 3 2 1 0 9

Library of Congress Cataloging in Publication Data

Kazmier, Leonard J.
    Basic statistics for business and economics.

    Includes index.
    1. Statistics. 2. Commercial statistics.
3. Economics–Statistical methods. I. Title.
HA29.K352   519.5'02'433   78-9294
ISBN 0-07-033445-5

To Your Success

STUDENTS: IF YOU WANT SOME EXTRA HELP . . .

This book was developed with special attention given to presenting statistical concepts and methods from a student-oriented viewpoint. However, if you want additional help, it will be worth your while to consider using the *Study Guide/Workbook to Accompany Basic Statistics for Business and Economics* by Norval F. Pohl and Leonard J. Kazmier. This supplement includes an overview of each chapter, a unique key-word diagram to help you master the concepts associated with statistical analysis, a summary of chapter content in simplified form, and "word" problems with step-by-step solutions. Your campus bookstore either has this manual in stock or can order it for you.

CONTENTS

PREFACE

This book covers the methods of statistical description, probability, statistical inference, and decision analysis typically included in the first course in business and economic statistics. The mathematical prerequisite is basic college algebra. The development of this book reflects a special concern about presenting statistical concepts in terms that the *student* can understand, and with a variety of applications examples. Although this edition is the first, many of the explanations, examples, and exercises have been extensively class-tested through three editions of the programmed text, *Statistical Analysis for Business and Economics* (McGraw-Hill, 1978).

Because statistical inference based on sample data is the cornerstone of modern applications of statistical analysis, the methods of sampling that can be used for inference are described in Chapter 1. Following this introduction, the remainder of the first 10 chapters are devoted to the description of data, then to the essential concepts in probability, and finally to the methods of interval estimation and hypothesis testing, which are the principal techniques of statistical inference.

Depending on course and instructor objectives, many different patterns of topic coverage can be chosen beyond the first 10 chapters. The number of topics included is greater than the number than can be covered in the typical first course specifically so that alternative selection of topics is made possible. The diagram on the next page indicates the relationships among the topics in the numbered chapters. Sections in the first 10 chapters not required for later material are labeled as "optional." In Chapters 11 through 18 many sections are optional, and the coverage in these chapters is based entirely on instructor preference.

Appendix A includes a description of the use of computers in statistical analysis. Also included in the back section of the book are the answers to most of the end-of-chapter exercises. This information provides the student with the opportunity to determine whether particular answers are correct before proceeding to other exercises.

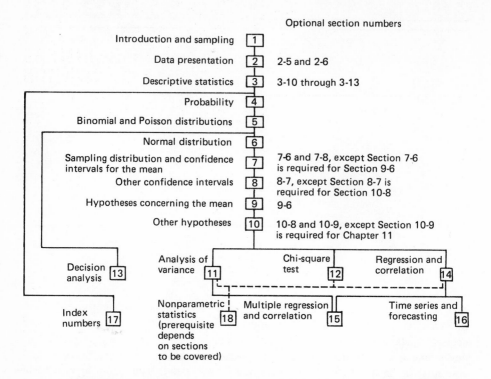

Optional section numbers

Introduction and sampling — 1

Data presentation — 2 — 2-5 and 2-6

Descriptive statistics — 3 — 3-10 through 3-13

Probability — 4

Binomial and Poisson distributions — 5

Normal distribution — 6

Sampling distribution and confidence intervals for the mean — 7 — 7-6 and 7-8, except Section 7-6 is required for Section 9-6

Other confidence intervals — 8 — 8-7, except Section 8-7 is required for Section 10-8

Hypotheses concerning the mean — 9 — 9-6

Other hypotheses — 10 — 10-8 and 10-9, except Section 10-9 is required for Chapter 11

Decision analysis — 13

Analysis of variance — 11

Chi-square test — 12

Regression and correlation — 14

Index numbers — 17

Nonparametric statistics (prerequisite depends on sections to be covered) — 18

Multiple regression and correlation — 15

Time series and forecasting — 16

A supplementary manual, *Study Guide/Workbook to Accompany Basic Statistics for Business and Economics* by Norval F. Pohl and Leonard J. Kazmier, is available for use with this book. This workbook is organized in parallel form to the text in terms of chapter-by-chapter topic coverage. Included are a broad-brush overview for each chapter, a summary of chapter content in simplified form, and a unique key-word diagram that helps the student to master the concepts associated with statistical analysis. The problems in the workbook are designed to develop a student's competence in solving "word" problems by incorporating a step-by-step structured solution for each application.

The author expresses gratitude to the several anonymous reviewers who made suggestions regarding the development of this book. Special thanks are extended to Professor Zenon S. Malinowski of the University of Connecticut, Storrs, for a particularly penetrating review of the manuscript, to Donald E. Chatham and Charles E. Stewart of the McGraw-Hill Book Company for effective editorial supervision, and to Rolfe W. Larson for his work on this project at Hemisphere Publishing Corporation. Finally, the author is indebted to the literary executor of the late Sir Ronald A. Fisher, F.R.S., to Dr. Frank Yates, F.R.S., and to the Longman Group Ltd., London, for permission to adapt and reprint Tables III, IV, and VI from their book, *Statistical Tables for Biological, Agricultural, and Medical Research* (6th edition, Longman, 1974).

Leonard J. Kazmier

BASIC STATISTICS
FOR BUSINESS
AND ECONOMICS

THE USE OF STATISTICS IN BUSINESS AND ECONOMICS

1-1   WHAT IS STATISTICS?

Statistics is concerned with the techniques by which information is collected, organized, analyzed, and interpreted. Typically, most information analyzed is quantitative data and, particularly, data collected by the process of sampling. However, the techniques of statistics are not limited to quantitative sample data but can also include the analysis of historical information and even the judgments of managers about such uncertain values as the level of market demand for a new product. The theme unifying the diverse applications of statistics in business and economics is that ultimately some *decision* is made. In this sense, the applications of statistics in business are mainly concerned with *decision making under conditions of uncertainty.*

1-2   WHY STUDY STATISTICS?

Techniques of statistics are now used in all fields of business and economics. Indeed, it is difficult to imagine a person functioning as a manager in any field of business today without a good foundation in statistical analysis. Of course, a manager may not be directly involved in formal statistical analysis as such. But the understanding of statistics is important for two distinct reasons. First, statistical concepts and techniques represent a way of thinking that serves as the basis for orderly comparison of decision alternatives and greater effectiveness in decision making. Second, the demands of management often require the interpretation of statistical results reported by others and evaluation of conflicting claims that may result from the analysis of the same data. No manager can afford to accept on faith the opinion of "experts," and therefore he or she will want a basic foundation in statistics to evaluate such opinions independently.

The following examples represent some of the most common applications of statistics in business and economics.

An auditor is concerned with verifying the financial records of a large organization. Because it is not possible to verify the accuracy of every account receivable, the auditor selects a sample of accounts based on the techniques of statistics and from the sample results either accepts the accuracy of the stated· amount of accounts receivable or continues with further sampling.

A production manager wishes to ascertain whether quality standards are being maintained. To accomplish this objective the production manager may have to test samples of the product and as a result of such tests may or may not have to make changes in the production process.

A personnel manager develops a new training program for sales personnel. Before implementing the program throughout the company, the personnel manager presents the program to a representative group of sales personnel and evaluates the results in comparison with other training and development methods.

A marketing manager is concerned about whether to market a new product. As a first step, the marketing manager could give a sample of the product to consumers for their use and evaluation. As another step before full-scale marketing, the marketing manager could carry out test marketing in limited geographic areas and then analyze the results to determine the likely level of overall demand.

An investment manager makes day-to-day decisions involving the choice of alternative investments. As the basis for these decisions, the investment manager incorporates the opinions of investment analysts and considers current governmental and business events as a basis for estimating the probability of various rates of return for each investment.

An economist needs to assess the impact of a proposed change in sales taxes in a given community in terms of consumer buying patterns. For his assessment the economist must first determine present buying patterns for different categories of consumers through field research. This determination will include interviews with samples of consumers in each major geographic area and in each income category.

The owner of a small business must decide how much of each item to order for inventory. Making this decision requires consideration of the likely level of demand, the cost of maintaining the item in inventory, and the cost of lost profit and lost goodwill if demand exceeds supply.

1-3   INTERNAL AND EXTERNAL DATA

Business data collected for analysis may be either internal or external, from the reference point of the individual firm. *Internal data*, data obtained within the firm itself, generally include such information as production levels, costs, and volume of sales. The internal records kept within a firm, such as the records pertaining to purchasing, receiving, sales, payroll, billing, and goods in process, serve as the primary source of internal data. The records maintained are concerned with both financial and nonfinancial data. For example, materials costs and payroll are essentially financial, while personnel records and quality-control data are nonfinancial.

External data, business data collected outside the firm, would include, for example, data on industry sales. When the data are available in published form, the source is considered as a *primary source* if it represents the original publication of the data. For example, the *Survey of Current Business*, published monthly by the Department of Commerce, is a primary source of statistics concerned with prices and volume of operations in a large number of industries. A *secondary source* of data is one that reproduces data from a primary source, sometimes along with other data being reported for the first time. Generally, external business data are more timely when obtained from primary rather than secondary sources. An example of a widely used secondary source of data is the *Statistical Abstract of the United States*, published annually by the Department of Commerce, which contains data from a variety of governmental and nongovernmental primary sources.

1-4   DESCRIPTIVE STATISTICS

Descriptive statistics is the collection of statistical techniques used to summarize and describe data and other types of information. For example, even though the financial page of a newspaper reports all price changes for stock issues traded on the New York Stock Exchange on a given day, it would be very difficult for the typical reader to interpret the overall price changes that day without some kinds of summary values. The *Dow Jones Industrial Average* and the *New York Stock Exchange Composite Index* are examples of descriptive values that summarize price data and therefore make price changes more meaningful.

In general, the methods of descriptive statistics include graphic techniques as well as quantitative summary values. For example, *bar charts, line graphs,* and *pie charts* can be used to portray business and economic data. The typical corporate annual report includes a variety of such graphic methods. Chapter 2 describes a number of techniques, including summary tables, charts, and graphs, by which data can be presented. The principal quantitative summary values used to describe sets of data are *measures of average* and *measures of dispersion*, or variability, in the data set. Again, the *Dow Jones Industrial Average* describes the price change in a selected group of industrial common stock issues, while the range of stock prices given on the financial page indicates how much a given stock price varied during the day. Chapter 3 presents the principal statistical measures of average and of dispersion for collections of data.

1-5   INFERENTIAL STATISTICS

Inferential statistics includes those techniques by which decisions about a statistical population can be made without all elements in the population having been observed or measured. Typically, the observed measurements in a random sample serve as the basis for statistical inference. In statistics a *population*, or universe, is the set of all elements that belong to a defined group. For example, all convenience markets in a given metropolitan area could be defined as the population of interest. A *sample* is a subset of elements taken from a defined population. A *random sample* is a sample that conforms to certain requirements such that probability concepts can be used in interpreting the sample results. For example, based on sales figures obtained from a random sample of convenience markets, we can estimate that the sales figures for all markets are within certain designated limits with a degree of confidence defined on the basis of applying probability concepts. The next section of this chapter describes the techniques by which a random sample can be obtained.

The summary values used to describe a sample are called *sample statistics*. In contrast, summary values for a population are called *population parameters*. Thus, the average weekly sales figure for a sample of convenience markets is a sample statistic, while the average sales figure for the population of convenience markets in the given metropolitan area of interest is a population parameter. In statistical inference, we typically wish to make some decision about a population parameter, based on the observed value of a sample statistic. Because such a decision is made under conditions of uncertainty, statistical inference always involves the application of probability concepts. For this reason, Chapters 4 through 6 are devoted to probability and probability distributions. The techniques covered in the remainder of this book are concerned with the application of these concepts.

The only circumstance in which probability concepts are not required is when all measurements or observations in the defined population are available. In this circumstance we might still be interested in the application of the techniques of descriptive statistics, but we would have no need for the techniques of statistical inference. When all the population measurements or observations are obtained, the process is called a *census*. Thus the national census carried out every 10 years in the United States involves an attempt to enumerate and describe all people in the country. Because of time and cost considerations, a complete census is not practical in many decision situations in business, and therefore the techniques of sampling and statistical inference are used.

1-6 METHODS OF SAMPLING

In general, there are three types of samples: convenience samples, judgment samples, and random samples. A *convenience sample* includes the most easily accessible measurements or observations, as implied by the word "convenience." For example, taking an opinion poll at a downtown intersection would be a convenience sample. A *judgment sample* is one in which the individual selecting the sample items uses experience as the basis for choosing the items to be included in the sample, with the objective being to make the sample as representative of the population as possible. An example is an accountant who chooses only certain records for a sample audit based on the judgment that these records are representative of the records in general. A *random sample* is a sampling procedure by which every element in the population has a known, and usually equal, chance of being chosen for inclusion in the sample.

Any of these three general types of samples could result in the selection of a representative sample of the population of interest, or the *target population.* However, only for a random sample can the *sampling error*, or variations due to sampling, be described on the basis of known probability concepts. The sampling variations associated with a convenience sample or a judgment sample cannot be described or anticipated on the basis of probability concepts, and therefore such sample results *cannot* be used as the basis for statistical inference.

Because the concepts of probability can only be applied to a random sample, such a sample is often also called a *probability sample.* In addition, because only a random sample can be used as the basis for statistical inference, it is often referred to as a *scientific sample.* There are in fact a number of specific methods, or sample designs, by which a random sample can be obtained. In the remainder of this section, we describe four such methods.

A *simple random sample* is one in which each item is selected entirely on the basis of chance. The result is that every element in the population has an equal chance of being included in the sample, and all possible samples of a given size n are equally likely to be selected. Chance selection does not imply arbitrary selection; rather, the elements are chosen on the basis of some randomizing procedure. By the preferred procedure, each element in the population is assigned a serial number, and the sample elements are then chosen by use of a *table of random numbers* or by use of a random-number generator on a computer. Table B-1 is an example of such a table. As an example of the use of a table of random numbers, suppose a population has 897 elements numbered 001 to 897 and we wish to take a sample of 50 elements. We would enter the table "blindly" by literally closing our eyes and pointing to a starting position. Then we would read the digits in groups of three, reading either to the right, left, downward, or upward, and choose the elements represented by those code numbers. Any unassigned code numbers would be ignored (000 and any value above 897 in our example). Also, we would ignore any code number that occurs a second time by chance. When we have selected 50 elements for the sample, we have completed the sample selection process. Although we simply refer to the samples in the remainder of the book as "random samples," the computational procedures presented are based on the assumption that the simple random-sampling method was used.

A *systematic sample* is one in which we select the sample elements from the population at a uniform interval of a listed order or at uniform points in time or distance. For example, we can take a 10 percent sample of all telephone subscribers listed in a directory by starting at a blind-choice point in the first 10 names and then choosing every 10th name thereafter. Technically, systematic sampling differs from simple random sampling in that each combination of elements does not have an equal chance of being selected. For example, if every 10th sequentially numbered element is chosen for a systematic sample, the elements numbered 233 and 235 could not both be included in the same sample. If systematic sampling is used, a particular concern is to avoid any periodic or cyclical factor that would lead to the inclusion of a systematic error in the sample results. For example, if every 10th house is at a corner location, a survey of households directed at the adequacy of street lighting would include a systematic bias if every 10th household were included in the survey. In this case, either all of the households included in the survey would be at a corner location or none of them would be at a corner location. When the order of listing of the population members can be assumed to be random in respect to the variable of interest (for example, wage rates of employees listed alphabetically), the results associated with systematic samples generally are analyzed with the same computational methods used with simple random samples.

A third type of sampling plan that results in a random sample being obtained is a *stratified sample.* In stratified sampling we classify the elements in the target population into separate groups, or strata, on the basis of characteristics associated with the variables being studied. The objective is that the several strata be different from one another in respect to the variable being studied but that the elements within a given stratum be similar to one another. After such classification, a simple random sample is taken from each stratum separately, and then the sample results are combined for analysis. For example, in a study of student attitude toward on-campus housing, if it is believed general differences exist between undergraduate and graduate students in this regard, a stratified sampling plan would be useful.

One obvious advantage of stratified sampling is that we can assure proportionate representation of each important subgroup in the population by taking the same percentage sample from each stratum. What is not so obvious is that by taking subsamples that are *not* proportionate, stratified sampling, as compared with simple random sampling, makes it possible to reduce overall sample size. For example, suppose 1,000 items in inventory are classified as low cost and 50 items classified as high cost. A 10 percent sample of the 1,000 low-cost items may be sufficient to estimate the average cost of these items at a required degree of confidence. (The statistical concept of "degree of confidence" is explained in Chapter 6.) But a 10 percent sample taken from just 50 items would probably be inadequate. Use of stratified sampling would make it possible to take a 10 percent sample of the large number of low-cost items while taking something like a 30 percent sample of the smaller number of high-cost items. Indeed, we could even take a 100 percent sample (census) of the high-cost items. In contrast, use of simple random sampling would force us to take a larger total sample size to include an adequate number of high-cost items in the sample.

A *cluster sample* is the last of the methods of random sampling we consider. A cluster sample is one in which the elements in the target population are selected in groups rather than individually at the initial step in sampling. The groups to be included in the sample are selected by simple random sampling. Thus each group in the target population should be assigned a serial number, and then the sample groups can be selected by reference to a table of random numbers. Cluster sampling is often used when the elements in the population are not easily identified individually but are grouped together (clustered) and more easily identified as members of the cluster. For example, if we wish to study the hourly wage rates being paid in a large metropolitan area, it would be difficult to obtain a listing of all individual wage earners. However, we could randomly sample the firms in which the people work, which would represent clusters of employees. When cluster groups being sampled are differentiated according to geographic location, as they often are in political polling, cluster sampling is called *area sampling*. The advantage of area cluster sampling here is that when entire residential blocks are sampled as clusters, the travel time and cost of sampling are reduced.

If all the elements (wage earners, registered voters, etc.) in the sampled clusters are included in the sample, the procedure is called *single-stage sampling*. In contrast, *multistage sampling* involves further simple random sampling within each cluster. Political polls typically follow a multistage-sampling design. For example, residential blocks can be randomly selected within each precinct; then particular homes might be randomly selected within each block, with all registered voters in the selected homes then being interviewed.

1-7 SUMMARY

We began this chapter by defining the term "statistics" and giving some examples of the application of statistical techniques in business and economics. The relatively rapid development of computers and computer programs during the past 20 years has substantially increased the application of statistical techniques because automation has substantially reduced, if not eliminated, the computational burden. Yet, the ease of such use makes it all the more imperative that managers, as users of statistical analysis, have a fundamental knowledge of the assumptions associated with the techniques of statistical analysis, the meaning of the results, and the limitations of the results. It is the fundamental objective of this book to give you sufficient information to develop such an understanding.

As indicated in this chapter, the methods of descriptive statistics are concerned with helping to make data more understandable by presenting such data in standard types of tables and graphs and by calculating certain summary measures for such data. Chapter 2 is concerned with data presentation, while Chapter 3 is concerned with the summary values that can be used to describe data.

The methods of statistical inference are concerned with generalizing the results of a sample to a target population of interest. Because the concepts of probability serve as the basis for such inference, Chapters 4 and 5, which follow the two chapters on descriptive statistics, cover probability and probability distributions. Most of the remaining chapters are concerned with specific methods of statistical inference.

Finally, because the methods of statistical inference can only be applied when a random sample has been collected, we have given our attention in this chapter to a description of sampling methods. The specific methods described that qualify as random, or probability, samples are *simple random sampling, systematic sampling, stratified sampling,* and *cluster sampling.* Our computational methods are all based on the assumption that a simple random sample has been obtained, although these methods also are applied to systematic samples when the order of listing of population elements can be assumed to be random in respect to the measurements of interest. The analysis of sample results based on the other methods often requires specialized variations of the formulas presented in this book and are included in more advanced books on sampling design.

EXERCISES

1-1 Indicate which of the following terms or operations are associated with a sample or sampling (*S*) and which are associated with the analysis of population data (*P*).

   P (*a*) Group measures called *parameters*
   S (*b*) Group measures called *statistics*
   P (*c*) Universe
   P (*d*) Census
   S (*e*) Application of probability concepts
   S (*f*) Use of inferential statistics
   P (*g*) Inspection of every item manufactured
   S (*h*) Judging the quality of a shipment of electronic components by testing 5 components randomly from every carton containing 100 components

1-2 Describe the difference between internal and external data, and explain why decisions in a firm or organization typically need to be based on analyses of both types of data.

1-3 One can say that statistical inference includes an interest in statistical description as well, since the ultimate purpose of statistical inference is to describe population data. How, then, does statistical inference differ from statistical description? Discuss.

1-4 A description of a population of values based on a sample inevitably includes the possibility of sampling error, since a sample is rarely exactly representative of a population. If a manager has the option of taking a "hurried" census of the data, as contrasted with taking a sample, would this solve the problem of error being included in the statistical description? Discuss.

1-5 For the purpose of statistical inference a representative sample is desired. Yet, the techniques of statistical inference require that a random sample be obtained. Why?

1-6 In a given statistical investigation, suppose the sampled population is different from the target population. Why is it generally inappropriate simply to redefine the target population so that it is the same as the sampled population?

1-7 Distinguish among (*a*) convenience, (*b*) judgment, and (*c*) random sampling by describing how an auditor might use each type in investigating the accuracy of a large number of spare-parts inventory figures.

1-8 Compare systematic sampling with simple random sampling. Why is systematic sampling generally the easier procedure? Under what circumstances is the use of systematic sampling questionable?

1-9 Both stratified sampling and cluster sampling involve certain groupings of elements (members) of a population. Describe the main differences between these sampling procedures.

1-10 An oil company wants to determine the factors affecting consumer choice of gasoline service stations in a test area and therefore has obtained the names and addresses of all registered car owners residing in the area. Describe how this list could be used to obtain a random sample by each of the four random-sampling methods described in this chapter.

DATA PRESENTATION

2-1 FREQUENCY DISTRIBUTIONS

When a relatively large number of observations or measurements has been made, it is often useful to organize the data into classes according to the magnitude of the measurements. Grouping the data into classes makes the interpretation of the results easier and also provides the basis for portraying the results graphically, as demonstrated in this chapter. A *frequency distribution* is a table in which possible values for a variable are grouped into classes and the number of observed values that belong in each class is recorded. Data organized in a frequency distribution are called *grouped data.* In contrast, for *ungrouped data* every individual observed value of the random variable is listed. Regardless of whether or not the data are grouped, the collection of values may be for either a sample or a population.

It will be useful to refer to an example as we define some of the terms associated with frequency distributions. Table 2-1 lists the heights of a sample of 50 men students at a university. Since each individual measurement is separately listed in this table, the data can be described as being ungrouped data.

From the measurements reported in Table 2-1, suppose a particular student's

Table 2-1 Heights of 50 men students measured to the nearest inch (ungrouped data)

				Height, in.					
67	73	71	74	61	68	70	70	66	73
68	67	72	69	71	69	76	70	72	71
77	69	71	74	66	68	70	72	72	70
71	70	64	65	70	69	72	75	66	67
70	72	67	70	71	68	66	73	69	67

(Source: Sample data.)

height was 70.5 inches and, as indicated in the table, the height is to be recorded to the nearest inch. Should 70.5 be recorded as 70 or as 71? In statistics, the so-called *even-digit rule* is used to resolve such problems. By this rule, when the remainder to be rounded is exactly midway between two values, the measurement is rounded to the nearest *even* value. Thus 70.5 inches would be rounded to 70. Similarly if package weights are recorded to the nearest *tenth* of an ounce, 31.65 ounces would be recorded as 31.6 ounces. By applying this rule as a matter of practice, the additions resulting from rounding will tend in the long run to counterbalance the subtractions from rounding.

The measurements listed in Table 2-1 are not particularly easy to interpret, owing to the absence of any organization of the data. In contrast, Table 2-2 is a frequency distribution for the measurements presented in Table 2-1. Although we lose the identification of the specific value of each measurement when data are grouped, the advantage of a frequency distribution is that such a table makes it easier to interpret the reported values. For each class in a frequency distribution, the lower and upper *class limits* identify the values included in the class. For example, the class limits for the first class of measurements reported in Table 2-2 are 60 to 62 inches, inclusive. Note that class limits are always stated in the same units as the level of measurement precision being used (nearest inch in this case). The *class frequency f* indicates the number of observed values for each class of the frequency distribution.

In addition to being described by inclusive class limits, each class of a

Table 2-2 Heights of 50 men students, measured to the nearest inch (grouped data)

Height, in.	No. of students *f*
60–62	1
63–65	2
66–68	13
69–71	20
72–74	11
75–77	3

Table 2-3 Class boundaries and midpoints for the heights of 50 men students

Class limits, in.	Class boundaries, in.	Midpoint M, in.
60–62	59.5–62.5	61
63–65	62.5–65.5	64
66–68	65.5–68.5	67
69–71	68.5–71.5	70
72–74	71.5–74.5	73
75–77	74.5–77.5	76

frequency distribution also can be described by the class boundaries associated with the class, by the class interval, and by the class midpoint. *Class boundaries* are the specific points along a measurement scale that separate adjoining classes (refer to Table 2-3). The lower and upper boundaries of the first class listed in Table 2-3 are 59.5 and 62.5, respectively. Because the upper boundary of the first class is the exact point separating the value in this class from the next adjoining class, it follows that the lower boundary of the second class in Table 2-3 should also be at the value 62.5. Thus, class boundaries are usually stated with one additional digit of precision as compared with the level of measurement. These boundaries are needed for the construction of certain graphs described in this chapter and in relation to the computation of certain summary measures for frequency distributions, as described in Chapter 3.

The *class interval i* indicates the number of measurement units, or range of values, included in each class. The class interval is determined by subtracting the lower class boundary from the upper class boundary for the class. Thus, we can say

$$i = B_U - B_L \tag{2-1}$$

For the first class in Table 2-3, $i = 62.5 - 59.5 = 3$. With respect to this frequency distribution, all classes have the same class interval.

Finally, the *class midpoint M* can be determined by adding one-half of the class interval to the lower boundary of the class:

$$M = B_L + 0.5i \tag{2-2}$$

As reported in Table 2-3, the midpoint of the first listed class is

$$M = 59.5 + 0.5(3) = 59.5 + 1.5 = 61$$

Having described the major characteristics of frequency distributions, we now direct our attention to how the frequency distribution is constructed for a set of ungrouped values. For graphic and computational purposes, it is generally desirable that all class intervals in a given frequency distribution be equal. Once we decide on the number of classes desired, we can determine the approximate class interval by

$$\sim i = \frac{H - L}{k} \tag{2-3}$$

where H = highest observed value

L = lowest observed value

k = number of desired classes

For the ungrouped heights in Table 2-1, we find that the largest observed value is 77 inches and the smallest observed value is 61 inches. If we desire six classes (as we did for Table 2-2), the approximate class interval to be used is

$$\sim i = \frac{H - L}{k} = \frac{77 - 61}{6} = \frac{16}{6} = 2.67$$

After the approximate (fractional) interval size is determined, it is rounded up according to the level of measurement being used. For example, if measurement is to the nearest 10th, the interval size would be rounded up to the next tenth (with our result, to 2.7). However, our measurements were taken to the nearest inch; therefore the class interval was rounded up to the whole number 3. We then set the lower class limit of the first class so that the lowest observed value will be included in the class, and we ascertain also that the highest observed value will be included in the last class of the frequency distribution. For the frequency distribution in Table 2-2, the first defined class, 60–62, does include the lowest observed value, 61, and the sixth (last) defined class, 75–77, does include the largest observed value, 77. Of course, we could have chosen to begin the first class at the lower limit of 61, in which case the class limits for the first class would have been 61–63, and the class limits for the last class would have been 76–78.

2-2 HISTOGRAMS, FREQUENCY POLYGONS, AND FREQUENCY CURVES

A *histogram* is a bar graph of a frequency distribution. Figure 2-1 is a histogram for the frequency distribution given in Table 2-2. As indicated in Figure 2-1, typically the class boundaries are identified along the horizontal axis of the graph, while the

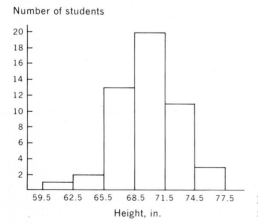

Figure 2-1 Histogram for the heights of 50 men students.

number of observations, or frequencies, are identified along the vertical axis. Thus, the width of each bar in the histogram indicates the class interval, while the height of each bar indicates the frequency of observations, or measurements, in that class.

Another way of graphically portraying a frequency distribution is by means of a *frequency polygon*, which can be described as being a line graph of a frequency distribution. As indicated in Figure 2-2, typically the class midpoints are identified along the horizontal axis of the frequency polygon. The number of observations in each class is graphically plotted above the midpoint for the class, and then these plotted points are joined by a series of line segments to form a "many-sided figure," or polygon. Because we want the polygon to form a closed figure with the horizontal axis, it is necessary to identify an additional class midpoint at the lower end of the polygon and an additional midpoint at the upper end of the polygon. Thus, in Figure 2-2 the additional midpoints, which are not included in the original frequency distribution, are 58 and 79. Of course, for each of these two classes the observed frequency is 0, and this fact is indicated graphically in Figure 2-2.

A *frequency curve* can be described as being a smoothed frequency polygon. Thus, if we were to smooth the polygon in Figure 2-2, the result would be a frequency curve. The form of a frequency curve can be described in two ways: in terms of its departure from symmetry, which is called *skewness*, and in terms of its degree of peakedness, which is called *kurtosis*. A symmetrical frequency curve is one for which the right half of the curve is the mirror image of the left half of the curve. The concepts of skewness and kurtosis are important because they are used to describe probability curves, beginning with our description of probability distributions in Chapter 5, as well as frequency curves.

In terms of skewness, a frequency curve can be

1. *Negatively skewed*, i.e., nonsymmetrical with the longer "tail" of the frequency curve to the left
2. *Symmetrical*

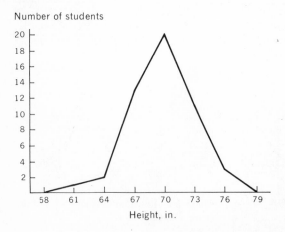

Figure **2-2** Frequency polygon for the heights of 50 men students.

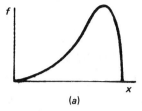 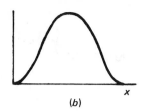 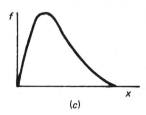

(a)   (b)   (c)

Figure 2-3 Types of frequency curves in terms of skewness. (a) Negatively skewed. (b) Symmetrical. (c) Positively skewed.

3. *Positively skewed*, i.e., nonsymmetrical with the longer tail of the frequency curve to the right

Figure 2-3 illustrates the general appearance of these three types of distributions. In terms of kurtosis, a frequency curve can be

1. *Platykurtic*, i.e., flat, with the number of observed values distributed relatively evenly across the classes
2. *Mesokurtic*, i.e., neither flat nor peaked in respect to the general appearance of the frequency curve
3. *Leptokurtic*, i.e., peaked, with a large number of observed values concentrated within a narrow range of the possible values of the variable being measured

Figure 2-4 illustrates the general appearance of these three types of curves.

2-3 CUMULATIVE-FREQUENCY DISTRIBUTIONS

A *cumulative-frequency distribution* identifies the cumulative number of observations below the upper boundary of each class in the distribution. The cumulative frequency (cf) for a class is determined by adding the observed frequency for that class to the cumulative frequency for the preceding class. Table 2-4 illustrates the calculation of cumulative frequencies for the frequency distribution in Table 2-2. Note that the cumulative frequency for the last class always equals the total number of observations.

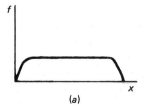 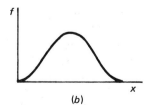 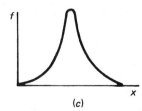

(a)   (b)   (c)

Figure 2-4 Types of frequency curves in terms of kurtosis. (a) Platykurtic. (b) Mesokurtic. (c) Leptokurtic.

Table 2-4 Calculation of cumulative frequencies for the 50 heights reported in Table 2-2

Height, in.	Upper class boundary, in.	relative f dist No. of students f	Cumulative frequency cf dist
60–62	62.5	1	1
63–65	65.5	2	$1 + 2 = 3$
66–68	68.5	13	$3 + 13 = 16$
69–71	71.5	20	$16 + 20 = 36$
72–74	74.5	11	$36 + 11 = 47$
75–77	77.5	3	$47 + 3 = 50$
Total		50	

A cumulative-frequency distribution can be portrayed graphically by a *cumulative-frequency polygon.* This line graph is more frequently called an *ogive* (pronounced: "ō-jīve"). The ogive for the cumulative-frequency distribution in Table 2-4 is presented in Figure 2-5. When such a line graph is smoothed, it is called an *ogive curve.*

2-4 RELATIVE–FREQUENCY DISTRIBUTIONS

A *relative-frequency distribution* is one in which the number of observations for each class is converted into a relative frequency by dividing it by the total number of observations in the entire distribution. Each relative frequency is thus a proportion. One particular reason for interest in relative-frequency distributions is that the cumulative distribution and ogive for such a distribution indicate the cumulative proportions of observations for various possible values of the variable being measured. Table 2-5 presents the relative frequencies and the cumulative proportions for the frequency distribution of heights in Table 2-2. For example, the

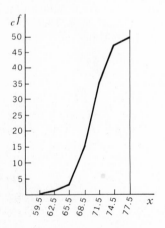

Figure 2-5 Ogive for the heights of 50 men students.

Table 2-5 Relative frequencies and cumulative proportions for the 50 heights reported in Table 2-2

Height, in.	Observed frequency f	Relative frequency	Cumulative proportion
60–62	1	0.02	0.02
63–65	2	0.04	0.06
66–68	13	0.26	0.32
69–71	20	0.40	0.72
72–74	11	0.22	0.94
75–77	3	0.06	1.00
Total	50	1.00	

relative frequency of 0.02 reported for the first class was obtained by dividing the observed frequency for that class (1) by the total number of students (50).

Because the ogive for a relative-frequency distribution indicates the cumulative proportion of the observed values located below any designated point, this curve can be used as the graphic basis for determining the percentile point associated with any measured value and vice versa. A *percentile* value indicates the percentage of observed measurements below the designated measurement. For example, if a test score of 73 is at the ninetieth percentile point, this would indicate that 90 percent of the test scores are below a score of 73.

Figure 2-6 presents the relative-frequency ogive for the data in Table 2-5. Because we wish to demonstrate the graphic determination of percentile points, the vertical axis is stated in terms of percent rather than proportion. As illustrated in the figure, we determine the approximate percentile point for the designated height of 70 inches by entering the vertical (dashed) line from the horizontal axis value of 70 up

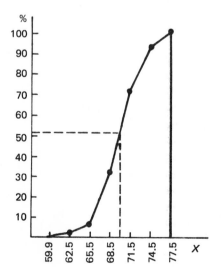

Figure 2-6 Percentage ogive illustrating the graphic determination of the percentile point associated with the height of 70 inches.

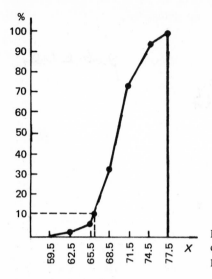

Figure 2-7 Percentage ogive illustrating the graphic determination of the height at the tenth percentile point.

to the ogive and then read the percentile point on the vertical axis by entering the horizontal (dashed) line from the ogive to the vertical axis. In this example, we see that the approximate percentile point associated with a height of 70 inches for the group of men students is 52. Thus, approximately 52 percent of the students in this group are below a height of 70 inches. Of course, a larger graph and the use of lined graph paper would enable us to make more accurate readings.

Suppose we wish to determine the measured value associated with a designated percentile point. The graphic process is essentially the same as the one described above, except that we begin by reference to the vertical axis of the percentage ogive. As illustrated in Figure 2-7, to determine the measured value at the 10th percentile point we first enter the horizontal (dashed) line from the percentage value of 10 to the ogive, and then enter the vertical (dashed) line down to the horizontal axis. As indicated, the approximate height at the tenth percentile point is 66 inches, which means that approximately 10 percent of the students in this group are below the height of 66 inches. In Chapter 3 we describe the algebraic basis for determining percentile points for both ungrouped and grouped data.

2-5 "AND–UNDER" FREQUENCY DISTRIBUTIONS

Consider the class limits identified in the first column of Table 2-6. For such "and-under" classes the class boundaries are defined to be at the stated class limits. Thus, for the first class in this distribution, the lower and upper class boundaries are 18.0 and 20.0, respectively. Except for this difference, the data grouped in an *and-under* type of frequency distribution are analyzed and interpreted in the same way as described in Section 2-1.

Table 2-6 Ages of a sample of applicants for a training program

Age	No. of applicants
18 and under 20	5
20 and under 22	18
22 and under 24	10
24 and under 26	6
26 and under 28	5
28 and under 30	4
30 and under 32	2
Total	50

2-6 BAR CHARTS, LINE GRAPHS, AND PIE CHARTS

The graphic techniques described in the preceding sections of this chapter are used only with data grouped in a frequency distribution. The graphic techniques described in this section, however, can be used whenever data can be classified into any types of categories, and therefore these descriptive techniques have a broad range of applications. It is our purpose here to provide a "sampler" of such graphic techniques, rather than a compendium of techniques. The typical corporate annual report includes a variety of such graphic displays.

A *bar chart* depicts amounts for different categories of data by a series of bars. The bars can be portrayed either horizontally or vertically for each category. Table 2-7 presents selected financial results for Delta Airlines, Inc., for the period 1973–1977. A vertical bar chart portraying the per-share net income for the company during this period is presented in Figure 2-8.

A *component bar chart* portrays subdivisions within the bars on the chart. Often, such subdivisions of each bar are color coded. Figure 2-9 is a component bar chart that shows the allocation of the annual earnings to dividends D and retained earnings R for Delta Airlines during the 1973–1977 period.

Whenever the categories of data represent time segments, as for the data in Table 2-7, the data can also be graphically portrayed by means of a *line graph*. A line graph portrays changes in amounts with respect to time by a series of line segments. Figure 2-10 presents the line graph for the net-income data in Table 2-7.

Table 2-7 Per-share net income, dividends, and retained earnings for Delta Airlines, Inc. (1973–1977)

Source	1973	1974	1975	1976	1977
Net income, $	3.32	4.56	2.61	3.53	4.65
Dividends, $	0.50	0.60	0.60	0.60	0.70
Retained earnings, $	2.82	3.96	2.01	2.93	3.95

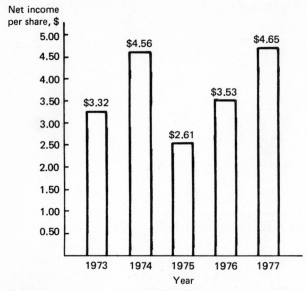

Figure 2-8 Bar chart for per-share net income for Delta Airlines, Inc., 1973–1977.

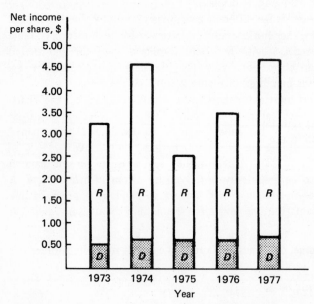

Figure 2-9 Component bar chart depicting the allocation of annual earnings for Delta Airlines, Inc., 1973–1977 (D = dividends; R = retained earnings). *(Source of data: Table 2-7.)*

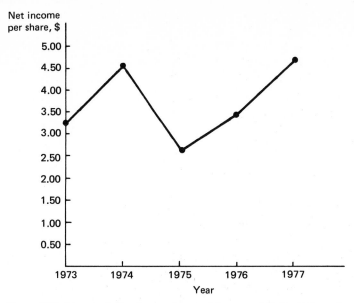

Figure 2-10 Line graph for the per-share net income of Delta Airlines, Inc., 1973–1977.

Finally, a *pie chart* which is a particularly appropriate graphic device for showing the divisions of a total amount, while a *percentage pie chart* portrays the subdivisions as percentages of the total amount. Table 2-8 presents the percentage of car sales in 1976 and in 1977 by the major domestic car makers and by imported cars. Figure 2-11 is the percentage pie chart for the 1977 sales data. This type of pie chart is useful as a visual comparison of the percentages.

Table 2-8 Automobile sales statistics: percentage of market for 1976 and 1977

Source	1976	1977
General Motors*	47.5	46.1
Ford*	22.3	22.9
Chrysler*	12.9	10.9
American Motors	2.5	1.7
Imports	14.8	18.4

(*Source: Wall Street Journal*, January 6, 1978, p. 16.)
*Excludes foreign cars sold by these makers.

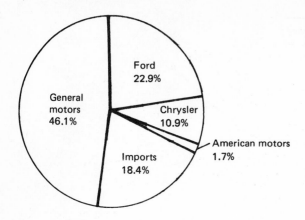

Figure 2-11 Percentage pie chart for 1977 automobile sales.

2-7 SUMMARY

In this chapter we have considered a number of descriptive techniques associated with the presentation of statistical data. Thus, data can be organized and presented more meaningfully by the grouping of the data into *frequency distributions.* Such distributions can be graphically portrayed by *histograms, frequency polygons,* and *frequency curves.* The form of a frequency curve, and thus of the underlying frequency distribution as well, can be described in terms of *departures from symmetry,* called *skewness,* and *degree of peakedness,* called *kurtosis.*

A cumulative frequency distribution can be portrayed graphically by an *ogive* or an *ogive curve.* When the cumulative distribution is for a relative-frequency distribution, the ogive indicates the cumulative proportion of values below any designated point. Such an ogive is useful for determining the percentile value, or point, associated with any designated measurement value in the distribution.

Bar charts, line graphs, and *pie charts* are also used for the statistical presentation of quantitative information. Compared with the other methods of graphic description presented in this chapter, the use of these techniques is not limited to data that have been grouped in frequency distributions.

FORMULAS

(2-1) $i = B_U - B_L$ — Class interval for a class in a frequency distribution.

(2-2) $M = B_L + 0.5i$ — Midpoint of a class in a frequency distribution.

(2-3) $\sim i = \dfrac{H - L}{k}$ — Approximate interval size to be used in constructing a frequency distribution.

EXERCISES

2-1 Given the following frequency distribution, identify the class boundaries for each class and determine the size of the class interval i.

Class limits	Observed frequency f	cf	rf	cf
3–5	1	1	.07	.07
6–8	2	3	.14	.21
9–11	2	5	.14	.35
12–14	5	10	.36	.71
15–17	4	14	.29	1.00

2-2 Construct the histogram for the frequency distribution in Exercise 2-1.

2-3 Construct the frequency polygon for the frequency distribution in Exercise 2-1.

2-4 Describe the frequency curve in terms of skewness for the data in Exercise 2-3.

2-5 Construct the ogive for the frequency distribution in Exercise 2-1.

2-6 Construct a percentage ogive for the frequency distribution in Exercise 2-1. From the graph
(a) What is the approximate percentile point associated with a measured value of 15?
(b) What is the approximate measured value at the fiftieth percentile point?

2-7 The following data report the dollar sales of three products according to region, in thousands of dollars. Using vertical bars, construct a bar chart depicting total sales by region.

Product group	Sales by region, $1,000s			Total sales, $1,000s
	East	Midwest	West	
A	50	55	70	175
B	70	40	80	190
C	30	40	20	90
Total	150	135	170	455

2-8 Construct a component bar chart to illustrate the product breakdown of sales by region for the data in Exercise 2-7, using horizontal bars.

2-9 Construct a pie chart illustrating total sales by product for the data of Exercise 2-7.

2-10 Given the following data for sales, in thousands of dollars construct a line graph illustrating total sales by year.

Product group	Sales by year, $1,000s				Total sales, $1,000s
	1976	1977	1978	1979	
A	120	170	160	175	625
B	160	160	180	190	690
C	10	30	60	90	190
Total	290	360	400	455	1,505

2-11 The following table presents the amounts of 40 personal loans in a consumer finance company. Suppose we wish to arrange the loan amounts in a frequency distribution with a total of seven classes. Assuming equal class intervals, what would be a convenient class interval for this frequency distribution?

Amounts of 40 personal loans, $

900	1,000	300	2,000
500	550	1,100	1,000
450	950	300	2,000
1,900	600	1,600	450
1,200	750	1,500	750
1,250	1,300	1,000	850
2,500	850	1,800	600
550	350	900	3,000
1,650	1,400	500	350
1,200	700	650	1,500

2-12 Construct the frequency distribution for the data in Exercise 2-11, beginning the first class at a lower class limit of $300 and using a class interval of $400.

2-13 Prepare a histogram for the frequency distribution constructed in Exercise 2-12.

2-14 Construct a frequency polygon and frequency curve for the frequency distribution constructed in Exercise 2-12.

2-15 Describe the skewness of the frequency curve constructed in Exercise 2-14.

2-16 Construct a cumulative-frequency distribution for the frequency distribution constructed in Exercise 2-12, and construct an ogive for these data.

2-17 Construct the percentage ogive for the frequency distribution in Exercise 2-12. From the graph
(a) What is the approximate percentile point for a loan amount of $2,000?
(b) What is the approximate loan value at the thirtieth percentile point?

2-18 From the frequency distribution in Table 2-6, determine
(a) The lower limit of the last class
(b) The upper limit of the last class
(c) The lower boundary of the last class
(d) The upper boundary of the last class
(e) The midpoint of the last class

2-19 Construct a frequency polygon for the frequency distribution in Table 2-6.

2-20 The following data are taken from the *Arizona Statistical Review*, published by the Valley National Bank (32d ed., 1976). Determine the class boundaries for each class of this relative-(percentage) frequency distribution.

Age breakdown of Phoenix area population compared with the U.S. population (1975)

Age group	Phoenix area, %	United States, %
Under 5	8.9	7.5
5 and under 18	24.5	23.6
18 and under 45	37.4	38.0
45 and under 65	19.2	20.4
65 and over	10.0	10.5

2-21 Notice that a constant interval size is not used in the frequency distribution in Exercise 2-20. Identify the interval size associated with each class. Using this distribution as an example, why do you think unequal interval sizes are frequently used in statistical reports?

2-22 The data in the table below are taken from the Survey of *Current Business* published by the U.S. Department of Commerce. Construct a vertical bar chart for these data.

Construction of new one-family structures in the United States, 1972–1977

Year	Housing starts, 1000s
1972	1,349
1973	1,132
1974	888
1975	892
1976	1,162
1977	1,451

2-23 Construct a line graph for the housing starts for single-family structures reported in Exercise 2-22.

2-24 The following data are taken from the annual report of the Clark Equipment Company for 1977. Construct a line chart that indicates the income per share for 1970–1977.

Year	Income per share, $	Dividends per share, $
1970	2.92	1.40
1971	2.37	1.40
1972	3.01	1.45
1973	4.06	1.51
1974	3.68	1.60
1975	3.43	1.60
1976	4.97	1.70
1977	4.39	1.70

2-25 For the per-share data in Exercise 2-24, construct a component bar chart that depicts dividends per share and retained earnings per share for the eight-year period, using vertical bars.

2-26 For the per-share data in Exercise 2-24, construct a percentage pie chart depicting the percentage of income paid as dividends and the percentage retained in the firm during the three-year period 1970–1972. Construct a similar percentage pie chart for the three-year period 1975–1977. Observe the difference between the two pie charts.

THREE

DESCRIPTIVE MEASURES FOR POPULATIONS AND SAMPLES

3-1 THE USE OF THE SUMMATION SIGN

In statistics, the uppercase Greek letter Σ (read: "sigma") is used to designate the summation of a series of values, and therefore this symbol can be read as "sum of." Because this summation symbol is frequently used in the calculation of the descriptive measures presented in this chapter, it is important that you understand the kind of summation required in several basic types of situations.

To begin with, the summation of a series of n values for variable X can be denoted by the formula

$$\sum_{i=1}^{n} X_i = X_1 + X_2 + \cdots + X_n \tag{3-1}$$

For example, given the collection of six values $X_1 = 5$, $X_2 = 8$, $X_3 = 9$, $X_4 = 12$, $X_5 = 14$, and $X_6 = 20$, the summation is designated by

$$\sum_{i=1}^{6} X = 5 + 8 + 9 + 12 + 14 + 20 = 68$$

where i indicates the position of each value in the series, the number below the summation sign identifies the position of the first value being summed, and the number above the summation sign indicates the position of the last value being summed. Thus, the summation of the middle four values in the above series (eliminating the first and last values from consideration) is

$$\sum_{i=2}^{5} X = 8 + 9 + 12 + 14 = 43$$

Because we typically sum all the values in the collection rather than summing only designated values, the general summation formula can be simplified by eliminating the references to the positions of the values being summed. In this text, we generally sum all values in each example, and thus we use the simplified formula

$$\Sigma X = X_1 + X_2 + \cdots + X_n \tag{3-2}$$

The summation of squared values for a variable X is denoted by

$$\Sigma X^2 = X_1^2 + X_2^2 + \cdots + X_n^2 \tag{3-3}$$

For example, the *sum of the squares* for the collection of values 5, 8, 9, 12, 14, and 20 is

$$\Sigma X^2 = 5^2 + 8^2 + 9^2 + 12^2 + 14^2 + 20^2 = 25 + 64 + 81 + 144 + 196 + 400 = 910$$

Another frequent operation in statistics is that of obtaining a *square of the sum*, which you should clearly differentiate from the sum of the squares described above. The square of the sum of n values for a variable X is denoted by

$$(\Sigma X)^2 = (X_1 + X_2 + \cdots + X_n)^2 \tag{3-4}$$

Thus, to determine the square of the sum, we simply sum the n values of the variable and then square this sum. For example, for the collection of values described above we have

$$(\Sigma X)^2 = (5 + 8 + 9 + 12 + 14 + 20)^2 = 68^2 = 4,624$$

Thus, ΣX^2 is *not* equal to $(\Sigma X)^2$.

When verbal reference is made to statistical formulas, the sum of the squares ΣX^2 is read as "sum of X squared," whereas the square of the sum, $(\Sigma X)^2$ is read as "sum of X *quantity* squared." The word "quantity" indicates that it is the quantity within the parentheses, and not each individual value, that is squared.

Another useful rule is that the sum of a series of constant values is simply the number of values multiplied by the constant c; that is,

$$\Sigma c = nc \qquad (3\text{-}5)$$

For example, given the collection of six values 8, 8, 8, 8, 8, and 8, the sum of these values is

$$\Sigma c = nc = (6)(8) = 48$$

When a series of values is to be multiplied by a constant and the products summed, the correct sum can also be obtained by multiplying the sum of the values by the constant. The formula representing this procedure is

$$\Sigma cX = c\Sigma X \qquad (3\text{-}6)$$

For example, the amount of a chemical held in five separate containers has been measured to the nearest ounce, and we wish to determine the total number of grams of the chemical. The number of ounces are 10, 14, 17, 20, and 23. Instead of converting each of these ounces to grams by multiplying by the constant 28.35, we can sum the ounces first and then convert the sum to grams:

$$\Sigma cX = c\Sigma X = 28.35(10 + 14 + 17 + 20 + 23) = 28.35(84) = 2,381.4 \text{ grams}$$

Finally, we can recognize that the summation of a series of sums is the sum of the summation of each variable. This idea is represented by

$$\Sigma(X + Y) = \Sigma X + \Sigma Y \qquad (3\text{-}7)$$

For example, suppose that employees A, B, and C have devoted the number of hours to projects X and Y indicated in Table 3-1. To determine the total number of hours devoted to the two projects, we can first sum the hours for each employee (the "Total no. of hours" column in Table 3-1) and then take the sum of these totals. However, the same answer is obtained by

$$\Sigma(X + Y) = \Sigma X + \Sigma Y = 320 + 470 = 790$$

Table 3-1 Hours devoted to projects X and Y by employees A, B, and C

Employee	Project hours		Total no. of hours
	X	Y	
A	120	180	300
B	60	200	260
C	140	90	230
	$\Sigma X = 320$	$\Sigma Y = 470$	790

Although the use of Formula (3-7) does not save a substantial amount of computational effort in this simplified example, application of this formula to more complex data situations involving several variables does simplify computational requirements.

3-2 MEASURES OF AVERAGE: THE MEAN AND THE WEIGHTED MEAN

In statistical description, an *average* is some one value used to represent, and be typical of, all the values in a collection. Based on the mathematical standard applied, several types of averages can in fact be used to represent a collection of values.

The *arithmetic mean*, or simply, *mean*, is the type of average with which you are most familiar. Computationally, it is sum of all of the values in a collection divided by the number of values.

At this point it is appropriate to observe that in statistical analysis a descriptive measure of a population, or a *population parameter*, typically is represented by a Greek letter, whereas a descriptive measure of a sample, or a *sample statistic*, is represented by an italicized Roman letter. Thus, the arithmetic mean for a population of values is represented by the Greek letter μ (read: "mū"), whereas the arithmetic mean for a sample is represented by $\bar{X}$ (read: "X bar"). The respective formulas are

Population mean:
$$\mu = \frac{\Sigma X}{N} \tag{3-8}$$

Sample mean:
$$\bar{X} = \frac{\Sigma X}{n} \tag{3-9}$$

In the numerator of Formulas (3-8) and (3-9) ΣX indicates that all of the values in the collection are summed, as explained in Section 3-1. The difference in the denominators is because in statistical analysis N is generally used to indicate the number of population values, while n is used to indicate the number of sample values. Thus, in this text *population size* is always designated by N and *sample size* is always designated by n.

For example, the following scores, arranged in ascending order, were earned by 12 students in a statistics course: 37, 59, 71, 75, 78, 78, 81, 86, 88, 92, 95, and 96. Considering this group to be a statistical population, the arithmetic mean is

$$\mu = \frac{\Sigma X}{N} = \frac{936}{12} = 78.8$$

(*Note:* Throughout this book descriptive measures are calculated to one additional digit, or decimal position, as compared with the values in the collection. Thus, the test scores just described are reported to the nearest whole number, and therefore the mean is reported to the first place beyond the decimal point.)

The *weighted mean*, or *weighted average*, is an arithmetic mean in which each

Table 3-2 Courses completed and grades earned in a given semester

Course	Credit hours	Grade
American literature	3	C
Mathematical analysis	4	A
Psychology	3	B
Survey of music	2	D
Basic accounting	4	A

value in the collection is not simply summed, but is weighted according to its importance. The formulas for the population and sample weighted means are identical, and in each case the sum of the weighted values is divided by the sum of the weights:

$$\mu_w \text{ or } \bar{X}_w = \frac{\Sigma wX}{\Sigma w} \tag{3-10}$$

For example, suppose we wish to calculate a student's grade point average for the semester in which the student completed a 16-credit-hour load. Table 3-2 reports the pertinent data. Where $A = 4.0$, $B = 3.0$, $C = 2.0$, and $D = 1.0$, the *unweighted* arithmetic mean is

$$\mu = \frac{\Sigma X}{N} = \frac{2.0 + 4.0 + 3.0 + 1.0 + 4.0}{5} = \frac{14.0}{5} = 2.80$$

But this grade point average, which is in the C+ range, is incorrect because it does not take into consideration the different hours of credit for the five courses. The correct procedure is to calculate the weighted mean with the credit hours used as the weights:

$$\mu_w = \frac{\Sigma wX}{\Sigma w} = \frac{3(2.0) + 4(4.0) + 3(3.0) + 2(1.0) + 4(4.0)}{3 + 4 + 3 + 2 + 4} = \frac{49.0}{16} = 3.06$$

Note that now the grade point average is in the B range.

3-3 MEASURES OF AVERAGE: THE MEDIAN AND THE MODE

The *median* for a collection of values is the value at the middle of the group when all of the values in the group are arranged in ascending order. When the group has an odd number of values, one value is always at the middle. For example, in an ordered set of five values, the third value is at the middle. For a collection with an even number of values, the median is assumed midway between the two middle values; that is, in an ordered set of six values the median is midway between the third and fourth values.

When the collection contains a large number of values, the following formula determines the position of the median in the ordered-group of values:

$$\text{Med} = X_{(n/2)+(1/2)} \tag{3-11}$$

For example, the 12 test scores described in the preceding section arranged in ascending order were 37, 59, 71, 75, 78, 78, 81, 86, 88, 92, 95, and 96. The position of the median in this group of values is

$$\text{Med} = X_{(12/2)+(1/2)} = X_{6.5}$$

Therefore the value of the median is the value midway between the sixth and seventh values in the ordered set, or in this case, halfway between 78 and 81. Since the difference between 78 and 81 is 3, the median is

$$\text{Med} = X_{6.5} = 78 + 0.5(3) = 78 + 1.5 = 79.5$$

The mode is the value that occurs most frequently in a collection of values. For a small group of values, it is possible that no value is repeated and therefore that no mode is available as a measure of average. For the test scores described above, for which the median is 79.5, the mode is 78.0 because 78 is the only test score that occurred more than once. Thus, for a small group of values, the mode is generally unreliable as an indicator of the average, or typical, value. If one mode clearly exists for a data set, the distribution of values is described as being *unimodal.* When two nonadjoining values have relatively high frequencies, the distribution of values is described as *bimodal.* Similarly, distributions with several modes are called *multimodal.* Figure 3-1 portrays the general forms of a unimodal and bimodal distribution of values. If more than one mode exists, no one measure of average may truly describe the "typical" value for the group.

3-4 SKEWNESS AND THE RELATIONSHIP AMONG THE MEAN, MEDIAN, AND MODE

As described in Section 2-2, a *negatively skewed* frequency curve has a tail to the left and a *positively skewed* frequency curve has a tail to the right. For a *symmetrical* distribution of values, the two halves of the associated frequency curve are mirror images. In a unimodal and symmetrical distribution the values of the mean,

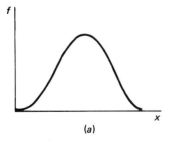
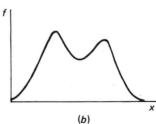

Figure 3-1 Types of distributions of values. (*a*) Unimodal distribution. (*b*) Bimodal distribution.

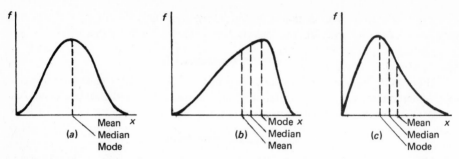

Figure 3-2 Relationships among the mean, median, and mode. (*a*) Symmetrical. (*b*) Negatively skewed. (*c*) Positively skewed.

median, and mode are all at the same value, as indicated in Figure 3-2*a*. On the other hand, for a negatively skewed distribution the mean has a lower value than either the median or mode with the mode generally having the largest value, as indicated in Figure 3-2*b*. For a positively skewed distribution the mean has the highest value of the three measures of average, as indicated in Figure 3-2*c*.

Because the mode is the least reliable measure of average for a small collection of values, the relationship between the mean and median is generally used as an indicator of skewness. When the mean is larger than the median, the distribution is positively skewed; when the mean is smaller than the median, the distribution is negatively skewed. For example, the test scores reported in Sections 3-2 and 3-3 have a mean of 78.0 and a median of 79.5. Therefore, this small group of scores would be negatively skewed.

Inspection of the 12 scores reported in Sections 3-2 and 3-3 indicates that the difference between the mean and median, and thus the negative skewness, is attributable to the one extremely low test score of 37. If this score were removed from the group, the median would be 81.0 and the mean, $\mu = 81.7$, would in fact become larger than the median. The mean is always more affected by extremely low or high values in the collection, and therefore for nonsymmetrical distributions the median is considered a better measure of average for statistical description. However, in statistical inference the principal probability distributions that we shall employ are symmetrical, and therefore in the analysis of such applications of statistics the use of the arithmetic mean is preferred.

3-5 MATHEMATICAL CRITERIA ASSOCIATED WITH THE MEAN, MEDIAN, AND MODE

In the preceding sections of this chapter we described how the mean, median, and mode differ as measures of average. Each of these measures can be considered a type of average because each one is in some manner "typical" and thus can be used to represent all the values in a collection. However, each one is typical by satisfying a different mathematical criterion, or standard, as to what constitutes an "average."

The *mode* is typical in that it is the "most frequent" value in the group. As such, it satisfies the criterion that, when used as the estimator of every value in the group, the number of estimation errors is minimized. Symbolically, this criterion can be represented by $N_e = $ min.

The *median* is typical of an entire collection of values in that it is the middle value. As such, it satisfies the criterion that the *sum of the absolute values of the errors* be minimized. Symbolically, this criterion can be represented by $\Sigma|e| = $ min. Thus, if we were to select different values to be used as the average and, for each average, took the sum of the absolute values of the differences between that average and every value in the collection, the smallest sum would be associated with the median value in the group. Any other value would have a larger sum of the absolute values of the errors.

Finally, the *mean* is typical in that if each value in the group were equal to the mean, the total of all the values in the collection would be unchanged (i.e., $\Sigma X = n\bar{X}$ or $\Sigma X = n\mu$). As such, this average satisfies the mathematical criterion that the *sum of the squared errors* be minimized. Symbolically, this criterion can be represented by $\Sigma e^2 = $ min. From the standpoint of this criterion, the arithmetic mean is the "correct" measure of average because any other value would have a higher sum of squared errors associated with it.

Thus the three main types of averages are all mathematically legitimate because each one satisfies a specific mathematical criterion. Of the three criteria we described, the objective of minimizing the sum of the squared errors is also the criterion underlying the development of many of the techniques of analysis in inferential statistics. This criterion is generally called the *least-squares criterion*. Because the mean is the measure of average that satisfies the least-squares criterion, it is mathematically consistent with the principal techniques of statistical inference.

3-6 QUARTILES AND PERCENTILES

Where the *median* is the point at which a distribution is divided into two halves, in terms of the frequency of the observed values on the two sides of the point, the *quartiles* divide the distribution into four quarters, and the *percentiles* divide the distribution into 100 parts. The formulas that can be used to determine the positions of the three quartile points Q_1, Q_2, Q_3, are variations of the formula for locating the position of the median in an ordered set of values:

First quartile: $\qquad\qquad\qquad Q_1 = X_{(n/4)+(1/2)}$ $\qquad\qquad\qquad$ (3-12)

Second quartile: $\qquad\qquad\qquad Q_2 = X_{(n/2)+(1/2)}$ $\qquad\qquad\qquad$ (3-13)

Third quartile: $\qquad\qquad\qquad Q_3 = X_{(3n/4)+(1/2)}$ $\qquad\qquad\qquad$ (3-14)

The value of Q_1 is the point below which 25 percent of the values are located, Q_2 is the point below which 50 percent of the values are located, and, Q_3 is the point below which 75 percent of the values are located. Thus the value of Q_2 is also the value of the median for the collection of values. As an example of computing Q_1 for a small group of values, the test scores reported in Sections 3.2 and 3.3 were 37, 59, 71, 75, 78, 78, 81, 86, 88, 92, 95, and 96. The position of the first quartile point in this ordered set of values is

$$Q_1 = X_{(n/4)+(1/2)} = X_{(12/4)+(1/2)} = X_{3.5}$$

Therefore, the first quartile point is midway between the third and fourth values in the ordered group, or halfway between 71 and 75:

$$Q_1 = X_{3.5} = 71 + 0.5(4) = 71 + 2.0 = 73.0$$

A *percentile point* indicates the value such that the designated percentage of the values in the ordered group are below that value. The position of the value associated with any percentile point can be determined by substituting the percentile point of interest for "per" in the general formula

$$P_{per} = X_{\{[per(n)]/100\}+(1/2)} \tag{3-15}$$

For example, for the small, ordered set of test scores reported above the position of the tenth percentile point is

$$P_{per} = X_{\{[per(n)]/100\}+(1/2)} = X_{\{[10(12)]/100\}+(1/2)} = X_{1.2+0.5} = X_{1.7}$$

Therefore, the position of the tenth percentile point is seven-tenths the distance between the first and second values, 37 and 59, in the ordered set. Since the difference between these two values is 22, the value at the tenth percentile point is

$$P_{10} = X_{1.7} = 37 + 0.7(22) = 37 + 15.4 = 52.4$$

As descriptive measures of location, percentile points are particularly useful when a large collection of measurements is involved. They are often used to aid in the interpretation of nationally standardized achievement tests. In this context a percentile of 60 associated with a reported test score indicates that 60 percent of the test scores were below the reported score.

3-7 MEASURES OF DISPERSION: THE RANGE AND MODIFIED RANGES

Whereas a measure of average identifies the typical value in a collection of values, it does not provide any information about the extent to which the values differ from one another. Knowledge about the variability among the values may be even more important than knowing the average of the values. Therefore, various measures of variability, or dispersion, have been developed in statistical analysis.

The *range R* is the difference between the highest and lowest observed values in a collection of values. Where H represents the highest observed value and L represents the lowest observed value, the formula is

$$R = H - L \tag{3-16}$$

For example, for the test scores reported in the preceding section the range is

$$R = H - L = 96 - 37 = 59.0$$

A *modified range* is a range for which a designated percent of the extreme values at the two ends of the distribution are eliminated from consideration, thus providing a more reliable measure of variability than the range. Typical modified ranges are the *middle 50 percent, middle 80 percent,* and *middle 90 percent* ranges. The procedure by which a modified range is determined is first to determine the values at the two percentile points involved and then take the difference between these two values. For example, the middle 80 percent range requires the elimination of 10 percent of the values at each end of the distribution, and thus we first determine the values at the 10th and 90th percentile points. For the 12 test scores reported in the preceding section, we determined that $P_{10} = 52.4$. The test scores were 37, 59, 71, 75, 78, 78, 81, 86, 88, 92, 95, and 96. Solving now for P_{90}:

$$P_{90} = X_{\{[90(12)]/100\} + (1/2)} = X_{11.3} = 95 + 0.3(1.0) = 95.3$$

Therefore, the middle 80 percent range is

$$\text{Middle } 80\% \ R = P_{90} - P_{10} = 95.3 - 52.4 = 42.9$$

The general advantage of the range and the modified ranges as measures of dispersion is that they are relatively easy to interpret, and therefore are particularly useful when statistical methods are applied for statistical description. However, when the methods of statistics are applied for statistical inference, the variance and standard deviation, described in the next section, are the more useful measures of dispersion.

3-8 MEASURES OF DISPERSION: THE VARIANCE AND STANDARD DEVIATION

The *variance* is a measure of dispersion that takes into consideration the difference between each value in a data set and the mean of the group. Each difference is squared, and then the mean of these squared differences is determined. Thus, in words the variance can be defined as being "the average of the squared deviations from the mean." For a population of values the variance is represented by the lowercase Greek σ^2 (read: "sigma squared"), and the basic formula for the *population variance* is

$$\sigma^2 = \frac{\Sigma(X - \mu)^2}{N} \tag{3-17}$$

One difficulty associated with interpreting the value of the variance is that it is in squared units of the variable. For this reason, the positive square root of the variance, called the *standard deviation*, is more frequently reported. The population standard deviation is represented by σ and the formula is

$$\sigma = \sqrt{\frac{\Sigma(X-\mu)^2}{N}} \qquad (3\text{-}18)$$

As the term is used in most statistics books, a *sample variance* is not simply the variance of a sampled group. Rather, it is an estimator of the population variance for the population from which a random sample was obtained. The formula for the sample variance differs from the formula for the population variance in that a correction for biasedness is included in the denominator of the sample variance formula. This matter is considered further in Section 7-1, Point Estimation. The sample variance is represented by the symbol s^2, and the formula is

$$s^2 = \frac{\Sigma(X-\bar{X})^2}{n-1} \qquad (3\text{-}19)$$

The sample standard deviation is represented by the symbol s and the formula is

$$s = \sqrt{\frac{\Sigma(X-\bar{X})^2}{n-1}} \qquad (3\text{-}20)$$

As an example of determining the variance and standard deviation, let us again consider the 12 test scores reported in previous sections of this chapter. The 12 scores were defined as constituting a statistical population, and the population mean for this group of values was determined to be $\mu = 78.0$ in Section 3-2. Table 3-3 presents the worksheet for calculating the variance and standard deviation. Referring to this table, we determine the variance by the use of Formula (3-17):

$$\sigma^2 = \frac{\Sigma(X-\mu)^2}{N} = \frac{3{,}082.00}{12} = 256.83$$

Table 3-3 Worksheet for calculating the variance and standard deviation for a population of 12 test scores

X	$X-\mu$	$(X-\mu)^2$
37	−41.0	1,681.00
59	−19.0	361.00
71	−7.0	49.00
75	−3.0	9.00
78	0.0	0.00
78	0.0	0.00
81	3.0	9.00
86	8.0	64.00
88	10.0	100.00
92	14.0	196.00
95	17.0	289.00
96	18.0	324.00
	$\Sigma(X-\mu)^2 =$	3,082.00

Similarly, we determine the value of the standard deviation by the use of Formula (3-18):

$$\sigma = \sqrt{\frac{\Sigma(X - \mu)^2}{N}} = \sqrt{\frac{3,082.00}{12}} = \sqrt{256.83} \approx 16.0$$

In this example, use of the basic formulas was relatively easy because the mean happened to be an integer (whole number). When the mean is at some fractional value, and especially when a large collection of values is involved, determining the difference between every value and the mean can be cumbersome. For this reason, alternative *computational formulas* have been developed for the population and sample variance and standard deviation that do not require each such difference to be determined. In this respect, the basic formulas used thus far are called *deviations formulas* because they require the determination of the difference (deviation) between each observed value and the mean of the collection of values.

Because the standard deviation rather than the variance is the more frequently used measure of dispersion, henceforth in this chapter we refer to alternative formulas for the standard deviation only. Of course, the variance is always simply the square of the standard deviation. The computational formulas for the standard deviation, which generally simplify the calculations, are

Population standard deviation: $\qquad \sigma = \sqrt{\frac{\Sigma X^2}{N} - \left(\frac{\Sigma X}{N}\right)^2}$ $\qquad\qquad$ (3-21)

Sample standard deviation: $\qquad s = \sqrt{\frac{\Sigma X^2 - (\Sigma X)^2/n}{n-1}}$ $\qquad\qquad$ (3-22)

Table 3-4 presents the worksheet for calculating the standard deviation for our population of 12 test scores by using the computational formula. When Formula (3-21) is applied, the population standard deviation is

$$\sigma = \sqrt{\frac{\Sigma X^2}{N} - \left(\frac{\Sigma X}{N}\right)^2} = \sqrt{\frac{76,090}{12} - \left(\frac{936}{12}\right)^2} = \sqrt{6,340.83 - (78.0)^2}$$

$$= \sqrt{6,340.83 - 6,084.00} = \sqrt{256.83} \approx 16.0$$

This answer corresponds with the value obtained by the deviations formula. Any slight difference in the answers would be from rounding error, and in fact such possible error is associated with the deviations formulas, rather than with the computational formulas, because the deviations formulas require that the differences may have to be rounded.

3-9 USE OF THE STANDARD DEVIATION

Because of its use in statistical inference, the standard deviation is the most important measure of dispersion. For this reason, it is used with a number of

Table 3-4 Worksheet for calculating the standard deviation using the computational formula

X	X^2
37	1,369
59	3,481
71	5,041
75	5,625
78	6,084
78	6,084
81	6,561
86	7,396
88	7,744
92	8,464
95	9,025
96	9,216
$\Sigma X = 936$	$\Sigma X^2 = 76,090$

analytical techniques in later chapters. Although it would be premature to attempt any detailed description of these techniques at this point, as a preview of such applications consider a distribution of values that is both symmetrical and mesokurtic (neither flat nor peaked). In statistical analysis, the frequency curve associated with such a distribution is called a *normal curve* and can be described as being bell-shaped. For *normally distributed values* approximately 68 percent are within one standard deviation of the mean, and approximately 95 percent of the values are within two standard deviations of the mean. Figure 3-3 portrays these relationships graphically. Note that "normal" does not imply that such distributions are to be generally expected. The use of the normal distribution in a wide range of statistical applications is justified mathematically on the basis of the central-limit theorem, described in Section 7-2.

As a brief example of the general application of the normal distribution, suppose that the accounts receivable in a building-materials firm are normally distributed with a mean of $620 and a standard deviation of $200. It then follows

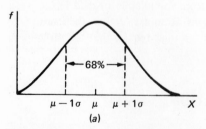
(a)

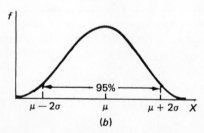
(b)

Figure 3-3 Percentage of values included within (*a*) one and (*b*) two standard deviation units from the mean for normally distributed variables.

that approximately 68 percent of the accounts are within $200 of the mean, or between $420 and $820. Similarly, approximately 95 percent of the accounts are within $400 of the mean, or between $220 and $1,020.

3-10   MEASURES OF AVERAGE FOR GROUPED DATA

When data have been grouped in a frequency distribution and the original individual values are not available, the three principal types of averages can be approximated on the basis of the frequency distribution. In this section we present the formulas for the mean, median, and mode to be used with grouped data and illustrate their application.

To compute the mean, we use the midpoint M of each class as an approximation of all values included in the class. Where f represents the observed frequency of values in each class, the respective formulas for the population and sample mean are

Population mean:
$$\mu = \frac{\Sigma fM}{N} \tag{3-23}$$

Sample mean:
$$\bar{X} = \frac{\Sigma fM}{n} \tag{3-24}$$

Computationally, in both Formulas (3-23) and (3-24), each class midpoint is multiplied by the observed frequency for the class, and then the sum of these products is divided by the number of observations included in the frequency distribution. For example, refer to Table 3-5, which repeats the sample data that were grouped and used for illustrative purposes throughout Chapter 2. When Formula (3-24) is applied, the sample mean for these grouped data is

$$\bar{X} = \frac{\Sigma fM}{n} = \frac{3,491.0}{50} = 69.82 \approx 69.8 \text{ inches}$$

To determine the median for grouped data, we first need to determine the class that contains the median and then by interpolation determine the position of the

Table 3-5 Heights of a sample of 50 men students

Height, in.	Class midpoint M, in.	No. of students f	fM	Cumulative frequency cf
60–62	61.0	1	61.0	1
63–65	64.0	2	128.0	3
66–68	67.0	13	871.0	16
69–71	70.0	20	1,400.0	36
72–74	73.0	11	803.0	47
75–77	76.0	3	228.0	50
		$n = 50$	$\Sigma fM = 3,491.0$	

median within the class. The class that contains the median is the first class for which the cumulative frequency equals or exceeds one-half of the sample (or population) size. Once this class is identified, the specific value of the median is determined by

$$\text{Med} = B_L + \left[\frac{(n/2) - \text{cf}_b}{f_c}\right] i \qquad (3\text{-}25)$$

where B_L = lower boundary of the class containing the median

n = total number of observations in the frequency distribution (N for a population)

cf_b = cumulative frequency in the class preceding ("before") the class containing the median

f_c = number of observations in the class containing the median

i = size of the class interval

For example, the class containing the median for the data in Table 3-5 is the fourth class (the class limits 69–71) because this class is the first for which the cumulative frequency (36) exceeds $n/2$, or 25. The median is

$$\text{Med} = B_L + \left[\frac{(n/2) - \text{cf}_b}{f_c}\right] i = 68.5 + \left(\frac{25 - 16}{20}\right) 3 = 68.5 + \left(\frac{9}{20}\right) 3 = 68.5 + 1.35$$

$$= 69.85 \approx 69.8 \text{ inches}$$

The grouped-data formula for determining the mode for a collection of values requires that all classes in the frequency distribution have equal class intervals. The procedure is first to identify the class with the highest observed frequency and then to approximate the position of the mode in this class by

$$\text{Mode} = B_L + \left(\frac{d_1}{d_1 + d_2}\right) i \qquad (3\text{-}26)$$

where B_L = lower boundary of the class containing the mode

d_1 = difference between the frequency in the modal class and frequency in the preceding class

d_2 = difference between the frequency in the modal class and frequency in the following class

i = size of the class interval

For the data in Table 3-5, the modal class is the fourth class, with the class limits 69–71 because the observed frequency of observations of 20 for this class is higher than the frequency for any other class. The mode is

$$\text{Mode} = B_L + \left(\frac{d_1}{d_1 + d_2}\right) i = 68.5 + \left[\frac{20 - 13}{(20 - 13) + (20 - 11)}\right] 3 = 68.5 + \left(\frac{7}{7 + 9}\right) 3$$

$$= 68.5 + \left(\frac{7}{16}\right) 3 = 68.5 + 1.31 = 69.81 \approx 69.8 \text{ inches}$$

For these grouped data, note that the mean, median, and mode are all about equal in value. Therefore, the distribution is essentially symmetrical, as can also be seen by scanning the pattern of class frequencies in Table 3-5.

3-11   QUARTILES AND PERCENTILES FOR GROUPED DATA

For grouped data, the formulas for the quartiles and percentiles are similar to the grouped-data formula for the median. In determining any of these values, we first must identify the class that contains the point of interest. For example, the first quartile is located in the first class for which the cumulative frequency equals or exceeds one-quarter of the sample (or population) size. Then by interpolation we determine the specific value at any quartile or percentile using one of the following formulas:

First quartile:
$$Q_1 = B_L + \left[\frac{(n/4) - cf_b}{f_c} \right] i \qquad\qquad (3\text{-}27)$$

Second quartile:
$$Q_2 = B_L + \left[\frac{(n/2) - cf_b}{f_c} \right] i \qquad\qquad (3\text{-}28)$$

Third quartile:
$$Q_3 = B_L + \left[\frac{(3n/4) - cf_b}{f_c} \right] i \qquad\qquad (3\text{-}29)$$

Percentile:
$$P_{per} = B_L + \left[\frac{(per(n)/100) - cf_b}{f_c} \right] i \qquad\qquad (3\text{-}30)$$

For example, for the heights of the sample of 50 men students in Table 3-5 the value at the first quartile of the frequency distribution is

$$Q_1 = B_L + \left[\frac{(n/4) - cf_b}{f_c} \right] i = 65.5 + \left(\frac{12.5 - 3}{13} \right) 3 \approx 67.7 \text{ inches}$$

Similarly, the value at the ninetieth percentile point of the distribution is

$$P_{90} = B_L + \left[\frac{90(n)/100 - cf_b}{f_c} \right] i = 71.5 + \left(\frac{45 - 36}{11} \right) 3 \approx 74.0 \text{ inches}$$

3-12   THE RANGE AND MODIFIED RANGES FOR GROUPED DATA

The range for data grouped in a frequency distribution is the difference between the upper boundary of the highest class, $B_U(H)$, and the lower boundary of the lowest value class, $B_L(L)$. Thus, the range for grouped data is

$$R = B_U(H) - B_L(L) \qquad (3\text{-}31)$$

For example, the range for the data in Table 3-5 is

$$R = B_U(H) - B_L(L) = 77.5 - 59.5 = 18.0 \text{ inches}$$

The modified ranges for grouped data, such as the middle 90 percent range, are determined in the same way as for data not grouped in a frequency distribution, as described in Section 3-6. The only difference is that the required percentile or quartile values are determined by the grouped-data formulas described in Section 3-11.

3-13   THE STANDARD DEVIATION FOR GROUPED DATA

As is true for data not grouped in a frequency distribution, the variance or standard deviation of a *sample* is distinguished from that of a *population*. As before (Section 3-8), the sample variance includes a correction factor so that it is an unbiased estimator of the variance of the population from which the sample was randomly selected. Also, as was the case for ungrouped data, so-called deviations formulas and computational formulas are available, and the variance is the square of the standard deviation. The *deviations formulas* for determining the population and sample standard deviations for grouped data are

Population standard deviation: $\quad \sigma = \sqrt{\dfrac{\Sigma f(M - \mu)^2}{N}} \qquad (3\text{-}32)$

Sample standard deviation: $\quad s = \sqrt{\dfrac{\Sigma f(M - \bar{X})^2}{n - 1}} \qquad (3\text{-}33)$

Table 3-6 is the worksheet for calculating the sample standard deviation for the heights reported in Table 3-5 by use of the deviations formula. The sample mean for these data was determined to be $\bar{X} = 69.8$ inches in Section 3-9. Note from this worksheet that the deviations formula requires that the difference (deviation) between each class midpoint and the mean of the distribution be determined. The sample standard deviation for the measures of height is

$$s = \sqrt{\frac{\Sigma f(M - \bar{X})^2}{n - 1}} = \sqrt{\frac{475.40}{50 - 1}} = \sqrt{9.7020} \approx 3.1 \text{ inches}$$

The computational formulas for the standard deviation do not require the determination of the difference between each class midpoint and the mean. The computational formulas are

Population standard deviation: $\quad \sigma = \sqrt{\dfrac{\Sigma f M^2}{N} - \left(\dfrac{\Sigma f M}{N}\right)^2} \qquad (3\text{-}34)$

Sample standard deviation: $\quad s = \sqrt{\dfrac{\Sigma f M^2 - [(\Sigma f M)^2 / n]}{n - 1}} \qquad (3\text{-}35)$

Table 3-6 Worksheet for calculating the sample standard deviation for grouped data by use of the deviations formula

Height, in.	Class midpoint M, in.	No. of students f	$(M - \bar{X})$	$(M - \bar{X})^2$	$f(M - \bar{X})^2$
60–62	61.0	1	−8.8	77.44	77.44
63–65	64.0	2	−5.8	33.64	67.28
66–68	67.0	13	−2.8	7.84	101.92
69–71	70.0	20	0.2	0.04	0.80
72–74	73.0	11	3.2	10.24	112.64
75–77	76.0	3	6.2	38.44	115.32
		$n = 50$			$\Sigma f(M - \bar{X})^2 = 475.40$

Table 3-7 is the worksheet for calculating the sample standard deviation for the heights reported in Table 3-5 by use of the computational formula. Referring to this table for the required values, one can calculate the sample standard deviation as

$$s = \sqrt{\frac{\Sigma fM^2 - (\Sigma fM)^2/n}{n-1}} = \sqrt{\frac{244,217.0 - (3,491.0)^2/50}{50-1}}$$

$$= \sqrt{\frac{244,217.00 - 243,741.62}{49}} = \sqrt{9.7016} \approx 3.1 \text{ inches}$$

This answer corresponds to the value of the sample standard deviation obtained by the deviations formula. The slight difference under the radical, just before the final answer of 3.1, is because use of the deviations formula leads to a slight rounding error when the rounded value of the mean is subtracted from each class midpoint. Also, note that the worksheet in Table 3-7 need not have included the determination of the sum ΣfM if the mean for the frequency distribution had already been calculated, because this value would have been determined for the calculation of the mean.

Table 3-7 Worksheet for calculating the sample standard deviation for grouped data by use of the computational formula

Height, in.	Class midpoint M, in.	No. of students f	fM	M^2	fM^2
60–62	61.0	1	61.0	3,721.0	3,721.0
63–65	64.0	2	128.0	4,096.0	8,192.0
66–68	67.0	13	871.0	4,489.0	58,357.0
69–71	70.0	20	1,400.0	4,900.0	98,000.0
72–74	73.0	11	803.0	5,329.0	58,619.0
75–77	76.0	3	228.0	5,776.0	17,328.0
		$n = 50$	$\Sigma fM = 3,491.0$		$\Sigma fM^2 = 244,217.0$

3-14 SUMMARY

In this chapter we presented a variety of measures to describe collections of values, both when all the individual values are available and when the values are grouped in a frequency distribution. The descriptive measures obtained with grouped-data formulas are approximations of the values that would be determined if all the individual values were available.

The *measures of average* we considered include the *mean*, the *weighted mean*, the *median*, and the *mode*. For general descriptive purposes one serious difficulty with using the mean to be representative of all values in a collection is that it is the measure of average most affected by a few extremely high (or low) values in the group. For this reason, either the median or mode is a better measure of average for nonsymmetrical distributions of values. Also, for relatively small collections of values, because of the unreliability of the mode, the median is generally preferred. However, in the techniques of statistical inference that constitute most of this book, the analysis will generally involve symmetrical distributions of values, and in such applications the mean is the preferred measure of average. Further, because the mean is the measure of average that satisfies the *least-squares criterion*, it is consistent with the mathematical standard underlying the principal methods of statistical inference.

Quartiles and *percentiles* are also summary values that describe certain characteristics of a collection of values. Where the median, at the second-quartile or fiftieth percentile point of a distribution of values, is one of the principal measures used to describe characteristics of a collection of values, the values associated with such other points as the first quartile and the ninetieth percentile can also be useful for descriptive purposes.

The *measures of dispersion*, or variability, easiest to interpret for descriptive purposes are the *range* and the *modified ranges*, such as the middle 90 percent range. However, in statistical inference the most important measures of dispersion are the *variance* and its positive square root, the *standard deviation*. As defined in this text, the sample variance is not simply a descriptive value for a sample but rather is an unbiased estimator of the variance of the sample population. For this reason, the formula for the sample variance differs from the formula for the population variance in that a correction for biasedness is included. Because the basic formulas for the variance and standard deviation require that the difference between each value (or class midpoint) and the mean of the collection of values be determined, these basic formulas are called *deviations formulas*. On the other hand, the *computational formulas* for the variance and standard deviation are generally easier to use because they do not require the determination of such differences. The standard deviation is used particularly in respect to normally distributed variables, which are both symmetrical and mesokurtic and have associated frequency curves that are bell-shaped.

FORMULAS

(3-1) $\displaystyle\sum_{i=1}^{n} X_i = X_1 + X_2 + \cdots + X_n$ Summation of n values.

(3-2) $\Sigma X = X_1 + X_2 + \cdots + X_n$ Simplified expression for the summation of n values.

(3-3) $\Sigma X^2 = X_1^2 + X_2^2 + \cdots + X_n^2$ Sum of squares for a collection of values.

(3-4) $(\Sigma X)^2 = (X_1 + X_2 + \cdots + X_n)^2$ Square of the sum for a collection of values.

(3-5) $\Sigma c = nc$ Sum of a series of constant values (the number of values multiplied by the constant).

(3-6) $\Sigma c X = c \Sigma X$ When a series of values is to be multiplied by a constant and then summed, this sum is equal to the sum of the values multiplied by the constant.

(3-7) $\Sigma(X + Y) = \Sigma X + \Sigma Y$ Sum of a series of sums (equal to the sum of the summation of each variable).

(3-8) $\mu = \dfrac{\Sigma X}{N}$ Population mean.

(3-9) $\bar{X} = \dfrac{\Sigma X}{n}$ Sample mean.

(3-10) μ_w or $\bar{X}_w = \dfrac{\Sigma w X}{\Sigma w}$ Weighted mean for a population or a sample.

(3-11) $\text{Med} = X_{(n/2)+(1/2)}$ Position of the median in an ordered group of values (population or sample).

(3-12) $Q_1 = X_{(n/4)+(1/2)}$ Position of the first quartile in an ordered group of values.

(3-13) $Q_2 = X_{(n/2)+(1/2)}$ Position of the second quartile in an ordered group of values.

(3-14) $Q_3 = X_{(3n/4)+(1/2)}$ Position of the third quartile in an ordered group of values.

(3-15) $P_{\text{per}} = X_{\{[\text{per}(n)]/100\}+(1/2)}$

Position of a designated percentile point in an ordered group of values.

(3-16) $R = H - L$

The range.

(3-17) $\sigma^2 = \dfrac{\Sigma(X - \mu)^2}{N}$

Population variance, deviations formula.

(3-18) $\sigma = \sqrt{\dfrac{\Sigma(X - \mu)^2}{N}}$

Population standard deviation, deviations formula.

(3-19) $s^2 = \dfrac{\Sigma(X - \bar{X})^2}{n - 1}$

Sample variance, deviations formula.

(3-20) $s = \sqrt{\dfrac{\Sigma(X - \bar{X})^2}{n - 1}}$

Sample standard deviation, deviations formula.

(3-21) $\sigma = \sqrt{\dfrac{\Sigma X^2}{N} - \left(\dfrac{\Sigma X}{N}\right)^2}$

Population standard deviation, computational formula.

(3-22) $s = \sqrt{\dfrac{\Sigma X^2 - [(\Sigma X)^2]/n}{n - 1}}$

Sample standard deviation, computational formula.

(3-23) $\mu = \dfrac{\Sigma fM}{N}$

Population mean for data grouped in a frequency distribution.

(3-24) $\bar{X} = \dfrac{\Sigma fM}{n}$

Sample mean for grouped data.

(3-25) $\text{Med} = B_L + \left[\dfrac{(n/2) + \text{cf}_b}{f_c}\right]i$

Median for grouped data (population or sample).

(3-26) $\text{Mode} = B_L + \left(\dfrac{d_1}{d_1 + d_2}\right)i$

Mode for grouped data.

(3-27) $Q_1 = B_L + \left[\dfrac{(n/4) - \text{cf}_b}{f_c}\right]i$

First quartile for grouped data.

(3-28) $Q_2 = B_L + \left[\dfrac{(n/2) - \text{cf}_b}{f_c}\right]i$

Second quartile for grouped data.

(3-29) $Q_3 = B_L + \left[\dfrac{(3n/4) - \text{cf}_b}{f_c}\right]i$

Third quartile for grouped data.

(3-30) $P_{\text{per}} = B_L + \left[\dfrac{(\text{per}(n)/100) - \text{cf}_b}{f_c}\right]i$

Value at a designated percentile point for grouped data.

(3-31) $R = B_U(H) - B_L(L)$ Range for grouped data.

(3-32) $\sigma = \sqrt{\dfrac{\Sigma f(M - \mu)^2}{N}}$ Population standard deviation, deviations formula for grouped data.

(3-33) $s = \sqrt{\dfrac{\Sigma f(M - \bar{X})^2}{n - 1}}$ Sample standard deviation, deviations formula for grouped data.

(3-34) $\sigma = \sqrt{\dfrac{\Sigma fM^2}{N} - \left(\dfrac{\Sigma fM}{N}\right)^2}$ Population standard deviation, computational formula for grouped data.

(3-35) $s = \sqrt{\dfrac{\Sigma fM^2 - (\Sigma fM)^2/n}{n - 1}}$ Sample standard deviation, computational formula for grouped data.

EXERCISES

3-1 For the data below, reporting employees' absences in a particular department during a three-month period, determine the values of the (a) mean, (b) median, and (c) mode. The number of days absent is reported to the nearest half day and the data are considered to be a statistical population.

Employee ID number	No. of days absent
001	5.0
002	0.0
003	1.5
004	3.0
005	1.0
006	2.0
007	9.0
008	5.5
009	1.0
010	4.0
011	2.0
012	2.0

3-2 Comment on and interpret the differences in the values of the mean, median, and mode computed in Exercise 3-1. Which of these values best represents the "typical" number of days that employees were absent?

3-3 Compute and interpret the values at (a) Q_1, (b) Q_2, and (c) Q_3 for the data in Exercise 3-1.

3-4 Determine the (a) range R and (b) the middle 90 percent range for the data in Exercise 3-1.

3-5 Determine the value of the population standard deviation σ for the data in Exercise 3-1 by using the deviations form of the formula.

3-6 Determine the population standard deviation σ for the data in Exercise 3-1 by using the computational formula.

3-7 The following table reports the number of components assembled during a series of working days considered to be a statistical population. Determine the values of the (a) mean, (b) median, and (c) mode for these data.

Day	Units assembled
1	8
2	7
3	7
4	6
5	8
6	7
7	9
8	7
9	6
10	6

3-8 Compute and interpret the values of (a) Q_1 and (b) Q_3 for the data in Exercise 3-7.

3-9 Determine the value of the (a) range R and (b) middle 50 percent range for the data in Exercise 3-7.

3-10 Compute the population standard deviation σ for the data in Exercise 3-7, using the deviations form of the formula.

3-11 The table below reports the profit margin for three product groups, A, B, and C, and the dollar sales for each product during a particular three-month period.
 (a) Determine the unweighted mean profit margin.
 (b) Determine the weighted mean that incorporates the dollar sales for each product.
 (c) Which arithmetic mean is the correct one?

Product line	Profit margin, %	Sales, $
A	10.3	1,000,000
B	8.1	4,000,000
C	4.2	8,000,000

3-12 The number of cars sold by each of the 10 salesmen in an automobile dealership during a particular month, arranged in ascending order, is 2, 4, 7, 10, 10, 10, 12, 12, 14, 15. Considering the month to be the statistical population of interest, determine the (a) mean, (b) median, and (c) mode for the number of cars sold.

3-13 Which value in Exercise 3-12 best describes the "typical" sales volume per salesperson?

3-14 For the data in Exercise 3-12, determine the values at the (a) first quartile Q_1 and (b) thirtieth percentile point P_{30} for these sales amounts.

3-15 For the data in Exercise 3-12, determine the (a) range R and (b) middle 80 percent range.

3-16 Determine the standard deviation σ for the data in Exercise 3-12 by using the deviations formula and considering the group of values as constituting a statistical population.

3-17 The weights of a random sample of outgoing packages in a mailroom, weighed to the nearest ounce, are found to be 21, 18, 30, 12, 14, 17, 28, 10, 16, and 25 ounces. Determine the (a) mean, (b) median, and (c) mode for these weights.

3-18 For the data in Exercise 3-17 determine the weights at the (a) third quartile Q_3 and (b) seventieth percentile P_{70} point.

3-19 Determine the (*a*) range *R* and (*b*) middle 50 percent range for the weights reported in Exercise 3-17.

3-20 Determine the sample standard deviation for the data in Exercise 3-17 by use of the computational version of the formula.

3-21 The following examination scores, arranged in ascending order, were achieved by 20 students enrolled in a decision analysis course: 39, 46, 57, 65, 70, 72, 72, 75, 77, 79, 81, 81, 84, 84, 84, 87, 93, 94, 97, 97. Considering this group to be the statistical population of interest, determine the (*a*) mean, (*b*) median, and (*c*) mode for these scores.

3-22 Describe the distribution of test scores in Exercise 3-21 in terms of skewness.

3-23 Determine the values at the (*a*) second quartile and (*b*) fiftieth percentile point for the scores in Exercise 3-21.

3-24 Determine the (*a*) range *R* and (*b*) the middle 90 percent range for the scores in Exercise 3-21.

3-25 Considering the examination scores in Exercise 3-21 to be a statistical population, determine the standard deviation by use of
  (*a*) The deviations formula
  (*b*) The alternative computational formula

3-26 Suppose the retail prices of selected items have changed as indicated in the table below.
  (*a*) Determine the mean percentage change in retail prices *without* reference to the average expenditures included in the table.
  (*b*) Determine the mean percentage change by weighting the percent increase for each item by the average amount per month spent on that item before the increase.
  (*c*) Which mean percentage price is more appropriate as a measure of the impact of the price changes on the particular consumers in this group? Why?

Item	Increase, %	Average expenditure/mo (before increase), $
Apparel	2.1	30.00
Gasoline	9.5	50.00
Ground beef	3.2	30.00
Milk	4.0	20.00

3-27 Describe the similarities and the differences among the median, quartiles, and percentiles as descriptive measures of position.

3-28 Throughout the remainder of this book the mean is used as the measure of average. Why, then, is it worthwhile to describe the median and the mode in this chapter?

3-29 In an academic grading system in which A = 4.0, B = 3.0, C = 2.0, D = 1.0, and E = 0.0, a group of students has the grade point averages reported in the following table. Compute the values of the (*a*) population mean, (*b*) median, and (*c*) mode for this distribution of grade point values.

Grade point average	No. of students *f*
1.0–1.4	3
1.5–1.9	4
2.0–2.4	8
2.5–2.9	12
3.0–3.4	5
3.5–3.9	3

3-30 Comment upon and interpret the differences in the values of the mean, median, and mode in Exercise 3-29.

3-31 Compute and interpret the values of (a) Q_1 and (b) Q_3 for the data in Exercise 3-29.

3-32 Determine the value at the sixtieth percentile point for the data in Exercise 3-29, and interpret this value.

3-33 Compute the (a) range R and (b) middle 90 percent range for the data in Exercise 3-29.

3-34 For the data of Exercise 3-29, compute the value of the population standard deviation σ using the deviations form of the formula.

3-35 For the data of Exercise 3-29, compute the value of the population standard deviation σ using the so-called computational formula. Compare your answer to the answer you obtained in Exercise 3-34.

3-36 The following frequency distribution reports operating-profit figures for a given month for a group of photoprocessing outlets, reported to the nearest dollar. Considering this to be a statistical population, compute the average profit for the month in terms of the (a) mean, (b) median, and (c) mode.

Monthly operating profit, $	Frequency f
0–499	12
500–999	14
1,000–1,499	8
1,500–1,999	2

3-37 Compute the values of (a) Q_1 and (b) Q_3 for the data in Exercise 3-11.

3-38 Determine the value at the ninetieth percentile point for the data in Exercise 3-36.

3-39 Determine the (a) range R and (b) middle 80 percent range for the data in Exercise 3-36.

3-40 For the data of Exercise 3-36, compute the value of the standard deviation σ using the computational formula.

3-41 Given the frequency distribution in the table below, compute the (a) mean, (b) median, and (c) mode of the loan amounts.

Amounts of a sample of 40 personal loans

Loan amount, $	No. of loans
300–699	13
700–1,099	11
1,100–1,499	6
1,500–1,899	5
1,900–2,299	3
2,300–2,699	1
2,700–3,099	1
Total:	40

3-42 Describe the form of the frequency distribution of personal loan amounts in Exercise 3-41.

3-43 For the loan amounts reported in Exercise 3-41 determine the values at the (a) second quartile Q_2 and (b) ninety-fifth percentile P_{95} point.

3-44 For the loan amounts reported in Exercise 3-41 determine the (a) range and (b) middle 50 percent range for the amounts of personal loans.

3-45 Determine the sample standard deviation s for the data in Exercise 3-41 by using the computational formula.

3-46 Briefly explain why descriptive measures calculated on the basis of grouped data are considered to be approximations.

PROBABILITY

4-1 WHAT IS PROBABILITY?

The field of probability analysis owes its early development to the interest of European mathematicians in games of chance during the latter part of the seventeenth century. Since then, the concepts of probability have become the foundation for the development of the techniques of statistical inference that are used in many fields of basic and applied research, including economic analysis and managerial decision making.

Before describing the historical approaches to probability, it is useful to define several terms that are used in probability analysis. To begin, an *event* is an uncertain outcome of an observation or experiment. For example, if a salesperson calls on two prospective customers, the outcome, "two sales," is one of the events that can occur. Events are also differentiated as being either elementary or composite. An *elementary event* represents one particular elementary outcome. For example, when two calls are made, the outcome, "two sales," is an elementary event, because there is only one specific sequence of outcomes in the two calls that represents the completion of two

123.456
12 3456
10 10
10 10
10 10

4-1 WHAT IS PROBABILITY   53

sales. On the other hand a *composite event* includes more than one elementary outcome of the observation. For example, when two calls are made, the event, "one sale," is a composite event, because it can occur either by the sequence of a sale being made with the first prospect followed by a nonsale or with a nonsale followed by a sale. Each of these two sequences is itself an elementary outcome. In this text the term "event" will designate either an elementary or composite event, according to the context. Finally, in the language of set theory in mathematics the complete listing of the events that can occur in an observation or experiment is called the *sample space*, and such a listing is described as an *exhaustive* listing of the events. Thus for our example of making two sales calls the sample space includes the possibility of 0, 1, or 2 sales being completed.

Historically, three different approaches, the classical approach, the relative-frequency approach, and the subjective approach, have been developed for defining probability, and these approaches determine how probability values are determined and interpreted.

By the *classical approach* to probability, if a possible elementary outcomes are favorable to an event A and b possible outcomes are unfavorable to the occurrence of A and all outcomes are equally likely and mutually exclusive, the probability that event A will occur is

$$P(A) = \frac{a}{a+b} \qquad (4\text{-}1)$$

By "mutually exclusive" we mean that the occurrence of any one outcome precludes the possibility of any other outcome occurring in the same trial, or observation, as explained further in Section 4-3. This requirement, and especially the requirement that the elementary outcomes be equally likely, results in the classical approach being particularly applicable to games of chance. Further, because this approach, when applicable, permits the determination of probability values before any sample results are observed, it has also been called the *a priori approach*. As an example of using the classical approach to determining a probability value, suppose a well-shuffled deck of cards contains 13 spades, 13 hearts, 13 diamonds, and 13 clubs; the probability that a randomly selected card is a heart is

$$P(H) = \frac{a}{a+b} = \frac{13}{13+39} = \frac{13}{52} = \frac{1}{4} = 0.25$$

By the *relative-frequency approach* to probability, the probability value is determined on the basis of the proportion of times that a favorable outcome occurs in a set of sample observations, or trials. No prior assumption about the likelihood of each possible outcome is required. Because this approach to determining probability values is based on the collection and analysis of data, it has also been called the *empirical approach*. The approach is useful in situations in which sample data relating to the event of interest can be collected. Thus, the probability that event A will occur is

$$P(A) = \frac{\text{no. of observations of } A}{\text{sample size } n} \qquad (4\text{-}2)$$

For example, suppose we wish to determine the probability that an individual with a given educational background will succeed in the industrial apprenticeship program of a large company. Of 200 randomly sampled individuals who had this background of achievement in the past, 150 succeeded in the program. Therefore the probability of success S is

$$P(S) = \frac{150}{200} = \frac{3}{4} = 0.75$$

Because the relative-frequency approach is based on sample data and not a priori knowledge, the probability value is an estimate of the exact probability. However, as the number of observations is increased, the observed relative frequency of an event tends to become stable. This result is often referred to as the *law of large numbers.* For example, Figure 4-1 portrays the observed relative frequency of heads occurring in 300 tosses of a fair coin. As the number of tosses of the coin increases, the relative frequency of heads stabilizes at about 0.50.

In terms of the interpretation of probability values both the classical and relative-frequency approaches yield objective probability values; that is, the probability value is interpreted as indicating the long-run relative rate of occurrence of the event. For example, if the probability of drawing a heart from a well-shuffled deck of cards is 0.25, we would expect that about 25 hearts would occur in 100 such trials. Similarly, if the probability of success in the apprenticeship program is 0.75, we would expect that about 75 out of 100 sampled individuals with the designated background will succeed. Thus, application of objective probability values involves "playing with the odds"; in other words, although certain repeated decisions will not always be correct we know the long-run rate of success favors the decisions.

A third approach to probability is the *subjective approach.* This approach is applicable when the process generating the events cannot be known on an a priori basis and results cannot be sampled. This situation particularly exists when there is

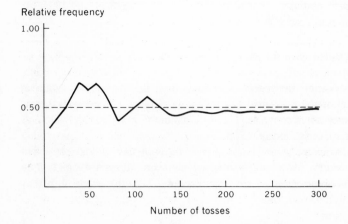

Figure 4-1 Relative frequency of heads occurring in 300 tosses of a fair coin.

only one opportunity for the occurrence of an event, such as the probability of rain tomorrow or the probability that there will be a strike in the automobile industry at the next contract negotiations. By the subjective approach, the probability of an event is the *degree of belief* by an individual in respect to the event, based on all available evidence. Of course, the validity of such a judgment is associated with the expertise and knowledge acquired by the individual making the judgment. Thus, the meteorologist considers continental weather patterns and recent weather changes in making a forecast, while a labor economist would consider the state of the economy, levels of profits in the industry, comparative interindustry wage rates, and a number of other factors in estimating the probability of a labor dispute. Because the probability value is a personal judgment, this approach has also been called the *personalistic approach.* This approach has been developed relatively recently and is associated with statistical decision analysis, described in Chapter 13.

4-2 EXPRESSING PROBABILITY

As indicated by our examples in the preceding section, the symbol P is used to designate the probability of an event. Thus, $P(A)$ designates the probability that event A will occur in a single observation, or trial. The smallest value that a probability statement can have is 0, indicating that the event is impossible. The largest value that a probability statement can have is 1, indicating that the event is certain to occur. Thus, the limits of a probability value are

$$0 \leqslant P(A) \leqslant 1 \qquad (4\text{-}3)$$

An event must either occur or not occur in a given observation, or trial. The sum of the probability of occurrence plus the probability of nonoccurrence thus always equals 1. Therefore, where A' (read: "not A") designates the nonoccurrence of event A, we have

$$P(A) + P(A') = 1 \qquad (4\text{-}4)$$

The probability of an event can be portrayed graphically by means of a *Venn diagram,* a diagram associated with set theory in mathematics. In a Venn diagram an enclosed figure represents a *sample space*, which is the set of all possible events, and portions of the area within the space are designated to represent particular elementary events or classes of events. For example, Figure 4-2 represents the probabilities of occurrence of two events A and A'. Because $P(A) + P(A') = 1$, the entire area in the sample space is allocated.

Another principle associated with the numeric value of probabilities is that the sum of the probability values for all mutually exclusive and exhaustive events that can occur in a particular observation, or trial, must equal 1. This condition indicates that one of the identified events must occur. Symbolically, this principle can be represented by the equation

$$\Sigma P(X) = 1 \qquad (4\text{-}5)$$

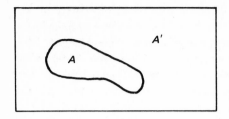

Figure 4-2 Venn diagram illustrating that $P(A) + P(A') = 1$.

As an alternative to probability values, probabilities can also be expressed in terms of *odds*. The *odds ratio* favoring the occurrence of an event is defined as

$$\text{Odds} = \text{no. of favorable outcomes}:\text{no. unfavorable outcomes} \qquad (4\text{-}6)$$

Since the odds ratio designates the ratio of favorable-to-unfavorable outcomes, in contrast to the classical approach where a probability value is the total number of favorable outcomes divided by the total number of elementary outcomes, given the odds ratio we can readily determine the probability value and vice versa. Given the odds favoring an event A as being $a:b$, the probability of A is

$$P(A) = \frac{a}{a+b} \qquad (4\text{-}7)$$

For example, if the odds ratio that a new product will succeed is $3:2$ (three chances of success to two chances of failure), the probability of success is

$$P(A) = \frac{a}{a+b} = \frac{3}{3+2} = \frac{3}{5} = 0.60$$

To convert a probability value to an odds ratio favoring an event A, we take the ratio of the probability of the event to the (complementary) probability that the event will not occur and then adjust the ratio so that it is expressed in the lowest integer (whole number) values:

$$a:b = P(A):1 - P(A) \qquad (4\text{-}8)$$

For example, if the probability that a new product will be profitable in the first year is 0.20, the odds ratio favoring profitability is

$$a:b = P(\text{profit}):1 - P(\text{profit}) = 0.20:0.80 = 1:4$$

4-3 MUTUALLY EXCLUSIVE EVENTS, NONEXCLUSIVE EVENTS, AND THE RULES OF ADDITION

Two or more events are *mutually exclusive*, or disjoint, if they cannot occur together; that is, the occurrence of one event precludes the occurrence of the other event (or events). For example, if a heart is drawn from a deck of cards, the card cannot also be a spade. A purchaser of one vehicle at a dealership who has bought a station wagon cannot also have bought a van.

Two or more events are *nonexclusive*, or joint, if the events can occur together. For example, if a heart is drawn from a deck of cards, it is possible for the card also to be a king. If a purchaser has bought a station wagon, it is also possible to have purchased tinted windows as an option. Whether two designated events are mutually exclusive is important in applying the rules of addition, which we now present.

The rules of addition are used when we wish to determine the probability of either one event or another event (or both) occurring in a given observation. For the two events A and B we designate the probability of either event occurring as $P(A$ or $B)$. In the language of set theory in mathematics this condition is called the *union* of A and B, and the probability is designated by $P(A \cup B)$ (read: "probability of A union B"). For two events that are mutually exclusive, the rule of addition is

$$P(A \text{ or } B) = P(A) + P(B) \tag{4-9}$$

Thus, for mutually exclusive events we simply add the two probability values to determine the probability of either event occurring. For example, if the probability that a purchaser buys a station wagon is $P(S) = 1/6$, and the probability that he buys a van is $P(V) = 1/12$, the probability that a randomly selected purchaser buys either a station wagon or a van is

$$P(S \text{ or } V) = P(S) + P(V) = 1/6 + 1/12 = 3/12 = 1/4 = 0.25$$

For events that are not mutually exclusive the probability of either event (or both events) occurring in a random trial is determined by adding the probability values for the two events and then subtracting the probability of the joint occurrence of the two events from the sum. For the two events A and B, we designate the probability of the joint occurrence of these two events as $P(A$ and $B)$. In the language of set theory in mathematics this is called the *intersection* of A and B, and the probability is designated by $P(A \cap B)$ (read: "probability of A intersect B"). Thus, the rule of addition for events that are not mutually exclusive but can occur together is

$$P(A \text{ or } B) = P(A) + P(B) - P(A \text{ and } B) \tag{4-10}$$

Formula (4-10) is also called the *general rule of addition* because for mutually exclusive events the last term would always be equal to zero; under such circumstances the formula is equivalent to Formula (4-9) for mutually exclusive events. If this rule is applied, the probability that a randomly selected card from a deck of 52 playing cards will be either a heart (H) or a king (K) is

$$P(H \text{ or } K) = [P(H) + P(K)] - P(H \text{ and } K) = (13/52 + 4/52) - 1/52 = 16/52$$
$$= 4/13 \approx 0.31$$

(where the symbol "$\approx$" means "approximately equal to").

The basis for the probability values substituted in the formula in the above example is that 13 of the 52 cards are hearts, 4 of the 52 cards are kings, and 1 card of the 52 is both a heart and a king.

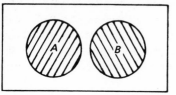 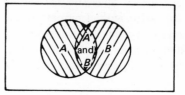

Figure 4-3 Venn diagrams. (*a*) Mutually exclusive events. (*b*) Events that are not mutually exclusive.

As another example, the probability that a purchaser buys a station wagon is $P(S) = 1/6$, the probability that tinted windows are included as an option is $P(T) = 1/4$, and the probability that the purchaser buys both is $P(S \text{ and } T) = 1/12$. The probability that a randomly selected purchaser either bought a station wagon or included tinted windows in the vehicle purchased (or both) is

$$P(S \text{ or } T) = [P(S) + P(T)] - P(S \text{ and } T) = (1/6 + 1/4) - 1/12$$
$$= (2/12 + 3/12) - 1/12 = 4/12 = 1/3 \approx 0.33$$

Note that we have emphasized that for events that are not mutually exclusive, $P(A \text{ or } B)$ includes the possibility that the two events occur together *even though this probability of joint occurrence is subtracted in the general rule of addition.* Figures 4-3*a* and 4-3*b* are Venn diagrams for two events that are mutually exclusive and that are not mutually exclusive, respectively. Referring to Figure 4-3*a*, we see that the probability of *A* or *B* occurring is conceptually equivalent to adding the proportions of area that represent events *A* and *B* in the sample space. In Figure 4-3*b*, however, for events that are not mutually exclusive, we see that event sets *A* and *B* overlap, and some of the elementary events are in the area *intersecting A* and *B*. If we conceptually add the two proportions of area for *A* and *B*, the area of intersection is included twice in the sum, once as part of *A* and once as part of *B*. In this respect, the rationale of subtracting $P(A \text{ and } B)$ in the general rule of addition is not to eliminate the possibility of joint occurrence from the definition of $P(A \text{ or } B)$ but rather to correct the sum of the probabilities for the duplicate addition of this area of intersection.

4-4 INDEPENDENT EVENTS, DEPENDENT EVENTS, AND CONDITIONAL PROBABILITY

Two events are *independent* if the occurrence or nonoccurrence of one event has no effect on the probability of occurrence of the other event. Two events are *dependent* when the occurrence or nonoccurrence of one event *does* affect the probability of occurrence of the other event. Often the events of interest occur in the context of separate trials, or observations. For example, the outcomes associated with tossing a coin twice in succession are independent events because whether a head or a tail occurs on the first toss has no effect on the probability of a head or a tail occurring on the second toss. On the other hand, if two cards are randomly selected *without replacement* from a deck of 52 playing cards, the two events (possible cards drawn) are dependent events. The probability of a king being obtained on the first draw is 4/52. But if a king is removed from the deck on the first draw, the probability that a king will be obtained on the second draw of a card is 3/51.

When two events are dependent, the probability of a second event, given that a first event has occurred, is called *conditional probability*. The expression $P(B|A)$ (read: "probability of B given A") designates the probability of event B given that event A has occurred. Conditional probability expressions are required only in the context of dependent events because for independent events the probability value associated with an event is unaffected by the possible occurrence of the other event of interest. Therefore, one approach by which we can test for the independence of two events is to compare the simple (unconditional) probability of either event to the conditional probability value for that event. Thus, a test for the independence of two events is

$$P(B) \overset{?}{=} P(B|A) \qquad (4\text{-}11)$$

or
$$P(A) \overset{?}{=} P(A|B) \qquad (4\text{-}12)$$

For example, for a given year suppose that 90 percent of the firms whose securities are listed on the New York Stock Exchange earned a profit. Thus, based on the classical approach to probability, we can say that the probability of a randomly selected firm earning a profit is $P(A) = 0.90$. Now, suppose that in the same year the percentage of firms in the chemical industry that earned a profit is 70 percent. Therefore, the probability of a profit given that a firm is in the chemical industry is $P(A|B) = 0.70$. Now, we can determine whether the two events "earned a profit" and "in the chemical industry" are independent by the comparison:

$$P(A) \overset{?}{=} P(A|B)$$

$$0.90 > 0.70$$

Therefore, the two events are dependent. Whether a firm is in the chemical industry does affect the probability that the firm earned a profit in the given year.

If the simple probability of a first event $P(A)$ and the joint probability of two events $P(A \text{ and } B)$ are known or can be obtained, the conditional probability $P(B|A)$ can be determined by

$$P(B|A) = \frac{P(A \text{ and } B)}{P(A)} \qquad (4\text{-}13)$$

Repeating an earlier example in this section, suppose the probability that a vehicle purchaser buys a station wagon is $P(S) = 1/6$, the probability that tinted windows are included as an option is $P(T) = 1/4$, and the probability that the purchaser both buys a station wagon and includes tinted windows as an option is

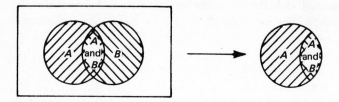

Figure 4-4 Venn diagram illustrating the rationale for the formula $P(B|A) = P(A \text{ and } B)/P(A)$.

$P(S$ and $T) = 1/12$. Then the probability that the purchaser includes the tinted-windows option, *given that a station wagon is bought*, is

$$P(T|S) = \frac{P(T \text{ and } S)}{P(S)} = \frac{1/12}{1/6} = \frac{1/12}{2/12} = \frac{1}{2} = 0.50$$

Note that $P(T \text{ and } S) = P(S \text{ and } T)$.

Similarly, the probability that a purchaser buys a station wagon, given that the tinted-windows option is included in the purchase, is

$$P(S|T) = \frac{P(S \text{ and } T)}{P(T)} = \frac{1/12}{1/4} = \frac{1/12}{3/12} = \frac{1}{3} = 0.33$$

The rationale underlying Formula (4-13) for determining a conditional probability value is illustrated by the Venn diagram in Figure 4-4. Referring to the left portion of this figure, suppose we want to determine the conditional probability of B given that A has occurred $P(B|A)$. Then given that A has occurred, it follows that the original Venn diagram (sample space) is reduced to the smaller diagram in the right portion of the figure. That is, the entire remaining sample space* represents the occurrence of A, and a portion of the remaining sample space includes A *and* B. Now, from the classical approach to determining a probability value we can say that the probability of B given A in the reduced sample is the ratio of the number of elementary events including B (the A *and* B area) to the total number of elementary events (the A area). The result is

$$P(B|A) = \frac{P(A \text{ and } B)}{P(A)}$$

which is Formula (4-13).

4-5 THE RULES OF MULTIPLICATION AND THE JOINT OCCURRENCE OF TWO EVENTS

The rules of multiplication are used to determine the probability of the joint occurrence of two (or more) events. For two events A and B, this is often called

---

*Remember that the sample space is the set of all possible events in a Venn diagram.

the *intersection* of A and B, as indicated in Section 4-3, and can be represented by $P(A \cap B)$ or by $P(A$ and $B)$. For two independent events the rule of multiplication is

$$P(A \text{ and } B) = P(A)P(B) \qquad (4\text{-}14)$$

The respective outcomes associated with two tosses of a coin are in fact independent events because the occurrence of a particular outcome on one toss does not affect the probability values associated with the second toss. Therefore, by Formula (4-14) the probability of observing two heads in two tosses of a fair coin is

$$P(H \text{ and } H) = P(H)P(H) = 1/2 \times 1/2 = 1/4 = 0.25$$

Just as Venn diagrams are useful for representing the events associated with a single trial, or observation, *tree diagrams* are useful for portraying the events in a sequence of trials, or observations. Figure 4-5 presents the tree diagram for two successive tosses of a fair coin. As is typical of such diagrams, the possible events associated with each trial are identified along with their probabilities of occurrence.

By reference to Figure 4-5, we see that four sequences of joint events are possible: H and H, H and T, T and H, and T and T. By the rule of multiplication for independent events, the probability of joint occurrence for any one of these sequences is $1/2 \times 1/2 = 1/4$, or 0.25, as indicated to the right of the tree diagram. Since these are mutually exclusive sequences and all possible sequences have been identified, by the rule of addition the sum of the four probabilities in the right portion of Figure 4-5 should be 1.00, which it is. Also, note that if we wish to determine the probability of observing one head and one tail *in any order* in two tosses of a coin, the probability values of the two sequences that include one head and one tail are added:

$$P \text{ (one head and one tail)} = P(H \text{ and } T) + P(T \text{ and } H) = 0.25 + 0.25 = 0.50$$

Outcome of first toss	Outcome of second toss	Joint event	Probability of joint event
1/2 H	1/2 H	H and H	0.25
	1/2 T	H and T	0.25
1/2 T	1/2 H	T and H	0.25
	1/2 T	T and T	0.25
			1.00

Figure 4-5 Tree diagram for two tosses of a fair coin (independent events).

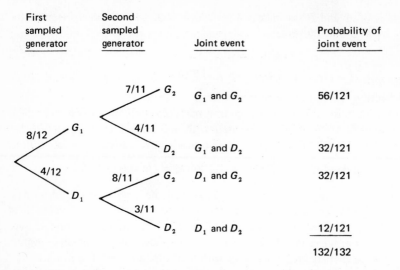

First sampled generator	Second sampled generator	Joint event	Probability of joint event
	7/11 G_2	G_1 and G_2	56/121
8/12 G_1	4/11		
		D_2 G_1 and D_2	32/121
4/12	8/11 G_2	D_1 and G_2	32/121
D_1	3/11		
		D_2 D_1 and D_2	12/121
			132/132

Figure 4-6 Tree diagram for the sampling of 2 generators from a shipment of 12 generators (dependent events).

For dependent events the probability of the joint occurrence of events A and B is the product of the simple (unconditional) probability of one event by the conditional probability of the other event, given that the first event has occurred. Thus, for dependent events the rule of multiplication is

$$P(A \text{ and } B) = P(A)P(B|A) \qquad (4\text{-}15)$$

or

$$P(A \text{ and } B) = P(B)P(A|B) \qquad (4\text{-}16)$$

This rule is often called the *general rule of multiplication*, because for independent events the conditional probability value in either Formula (4-15) or (4-16) would be equal to the simple probability value. That is, for independent events, $P(B|A) = P(B)$ and $P(A|B) = P(A)$, which would make either Formula (4-15) or (4-16) the same as Formula (4-14).

As an example of using the general rule of multiplication, suppose a shipment of 12 generators includes 8 good generators G and 4 defective generators D. Given 2 randomly selected generators, the sequence of possible outcomes and the associated probabilities are portrayed by the tree diagram in Figure 4-6. In this diagram, the subscripts indicate the sequential position of each outcome. Based on the general rule of multiplication, the probability that both of the randomly selected generators are good is

$$P(G_1 \text{ and } G_2) = P(G_1)P(G_2|G_1) = 8/12 \times 7/11 = 56/132 = 14/33 \approx 0.42$$

If the probability of the joint occurrence of two events is available directly without use of a multiplication rule, as an alternative to Formulas (4-11) and (4-12) the independence of two events A and B can be tested by observing whether the joint probability value corresponds to the value that would be obtained by using the rule of multiplication for independent events:

$$P(A \text{ and } B) \overset{?}{=} P(A)P(B) \qquad (4\text{-}17)$$

For example, we have established the probability that a vehicle purchaser buys a station wagon is $P(S) = 1/6$, the probability that tinted windows are bought as an option is $P(T) = 1/4$, and the probability that the purchaser buys a station wagon and includes the tinted-window option is $P(S \text{ and } T) = 1/12$. We test for the independence of these two events as follows:

$$P(S \text{ and } T) \overset{?}{=} P(S)P(T)$$

$$1/12 \overset{?}{=} 1/6 \times 1/4$$

$$1/12 > 1/24$$

Therefore, the two events are dependent events. The probability of these two events occurring together is greater than it would be for two independent events.

4-6 BAYES' THEOREM

In its simplest form, Bayes' theorem is concerned with determining the conditional probability of event A given that event B has occurred. Therefore, it is an algebraic variation of Formula (4-13) for determining a conditional probability value, as described in Section 4-4. The general formula representing Bayes' theorem is

$$P(A|B) = \frac{P(A \text{ and } B)}{P(B)} \qquad (4\text{-}18)$$

The special importance of Bayes' theorem is that it is used to determine the probability for the *first* of two sequential events given that the *second* event has been observed. In the context of the application of this theorem the joint probability $P(A \text{ and } B)$ and the simple probability $P(B)$ generally would not be available directly. Therefore the computational formula for Bayes' theorem is useful:

$$P(A|B) = \frac{P(A)P(B|A)}{P(A)P(B|A) + P(A')P(B|A')} \qquad (4\text{-}19)$$

As a simplified example of the application of Bayes' theorem suppose that box 1 contains two dimes and three nickels while box 2 contains four dimes and one nickel. A box is chosen randomly, and then a coin is chosen randomly from the box. The coin is a dime. Given this information, what is the probability that the box chosen is box 1? As indicated in the tree diagram in Figure 4-7, the simple probability of box 1 is $P(\text{box } 1) = 0.50$. However, given the sample result, the conditional probability is $P(\text{box } 1|\text{dime})$. With Bayes' formula, this is

$$P(\text{box } 1|\text{dime}) = \frac{P(\text{box } 1)P(\text{dime}|\text{box } 1)}{P(\text{box } 1)P(\text{dime}|\text{box } 1) + P(\text{box } 2)P(\text{dime}|\text{box } 2)}$$

$$= \frac{(0.50)(0.40)}{(0.50)(0.40) + (0.50)(0.80)} = \frac{0.20}{0.60} = \frac{1}{3} \doteq 0.33$$

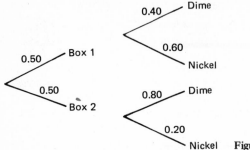

Figure 4-7 Tree diagram for the coin example.

Bayes' theorem is important in statistical decision analysis, explained in Section 13-1, because it provides the basis for revising so-called prior probabilities based on sample information. In this context the "prior" probabilities are the simple (unconditional) probabilities prior to the sample information, while the *posterior probabilities* are the conditional probabilities given the sample result. As an example that illustrates this idea of sampling more directly, suppose that a manufacturing process is either "in control," with a proportion of defective pieces of 0.05, or "out of control," with a proportion of defective pieces of 0.20. Based on historical data, the process is known to be in control 90 percent of the time and out of control 10 percent of the time. Suppose one item is randomly sampled from the process and is found to be defective. This sampling situation is represented by the tree diagram in Figure 4-8 in which C indicates the process is in control and C' indicates the process is out of control, while D indicates a defective item, and D' indicates a nondefective item. Of course, the probability of a randomly selected item being defective is dependent on whether the process is in control or out of control, and the probability is equal to the proportion of defective pieces associated with each of these two possible states. Where the prior probability of the process being in control is $P(C) = 0.90$, given that the one sampled item is defective, the posterior probability of the process being in control is

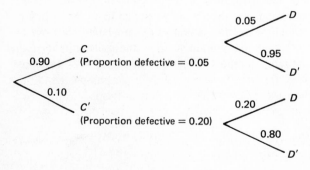

Figure 4-8 Tree diagram for the sampling example.

$$P(C|D) = \frac{P(C)P(D|C)}{P(C)P(D|C) + P(C')P(D|C')} = \frac{(0.90)(0.05)}{(0.90)(0.05) + (0.10)(0.20)}$$

$$= \frac{0.045}{0.045 + 0.02} = \frac{0.045}{0.065} \approx 0.69$$

Thus, in this example, given the adverse sample result, the posterior probability that the process is in control is substantially reduced as compared with the prior probability. Of course, we would expect a reduction in the posterior probability value, and we would be inclined to make such an adjustment intuitively upon seeing that the one sampled item is defective. However, Bayes' formula provides the basis for determining the mathematically correct posterior probability value.

4-7 SUMMARY

In this chapter we introduced you to the basic concepts in probability and to certain rules and methods of analysis useful in statistical applications.

Development of the concepts of probability has resulted in three principal approaches by which probability values can be formulated and interpreted. The *classical approach* is applicable when each elementary event can be assumed to be equally likely and the events are mutually exclusive. The *relative-frequency approach* is appropriate when elementary events cannot be assumed to be equally likely, but a random sample of events can be obtained from the target population. The *subjective approach* is appropriate when equal likelihood cannot be assumed and the population cannot be sampled, typically because the event either will or will not occur on only a single occasion, thereby making it not possible to use either the classical or relative frequency approach. Both the classical and relative-frequency approaches result in objective probability values that are interpreted in terms of long-run expected frequencies, whereas subjective probability values are interpreted in terms of the *degree of belief* that an event will happen.

The *rules of addition* are useful when we wish to determine the probability of one event *or* another event (or both events) occurring by chance. Where the general rule of addition applies to any sampling situation, the simplified special rule of addition applies when the two events are mutually exclusive events. In contrast, the *rules of multiplication* are useful when we wish to determine the probability of the joint occurrence of two events. Whereas the general rule of multiplication applies to any situation, the simplified special rule of multiplication applies when the two events are independent events. Only with dependent events do we need to be concerned with *conditional probability* because only in dependent events is the probability of one event affected by whether the other event has occurred.

Mathematically, Bayes' theorem is simply the formula by which a conditional probability value is determined. However, the special importance of this theorem is that it represents the method by which the probability that an event in a first sequential position has occurred can be determined by the occurrence (or nonoccurrence) of an event in a second sequential position. In statistical analysis, this theorem provides the basis for combining sample information with information available prior to a sample, as explained further in Chapter 13 on statistical decision analysis.

FORMULAS

(4-1) $P(A) = \dfrac{a}{a + b}$

Probability of an event determined by the classical, or a priori, approach.

(4-2) $P(A) = \dfrac{\text{no. of observations of } A}{\text{sample size } n}$

Probability of an event determined by the relative-frequency, or empirical, approach.

(4-3) $0 \leqslant P(A) \leqslant 1$

Limits of a probability value.

(4-4) $P(A) + P(A') = 1$

Probability of the occurrence of an event plus the probability of nonoccurrence of the same event always equals 1.

(4-5) $\Sigma P(X) = 1$

Sum of the probability values for all mutually exclusive and exhaustive events must equal 1.

(4-6) Odds = no. of favorable outcomes : no. of unfavorable outcomes

Odds ratio favoring the occurrence of an event.

(4-7) $P(A) = \dfrac{a}{a + b}$

Probability of an event A, given that the odds ratio favoring occurrence of the event is $a : b$.

(4-8) $a : b = P(A) : 1 - P(A)$

Odds ratio favoring an event A, given $P(A)$.

(4-9) $P(A \text{ or } B) = P(A) + P(B)$

Rule of addition for two events that are mutually exclusive.

(4-10) $P(A \text{ or } B) = P(A) + P(B)$
$- P(A \text{ and } B)$

General rule of addition.

(4-11) $P(B) \overset{?}{=} P(B|A)$

Test for the independence of two events.

(4-12) $P(A) \overset{?}{=} P(A|B)$

Test for the independence of two events.

(4-13) $P(B|A) = \dfrac{P(A \text{ and } B)}{P(A)}$

Conditional probability of event B, given that event A has occurred.

(4-14) $P(A \text{ and } B) = P(A)P(B)$

Rule of multiplication for two independent events.

(4-15) $P(A \text{ and } B) = P(A)P(B|A)$

General rule of multiplication.

(4-16) $P(A \text{ and } B) = P(B)P(A|B)$

General rule of multiplication.

(4-17) $P(A \text{ and } B) \overset{?}{=} P(A)P(B)$

Test for the independence of two events.

(4-18) $P(A|B) = \dfrac{P(A \text{ and } B)}{P(B)}$

Bayes' theorem.

(4-19) $P(A|B) = \dfrac{P(A)P(B|A)}{P(A)P(B|A) + P(A')P(B|A')}$

Computational formula for Bayes' theorem.

EXERCISES

4-1 An inspector randomly samples 50 transistors manufactured during one day and finds that two are defective.

(*a*) What is the probability that an electronic device containing one such transistor will be inoperative because the transistor is defective?

(*b*) What approach and method did you use in arriving at the probability value?

4-2 (*a*) What is the probability that the sum of the dots showing on the face of two dice is seven?

(*b*) What approach and method did you use in arriving at the probability value?

4-3 A financial analyst estimates that the chances are two in three that bond prices will decline during the coming month.

(*a*) Based on his assessment, what is the probability that bond prices will decline during the coming month?

(*b*) What approach and method did you use in arriving at this probability value?

4-4 For each of the following reported odds ratios determine the equivalent probability value, and for each of the reported probability values determine the equivalent odds ratio.

(*a*) A purchasing agent estimates that the odds are $2:1$ that a shipment will arrive on schedule.

(*b*) The probability that a new component will not function properly when assembled is assessed as being $P = 1/5$.

(*c*) The odds that a new product will succeed are estimated as being $3:1$.

(*d*) The probability that the home team will win the opening game of the season is assessed as being $1/3$.

4-5 For each of the following reported odds ratios determine the equivalent probability value, and for each of the reported probability values determine the equivalent odds ratio.

(*a*) Probability of $P = 2/3$ that a target delivery date will be met.

(*b*) Probability of $P = 9/10$ that a new product will exceed the break-even sales level.

(*c*) Odds of $1:2$ that a competitor will achieve a technological breakthrough.

(*d*) Odds of $5:1$ that a new product will be profitable.

4-6 The following table indicates the probabilities associated with the possible demand levels for color TV sets in a particular appliance store during the next three-month period.

No. of sets	<50	50–99	100–149	150–199	>200
Probability	0.20	0.40	0.20	0.10	0.10

   (*a*) What is the probability that fewer than 100 sets will be demanded?
   (*b*) What is the probability that at least 50 but not more than 199 sets will be demanded?

4-7 A personnel manager has found it useful to categorize engineering job applicants according to (1) whether they have earned a college degree in engineering and (2) whether they have had relevant work experience. In a large number of such job applicants 70 percent have the degree with or without any work experience, and 60 percent have work experience with or without the degree. Fifty percent of the applicants have both the degree and relevant work experience. Construct a Venn diagram to portray the probabilities associated with sampling one applicant from this group using *D* for degree completion and *W* for work experience.

4-8 For the situation described in Exercise 4-7
   (*a*) Determine the probability that a randomly selected job applicant has either the degree or relevant work experience.
   (*b*) What is the probability that the applicant has neither the degree nor work experience?

4-9 During a six-month period two-thirds of a large number of common stock issues have advanced in market price or remained unchanged, while one-third have declined in price. If three common stock issues are randomly selected, construct a tree diagram illustrating the probabilities of price advances and price declines for the three stocks using *A* to signify that the price of the stock has advanced or remained unchanged and *D* to signify a price decline. (*Hint:* Construct a three-step diagram, left to right.)

4-10 Refer to Exercise 4-9.
   (*a*) What is the probability that all three of the randomly chosen stock issues experienced a decline in price?
   (*b*) What is the probability that *at least* one of the stock issues declined in price?
(*Hint:* Only one path in the tree diagram does *not* satisfy this requirement; hence the probability of this particular sequence of outcomes can be subtracted from 1.0 to obtain the answer.)

4-11 The probability of a general rise in consumer demand for home air-conditioning units next year is estimated to be 0.70. If this increase in demand materializes, the probability is 0.80 that the sales volume of a particular company will increase. If the rise does not occur, the probability is 0.50 that the company's sales volume will increase. Construct a tree diagram illustrating the various possible outcomes and the associated probabilities using *R* and *R'* for a rise and no rise in general demand, respectively, and *I* and *I'* for an increase and no increase in company sales, respectively.

4-12 For the situation described in Exercise 4-11 what is the probability that demand will rise, accompanied by an increase in company sales volume?

4-13 Of 1,000 assembled components, 10 have a wiring defect and 20 have a structural defect. There is good reason to assume that no component has both defects. What is the probability that a randomly chosen component will have either type of defect?

4-14 Of 500 employees, 200 participate in a company's profit-sharing plan *P*, 400 have major-medical insurance coverage *M*, and 200 employees participate in both programs. Construct a Venn diagram to portray the events designated *P* and *M*.

4-15 Refer to the Venn diagram prepared in Exercise 4-14.
   (*a*) What is the probability that a randomly selected employee will be a participant in at least one of the two programs?

(*b*) What is the probability that a randomly selected employee will not be a participant in either program?

4-16 The probability that a new marketing approach will be successful S is 0.60. The probability that the expenditure for developing the approach can be kept within the original budget B is 0.50. The probability that both of these objectives will be achieved is estimated at 0.30. What is the probability that at least one of these objectives will be achieved?

4-17 For the two events described in Exercise 4-16 determine whether the events are independent or dependent.

4-18 On the average a salesperson completes a sale with 10 percent of potential customers contacted. If the salesperson randomly selects two potential customers from a list of potential customers and calls on them, construct the tree diagram that indicates the probabilities associated with the various sequences of outcomes using S for sale and S' for no sale.

4-19 For the situation in Exercise 4-18
(*a*) What is the probability that both calls will result in sales?
(*b*) What is the probability that the two calls will result in exactly one sale?

4-20 Three of eight account reports prepared by a bank teller contain a procedural error. If an auditor samples two of the eight accounts, construct the tree diagram that indicates the probabilities associated with the various sequences of outcomes using E for obtaining an account report containing the error and E' for obtaining an account report without an error.

4-21 For the sampling situation in Exercise 4-20
(*a*) What is the probability that neither of the accounts sampled contains a procedural error?
(*b*) What is the probability that at least one of the accounts contains a procedural error?

4-22 During a particular period 80 percent of the common stock issues in an industry that includes 10 companies has increased in market value. If an investor chooses two of these issues randomly, what is the probability that both issues will increase in market value during this period?

4-23 For the situation described in Exercise 4-22 suppose an investor chooses three of these stock issues randomly. Construct a tree diagram to portray the various possible results for the sequence of three stock issues.

4-24 Referring to the tree diagram prepared in Exercise 4-23, determine each of the following probabilities.
(*a*) Only one of the three issues will increase in market value.
(*b*) Exactly two issues will increase in market value.
(*c*) At least two issues will increase in market value.

4-25 Box A is known to contain one penny P and one dime D while box B contains two dimes. A box is chosen randomly, and then a coin is randomly selected from the box.
(*a*) Construct a tree diagram to portray this situation involving sequential events.
(*b*) If box A is selected in the first step, what is the probability that a dime D will be selected in the second step?
(*c*) If a dime D is selected in the second step, what is the probability that it came from box A?
(*d*) If a penny P is selected in the second step, what is the probability that it came from box A?

4-26 Suppose there are two urns U_1 and U_2. U_1 contains two red tokens and one green token, while U_2 contains one red token and two green tokens.
(*a*) An urn is randomly selected, and then one token is randomly selected from the urn. The token is red. What is the probability that the urn selected was U_1?
(*b*) An urn is randomly selected, and then two tokens are randomly selected (without

replacement) from the urn. The first token is red and the second token is green. What is the probability that the urn selected was U_1?

4-27 Refer to the urns described in Exercise 4-26.

(a) Suppose an urn is randomly selected, and then two tokens are randomly selected (without replacement) from the urn. Both tokens are red. What is the probability that the urn selected was U_1?

(b) Suppose an urn is randomly selected and then two tokens are randomly selected but with the first selected token being replaced back in the urn before the second token is drawn. Both tokens are red. What is the probability that the urn selected was U_1?

4-28 If a manufacturer plans a major change in the new model of his product, the probability is 0.70 that production-line modifications will begin before September 1. On the other hand, if the manufacturer does not plan a major change, the probability is only 0.20 that production-line modifications will begin before September 1. In terms of the historical pattern of model changes, it is estimated that the probability is approximately 40 percent that a major model change is planned for this year.

(a) Construct a tree diagram to represent the possible outcomes in this situation, which involves dependent events. In your diagram use M to signify a major change in the new model, M' for no major change, L for production-line modifications being made before September 1, and L' for the production-line changes not being made before September 1.

(b) Refer to your tree diagram. If the manufacturer has decided not to make a major model change, what is the probability that production-line modifications are *not* begun before September 1?

4-29 For the uncertain situation described in Exercise 4-28 suppose we observe that production-line modifications have in fact begun before September 1.

(a) What is the prior probability that the manufacturer has decided to make a major change in the new model?

(b) What is the posterior probability that the manufacturer has decided to make a major change in the new model?

4-30 Eighty percent of the vinyl material received from vendor A is of exceptional quality, while only 50 percent of the vinyl material received from vendor B is of exceptional quality. However, the manufacturing capacity of vendor A is limited, and for this reason only 40 percent of the vinyl material purchased by a firm comes from vendor A. The other 60 percent comes from vendor B. An incoming shipment of vinyl material is inspected, and it is found to be of exceptional quality. What is the probability that it comes from vendor A?

DISCRETE PROBABILITY DISTRIBUTIONS

5-1 WHAT IS A RANDOM VARIABLE?

A *random variable* is a numerical event whose value is determined by a chance process, an event not under the direct control of the observer. In this respect, the amount of advertising expenditure is a variable, but it is not a random variable. The expenditure can be at a number of possible values, but the level is chosen and is not associated with a chance process. On the other hand, the level of sales for a product is a random variable, because this level is not under the direct control of any observer.

Random variables can be either discrete or continuous. A *discrete random variable* is one that can assume only a countable number of different values. In applied statistics discrete random variables generally only assume integer (whole number) values and are associated with the process of *counting*. Thus, the number of defective items in a production run and the number of firms that purchased a new computer system are discrete random variables. In contrast, a *continuous random variable* is one that can assume any value along a scale of values. In applied statistics continuous random variables are associated with the process of *measuring*. Thus, the weights of packages of breakfast cereal and the diameters of bearings being manufactured are examples of continuous random variables.

Strictly speaking, a monetary amount, such as dollar amount of sales, is a discrete variable, because the actual amount is at some whole-penny amount. However, we treat variables that involve monetary amounts as continuous random variables throughout this text. On the other hand, even though the *number of customers* served at a store is a discrete random variable, note that the *average number* of customers per store is a continuous random variable. Although the individual counts are discrete values, the average can be at any point along a scale of values and is thus a continuous random variable.

5-2   DISCRETE PROBABILITY DISTRIBUTIONS

For a discrete random variable all possible values of the variable can be listed in a table with the associated probabilities for the several numeric events. Such a table represents the discrete probability distribution for the variable. For example, suppose that for a given week the 20 sales representatives employed by an encyclopedia publisher sold the number of encyclopedia sets reported in Table 5-1. The number of encyclopedia sets sold is the random variable and therefore is designated by the symbol X in column 1. The observed frequencies (number of sales representatives) in column 2 of the table are used to determine the probabilities in column 3 by the classical approach to determining probability values, as described in Section 4-1. Thus, for the given week 4 sales representatives of the 20 sold no encyclopedias, and therefore the probability that a randomly sampled sales representative sold no encyclopedia in the given week is $4/20 = 0.20$. Because the sum of the probabilities for all of the possible events (sets sold) equals 1.0, we can recognize that the probability distribution is complete.

In addition to being presented as a table, a discrete probability distribution can also be presented graphically by a chart. The chart that portrays the probabilities for all the possible values of a discrete random variable is called the *probability mass function* (PMF) for the discrete variable. Figure 5-1 is the probability mass function for the probability distribution presented in Table 5-1.

Table 5-1   Number of encyclopedia sets sold by 20 sales representatives

No. sets sold, X	No. of sales representatives	Probability $P(X)$
0	4	0.20
1	6	0.30
2	3	0.15
3	2	0.10
4	2	0.10
5	2	0.10
6	1	0.05
Total	20	1.00

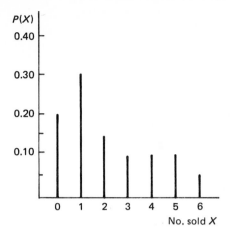

Figure 5-1 Probability mass function for the number of encyclopedia sets sold.

Just as for collections of sample and population data, a probability distribution can be described by determining the mean and the variance for the probability distribution. Calculation of the mean and variance for data sets is described in Chapter 3. The mean for a probability distribution is called the *expected value.* For a discrete random variable X the expected value is denoted by $E(X)$. It is essentially a weighted average of all of the possible values of the random variable, with the probability values used as the weights. Because the sum of the weights (probabilities) for a probability distribution is always equal to 1.00, Formula (3-10) for the weighted mean can be simplified, resulting in the following general formula for determining the expected value for a discrete probability distribution:

$$E(X) = \Sigma XP(X)$$ (5-1)

Table 5-2 presents the procedure for determining the expected value for the probability distribution given in Table 5-1. The expected value for the number of encyclopedia sets sold is 2.1.

Table 5-2 Calculation of the expected value for the number of encyclopedia sets sold

No. sets sold X	Probability $P(X)$	Weighted value $XP(X)$
0	0.20	0.0
1	0.30	0.3
2	0.15	0.3
3	0.10	0.3
4	0.10	0.4
5	0.10	0.5
6	0.05	0.3
	1.00	$E(X) = 2.1$

The variance for a discrete random variable X is denoted by $V(X)$. The general deviations form of the formula for the variance of a discrete probability distribution is

$$V(X) = \Sigma[X - E(X)]^2 P(X) \qquad (5\text{-}2)$$

The computational version of the formula for the variance of a discrete probability distribution does not require the determination of the deviation of each possible value of the random variable from the expected value (mean) of the distribution. The computational formula for the variance is

$$V(X) = \Sigma X^2 P(X) - [\Sigma X P(X)]^2 \qquad (5\text{-}3)$$

Note that the second term in Formula (5-3) is simply the expected value squared. Table 5-3 presents the calculation of all the other values needed in Formulas (5-2) and (5-3). Columns 2 through 5 present the calculation of the variance by Formula (5-2). That is, each deviation is determined in column 3; each deviation is then squared in column 4; the squared deviation is then multiplied by the respective probability value (from column 2) in column 5; and finally the sum of column 5 is the variance for this discrete probability distribution, which is $V(X) = 3.29$.

The calculations in columns 6 and 7 of Table 5-3 are needed for computing the variance by the computational formula, Formula (5-3). With $\Sigma X P(X) = E(X) = 2.1$ (from Table 5-2), the variance is

$$V(X) = \Sigma X^2 P(X) - [\Sigma X P(X)]^2$$

$$V(X) = 7.70 - 2.1^2 = 7.70 - 4.41 = 3.29$$

As was true for the calculation of the variance and standard deviation for sets of data in Chapter 3, the computational version of the formula is generally easier to use than the general deviations formula. Further, rounding errors are minimized with the computational formula because the deviation of each possible value of the random variable from the expected value of the probability distribution is not required.

Table 5-3 Worksheet for calculation of the variance by both the general deviations formula and the computational formula

No. sets sold X	$P(X)$	$X - E(X)$	$[X - E(X)]^2$	$[X - E(X)]^2 P(X)$	X^2	$X^2 P(X)$
0	0.20	−2.1	4.41	0.8820	0	0.00
1	0.30	−1.1	1.21	0.3630	1	0.30
2	0.15	−0.1	0.01	0.0015	4	0.60
3	0.10	0.9	0.81	0.0810	9	0.90
4	0.10	1.9	3.61	0.3610	16	1.60
5	0.10	2.9	8.41	0.8410	25	2.50
6	0.05	3.9	15.21	0.7605	36	1.80
				$V(X) = 3.2900$		$\Sigma X^2 P(X) = 7.70$

In this section we have described the general characteristics of any discrete probability distribution. In applied statistics certain standard probability distributions are used as models for a wide variety of decision-analysis situations because of underlying similarities among these situations that make a common method of analysis possible. Essentially, what we are saying is that every decision- or data-analysis situation is *not* unique in terms of the probability model that can be used, and much of the work in applied statistics is concerned with identifying the underlying similarities in different analysis situations so that common probability models (probability distributions) and common methods of analysis can be employed. In discrete probability distributions, two frequently used standard models are the binomial probability distribution and the Poisson probability distribution. These standard distributions are described in the following two sections.

5-3   THE BINOMIAL DISTRIBUTION

The binomial probability distribution is appropriate as a probability model when the numeric events of interest are discrete and occur in the context of a Bernoulli process. A *Bernoulli process* is a sampling process in which

1. Only two mutually exclusive outcomes are possible in each trial, or observation. Conventionally these two outcomes are often designated as *success* and *failure*.
2. The outcomes in the series of trials, or observations, constitute *independent events*; that is, the occurrence of a success in one observation does not affect the probability of success in the next (random) observation.
3. The probability of success p in each trial remains constant from trial to trial; that is, the process is *stationary*.

The objective of using the binomial distribution is to determine the probability values for the various possible numbers of successes, given a designated number of trials (or number of randomly sampled items) and the probability of success in each trial. Thus, the random variable for the overall Bernoulli process is the number of successes X, while the two values needed to determine the probability $P(X)$ for each possible number of successes is the number of trials, or observations, n and the probability of success p in each trial. In this respect the binomial distribution is really an entire family of distributions because the probability distribution is different for every combination of sample size n and probability of success p in each sample observation, or trial. The existence of an entire family of binomial distributions is one of the factors that makes this probability distribution useful in a variety of applications in statistical analysis.

Because a Bernoulli process involves a sequence of trials, the process can be represented by a tree diagram, with each step or branch in the diagram representing a trial, or sampled item. Then, by the appropriate application of the rules of probability presented in Chapter 4, the probability value associated with any designated number of successes can be determined by reference to this diagram. As a simple example of this approach, suppose a fair coin is tossed three times. Figure 5-2 is the tree diagram representing the sequence of outcomes that can occur in three tosses of a fair coin. Applying the rule of multiplication for independent events gives the probability of each sequence, which is posted in the right portion of the diagram.

Now, suppose we wish to determine the probability of exactly two heads occurring in three tosses of a fair coin. By reference to Figure 5-2 we see that there are three sequences that include exactly two heads: $H, H, T; H, T, H$; and T, H, H. Each sequence has a probability of occurring of 0.125. Because the different sequences are mutually exclusive, by the rule of addition for mutually exclusive events the probability of observing exactly two heads in any sequence is the sum of the three probability values: $0.125 + 0.125 + 0.125 = 0.375$.

By a similar process the probability of observing zero heads, one head, and three heads can also be determined from the tree diagram in Figure 5-2. If we list these outcomes and the associated probabilities in a table, the listing constitutes the complete binomial probability distribution for this Bernoulli sampling situation. Table 5-4 presents the binomial distribution. As is true for any discrete probability distribution, note that the sum of the probabilities is 1.

Obviously, constructing a tree diagram and calculating binomial probabilities by

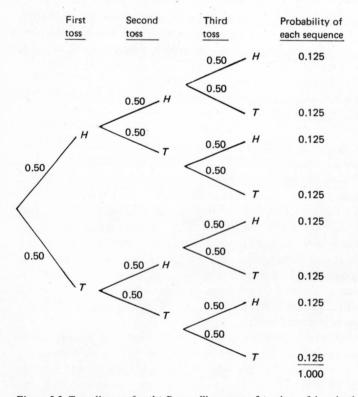

Figure 5-2 Tree diagram for the Bernoulli process of tossing a fair coin three times.

Table 5-4 Binomial probability distribution for the number of heads observed in three tosses of a fair coin

No. of heads X	Probability $P(X)$
0	0.125
1	0.375
2	0.375
3	0.125
Total	1.000

the approach illustrated above can be very cumbersome if a relatively large number of Bernoulli trials is involved. However, the binomial probability distribution can be determined algebraically by expanding the binomial $(q + p)^n$, where p is the probability of success in each Bernoulli trial, q is the probability of failure in each trial, and n is the number of trials. For example, for a sample size of three (such as tossing a coin three times) the expansion is

$$(q + p)^3 = q^3 + 3q^2 p + 3qp^2 + p^3$$

Now, let us demonstrate what each term in the binomial expansion represents from the example of tossing a fair coin three times. Look at Table 5-5. The first term in the expansion (q^3) is the probability of 0 successes, the second term $(3q^2 p)$ is the probability of 1 success, and so forth. Furthermore, by reference to the tree diagram in Figure 5-2, note that the coefficient included in each term always indicates the number of sequences by which the designated event can occur, and the rest of the term is essentially the rule of multiplication for the independent events. For example, consider the probability of observing exactly two heads in three tosses of a fair coin. The term in the binomial expansion for the probability of this event is $3qp^2$, as indicated in Table 5-5. The 3 in this term indicates that exactly two heads can occur by three different sequences, and qp^2 indicates that the probability of each of these sequences is $(0.50)(0.50)^2 = 0.125$. These values correspond to the observations we made concerning the tree diagram in Figure 5-2.

Any given term of a binomial expansion can be determined by Formula (5-4) in

Table 5-5 Probability distribution for the number of heads observed in three tosses of a fair coin as related to the terms of the expansion of the binomial $q + p$

No. of heads	Associated binomial term	Probability
0	q^3	$(0.50)^3 = 0.125$
1	$3q^2 p$	$3(0.50)^2(0.50) = 0.375$
2	$3qp^2$	$3(0.50)(0.50)^2 = 0.375$
3	p^3	$(0.50)^3 = 0.125$

which X identifies the designated number of successes to which the probability value applies:

$$P(X|n, p) = \frac{n!}{X!(n-X)!} p^X q^{n-X} \tag{5-4}$$

For example, if a fair coin is tossed three times, the probability of observing exactly two heads is

$$P(X = 2|n = 3, p = 0.50) = \frac{n!}{X!(n-X)!} p^X q^{n-X} = \frac{3!}{2!(3-2)!} (0.50)^2 (0.50)^{3-2}$$

$$= \frac{3 \times 2 \times 1}{(2 \times 1)(1)} (0.25)(0.50) = 3(0.125) = 0.375$$

(Note that the symbol ! indicates a factorial.)

Recall that in mathematics $0! = 1$ (*not* zero) and that any number raised to the zero power also equals 1. To demonstrate, let us determine the probability of observing three heads in three tosses of a fair coin:

$$P(X = 3|n = 3, p = 0.50) = \frac{n!}{X!(n-X)!} p^X q^{n-X} = \frac{3!}{3!(3-3)!} (0.50)^3 (0.50)^{3-3}$$

$$= \frac{3 \times 2 \times 1}{(3 \times 2 \times 1)0!} (0.125)(0.50)^0 = \frac{3 \times 2 \times 1}{(3 \times 2 \times 1)(1)} (0.125)(1)$$

$$= 0.125$$

For convenience, Table B-2 provides binomial probability values for $n = 1$ through $n = 30$ for various values of p. Therefore, you will be able to obtain most required binomial probability values from this table rather than having to calculate them by Formula (5-4). For example, the probability distribution in Table 5-5 can be seen in Table B-2 by going down to $n = 3$ along the left column of the table and then looking under the column heading $p = 0.50$ (the last column).

When the binomial distribution is used, it is typically because we wish to determine the probability of "X or more" successes or "X or fewer" successes. Of course, in determining these types of probabilities, we need to sum several binomial probability values. For example, suppose the probability is 0.05 that a randomly sampled vehicle owner has a van. What is the probability that we will observe two or more van owners in a random sample of $n = 20$ vehicle owners? Referring to Table B-2 for the required probability values, we have

$$P(X \geqslant 2|n = 20, p = 0.05) = P(X = 2) + P(X = 3) \ldots$$

$$= 0.1887 + 0.0596 + 0.0133 + 0.0022 + 0.0003 = 0.2641$$

If the number of individual probability values to be summed is large, it is sometimes easier to determine the complementary probability value and to subtract this value from 1. For the example above we would do this as follows:

$$P(X \geqslant 2|n = 20, p = 0.05) = 1 - P(X \leqslant 1|n = 20, p = 0.05)$$

$$= 1 - [P(X = 0) + P(X = 1)] = 1 - (0.3585 + 0.3774)$$

$$= 1 - 0.7359 = 0.2641$$

Finally, with respect to Table B-2 you may have noticed that the values of p in the table do not exceed $p = 0.50$. How do we determine binomial probabilities for $p > 0.50$? The general procedure is to restate the problem in terms of the required number of failures rather than the required number of successes. Where $X' =$ not $X = n - X$ and $q = 1 - p$, the formula for restating a problem in terms of the number of failures is

$$P(X|n, p) = P(X'|n, q) \qquad (5\text{-}5)$$

For example, suppose the probability is 0.90 that a shipment will be received before the target date. What is the probability that of 15 randomly selected shipments exactly 12 will be received before the target date? The formulation of this probability in the binomial format is $P(X = 12|n = 15, p = 0.90)$. But because Table B-2 does not report binomial probability values for $p = 0.90$, we restate the problem as follows and then use values of X' and q in Table B-2:

$$P(X|n, p) = P(X'|n, q)$$

$$P(X = 12|n = 15, p = 0.90) = P(X' = 3|n = 15, q = 0.10) = 0.1285$$

In this example, note that 12 successes is the same as 3 failures in the sample of 15 shipments. The procedure for restating a cumulative binomial probability in the "less-than-or-equal-to" or "greater-than-or-equal-to" types of application is similar to the transformation for the individual probability value. In a cumulative probability value, an additional factor is that the inequality symbol is also reversed. For example, suppose that we want to determine the probability that *at least* 12 shipments have been received before the target date. The solution is

$$P(X \geqslant 12|n = 15, p = 0.90) = P(X' \leqslant 3|n = 15, q = 0.10)$$

$$= P(X' = 0) + P(X' = 1) + P(X' = 2) + P(X' = 3)$$

$$= 0.2059 + 0.3432 + 0.2669 + 0.1285 = 0.9445$$

In this example, at least 12 successes is the same as three or fewer failures in the sample of 15 shipments.

Because the binomial distribution is a discrete probability distribution, the mean and variance can be determined by Formulas (5-1) and (5-2), as described in Section 5-2. However, given that a discrete random variable is a binomial variable, the mean and variance can be determined more easily by the following special formulas which can be derived from Formulas (5-1) and (5-2):

$$E(X) = np \qquad (5\text{-}6)$$

$$V(X) = npq \qquad (5\text{-}7)$$

Thus, for the example in which the probability that a shipment will be received before the target date is 0.90, if 15 shipments are randomly selected, the mean and variance of the number of shipments received before the target date are, respectively,

$$E(X) = np = 15(0.90) = 13.5$$

and
$$V(X) = npq = 15(0.90)(0.10) = 1.35$$

5-4 THE POISSON DISTRIBUTION

The Poisson probability distribution is appropriate as a probability model when the numeric events of interest are discrete and occur in the context of a Poisson process. A *Poisson process* is a sampling process in which

1. The events occur in a continuum of time or space, and at any particular point in time (or space) the event either occurs or does not occur.
2. Whether the event occurs in a particular segment of time (or space) does not affect the probability of the event occurring in the next segment of time (or space); that is, the events are *independent events.*
3. The probability of an event occurring is the same for all equal-sized segments of time (or space); that is, the process is stationary.

As you can see by the above description, the Poisson process is very similar to the Bernoulli process described in Section 5-3, except that events occur in the context of a continuum of time or space instead of in the context of trials, or observations. Examples of discrete random variables that follow a Poisson probability distribution are the number of telephone calls arriving at a switchboard during a designated period of time and the number of defects in a roll of sheet steel of designated length.

The objective of using the Poisson probability distribution is to determine the probabilities of various numbers of events, given the length of the time or space dimension. Having designated the length of the time or space dimension of interest, the only other value required to determine a Poisson probability value is the mean number of events for this specified dimension, which is represented by the lowercase Greek letter λ (read: "lambda"). The general formula for determining the probability of a designated number of events X for a Poisson distribution is

$$P(X|\lambda) = \frac{\lambda^X e^{-\lambda}}{X!} \tag{5-8}$$

In Formula (5-8) $e = 2.7183$ and is the base of natural logarithms. Values of $e^{-\lambda}$ for various values of λ can be determined from standard tables. However, for applications purposes it is more convenient to use a table of Poisson probabilities. Table B-3 is a table of Poisson probabilities for values of λ ranging from 0.1 to 10.0. The Poisson distribution is thus a family of discrete probability distributions with a different distribution being associated with each different value of λ. As an example of using Table B-3, if an average of 2.0 calls per minute arrives at a switchboard during a designated time interval, the probability that exactly three calls will arrive in a randomly sampled minute during the interval is determined by looking in Table B-3 under the column headed $\lambda = 2.0$ and then observing the value in the row corresponding to $X = 3$ in the left margin of the table. The probability is

$$P(X = 3|\lambda = 2.0) = 0.1804$$

As for the binomial distribution in Section 5-3, the Poisson distribution typically involves determining the probability of "X or more" or "X or fewer" successes. We do this by summing the appropriate probability values. For example, given an average of $\lambda = 2.0$ calls per minute, the probability of three or more calls being received during a randomly selected minute is

$$P(X \geqslant 3 | \lambda = 2.0) = P(X = 3) + P(X = 4) + \cdots$$

$$= 0.1804 + 0.0902 + 0.0361 + 0.0120 + 0.0034 + 0.0009 + 0.0002$$

$$= 0.3232$$

If the time (or space) interval of interest is not one measurement unit in length, then because the Poisson process is stationary, the mean for such an interval is always proportional to the designated number of interval units of interest. *This fact is important because the mean used in the table of Poisson probabilities must be applicable to the designated time or space dimension.* For example, given an average of $\lambda = 2.0$ calls per minute, the probability of exactly five calls being received during a randomly selected three-minute interval is

$$P(X = 5 | \lambda = 6.0) = 0.1606$$

In the above example, because three minutes is three times the reference time interval of one minute, the average $\lambda = 6.0$ for three minutes is three times the average $\lambda = 2.0$ for one minute. Similarly, if the period of interest is shorter than the reference-time interval, the average is correspondingly smaller. For example, given an average of $\lambda = 2.0$ calls per minute, the probability of no calls being received during a randomly selected one-half minute interval is

$$P(X = 0 | \lambda = 1.0) = 0.3679$$

If a discrete random variable is a Poisson variable, the expected value $E(X)$ and variance $V(X)$ are both equal to the mean number of events for the time or space dimension of interest:

$$E(X) = \lambda \tag{5-9}$$

$$V(X) = \lambda \tag{5-10}$$

5-5 POISSON APPROXIMATION OF BINOMIAL PROBABILITIES

When the probability of success p for a binomial probability distribution is very small (or the probability of failure q is very small) and the sample size n is relatively large, tabled values for required binomial probability values frequently are not available. Further, the computation of binomial probabilities by the general formula would be very tedious. Fortunately, the Poisson probability distribution can be used to approximate binomial probabilities when p (or q) is small and n is large. The rule of thumb used in this text is that such approximation is acceptable when $n \geqslant 30$ and $np < 5$ (or $nq < 5$).

The mean of the Poisson distribution used to approximate binomial probabilities is

$$\lambda = np \tag{5-11}$$

Let us cite an example for which we can determine both the correct binomial probability value and the Poisson approximation of this value. Suppose it is known that 1 percent of the items being produced in a manufacturing process are defective. If 30 items are randomly selected, the binomial probability value that no item will be defective is, from Table B-2,

$$P(X = 0 | n = 30, p = 0.01) = 0.7397$$

For the Poisson approximation of this binomial probability value

$$\lambda = np = (30)(0.01) = 0.3$$

From Table B-3, the Poisson approximation of the binomial probability value is

$$P(X = 0 | \lambda = 0.3) = 0.7408$$

Thus, the approximation is within 0.0011 of the correct probability value.

5-6 SUMMARY

In this chapter, we began by describing *random variables* in general and differentiating *discrete random variables* from *continuous random variables*. In applied statistics discrete random variables typically are associated with the process of *counting*, while continuous random variables are associated with the process of *measuring*.

For a discrete random variable a *discrete probability distribution* can be presented by a table that lists all possible values of the variable along with corresponding probabilities. The graphic presentation of a discrete probability distribution is called the *probability mass function* (PMF). A discrete probability distribution can also be described by determining the *expected value* and *variance* for the distribution.

The *binomial distribution* is a family of discrete probability distributions in which an observed number of "successes" occurs in the context of a *Bernoulli process*. In such a process

1. Only two outcomes are possible in each trial, or sampled item.
2. The series of trials represent independent events.
3. The process is stationary, with the probability of success remaining constant from trial to trial.

Every different possible combination of sample size n (number of trials) and probability of success p in the Bernoulli process has a different binomial probability distribution. Table B-2 provides binomial probability values for $n = 1$ through $n = 30$ for various values of p.

The *Poisson distribution* is appropriate as a discrete probability model when the events occur in the context of a *Poisson process*. In such a process

1. The events occur in a time or space continuum.
2. The events are independent.
3. The process is stationary.

The Poisson distribution is a family of discrete probability distributions, with a different probability distribution being associated with each different value of the mean number of events λ for a designated time or space interval. Table B-3 provides Poisson probability values for $\lambda = 0.1$ through $\lambda = 10.0$.

When the probability of success p for a binomial probability distribution is very small (or q is very small) and the sample size n is relatively large, Poisson probability values can be used as approximations of the required binomial probabilities. The rule of thumb used in this text is that such approximation is acceptable when $n \geqslant 30$ and $np < 5$ (or $nq < 5$).

FORMULAS

(5-1) $E(X) = \Sigma X P(X)$

Expected value (mean) for a discrete probability distribution.

(5-2) $V(X) = \Sigma [X - E(X)]^2 P(X)$

Deviations formula for the variance of a discrete probability distribution.

(5-3) $V(X) = \Sigma X^2 P(X) - [\Sigma X P(X)]^2$

Computational formula for the variance of a discrete probability distribution.

(5-4) $P(X|n, p) = \dfrac{n!}{X!(n-X)!} p^X q^{n-X}$

Probability of a designated number of successes in a binomial probability distribution.

(5-5) $P(X|n, p) = P(X'|n, q)$

Restating a binomial probability statement in terms of the designated number of failures; used when $p > 0.50$.

(5-6) $E(X) = np$

Expected value for a binomial probability distribution.

(5-7) $V(X) = npq$

Variance for a binomial probability distribution.

(5-8) $P(X|\lambda) = \dfrac{\lambda^X e^{-\lambda}}{X!}$

Probability of a designated number of events occurring in a Poisson probability distribution.

(5-9) $E(X) = \lambda$

Expected value for a Poisson probability distribution.

(5-10) $V(X) = \lambda$

Variance for a Poisson probability distribution.

(5-11) $\lambda = np$

Mean used with the Poisson probability distribution when this distribution is used to approximate binomial probabilities; such approximation is acceptable when $n \geqslant 30$ and $np < 5$ (or $nq < 5$).

EXERCISES

5-1 Given that 70 percent of the television viewers tuned in to a certain program also watch the sponsor's commercial, suppose that a sample of three randomly chosen viewers are interviewed regarding the commercial. Develop the probability distribution for the number who actually saw the commercial by the use of a tree diagram designating those who watched the commercial by a W and those who did not watch it by W'.

5-2 Develop the probability distribution for the situation described in Exercise 5-1 by expanding the binomial $(q + p)^n$.

5-3 Determine the probability distribution for the situation described in Exercise 5-1 by use of the table of binomial probabilities.

5-4 Determine the following probabilities by use of the table of binomial probabilities.
   (a) $P(X = 5 | n = 10, p = 0.20)$
   (b) $P(X \leqslant 3 | n = 15, p = 0.10)$
   (c) $P(X > 15 | n = 20, p = 0.30)$
   (d) $P(X = 7 | n = 15, p = 0.70)$
   (e) $P(X \geqslant 8 | n = 10, p = 0.80)$

5-5 If 60 percent of the employees in a large firm are in favor of union representation, what is the probability that fewer than half of a random sample of 20 employees will be in favor of such representation?

5-6 On the average a sale is completed with 10 percent of the potential customers contacted. Construct a tree diagram to develop the probability distribution of the number of sales completed, given that a sample of four customers are called on. Use S for a completed sale and S' for no sale.

5-7 Develop the probability distribution for the situation described in Exercise 5-6 by use of the formula for determining binomial probabilities.

5-8 Determine the probability distribution for the situation described in Exercise 5-6 by reference to the table of binomial probabilities.

5-9 Because of economic conditions, 30 percent of the accounts receivable in a large company are overdue. If an accountant takes a random sample of four accounts, determine the following probabilities by constructing a tree diagram using O for overdue and O' for not overdue.
   (a) None of the sample accounts is overdue.
   (b) Two of the sample accounts are overdue.
   (c) At least three of the sample accounts are overdue.

5-10 Determine the probabilities in Exercise 5-9 by use of the formula for determining binomial probabilities.

5-11 Determine the probabilities in Exercise 5-9 by reference to the table of binomial probabilities.

5-12 Given the probability of 0.05 that a milling machine is inoperative, construct the probability mass function illustrating the probability of various numbers of milling machines being inoperative at a randomly selected point in time. There are eight milling machines in all.

5-13 For the situation in Exercise 5-12 suppose that the production schedule is disrupted if fewer than eight milling machines are operating. What minimum number of milling machines should be installed so that the probability is at least 0.90 that at least eight machines will be operative at any particular point in time?

5-14 Determine the following probabilities by use of the table of binomial probabilities.
(a) $P(X = 0 | n = 8, p = 0.30)$
(b) $P(X = 4 | n = 10, p = 0.60)$
(c) $P(X \leqslant 5 | n = 5, p = 0.50)$
(d) $P(X < 3 | n = 6, p = 0.40)$
(e) $P(X \geqslant 7 | n = 10, p = 0.90)$

5-15 The nature of a process is such that when it is in control only 5 percent defectives are produced, while when it is out of control 20 percent defectives are produced. A random sample of 10 items includes 2 defective items.
(a) Determine the probability of obtaining this sample result given that the process is in control.
(b) Determine the probability of obtaining this sample result given that the process is out of control.
(c) Based on the sample result, is it more likely that the process is in control or out of control? $P(x \geq 8 / n = 10, p = .60) \quad P(x \leq 2 / n = 10 \quad p = .40)$

5-16 During a six-month period 60 percent of the common stocks listed on the New York Stock Exchange increased in market value and 40 percent decreased in market value or were unchanged. Of the 10 stocks that were highly recommended by a stock advisory service, 8 increased in market value during this period. What is the probability that at least 8 of 10 randomly selected stock issues would have increased in value during this period?

5-17 Determine the following probabilities by use of the table of Poisson probabilities. $\frac{10!}{8!} \frac{10.5}{2!}$
(a) $P(X = 5 | \lambda = 5.0)$ $\frac{10!}{10!8!}(.6)^8(.4)^2 + \frac{10!}{9!1!}(.6)^8(.4)^2$
(b) $P(X \geqslant 7 | \lambda = 4.0)$ $\frac{5}{10.9}$
(c) $P(X > 5 | \lambda = 2.5)$ $10 (.6)^9(.4) + \frac{5}{2!}$
(d) $P(X < 3 | \lambda = 3.0)$ $1 (.6)^{10}$
(e) $P(X \leqslant 3 | \lambda = 6.0)$ .1512

5-18 If an average of 40 service calls are required during a typical eight-hour shift in a manufacturing plant,
(a) What is the probability that more than 10 service calls will be required during a particular hour?
(b) What is the probability that no service calls will be required during a particular hour?

5-19 Determine the following probabilities by use of the table of Poisson probabilities.
(a) $P(X = 0 | \lambda = 1.0)$
(b) $P(X = 5 | \lambda = 2.0)$
(c) $P(X \geqslant 5 | \lambda = 1.5)$
(d) $P(X > 8 | \lambda = 4.0)$
(e) $P(X < 2 | \lambda = 5.0)$

5-20 On the average six people per hour use a self-service banking facility during the prime shopping hours in a department store.
(a) What is the probability that six people will use the facility during a randomly selected hour?

(b) What is the probability that fewer than five people will use the facility during a randomly selected hour?

(c) What is the probability that no one will use the facility during a 10-minute interval?

(d) What is the probability that no one will use the facility during a five-minute interval?

5-21 Suppose that the manuscript for a textbook has a total of 50 errors or mistypes included in the 500 pages of material, and the errors are distributed randomly throughout the text.

(a) What is the probability that a chapter covering 30 pages has two or more errors?

(b) What is the probability that a chapter covering 50 pages has two or more errors?

(c) What is the probability that a randomly selected page has no error?

5-22 On the average 10 trucks per day arrive at a loading dock and require a half-day to either load or unload. The arrival times are randomly distributed throughout the day. If seven loading spaces are available,

(a) What is the probability that seven loading spaces will not be sufficient to handle the trucks arriving at the dock during the first half of the working day, assuming that all docks are available at the beginning of each day?

(b) What is the probability if an additional loading space is constructed?

5-23 It is known that billing entries by new employees before internal verification and correction include a 1 percent error rate.

(a) Given a random sample of $n = 10$ billing entries completed by a new employee, what is the probability that these billings have no errors?

(b) What would be your assessment of the employee's work if 2 or more of the 10 billing entries include an error?

5-24 For the situation described in Exercise 5-23 suppose a random sample of 200 billing entries is inspected. What is the probability that the sample will include four or more entries with errors?

5-25 The percentage of items that are temporarily out of stock is 5 percent in a mail-order firm. Given that an order for eight randomly selected items is placed, what is the probability that all the items are in stock?

5-26 For the situation described in Exercise 5-25 if 80 items are randomly selected, what is the probability that two or fewer are out of stock?

THE NORMAL PROBABILITY DISTRIBUTION

6-1 CONTINUOUS PROBABILITY DISTRIBUTIONS

As explained in Section 5-1, a continuous random variable can assume any value along a scale of values. For such probability distributions one cannot list all possible values of the variable with corresponding probabilities, because there is an infinite number of different measurements that can occur for such a distribution. Instead, the general approach is to define a continuous probability distribution by a *probability density function* (PDF). This mathematical expression indicates the value of the function $f(X)$ given a value of the random variable X. When the probability density function values are plotted on a graph, the resulting curve is itself referred to as the probability density function, or more simply, as the *probability curve*.

For a function (or curve) to qualify as a probability density function it is required that

1. The density function value (height of the probability curve) can never be zero within the range of values specified by the function; that is, $f(X) > 0$.
2. The total area under the density function must be equal to 1.0.

Given a probability density function, the probability that a continuous random variable will have a value within a designated interval of values is equal to the proportion of area under the curve associated with that interval. For example,

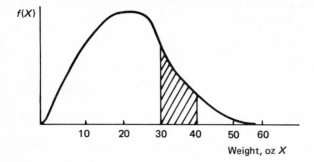

Figure 6-1 Probability density function for the weights of packages handled in a mailroom.

consider the probability curve portrayed in Figure 6-1, which represents the continuous probability distribution for the weights of packages handled in a mailroom. The probability that a randomly selected package weighs between 30 and 40 ounces is equal to the proportion of area between 30 and 40 under the density function.

Mathematically it is not possible to determine a probability value for one specific value of a continuous random variable, because there can be no area under the curve associated with a point on the horizontal axis. Thus, the probability that a randomly selected package will weigh exactly 36 ounces is 0. However, if by "exactly 36 ounces" we mean as measured to the nearest ounce, it is understood that an interval of possible values exists that extends from 35.5 to 36.5 ounces, and the probability associated with this interval *can* be determined.

In mathematics the area between two designated values for a probability density function is determined by applying the method of integration from calculus. However, several standard, continuous probability distributions serve as probability models for a variety of applications in statistical analysis, and tables of probability values have been prepared for these distributions. Therefore, it is seldom necessary for an applied statistician to determine probability values from a probability density function as such. In the following section we describe the most important continuous probability model in statistical analysis: the normal probability distribution.

6-2 THE NORMAL PROBABILITY DISTRIBUTION

The normal probability distribution is a continuous probability distribution that is both symmetrical and mesokurtic. As explained in Section 2-2, a *symmetrical distribution* is a distribution that is neither negatively nor positively skewed, but rather, each half of the distribution is a mirror-image of the other half. A *mesokurtic distribution* is a distribution that is neither flat nor peaked, in terms of the concentration of values with respect to the midpoint of the distribution. As explained in Section 3-4, for any unimodal symmetrical distribution, as is the case for the normal distribution, the mean, median, and mode are all at the same value. As indicated in Section 3-9, the measure of dispersion particularly useful in conjunction with the normal probability distribution is the standard deviation. The probability curve representing the normal probability distribution can be described as bell-shaped, as exemplified by the probability density function in Figure 6-2.

The normal probability distribution is important in statistical inference for three reasons:

1. The measurements obtained in many random processes are known to have distributions similar to this distribution.
2. Normal probabilities can often be used to approximate other probability distributions, such as the binomial and Poisson distributions. These relationships are explained and illustrated in Sections 6-3 and 6-4.
3. Distributions of certain sample statistics, such as the sample mean, are approximately normally distributed when the sample size is relatively large, regardless of the distribution of the population from which the sample was obtained. This result is called the *central-limit theorem*, which is explained further in Section 7-2.

For the normal probability distribution, the height of the probability density function, or probability curve, that corresponds with a value X of the random variable is

$$f(X) = \frac{e^{-[(X-\mu)^2/2\sigma^2]}}{\sqrt{2\pi\sigma^2}}$$ (6-1)

where π = constant 3.1416
   e = constant 2.7183
   μ = mean of the normal probability distribution
   σ = standard deviation of the distribution

You will probably be relieved to read that we shall *not* be involved in using the above density-function formula. However, one observation we can make concerning the density function for the normal probability distribution is that since π and e are constants, the normal probability distribution is different for every possible combination of the values of μ and σ. Therefore, only the values of the mean and standard deviation are required to define completely any normal probability distribution. Just as for the binomial and Poisson probability distribu-

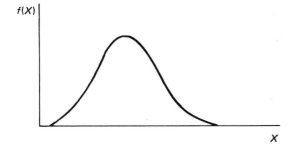

f(X)

X

Figure 6-2 General form of the normal probability distribution.

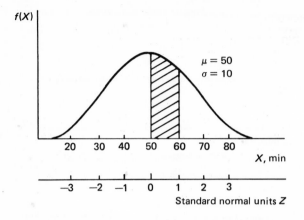

Figure 6-3 Normal probability curve portraying $P(50 \leqslant X \leqslant 60)$.

tions, the normal distribution is a whole family of distributions, all having symmetrical and mesokurtic probability curves.

Since every different combination of μ and σ results in a different normal probability distribution, tables of normal probability values are based on one particular distribution: the *standard normal distribution*. This distribution is the normal probability distribution with $\mu = 0$ and $\sigma = 1$. Any value X from a normal probability distribution can be converted into the equivalent value z for the standard normal distribution by

$$z = \frac{X - \mu}{\sigma} \tag{6-2}$$

Table B-4 indicates the areas for various intervals of values for the standard normal probability distribution, with the lower boundary of the interval always being at the mean of the distribution. Converting designated values of the normally distributed variable X into standard normal values z makes use of this table possible and thereby makes it unnecessary to use Formula (6-1) and related mathematical methods to calculate normal probabilities.

For example, suppose the time required for equipment repairs by company maintenance personnel is normally distributed with a mean of $\mu = 50$ minutes with a standard deviation of $\sigma = 10$ minutes. What is the probability that a randomly chosen piece of equipment will require between 50 and 60 minutes to repair? Figure 6-3 portrays the probability curve for this problem and also indicates the relationship between the minutes X scale and the standard normal z scale. Further, the area under the curve corresponding to the interval between 50 and 60 minutes has been shaded.

The lower boundary of the interval of interest is at the mean of the distribution and therefore is at the value $z = 0$. The upper boundary of the designated interval in terms of the z value is

$$z = \frac{X - \mu}{\sigma} = \frac{60 - 50}{10} = 1.0$$

Reference to Table B-4 shows that

$$P(0 \leqslant z \leqslant 1.0) = 0.3413$$

Therefore,

$$P(50 \leqslant X \leqslant 60) = 0.3413$$

Of course, most problems will not be concerned with intervals that have the lower boundary at the mean of the distribution. Nevertheless, Table B-4 can be used with any type of problem involving the normal probability distribution by the addition or subtraction of appropriate areas under the curve. For each problem you will usually find it useful to draw a small normal curve on which the area of interest is identified. Following are example problems.

Given a normally distributed variable with $\mu = 50$ and $\sigma = 10$, the probability that X is greater than 70, $P(X > 70)$, is represented in Figure 6-4. Note that the total proportion of area to the right of the mean of 50 in Figure 6-4 is 0.5000. Therefore, if we determine the proportion of area between the mean and 70, we can subtract this value from 0.5000 to obtain the probability that X is greater than 70. The solution is

$$z = \frac{X - \mu}{\sigma} = \frac{70 - 50}{10} = 2.0$$

$$P(X > 70) = P(z > 2.0) = 0.5000 - P(0 \leqslant X \leqslant 70) = 0.5000 - 0.4772 = 0.0228$$

Incidentally, if the required probability in the example above had been that X is greater than or *equal* to 70, $P(X \geqslant 70)$, the answer would be identical to the answer determined above. As for any continuous probability distribution, whether a particular specific value (point) is included in the interval does not change the probability associated with the interval of values. As explained in Section 6-1, the probability that a continuous random variable has one specific value is 0, because there is no area under the probability curve associated with a point on the horizontal axis. In the above example $P(X = 70) = 0$.

Given a normally distributed variable with $\mu = 50$ and $\sigma = 10$, the probability that

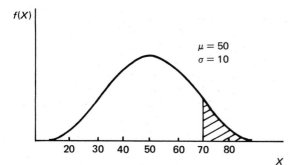

Figure 6-4 Normal probability curve portraying $P(X > 70)$.

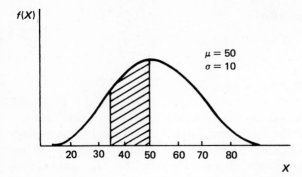

Figure 6-5 Normal probability curve portraying $P(35 \leqslant X \leqslant 50)$.

X is between 35 and 50 inclusive, $P(35 \leqslant X \leqslant 50)$, is represented in Figure 6-5. The probability is

$$z = \frac{X - \mu}{\sigma} = \frac{35 - 50}{10} = -1.5$$

$$P(35 \leqslant X \leqslant 50) = P(-1.5 \leqslant z \leqslant 0) = 0.4332$$

In this example, because the normal probability curve is symmetrical, we determine the probability in Table B-4 by reference to the equivalent positive value of z.

Given a normally distributed variable with $\mu = 50$ and $\sigma = 10$, the probability that X is between 40 and 70, $P(40 \leqslant X \leqslant 70)$, is presented in Figure 6-6. In this example two values of z have to be calculated, and then the proportion of area to the left of the mean and to the right of the mean is summed:

$$z_1 = \frac{X_1 - \mu}{\sigma} = \frac{40 - 50}{10} = -1.0$$

$$z_2 = \frac{X_2 - \mu}{\sigma} = \frac{70 - 50}{10} = 2.0$$

$$P(40 \leqslant X \leqslant 70) = P(-1.0 \leqslant z \leqslant 2.0) = P(-1.0 \leqslant z \leqslant 0) + P(0 \leqslant z \leqslant 2)$$

$$= 0.3413 + 0.4772 = 0.8185$$

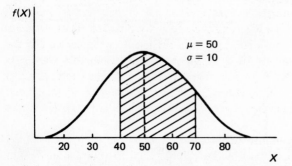

Figure 6-6 Normal probability curve portraying $P(40 \leqslant X \leqslant 70)$.

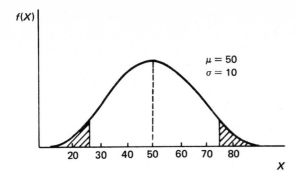

Figure 6-7 Normal probability curve portraying $P[(X < 25$ or $(X > 75)]$.

Given a normally distributed variable with $\mu = 50$ and $\sigma = 10$, the probability that X is either less than 25 or greater than 75, $P[(X < 25)$ or $(X > 75)]$, is portrayed in Figure 6-7. In this example the proportion of area in the two tails of the distribution is summed:

$$z_1 = \frac{X_1 - \mu}{\sigma} = \frac{25 - 50}{10} = -2.5$$

$$z_2 = \frac{X_2 - \mu}{\sigma} = \frac{75 - 50}{10} = 2.5$$

$$P[(X < 25) \text{ or } (X > 75)] = P[(z < -2.5) \text{ or } (z > 2.5)]$$

where
$$P(z < -2.5) = 0.5000 - P(-2.5 \leqslant z \leqslant 0) = 0.5000 - 0.4938$$
$$= 0.0062$$
$$P(z > 2.5) = 0.5000 - P(0 \leqslant z \leqslant 2.5) = 0.5000 - 0.4938$$
$$= 0.0062$$
$$P[(z < -2.5) \text{ or } (z > 2.5)] = P(z < -2.5) + P(z > 2.5)$$
$$= 0.0062 + 0.0062 = 0.0124$$

6-3 NORMAL APPROXIMATION OF BINOMIAL PROBABILITIES

When the number of observations, or trials, n in a Bernoulli process is relatively large and p is *not* small, the normal probability distribution can be used to approximate binomial probabilities. The rule of thumb in this text is that such approximation is acceptable when $n \geqslant 30$ and both $np \geqslant 5$ and $nq \geqslant 5$. Thus, neither p nor its complement q should be small. Recall that in Section 5-5 we indicated that the Poisson distribution can be used to approximate binomial probabilities when n is relatively large ($n \geqslant 30$) and $np < 5$ (or $nq < 5$). Therefore, when the sample size n in a Bernoulli process is relatively large, either the Poisson distribution or the normal distribution can be used to approximate binomial probabilities not available in the table of binomial probabilities.

Using normal curve probabilities as approximations of binomial probabilities implies that the probability mass function for the binomial distribution approaches the form of the probability density function for the normal distribution as sample size is increased. Figure 6-8 presents modified probability mass functions for the binomial probability distributions based on $n = 5$, $n = 10$, and $n = 30$, with $p = 0.50$. Each probability mass function is presented as a series of bars rather than as a series of vertical lines as in Chapter 5. The lower and upper boundaries for each bar can be thought of as the class boundaries for that outcome. Using a series of bars enhances the comparison of the binomial distribution with the normal distribution. In comparing these three figures we see that the probability mass function most similar to the normal probability distribution is the one for $n = 30$.

Because $p = 0.50$, all the binomial probability distributions portrayed in Figure 6-8 are symmetrical. With p at some other value, the binomial probability distribution based on a relatively small sample size n will not be symmetrical.

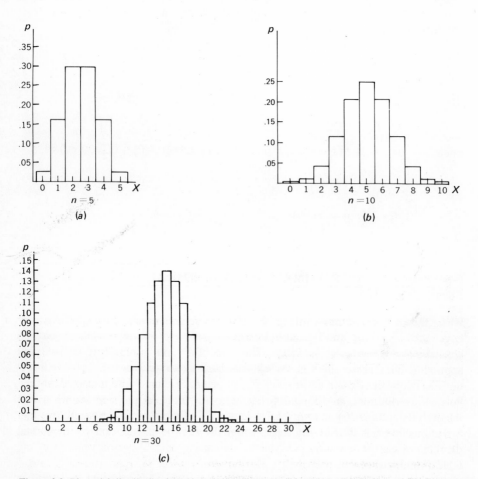

Figure 6-8 Binomial distributions with $p = 0.50$ for (a) $n = 5$, (b) $n = 10$, and (c) $n = 30$.

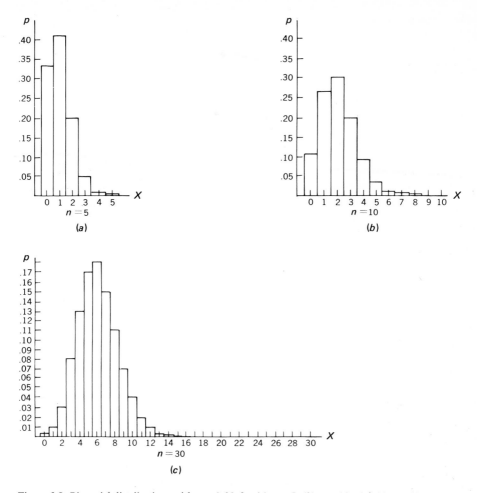

Figure 6-9 Binomial distributions with $p = 0.20$ for (a) $n = 5$, (b) $n = 10$, and (c) $n = 30$.

However, as n is increased, the probability mass function becomes approximately symmetrical and approaches the normal probability distribution in form. To illustrate this point, let us consider several binomial probability distributions for $p = 0.20$. Figure 6-9 presents the bar charts for $n = 5$, $n = 10$, and $n = 30$. While the figures for $n = 5$ and $n = 10$ portray distributions that clearly are not symmetrical, for $n = 30$ the distribution is approximately symmetrical and is similar in form to the normal probability distribution. On this general basis the normal probability distribution can be used to approximate binomial probabilities when $n \geqslant 30$, $np \geqslant 5$, and $nq \geqslant 5$.

When the normal probability distribution is used to approximate binomial probabilities, the mean and standard deviation for the normal approximation are based on the expected value and variance for the binomial distribution, as given in Section 5-3. The mean number of successes for a binomial distribution is

$$\mu = np \qquad (6\text{-}3)$$

The standard deviation of the number of successes in a binomial probability distribution is

$$\sigma = \sqrt{npq} \qquad (6\text{-}4)$$

Before we use Formulas (6-3) and (6-4) to determine normal approximation of binomial probabilities, one more matter has to be considered. When we use a normal probability value as an approximation of a binomial probability, we are substituting a continuous probability distribution for a discrete probability distribution. This substitution difference requires a *correction for continuity* in the approximation procedure, which is best explained by an example. Suppose we wish to determine the normal approximation for the binomial probability of obtaining 20 or more heads in 30 tosses of a fair coin. The pertinent binomial probability distribution is the distribution presented in Figure 6-8c. The actual binomial probability value from Table B-2 is $P(X \geqslant 20 | n = 30, \ p = 0.50) = 0.0494$. For the normal approximation we first determine the mean and standard deviation:

$$\mu = np = 30(0.50) = 15.0$$

and $\qquad\qquad \sigma = \sqrt{npq} = \sqrt{30(0.50)(0.50)} = \sqrt{7.50} = 2.74$

To determine the appropriate normal approximation, we need to interpret "20 or more" as if values on a continuous scale are represented; that is, each possible number of successes, or counts, is considered a category of measurements. From this standpoint "20 or more" is a set of outcomes that has a lower class boundary of 19.5, because this is the point that serves as the boundary between 19 successes and 20 successes. Figure 6-10 portrays the normal approximation of this binomial

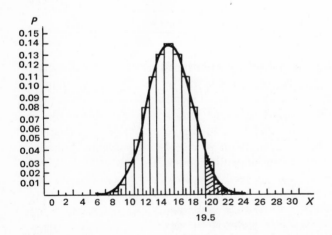

Figure 6-10 Normal approximation for the binomial probability $P(X \geqslant 20 | n = 30, \ p = 0.50)$.

probability value, including the correction for continuity. Therefore, we determine the approximation as follows:

$$P_{bin}(X \geq 20 | n = 30, p = 0.50) \approx P_{norm}(X \geq 19.5 | \mu = 15.0, \sigma = 2.74)$$

where $z = (X - \mu)/\sigma = (19.5 - 15.0)/2.74 = 4.5/2.74 = 1.64$

$$P_{norm}(X \geq 19.5 | \mu = 15.0, \sigma = 2.74) = P(z \geq 1.64) = 0.5000 - 0.4495 = 0.0505$$

In the preceding example the approximation of 0.0505 differs by just 0.0011 from the actual binomial probability of 0.0494. Without the correction for continuity the approximation would not be as good. (In fact, the approximation would be 0.0344, which is off by 0.0150.)

When the normal probability distribution is used to approximate binomial probabilities, the correction for continuity will always involve either adding or subtracting 0.5 to the number of successes specified in the binomial probability statement. The logic associated with the approximation generally makes it obvious whether the 0.5 should be added or subtracted, as in our example above. However, this logic can be summarized in the following rules for applying the correction for continuity:

1. Add 0.5 to X_i when $P(X \leq X_i)$ is required.
2. Add 0.5 to X_i when $P(X > X_i)$ is required.
3. Subtract 0.5 from X_i when $P(X \geq X_i)$ is required.
4. Subtract 0.5 from X_i when $P(X < X_i)$ is required.

As another example of the use of the normal probability distribution to approximate a binomial probability, let us determine the probability that 3 or fewer components in a sample of 30 components will be defective, given that the probability of a defective component is $p = 0.20$. The pertinent binomial distribution is the distribution presented in Figure 6-9c. The actual binomial probability value from Table B-2 is $P(X \leq 3 | n = 30, p = 0.20) = 0.1227$. For the normal approximation the mean and the standard deviation are

$$\mu = np = 30(0.20) = 6.0$$

and

$$\sigma = \sqrt{npq} = \sqrt{30(0.20)(0.80)} = \sqrt{4.80} = 2.19$$

Therefore, the normal approximation of the binomial probability value is

$$P_{bin}(X \leq 3 | n = 30, p = 0.20) \approx P_{norm}(X \leq 3.5 | \mu = 6.0, \sigma = 2.19)$$

where $z = (X - \mu)/\sigma = (3.5 - 6.0)/2.19 = -2.5/2.19 = -1.14$.

$$P_{norm}(X \leq 3.5 | \mu = 6.0, \sigma = 2.19) = P(z \leq -1.14) = 0.5000 - 0.3729 = 0.1271$$

In the preceding example the difference between the actual binomial probability of 0.1227 and the normal approximation of 0.1271 is just 0.0044. Of course, in both examples above use of the normal approximation was warranted because the sample size was $n \geq 30$ (in both examples it was exactly 30), and in both examples $np \geq 5$ and $nq \geq 5$.

6-4 NORMAL APPROXIMATION OF POISSON PROBABILITIES

When the mean λ of a Poisson probability distribution is relatively large, the normal probability distribution can be used to approximate Poisson probabilities. Such approximation is generally considered to be acceptable when $\lambda \geqslant 10.0$. For this reason tabled values for Poisson probabilities typically are not given for $\lambda > 10.0$.

The mean and standard deviation used with the normal approximation are based on the expected value and variance for the number of events in the Poisson probability distribution, as identified in Section 5-4. The mean and the standard deviation of the number of events in a Poisson probability distribution are, respectively,

$$\mu = \lambda t \tag{6-5}$$

$$\sigma = \sqrt{\lambda} \tag{6-6}$$

Exactly as for the normal approximation of binomial probabilities, a *correction for continuity* should be used with the normal approximation of Poisson probabilities. Again, the logic of the probability statement will indicate whether the 0.5 correction factor should be added or subtracted, but the list of rules given in Section 6-3 applies for the normal approximation of Poisson probabilities as well.

For example, suppose we wish to determine the probability that 15 or more maintenance calls will be required on a randomly selected day, given a Poisson sampling process with an average of $\lambda = 10$ calls per day. The actual Poisson probability value from Table B-3 is $P(X \geqslant 15 | \lambda = 10.0) = 0.0835$. For the normal approximation the mean and the standard deviation are

$$\mu = \lambda = 10.0 \quad \text{and} \quad \sigma = \sqrt{\lambda} = \sqrt{10.0} = 3.16$$

Therefore, the normal approximation of the Poisson probability value is

$$P_{\text{Pois}}(X \geqslant 15 | \lambda = 10.0) \approx P_{\text{norm}}(X \geqslant 14.5 | \mu = 10.0, \sigma = 3.16)$$

where $z = (X - \mu)/\sigma = (14.5 - 10.0)/3.16 = 4.5/3.16 = 1.42$

$$P_{\text{norm}}(X \geqslant 14.5 | \mu = 10.0, \sigma = 3.16) = P(z \geqslant 1.42) = 0.5000 - 0.4222 = 0.0778$$

In this example the difference between the actual Poisson probability of 0.0835 and the normal approximation of 0.0778 is just 0.0057. Again, this type of approximation is considered to be acceptable when $\lambda \geqslant 10.0$.

6-5 SUMMARY

The probability distribution for a continuous random variable is represented by a *probability density function* (PDF). The density-function value for each possible value of the variable X is $f(X)$ and is graphically represented as a probability curve. For any continuous random variable the probability that a value within a designated

$\lambda = \lambda +$

interval of values will occur is equal to the area under the probability density function for that interval of values. The total area under a probability curve is always 1.0.

The *normal probability distribution* is the most important continuous probability model in applied statistics. It is important because

1. Many measurements are approximately normally distributed.
2. Normal probabilities are often used to approximate other probability values.
3. Certain sample statistics, such as the sample mean, are normally distributed regardless of the population distribution.

The normal distribution is a family of continuous probability distributions, with a different distribution being possible for every different combination of values of the mean μ and standard deviation σ. However, all the distributions are symmetrical and mesokurtic and can be graphically represented as bell-shaped probability curves.

Table B-4 reports probabilities for values of the *standard normal probability distribution*, for which $\mu = 0$ and $\sigma = 1.0$. Any normally distributed variable can be converted into the equivalent standard-normal value z by

$$z = \frac{X - \mu}{\sigma}$$

The normal probability distribution can be used to approximate binomial probability values when $n \geqslant 30$, $np \geqslant 5$, and $nq \geqslant 5$. This rule of thumb is based on the fact that unless p or its complement q is very small, the form of the binomial probability distribution approaches the form of the normal probability distribution as sample size is increased. Recalling (from Chapter 5) that the Poisson probability distribution can be used to approximate binomial probabilities when $n \geqslant 30$ and $np < 5$ (or $nq < 5$), it is always possible to obtain a generally acceptable approximation of binomial probabilities when the sample is relatively large ($n \geqslant 30$) and tabled values may not be available. When determining a normal approximation for a binomial probability, a *correction for continuity* should be used as a reflection of the fact that a continuous probability distribution serves as the basis for approximating a probability for a discrete random variable.

The normal probability distribution can be used to approximate Poisson probability values when $\lambda \geqslant 10.0$. As for the approximation of binomial probabilities, the correction for continuity should be used in conjunction with such approximations.

FORMULAS

(6-1) $\quad f(X) = \dfrac{e^{-[(X - \mu)^2/2\sigma^2]}}{\sqrt{2\pi\sigma^2}}$
Probability density function for the normal probability distribution.

(6-2) $\quad z = \dfrac{X - \mu}{\sigma}$
Conversion of a normal random variable X to the equivalent standard normal random variable z.

(6-3) $\mu = np$

Mean number of successes for a binomial probability distribution, used for normal approximation of a binomial probability value.

(6-4) $\sigma = \sqrt{npq}$

Standard deviation of the number of successes for a binomial probability distribution, used for normal approximation of a binomial probability value.

(6-5) $\mu = \lambda$

Mean number of events for a Poisson probability distribution, used for normal approximation of a Poisson probability value.

(6-6) $\sigma = \sqrt{\lambda}$

Standard deviation of the number of events for a Poisson probability distribution, used for normal approximation of a Poisson probability value.

EXERCISES

6-1 Determine each of the following probabilities by use of the table of areas under the normal curve.

(a) $P(90 \leqslant X \leqslant 100 | \mu = 90, \sigma = 15)$
(b) $P(X > 110 | \mu = 90, \sigma = 15)$
(c) $P(X \leqslant 60 | \mu = 90, \sigma = 15)$
(d) $P(80 \leqslant X \leqslant 110 | \mu = 90, \sigma = 15)$
(e) $P[(X < 60) \text{ or } (X > 120) | \mu = 90, \sigma = 15]$

6-2 The time required for equipment repairs carried out by company maintenance personnel follows a normal distribution with a mean of 53.0 minutes and a standard deviation of 9.0 minutes.

(a) What is the probability that a randomly chosen repair job will require less than 50 minutes?

(b) What is the probability that it will require at least one hour?

6-3 For the situation described in Exercise 6-2, suppose a member of the maintenance staff is given three randomly selected repair jobs. What is the probability that each job requires at least one hour?

6-4 A review of a large number of investment portfolios indicates that for the preceding calendar year the average return on an investment of $10,000 was $750 with a standard deviation of $150. The above return includes capital gains as well as interest and dividend payments.

(a) If the portfolio yields are approximately normally distributed, what is the probability that a portfolio selected randomly from this group has a yield of less than $500 for the year?

(b) What is the probability that the yield was at least $900?

6-5 For the situation in Exercise 6-4 three portfolios included in the group studied were recommended by the same advisory service. Based on chance alone, what is the probability associated with all three portfolios each yielding a return of $800 or more for the year?

6-6 The useful life of a certain brand of steel-belted radial tires has been found to follow a normal distribution with $\mu = 38,000$ miles and $\sigma = 3,000$ miles.

(a) What is the probability that a randomly selected tire will have a useful life of at least 35,000 miles?

(b) What is the probability that a randomly selected tire will last more than 45,000 miles?

6-7 The useful life of a certain brand of steel-belted radial tire has been found to follow a normal distribution with $\mu = 38,000$ miles and $\sigma = 3,000$ miles. A dealer orders 500 tires for resale.

(a) Approximately what number of tires will last between 40,000 and 45,000 miles?

(b) Approximately what number of tires will last 40,000 miles or more?

6-8 The useful life of a certain brand of steel-belted radial tire has been found to follow a normal distribution with $\mu = 38,000$ miles and $\sigma = 3,000$ miles. An individual buys four of these tires.

(a) What is the probability that all four tires will last at least 38,000 miles each?

(b) What is the probability that all four tires will last at least 35,000 miles each?

6-9 The performance on a nationally standardized aptitude test in a certain professional field is reported in the form of transformed values having a mean of 500 with a standard deviation of 100. Given that the scores are approximately normally distributed,

(a) What percentage of the results are between 350 and 650?

(b) Of 10,000 test results, how many would we expect to have a score of 700 or higher?

6-10 For the situation described in Exercise 6-9 suppose that the top 10 percent of the scores are regarded as being distinctly superior. What is the lowest score required to be included in this category? (*Hint:* For this kind of problem you have to use Table B-4 in the reverse of the usual direction. That is, the proportion to be included in the upper tail of the distribution is known, and on this basis the z value is obtained from the table and is then used to solve for the unknown value of X.)

6-11 The amount of time required per individual at a bank teller's window has been found to be approximately normally distributed with $\mu = 130$ seconds and $\sigma = 45$ seconds.

(a) What is the probability that a randomly selected individual will require less than 100 seconds to complete his or her transactions?

(b) What is the probability that a randomly selected individual will spend between 2.0 and 3.0 minutes at the teller's window?

6-12 The amount of time required per individual at a bank teller's window is approximately normally distributed with $\mu = 130$ seconds and $\sigma = 45$ seconds.

(a) Within what length of time do the 20 percent of individuals with simple transactions complete their business at the window?

(b) At least what length of time is required for the individuals in the top 5 percent of required time?

6-13 Newsstand sales for a weekly news magazine averaged 52,340 copies per week with a standard deviation of 2,850 copies. The distribution of sales for the weeks included in the analysis, which excluded the weeks that include major national holidays, is approximately normal. What is the probability that 5,000 or more copies will be unsold in a randomly selected week without a holiday if the publisher distributes 55,000 copies to newsstands?

6-14 For the situation described in Exercise 6-13 suppose the publisher requires a probability no larger than 0.05 that the newsstands will run out of all copies for sale. What total number of copies should the publisher distribute?

6-15 It is known that billing entries by new employees, before internal verification and correction, include a 5 percent error rate.

(a) Given a sample of 10 billing entries completed by a new employee, what should be the probability that no errors are included?

(b) What would be your interpretation of the situation if three or more errors are included in the sample of 10?

6-16 For the situation described in Exercise 6-15 suppose a sample of 200 billing entries is inspected.

(a) What is the probability that 10 or more contain an error?

(b) What is the probability that 15 or more contain an error?

6-17 If an average of three calls arrives at a switchboard during five-minute intervals, what is the probability that five or more calls will be received during a randomly chosen five-minute interval?

6-18 For the situation described in Exercise 6-17 what is the probability that fewer than 30 calls will be received at the switchboard during a randomly chosen hour?

6-19 The percentage of items that are "temporarily out of stock" is known to be 10 percent during the peak sales season in a mail-order firm. Given that an order for eight randomly selected items is placed, what is the probability that all of the items are in stock?

6-20 For the mail-order example given in Exercise 6-19 suppose 80 randomly selected items are ordered.

(a) What is the probability that all the items are in stock?

(b) What is the probability that four or fewer items are temporarily out of stock?

6-21 During the six-hour period between the morning and afternoon peaks, an average of three cars enters an automobile service station during each 15-minute interval. What is the probability that six or more cars enter the service station in a randomly selected 15-minute interval during the six-hour period?

6-22 For the situation described in Exercise 6-21 what is the probability that 80 or more cars will enter the station for service during the entire six-hour period?

SEVEN

SAMPLING DISTRIBUTIONS AND CONFIDENCE INTERVALS FOR THE POPULATION MEAN

7-1 POINT ESTIMATION

In *point estimation* a single numeric value based on sample data is used to estimate the value of a population parameter. A number of criteria can be used by mathematical statisticians to choose appropriate estimators of population parameters based on sample data. One of the most important characteristics of an estimator is that it be unbiased. An *unbiased estimator* is a sample statistic for which the expected value is equal to the parameter being estimated. In this context the *expected value* is the long-run average value of the estimator.

Table 7-1 presents the unbiased point estimators used in our coverage of statistical estimation. Each of these estimators is the sample statistic that corresponds to the parameter being estimated. For instance the sample mean $\bar{X}$ is the appropriate point estimator of the population mean μ. However, note that the formula for the sample variance includes a correction for biasedness, as indicated in Section 3-8. That is, while

Table 7-1 Frequently used unbiased point estimators

Population parameter	Estimator
Mean, μ	$\bar{X} = \dfrac{\Sigma X}{n}$
Total quantity in a population of values $N\mu$	$N\bar{X}$
Difference between the means of two populations $\mu_1 - \mu_2$	$\bar{X}_1 - \bar{X}_2$
Variance σ^2	$s^2 = \dfrac{\Sigma(X - \bar{X})^2}{n-1}$
Standard deviation σ	$s = \sqrt{s^2}$
Proportion π	$\hat{p} = \dfrac{X}{n}$
Total number included in a category of the population $N\pi$	$N\hat{p}$
Difference between the proportions included in two populations $\pi_1 - \pi_2$	$\hat{p}_1 - \hat{p}_2$

the formula for the *population* variance has N in the denominator, the formula for the sample variance has $n-1$ rather than n in the denominator. Without this difference the sample variance would be a biased estimator of the population variance, and the expected value of the estimator would be smaller than the population variance σ^2. Incidentally, although s^2 is corrected for biasedness and thus is an unbiased estimator of σ^2, its square root s is *not* thereby an unbiased estimator of σ. However, the remaining biasedness in s as an estimator of σ is minor and is generally ignored by practicing statisticians.

The two parameters whose meaning may not be entirely clear to you are "total quantity in a population" and "total number included in a category of the population." Let us give examples of these two population values. Suppose that of a population of 100 drugstores a sample of 25 stores chosen at random has an average inventory investment of $150 in a particular product. It then follows that the unbiased estimate of the population mean μ is the sample mean $\bar{X} = \$150$. Now, what is the estimate of the total value (*total quantity*) of the inventory in all 100 stores? The actual value is the number of stores in the population times the actual mean dollar value of inventory per store in the population $N\mu$. The unbiased point estimate of this unknown total value is the number of stores in the population times the sample mean, that is, $N\bar{X}$. Note that $n\bar{X}$ would be the total value of the inventory only in the sample stores. For this example the estimated total inventory value is

$$N\bar{X} = 100(\$150) = \$15,000$$

Instead of assessing the value of a product held in inventory, suppose we simply determine whether each of the drugstores in the sample of 25 stores carries the product. If 20 of 25 stores carry the product, we calculate the sample proportion by

$$\hat{p} = \frac{X}{n} \qquad (7\text{-}1)$$

where $\hat{p}$ = sample proportion (read: "p hat")
$\quad X$ = observed number of successes
$\quad n$ = sample size

We need to make several points concerning Formula (7-1) before we continue with our example. The hat symbol in statistics always indicates an estimator of a population parameter. However, the hat is often omitted when the symbol itself is understood to designate an estimator (such as for our definition of the standard deviation s). We include the hat in $\hat{p}$, however, to clearly differentiate this estimator from p as used to indicate the probability of success for a binomial probability distribution, as explained in Section 5-3.

Continuing with our example, we see that our sample proportion is $\hat{p} = X/n = 20/25 = 0.80$. Thus, the unbiased point estimate of the proportion of the population of 100 drugstores that carry the product is $p = 0.80$. Now, what is the estimate of the total number of drugstores that carry the product in the population of 100 stores? Where the total number is the number of stores in the population times the true (population) proportion $N\pi$, the unbiased point estimate of this total number is $N\hat{p}$. Thus, for this example the estimated total number of drugstores that carry the product is

$$N\hat{p} = 100(0.80) = 80$$

7-2 SAMPLING DISTRIBUTION OF THE MEAN

In Chapter 6 the normal probability distribution was used to determine probabilities for normally distributed individual measurements, given the mean and the standard deviation of the distribution. Symbolically, the variable was the measurement X, with population mean μ and population standard deviation σ. In contrast to such distributions of individual measurements a *sampling distribution* is a probability distribution for the possible values of a *sample statistic*, such as the sample mean. Thus, the *sampling distribution of the mean* is the probability distribution for the possible values of the sample mean $\bar{X}$, given the mean of the population μ, the population standard deviation σ, and the size of the random sample n.

Note that the sampling distribution of the mean is *not* the *sample distribution*, which is the distribution of the measured values X in the random sample. Rather, the sampling distribution of the mean is the probability distribution for $\bar{X}$, the sample *mean*. In this regard a sampling distribution of the mean generally is not determined by collecting a large number of sample mean values. Typically, a single random sample of some size n has been collected and only a single sample mean $\bar{X}$ will be determined. But the use of this sample mean in statistical estimation (covered in this chapter) and in hypothesis testing (covered in Chapter 9) is based on the use of the sampling distribution of the mean.

For any given sample size n taken from a population with mean μ and standard deviation σ, the value of the sample mean $\bar{X}$ would vary from sample to sample if several separate random samples were obtained from the population. This variability serves as the basis for the sampling distribution. The sampling distribution of the mean is described by determining the expected value $E(\bar{X})$, or mean, of the sampling distribution of the mean, and the standard deviation of the mean $\sigma_{\bar{X}}$. Because this standard deviation indicates the accuracy of the sample mean as an unbiased point estimator of the population mean μ, this standard deviation of the mean $\sigma_{\bar{X}}$ is called the *standard error of the mean*. Therefore, the term *standard error* will always serve to indicate that the standard deviation is for a sampling distribution of a sample statistic, such as the sample mean. Mathematically, the expected value of the mean $E(\bar{X})$ and the standard error of the mean $\sigma_{\bar{X}}$ are defined, respectively by

$$E(\bar{X}) = \mu \tag{7-2}$$

and
$$\sigma_{\bar{X}} = \frac{\sigma}{\sqrt{n}} \tag{7-3}$$

Thus, the mean of the sampling distribution of the mean, as a probability distribution, is in fact equal to the population mean. The standard error of the distribution is equal to the population standard deviation σ divided by the square root of the sample size n. One implication of the formula for the standard error of the mean is that this value would always be smaller than the population standard deviation σ (given that $n > 1$). We would intuitively expect this implication since several sample means would tend to be closer to one another in value than would several randomly selected individual measurements. Further, the larger the common sample size n for each sample mean, the closer would the sample means tend to be to one another in value, thus resulting in a smaller value for the standard error of the mean $\sigma_{\bar{X}}$.

As an example of a sampling distribution of the mean, suppose the mean of a large population of measurements is $\mu = 100.0$ and the population standard deviation is $\sigma = 15.0$. For a sample of size $n = 36$ the expected value and standard error for the sampling distribution are, respectively,

$$E(\bar{X}) = \mu = 100.0$$

and
$$\sigma_{\bar{X}} = \frac{\sigma}{\sqrt{n}} = \frac{15.0}{\sqrt{36}} = \frac{15.0}{6} = 2.5$$

When a sample mean is based on a random sample taken from a population that is finite, a *finite correction factor* is required in conjunction with Formula (7-3) for the standard error of the mean. However, the correction is negligible if the sample is but a small portion of the total population of items. The rule of thumb we use is that the finite correction factor may be omitted when the sample size is less than 5 percent of the population size, that is, when $n < 0.05N$. The formula for the standard error of the mean that includes the finite correction factor is

$$\sigma_{\bar{X}} = \frac{\sigma}{\sqrt{n}} \sqrt{\frac{N-n}{N-1}} \qquad (7\text{-}4)$$

If the standard deviation σ is not known, the standard error of the mean can be estimated by using the sample standard deviation s in place of σ in the standard formula. Recall that the formula for the sample standard deviation includes a correction factor specifically so that this sample statistic s can be used as an estimator of the population standard deviation σ. To differentiate the estimated standard error of the mean based on use of the sample standard deviation from one based on a known σ, we designate the estimated standard error by the symbol $s_{\bar{X}}$ in this text. The basic formula for the estimated standard error of the mean is

$$s_{\bar{X}} = \frac{s}{\sqrt{n}} \qquad (7\text{-}5)$$

The formula for the estimated standard error of the mean that includes the finite correction factor is

$$s_{\bar{X}} = \frac{s}{\sqrt{n}} \sqrt{\frac{N-n}{N-1}} \qquad (7\text{-}6)$$

As an example of using the sample standard deviation to estimate the value of the standard error of the mean, suppose an auditor takes a random sample of size $n = 15$ accounts from a population of 200 accounts receivable. The standard deviation of the distribution of the receivable amounts for the entire population of 200 accounts is not known. However, the standard deviation of the sample is $s = \$63.00$. Note that because the sample size is more than 5 percent of the population size [i.e., $15 > 0.05(200)$] the finite correction factor is required in estimating the standard error of the mean. The standard error is

$$s_{\bar{X}} = \frac{s}{\sqrt{n}} \sqrt{\frac{N-n}{N-1}} = \frac{63.00}{\sqrt{15}} \sqrt{\frac{200-15}{200-1}} = 16.27\sqrt{.9296} = 16.27(.9642) = \$15.69$$

Having considered how the standard error of the mean is calculated or estimated, we now turn our attention to the importance of this standard error in statistical inference. As we shall demonstrate in both this chapter and the chapters that follow, the standard error of the mean provides the principal basis for statistical inference for an unknown population mean. The standard error of the mean is of course a standard-deviation value. Now, as you are aware from Chapter 6 on the normal probability distribution, the standard deviation is the measure of dispersion that is particularly useful when the variable of concern is normally distributed. Therefore, it follows that the standard error of the mean is particularly useful when the sampling distribution of the mean is approximately a normal distribution. Along these lines it is in fact true that when a population is normally distributed, the sampling distribution of the mean based on any sample size taken from that population will also be normally distributed. Figure 7-1 portrays a normally distributed population of values and three sampling distributions of the mean based on $n = 2$, $n = 5$, and $n = 30$, respectively. As the sample size is increased, the standard error of the mean becomes smaller, and thus the distribution becomes narrower with respect to the fixed scale of values on the horizontal axis. However, statistically speaking all the distributions in Figure 7-1 are both symmetrical and mesokurtic and are thus normal distributions.

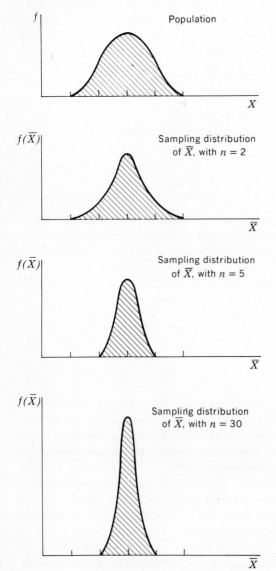

Figure 7-1 A normally distributed population of values and associated sampling distributions of the mean.

Although the sampling distribution of the mean will be normally distributed when the sampled population is normally distributed, many data populations of interest in business and economics are *not* normally distributed. However, a theorem in statistics that results in a wide applicability of the standard error of the mean is the central-limit theorem:

Central-limit theorem As the sample size is increased, the sampling distribution of the mean approaches the normal distribution in form, regardless of the form of the population distribution.

For practical purposes the sampling distribution of the mean can be assumed to be approximately normal, regardless of the population distribution whenever the sample size is $n \geqslant 30$. For this reason a sample of size $n \geqslant 30$ is generally considered to be a *large sample* in statistical inference, whereas a sample of $n < 30$ is considered to be a *small sample*. Because the central-limit theorem makes it possible to use the normal probability distribution in a wide variety of decision problems involving an unknown population mean, it is perhaps the most important theorem in applied statistics.

As an illustration of the implications of the central-limit theorem, consider the population of values and the associated sampling distributions of the mean portrayed in Figure 7-2. In this example the population distribution is rectangular and is clearly not normally distributed. Yet, by the time the sample size is $n = 30$ the sampling distribution *does* approximate the normal distribution in form. Therefore for the sampling distribution based on $n = 30$ in Figure 7-2, the standard error of the mean can be used in conjunction with the normal distribution to determine the probabilities of various values occurring for the sample mean.

In using the normal probability distribution in conjunction with the sampling distribution of the mean, we first convert the value of the sample mean $\bar{X}$ of interest into a value z on the standard normal distribution. If the population standard deviation σ is known, the standard error of the mean $\sigma_{\bar{X}}$ is the measure of dispersion for the sampling distribution, and the value of $\bar{X}$ is converted into z by

$$z = \frac{\bar{X} - \mu}{\sigma_{\bar{X}}} \qquad (7\text{-}7)$$

In Formula (7-7) note that μ is designated as the mean of the sampling distribution of the mean because $E(\bar{X}) = \mu$, as indicated in Formula (7-2). Further, note that the divisor in Formula (7-7) is the standard error of the mean $(\sigma_{\bar{X}})$ because this measure of dispersion is appropriate for the sampling distribution of the mean. In Chapter 6, Formula (6-2) for converting a value of the random variable X into the standard normal value z involved division by σ because this measure of dispersion is appropriate for a population of *individual* values.

As an example of using the normal probability distribution with a sampling distribution of the mean, an auditor takes a random sample of $n = 50$ accounts from a large population of accounts receivable in a firm. The standard deviation of the population of such accounts is known to be $\sigma = \$45.00$. If the true mean value

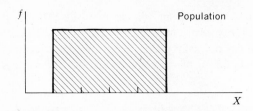

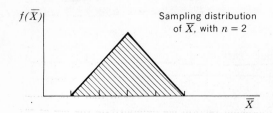

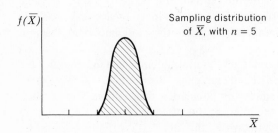

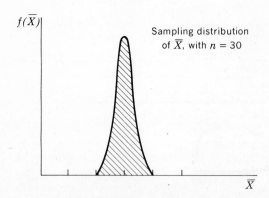

Figure 7-2 A population with a rectangular distribution of values and associated sampling distributions of the mean.

of all of the accounts receivable for the population is $\mu = \$200.00$, what is the probability that the sample mean will be less than or equal to $\$190.00$? First we determine the expected value (mean) of the sampling distribution and the standard error of the mean:

$$E(\bar{X}) = \mu = \$200.00$$

$$\sigma_{\bar{X}} = \frac{\sigma}{\sqrt{n}} = \frac{45.00}{\sqrt{50}} = \$6.36$$

Then
$$z = \frac{\bar{X} - \mu}{\sigma_{\bar{X}}} = \frac{190 - 200}{6.36} = \frac{-10}{6.36} = -1.57$$

$$P(\bar{X} \leqslant 190 | \mu = 200.00, \sigma_{\bar{X}} = 6.36) = P(z \leqslant -1.57) = 0.5000 - 0.4418$$

$$= 0.0582 \approx 0.06$$

In concluding this section on the sampling distribution of the mean, we have observed that the central-limit theorem justifies the use of the normal distribution with such sampling distributions when the sample is "large" ($n \geqslant 30$), regardless of the distribution of the population values. If the population is normally distributed, the normal probability distribution can be used in conjunction with sampling distributions of the mean for small samples ($n < 30$) as well. However, for the normal probability distribution to be used for small samples σ must be known and not estimated by the sample standard deviation s. The requirement that σ be known is explained in Section 7-5. In the following section we demonstrate the use of the standard error of the mean and the concept of the sampling distribution of the mean to estimate an unknown population mean with confidence intervals.

7-3 CONFIDENCE INTERVALS FOR THE MEAN USING THE NORMAL DISTRIBUTION

The methods of interval estimation in this section are based on the assumption that the normal probability distribution can be used with the sampling distribution of the mean. As indicated in Section 7-2, this assumption is warranted

1. When $n \geqslant 30$, because of the central-limit theorem
2. When $n < 30$, but the population is normally distributed and σ is known

Although the single value of a sample mean is useful as an unbiased point estimator of the population mean, as explained in Section 7-1, there is no way of expressing the degree of accuracy of a point estimator. Because a point estimator is on a continuous scale of measurement, the probability that a point estimator of the population mean will be *exactly* correct is $P = 0$. As explained in Section 6-1, a precise point value occupies no area under the probability density function for that variable. As contrasted with a point estimate, a *confidence interval* for the mean is an estimation interval for the population mean in respect to which a measure of accuracy for the interval can be determined. The *degree of confidence* for a confidence interval indicates the percentage of such intervals (in the long run) that include the true value of the parameter being estimated.

A confidence interval for estimating the value of the population mean μ is constructed with the unbiased estimator $\bar{X}$ positioned at the center of the estimation interval. When use of the normal probability distribution is warranted, the confidence interval for estimating the population mean is determined by one of the two following general formulas, depending on whether σ is known (and thus $\sigma_{\bar{X}}$

has been determined) or σ is unknown (and thus the standard error of the mean is estimated by $s_{\bar{X}}$):

$$\text{Conf. int. for } \mu = \bar{X} \pm z\sigma_{\bar{X}} \qquad (7\text{-}8)$$

or $$\text{Conf. int. for } \mu = \bar{X} \pm zs_{\bar{X}} \qquad (7\text{-}9)$$

The value of z used in either Formula (7-8) or (7-9) designates the proportion of area under the normal probability distribution and thus the degree of confidence associated with the estimation interval. The most frequently used confidence intervals are the 90 percent, 95 percent, and 99 percent confidence intervals. The values of z to be used in Formula (7-8) or (7-9) to define such intervals are given in Table 7-2.

We can verify the accuracy of the z values given in Table 7-2 by reference to Table B-4 for the standard normal distribution. For example, if we look up the area associated with a z value of 1.96, the area given in the table is 0.4750. This is the proportion of the area under the curve included between μ and $\mu + 1.96\sigma$ (or in the sampling distribution of the mean, between μ and $\mu + 1.96\sigma_{\bar{X}}$). Because the normal probability distribution is symmetrical, the area included in the interval $\mu \pm 1.96\sigma$ is two times the area to the right of the mean. Therefore, the area under the probability curve associated with the interval $\mu \pm 1.96\sigma_{\bar{X}}$ for the sampling distribution is $2 \times 0.4750 = 0.9500$.

But what we have thus far demonstrated is that the interval $\mu \pm 1.96\sigma_{\bar{X}}$, with the *population mean* μ at the center of the interval, will include 95 percent of the sample means within this interval in the long run. What we now need to demonstrate is why we can consider an interval such as $\bar{X} \pm 1.96\sigma_{\bar{X}}$, with the *sample mean* $\bar{X}$ at the center of the interval, as being a 95 percent confidence interval. Consider Figure 7-3, which portrays the values of the means of several random samples taken from the same population. As indicated in Figure 7-3, the values of the several sample means tend to cluster symmetrically in respect to the values of the several sample means tend to cluster symmetrically with respect to the would expect 95 percent of the sample means to be within the limits $\mu \pm 1.96\sigma_{\bar{X}}$, designated by the dashed lines in Figure 7-3.

Now consider Figure 7-4. This figure is the same as Figure 7-3, except now we have designated the 95 percent confidence intervals that would be defined based on each of the eight sample means. Of course, in any given sampling study we would typically have only one sample mean and therefore only one confidence interval.

Table 7-2 Selected areas under a normally distributed sampling distribution of the mean

Value of z	Area in the interval $\mu \pm z\sigma_{\bar{X}}$
1.65	0.90
1.96	0.95
2.58	0.99

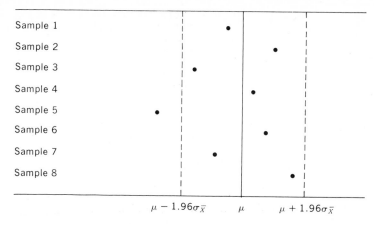

Figure 7-3 Values of several sample means in relation to the population mean.

Nevertheless, in Figure 7-4 notice that most of the confidence intervals overlap the value of the population mean μ and therefore include this value within the limits of the defined confidence interval. But one confidence interval (for sample 5) does not include the value of the population mean within the limits of the confidence interval. Further, note that the sample mean for sample 5 is outside of the interval $\mu \pm 1.96\sigma_{\bar{X}}$ represented by the dashed lines. Therefore, because 95 percent of the sample means (in the long run) lie within the limits of $\mu \pm 1.96\sigma_{\bar{X}}$, it follows that the confidence interval $\bar{X} \pm 1.96\sigma_{\bar{X}}$ includes the population mean within the limits of the confidence interval 95 percent of the time, in the long run. It is precisely on this basis that such an estimation interval is designated the 95 percent confidence interval, and the limits that define such an interval are called *confidence limits*.

Having presented the logical foundation for defining confidence intervals for the mean, let us now give an example of defining such an interval. Suppose that 50

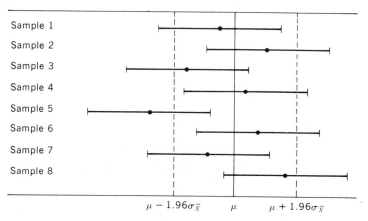

Figure 7-4 Ninety-five percent confidence intervals for several sample means taken from the same population.

hourly employees are randomly selected in a firm employing 800 hourly employees, and we find that the average weekly wage for the sample of employees is $\bar{X} = \$245.60$ with the sample standard deviation $s = \$26.45$. We cannot assume that the weekly wages are normally distributed. If we wish to define the 95 percent confidence interval for estimating the population mean, we note that because $n \geqslant 30$, use of the normal distribution is warranted. We also note that use of the finite correction factor is required in estimating the value of the standard error of the mean, because $n > 0.05N$. Therefore the 95 percent confidence interval for the mean is determined as follows:

$$95\% \text{ conf. int.} = \bar{X} \pm z s_{\bar{X}}$$

where $\bar{X} = \$245.60$

$\quad s_{\bar{X}} = s/\sqrt{n}\sqrt{(N-n)/(N-1)} = 26.45/\sqrt{50}\sqrt{(800-50)/(800-1)}$

$\quad\quad = 3.74(0.969) = \$3.62$

$\quad z = 1.96$

$\bar{X} \pm z s_{\bar{X}} = 245.60 \pm 1.96(3.62) = 245.60 \pm 7.10 = \$238.50 \text{ to } \$252.70$

Thus, with 95 percent confidence we can state that the mean weekly wage for all 800 hourly employees is between $238.50 and $252.70. Suppose we wish to define a 90 percent confidence interval, instead of the 95 percent confidence interval defined above. Based on the same sample data, the 90 percent confidence interval is determined as follows:

$$90\% \text{ conf. int.} = \bar{X} \pm z s_{\bar{X}}$$

where $\bar{X} = \$245.60$

$\quad s_{\bar{X}} = \$3.62$ (calculated above)

$\quad z = 1.65$

$\bar{X} \pm z s_{\bar{X}} = 245.60 \pm 1.65(3.62) = 245.60 \pm 5.97 = \$239.63 \text{ to } \$251.57$

Note that this interval is more precise (narrower) than the 95 percent confidence. However, the "trade-off" is that we can be only 90 rather than 95 percent confident that the interval includes the value of the population mean.

7-4   DETERMINING THE REQUIRED SAMPLE SIZE

Suppose the desired size of a confidence interval for estimating the population mean and the desired degree of confidence to be associated with the interval are stipulated before a sample is collected. If the population standard deviation σ is known or can be estimated (perhaps from other studies involving similar variables), the minimum required sample size n based on use of the normal distribution can be determined by

$$n = \left(\frac{z\sigma}{E}\right)^2 \tag{7-10}$$

where z = value used for the stipulated degree of confidence

σ = standard deviation of the population (or estimate thereof)

E = plus-or-minus error factor allowed in the interval (always one-half the total confidence interval)

When Formula (7-10) is used, a fractional result is always rounded up to the next whole number because otherwise the sample would not be large enough to achieve the confidence-interval objectives. Further, unless the population is normally distributed and σ is known, any computed sample size less than 30 should be increased to 30 so that the central-limit theorem can serve as the justification for using the normal probability distribution.

The derivation of Formula (7-10) is algebraically quite simple, and based on the definition of E, is the plus-and-minus error factor allowed in the estimation interval. That is, where the general confidence interval for the mean is $\bar{X} \pm z\sigma_{\bar{X}}$,

$$E = z\sigma_{\bar{X}}$$

Continuing

$$E = z\frac{\sigma}{\sqrt{n}} \qquad E = \frac{z\sigma}{\sqrt{n}}$$

$$\sqrt{n} = \frac{z\sigma}{E} \qquad n = \left(\frac{z\sigma}{E}\right)^2$$

Note that the formula for sample size n is derived by using the formula for the standard error of the mean without any finite correction factor. If Formula (7-10) is used with a finite population, the sample size obtained is in fact larger than the minimum required sample size.

As an example of applying the formula for sample size suppose an economist wishes to estimate the average weekly earnings per employed worker in a large metropolitan area. The economist stipulates that a 99 percent confidence interval should be defined and that the interval estimate should be within ±$5.00 of the true (population) mean at this degree of confidence. Based on studies in other similar metropolitan areas, the standard deviation of weekly earnings is estimated as σ_{est} = $30.00. From this information the required sample size is

$$n = \left(\frac{z\sigma}{E}\right)^2 = \left[\frac{(2.58)(30.00)}{5.00}\right]^2 = 15.48^2 = 239.63 = 240$$

If the economist is satisfied with an estimate within $10.00 of the true mean and with 95 percent confidence, the required sample size is

$$n = \left(\frac{z\sigma}{E}\right)^2 = \left[\frac{(1.96)(30.00)}{10.00}\right]^2 = 5.88^2 = 34.57 = 35$$

7-5   USE OF STUDENT'S t DISTRIBUTION

In Section 7-3 we indicated that use of the normal distribution for defining confidence intervals for the population mean is appropriate for any large sample ($n \geqslant 30$) because of the central-limit theorem and is appropriate for a small sample ($n < 30$) only if the population is normally distributed and the population standard deviation σ is known. In this section we consider the situation in which the sample is small and the population is normally distributed, but σ is not known.

Regardless of the sample size or whether the population standard deviation σ is known, if a population is normally distributed, the sampling distribution of the mean associated with a sample of any size will also be normally distributed. However, in the process of inference the observed sample mean is converted into a standard value, and *herein lies the problem.* If σ is unknown, the conversion formula is

$$\text{Standard value} = \frac{\bar{X} - \mu}{s_{\bar{X}}}$$

In the conversion formula just given, assuming that the sampling distribution of the mean is normal, subtracting a constant from every sample mean and dividing by a constant would also result in a normally distributed variable. But in the conversion formula, the divisor is *not* in fact a constant because the value of $s_{\bar{X}}$ will vary according to each sample standard deviation s. Therefore, unlike the standard formula, Formula (7-7), in which the divisor is the constant $\sigma_{\bar{X}}$, the conversion does *not* result in the standard normal variable z. Instead, the converted value has a platykurtic (flat) distribution in contrast to the normal distribution, which is mesokurtic (neither peaked nor flat). However, like the standard normal variate z, this converted value also has a mean of zero and a symmetrical distribution. Because W. S. Gosset, who first described this distribution mathematically, published his work under the name "Student," this distribution has come to be called "Student's t distribution." Figure 7-5 portrays the general comparison between the forms of the standard normal distribution and the t distribution. Thus, the conversion formula we are considering results in a value of t being calculated as follows:

$$t = \frac{\bar{X} - \mu}{s_{\bar{X}}} \tag{7-11}$$

In contrast to the standard normal distribution, where z is one particular

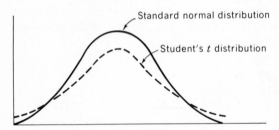

Standard normal distribution

Student's t distribution

Figure 7-5 The form of Student's t distribution compared with that of the standard normal distribution.

normal distribution with mean $\mu = 0$ and standard deviation $\sigma = 1$, the t distribution is in fact a family of distributions. A different t distribution is associated with each *degree of freedom* df. In statistical inference concerning a single random sample, such as when the sample mean is used as the basis for constructing a confidence interval for the population mean, the degrees of freedom are always equal to df $= n - 1$.

The concept of degrees of freedom is used in several areas of statistical analysis. Essentially, the number of degrees of freedom indicates the number of values that are free to vary in a random sample. In general the number of degrees of freedom lost is equal to the number of population parameters estimated as the basis for a statistical inference procedure. For example, given that the population standard deviation σ is unknown, the sample standard deviation s is calculated as an estimator of σ by using the sample mean as the estimator of μ [recall that $s = \sqrt{(X - \bar{X})^2/(n-1)}$]. Therefore, when the estimated standard error of the mean $(s_{\bar{X}} = s/\sqrt{n})$ is used in statistical inference, one degree of freedom was lost in the earlier step of computing the sample standard deviation.

As a simple example to illustrate why one degree of freedom is lost when a parameter estimate, such as the mean, serves as the basis for inference in conjunction with a random sample, suppose we have a random sample of only two measurements X_1 and X_2. If the sample mean $\bar{X}$ is identified as being equal to 7.0, then of course X_1 and X_2 can have various combinations of values such that the mean of the two values is $\bar{X} = 7.0$. But suppose we observe the value of the variable X_1 and it is $X_1 = 3$. Having observed the value of X_1, we see then that X_2 is *not* in fact free to vary because X_2 must have a value such that $\bar{X} = 7.0$ (in this example $X_2 = 11$). Thus one degree of freedom is lost with each parameter estimated on the basis of sample results.

For interval estimation, the value of t from Student's t distribution is used instead of z when such use is warranted. Again, the assumptions are a normally distributed population and σ unknown. However, for practical purposes approximate normality of the population is sufficient. Further, if the degrees of freedom are large (df $\geqslant 29$), the t distribution is close to the standard normal distribution, and values of z can be used in place of values of t. Thus, as sample size is increased, the t distribution becomes less platykurtic. Note that substitution of the standard normal values z for values of t has nothing to do with the central-limit theorem because given the assumption of a normal distribution, the sampling distribution of the mean is normal regardless of sample size. If a sample is large ($n \geqslant 30$) and σ is not known, technically the t distribution is always appropriate regardless of the form of the population distribution. With a large sample the sampling distribution of the mean will always be approximately normal, but the ratio $(\bar{X} - \mu)/s_{\bar{X}}$ is a t statistic because $s_{\bar{X}}$ is not a constant. However, it is a rather convenient coincidence that samples of approximately the same size justify use of both the normal distribution and values of z in place of values of t. Therefore, only when df < 29 do we consider it necessary to use Student's t distribution in this text.

Table B-5 presents values for Student's t distribution according to the degrees of freedom. Note that the values of t reported in this table indicate the area in the upper "tail" for this probability density function rather than the area between the mean and a designated value as in Table B-4 for the normal distribution. When using the table for interval estimation, we therefore recognize that for a 95 percent confidence interval, for example, an area of 0.025 should be left in each tail of the distribution. Therefore, the standard formula to define the confidence interval for the population mean when the population is normally distributed, σ is unknown, and df <29 (i.e., $n < 30$) is

$$\text{Conf. int. for } \mu = \bar{X} \pm t_{df} s_{\bar{X}} \qquad (7\text{-}12)$$

As an example of using Formula (7-12), suppose that in the production of size D cells for use as flashlight batteries, the mean operating life for a random sample of $n = 9$ batteries is $\bar{X} = 20.0$ hours with a sample standard deviation of $s = 3.0$ hours. Battery life is assumed to be approximately normally distributed. The 95 percent confidence interval for estimating the mean life of all size D batteries would then be

$$95\% \text{ conf. int.} = \bar{X} \pm t_{df} s_{\bar{X}}$$

where $\bar{X} = 20.0$

$t_{df} = t_{n-1} = t_8 = 2.306$

$s_{\bar{X}} = s/\sqrt{n-1} = 3.0/\sqrt{9} = 1.00$

$95\% \text{ conf. int.} = \bar{X} \pm t_{df} s_{\bar{X}} = 20.0 \pm 2.306(1.00) = 20.0 \pm 2.3 = 17.7 \text{ to } 22.3 \text{ hours}$

Similarly, the 90 percent confidence interval for estimating the population mean is

$$90\% \text{ conf. int.} = \bar{X} \pm t_{df} s_{\bar{X}}$$

where $\bar{X} = 20.0$

$t_8 = 1.860$

$s_{\bar{X}} = 1.00$

$90\% \text{ conf. int.} = \bar{X} \pm t_{df} s_{\bar{X}} = 20.0 \pm 1.860(1.00) = 20.0 \pm 1.9 = 18.1 \text{ to } 21.9 \text{ hours}$

On the other hand, suppose the sample size is in fact $n = 90$ and we wish to define the 90 percent confidence interval for estimating the population mean. Because $n \geqslant 30$, the standard normal distribution can substitute for the t distribution.

$$90\% \text{ conf. int.} = \bar{X} \pm z s_{\bar{X}} = 20.0 \pm 1.65 \left(\frac{3.0}{\sqrt{90}} \right) = 20.0 \pm 1.65(0.316) = 20.0 \pm 0.5$$

$$= 19.5 \text{ to } 20.5 \text{ hours}$$

7-6 USE OF CHEBYSHEV'S INEQUALITY

When the sample is small ($n < 30$) and the population *cannot* be assumed to be normally distributed, neither the normal probability distribution nor Student's t

distribution can be used to define a confidence interval for estimating the population mean. However, a general theorem developed by the Russian mathematician Chebyshev is useful:

Chebyshev's theorem The proportion of measurements in a set of data that lies within k standard deviations of the mean is not less than $1 - 1/k^2$, where $k \geqslant 1$.

As applied to the sampling distribution of the mean, the probability that a sample mean will lie within k standard error units from the population mean is

$$P(|\bar{X} - \mu| \leqslant k\sigma_{\bar{x}}) \geqslant 1 - \frac{1}{k^2} \qquad (7\text{-}13)$$

Formula (7-13) is generally referred to as *Chebyshev's inequality*. Note that it is based on the assumption that σ is known, and thus $\sigma_{\bar{x}}$ appears in the formula. If $\sigma_{\bar{x}}$ cannot be calculated, the estimator $s_{\bar{x}}$ can be used in Chebyshev's inequality but with some risk because of the fluctuation of this value for small samples. In fact Chebyshev's inequality is rarely used for defining confidence intervals, mainly because such intervals are generally too wide to be of practical value in decision making. But this inequality is the only appropriate basis for defining a confidence interval for estimating the mean if the population is not normally distributed and the sample is small ($n < 30$).

In using Chebyshev's inequality to define a confidence interval for the mean, the procedure is to set $1 - 1/k^2$ equal to the desired degree of confidence, solve for k, and then define the interval using either Formula (7-14) or (7-15), according to whether the population standard deviation σ is known:

$$\text{Conf. int. for } \mu = \bar{X} \pm k\sigma_{\bar{x}} \qquad (7\text{-}14)$$

or

$$\text{Conf. int. for } \mu = \bar{X} \pm ks_{\bar{x}} \qquad (7\text{-}15)$$

As an example of applying Chebyshev's inequality, suppose the mean operating life of a random sample of $n = 9$ size D flashlight cells is $\bar{X} = 20.0$ with a sample standard deviation of $s = 3.0$ hours, as in the example in Section 7-5. Unlike the previous example using the t distribution, however, the population is not assumed to be approximately normally distributed. Specifically, because battery life is particularly affected by improper formulation of materials, we suspect the population distribution is bimodal, with one mode reflecting the lifetime of defective batteries and the other mode reflecting the lifetime of correctly formulated batteries. What is the interval of hours such that confidence is at least 95 percent that the mean for the population of size D batteries (the entire production run) is included within the interval? To use Chebyshev's inequality, we first solve for k:

$$1 - \frac{1}{k^2} = 0.95$$

$$\frac{1}{k^2} = 1 - 0.95 = 0.05$$

$$0.05k^2 = 1$$

$$\frac{1}{.05} = 20$$

$$k^2 = 20$$

$$k = \sqrt{20} = 4.472 \text{ standard-error units}$$

Then, using Formula (7-15):

$$\text{Conf. int.} = \bar{X} \pm ks_{\bar{X}} = 20.0 \pm (4.472)\frac{3.0}{\sqrt{9}} = 20.0 \pm 4.5 = 15.5 \text{ to } 24.5 \text{ hours}$$

This confidence interval is considerably wider than the 95 percent confidence interval of 17.7 to 22.3 hours based on use of the t distribution in Section 7-5. However in the interval we have just defined, note that the confidence interval is *at least* 95 percent. That is, it would be a 95 percent confidence interval for even the most adverse population distribution. The degree of confidence would be higher (but unknown) given, say, a unimodal population.

7-7 SUMMARY TABLE FOR INTERVAL ESTIMATION OF THE POPULATION MEAN

In this chapter we described the conditions under which the normal distribution, Student's t distribution, and Chebyshev's inequality can serve as the basis for defining a confidence interval for the population mean. Table 7-3 summarizes the appropriate determination of such confidence intervals.

7-8 CONFIDENCE INTERVALS FOR ESTIMATING THE TOTAL QUANTITY

As explained in Section 7-1, when the total quantity in a population can be designated by $N\mu$, the unbiased point estimate of that quantity is $N\bar{X}$. For example,

Table 7-3 Interval estimation of the population mean

Population distribution	Sample size n	σ known	σ unknown
Normal	Large ($n \geqslant 30$)	$\bar{X} \pm z\sigma_{\bar{X}}$	$\bar{X} \pm zs_{\bar{X}}$[†]
	Small ($n < 30$)	$\bar{X} \pm z\sigma_{\bar{X}}$	$\bar{X} \pm ts_{\bar{X}}$
Not normal	Large ($n \geqslant 30$)	$\bar{X} \pm z\sigma_{\bar{X}}{}^{*}$	$\bar{X} \pm zs_{\bar{X}}{}^{*,†}$
	Small ($n < 30$)	$\bar{X} \pm k\sigma_{\bar{X}}{}^{**}$	$\bar{X} \pm ks_{\bar{X}}{}^{**,§}$

[*]The central-limit theorem is invoked.
[**]The value $1 - 1/k^2$ is defined using Chebyshev's inequality.
[†]z is used as an approximation of t.
[§]Some statisticians consider this interval unreliable because of the fluctuation in the value of $s_{\bar{X}}$ for small samples.

in Section 7-1 we estimated the total value of an item held in the inventory of a population of 100 stores by observing that the mean value for a sample of $n = 25$ stores was $\bar{X} = \$150$ and then estimating the total value of this item in all 100 stores as being

$$N\bar{X} = 100(\$150) = \$15,000$$

To define a *confidence interval* for a total quantity, we first define the confidence interval for the mean and then multiply the confidence limits by the population size N. The specific formula depends on whether the normal distribution, the t distribution, or Chebyshev's inequality serves as the appropriate basis for defining the confidence interval for the mean, as summarized in Section 7-7. The general formula for defining such confidence limits is

$$\text{Conf. int. for total quant.} = N(\text{conf. limits for the mean}) \qquad (7\text{-}16)$$

Let us consider the earlier example of estimating the average weekly wages in Section 7-3. Based on a random sample of $n = 50$ employees taken from the $N = 800$ hourly employees in the firm, we determined that the 95 percent confidence interval for the population mean is defined by the interval \$238.50 to \$252.70. Therefore, the estimate of the total of the weekly wage amount paid to all 800 employees is

$$N(\text{conf. limits for the mean}) = 800(\$238.50 \text{ to } \$252.50) = \$190,800 \text{ to } \$202,000$$

Therefore, for this example we can say with a 95 percent degree of confidence that the total weekly wage payroll for this company is between \$190,800 and \$202,000.

7-9 SUMMARY

We began this chapter by considering *point estimation*, which involves the calculation of a single numeric value based on sample data in order to estimate the value of a population parameter. One of the most important criteria used by statisticians in choosing a point estimator is that it be unbiased. "Unbiased" means that the expected (long-run) value of the estimator is equal to the value of the parameter being estimated.

The concept of the *sampling distribution* provides the basis for statistical inference when sample results are analyzed. The *sampling distribution of the mean*, for example, is the probability density function that describes the distribution of the possible values of a sample mean. The expected value (mean) of this distribution is in fact equal to the population mean μ from which the sample is chosen. Because the standard deviation of this sampling distribution indicates the accuracy of the sample mean $\bar{X}$ as an unbiased estimator of the population mean μ, it is called the *standard error of the mean.*

A theorem of fundamental importance in applied statistics is the *central-limit theorem*, which states that as the sample size is increased the sampling distribution of the mean approaches the normal distribution regardless of the population distribution. This theorem makes it possible to use the normal probability distribution with the sampling distribution of the mean for a variety of populations. Because a sample size of $n \geqslant 30$ is considered large enough to invoke the central-limit theorem, a sample of $n \geqslant 30$ generally is considered to be a "large sample."

A *confidence interval* is an estimation interval for a population parameter such that a degree of confidence can be associated with the interval. The degree of confidence indicates the percentage of such intervals (in the long run), which include the true value of the parameter being estimated. In Section 7-3 we explained and illustrated the rationale by which the concept of the sampling distribution of the mean can be applied to construct confidence intervals for the population mean based on use of the normal probability distribution.

Depending on whether the population is normally distributed, whether the sample is large ($n \geqslant 30$) or small ($n < 30$), and whether the population standard deviation σ is known, either the normal distribution, Student's t distribution, or Chebyshev's inequality serves as the appropriate basis for defining a confidence interval for the mean. Table 7-3 in Section 7-7 of this chapter is a summary table for determining the basis for such interval estimation.

Just as the concept of the sampling distribution of the mean has served as the basis for defining confidence intervals for the population mean in this chapter, so will the sampling distributions for other sample statistics serve as the basis for defining confidence intervals for other population parameters in Chapter 8. Further, the concept of the sampling distribution also serves as the basis for the method of statistical inference called *hypothesis testing*, which is introduced in Chapter 9.

FORMULAS

(7-1) $\hat{p} = \dfrac{X}{n}$

Sample proportion.

(7-2) $E(\bar{X}) = \mu$

Expected value (mean) of the sampling distribution of the mean.

(7-3) $\sigma_{\bar{X}} = \dfrac{\sigma}{\sqrt{n}}$

Standard error of the mean, which is the standard deviation of the sampling distribution of the mean.

(7-4) $\sigma_{\bar{X}} = \dfrac{\sigma}{\sqrt{n}} \sqrt{\dfrac{N-n}{N-1}}$

Standard error of the mean for a sample taken from a finite population; the finite correction factor may be omitted if $n < 0.05N$.

(7-5) $s_{\bar{X}} = \dfrac{s}{\sqrt{n}}$

Estimated value of the standard error of the mean when the population standard deviation σ is not known.

$$(7\text{-}6) \quad s_{\bar{X}} = \frac{s}{\sqrt{n}} \sqrt{\frac{N-n}{N-1}}$$

Estimated value of the standard error of the mean for a finite population; the finite correction factor may be omitted if $n < 0.05N$.

$$(7\text{-}7) \quad z = \frac{\bar{X} - \mu}{\sigma_{\bar{X}}}$$

Conversion of the value of a sample mean $\bar{X}$ into the equivalent value of z on the standard normal distribution, applicable when the population is normally distributed or when $n \geq 30$ (central-limit theorem).

$$(7\text{-}8) \quad \text{Conf. int. for } \mu = \bar{X} \pm z\sigma_{\bar{X}}$$

Confidence interval for the population mean based on use of the normal distribution when the population standard deviation σ is known.

$$(7\text{-}9) \quad \text{Conf. int. for } \mu = \bar{X} \pm zs_{\bar{X}}$$

Confidence interval for the population mean based on use of the normal distribution when the population standard deviation σ is not known but $n \geq 30$.

$$(7\text{-}10) \quad n = \left(\frac{z\sigma}{E}\right)^2$$

Minimum required sample size for defining a confidence interval at a stipulated degree of confidence and with a stipulated size (error factor), based on use of the normal distribution.

$$(7\text{-}11) \quad t = \frac{\bar{X} - \mu}{s_{\bar{X}}}$$

Conversion of the value of a sample mean $\bar{X}$ into the equivalent value of t on Student's t distribution, applicable when the population is approximately normally distributed and σ is unknown.

$$(7\text{-}12) \quad \text{Conf. int. for } \mu = \bar{X} \pm t_{\text{df}}s_{\bar{X}}$$

Confidence interval for the population mean based on use of Student's t distribution, appropriate when the population is approximately normally distributed and σ is unknown; values of z can be used to approximate values of t when df ≥ 29 (i.e., $n \geq 30$).

(7-13) $P(|\bar{X} - \mu| \leqslant k\sigma_{\bar{X}}) \geqslant 1 - \dfrac{1}{k^2}$

Chebyshev's inequality, which indicates the minimum probability that the value of a sample mean will be within k standard-error units of the population mean regardless of the sampling distribution of the mean, applicable when the population is not normally distributed and the sample is small $(n < 30)$.

(7-14) Conf. int. for $\mu = \bar{X} \pm k\sigma_{\bar{X}}$

Confidence interval for the population mean based on use of Chebyshev's inequality, appropriate when the population is not normally distributed, the sample is small $(n < 30)$, and σ is known.

(7-15) Conf. int. for $\mu = \bar{X} \pm ks_{\bar{X}}$

Confidence interval for the population mean based on use of Chebyshev's inequality, appropriate when the population is not normally distributed, the sample is small $(n < 30)$, and σ is unknown.

(7-16) Conf. int. for total quant.

$= N(\text{conf. limits for the mean})$

Confidence interval for estimating the total quantity in a population.

EXERCISES

7-1 In a facility manufacturing television picture tubes suppose it is known that the average (mean) operating life of the tubes is 10,000 hours with a standard deviation of 300 hours.

(*a*) For samples of 36 television tubes each what is the standard error of the sampling distribution of the mean?

(*b*) Interpret the meaning of the value that you have computed.

7-2 For the situation in Exercise 7-1 suppose we have no information about the population parameters. However, for one sample size of 36 television tubes we obtain a mean operating life of 9,800 hours with a sample standard deviation of 320 hours. On the basis of the sample results,

(*a*) Estimate the value of the population mean.

(*b*) Estimate the value of the standard error of the mean.

7-3 For a random sample of 25 stock issues taken from a listing of 257 over-the-counter issues, the market price has advanced by an average (mean) of $3.00 per share during a fiscal quarter with a standard deviation of 50 cents

(*a*) What is the best (point) estimate of the mean price change for all 257 stock issues?

(*b*) For a sample of size 25 what is the estimated value of the standard error of the mean?

7-4 Assuming the sample in Exercise 7-3 was taken from a large number of over-the-counter issues,

(a) What is the best (point) estimate of the mean price change for all stock issues?

(b) For a sample of size 25 what is the estimated value of the standard error of the mean?

(c) Indicate the implications of any differences in the numerical results between the answers to Exercise 7-3a and 7-3b and Exercise 7-4a and 7-4b.

7-5 It is known that the variance of the amounts in a large number of accounts receivable is $225. If a sample of 25 accounts is taken, determine the value of the standard error of the mean to be used in interpreting the sample results.

7-6 Suppose the sample in Exercise 7-5 is 200 accounts receivable. Determine the value of the standard error of the mean and compare it with the value computed in Exercise 7-5.

7-7 A simple random sample of 50 ball bearings taken from a large number being manufactured has a mean weight of 1.5 ounces per bearing with a standard deviation of 0.1 ounce.

(a) What is the best estimate of the average per-bearing weight of all bearings being manufactured?

(b) Estimate the value of the standard error of the mean.

7-8 Suppose that the 50 sampled bearings in Exercise 7-7 are taken from a particular production run that includes just 150 bearings as the total population.

(a) What is the best estimate of the average per-bearing weight for the 150 bearings?

(b) Estimate the value of the standard error of the mean and compare it with your answer in Exercise 7-7b.

7-9 The mean dollar value of the sales amounts per retail outlet handling a particular consumer product last year is known to be $\mu = \$3,400$ with a standard deviation of $\sigma = \$200$. If a large number of outlets handle the product, determine the standard error of the mean for a sample of size $n = 25$.

7-10 For the sampling situation in Exercise 7-9 suppose only 100 retail outlets handle the product.

(a) Determine the standard error of the mean for the sample of $n = 25$.

(b) Compare your answer with the answer to Exercise 7-9.

7-11 A marketing research analyst collects data for a random sample of 100 customers of the 500 who purchased a particular "coupon special." The 100 people in the sample spent an average (mean) of $27.00 in the store with a standard deviation of $8.00, and 70 percent of the customers in the sample made at least one other purchase in addition to the coupon special. Based on these results, identify the best single estimate for each of the following parameter values.

(a) Mean purchase amount by all 500 customers who purchased the coupon special.

(b) The standard deviation of the distribution of purchase amounts by the 500 customers.

(c) Total amount of purchases by the 500 customers.

(d) The number of customers of the 500 who made at least one other purchase in addition to the coupon special.

7-12 In a department store an auditor finds that 49 randomly chosen charge accounts of a total of 3,000 such accounts have a mean debit balance of $53.00 with a standard deviation of $14.00.

(a) Estimate the mean account balance of all charge accounts, using 90 percent confidence limits.

(b) Estimate the mean balance of all accounts, using 95 percent confidence limits.

(c) Estimate the mean balance of all accounts, using 99 percent confidence limits.

(d) Which one of the three estimates do you consider to be most useful? Why?

7-13 For the data of Exercise 7-12

(a) Estimate the total balance due for all 3,000 charge accounts, using 90 percent confidence limits

(b) Estimate the total balance due for all 3,000 charge accounts, using 95 percent confidence limits

(c) Estimate the total balance due for all 3,000 charge accounts, using 99 percent confidence limits

7-14 For the data in Exercise 7-11

(a) Determine the 95 percent confidence intervals for estimating the mean purchase amount for all 500 customers.

(b) Determine the 95 percent confidence interval for the total purchase amount for all 500 customers.

7-15 A random sample of 50 firms taken from an industry with 1,200 firms has an average (mean) number of employees of 77.5 with a standard deviation of 20 employees.

(a) Estimate the average number of employees per firm in the entire industry, using 90 percent confidence limits.

(b) Estimate the average number of employees per firm in the entire industry, using 95 percent confidence limits.

(c) Estimate the average number of employees per firm in the entire industry, using 99 percent confidence limits.

7-16 Using the data of Exercise 7-15 estimate the total number of employees working in this industry, using 95 percent confidence limits.

7-17 The mean diameter of a sample of $n = 100$ rods in a shipment is 2.350 centimeters, with a standard deviation of 0.050 centimeter. Estimate the mean diameter of all rods included in the shipment if the shipment contains 500 rods, using a 99 percent confidence interval.

7-18 For the shipment of rods described in Exercise 7-17 the mean weight per rod for the sample of 100 rods is 84.50 grams with a standard deviation of 2.50 grams. Estimate the total weight of the entire shipment (exclusive of packing materials), using a 99 percent confidence interval.

7-19 As purchasing agent for a large company, you arrange to obtain a random sample of 49 General Electric 100-watt fluorescent bulbs and to have these installed in certain work areas that include unusual (excessive) temperature conditions. Later follow-up indicates that the mean bulb life is 650 hours with a standard deviation of 50 hours.

(a) What is the best point estimate of mean bulb life of all General Electric 100-watt fluorescent bulbs when subjected to the excessive temperature conditions?

(b) What is the standard error of the sampling distribution of the mean? Describe what this value signifies.

(c) Determine the lower and upper limits for the 80 percent confidence interval for estimating the value of the population mean.

7-20 An alumni association contacts a sample of 300 members of the class of 1970 and obtains information regarding their current income status. There were 1,000 graduates in 1970. The average annual income for the sample of 300 is $20,000 with a standard deviation of $3,500.

(a) What kind of information would you need to have about the sample and the way the information was obtained before you would proceed to use statistical estimation with these sample data?

(b) Assuming that the requirements associated with statistical inference are satisfied, determine the 95 percent confidence interval for estimating the mean annual income for members of the class of 1970.

7-21 In a small firm employing 100 people a random sample of 25 employees earn an average hourly wage of $6.75 with a standard deviation of 25 cents. Estimate the average hourly wage of all 100 employees to the nearest cent, using 95 percent confidence limits. The wages are assumed to be approximately normally distributed.

7-22 Referring to Exercise 7-21, suppose the wages cannot be assumed to be normally distributed. What is the confidence interval such that there is at least 95 percent confidence that the average hourly wage is within this interval of values?

7-23 A random sample of $n = 10$ No. 303 cans of peas is taken in a canning plant, and the mean weight for the drained peas is found to be $\bar{X} = 11.0$ ounces with a standard deviation of $s = 0.30$ ounce. Assuming that the weights are approximately normally distributed, estimate the average drained weight of the peas contained in No. 303 cans, using 95 percent confidence limits.

7-24 Referring to Exercise 7-23, suppose the weights are not assumed to be approximately normally distributed. What is the confidence interval such that there is at least 95 percent confidence that the true mean weight is within this interval of weights?

7-25 An analyst in a personnel department randomly selects the records of 16 hourly employees and finds that the mean wage rate per hour is $5.50. The wage rates in the firm are assumed to be approximately normally distributed. If the standard deviation of the wage rates is known to be $1.00, estimate the mean wage rate in the firm, using an 80 percent confidence interval.

7-26 Referring to Exercise 7-25, suppose that the standard deviation of the population is not known, but that the standard deviation of the sample is $1.00. Estimate the mean wage rate in the firm, using an 80 percent confidence interval.

7-27 In Exercise 7-25 suppose that the wage rates cannot be assumed to be normally distributed. Define the confidence interval for the population mean such that there is at least an 80 percent chance that the mean wage rate for the population is within this interval.

7-28 From historical records the standard deviation of the sales level per retail outlet for a consumer product is known to be $\sigma = \$200$, and the population of sales amounts per outlet is assumed to be approximately normally distributed. What is the minimum sample size required to estimate the mean sales per outlet within $100 and with 95 percent confidence?

7-29 Referring to Exercise 7-28, what is the minimum sample size if the population is *not* assumed to be normally distributed?

7-30 An analyst wishes to estimate the mean hourly wage of workers in a particular company within 25 cents and with 90 percent confidence. The standard deviation of the wage rates is estimated as being no larger than $1.00. What is the number of personnel records that should be sampled, as a minimum, to satisfy this research objective?

CHAPTER

EIGHT

OTHER CONFIDENCE INTERVALS

8-1 CONFIDENCE INTERVALS FOR THE DIFFERENCE BETWEEN MEANS USING THE NORMAL DISTRIBUTION

Often, there is an interest in estimating the difference between the means of two populations, such as the difference between the average household incomes in two communities. As indicated in Section 7-1, the unbiased point estimate of the true difference $(\mu_1 - \mu_2)$ is the difference between the sample means $(\bar{X}_1 - \bar{X}_2)$, where each sample is a random sample taken from the respective target population. The confidence interval is constructed similarly to the method used for estimating the mean, except that the relevant standard-error value used here is the *standard error of the difference between means.* As in Section 7-2 for estimating the mean, because of the central-limit theorem, use of the normal probability distribution is always appropriate when each of the two sample sizes is large $(n \geqslant 30)$. If one or

128

both of the samples are small ($n < 30$), use of the normal distribution is appropriate only if the populations are normally distributed and the value of each population standard deviation σ is known.

Depending on whether the population standard deviations are known, the general formula for estimating the difference between the means of two populations by using a confidence interval is

$$\text{Conf. int.} = \bar{X}_1 - \bar{X}_2 \pm z\sigma_{\bar{X}_1 - \bar{X}_2} \tag{8-1}$$

or

$$\text{Conf. int.} = \bar{X}_1 - \bar{X}_2 \pm zs_{\bar{X}_1 - \bar{X}_2} \tag{8-2}$$

When the standard deviations of the two populations are known, the standard error of the difference between means is

$$\sigma_{\bar{X}_1 - \bar{X}_2} = \sqrt{\sigma_{\bar{X}_1}^2 + \sigma_{\bar{X}_2}^2} \tag{8-3}$$

When the standard deviations of the two populations are not known, the estimated standard error of the difference between means is

$$s_{\bar{X}_1 - \bar{X}_2} = \sqrt{s_{\bar{X}_1}^2 + s_{\bar{X}_2}^2} \tag{8-4}$$

The value of each standard error of the mean required in Formulas (8-3) and (8-4) is determined by one of the formulas given in Section 7-2, including the possible use of the finite correction factor.

As an example suppose that the average monthly household income for a random sample of $n_1 = 40$ households in one large community is $\bar{X}_1 = \$1,900$ with $s_1 = \$540$. In another large community the average household income for a sample of $n_2 = 30$ households is $\bar{X}_2 = \$1,600$ with $s_2 = \$420$. The 95 percent confidence interval for estimating the difference between the mean monthly household income in the two communities is

$$95\% \text{ conf. int.} = \bar{X}_1 - \bar{X}_2 \pm zs_{\bar{X}_1 - \bar{X}_2}$$

where
$$\bar{X}_1 - \bar{X}_2 = \$1,900 - \$1,600 = \$300$$
$$z = 1.96$$
$$s_{\bar{X}_1} = s_1/\sqrt{n} = 540/\sqrt{40} = \$85.38$$
$$s_{\bar{X}_2} = s_2/\sqrt{n} = 420/\sqrt{30} = \$76.68$$
$$s_{\bar{X}_1 - \bar{X}_2} = \sqrt{s_{\bar{X}_1}^2 + s_{\bar{X}_2}^2} = \sqrt{85.38^2 + 76.68^2} = \sqrt{13,169.566}$$
$$= \$114.76$$
$$\bar{X}_1 - \bar{X}_2 \pm zs_{\bar{X}_1 - \bar{X}_2} = \$300 \pm \$1.96(114.76) = \$300 \pm \$225 = \$75 \text{ to } \$525$$

Thus, with 95 percent confidence we can state that the average monthly household income in the first community is greater than the average monthly household income in the second community by between $75 and $525. Note that we did not identify the number of households in each community but rather assumed that each sample constitutes less than 5 percent of the population size. As explained in Section 7-2, under these circumstances use of the finite correction factor is not required.

8-2 CONFIDENCE INTERVALS FOR THE DIFFERENCE BETWEEN MEANS USING STUDENT'S t DISTRIBUTION

As explained in Section 7-5, use of Student's t distribution is appropriate when

1. The samples are small $(n < 30)$.
2. The population standard deviations σ are not known.
3. The populations are assumed to be approximately normally distributed.

However, if the t distribution is to be used to estimate the difference between the means of two populations, one additional assumption is required: that the two (unknown) population standard deviations are equal. The implication of this additional requirement is that the standard error of the difference between means should be based on a pooled estimate of the variance of the two populations. The pooled estimate of the variance is a weighted average of the two sample variances, with the degrees of freedom associated with each sample being used as the weights:

$$\hat{\sigma}^2 = \frac{(n_1 - 1)s_1^2 + (n_2 - 1)s_2^2}{n_1 + n_2 - 2} \tag{8-5}$$

Based on the assumption that the population standard deviations are equal, the estimated value of the standard error of the difference between means is

$$\hat{\sigma}_{\bar{X}_1 - \bar{X}_2} = \sqrt{\frac{\hat{\sigma}^2}{n_1} + \frac{\hat{\sigma}^2}{n_2}} \tag{8-6}$$

Note that the symbol used for the estimated standard error of the difference based on a pooled estimate of the standard deviation is $\hat{\sigma}_{\bar{X}_1 - \bar{X}_2}$ to differentiate this standard error from the estimated standard error $s_{\bar{X}_1 - \bar{X}_2}$ [Formula (8-4)], which is not based on the assumption that the population standard deviations are equal. If the two sample sizes are equal, however, both Formula (8-4) and Formula (8-6) yield the same numeric result.

When estimating the difference between means by a confidence interval, the degrees of freedom to be used in conjunction with the t distribution are $df = n_1 + n_2 - 2$, and the confidence interval is defined by

$$\text{Conf. int.} = \bar{X}_1 - \bar{X}_2 \pm t_{df}\hat{\sigma}_{\bar{X}_1 - \bar{X}_2} \tag{8-7}$$

For example, suppose that for a random sample of $n_1 = 12$ bulbs of a particular brand the mean bulb life is found to be $\bar{X}_1 = 3{,}400$ hours with a sample standard deviation of $s_1 = 240$ hours. For another brand of bulbs a random sample of $n_2 = 8$ bulbs has a mean life of $\bar{X}_2 = 2{,}800$ hours with $s_2 = 210$ hours. The distribution of bulb life is assumed to be approximately normal for the two populations (brands) of bulbs and the standard deviations of the two populations are assumed to be equal. The 90 percent confidence interval for estimating the difference between the mean bulb life for the two brands is

$$90\% \text{ conf. int.} = \bar{X}_1 - \bar{X}_2 \pm t_{df}s_{\bar{X}_1 - \bar{X}_2}$$

where $\qquad \bar{X}_1 - \bar{X}_2 = 3{,}400 - 2{,}800 = 600$ hours

$$t_{df} = t_{n_1 + n_2 - 2} = t_{18} = 1.734$$
$$\hat{\sigma}^2 = [(n_1 - 1)s_1^2 + (n_2 - 1)s_2^2]/(n_1 + n_2 - 2)$$
$$= [(12 - 1)(240)^2 + (8 - 1)(210)^2]/(12 + 8 - 2)$$
$$= 942{,}300/18 = 52{,}350$$
$$\hat{\sigma}_{\bar{X}_1 - \bar{X}_2} = \sqrt{\hat{\sigma}^2/n_1 + \hat{\sigma}^2/n_2} = \sqrt{52{,}350/12 + 52{,}350/8}$$
$$= \sqrt{10{,}906.25} = 104.43$$

$\bar{X}_1 - \bar{X}_2 \pm t_{df}\hat{\sigma}_{\bar{X}_1 - \bar{X}_2} = 600 \pm 1.734(104.43) = 600 \pm 181 = 419$ to 781 hours

Therefore, with 90 percent degree of confidence we can state that the first brand of bulbs has a 419-to-781-hour longer average bulb life than the second brand.

As explained in Section 7-5, the standard normal value z can be used as an approximation of a required value of t when df $\geqslant 29$. Thus, in the estimation of the difference between two means it is possible that each sample is small ($n < 30$) but that the degrees of freedom associated with the confidence interval are large enough that use of the normal distribution as an approximation for Student's t distribution is warranted (because df $= n_1 + n_2 - 2$). *However, in such small-sample applications note that because the central-limit theorem cannot be invoked, the two populations must be assumed to be normally distributed.* That is, use of a z value when df $\geqslant 29$ is warranted only as an approximation for a value of t, and use of the t distribution is based on the assumption that the populations are normally distributed. Of course, if each sample is large ($n \geqslant 30$), the central-limit theorem can be invoked, the normality assumption is not required, and the standard normal z values can be used because the degrees of freedom are large. For simplicity in analysis, the prescription is to take large samples when it is possible to do so.

8-3 CONFIDENCE INTERVALS FOR THE POPULATION PROPORTION

As indicated in the point-estimation formulas in Table 7-1, a proportion is essentially a converted count of the number of successes. A sample proportion is the observed number of successes divided by the size of the random sample. Thus, as previously defined in Formula (7-1), the sample proportion is

$$\hat{p} = \frac{X}{n} \qquad (8\text{-}8)$$

Similarly, where X designates the observed number of successes, the population proportion is

$$\pi = \frac{X}{N} \qquad (8\text{-}9)$$

Because the number of successes, which is converted into a proportion, follows the binomial distribution (as explained in Section 5-3), the sampling distribution of a proportion also follows the binomial distribution in its form. However, the process associated with constructing a confidence interval for an unknown population proportion π based on use of the binomial distribution is mathematically complex. For this reason as well as because quite a large sample is required to construct confidence intervals for π that are precise enough to have practical value, applications-oriented textbooks in statistics all use the normal probability distribution as an approximation of the binomial probability distribution for constructing such confidence intervals.

In Section 6-3 we stated that the rule in this text is that the normal approximation of binomial probability values is acceptable when $n \geq 30$, $np \geq 5$, and $nq \geq 5$. But note that in this rule the probability of success p in the Bernoulli process is assumed to be known and that p is essentially the same parameter that we now designate as π. That is, the true proportion π in the population serves as the basis for the probability of success p in the binomial sampling. But with π (and p) being unknown, the estimator $\hat{p}$ is used as the basis for estimating the standard error of the proportion. Given this type of application, the rule we follow is that the normal probability distribution can be used with the estimated standard error of the proportion when $n \geq 100$, $n\hat{p} \geq 5$, and $n(1 - \hat{p}) \geq 5$. A sample of $n \geq 30$ is often called a "large sample" in statistics, and a sample of $n \geq 100$ is often called a "very large sample."

Given an observed sample proportion $\hat{p}$, the estimated standard error of the proportion is

$$s_{\hat{p}} = \sqrt{\frac{\hat{p}(1 - \hat{p})}{n}} \tag{8-10}$$

If the population from which the random sample has been taken is finite, use of the finite correction factor is appropriate, as it was in computing the standard error of the mean in Section 7-2. As before, however, use of this correction factor is not considered necessary if the sample size is less than 5 percent of the population size, that is, if $n < 0.05N$. The formula for the standard error of the proportion that includes the finite correction factor is

$$s_{\hat{p}} = \sqrt{\frac{\hat{p}(1 - \hat{p})}{n}} \sqrt{\frac{N - n}{N - 1}} \tag{8-11}$$

Finally, the confidence interval for estimating a population proportion is

$$\text{Conf. int. for } \pi = \hat{p} \pm z s_{\hat{p}} \tag{8-12}$$

As an example of estimating an unknown population proportion, suppose that a random sample of $n = 100$ people are interviewed in a large metropolitan area, and 65 of them indicate they are in favor of a particular federal program. Thus, the sample proportion is

$$\hat{p} = \frac{X}{n} = \frac{65}{100} = 0.65$$

The estimated standard error of the proportion is

$$s_{\hat{p}} = \sqrt{\frac{\hat{p}(1-\hat{p})}{n}} = \sqrt{\frac{0.65(0.35)}{100}} = \sqrt{\frac{0.2275}{100}} = 0.048$$

The 95 percent confidence interval for estimating the proportion of all people in the metropolitan area in favor of the program is

$$\hat{p} \pm z s_{\hat{p}} = 0.65 \pm 1.96(0.048) = 0.65 \pm 0.09 = 0.56 \text{ to } 0.74$$

As a variation of the example above, suppose the sample of 100 people was obtained from a small community of 500 people. The finite correction factor is then required in estimating the standard error of the proportion (because $n > 0.05N$):

$$s_{\hat{p}} = \sqrt{\frac{\hat{p}(1-\hat{p})}{n}} \sqrt{\frac{N-n}{N-1}} = \sqrt{\frac{(0.65)(0.35)}{100}} \sqrt{\frac{500-100}{500-1}}$$

$$= \sqrt{\frac{0.2275}{100}} \sqrt{\frac{400}{499}} = 0.043$$

The 95 percent confidence interval in this example is somewhat more precise (narrower) than that for the large metropolitan area:

$$\hat{p} \pm z s_{\hat{p}} = 0.65 \pm 1.96(0.043) = 0.65 \pm 0.08 = 0.57 \text{ to } 0.73$$

Finally, we can observe that any estimation problem in which a confidence interval for a percentage is required can be handled as an estimate for a proportion. Then the confidence limits for the population proportion can simply be changed to percentages. For instance in the preceding example we determined that with 95 percent confidence we can say the true proportion of people in the small community in favor of the federal program is between 0.57 and 0.73. Therefore, it directly follows that the percentage of people in the community in favor of the program is between 57 and 73 percent.

8-4   DETERMINING THE REQUIRED SAMPLE SIZE FOR ESTIMATING THE PROPORTION

The minimum required sample size for estimating a population proportion can be determined by specifying the degree of confidence required, by specifying the acceptable plus-and-minus error (always one-half of the confidence interval), and by making an initial general estimate of π, the unknown population proportion. The formula is

$$n = \frac{z^2 \pi (1-\pi)}{E^2} \tag{8-13}$$

A key area of difficulty with respect to Formula (8-13), of course, is that we must make an initial estimate of the very parameter value π for which the confidence interval is to be defined. To assure that the sample size determined is large enough to satisfy the confidence-interval specification, we want our general estimate of π to be conservative. But what is "conservative" in this context? The answer is, if π is expected to be small (such as for a true proportion of defectives) the *largest* reasonable estimate for π should be made. On the other hand, if π is expected to be large (such as the proportion of company employees who completed high school), the *lowest* reasonable estimate should be used. These rules are appropriate because the minimum sample size required is largest when $\pi = 0.50$. The required sample size is largest when $\pi = 0.50$ because the standard error of the proportion is largest when $\pi = 0.50$.

As an example of determining sample size, suppose we wish to estimate the proportion of people in a large metropolitan area who favor a new federal program. Because of the nature of the program, we believe that a large majority favor the program, and certainly at least 80 percent favor it, i.e., $\pi \geqslant 0.80$. Given that we want to construct a 90 percent confidence interval and to have the estimate of π be accurate within ± 0.05, the minimum required sample size is

$$n = \frac{z^2 \pi (1 - \pi)}{E^2} = \frac{(1.65)^2 (0.80)(0.20)}{(0.05)^2} = \frac{0.4356}{0.0025} = 174.24 = 175$$

But suppose there is no basis for making an initial estimate of the unknown population proportion π. Because the minimum sample size is largest when $\pi = 0.50$, this value can be used as the conservative general estimate. Given this general estimate, Formula (8-11) can be simplified as follows:

$$n = \frac{z^2 (0.50)(1 - 0.50)}{E^2}$$

$$n = \left[\frac{z(0.50)}{E} \right]^2$$

$$n = \left(\frac{z}{2E} \right)^2 \tag{8-14}$$

As before, suppose we wish to estimate the proportion of people in a large metropolitan area in favor of a particular federal program with a 90 percent confidence interval and within ± 0.05. However, we have no basis for an initial general estimate of the population proportion π. The minimum required sample size is

$$n = \left(\frac{z}{2E} \right)^2 = \left[\frac{1.65}{2(0.05)} \right]^2 = (16.5)^2 = 272.25 = 273$$

Thus, the minimum sample size of $n = 273$ is larger than the minimum of $n = 175$ in the preceding example in which we made the initial general estimate $\pi = 0.80$.

When solving for sample size, we always round any fractional result up to the next whole number. Further, in the context of estimating a population proportion, any computed sample size below 100 should be increased to 100 because Formulas (8-13) and (8-14) are based on use of the normal distribution. As indicated in Section 8-3, use of the normal distribution for estimating a population proportion is considered acceptable when $n \geqslant 100$, $np \geqslant 5$, and $n(1 - \hat{p}) \geqslant 5$.

8-5 CONFIDENCE INTERVALS FOR ESTIMATING THE TOTAL NUMBER

As explained in Section 7-1, where $\hat{p}$ is the unbiased point estimate of a population proportion, the unbiased point estimate of the total number (of items, of people, etc.) in a particular category of the population is $N\hat{p}$. For instance, in addition to estimating the *proportion* of people who favor a federal program we may want to estimate the *total number* of people who favor the program. The confidence interval for a total number is determined simply by multiplying the confidence limits for estimating the population proportion by the population size N. Assuming that use of the normal probability distribution is appropriate, as explained in Section 8-3, the confidence interval for the total number is determined by

$$\text{Conf. int.} = N(\hat{p} \pm z s_{\hat{p}}) \qquad (8\text{-}15)$$

The idea of estimating a total number is similar to that of estimating a total quantity, except that the confidence interval for a total quantity is determined by multiplying the confidence limits for estimating the mean by N, as explained in Section 7-8. In both cases the procedure is meaningful only for finite populations.

As an example of determining a confidence interval for a total number, suppose that 65 of a random sample of $n = 100$ people in a small community with $N = 500$ people are in favor of a federal program. In Section 8-3 we determined the 95 percent confidence interval for the population proportion to be

$$\hat{p} \pm z s_{\hat{p}} = 0.65 \pm 1.96(0.043) = 0.57 \text{ to } 0.73$$

The 95 percent confidence interval for estimating the total number of people out of the 500 in favor of the program is

$$N(\hat{p} \pm z s_{\hat{p}}) = 500(0.57 \text{ to } 0.73) = 285 \text{ to } 365 \text{ people}$$

8-6 CONFIDENCE INTERVALS FOR THE DIFFERENCE BETWEEN TWO POPULATION PROPORTIONS

As indicated in Section 7-1, the unbiased point estimate for the difference between the proportions in two populations $\pi_1 - \pi_2$ is the difference between the two sample proportions $\hat{p}_1 - \hat{p}_2$, with each sample being a random sample from the respective population. Construction of a confidence interval involves use of the standard error of the difference between proportions, conceptually very similar to the standard error of the difference between means described in Section 8-1. The formula for estimating the standard error of the difference between proportions is

$$s_{\hat{p}_1 - \hat{p}_2} = \sqrt{s_{\hat{p}_1}^{\,2} + s_{\hat{p}_2}^{\,2}} \tag{8-16}$$

Use of the normal distribution to define a confidence interval for the difference between proportions is the same as presented in Section 8-4 on estimating a population proportion, except that two samples are involved. That is, *each* of the samples must satisfy the requirement that $n \geqslant 100$, $n\hat{p} \geqslant 5$, and $n(1 - \hat{p}) \geqslant 5$. With these assumptions satisfied the confidence interval for estimating the difference between two population proportions can be determined by the formula

$$\text{Conf. int.} = \hat{p}_1 - \hat{p}_2 \pm z s_{\hat{p}_1 - \hat{p}_2} \tag{8-17}$$

For example, suppose 65 out of a random sample of $n_1 = 100$ people in one large metropolitan area are in favor of a particular federal program, while 110 out of a random sample of $n_2 = 200$ people in another large metropolitan area are in favor of the program. The 99 percent confidence interval for estimating the true difference between the proportions of people in the two metropolitan areas in favor of the program is determined as follows:

$$\text{Conf. int.} = \hat{p}_1 - \hat{p}_2 \pm z s_{\hat{p}_1 - \hat{p}_2}$$

where $\hat{p}_1 - \hat{p}_2 = 65/100 - 110/200 = 0.65 - 0.55 = 0.10$

$z = 2.58$

$s_{\hat{p}_1}^{\,2} = \hat{p}_1(1 - \hat{p}_1)/n_1 = (0.65)(0.35)/100 = 0.0022750$

$s_{\hat{p}_2}^{\,2} = \hat{p}_2(1 - \hat{p}_2)/n_2 = (0.55)(0.45)/200 = 0.0012375$

$s_{\hat{p}_1 - \hat{p}_2} = \sqrt{s_{\hat{p}_1}^{\,2} + s_{\hat{p}_2}^{\,2}} = \sqrt{0.0022750 + 0.0012375} = 0.05927 \approx 0.06$

Conf. int. $= 0.10 \pm 2.58(0.06) = 0.10 \pm 0.15 = -0.05$ to 0.25

Therefore, at the 99 percent degree of confidence the lower limit indicates that the first population proportion is *smaller* than the second by 0.05, while the upper limit indicates that the first population proportion is *larger* by 0.25. Note that the possibility of no difference between the two population proportions is included in this confidence interval.

8-7 THE χ^2 (CHI–SQUARE) DISTRIBUTION AND CONFIDENCE INTERVALS FOR THE VARIANCE AND STANDARD DEVIATION

Just as the sampling distribution of the mean serves as the basis for constructing confidence intervals for estimating the population mean μ, so also the sampling distribution of the ratio $(n - 1)s^2/\sigma^2$ serves as the basis for constructing confidence intervals for estimating the population variance σ^2. Given a normally distributed population of values, this ratio is distributed as the χ^2 (*chi-square*) (pronounced: "kī-square") *distribution*. As is true for Student's t distribution, the χ^2 distribution is in fact a family of probability distributions, with a different distribution for each degree of freedom df. In the context of estimating an unknown population variance, df $= n - 1$. Thus,

$$\frac{(n-1)s^2}{\sigma^2} = \chi^2_{df} \qquad (8\text{-}18)$$

Let us consider the individual values included in the above ratio. Because the sample variance s^2 is the unbiased estimator of the population variance σ^2, the long-run expected value of the ratio is equal to $n - 1$, or the degrees of freedom. However, for any particular sample the sample variance of course is unlikely to be exactly equal to the value of the population variance. The fact that this ratio can be shown to follow the χ^2 distribution provides us with the opportunity to use a standard probability model for inferences concerning the population variance.

The family of χ^2 distributions is not symmetrical but, rather, is positively skewed. Therefore construction of a confidence interval for estimating the population variance σ^2 requires the use of two different values of χ^2 rather than the one value of z (or t) used in the plus-and-minus approach to constructing confidence intervals for the population mean. The formula to construct a confidence interval for the population variance is

$$\frac{(n-1)s^2}{\chi^2_{df,U}} \leqslant \sigma^2 \leqslant \frac{(n-1)s^2}{\chi^2_{df,L}} \qquad (8\text{-}19)$$

Table B-6 indicates the areas for the χ^2 distribution corresponding to various degrees of freedom. In Formula (8-19) the subscripts U and L stand for upper and lower, respectively, and identify the upper-tail and lower-tail probabilities for the particular χ^2 distribution that serves as the basis for constructing the confidence interval. For instance, for a 90 percent confidence interval the lowest 5 percent and highest 5 percent of the χ^2 distribution are excluded, thereby leaving the middle 90 percent.

As an example of constructing a 95 percent confidence interval for estimating the population variance, suppose the mean operating life for a random sample of $n = 9$ size D batteries is $\bar{X} = 20.0$ hours with a sample standard deviation of $s = 3.0$. Battery life is assumed to be approximately normally distributed. In Section 7-5 we used these sample results to construct a confidence interval for the population mean by use of Student's t distribution. The 95 percent confidence interval for estimating the variance of the population is

$$\frac{(n-1)s^2}{\chi^2_{8,U\,0.025}} \leqslant \sigma^2 \leqslant \frac{(n-1)s^2}{\chi^2_{8,L\,0.025}}$$

$$\frac{(9-1)(9.0)}{17.53} \leqslant \sigma^2 \leqslant \frac{(9-1)(9.0)}{2.18}$$

$$4.1 \leqslant \sigma^2 \leqslant 33.0$$

The required χ^2 value for the upper 0.025 in this example is obtained directly from Table B-6, which reports upper-tail proportions of area. To obtain the χ^2

value for the lower 0.025 it is necessary to look under the "0.975" column in Table B-6, because $1.000 - 0.975 = 0.025$. The wide confidence interval in this example reflects the small size of the sample. Also, with $s^2 = 9.0$ note the nonsymmetric nature of the above confidence interval. Unlike the confidence intervals based on the normal and t distributions, the unbiased estimator $s^2 = 9.0$ is not at the midpoint of the above confidence interval.

Although it is appealing to believe that the square root of the confidence limits for estimating the variance provides the correct confidence interval for estimating the population standard deviation, recall that while s^2 is an unbiased estimator of σ^2, s is in fact not an unbiased estimator of σ (as indicated in Section 7-1). However, the determination of exact confidence limits for the population standard deviation is mathematically complex. Because of the complexity of determining exact confidence limits and because the square root of the confidence limits for the variance usually provides an acceptable estimate of the confidence limits for the standard deviation for most applications, the confidence interval for the standard deviation is estimated by

$$\sqrt{\frac{(n-1)s^2}{\chi^2_{df,U}}} \leqslant \sigma \leqslant \sqrt{\frac{(n-1)s^2}{\chi^2_{df,L}}} \tag{8-20}$$

Thus, for the preceding example in which we estimated the variance of battery life, the approximate 95 percent confidence interval for estimating the population standard deviation is

$$\sqrt{\frac{(n-1)s^2}{\chi^2_{8,U0.025}}} \leqslant \sigma \leqslant \sqrt{\frac{(n-1)s^2}{\chi^2_{8,L0.025}}}$$

$$\sqrt{\frac{(9-1)(9.0)}{17.53}} \leqslant \sigma \leqslant \sqrt{\frac{(9-1)(9.0)}{2.18}}$$

$$\sqrt{4.11} \leqslant \sigma \leqslant \sqrt{33.03}$$

$$2.0 \leqslant \sigma \leqslant 5.7$$

In conclusion, note that when a confidence interval is constructed for the population variance or the population standard deviation, a necessary assumption is that the population being sampled is normally distributed. Only for a normally distributed population is the ratio $(n-1)s^2/\sigma^2$ distributed as the χ^2 distribution.

8-8 SUMMARY

In this chapter we presented the basis for defining confidence intervals for several different population parameters. In every case we begin with the sample statistic that is the unbiased *point estimator* of the population parameter, and then we use our knowledge about the *sampling distribution* associated with the statistic to construct a *confidence interval.* The different sampling distributions of interest in this chapter follow the normal distribution, Student's t distribution, or the χ^2 distribution.

Confidence intervals for estimating the *difference between the means of two populations* are constructed by first determining the difference between the means of two samples taken from the populations of interest and calculating the estimated *standard error of the difference between means.* The normal probability distribution is used if (1) both samples are large ($n \geqslant 30$) or (2) one or both of the samples are small, but the populations are assumed to be normally distributed and the population standard deviations σ are known. Student's t distribution is used when (1) the population standard deviations are not known, (2) one or both of the samples are small ($n < 30$), (3) the populations are normally distributed, and (4) the population standard deviations are equal. Finally, given that the t distribution is appropriate, the normal distribution can be used to approximate values of t when df $\geqslant 29$.

Confidence intervals for estimating the *population proportion* are constructed with the sample proportion $\hat{p}$ as the unbiased point estimator, while the *standard error of the proportion* is used with the normal probability distribution. Use of the normal probability model for constructing confidence intervals for the population proportion is appropriate when $n \geqslant 100$, $n\hat{p} \geqslant 5$, and $n(1 - \hat{p}) \geqslant 5$.

Confidence intervals for estimating a *total number* in a particular category of a population are simply a variation of confidence intervals for proportions. Confidence limits for a total number are determined by multiplying the confidence limits for the population proportion by the population size N.

Confidence intervals for the *difference between two population proportions* are constructed by first determining the difference between the proportions in two samples taken from the populations of interest and calculating the estimated *standard error of the difference between proportions.* Use of the normal probability model is appropriate when, for each sample, $n \geqslant 100$, $n\hat{p} \geqslant 5$, and $n(1 - \hat{p}) \geqslant 5$.

Confidence intervals for the population *variance* and population *standard deviation* are based on use of the χ^2 distribution. Use of this probability distribution is based on the assumption that the population is normally distributed.

FORMULAS

(8-1) Conf. int. $= \bar{X}_1 - \bar{X}_2 \pm z\sigma_{\bar{X}_1 - \bar{X}_2}$

Confidence interval for estimating the difference between the means of two populations when the two population standard deviations are known and (1) the populations are normally distributed or (2) each sample size is $n \geqslant 30$.

(8-2) Conf. int. $= \bar{X}_1 - \bar{X}_2 \pm zs_{\bar{X}_1 - \bar{X}_2}$

Confidence interval for estimating the difference between the means of two populations when the population standard deviations are not known and (1) each sample size is $n \geqslant 30$ or (2) one or both sample sizes are $n < 30$, each population is assumed to be normally distributed, and df $\geqslant 29$ (z used as an approximation of t).

(8-3) $\sigma_{\bar{X}_1 - \bar{X}_2} = \sqrt{\sigma_{\bar{X}_1}{}^2 + \sigma_{\bar{X}_2}{}^2}$

Standard error of the difference between means when the standard deviations of the two populations are known.

(8-4) $s_{\bar{X}_1 - \bar{X}_2} = \sqrt{s_{\bar{X}_1}{}^2 + s_{\bar{X}_2}{}^2}$

Estimated standard error of the difference between means when the standard deviations of the two populations are not known and not assumed to be equal.

(8-5) $\hat{\sigma}^2 = \dfrac{(n_1 - 1)s_1^2 + (n_2 - 1)s_2^2}{n_1 + n_2 - 2}$

Pooled estimate of the population variance based on two sample variances.

(8-6) $\hat{\sigma}_{\bar{X}_1 - \bar{X}_2} = \sqrt{\dfrac{\hat{\sigma}^2}{n_1} + \dfrac{\hat{\sigma}^2}{n_2}}$

Estimated standard error of the difference between means when the population standard deviations are unknown but assumed to be equal, a necessary assumption when the t distribution is to be used to construct the confidence interval.

(8-7) Conf. int. $= \bar{X}_1 - \bar{X}_2 \pm t_{\mathrm{df}} \sigma_{\bar{X}_1 - \bar{X}_2}$

Confidence interval for estimating the difference between the means of two populations when the population standard deviations are not known, one or both sample sizes are $n < 30$, and each population is approximately normally distributed; z can be used as an approximation of t when df $\geqslant 29$.

(8-8) $\hat{p} = \dfrac{X}{n}$

Sample proportion.

(8-9) $\pi = \dfrac{X}{N}$

Population proportion.

(8-10) $s_{\hat{p}} = \sqrt{\dfrac{\hat{p}(1 - \hat{p})}{n}}$

Estimated value of the standard error of the proportion when the population proportion π is not known.

(8-11) $s_{\hat{p}} = \sqrt{\dfrac{\hat{p}(1 - \hat{p})}{n}} \sqrt{\dfrac{N - n}{N - 1}}$

Estimated value of the standard error of the proportion for a finite population; the finite correction factor can be omitted when $n < 0.05N$.

(8-12) Conf. int. for $\pi = \hat{p} \pm z s_{\hat{p}}$

Confidence interval for estimating a population proportion when $n \geqslant 100$, $n\hat{p} \geqslant 5$, and $n(1 - \hat{p}) \geqslant 5$.

(8-13) $n = \dfrac{z^2 \pi(1 - \pi)}{E^2}$

Minimum required sample size for estimating a population proportion; any computed sample size below 100 should be increased to 100.

(8-14) $n = \left(\dfrac{z}{2E}\right)^2$

Minimum required sample size for estimating a population proportion when no initial estimate of π can be made; any computed sample size below 100 should be increased to 100.

(8-15) Conf. int. $= N(\hat{p} \pm z s_{\hat{p}})$

Confidence interval for estimating the total number in a particular category of the population.

(8-16) $s_{\hat{p}_1 - \hat{p}_2} = \sqrt{s_{\hat{p}_1}{}^2 + s_{\hat{p}_2}{}^2}$

Estimated standard error of the difference between two population proportions, given that the two population proportions are not known.

(8-17) Conf. int. $= \hat{p}_1 - \hat{p}_2 \pm z s_{\hat{p}_1 - \hat{p}_2}$

Confidence interval for the difference between two population proportions, given that for each sample $n \geqslant 100$, $n\hat{p} \geqslant 5$, and $n(1 - \hat{p}) \geqslant 5$.

(8-18) $\dfrac{(n - 1)s^2}{\sigma^2} = \chi^2_{\text{df}}$

Mathematical basis by which the χ^2 distribution can be used for statistical inference concerning the population variance σ^2, given a normally distributed population of values.

(8-19) $\dfrac{(n-1)s^2}{\chi^2_{df,U}} \leqslant \sigma^2 \leqslant \dfrac{(n-1)s^2}{\chi^2_{df,L}}$ Confidence interval for estimating the population variance for a normally distributed population.

(8-20) $\sqrt{\dfrac{(n-1)s^2}{\chi^2_{df,U}}} \leqslant \sigma \leqslant \sqrt{\dfrac{(n-1)s^2}{\chi^2_{df,L}}}$ Approximate confidence interval for estimating the population standard deviation for a normally distributed population.

EXERCISES

8-1 For two retail outlets an auditor finds that the mean charge account balance for a random sample of 50 accounts taken at one store is $445.18 with an associated sample standard deviation of $15.75 and that at the other store the mean account balance for 50 accounts is $454.84 with a sample standard deviation of $20.10. Using 95 percent confidence limits, estimate the difference between the mean account balances at the two stores.

8-2 For a sample of 50 firms taken from a total of 380 firms in a particular industry the mean number of employees per firm is $\bar{X}_1 = 420.4$ with $s_1 = 55.7$. In a second industry that includes 200 firms, the mean number of employees in a sample of 50 firms is $\bar{X}_2 = 392.5$ employees with $s_2 = 87.9$. Using a 95 percent confidence interval, estimate the difference in the mean number of employees per firm in the two industries.

8-3 Construct the 99 percent confidence interval for the difference between the means in Exercise 8-2.

8-4 For a sample of 30 employees in one large firm the mean hourly wage is $\bar{X}_1 = \$7.50$ with $s_1 = \$1.00$. In a second large firm the mean hourly wage for a sample of 40 employees is $\bar{X}_2 = \$7.05$ with $s_2 = \$1.20$. Using a 90 percent confidence interval, estimate the difference between the mean hourly wage at the two firms.

8-5 A random sample of 10 No. 303 cans of peas is taken in one canning plant, and the mean weight of the drained peas is found to be $\bar{X}_1 = 11.0$ ounces with a standard deviation of $s_1 = 0.30$ ounce. At another plant 10 randomly selected cans of peas have a mean drained weight of $\bar{X}_2 = 10.8$ ounces with a standard deviation of $s_2 = 0.20$ ounce. Assuming the weights in both populations are normally distributed and the population standard deviations are equal, use a 90 percent confidence interval to estimate the difference between the average weight of peas being packed in No. 303 cans at the two plants.

8-6 For one consumer product the mean dollar sales per retail outlet last year in a sample of $n_1 = 10$ stores was $\bar{X}_1 = \$3,425$ with $s_1 = \$200$. For a second product the mean dollar sales per outlet for a sample of $n_2 = 12$ stores was $\bar{X}_2 = \$3,250$ with $s_2 = \$175$. The sales amounts per outlet are assumed to be approximately normally distributed for both products, and the population standard deviations are assumed to be equal. Using a 99 percent confidence interval, estimate the difference between the mean dollar sales per retail outlet for the two products.

8-7 Suppose the two sample sizes in Exercise 8-6 were $n_1 = 20$ and $n_2 = 24$. What are the limits for the 99 percent confidence interval in this case?

8-8 In a sample of 100 graduate business students randomly selected at several major universities offering M.B.A. programs, 60 earned their undergraduate degree in one of the social sciences. Estimate the proportion of all graduate business students in the universities surveyed who earned their undergraduate degrees in the social sciences

(a) Using 90 percent confidence limits

(*b*) Using 95 percent confidence limits

(*c*) Using 99 percent confidence limits

8-9 For the sampling study described in Exercise 8-8 suppose that before the data were collected, it was specified that the 95 percent confidence interval should be within ±0.08 of the true proportion. No preliminary estimate of the proportion of students with degrees in the social sciences is available. Determine the size of the random sample that should be obtained.

8-10 For the data of Exercise 8-8, if a total of 5,480 students are enrolled in the graduate programs studied, estimate the total number who have undergraduate degrees in the social sciences, using 95 percent confidence limits.

8-11 A superintendent of schools in a small community is concerned about the proportion of voters who are likely to vote in favor of a school bonding proposal to be included in the next general election. To obtain a sampling of voter attitudes the superintendent arranges to poll a systematic random sample of 2 percent of the 6,500 registered voters in the community. Of the 130 voters sampled, 76 indicate that they will vote for the proposal. Using 95 percent confidence limits, determine the confidence intervals that can be used to estimate (*a*) the proportion of voters in favor of the proposal and (*b*) the total number of voters in favor of the proposal.

8-12 Of a sample of 100 firms in a particular industry that includes 1,200 firms, suppose that the employees of 40 of the firms belong to a national labor union. Using a 90 percent confidence interval,

(*a*) Estimate the percentage of all 1,200 firms whose employees belong to a national labor union.

(*b*) Estimate the total number of firms whose employees belong to a national labor union.

8-13 In another industry consisting of 1,000 firms, 60 of a sample of 100 firms are unionized. Using 90 percent confidence limits, estimate the difference between the proportion of firms whose employees are represented by a labor union in this industry and the proportion in the industry described in Exercise 8-12.

8-14 For a random sample of 150 households in a large metropolitan area the number of households in which at least one adult is currently unemployed and seeking a full-time job is 12. Using a 95 percent confidence interval, estimate the proportion of households in the area in which at least one adult is unemployed.

8-15 For the sampling study described in Exercise 8-14 suppose that before any data are collected we specify that the 95 percent confidence interval should be within 0.05 of the population proportion. As an initial general estimate we believe that the population proportion is no less than $\pi = 0.05$ and no greater than $\pi = 0.10$. Determine the size of the random sample that should be collected.

8-16 In attempting to assess voter sentiment regarding a state bonding proposal, a legislator has a random sample of 200 people polled in each of two districts containing a large number of voters. In the first district 120 of the 200 people interviewed expressed their approval of the proposal, and in the second district 100 of the 200 people interviewed expressed approval. Using 95 percent confidence limits, estimate the difference between the percentage of people in the two districts supporting the bonding proposal.

8-17 An internal auditor wishes to estimate the proportion of correct inventory records by choosing a random sample of such records and comparing each record with the physical inventory. This manufacturing company has a large number of inventory items, and based on previous data the auditor believes the proportion of records that are exactly correct will range between 0.80 and 0.90. If the 95 percent confidence interval should be within ±0.03 of the true proportion of correct accounts, determine the sample size that should be collected to make this interval estimate.

8-18 In reference to Exercise 8-17, suppose another internal auditor who is not so demanding specifies that the 95 percent confidence interval should be within ±0.10 of the true proportion. Determine the sample size that should be collected to make this interval estimate.

8-19 For a particular consumer product the mean dollar sales per retail outlet last year in a sample of $n = 10$ stores was $\bar{X} = \$3,425$ with $s = \$200$. The sales amounts per outlet are assumed to be approximately normally distributed. Estimate the (a) variance and (b) standard deviation of dollar sales of this product in all stores last year, using a 90 percent confidence interval.

8-20 A random sample of $n = 10$ No. 303 cans of peas is taken in a canning plant, and the mean weight for the drained peas is found to be $\bar{X} = 11.0$ ounces with a standard deviation of $s = 0.30$ ounce. The weights in the population are assumed to be normally distributed. In Exercise 7-23 these sample results were used to construct the 95 percent confidence limits for the population mean. Now use these sample results as the basis for constructing the 95 percent confidence limits for the (a) population variance and (b) population standard deviation.

8-21 Suppose the sample size in Exercise 8-20 was $n = 30$ instead of $n = 10$. Construct the 95 percent confidence limits for the (a) population variance and (b) population standard deviation. Compare your confidence intervals with those defined in Exercise 8-20.

TESTING HYPOTHESES CONCERNING THE POPULATION MEAN

9-1 BASIC STEPS IN HYPOTHESIS TESTING

The general idea underlying hypothesis testing is that we begin with a designated (hypothesized) value for a population parameter, such as the population mean, and then we "test" this hypothesized value by collecting a random sample and comparing the appropriate sample statistic, such as the sample mean, to the hypothesized parameter value. If the sample statistic is "close" to the hypothesized parameter value, we do not reject the hypothesized value, but rather, we accept it as being correct. If the sample statistic is so different from the hypothesized parameter value that such a result is unlikely to occur by chance when the parameter has the hypothesized value, we reject the hypothesized value as being correct. Hypothesis testing differs from interval estimation as a method of statistical inference in that with interval estimation no value of the parameter is assumed before the sample is collected. Rather, the statistical objective is to estimate the unknown parameter value. In hypothesis testing, a parameter value is hypothesized before collection of sample data, typically because this hypothesized value represents some type of standard, and then sample data are collected to determine whether the hypothesized value should be rejected or should be accepted as being correct. With this overview in mind, let us consider seven basic steps included in hypothesis testing.

Step 1: Formulate the null hypothesis and the alternative hypothesis. The *null hypothesis* (H_0) specifies the parameter value to be tested. The *alternative hypothesis* (H_1) specifies the parameter value or values which are to be accepted if the null hypothesis is rejected. Which parameter value is designated as the null hypothesis and which value or values are designated as the alternative hypothesis are important, because in the process of hypothesis testing, the null hypothesis is given the benefit of the doubt. That is, the null hypothesis will be accepted unless the sample result clearly is inconsistent with it. On the other hand, the alternative hypothesis can only be accepted if the null hypothesis is rejected. Thus it is the null hypothesis that can be thought of as being the *principal hypothesis* because the decision procedure is carried out in reference to this hypothesized value. The word "null" was chosen by statisticians in reference to this principal hypothesis because what is being tested is the assumption that there is "no difference" between the parameter value specified in the null hypothesis and the actual value of the population parameter.

As an example of formulating a null hypothesis and an alternative hypothesis, suppose a chamber of commerce representative claims that the mean household income per month in a metropolitan area is $1,400. A prospective developer of a shopping center wishes to test this claim by contacting $n = 36$ households in the area, determining the average income in these households through confidential interviews, and comparing the obtained sample mean with the claimed mean. The developer wishes to reject the claim only if it is clearly contradicted by the sample result, and thus the claimed monthly mean of $1,400 is given the "benefit of the doubt" and is assigned to the null hypothesis. Therefore, the null and alternative hypotheses are

Hypotheses: $H_0: \mu = \$1,400$

$H_1: \mu \neq \$1,400$

As is true in the example above, the parameter values associated with the alternative hypothesis are always all possible values of the parameter that are not included in the null hypothesis. Thus in this example if we reject the null hypothesis, we accept the alternative hypothesis that the mean monthly household income in the metropolitan area is some value *other than* $1,400.

Step 2: Specify the level of significance to be used. The level of significance is the statistical standard used as the basis for rejecting the null hypothesis. If a 5 percent level of significance is specified, the null hypothesis is rejected only if the sample result is so different from the hypothesized parameter value that a difference of such magnitude or larger would occur by chance with a probability of 0.05 or less. Note that a level of significance implies that this level is the probability of the sample result, *given that the null hypothesis is in fact true.* That is, if the 5 percent level of significance is used as the basis for rejecting a null hypothesis, it follows that the probability is 0.05 of rejecting the null hypothesis when it is true. Called a *type I error*, this probability is always equal to the level of significance used as the standard for rejecting (or not rejecting) a null hypothesis. The probability of a type I error in hypothesis testing is designated by the lowercase Greek α (read: "alpha"), and thus α also designates the level of significance. The most frequently used levels of significance in hypothesis testing are the 5 percent and 1 percent levels.

In contrast to a type I error, the error of rejecting a true null hypothesis, a *type II error* is the error of accepting (not rejecting) a false null hypothesis. The probability of a type II error in hypothesis testing is designated by the lowercase Greek β (read: "beta"). Table 9-1 summarizes the types of decisions made in hypothesis testing and the consequences of these decisions. Thus, just as there are two types of errors, there are also two types of correct decisions: accepting a true null hypothesis and rejecting a false null hypothesis. Further, given that the null hypothesis is true, note that the probability of correct acceptance is the complement of the probability of a type I error (level of significance). Specifically, if the 5 percent level of significance is used, the probability of accepting a true null hypothesis is $1.00 - \alpha = 1.00 - 0.05 = 0.95$. Similarly, the probability of correctly rejecting a false null hypothesis is the complement of the probability of a type II error $(1.00 - \beta)$. The determination of the probability of a type II error is explained in Section 9-3.

Step 3: Select the test statistic. The test statistic is the value, based on the sample, used to determine whether the null hypothesis should be rejected or accepted. The obvious test statistic is the sample estimator of the parameter value being tested. For example, the value of the sample mean can serve as the test statistic for the hypothesized value of the population mean. However, the probability associated with a sample result is determined on the basis of the standard probability distribution applicable to the sampling distribution of the sample statistic. Therefore, it is generally more convenient to convert the sample statistic into a value on the appropriate standard distribution and to use this transformed value as the test statistic. For example, given that the sample distribution of the mean can be assumed to be normally distributed, we can convert the value of a sample mean into a z value; we then use this value of z as the test statistic. The procedure for this conversion of a sample mean $\bar{X}$ to a value z on the standard normal distribution and the subsequent interpretation of the obtained z value is presented in Section 9-2.

Step 4: Establish the critical value or values of the test statistic. Having specified the null and alternative hypotheses, the level of significance, and the test statistic to be used, we now establish the critical value(s) of the test statistic. There

Table 9-1 Consequences of decisions in hypothesis testing

Decision	Null hypothesis true	Null hypothesis false
Accept null hypothesis	Correct acceptance $(1 - \alpha)$	Type II error (β)
Reject null hypothesis	Type I error (α)	Correct rejection $(1 - \beta)$

may be one or two such values, as explained and illustrated in Section 9-2, depending on whether a so-called one-tail or two-tail test is involved. For either type of test, a *critical value* is in the same units of measurement as the test statistic and identifies the value of the test statistic that would lead to the rejection of the null hypothesis at the designated level of significance. Thus, this value is a "critical" value in the test procedure because it is the value with which the value of the test statistic is compared.

Step 5: *Determine the actual value of the test statistic.* For example, if the null hypothesis concerns the value of the population mean, a random sample is collected from the target population, and the sample mean is calculated. If the critical value was established as a z value, the sample mean is converted into a value of z.

Step 6: *Make the decision.* The obtained value of the sample statistic is compared with the critical value (or values) of the test statistic. The null hypothesis is then either rejected or not rejected. In the application of hypothesis testing in the sciences nonrejection of a null hypothesis does not automatically lead to acceptance of the null hypothesis. The reason is that the null hypothesis typically is associated with an explanatory theory, and nonrejection of the null hypothesis does not thereby "prove" the theory as being correct. However, in managerial decision analysis it is appropriate that either the null hypothesis is accepted or the alternative hypothesis is accepted. Of course, we recognize that there is a risk that we may be incorrect no matter what decision is made.

Step 7: *Take the appropriate managerial action.* The purpose of using hypothesis testing and other techniques of quantitative decision analysis in business and economics is associated with the need to take some form of managerial action, such as which of two versions of a product should be marketed or whether to certify an inventory balance as being correct. In this context the decision to do nothing, such as the decision not to buy a new type of machine or not to market a proposed new product, is itself a form of managerial action.

9-2 TESTING A HYPOTHESIZED VALUE OF THE MEAN USING THE NORMAL DISTRIBUTION

As explained in Section 7-2, the sampling distribution of the mean can be assumed to be normally distributed when (1) $n \geqslant 30$ because of the central-limit theorem or (2) $n < 30$ but the population is normally distributed. Because of the central-limit theorem, the normal probability distribution can serve as the basis for determining the critical value of the test statistic in testing a hypothesis concerning the population mean whenever the sample is large ($n \geqslant 30$). However, if a small sample is taken from a normally distributed population, use of the normal distribution to determine the critical value is appropriate only if the population standard deviation σ is known. This requirement is also explained in Section 7-2.

In hypothesis testing, a *two-tail test* is used when we are concerned about a possible deviation in *either* direction from the hypothesized value of the mean. If the sample mean is used as the test statistic, two critical values of the sample mean have to be defined: one that is less than the hypothesized value and one that is greater than the hypothesized value. The basic formula to determine these two critical values is similar to Formula (7-8) for defining a confidence interval for the population mean, except that the point of reference is the hypothesized value of the population mean μ_0 rather than the sample mean $\bar{X}$. Based on use of the normal probability distribution, the critical values of the sample mean for a two-tail test, according to whether σ is known, are defined by

$$\text{Critical } \bar{X} = \mu_0 \pm z\sigma_{\bar{X}} \qquad (9\text{-}1)$$

or
$$\text{Critical } \bar{X} = \mu_0 \pm zs_{\bar{X}} \qquad (9\text{-}2)$$

In Formulas (9-1) and (9-2) μ_0 indicates the value of the population mean specified in the null hypothesis, and the standard error of the mean (either $\sigma_{\bar{X}}$ or $s_{\bar{X}}$) is calculated using the formulas presented in Chapter 7, including the possibility that the use of the finite correction factor may be required. The value of z used depends on the level of significance; the proportion of area in the two tails of the sampling distribution corresponds to the level of significance, as illustrated in the following example.

In Section 9-1 the null hypothesis was that the mean household income per month in a metropolitan area is $1,400. Suppose we wish to test this hypothesis at the 5 percent level of significance and, based on data from other similar metropolitan areas, the population standard deviation for the distribution of income amounts is $\sigma = \$300$. Given that a random sample of $n = 36$ households is to be contacted and the metropolitan area is large (thus making use of the finite correction factor unnecessary), we determine the critical values of the sample mean as follows:

Hypotheses: $H_0: \mu = \$1,400$

$H_1: \mu \neq \$1,400$

Level of significance: $\alpha = 0.05$

Test statistic: $\bar{X}$, based on $n = 36$ and $\sigma = \$300$

$\text{Critical } \bar{X} = \mu_0 \pm z\sigma_{\bar{X}}$

where $\mu_0 = \$1,400$
$z = 1.96$
$\sigma_{\bar{X}} = \sigma/\sqrt{n} = 300/\sqrt{36} = 300/6 = \$50$

$\text{Critical } \bar{X} = \$1,400 \pm (1.96)(50) = \$1,400 \pm 98 = \$1,302 \text{ and } \$1,498$

Therefore, to reject the null hypothesis at the 5 percent level of significance the sample mean must have a value that is either below the critical limit of $1,302 or above the critical limit of $1,498. Figure 9-1 graphically portrays the sampling distribution of the mean and the regions of acceptance and rejection of the null hypothesis, given that the null hypothesis is true. As can be seen in this figure, a two-tail test has two regions of rejection. The z values of ± 1.96 are used to establish

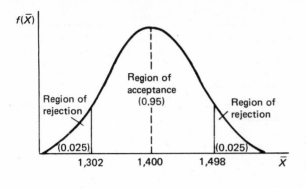

$f(\bar{X})$

Region of
acceptance
(0.95)

Region of
rejection

Region of
rejection

(0.025)

(0.025)

1,302   1,400   1,498 $\bar{X}$

Figure 9-1 Regions of acceptance and rejection of a null
hypothesis in critical values of the
sample mean.

the critical limits because for the standard normal distribution a proportion of 0.05
of the area is outside these limits and located in the two tails of the distribution,
which corresponds to the designated 5 percent level of significance. Since the
normal distribution is symmetrical, the area in each tail of Figure 9-1 is one-half of
0.05, or 0.025. Thus, given that the null hypothesis is true, the overall probability is
0.05 that the mean for a random sample of $n = 36$ households will be either below
$1,302 or above $1,498 for this example.

Instead of establishing the critical values in terms of the sample mean as such,
we would typically specify the critical values in z values. Table 9-2 lists the values
of z most frequently used as critical values in hypothesis testing. Note that for a
two-tail test there are always two critical values of z. For instance, for a two-tail
test at the 5 percent level of significance the critical values are at $z = \pm 1.96$. When
the value of a sample mean is determined, it is converted into a value of z so that it
can be compared with the critical value(s) of z. The conversion formula, according
to whether σ is known, is

$$z = \frac{\bar{X} - \mu_0}{\sigma_{\bar{X}}}$$ (9-3)

or

$$z = \frac{\bar{X} - \mu_0}{s_{\bar{X}}}$$ (9-4)

For the hypothesis-testing example regarding the mean monthly household
income, suppose the sample mean based on a sample of $n = 36$ households is
$1,250. By reference to the critical limits for the sample mean, as previously
determined and illustrated in Figure 9-1, we would reject the null hypothesis at the

Table 9-2 Critical values of z in hypothesis testing

Level of significance	One-tail test	Two-tail test
5%	1.65 (or −1.65)	± 1.96
1%	2.33 (or −2.33)	± 2.58

5 percent level of significance and accept the alternative hypothesis, that $\mu \neq \$1,400$. The same conclusion is reached by converting the observed sample mean into a z value and comparing this value with the critical values of z. The overall hypothesis-testing procedure is

Hypotheses: H_0: $\mu = \$1,400$

H_1: $\mu \neq \$1,400$

Level of significance: $\alpha = 0.05$

Critical $z = \pm 1.96$

$\sigma_{\bar{X}} = \$50$ (from the preceding example)

$\bar{X} = \$1,250$ (as given)

$$z = \frac{\bar{X} - \mu_0}{\sigma_{\bar{X}}} = \frac{1,250 - 1,400}{50} = \frac{-150}{50} = -3.00$$

This value of z is in the left-tail region of rejection of the hypothesis-testing model, as portrayed in Figure 9-2. Thus, the null hypothesis is rejected, and the alternative hypothesis ($\mu \neq \$1,400$) is accepted.

As illustrated by the example above, a two-tail test is appropriate when we are concerned about the possibility that the population mean is smaller *or* larger than the hypothesized value of the mean. In contrast a *one-tail test* is appropriate when we are concerned about possible deviations in only one direction from the hypothesized value of the mean. For instance, it is likely that the prospective developer of the shopping center is not concerned about the possibility that the average monthly household income is greater than $1,400, but only about the possibility that it might be less than $1,400. Giving the benefit of the doubt to the chamber of commerce claim that the average is $1,400 (or more), we find that the null and alternative hypotheses are

Hypotheses: H_0: $\mu \geqslant \$1,400$

H_1: $\mu < \$1,400$

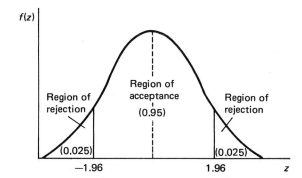

Figure 9-2 Regions of acceptance and rejection of a null hypothesis in critical z values.

As implied by the description of such a test, only one region of rejection is associated with a one-tail test. As illustrated in the example that follows, the region of rejection for a one-tail test is always in the tail of the distribution that represents support of the alternative hypothesis (in this example, in the lower tail). As for a two-tail test, the critical value can be established either by using the sample mean as the test statistic or by using the standard-normal z value. The required z values for significance at the 5 percent and 1 percent levels are given in Table 9-2 for both one-tail and two-tail tests. The critical values for one-tail tests differ from those for two-tail tests because for a one-tail test the designated proportion of area is all in *one* tail of the distribution. The general formula to establish the critical value of the sample mean as the test statistic for a one-tail test, according to whether σ is known, is

$$\text{Critical } \bar{X} = \mu_0 + z\sigma_{\bar{X}} \tag{9-5}$$

or

$$\text{Critical } \bar{X} = \mu_0 + zs_{\bar{X}} \tag{9-6}$$

In both Formulas (9-5) and (9-6) note that for a lower-tail test the value of z is negative, resulting in the subtraction of the second term from the hypothesized value of the mean.

Following up on our previous example, suppose the developer of the shopping center is only concerned about the possibility that the average monthly household income is less than the claimed value of \$1,400. As before, for a sample of $n = 36$ households the sample mean is $\bar{X} = \$1,250$. Using the sample mean as the test statistic, we carry out the test at the 5 percent level of significance as follows:

Hypotheses: $\qquad H_0: \mu \geqslant \$1,400$

$\qquad\qquad\qquad\qquad H_1: \mu < \$1,400$

Level of significance: $\qquad \alpha = 0.05$

Test statistic: $\qquad \bar{X}$, based on $n = 36$ and $\sigma = \$300$

$$\text{Critical } \bar{X} = \mu_0 + z\sigma_{\bar{X}}$$

where $\mu_0 = \$1,400$
$z = -1.65$
$\sigma_{\bar{X}} = \sigma/\sqrt{n} = 300/\sqrt{36} = 300/6 = \$50$

$$\text{Critical } \bar{X} = \$1,400 + (-1.65)(50) = \$1,400 - 82.50 = \$1,317.50$$
$$\bar{X} = \$1,250$$

As portrayed in Figure 9-3, the obtained sample mean is in the region of rejection of the null hypothesis at the 5 percent level of significance, and thus we accept the alternative hypothesis that $\mu < \$1,400$. The appropriate managerial action is not to develop the shopping center, given that the household income requirement is a critical factor in the decision.

If the standard normal z value is used as the test statistic, the critical value of z for a lower-tail test at the 5 percent level of significance is -1.65, as indicated in

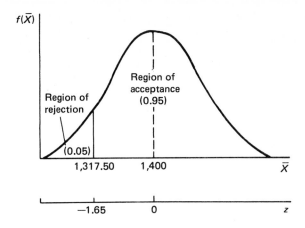

Figure 9-3 Regions of acceptance and rejection of the null hypothesis for a one-tail test.

Table 9-2. You should be able to verify this value by reference to Table B-4 for the standard normal distribution. Referring to this table, note that the area under the density function included between the mean and $z = 1.65$ is 0.4505 (which is the closest value to 0.4500 in the table, without going below 0.4500). Therefore the proportion of area remaining in the right tail of the distribution is $0.500 - 0.4505 = 0.0495$, as close as we can get to the specified significance level of $\alpha = 0.05$ without going over this value. Of course, in our example we are in the left tail of the distribution, but because the normal probability distribution is symmetrical the concept applies equally for negative values of z as for positive values of z. The z values equivalent to the critical value of the sample mean and the hypothesized value of the population mean for our example are shown in the lower portion of Figure 9-3. The z value equivalent to the observed sample mean of $\bar{X} = \$1,250$ is

$$z = \frac{\bar{X} - \mu_0}{\sigma_{\bar{X}}} = \frac{1,250 - 1,400}{50} = -3.00$$

Because this obtained value of z is in the region of rejection of the null hypothesis (it is less than the critical value $z = -1.65$), we reject the null hypothesis and accept the alternative hypothesis that $\mu < \$1,400$.

It may have occurred to you that if after a sample is collected, the sample mean is different from the hypothesized value of the population mean, it must be either smaller or larger than the hypothesized value. It cannot be both. Under what circumstances, then, do we use a two-tail test? Does it not follow that if the sample is smaller than the hypothesized value, we should use a lower-tail test; and that if the sample is larger than the hypothesized value, we should then use an upper-tail test? The answer for both situations is *no*. Consider again the overall hypothesis-testing procedure. Formulating the null and alternative hypotheses is the first step in hypothesis testing, *before any sample data are observed.* Formulating the null hypothesis or deciding on the level of significance to be used *after* observing the sample result is inappropriate. A sample result can be used as the basis for formulating a null hypothesis that is then tested by collecting *another* random sample. But a sample can never legitimately be used to test a hypothesis suggested by that same sample.

Therefore, whether a particular test should be a one-tail or two-tail test depends on whether we are concerned about deviations in only one direction or in either direction and not on the result associated with a particular sample. For example, for our hypothesis concerning average household income we concluded that a one-tail test was appropriate because the developer would cancel the project only if the income level in the area were not sufficient to support the proposed shopping center. On the other hand, suppose we are concerned with measuring the average net weight for a sample of packaged products, such as, say, 14-ounce bags of potato chips. From the management point of view discrepancies in weight in either direction are of concern. Weight less than the claimed weight could result in legal implications as well as the loss of customer goodwill. Weight greater than the claimed weight could result in lost profit as well as, ironically, loss of customer goodwill because the potato chips are more likely to be damaged in overpacked bags.

9-3 TYPE I AND TYPE II ERRORS IN HYPOTHESIS TESTING

In this section we consider type I and type II errors in one-tail tests only, because the discussion of type II errors for two-tail tests is more complicated and beyond the intended scope of this text. However, the basic concepts presented here apply to any type of hypothesis-testing situation.

As we indicated in Section 9-1 and in Table 9-1, the type I error is the error of rejecting a true null hypothesis. The probability of a type I error, designated by α, always equals the level of significance specified in the hypothesis-testing procedure, because by definition the area in the region of rejection of the null hypothesis is equal to the proportion of sample results that would occur in that region, *given that the null hypothesis is true.* For example, in Figure 9-3 the sampling distribution is constructed with respect to the true value of the population mean being $\mu = \$1,400$, which is the null-hypothesized value.

A *type II error* is the error of accepting a false null hypothesis, as also indicated in Table 9-1. Now, to determine the probability of a type II error it is necessary to consider *one* specific alternative value of the population mean as a point of reference. That is, the probability of a type II error is variable, depending on the actual alternative value of the population mean when the null hypothesis is false. In general, if the true value is close to the null-hypothesized value, the probability of type II error is high, whereas if the true value of the mean is very different from the null-hypothesized value, the probability of type II error is low. In intermediate and advanced books in statistics the functional relationship between the actual value of the mean μ in hypothesis testing and the probability of a type II error is described by developing a so-called operating characteristic (OC) curve. For our purposes and for most applications purposes we are not so concerned about the entire range of possible values of β; rather, we are concerned about the probability of a type II error, given one specific alternative value of the mean.

The specific alternative value chosen as the basis for computing the probability of type II error should reflect our judgment concerning the amount of difference from the null-hypothesized value that represents an important difference. For instance, in our example involving the average monthly household income, the null hypothesis was H_0: $\mu \geqslant \$1,400$. Now, given that a mean income of at least $\$1,400$ would lead to a development of the shopping center, is it likely that a true mean of $\mu = \$1,399$ should lead to rejection of the proposed project? A difference of just $\$1.00$ probably would not be that important. But based on the financial analysis underlying the income requirement, at some point the difference *does* become important. Let us say the difference is important if the true mean monthly household income is at (or below) $\mu_1 = \$1,300$. Then the probability of a type II error is equal to the probability that the null hypothesis is accepted, given that the alternative mean is $\mu_1 = \$1,300$. For our example, this probability indicates that the sample mean is at or above the critical value of $\bar{X} = \$1,317.50$, which is the region of acceptance of the null hypothesis. Thus, the probability of a type II error $= P(\bar{X} \geqslant \$1,317.50 | \mu_1 = \$1,300; \sigma_{\bar{X}} = \$50)$. We determine the probability of a type II error (β) as follows:

$$\beta = P(\bar{X} \geqslant \$1,317.50 | \mu_1 = \$1,300; \sigma_{\bar{X}} = \$50)$$

$$z = \frac{\bar{X} - \mu_1}{\sigma_{\bar{X}}} = \frac{1,317.50 - 1,300}{50} = \frac{17.5}{50} = 0.35$$

$$\beta = P(z \geqslant 0.35) = 0.5000 - 0.1368 = 0.3632 \approx 0.36$$

Figure 9-4 portrays the relationship between two sampling distributions: one based on the assumption that the null hypothesis is true and that $\mu = \$1,400$, the other based on the assumption that the null hypothesis is false and that $\mu = \$1,300$. Note that to determine the probability of a type II error, we must determine the critical value of the sample mean with respect to the null-hypothesized value and then determine the probability of acceptance of the null hypothesis, given the specific *alternative* value of the population mean.

As can be seen by studying Figure 9-4, if the probability of a type I error (α) is reduced (in this example, by lowering the critical $\bar{X} = \$1,317.50$), the probability of a type II error (β) would be increased, because the new critical $\bar{X}$ would be closer to the specific alternative value of the population mean μ_1 ($\$1,300$ in this example). Conversely, if we are willing to accept a higher probability of a type I error, given a particular sample size, the probability of a type II error would be reduced. The decision as to the relative magnitude of α and β should be associated with the relative cost associated with the two types of errors. For our example of the possible development of a shopping center it would appear that the probability of a type II error, $\beta = 0.36$, (the probability of developing the center when it should not be developed) is too large.

The probability of a type II error can be reduced *without* allowing the

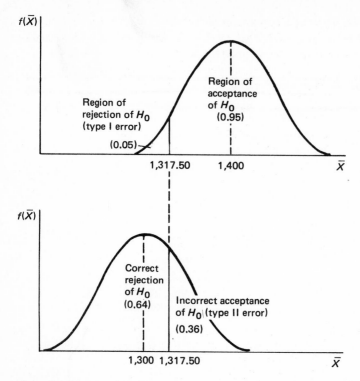

Figure 9-4 Type I and type II errors.

probability of a type I error to increase by increasing the sample size used in the testing procedure. A larger sample size results in a smaller standard error and thus results in less relative overlap between the sampling distribution associated with the value μ_0 and the sampling distribution associated with μ_1. The relationship between sample size and the standard error makes it possible to specify the level of both α and β before any sample data are collected and to use a sample size such that both standards can be satisfied. The procedure for determining the required sample size is presented in Section 9-4.

A final concept in hypothesis testing is the concept of power. The *power* associated with a statistical test is the probability that a null hypothesis will be rejected. The concept is usually applied in the context of the null hypothesis being false, and thus the power of a test is the probability of rejecting a false null hypothesis. As we shall see later in this book, and particularly in Chapter 18 on nonparametric statistical tests, different statistical testing procedures are often compared with one another by comparing their respective power to reject a false null hypothesis, given equal α levels. Because the power of a test is the complement of the probability of a type II error when the null hypothesis is false, the power of a test is determined by

$$\text{Power} = 1 - \beta \tag{9-7}$$

For the hypothesis-testing example concerned with the average monthly household income with $\mu_0 = \$1,400$, $\mu_1 = \$1,300$, and $\alpha = 0.05$, we determined that $\beta = 0.36$. Therefore the power of the statistical test procedure in this example is

$$\text{Power} = 1 - \beta = 1 - 0.36 = 0.64$$

9-4 DETERMINING THE REQUIRED SAMPLE SIZE

Before a sample is collected, the required sample size can be determined by specifying

1. The hypothesized value of the mean
2. A specific alternative value of the mean such that the amount of difference from the null-hypothesized value is considered important
3. The level of significance (α) to be used
4. The probability of a type II error (β)
5. The value of the population standard deviation (σ)

The formula for determining the minimum required sample size based on the use of the normal probability distribution in the statistical testing procedure is

$$n = \frac{(z_0 - z_1)^2 \sigma^2}{(\mu_1 - \mu_0)^2} \tag{9-8}$$

In Formula (9-8), z_0 is the critical value of z used in conjunction with the specified level of significance (α), while z_1 is the value of z with respect to the designated probability of a type II error (β). The value of σ must either be known or estimated on the basis of the known standard deviations for variables similar to the one being studied. If σ is estimated, which is typically the case, the conservative approach is to overestimate the value slightly rather than allow the value to be underestimated, because the smaller the value of σ, the smaller the required sample size. When solving for sample size, any fractional result should always be rounded to the next whole number. Further, unless σ is known and the population is normally distributed, any computed sample size below 30 should be increased to 30, so that use of the normal distribution is appropriate. Finally, we can state that Formula (9-8) can be used with respect to either a one-tail or a two-tail test. The only value that would differ is the value of z_0, as illustrated in the examples below.

As an example of applying Formula (9-8) to determine the required sample size for a one-tail test, let us use the following assigned values from our previous example (Section 9-3) concerning the possible development of a shopping center:

Hypotheses:
$$H_0: \mu \geqslant \$1,400$$
$$H_1: \mu < \$1,400$$
$$\mu_0 = \$1,400$$

$$\mu_1 = \$1,300$$

$$\alpha = 0.05$$

$$\beta = 0.10$$

$$\sigma = \$300$$

The minimum required sample size by which we can set the probabilities of a type I and type II error at 0.05 and 0.10, respectively, is then

$$n = \frac{(z_0 - z_1)^2 \sigma^2}{(\mu_1 - \mu_0)^2} = \frac{(-1.65 - 1.28)^2 (300)^2}{(1,300 - 1,400)^2} = \frac{(-2.93)^2 (300)^2}{(-100)^2} = \frac{772,641}{10,000} = 77.2641$$

$$= 78$$

Note that z_0 and z_1 would always have the opposite arithmetic signs before entry into Formula (9-8). Therefore, subtracting z_1 from z_0 always results in the two values being accumulated. If the accumulated value is a negative value, as in the example above, the process of squaring results in a positive value.

Suppose that the prospective developer of the shopping center is concerned about a deviation of $100 in *either* direction from the hypothesized average monthly household income of $1,400. A reason might be that while the center would not be developed if the income level is $1,300 or less, a different type of center would be developed if the income level is at least $1,500. Because any actual deviation can be only in one direction or the other, we can determine the minimum sample size by reference to either the negative *or* the positive deviation and then use the appropriate z_0 and z_1 values. As before, the values of z_0 and z_1 will always be accumulated. For our example, the two columns of values below are used to demonstrate that either solution procedure results in the same required sample size.

$$H_0: \mu = \$1,400$$

$$H_1: \mu \neq \$1,400$$

$\mu_0 = \$1,400$	$\mu_0 = \$1,400$
$\mu_1 = \$1,300$	$\mu_1 = \$1,500$
$\alpha = 0.05$	$\alpha = 0.05$
$\beta = 0.10$	$\beta = 0.10$
$\sigma = \$300$	$\sigma = \$300$

$$n = \frac{(z_0 - z_1)^2 \sigma^2}{(\mu_1 - \mu_0)^2}$$

$$= \frac{(-1.96 - 1.28)^2 (300)^2}{(1,300 - 1,400)^2} \quad \text{or} \quad \frac{[1.96 - (-1.28)]^2 (300)^2}{(1,500 - 1,400)^2}$$

$$= \frac{(-3.24)^2 (300)^2}{(-100)^2} \quad \text{or} \quad \frac{(3.24)^2 (300)^2}{(100)^2}$$

$$= \frac{944,784}{10,000} \quad \text{or} \quad \frac{944,784}{10,000}$$

$$= 94.4784 = 95$$

Thus, for a two-tail test the minimum required sample size such that $\alpha = 0.05$ and $\beta = 0.10$ is $n = 95$. Note that the value of z_0 is with respect to the two-tail hypothesis-testing procedure but that the value of z_1 is always with respect to the one-tail probability for the particular alternative value.

9-5 USE OF STUDENT'S t DISTRIBUTION

As explained in Section 7-5 on interval estimation, use of the t distribution in conjunction with the sampling distribution of the mean is appropriate when the sample is small ($n < 30$), the population is approximately normally distributed, and σ is not known. Under such circumstances the procedure used to test a hypothesized value of the population mean is identical to the procedure based on use of the normal distribution in Section 9-2, except that the critical value is a t value. The test statistic is

$$t = \frac{\bar{X} - \mu_0}{s_{\bar{X}}} \tag{9-9}$$

As an example of using the t distribution in hypothesis testing, suppose that the production standard in the manufacture of size D cells for use as flashlight batteries requires a mean life of $\mu \geqslant 22.0$ hours. A sample of $n = 9$ batteries has a sample mean life of $\bar{X} = 20.0$ hours with the sample standard deviation $s = 3.0$ hours. Battery life in general is known to be approximately normally distributed. Giving the benefit of doubt to the assumption that the production process is in control and using the 5 percent level of significance, we test the hypothesis that the population mean is at least 22.0 hours as follows:

Hypotheses: $\qquad\qquad\qquad\quad H_0 : \mu \geqslant 22.0$

$$H_1 : \mu < 22.0$$

Level of significance: $\qquad\qquad\quad \alpha = 0.05$

Critical value of test statistic: $\quad t_{\mathrm{df}=n-1} = t_8 = -1.860$

$$t = \frac{\bar{X} - \mu_0}{s_{\bar{X}}}$$

where $s_{\bar{X}} = s/\sqrt{n} = 3.0/\sqrt{9} = 1.0$.

$$t = \frac{20.0 - 22.0}{1.0} = \frac{-2.0}{1.0} = -2.00$$

Thus, the obtained t is in the region of rejection of the null hypothesis at the 5 percent level of significance, and the alternative hypothesis, that the mean battery life is less than 22.0 hours, is accepted.

As in Section 7-5 on interval estimation, the normal distribution can be used to approximate values of t when $df \geqslant 29$ (i.e., $n \geqslant 30$). Technically, the t distribution is also appropriate when the sample is large and $s_{\bar{X}}$ is used to estimate $\sigma_{\bar{X}}$, regardless of the form of the population. But $df \geqslant 29$ justifies using z as an approximation of t, as well as justifying use of the central-limit theorem. Therefore only when $df < 29$ do we consider it necessary to use Student's t distribution.

9-6 USE OF CHEBYSHEV'S INEQUALITY

As explained in Section 7-6 on interval estimation, use of Chebyshev's inequality in conjunction with the sampling distribution of the mean is appropriate when the sample is small $(n < 30)$ and the population is *not* assumed to be normally distributed. The form of Chebyshev's inequality that is appropriate in the context of hypothesis testing and that indicates the maximum probability that the sample mean is located more than k standard error units from the population mean is

$$P(|\bar{X} - \mu| > k\sigma_{\bar{X}}) \leqslant \frac{1}{k^2} \tag{9-10}$$

In the context of Chebyshev's inequality, according to whether σ is known, k is defined as

$$k = \frac{\bar{X} - \mu_0}{\sigma_{\bar{X}}} \tag{9-11}$$

or

$$k = \frac{\bar{X} - \mu_0}{s_{\bar{X}}} \tag{9-12}$$

The procedure followed in the test is that the sample mean is converted into a value of k as the test statistic, and the critical value of k is determined by setting $1/k^2$ equal to the significance level and then solving for the critical value of k:

$$\frac{1}{k^2} = \alpha \qquad k^2 = \frac{1}{\alpha}$$

$$\text{Critical } k = \pm \sqrt{\frac{1}{\alpha}} \tag{9-13}$$

As an example of using Chebyshev's inequality in hypothesis testing, suppose it is required that the average net weight of potato chips per bag be $\mu = 16.0$ ounces. On the basis of previous data, we know that $\sigma = 0.5$ ounce and that the distribution of weights cannot be assumed to follow the normal probability distribution. A random sample of $n = 10$ bags of chips has a mean weight of $\bar{X} = 15.8$ ounces. Giving the benefit of the doubt to the assumption that the process is in control, we formulate and test the null hypothesis at the 5 percent level of significance as follows.

Hypotheses: $H_0 : \mu = 16.0$

$H_1 : \mu \neq 16.0$

Level of significance: $\alpha = 0.05$

$$\text{Critical } k = \pm \sqrt{\frac{1}{\alpha}} = \sqrt{\frac{1}{0.05}} = \sqrt{20} = \pm 4.472$$

$$k = \frac{\bar{X} - \mu_0}{\sigma_{\bar{X}}}$$

where $\sigma_{\bar{X}} = \sigma / \sqrt{n} = 0.5 / \sqrt{10} = 0.158$.

$$k = \frac{15.8 - 16.0}{0.158} = \frac{-0.2}{0.158} = -1.266$$

Therefore, the obtained value of k is in the region of acceptance of the null hypothesis, and we cannot reject the hypothesis that the process is in control.

Any hypothesis-testing procedure based on Chebyshev's inequality must involve a two-tail test because the population distribution is not assumed to be symmetrical. Chebyshev's inequality is rarely used in hypothesis testing, because a relatively large difference between the values of the sample mean and the hypothesized mean is required to reject the null hypothesis. In this sense, the test is not sensitive to small differences. But this inequality is the only appropriate basis for testing a hypothesized value of the mean if the sample is small ($n < 30$) and the population is not normally distributed.

9-7 SUMMARY TABLE FOR TESTING A HYPOTHESIZED VALUE OF THE POPULATION MEAN

In this chapter we have described the conditions under which the normal probability distribution, Student's t distribution, and Chebyshev's inequality can

Table 9-3 Summary table for testing a hypothesized value of the population mean

Population	Sample size	σ known	σ unknown
Normally distributed	Large ($n \geqslant 30$)	$z = \dfrac{\bar{X} - \mu_0}{\sigma_{\bar{X}}}$	$z = \dfrac{\bar{X} - \mu_0}{s_{\bar{X}}}$ [†]
	Small ($n < 30$)	$z = \dfrac{\bar{X} - \mu_0}{\sigma_{\bar{X}}}$	$t = \dfrac{\bar{X} - \mu_0}{s_{\bar{X}}}$
Not normally distributed	Large ($n \geqslant 30$)	$z = \dfrac{\bar{X} - \mu_0}{\sigma_{\bar{X}}}$ [*]	$z = \dfrac{\bar{X} - \mu_0}{s_{\bar{X}}}$ [*,†]
	Small ($n < 30$)	$k^{**} = \dfrac{\bar{X} - \mu_0}{\sigma_{\bar{X}}}$ [**]	$k^{**} = \dfrac{\bar{X} - \mu_0}{s_{\bar{X}}}$ [**,§]

[*] Central limit theorem is invoked.
[**] Where $1/k^2$ is determined based on Chebyshev's inequality.
[†] z is used as an approximation of t.
[§] Some statisticians consider this test unreliable, because of the fluctuation in the value of $s_{\bar{X}}$ for small samples.

serve as the basis for testing a hypothesized value of the population mean. Table 9-3 summarizes the appropriate test statistics for such tests.

9-8 SUMMARY

The *basic steps* in any hypothesis-testing procedure in business and economics are

1. Formulate the null hypothesis and the alternative hypothesis.
2. Specify the level of significance to be used.
3. Select the test statistic.
4. Establish the critical value or values of the test statistic.
5. Determine the actual value of the test statistic.
6. Make the decision.
7. Take the appropriate managerial action.

The basis for establishing the critical value(s) of the test statistic when testing a hypothesized value of the population mean can be the normal probability distribution, Student's t distribution, or Chebyshev's inequality. Relevant factors are the size of the sample, whether the population is normally distributed, and whether the population standard deviation σ is known, as summarized in Table 9-3. A *two-tail test* is used when we are concerned about a possible deviation in either direction from the hypothesized value of the mean, while a *one-tail test* is used when we are concerned about a possible deviation in one direction only. Thus, two-tail tests have two regions of rejection, while one-tail tests have a region of rejection either in the lower tail *or* in the upper tail (not both) of the probability density model.

In hypothesis testing, a *type I error* is the probability of rejecting a true null hypothesis. The probability of a type I error is always equal to the level of significance and is designated by α. A *type II error* is the probability of accepting a false null hypothesis. The probability of a type II error depends on the value of the specific alternative hypothesis chosen as a point of reference and is designated by β. The *power* of a test is the probability that a false null hypothesis will be rejected and is equal to $1 - \beta$.

Given that the normal probability distribution will be used as the basis for the test, the levels of α and β in testing a hypothesized value of the mean can be designated before data collection, and the minimum required sample size can be determined. When this approach is used, the value of σ must be known or estimated. Any fractional value for the sample size is always rounded to the next whole number and because the procedure is based on use of the normal distribution, any computed sample size below 30 should be increased to $n = 30$, unless the population is normally distributed and σ is known.

Having established the basic concepts associated with hypothesis testing in this chapter, in the following chapter we consider tests concerned with several additional types of population parameters.

FORMULAS

(9-1) Critical $\bar{X} = \mu_0 \pm z\sigma_{\bar{X}}$

Critical limits of the sample mean for a two-tail test when σ is known, based on use of the normal probability distribution.

(9-2) Critical $\bar{X} = \mu_0 \pm zs_{\bar{X}}$

Critical limits of the sample mean for a two-tail test when σ is not known, based on use of the normal probability distribution ($n \geqslant 30$).

(9-3) $z = \dfrac{\bar{X} - \mu_0}{\sigma_{\bar{X}}}$

Conversion of an observed value of a sample mean into z when σ is known.

(9-4) $z = \dfrac{\bar{X} - \mu_0}{s_{\bar{X}}}$

Conversion of an observed value of a sample mean into z when σ is not known ($n \geqslant 30$).

(9-5) Critical $\bar{X} = \mu_0 + z\sigma_{\bar{X}}$

Critical limit of the sample mean for a one-tail test when σ is known, based on use of the normal probability distribution.

(9-6) Critical $\bar{X} = \mu_0 + zs_{\bar{X}}$

Critical limit of the sample mean for a one-tail test when σ is not known, based on use of the normal probability distribution ($n \geqslant 30$).

(9-7) Power $= 1 - \beta$

Probability of rejecting a null hypothesis that is in fact false, given a specific alternative hypothesis.

(9-8) $n = \dfrac{(z_0 - z_1)^2 \sigma^2}{(\mu_1 - \mu_0)^2}$

Minimum required sample size for testing a hypothesized value of the mean when the probability of a type I error (α) and the probability of a type II error (β) are specified.

(9-9) $t = \dfrac{\bar{X} - \mu_0}{s_{\bar{X}}}$

Conversion of a sample mean into a t value when this value is used as the test statistic.

(9-10) $P(|\bar{X} - \mu| > k\sigma_{\bar{x}}) \leqslant \dfrac{1}{k^2}$

The form of Chebyshev's inequality used in the context of testing a hypothesis concerning the population mean.

(9-11) $k = \dfrac{\bar{X} - \mu_0}{\sigma_{\bar{X}}}$

Conversion of a sample mean into the k test statistic when Chebyshev's inequality serves as the basis for testing a hypothesized value of the mean, given that σ is known.

(9-12) $k = \dfrac{\bar{X} - \mu_0}{s_{\bar{X}}}$

Conversion of a sample mean into the k test statistic when Chebyshev's inequality serves as the basis for testing a hypothesized value of the mean, given that σ is not known.

(9-13) $\quad$ Critical $k = \pm \sqrt{\dfrac{1}{\alpha}}$ $\qquad$ The critical limits of k when Chebyshev's inequality is used to test a hypothesis concerning the population mean.

EXERCISES

9-1 Describe how statistical estimation and hypothesis testing *differ* by considering
(*a*) The difference in the limits defined in the two procedures
(*b*) The type of problem, or application, for which each method would be used

9-2 Discuss the concept of a type I error by describing
(*a*) How the probability of such an error can be determined
(*b*) How the probability of such an error can be reduced
(*c*) Why a decision maker might choose not to reduce the probability of this type of error and might even choose to increase it

9-3 The manufacturer of three-way light bulbs claims that the bulbs have an average life of 2,500 hours. A sample of 36 bulbs has an average (mean) life of 2,325 hours with a standard deviation of 600 hours. Carry out a hypothesis-testing procedure by identifying the null and alternative hypotheses, identifying the critical z value(s) for the test at the 5 percent level of significance, and comparing the value of z for the sample data with the critical z value(s). Designate the manufacturer's claim as the null hypothesis.

9-4 In a decision problem such as that described in Exercise 9-3 the purchaser might not be concerned if the manufacturer's claim is exceeded but rather would be specifically concerned about the possibility that the bulbs do not live up to the claim. From this viewpoint repeat the analysis for the data of Exercise 9-3.

9-5 The manufacturer of a new car claims that the automobile will average at least 32 miles per gallon for general highway driving. For 49 test runs the car model averages 31.5 miles per gallon with a standard deviation of 2.3 miles per gallon. Designating the manufacturer's claim as the null hypothesis, can this claim be rejected at the 5 percent level of significance?

9-6 Before the highway tests were carried out, a consumer advocate claimed that the new car would average *no more than* 32 miles per gallon for general highway driving. Using the data of Exercise 9-5, test this claim at the 5 percent level of significance by designating the consumer advocate's claim as the null hypothesis. Briefly discuss the implications regarding which hypothesis in a decision-analysis situation is taken as the principal, or null, hypothesis to be tested.

9-7 With respect to the hypothesis-testing situation described in Exercise 9-5, suppose it is considered to be an important discrepancy if the actual average mileage is 31 miles per gallon (or less). Determine (*a*) the probability of a type II error and (*b*) the power associated with the statistical test.

9-8 Discuss the concept of a type II error by defining what it means and indicating how the probability of such an error can be determined.

9-9 A fertilizer company claims that the use of its product will result in a yield of at least 35 bushels of wheat per acre, on the average. Application of the fertilizer to a randomly selected 36 sample acres results in a yield of 33 bushels per acre with a standard deviation of 5.0 bushels. Designating the manufacturer's claim as the null hypothesis, can this claim be rejected at the 1 percent level of significance?

9-10 With respect to the null hypothesis in Exercise 9-9 suppose it is considered an important discrepancy if the actual average yield is at 32 bushels per acre (or less). Before the sample is collected, the population standard deviation is estimated to be $\sigma = 4.5$ bushels. Determine the minimum required sample size if it is desired that the probability of a type I error should not exceed 0.01 and the probability of a type II error should not exceed 0.02.

9-11 For a random sample of 50 firms from a particular industry the mean number of employees per firm is 420.4 with a sample standard deviation of 55.7. A total of 380 firms comprises this industry. Before the data were collected, it was hypothesized that the mean number of employees per firm in this industry would not exceed 408 employees. Test this hypothesis at the 5 percent level of significance.

9-12 Suppose the analyst in Exercise 9-11 neglected to use the finite correction factor in determining the value of the standard error of the mean. What would be the result of the test at the 5 percent level of significance?

9-13 A random sample of 30 employees at the secretary II level in a large organization take a standardized typing test. The sample results are $\bar{X} = 63.0$ words per minute with $s = 5.0$ words per minute. Test the null hypothesis that the secretaries in general do *not* exceed a typing speed of 60 words per minute, using the 1 percent level of significance.

9-14 With reference to Exercise 9-13 suppose it is considered an important difference from the hypothesized value of the mean if the average typing speed is at least 64.0 words per minute. Determine the probability of (*a*) a type I error and (*b*) a type II error.

9-15 The superintendent of a manufacturing department informs the plant personnel manager that he needs additional skilled operators who can assemble an average of at least three components per minute. Because several available applications have all had prior satisfactory work experience of a similar type in the company, the personnel manager believes that they all qualify. However, the superintendent decides to obtain a 30-minute sampling of work to identify any applicant clearly below the required standard. For a 30-minute work sample a particular applicant assembles an average (mean) of 2.8 components per minute with a standard deviation of 0.5 component per minute. Given the viewpoint that the applicants are considered acceptable unless the work sample clearly indicates otherwise, should this applicant be placed on the job? Use the 5 percent level of significance for your test. Is there any possible (statistical) difficulty with the sampling procedure used to collect the data?

9-16 In reference to the null hypothesis in Exercise 9-15 suppose it is considered an important difference if an applicant can assemble only 2.5 components (or less) per minute, on the average. Assuming that the standard deviation of the number of components assembled per minute is 0.5 for an applicant, what sample size, in minutes, should be collected so that $\alpha = 0.05$ and $\beta = 0.10$? Assume that the number of components assembled per minute is normally distributed.

9-17 For the situation described in Exercise 9-15, instead of assuming that the applicants are qualified unless the sample indicates otherwise, the personnel manager cautiously begins with the assumption that the applicants are *not* qualified and specifically that the number of components assembled is no greater than three units per minute. A particular applicant assembles an average of 3.1 units in the 30 minute period with a standard deviation of 0.6 unit per period. Given the viewpoint in this exercise, should this applicant be placed on the job? Use the 5 percent level of significance for your test.

9-18 Describe the situation in which it is appropriate to use the *t* distribution in testing a hypothesis concerning the population mean.

9-19 Each of a random sample of 10 packages of cereal has the contents, in ounces, listed in the table below.

Oz./package	11.8	11.7	12.1	11.9	12.0	12.0	11.7	12.0	11.8	12.0

(*a*) Compute the mean for this sample.
(*b*) Compute the sample standard deviation.

(c) Compute the standard error of the mean.

(d) Suppose the required minimum average weight per package is 12.0 ounces and the population of the weights is assumed to be normally distributed. On the basis of this sample, can we reject the hypothesis that this requirement is being satisfied at the 5 percent level of significance?

9-20 An industrial development advisor has claimed that the average hourly wage being paid in a small firm employing just 100 people is at least $6.85. For a random sample of $n = 25$ employees the average hourly wage is $\bar{X} = \$6.75$ with a sample standard deviation of 25 cents. The wage amounts are assumed to be approximately normally distributed in the population. Designating the industrial development advisor's claim as the null hypothesis, test the claim using the 5 percent level of significance.

9-21 Suppose the average net weight for No. 303 cans of peas being packed in a canning plant is specified to be 11.2 ounces (drained). A random sample of $n = 10$ cans of peas is taken, and the mean weight per can is found to be $\bar{X} = 11.0$ ounces with a standard deviation of $s = 0.30$ ounce. The weights being packed in general are known to be normally distributed. Assuming that we are concerned only about the alternative that the contents are underweight rather than overweight, test the null hypothesis that the average weight of drained peas per can in the sampled production run is at least 11.2 ounces, using the 5 percent level of significance.

9-22 A fast-foods chain will build a new outlet in a proposed location if at least 200 cars per hour pass the location during certain prime hours. For 20 randomly sampled hours during the prime periods, the average number of cars passing the location is $\bar{X} = 208.5$ with $s = 30.0$. The statistical population is assumed to be approximately normal. The management of the chain conservatively adopts the null hypothesis that the traffic volume does *not* satisfy their requirement, i.e., $H_0: \mu \leqslant 200.0$. Can this hypothesis be rejected at the 5 percent level of significance?

9-23 Suppose the sample results in Exercise 9-22 are based on a sample of $n = 50$ hours. Can the null hypothesis be rejected at the 5 percent level of significance?

9-24 An automatic dispenser for soft ice cream has been set to dispense 4.00 ounces of ice cream per serving. For a sample of $n = 10$ servings the average amount of ice cream is $\bar{X} = 4.05$ ounces with $s = 0.10$ ounce. The amounts being dispensed are assumed to be normally distributed. Basing the null hypothesis on the assumption that the process is in control, should the dispenser be reset as a result of a test at the 5 percent level of significance? 2 tail

9-25 With reference to the null hypothesis in Exercise 9-24 suppose it is considered an important discrepancy if the amount of soft ice cream being dispensed differs from the standard by 0.10 ounce (or more). The population standard deviation is $\sigma = 0.10$ and the population of weights is assumed to be normally distributed. What sample size should be observed, as a minimum, so that the probability of both a type I error and a type II error is set at 0.05?

9-26 A shipment of 100 defective machines has been received in a machine-repair department. For a random sample of 10 machines, the average repair time is $\bar{X} = 85.0$ minutes with $s = 15.0$ minutes. Test the null hypothesis $H_0: \mu = 100.0$ minutes, using the 10 percent level of significance and basing the test on the assumption that the distribution of repair time is approximately normal. 2 tail

9-27 The promotional literature for a franchise opportunity for a gift store includes the claim that the customers of established stores spend an average of at least $10 each on purchases. A prospective investor in the franchise offering visits an established store in a nearby city and observes the purchase amounts for 20 customers at randomly selected times during the period of the visit. The average (mean) purchase amount for the sample is $8.80 with a standard deviation of $3.85. Giving the "benefit of the doubt" to the promotional claim, determine if the claim can be rejected at the 5 percent level of significance. The sales amounts are assumed to be approximately normally distributed.

9-28 Suppose the distribution of weights in the population for the data in Exercise 9-24 cannot be assumed to be normally distributed. Test the null hypothesis specified in Exercise 9-24 using the (a) 5 percent level of significance and (b) 10 percent level of significance.

9-29 Suppose the distribution of repair time in Exercise 9-26 cannot be assumed to be approximately normally distributed. Test the null hypothesis $H_0 : \mu = 100.0$ at the (a) 5 percent level of significance and (b) 10 percent level of significance.

9-30 Based on historical data, the standard deviation of the amount of time spent per client in an income tax service office is $\sigma = 15$ minutes. The null hypothesis is established as $H_0 : \mu \leqslant 2$ hours per client. For a random sample of $n = 15$ clients the average time spent per client is $\bar{X} = 2$ hours, 10 minutes. Test the null hypothesis at the 5 percent level of significance assuming

  (a) The time spent per client in the population is normally distributed.
  (b) The time spent per client in the population is not normally distributed.

TEN

TESTING OTHER HYPOTHESES

10-1 TESTING THE DIFFERENCE BETWEEN TWO MEANS USING THE NORMAL DISTRIBUTION

The procedure associated with testing the difference between the means of two populations follows the basic steps in hypothesis testing described in Section 9-1. However, the relevant standard error is the standard error of the difference between means, as introduced in Section 8-1 on estimating the difference between two population means. Use of the normal distribution for testing the difference between two means is always appropriate when each of the two sample sizes is large $(n \geqslant 30)$, because the central-limit theorem can be invoked. If either sample is small $(n < 30)$, use of the normal distribution is appropriate only if that population is assumed to be normally distributed and the value of the population standard deviation σ is known.

As explained in Section 8-1, three formulas [Formulas (8-3), (8-4), and (8-6)] can be used to calculate or estimate the value of the standard error of the difference between means. For convenience, these formulas are repeated below.

When the two population standard deviations are known, the standard error of the difference between the means of the two samples, each taken from the respective population, is

$$\sigma_{\bar{X}_1 - \bar{X}_2} = \sqrt{\sigma_{\bar{X}_1}^2 + \sigma_{\bar{X}_2}^2} \qquad (8\text{-}3)$$

When the two population standard deviations are not known and not assumed to be equal, the standard error of the difference between means is estimated by

$$s_{\bar{X}_1 - \bar{X}_2} = \sqrt{s_{\bar{X}_1}^2 + s_{\bar{X}_2}^2} \qquad (8\text{-}4)$$

When the two population standard deviations are not known but are assumed to be equal, it is first required that a pooled estimate of the (common) population variance be made:

$$\hat{\sigma}^2 = \frac{(n_1 - 1)s_1^2 + (n_2 - 1)s_2^2}{n_1 + n_2 - 2} \qquad (8\text{-}5)$$

Then the standard error of the difference is estimated by

$$\hat{\sigma}_{\bar{X}_1 - \bar{X}_2} = \sqrt{\frac{\hat{\sigma}^2}{n_1} + \frac{\hat{\sigma}^2}{n_2}} \qquad (8\text{-}6)$$

When a difference between means is tested based on use of the normal distribution, the standard normal z value serves as the test statistic. The basic formula for converting an observed difference between two sample means into a value of z is

$$z = \frac{(\bar{X}_1 - \bar{X}_2) - (\mu_1 - \mu_2)_0}{\sigma_{\bar{X}_1 - \bar{X}_2}} \qquad (10\text{-}1)$$

As indicated in Formula (10-1), we can begin with any assumed difference $(\mu_1 - \mu_2)_0$ to be tested. However, the usual null hypothesis when the difference between means is tested is that there is no difference between the means of the two populations. Therefore, the numerator in Formula (10-1) can be simplified to recognize this factor. Consequently, the formulas to convert an observed difference between the means of two samples into the z test statistic are

$$z = \frac{\bar{X}_1 - \bar{X}_2}{\sigma_{\bar{X}_1 - \bar{X}_2}} \qquad (10\text{-}2)$$

use formula from Ralph

or
$$z = \frac{\bar{X}_1 - \bar{X}_2}{s_{\bar{X}_1 - \bar{X}_2}} \qquad (10\text{-}3)$$

or
$$z = \frac{\bar{X}_1 - \bar{X}_2}{\hat{\sigma}_{\bar{X}_1 - \bar{X}_2}} \qquad (10\text{-}4)$$

In testing the difference between two means, when it is the null hypothesis that there is no difference between the population means, it is often also the hypothesis that the two samples were obtained from the same statistical population. This means that $\sigma_1 = \sigma_2$ and that Formula (10-4) is used in such tests. The assumption that the two sample variances were obtained from the same population can itself be tested as the null hypothesis by the procedure described in Section 10-9.

As an example of testing the difference between means, suppose it is hypothesized that there is no difference between the average monthly household income in two large communities, even though they may differ in the variability (variance) of the income amounts. A random sample of $n_1 = 40$ households in the first community has a mean of $\bar{X}_1 = \$1,900$ with $s_1 = \$540$. For the second community a sample of $n_2 = 30$ households has a mean of $\bar{X}_2 = \$1,600$ with $s = \$420$. Using the 5 percent level of significance, we test the null hypothesis that there is no difference between the average monthly household income in the two communities as follows:

Hypotheses: $\qquad\qquad\qquad H_0 : \mu_1 = \mu_2$

$$H_1 : \mu_1 \neq \mu_2$$

Critical z $(\alpha = 0.05) = \pm 1.96$

$$\bar{X}_1 = \$1,900 \qquad \bar{X}_2 = \$1,600$$

$$s_1 = \$540 \qquad s_2 = \$420$$

$$n_1 = 40 \qquad n_2 = 30$$

$$z = \frac{\bar{X}_1 - \bar{X}_2}{s_{\bar{X}_1 - \bar{X}_2}}$$

where $\bar{X}_1 - \bar{X}_2 = \$1,900 - \$1,600 = \$300$

$s_{\bar{X}_1} = s_1 / \sqrt{n_1} = 540 / \sqrt{40} = \$85.38$

$s_{\bar{X}_2} = s_2 / \sqrt{n_2} = 420 / \sqrt{30} = \$76.68$

$s_{\bar{X}_1 - \bar{X}_2} = \sqrt{s_{\bar{X}_1}^2 + s_{\bar{X}_2}^2} = \sqrt{(85.38)^2 + (76.68)^2} = \sqrt{13,169.5668} = \$114.76$

$$z = \frac{300}{114.76} = 2.61$$

Thus, the obtained value of the test statistic z exceeds the positive critical value 1.96 and is in the region of rejection of the null hypothesis. Therefore we reject the null hypothesis that there is no difference between the average monthly household income levels in the two communities, and we accept the alternative hypothesis that there is a difference. Recall that these same data were used in Section 8-1 as the basis for defining a 95 percent confidence interval for estimating the difference between the two average income amounts. In that section we determined that the confidence limits for the 95 percent confidence interval were $75 and $525. That the 95 percent confidence interval does not include the value $0 within the interval is consistent with our rejection of the null hypothesis of no difference at the 5 percent level of significance in the present example.

Suppose that *before* the sample results in the above example were observed, it was believed that the average monthly income level in the first community was higher than the income amount in the second community. To subject this belief to a statistical test, we give the benefit of the doubt to the opposite possibility that the income amount in the first community is less than or equal to the income amount in the second community. We test this hypothesis at the 1 percent level of significance, again without assuming that the standard deviations of the two populations are equal, as follows:

Hypotheses:
$$H_0: \mu_1 \leqslant \mu_2$$
$$H_1: \mu_1 > \mu_2$$
$$\text{Critical } z \ (\alpha = 0.01) = 2.33$$
$$\text{Computed } z = 2.61 \text{ (from the preceding example)}$$

Therefore, at the 1 percent level of significance we reject the null hypothesis that the average monthly household income in the first community is less than or equal to the household income in the second community. Instead we accept the alternative hypothesis that the average monthly household income is greater in the first community. From this example notice that the belief we want to test should not generally be defined as the null hypothesis, because if we want to test a belief or a claim from a skeptical point of view, we should not give it the benefit of the doubt in the hypothesis-testing procedure.

10-2 TESTING THE DIFFERENCE BETWEEN TWO MEANS USING STUDENT'S t DISTRIBUTION

Use of Student's t distribution for testing the difference between two population means is appropriate when

1. The samples are small ($n < 30$)
2. The population standard deviations σ are not known
3. The populations are assumed to be approximately normally distributed

As was true in Section 8-2 on estimating the difference between two population means, an additional required assumption is that the standard deviations of the two populations are equal. Therefore, when the value of t is used as the test statistic, the standard error of the difference between means is always designated by $\hat{\sigma}_{\bar{X}_1 - \bar{X}_2}$

in this book and would be calculated by Formulas (8-5) and (8-6). The observed difference between the sample means is converted into a value of t by

$$t = \frac{\bar{X}_1 - \bar{X}_2}{\hat{\sigma}_{\bar{X}_1 - \bar{X}_2}} \qquad (10\text{-}5)$$

As in Section 8-2 on interval estimation, the degrees of freedom to be used in conjunction with the t distribution are $df = n_1 + n_2 - 2$. Also, values from the standard normal distribution z can be used to approximate required critical values of t when $df \geqslant 29$. However, note that if z is substituted for t, for any small $(n < 30)$ sample the corresponding population must be assumed to be approximately normally distributed, because the central-limit theorem cannot be invoked.

As an example of using the t distribution, the null hypothesis is that there is no difference between the mean bulb life of two brands of light bulbs. For a random sample of $n_1 = 12$ bulbs of one brand the mean bulb life is $\bar{X}_1 = 3,400$ hours with a sample standard deviation of $s_1 = 240$ hours. For the second brand of bulbs the mean bulb life for a sample of $n_2 = 8$ bulbs is $\bar{X}_2 = 2,800$ hours with $s_2 = 210$ hours. The distribution of bulb life is assumed to be approximately normal, and the standard deviations of the two populations are assumed to be equal. Using the 1 percent level of significance, we test the null hypothesis as follows:

Hypotheses:
$$H_0 : \mu_1 = \mu_2$$
$$H_1 : \mu_1 \neq \mu_2$$
$$df = n_1 + n_2 - 2 = 12 + 8 - 2 = 18$$

Critical t (df = 18, $\alpha = 0.01$) = ±2.878

$$\bar{X}_1 = 3,400 \qquad \bar{X}_2 = 2,800$$
$$s_1 = 240 \qquad s_2 = 210$$
$$n_1 = 12 \qquad n_2 = 8$$
$$t = \frac{\bar{X}_1 - \bar{X}_2}{\hat{\sigma}_{\bar{X}_1 - \bar{X}_2}}$$

where $\bar{X}_1 - \bar{X}_2 = 3,400 - 2,800 = 600$
$$\hat{\sigma}^2 = [(n_1 - 1)s_1^2 + (n_2 - 1)s_2^2]/(n_1 + n_2 - 2)$$
$$= [11(240)^2 + 7(210)^2]/(12 + 8 - 2) = 942,300/18 = 52,350$$
$$\hat{\sigma}_{\bar{X}_1 - \bar{X}_2} = \sqrt{\hat{\sigma}^2/n_1 + \hat{\sigma}^2/n_2} = \sqrt{52,350/12 + 52,350/8} = \sqrt{10,906.25}$$
$$= 104.43$$

$$t = \frac{600}{104.43} = 5.745$$

Because the value of the test statistic t exceeds the positive critical limit of 2.878, we reject the null hypothesis that there is no difference between the mean bulb life for the two brands of bulbs, and we accept the alternative hypothesis that there is a difference in mean bulb life.

10-3 TESTING THE DIFFERENCE BETWEEN TWO MEANS BASED ON PAIRED OBSERVATIONS

The procedures in Sections 10-1 and 10-2 are appropriate for data situations in which two random samples are independently obtained from their respective populations. However, in a comparison of two sample means such samples are often collected as pairs of values, and the two samples are therefore dependent samples rather than independent samples. For instance, in determining whether a training program influences productivity, an experimental design would involve dependent samples if the mean productivity figures being compared (tested) are for the same group of people, but before and after the program. In contrast, an experimental design would involve independent samples if the mean productivity figures of two different samples of people are compared, with one sample being taken from those who did not have the training and the other sample being taken from those who did have the training.

The dependent samples do not have to contain the same people in both groups, as in our before-and-after example above. Instead, the individuals (or other types of sampling units) can be matched so that for each individual in one sample group there is an individual in the other sample group with similar characteristics important to the experiment. Therefore, these types of samples are referred to as *paired observations*, or *matched pairs.*

As an example of a matched-pairs design, suppose we wish to compare the effectiveness of two different training approaches to the objective of improving productivity. The same individuals cannot participate in both programs, because they would then have more than one type of program experience. Before program assignment, however, pairs of individuals at the same level of productivity could be randomly chosen, and then one person from each pair would be randomly assigned to one type of program, and the other person would be assigned to participate in the other program. Again, this differs from two independent samples, in which case two groups of people would be randomly selected for each of the two types of programs without regard to previous levels of productivity.

The degree of experimental control for the paired-observations sampling design is greater than it is for independent samples. The result is a lower sampling error, and the test for the difference between means is more sensitive to detecting a difference that actually exists.

To test a hypothesis concerning the difference between the means of two populations in the case of paired observations, we first determine the difference d between each pair of values in the paired samples. Then we test the hypothesis regarding the assumed value of the population difference, with the usual hypothesis being that the average difference in the population is zero. Thus, the two sets of sample data are reduced to one set of d values, and from the standpoint of the computational procedure used the test is much like the one-sample test of a hypothesized value of a population mean, as described in Chapter 9.

The mean and standard deviation of the set of sample d values are obtained from the formulas presented in Chapter 3, except that d is substituted for X in the formulas. The mean difference for a sample of paired observations is

$$\bar{d} = \frac{\Sigma d}{n} \qquad (10\text{-}6)$$

The deviations formula and the computational formula for the standard deviation of the differences between the paired observations are, respectively,

$$s_d = \sqrt{\frac{\Sigma(d - \bar{d})^2}{n - 1}} \qquad (10\text{-}7)$$

$$s_d = \sqrt{\frac{\Sigma d^2 - n\bar{d}^2}{n - 1}} \qquad (10\text{-}8)$$

The standard error of the mean difference between paired observations is obtained by Formula (7-5) for estimating the standard error of the mean, except that the standard deviation in the numerator is the standard deviation of the sample d values rather than the sample X values:

$$s_{\bar{d}} = \frac{s_d}{\sqrt{n}} \qquad (10\text{-}9)$$

The test statistic used to test the difference between the means based on paired observations is the t statistic, because the standard error of the mean difference $s_{\bar{d}}$ is estimated on the basis of sample data and because the population distribution for d values generally can be assumed to be approximately normally distributed. The degrees of freedom are equal to the number of *pairs* of observed sample values minus one, or $n - 1$. Or to put it another way, the degrees of freedom are equal to the number of d values minus one. As before, the standard normal distribution z can be used to approximate required critical values of t when df ≥ 29 (i.e., when $n \geq 30$). The general form of the test statistic, where $\bar{D}_0$ is the hypothesized difference between the two means, is

$$t = \frac{\bar{d} - \bar{D}_0}{s_{\bar{d}}} \qquad (10\text{-}10)$$

As indicated earlier in this section, the usual hypothesis is that there is no difference between the means of the two populations; thus the test statistic simplifies to

$$t = \frac{\bar{d}}{s_{\bar{d}}} \qquad (10\text{-}11)$$

As an example of using paired observations to test the difference between means, a training director wishes to compare two training approaches for new machine operators. Approach A involves practice trials with operators who have already achieved high productivity, while approach B involves a lecture/discussion session with representatives from the work standards department. The training director matches 10 pairs of trainees according to age, experience, and level of productivity in the previous job assignment and randomly assigns one member of each pair to approach A and the other to approach B. During the week following the training session, the number of units produced per worker is recorded, and the results are reported in Table 10-1. Using the 5 percent level of significance, we test the hypothesis that there is no difference between the mean levels of productivity following the two approaches to training as follows:

Hypotheses: $\qquad H_0: \mu_A = \mu_B$ (or $\mu_d = 0$, or $\bar{D} = 0$)

$$H_1: \mu_A \neq \mu_B \text{ (or } \mu_d \neq 0, \text{ or } \bar{D} \neq 0)$$

Critical t (df = 9, $\alpha = 0.05$) = ± 2.262

$$\bar{X}_A = \frac{206}{10} = 20.6 \text{ units}$$

$$\bar{X}_B = \frac{197}{10} = 19.7 \text{ units}$$

$$t = \frac{\bar{d}}{s_{\bar{d}}}$$

where $\bar{d} = \Sigma d/n = 9/10 = 0.9$

$$s_d = \sqrt{(\Sigma d^2 - n\bar{d}^2)/(n-1)} = \sqrt{[57 - 10(0.9)^2]/(10-1)} = \sqrt{5.4333} = 2.33$$

$$s_{\bar{d}} = s_d/\sqrt{n} = 2.33/\sqrt{10} = 0.74$$

$$t = \frac{0.9}{0.74} = 1.216$$

Because the obtained value of the test statistic t is within the critical limits ± 2.262, the null hypothesis that there is no difference between the mean level of productivity with the two approaches to training cannot be rejected at the 5 percent level of significance.

Table 10-1 Productivity data and worksheet for computing the mean difference and the standard deviation of the difference

| Trainee pair | No. units produced | | Difference between pairs d | d^2 |
	Approach A	Approach B		
1	18	20	-2	4
2	20	19	1	1
3	25	21	4	16
4	21	22	-1	1
5	19	21	-2	4
6	26	22	4	16
7	16	15	1	1
8	20	18	2	4
9	19	16	3	9
10	22	23	-1	1
Total	206	197	9	57

Before the data in Table 10-1 were collected, the training director believed approach A was the superior approach to training. To test this belief, the training director gives the benefit of the doubt to approach B and formulates the null hypothesis $H_0: \mu_A \leqslant \mu_B$. Using the 5 percent level of significance, this one-tail test is carried out as follows:

Hypotheses:

$$H_0: \mu_A \leqslant \mu_B \text{ (or } \mu_d \leqslant 0, \text{ or } \bar{D} \leqslant 0)$$

$$H_1: \mu_A > \mu_B \text{ (or } \mu_d > 0, \text{ or } \bar{D} > 0)$$

$$\text{Critical } t \text{ (df} = 9, \alpha = 0.05) = 1.833$$

$$t = 1.216 \text{ (from the preceding example)}$$

Again, the obtained t statistic is in the region of acceptance of the null hypothesis. Thus, we cannot reject the null hypothesis that the mean productivity level associated with approach A is less than or equal to the mean productivity level associated with approach B.

10-4 TESTING A HYPOTHESIZED VALUE OF THE PROPORTION USING THE BINOMIAL DISTRIBUTION

When a sampling process represents a Bernoulli process, as described in Section 5-3, the binomial probability distribution serves as the basis for testing hypotheses for the population proportion. Recall that a Bernoulli process is one in which

1. There are two possible outcomes in each trial
2. The trials, or observations, are independent
3. The process is stationary with the probability of success in any trial being designated by p

In the present context the population proportion π serves as the value for the binomial probability p. That is, in testing a hypothesized value of the population proportion, we observe a sample result and determine the probability that such a sample result could have occurred by chance by determining the binomial probability associated with the result.

To take a simple situation in which the binomial distribution can be used in hypothesis testing, suppose that we formulate the null hypothesis that a coin is fair. We then toss the coin five times and observe that the coin lands heads all five times. Using the 10 percent level of significance, we test the null hypothesis as follows:

Hypotheses:

$$H_0: \pi = 0.50$$

$$H_1: \pi \neq 0.50$$

Critical outcomes $(\alpha = 0.10)$: $X = 0$ heads or $X = 5$ heads

As shown in Table 10-2, the extreme outcome in each "tail" of the distribution is

Table 10-2 Binomial probability distribution for the number of heads $P(X|n = 5, p = 0.50)$

No. of heads X	$P(X)$
0	0.0312
1	0.1562
2	0.3125
3	0.3125
4	0.1562
5	0.0312

$P(X = 0) = 0.0312$ and $P(X = 5) = 0.0312$. The sum of these two areas is $P = 0.0624$. If we consider the next outcome in each tail, the area in each tail is $P = 0.0312 + 0.1562 = 0.1874$, and the sum of two such tails would exceed the specified level of significance of 0.10. Therefore, the level of significance we use in the present two-tail test is $\alpha = 0.0624$.

Observed outcome: $X = 5$ heads

Therefore the null hypothesis is rejected at the specified 10 percent level (in fact, 6.24 percent level) of significance. Had we specified that the test be carried out at the 5 percent level of significance, the null hypothesis could not be rejected. As a two-tail test, no outcome is so divergent that the two-tail probability is 0.05 or less. The other point of interest in this example is that because the binomial probability distribution is a discrete probability model, it is not possible to carry out the test at exactly a standard level of significance, such as $\alpha = 0.10$. In our example the closest level without exceeding the specified 0.10 level is $\alpha = 0.0624$.

Typically, tests of proportions based on using the binomial probability distribution are one-tail tests. Therefore the sample results in only one direction are generally of concern. For example, suppose that before the sample result above was observed, we suspected that the coin might be biased in favor of heads. To test this belief without giving it the benefit of the doubt, we formulate the null hypothesis as follows:

Hypotheses: $H_0: \pi \leqslant 0.50$

$H_1: \pi > 0.50$

Critical outcome ($\alpha = 0.05$): $X = 5$ heads

(From Table 10-2 note that the actual one-tail level of significance is $\alpha = 0.0312$.)

Observed outcome: $X = 5$ heads

Therefore the null hypothesis is rejected, and the alternative hypothesis, that the coin is biased in favor of heads, is accepted.

As a broader example of using the binomial distribution in hypothesis testing, suppose that a college official claims that at least 30 percent of the students have part-time jobs. This claim is given the benefit of the doubt and therefore is designated as the null hypothesis. (As explained in Section 10-1, note that the benefit of the doubt generally is *not* given to a claim.) For a random sample of $n = 15$ students it is observed that only three of the students have part-time jobs. We test the null hypothesis at the 5 percent level of significance as follows:

Hypotheses: $\qquad\qquad\qquad\qquad H_0: \pi \geqslant 0.30$

$\qquad\qquad\qquad\qquad\qquad\qquad H_1: \pi < 0.30$

Critical outcomes ($\alpha = 0.05$): $\qquad X \leqslant 1$

(because $P(X \leqslant 1 | n = 15, \ p = 0.30) = 0.0352$, while $P(X \leqslant 2 | n = 15, \ p = 0.30) = 0.1268$).

Observed outcome: $\qquad\qquad\qquad X = 3$

Therefore the null hypothesis that a proportion of at least 0.30 of the students hold part-time jobs cannot be rejected at the 5 percent level (actually, the 3.52 percent level) of significance. With a larger sample the same relative sample result might indeed lead to rejection of the null hypothesis. We illustrate this point in Section 10-5.

10-5 TESTING A HYPOTHESIZED VALUE OF THE PROPORTION USING THE NORMAL DISTRIBUTION

As explained in Section 8-3 on confidence intervals for the population proportion, a proportion is essentially a converted count of the number of "successes" in a Bernoulli process. As explained in Section 6-3, the rule we use in this text is that the normal distribution can be used to approximate binomial probabilities when $n \geqslant 30$, $np \geqslant 5$, and $nq \geqslant 5$. Therefore, although the sampling distribution of the proportion follows the binomial distribution, in many data situations we can use the normal distribution to test a hypothesized value of the population proportion. In the context of hypothesis testing the hypothesized value of a population parameter is assumed to be correct until or unless it is rejected following an observed sample result. Because the hypothesized proportion π_0 serves as the basis for the Bernoulli probability p, in hypothesis testing we consider that use of the normal distribution is appropriate when $n \geqslant 30$, $n\pi_0 \geqslant 5$, and $n(1 - \pi_0) \geqslant 5$. The general formula for the standard error of the proportion used in hypothesis testing is

$$\sigma_{\hat{p}} = \sqrt{\frac{\pi_0(1 - \pi_0)}{n}} \qquad\qquad (10\text{-}12)$$

The formula for the standard error of the proportion that includes the finite correction factor is

$$\sigma_{\hat{p}} = \sqrt{\frac{\pi_0(1 - \pi_0)}{n}} \sqrt{\frac{N-n}{N-1}} \qquad\qquad (10\text{-}13)$$

As contrasted to the formulas for the standard error of the proportion presented in Chapter 8, on estimation [Formulas (8-10) and (8-11)] Formulas (10-12) and (10-13) include π_0 instead of $\hat{p}$. Again, the reason is that the hypothesized value of the proportion is accepted as correct until or unless it is rejected. Therefore π_0 serves as the basis for calculating the standard error of the proportion. Further, because the standard error is not based on using $\hat{p}$ as an estimator of π, the sample size required for normal approximation is $n \geqslant 30$ rather than the $n \geqslant 100$ required for interval estimation in Section 8-3.

The procedure for testing a hypothesis concerning the population proportion when the normal probability distribution is used is identical to the procedure for testing a hypothesis concerning the population mean, as described in Section 9-2, except that a hypothesized value of the proportion is involved. The formula to convert a sample proportion into a z value, which serves as the test statistic, is

$$z = \frac{\hat{p} - \pi_0}{\sigma_{\hat{p}}} \qquad (10\text{-}14)$$

In the preceding section the null hypothesis was formulated that at least 30 percent of the students attending a college hold part-time jobs; that is, H_0: $\pi \geqslant 0.30$. For a random sample of $n = 15$ students we observed that only three of them had jobs. Based on the binomial distribution, we could not reject the null hypothesis at the 5 percent level of significance, because the region of rejection was $X \leqslant 1$. Now, suppose that we modify this example by changing the sample size to $n = 75$, and we observe that 15 of these students hold part-time jobs. Note that for both the small and the large samples the proportion of students in the sample who hold part-time jobs is $\hat{p} = 0.20$; that is $3/15 = 0.20$ and $15/75 = 0.20$. In the present situation, however, we can use the normal probability distribution to test the hypothesis because the following rules are satisfied:

1. $n \geqslant 30$ (in this example, $n = 75$)
2. $n\pi_0 \geqslant 5$ [in this example, $n\pi_0 = 75(0.30) = 22.5$]
3. $n(1 - \pi_0) \geqslant 5$ [in this example, $n(1 - \pi_0) = 75(0.70) = 52.5$]

Using the 5 percent level of significance and assuming that use of the finite correction factor is not necessary because the sample size is less than 5 percent of the population size, we test the null hypothesis as follows:

Hypotheses: $\qquad\qquad\qquad H_0: \pi \geqslant 0.30$

$$H_1: \pi < 0.30$$

$$\text{Critical } z \ (\alpha = 0.05) = -1.65$$

$$z = \frac{\hat{p} - \pi_0}{\sigma_{\hat{p}}}$$

where $\hat{p} = X/n = 15/75 = 0.20$
$\qquad \pi_0 = 0.30$
$\qquad \sigma_{\hat{p}} = \sqrt{\pi_0(1 - \pi_0)/n}\ \sqrt{[0.30(0.70)]/75} = \sqrt{0.0028} = 0.053$

$$z = \frac{0.20 - 0.30}{0.053} = \frac{-0.10}{0.053} = -1.89$$

The obtained value of z is in the region of rejection of the null hypothesis. Therefore we reject the null hypothesis that the proportion of all students at the college who hold part-time jobs is equal to or greater than 0.30, and we accept the alternative hypothesis that the proportion is less than 0.30. As we noted at the beginning of this example, with a sample of $n = 15$ and $\hat{p} = 0.20$ we were not able to reject the null hypothesis, but with a sample of $n = 75$ and $\hat{p} = 0.20$ we now find that we do reject the null hypothesis. This difference illustrates that there is relatively less sampling error associated with a larger sample, and therefore a difference of the same relative magnitude with respect to the null-hypothesized value might not be significant for a small sample but be significant for the larger sample.

10-6 DETERMINING THE REQUIRED SAMPLE SIZE FOR TESTING THE PROPORTION

Before a sample is collected, the required sample size for testing a hypothesis concerning the population proportion based on use of the normal probability distribution can be determined by specifying

1. The hypothesized value of the proportion
2. A specific alternative value of the proportion such that the difference from the null-hypothesized value is considered important
3. The level of significance to be used (α)
4. The probability of a type II error permitted (β)

Based on this information, the formula for determining the minimum required sample size for testing a hypothesis concerning the population proportion is

$$n = \left[\frac{z_0 \sqrt{\pi_0(1 - \pi_0)} - z_1 \sqrt{\pi_1(1 - \pi_1)}}{\pi_1 - \pi_0} \right]^2 \qquad (10\text{-}15)$$

In Formula (10-15) z_0 is the critical value of z used with the specified level of significance (α), while z_1 is the value of z with respect to the designated probability of a type II error (β). As explained in Section 9-4, where we considered the required sample size for testing a hypothesized value of the mean, z_0 and z_1 will always have opposite arithmetic signs, and therefore the two identities in the numerator of Formula (10-15) will always be accumulated. As also explained in Section 9-4, Formula (10-15) can be used with respect to either a one-tail or a two-tail test. Any fractional sample size should always be rounded up to the next whole number. Further, because Formula (10-15) is based on use of the normal probability distribution, the sample size should always be large enough to satisfy three rules: (1) $n \geqslant 30$, (2) $n\pi_0 \geqslant 5$, and (3) $n(1 - \pi_0) \geqslant 5$.

Before collection of sample data, suppose we wish to test the null hypothesis that at least 30 percent of the students attending a college have part-time jobs, H_0: $\pi \geqslant 0.30$. We wish to carry out the test at the 5 percent level of significance and allow no more than a 10 percent probability of a type II error if the true proportion is in fact $\pi = 0.20$ (or less). The information for determining the minimum required sample size is

Hypotheses:
$$H_0: \pi \geqslant 0.30$$
$$H_1: \pi < 0.30$$
$$\pi_0 = 0.30$$
$$\pi_1 = 0.20$$
$$\alpha = 0.05$$
$$\beta = 0.10$$

The minimum required sample size is

$$n = \left[\frac{z_0\sqrt{\pi_0(1 - \pi_0)} - z_1\sqrt{\pi_1(1 - \pi_1)}}{\pi_1 - \pi_0} \right]^2$$

$$= \left[\frac{-1.65\sqrt{0.30(0.70)} - 1.28\sqrt{0.20(0.80)}}{0.20 - 0.30} \right]^2 = \left(\frac{-0.7561 - 0.5120}{-0.10} \right)^2$$

$$= (12.68)^2 = 160.8 = 161$$

10-7 TESTING THE DIFFERENCE BETWEEN TWO POPULATION PROPORTIONS

When we wish to test the hypothesis that the proportions in two populations are not different, the two sample proportions obtained are pooled for the purpose of determining the standard error of the difference between proportions. The pooled estimate of the population proportion is

$$\hat{\pi} = \frac{n_1\hat{p}_1 + n_2\hat{p}_2}{n_1 + n_2} \tag{10-16}$$

The standard error of the difference between proportions used with hypothesis testing is

$$\hat{\sigma}_{\hat{p}_1 - \hat{p}_2} = \sqrt{\frac{\hat{\pi}(1 - \hat{\pi})}{n_1} + \frac{\hat{\pi}(1 - \hat{\pi})}{n_2}} \tag{10-17}$$

Note that Formula (10-17) differs from the standard error of the difference between proportions defined in Formula (8-16) and used in constructing confidence intervals. The reason is that in constructing confidence intervals, the assumption is that there is a difference between the population proportions, and therefore each sample $\hat{p}$ is used as an estimator of the respective π. But in hypothesis testing the null hypothesis tested is that there is no difference between the population proportions. Therefore, it makes sense that the two sample proportions should be pooled as the basis for estimating the (common) population proportion. We designate the standard error of the difference between proportions which is used in hypothesis testing by $\hat{\sigma}_{\hat{p}_1 - \hat{p}_2}$, but the standard error used in constructing a confidence interval is designated by $s_{\hat{p}_1 - \hat{p}_2}$.

The observed difference between two sample proportions is converted into the z test statistic by

$$z = \frac{\hat{p}_1 - \hat{p}_2}{\hat{\sigma}_{\hat{p}_1 - \hat{p}_2}} \tag{10-18}$$

Because the application of Formula (10-18) is based on use of the normal probability distribution and the value of π is estimated on the basis of sample data, both samples have to be very large ($n \geqslant 100$), as explained in Section 8-6. Further, for each sample it is required that $n\hat{\pi} \geqslant 5$ and $n(1 - \hat{\pi}) \geqslant 5$. As is true for testing the difference between means in Section 10-1, hypotheses concerning differences between proportions can involve one-tail or two-tail tests.

As an example of testing the difference between proportions, suppose that we believe a higher proportion of students in the College of Business (π_1) holds part-time jobs as compared with students in the College of Education (π_2). To subject our belief to a critical test, we give the benefit of the doubt to the opposite possibility and designate the null hypothesis $H_0: \pi_1 \leqslant \pi_2$. For a random sample of $n_1 = 100$ students from the College of Business the number of students who hold part-time jobs is $X_1 = 30$. For a random sample of 150 students from the College of Education the number of students holding part-time jobs is $X_2 = 36$. The colleges have large enrollments; so use of finite correction factors is not required. Using the 5 percent level of significance, we test the null hypothesis as follows:

Hypotheses: $\qquad\qquad\qquad\qquad H_0: \pi_1 \leqslant \pi_2$

$$H_1: \pi_1 > \pi_2$$

Critical z ($\alpha = 0.05$) $= 1.65$

$n_1 = 100 \qquad\qquad\qquad\qquad n_2 = 150$

$X_1 = 30 \qquad\qquad\qquad\qquad X_2 = 36$

$$\hat{p}_1 = \frac{X_1}{n_1} = \frac{30}{100} = 0.30 \qquad \hat{p}_2 = \frac{X_2}{n_2} = \frac{36}{150} = 0.24$$

$$z = \frac{\hat{p}_1 - \hat{p}_2}{\hat{\sigma}_{\hat{p}_1 - \hat{p}_2}}$$

where $\hat{p}_1 - \hat{p}_2 = 0.30 - 0.24 = 0.06$

$\hat{\pi} = (n_1 \hat{p}_1 + n_2 \hat{p}_2)/(n_1 + n_2) = [100(0.30) + 150(0.24)]/(100 + 150)$

$$= 66/250 = 0.264$$

$$\hat{\sigma}_{\hat{p}_1 - \hat{p}_2} = \sqrt{\hat{\pi}(1 - \hat{\pi})/n_1 + \hat{\pi}(1 - \hat{\pi})/n_2}$$

$$= \sqrt{(0.264)(0.736)/100 + (0.264)(0.736)/150}$$

$$= \sqrt{0.001943 + 0.001295} = \sqrt{0.003238} = 0.057$$

$$z = \frac{0.06}{0.057} = 1.05$$

The obtained value of the z test statistic is in the region of acceptance of the null hypothesis. Therefore we cannot reject the hypothesis that the proportion of students in the College of Business who have part-time jobs is equal to or less than that in the College of Education.

10-8 TESTING A HYPOTHESIZED VALUE OF THE VARIANCE OR STANDARD DEVIATION USING THE χ^2 (CHI-SQUARE) DISTRIBUTION

As explained in Section 8-7, for a normally distributed population the ratio $(n-1)s^2/\sigma^2$ follows the χ^2 (chi-square) probability distribution, with a different χ^2 distribution being appropriate according to the degrees of freedom $(n-1)$ involved. Therefore, when a null hypothesis concerning the value of the variance has been formulated, the hypothesized value σ_0 replaces σ in the ratio and the observed value of the sample variance is converted into the χ^2 test statistic by

$$\chi^2 = \frac{(n-1)s^2}{\sigma_0^2} \tag{10-19}$$

The obtained value of the test statistic is then compared to the critical required value or values of χ^2, depending on whether a one-tail or two-tail test is involved. Typically, hypotheses concerning variances are concerned with one-tail tests. Table B-6 reports areas for the χ^2 distribution with respect to various degrees of freedom df. If the null hypothesis of interest concerns the value of the population standard deviation, for the purpose of the test the hypothesized value of the standard deviation is squared so that the value of the variance is tested.

As an example of testing a hypothesis concerning a population standard deviation, suppose that the production standard for the manufacture of light bulbs specifies that the standard deviation of bulb life should be no greater than $\sigma = 200$ (that is, H_0: $\sigma^2 \leqslant 40{,}000$). For a random sample of $n = 12$ bulbs the mean bulb life is $\bar{X} = 3{,}400$ hours with the sample standard deviation $s = 240$ hours. Bulb life is assumed to be approximately normally distributed. Giving the benefit of the doubt to the hypothesis that the manufacturing process is in control, we test the null hypothesis at the 5 percent level of significance as follows:

Hypotheses: H_0: $\sigma^2 \leqslant 40{,}000$

H_1: $\sigma^2 > 40{,}000$

$$\text{Critical } \chi^2 \ (df = 11, \ \alpha = 0.05) = 19.63$$

$$\chi^2 = \frac{(n-1)s^2}{\sigma_0^2} = \frac{(12-1)240^2}{40,000} = 15.84$$

Because the computed value of $\chi^2 = 15.84$ does not exceed the critical value $\chi^2 = 19.63$ for this one-tail test, the null hypothesis cannot be rejected. Therefore the managerial implication is that we accept the assumption that the process is in control in terms of the variance (standard deviation) of bulb life. Incidentally, in quality-control applications the assumption that the process is in control generally is given the benefit of the doubt and is designated as the null hypothesis, because tests are continuously made, and we would not want to keep stopping the process for needless adjustments.

10-9 THE F DISTRIBUTION AND TESTING THE DIFFERENCE BETWEEN TWO VARIANCES OR TWO STANDARD DEVIATIONS

It can be shown that when two samples are taken independently from the same normally distributed population, the ratio of the two sample variances s_1^2/s_2^2 is distributed as the F distribution, with a different F distribution being appropriate for every combination of the degrees of freedom df associated with the numerator and denominator of this ratio. For each of the two samples $df = n - 1$. Because this ratio is distributed as the F distribution, the F value is used as the test statistic when testing the hypothesis that two population variances are equal. If the null hypothesis states that two population standard deviations are equal, the two sample standard deviations are squared, and the test is carried out with respect to the hypothesis that the variances are equal. Thus, the test statistic used to test the null hypothesis that there is no difference between two population variances (or two population standard deviations) is

$$F = \frac{s_1^2}{s_2^2} \tag{10-20}$$

Now, if the two samples were obtained from the same population or from populations with equal variances, it follows that we would expect the ratio in Formula (10-20) to be about 1.0. In fact, the expected (long-run average) value of this ratio is not exactly 1.0 but is equal to $df_2/(df_2 - 2)$, for mathematical reasons that are beyond the scope of this book. In any event, any given pair of sample-variance values are not likely to be identical, even though the null hypothesis is true. About half the time the ratio will be larger than 1.0, and half the time it will be smaller than 1.0. The F distribution provides the basis for determining how large or how small this ratio should be to conclude that the difference between the sample variances is significant. Although it is a necessary assumption that the samples have been taken from normally distributed populations, the F test is relatively unaffected by departures from normality when each population is at least unimodal and the sample sizes are about equal.

Table B-7 reports the values of F that serve as the critical values for the upper 5 percent and 1 percent tail of the distribution. The degrees of freedom df in the numerator of the calculated F ratio are represented as the column headings in this table, while the degrees of freedom in the denominator are the row headings. The table does not provide lower-tail probabilities for two reasons: One is that the large majority of the applications of this table are associated with the technique called *analysis of variance*, described in Chapter 11, and in the context of such applications critical F values for only upper-tail probabilities are required. Another reason only upper-tail values of F are given in Table B-7 is that lower-tail values of F can be calculated on the basis of upper-tail values of F by the so-called reciprocal property of the F distribution. The F distribution is not a symmetrical distribution. However, the reciprocal property by which a lower-tail value can be obtained by reference to an upper-tail value is

$$F_{df_1, df_2, \text{lower}} = \frac{1}{F_{df_2, df_1, \text{upper}}} \tag{10-21}$$

We illustrate the use of Formula (10-21) in the following complete example of a two-tail test. In applying this formula, we determine the required lower-tail critical F value by taking the reciprocal of the equivalent upper-tail F value *but with the degrees of freedom reversed.*

In Section 10-2 on testing the difference between means by using the t distribution, we indicated that the standard deviations of the two populations must be equal. In the example in that section the sample standard deviation of bulb life for one brand of light bulbs was given as $s_1 = 240$ hours for a sample of $n_1 = 12$ bulbs, and the sample standard deviation for a second brand of bulbs was $s_2 = 210$ hours for a sample of $n_2 = 8$ bulbs. Using the 10 percent level of significance, we test the null hypothesis that there is no difference in the standard deviations of bulb life for the two brands of bulbs as follows:

Hypotheses: $H_0 : \sigma_1^2 = \sigma_2^2$

$$H_1 : \sigma_1^2 \neq \sigma_2^2$$

Critical $F_{11,7, \text{upper } 5\%} = 3.60$

$$\text{Critical } F_{11,7, \text{lower } 5\%} = \frac{1}{F_{7,11, \text{upper } 5\%}} = \frac{1}{3.01} = 0.33$$

$$F = \frac{s_1^2}{s_2^2} = \frac{240^2}{210^2} = \frac{57,600}{44,100} = 1.31$$

Since the computed F ratio of 1.31 is neither smaller than 0.33 nor larger than 3.60, it is in the region of acceptance of the null hypothesis. Therefore the hypothesis that the variances (standard deviations) of the two populations are equal cannot be rejected at the 10 percent level of significance.

Now that we have demonstrated the use of the reciprocal property to determine a critical value for the lower tail of the F distribution, an additional practical comment is in order. In practice there is never any real need for a lower-tail value of F. If a one-tail test is involved, you can always designate the two populations so that the test will be an upper-tail test. If a two-tail test is involved, you can simply place the larger sample variance over the smaller sample variance, ignoring the original identification of "sample 1" and "sample 2," and use the F table (Table B-7) in the usual way, with df_1 being the degrees of freedom for the numerator and df_2 being the degrees of freedom for the denominator. The effect will always be the same as using the reciprocal property to compute the lower-tail critical value.

10-10 SUMMARY

In this chapter we described the hypothesis-testing procedures for several types of population parameters. From the standpoint of the probability models, we have described the use of the normal probability distribution, Student's t distribution, the binomial distribution, the χ^2 distribution, and the F distribution.

The normal distribution is used to test a hypothesis concerning the *difference between the means* of two populations when both samples are large ($n \geqslant 30$). If either sample is small, that population must be normally distributed and the population standard deviation σ must be known. On the other hand, Student's t distribution is used to test a hypothesis concerning the difference between means when the samples are small ($n < 30$) and σ is not known. Required assumptions for the use of Student's t distribution are that the populations are approximately normally distributed and have the same standard deviation.

A special type of sampling design often used to test the difference between means is the *paired-observations*, or *matched-pairs*, design. Computationally, this hypothesis-testing procedure involves a one-sample test that the true average difference between the pairs of values is zero. As compared with obtaining two independent samples, the advantage of the design involving dependent samples is that the test is more sensitive to detecting a difference between the population means when such a difference exists.

When the sample is small, a hypothesis concerning the *population proportion* is tested by use of the binomial distribution. The hypothesized value of the proportion π_0 serves as the basis for the Bernoulli probability p with respect to the binomial distribution. The normal probability distribution can be used for such tests when $n \geqslant 30$, $n\pi_0 \geqslant 5$, and $n(1 - \pi_0) \geqslant 5$. Whereas the sample proportion $\hat{p}$ serves as the basis for the standard error of the proportion when constructing a confidence interval for the population proportion, the hypothesized value of the proportion π_0 serves as the basis of the standard error of the proportion in hypothesis testing.

Testing the difference between two population proportions using the normal probability distribution requires that both samples be very large ($n \geqslant 100$), because the true proportion π is not known, and the two sample proportions $\hat{p}_1$ and $\hat{p}_2$ are combined to form the estimate of $\hat{\pi}$. In hypothesis testing this pooled estimate serves as the basis for estimating the value of the standard error of the difference between proportions.

For hypotheses concerning the value of the *variance or standard deviation*, the test statistic is the ratio $(n-1)s^2/\sigma_0^2$. Given a normally distributed population, this ratio is distributed as the χ^2 distribution, with a different χ^2 distribution being appropriate according to the degrees of freedom df.

The test statistic for testing *the difference between two population variances* is s_1^2/s_2^2. Given that both populations (or the common population) are normally distributed, this ratio is distributed as the F distribution when the null hypothesis is true. A different F distribution is associated with every different combination of the degrees of freedom for the numerator and denominator of this ratio.

FORMULAS

(8-3) $\quad \sigma_{\bar{X}_1 - \bar{X}_2} = \sqrt{\sigma_{\bar{X}_1}{}^2 + \sigma_{\bar{X}_2}{}^2}$

Standard error of the difference between means when the standard deviations of the two populations are known.

(8-4) $\quad s_{\bar{X}_1 - \bar{X}_2} = \sqrt{s_{\bar{X}_1}{}^2 + s_{\bar{X}_2}{}^2}$

Estimated standard error of the difference between means when the standard deviations of the two populations are not known and not assumed to be equal.

(8-5) $\quad \hat{\sigma}^2 = \dfrac{(n_1 - 1)s_1^2 + (n_2 - 1)s_2^2}{n_1 + n_2 - 2}$

Pooled estimate of the population variance based on two sample variances.

(8-6) $\quad \hat{\sigma}_{\bar{X}_1 - \bar{X}_2} = \sqrt{\dfrac{\hat{\sigma}^2}{n_1} + \dfrac{\hat{\sigma}^2}{n_2}}$

Estimated standard error of the difference between means when the population standard deviations are unknown but are assumed to be equal.

(10-1) $\quad z = \dfrac{(\bar{X}_1 - \bar{X}_2) - (\mu_1 - \mu_2)_0}{\sigma_{\bar{X}_1 - \bar{X}_2}}$

General formula for computing the z test statistic when testing the difference between means.

(10-2) $\quad z = \dfrac{\bar{X}_1 - \bar{X}_2}{\sigma_{\bar{X}_1 - \bar{X}_2}}$

z test statistic for the null hypothesis that there is no difference between the population means, given that the two population standard deviations are known.

(10-3) $\quad z = \dfrac{\bar{X}_1 - \bar{X}_2}{s_{\bar{X}_1 - \bar{X}_2}}$

z test statistic for the null hypothesis that there is no difference between the population means, given that the two population

(10-4) $z = \dfrac{\bar{X}_1 - \bar{X}_2}{\hat{\sigma}_{\bar{X}_1 - \bar{X}_2}}$

standard deviations are not known and not assumed to be equal.

z test statistic for the null hypothesis that there is no difference between the population means, given that the two population standard deviations are not known but are assumed to be equal.

(10-5) $t = \dfrac{\bar{X}_1 - \bar{X}_2}{\hat{\sigma}_{\bar{X}_1 - \bar{X}_2}}$

t test statistic for null hypothesis that there is no difference between the population means; used when the samples are small ($n < 30$), the population σ values are equal but not known, and the populations are assumed to be normally distributed.

(10-6) $\bar{d} = \dfrac{\Sigma d}{n}$

Mean difference between paired observations when using such a sampling design to test the difference between two population means.

(10-7) $s_d = \sqrt{\dfrac{\Sigma(d - \bar{d})^2}{n - 1}}$

Standard deviation of the differences between paired observations, deviations formula.

(10-8) $s_d = \sqrt{\dfrac{\Sigma d^2 - n\bar{d}^2}{n - 1}}$

Standard deviation of the differences between paired observations, computational formula.

(10-9) $s_{\bar{d}} = \dfrac{s_d}{\sqrt{n}}$

Standard error of the mean difference between paired observations.

(10-10) $t = \dfrac{\bar{d} - \bar{D}_0}{s_{\bar{d}}}$

t test statistic for testing a hypothesis concerning the difference between means in the paired-observations design.

(10-11) $t = \dfrac{\bar{d}}{s_{\bar{d}}}$

t test statistic for the null hypothesis that there is no difference between the population means, using the paired-observations sampling design.

(10-12) $\sigma_{\hat{p}} = \sqrt{\dfrac{\pi_0(1-\pi_0)}{n}}$

Standard error of the proportion used in hypothesis testing.

(10-13) $\sigma_{\hat{p}} = \sqrt{\dfrac{\pi_0(1-\pi_0)}{n}}\sqrt{\dfrac{N-n}{N-1}}$

Standard error of the proportion used in hypothesis testing when the population is finite; the finite correction factor can be omitted when $n \leqslant 0.05N$.

(10-14) $z = \dfrac{\hat{p}-\pi_0}{\sigma_{\hat{p}}}$

z test statistic for testing a hypothesis concerning the population proportion.

(10-15)

$$n = \left[\dfrac{z_0\sqrt{\pi_0(1-\pi_0)} - z_1\sqrt{\pi_1(1-\pi_1)}}{\pi_1 - \pi_0}\right]^2$$

Minimum required sample size for testing a hypothesis concerning the population proportion; the minimum sample size must also satisfy the rules (1) $n \geqslant 30$, (2) $n\pi_0 \geqslant 5$, and (3) $n(1-\pi_0) \geqslant 5$ for the appropriate use of the normal probability distribution.

(10-16) $\hat{\pi} = \dfrac{n_1\hat{p}_1 + n_2\hat{p}_2}{n_1 + n_2}$

Pooled estimate of the population proportion based on two sample proportions.

(10-17) $\hat{\sigma}_{\hat{p}_1 - \hat{p}_2} = \sqrt{\dfrac{\hat{\pi}(1-\hat{\pi})}{n_1} + \dfrac{\hat{\pi}(1-\hat{\pi})}{n_2}}$

Standard error of the difference between proportions used to test the null hypothesis that there is no difference between the population proportions.

(10-18) $z = \dfrac{\hat{p}_1 - \hat{p}_2}{\hat{\sigma}_{\hat{p}_1 - \hat{p}_2}}$

z test statistic for the null hypothesis that there is no difference between the proportions in two populations.

(10-19) $\chi^2 = \dfrac{(n-1)s^2}{\sigma_0^2}$

χ^2 test statistic for testing a hypothesis concerning the population variance or population standard deviation for a normally distributed population.

(10-20) $F = \dfrac{s_1^2}{s_2^2}$

F test statistic for testing the null hypothesis that the variances or standard deviations of two normally distributed populations are equal.

$$(10\text{-}21) \quad F_{df_1, df_2, \text{lower}} = \frac{1}{F_{df_2, df_1, \text{upper}}}$$

The reciprocal property of the F distribution by which a lower-tail F value can be determined.

EXERCISES

10-1 A random sample of 64 bearings produced by a machine has a mean diameter of 0.24 inch with a standard deviation of 0.02 inch. Another batch of 64 bearings produced by the same machine the next day has a mean diameter of 0.25 inch with a standard deviation of 0.04 inch. Using the 5 percent level of significance, test the hypothesis that the machine is not out of adjustment with respect to the difference in average diameter of the bearings in the two samples.

10-2 For Exercise 10-1 suppose that when this machine goes out of adjustment, it invariably produces smaller bearings than those produced earlier. Giving the benefit of the doubt to the assumption that the process is in control, restate the null and alternative hypotheses for the problem presented in Exercise 10-1 and indicate the result of the test.

10-3 Application of one type of fertilizer to 36 sample acres results in an average yield of 33 bushels per acre with a standard deviation of 5.0 bushels. Another type of fertilizer results in an average yield of 34 bushels of wheat per acre on 36 randomly selected acres with a standard deviation of 6.0 bushels.

(*a*) Using the 5 percent level of significance, test the null hypothesis that the average yield for the two types of fertilizer does not differ.

(*b*) Suppose that before the sample data were collected, the null hypothesis was formulated that the average yield with the first type of fertilizer is equal to or better than that with the second type of fertilizer. Can this hypothesis be rejected at the 5 percent level of significance?

10-4 For a sample of 30 employees in one large firm the mean hourly wage is $\bar{X}_1 = \$7.50$ with $s_1 = \$1.00$. In a second large firm, the mean hourly wage for a sample of 40 employees is $\bar{X}_2 = \$7.05$ with $s_2 = \$1.20$. Using the 5 percent level of significance, test the hypothesis that there is no difference between the average wage rate being earned in the two firms.

10-5 In Exercise 10-4 suppose that the null hypothesis tested was that the average wage in the second firm is equal to or greater than the average wage rate in the first firm. Can this hypothesis be rejected at the 5 percent level of significance?

10-6 A random sample of 10 No. 303 cans of peas is taken in one canning plant and the mean weight of the drained peas is found to be $\bar{X}_1 = 11.0$ ounces with a standard deviation of $s_1 = 0.30$ ounce. At another plant 10 randomly selected cans of peas have a mean drained weight of $\bar{X}_2 = 10.8$ ounces with a standard deviation of $s_2 = 0.20$ ounce. Using a 5 percent level of significance, test the null hypothesis that there is no difference in the average weight being packed at the two plants. Identify the assumptions you have to make to carry out this test.

10-7 In respect to the situation described in Exercise 10-6, before any data were obtained, the null hypothesis formulated was $H_0: \mu_1 \leq \mu_2$. Test this hypothesis using the 5 percent level of significance.

10-8 For one consumer product the mean dollar sales per retail outlet last year in a sample of $n_1 = 10$ stores was $\bar{X}_1 = \$3,425$ with $s_1 = \$200$. For a second product the mean dollar sales per outlet in a sample of $n_2 = 12$ stores was $\bar{X}_2 = \$3,250$ with $s_2 = \$175$. The sales amounts per outlet are assumed to be approximately normally distributed for both products and the variances of the two populations are assumed to be equal. Using the 1 percent level of significance, test the null hypothesis that there is no difference between the mean dollar sales for the two products.

10-9 For the data reported in Exercise 10-8 suppose that the two sample sizes were $n = 20$ and $n = 24$. Using the 1 percent level of significance, test the difference between the two means assuming, as in Exercise 10-8, that the variances of the two populations are equal.

10-10 A manager is considering the purchase of several electronic calculators to be used for general computational purposes in the company offices. The price of two competitive models is comparable and the sales representative for each model claims that the model has features that will result in less time spent doing the computational work required in the offices. To compare the two machines, the manager obtains a "loaner" from each company and determines the time required to perform typical computational routines done in the office. Of course, in the comparison the manager was careful to use several equally skilled operators who do not have an established preference for one type of machine and who have had sufficient practice time to learn the use and unique features of each machine. For the first machine the mean time required for the computations was 13.5 minutes with a sample standard deviation of 3.5 minutes for 12 randomly selected employees. For the second machine the sample mean was 12.4 minutes with a standard deviation of 3.0 minutes for a separate sample of 12 randomly selected employees. Using the 5 percent level for the test, determine whether the difference between the sample means is statistically significant.

10-11 To compare two electronic calculators in conjunction with a planned purchase of several such units, a manager obtains a "loaner" from each company and has 10 operators use each machine to perform a standard set of computations typical of those encountered in the office. Of course, in carrying out the comparison, the manager was careful to use operators who did not have an established preference or skill with either type of machine. The manager randomly assigned five of the operators to use calculator A first, while the other five used calculator B first. The number of minutes required to perform the standard set of computations, to the nearest minute, are reported in the table below. Using the 5 percent level of significance, test the null hypothesis that there is no difference between the average number of minutes required to perform the calculations on the two machines.

Operator	Calculator A	Calculator B
1	12	10
2	16	17
3	15	18
4	13	16
5	16	19
6	10	12
7	15	17
8	17	15
9	14	17
10	12	14

Time required to perform calculations, min

10-12 A salesperson claims that on the average 30 percent of the prospects contacted placed orders. For a random sample of 10 prospects the salesperson obtains just one order. Designating the salesperson's claim as the null hypothesis and using the 5 percent level of significance, state whether this hypothesis can be rejected.

10-13 For the claim in Exercise 10-12 suppose that the salesperson obtains orders from 20 of 100 randomly selected prospects.
(a) At the 5 percent level of significance can the salesperson's claim be rejected?
(b) At the 1 percent level of significance can the salesperson's claim be rejected?

10-14 A magazine publisher is considering the publication of a special annual issue to be offered to subscribers only. The anticipated selling price and costs are such that at least 20 percent of the 95,000 subscribers would have to purchase the special issue to make it economically justifiable. Therefore the publisher has decided to prepare the annual issue only if the response to a preliminary offer to a sample of the subscribers makes it unlikely (probability less than 0.05) that the percentage of all subscribers who will buy the special issue is less than or equal to 20 percent. In other words, the publisher conservatively assumes that the true percentage is less than or equal to 20 percent and is willing to make a positive commitment only if the sample indicates otherwise. For a random sample of 250 subscribers, 62 of the subscribers order the special issue. Determine whether the publisher should prepare the annual issue.

10-15 For the situation described in Exercise 10-14 suppose that the publisher considers it an important difference from the null hypothesis if 25 percent (or more) of the subscribers order the annual issue.
(a) What sample size should be collected as a minimum if the publisher stipulates that the probability of a type I error should be no larger than $\alpha = 0.01$ and the probability of a type II error should be no larger than $\beta = 0.10$?
(b) What is the minimum sample size if the publisher stipulates that $\alpha = 0.10$ and $\beta = 0.10$?

10-16 A producer of a television special expected that 40 percent (or more) of the viewing audience would watch the show in a particular metropolitan area. A random sample of twenty households with television sets turned on yields only six households watching the show. Based on this limited sample and designating the producer's expectation as the null hypothesis, can the null hypothesis be rejected at the 10 percent level of significance?

10-17 In relation to Exercise 10-16 the sample is expanded so that 100 households with sets turned on are contacted. Of the 100 households, 30 households are tuned in to the special. If the 10 percent level of significance is used, can the null hypothesis that 40 percent (or more) of the households would watch the program be rejected?

10-18 For the television special described in Exercises 10-16 and 10-17, suppose that before any sample was obtained the producer indicated that it would be an important difference from the hypothesis if 30 percent or less of the viewing audience watched the show. Determine the minimum sample size required if it is stipulated that $\alpha = 0.05$ and $\beta = 0.05$.

10-19 For the television special described in Exercises 10-16 and 10-17, it was suggested that the program might appeal differently to urban versus suburban residents, but there was a difference of opinion among the production staff regarding the direction of the difference. For a random sample of 100 urban households 40 reported watching the show; for a random sample of 100 suburban households 50 reported watching the show. Can this difference be considered significant at the 5 percent level?

10-20 Based on historical data, the standard deviation of the amount of time spent per client in an income tax service office is assumed to be no greater than $\sigma = 15$ minutes, and this assumption is designated as the null hypothesis. For a random sample of $n = 15$ clients the average time spent per client is $\bar{X} = 2$ hours, 10 minutes, with the sample standard deviation $s = 20$ minutes. The time spent per client is assumed to be approximately normally distributed. Test the null hypothesis using the (a) 5 percent and (b) 1 percent levels of significance for the test.

10-21 The manufacturer of three-way light bulbs claims that the bulbs have an average life of at least 2,500 hours, with the standard deviation of bulb life being no greater than 500 hours. Bulb life is assumed to be normally distributed. For a sample of $n = 20$ bulbs the mean bulb life is $\bar{X} = 2,439$ hours with a standard deviation of $s = 541$ hours. Designating the manufacturer's claim about the standard deviation as the null hypothesis, test this claim at the (a) 5 percent and (b) 1 percent levels of significance.

10-22 Using the 10 percent level of significance, test the null hypothesis that the two samples in Exercise 10-6 were obtained from populations with equal variances.

10-23 Using the 2 percent level of significance for your test, test the null hypothesis that the two samples in Exercise 10-8 were obtained from populations with equal variances.

10-24 In many reported studies it is implied that results that are "statistically significant" are thereby important. Discuss the appropriateness of this interpretation by considering the meaning of "significant" in the context of hypothesis testing.

ELEVEN

ANALYSIS OF VARIANCE

11-1 OBJECTIVES AND ASSUMPTIONS FOR THE ANALYSIS OF VARIANCE

The technique called *analysis of variance* serves as the foundation for a variety of statistical-analysis models related to the design of experiments. In the simplest application of the procedure the analysis of variance permits us to test the hypothesis that the means of several populations do not differ. In this respect the analysis of variance is an extension of the tests for differences between two means, as described in Chapter 10. In fact, the two principal assumptions underlying the use of the analysis of variance are the same assumptions as are required when the t distribution is used to test the difference between means. These assumptions are that the populations are normally distributed and have equal variances. In analysis of variance the latter assumption is called *homogeneity of variance*. Because the null hypothesis is that the several population means are equal, the assumption of homogeneity of variance means that for practical purposes the test is concerned with the hypothesis that the several means came from the same population. The same population is involved because any normally distributed population is completely defined by the mean and variance.

In this chapter we describe in detail only the simplest model of the analysis of variance: the *one-factor completely randomized design.* Therefore, the coverage in this chapter represents only an introduction to this technique of analysis. However, a fundamental understanding of the basic design is necessary to understand the more complex designs, which are extensions of the basic model. Entire textbooks are devoted to the various design models available in the analysis of variance.

Since the null hypothesis concerns the equality of population means, why is the technique of analysis called analysis of *variance*? As we demonstrate in the following section, it is the F test for testing the difference between two variances, as described in Section 10-9, that serves as the statistical basis for testing the null hypothesis that the several population means are equal. The basic rationale and the procedures of the analysis of variance were developed by the British statistican Sir Ronald A. Fisher. In recognition of this achievement, the F distribution was named in his honor.

11-2 THE BASIC RATIONALE ASSOCIATED WITH TESTING DIFFERENCES AMONG SEVERAL POPULATION MEANS

In this section we describe the conceptual rationale underlying the analysis of variance by illustrating the application of this method in a step-by-step manner. The concepts developed in this section are not necessarily easy or immediately obvious. But once you understand why the F test serves as the basis for testing the differences among several means, you can extend your understanding to more complex designs in the analysis of variance. Further, the steps described in this section are not generally carried out this way in an actual application of the analysis of variance. Computational formulas and summary tables that minimize the required calculations are used instead, and these are introduced in Section 11-3. If the step-by-step approach is studied first, however, the conceptual approach underlying the analysis of variance can be given primary attention.

Suppose it is the null hypothesis that the mean levels of achievement for three different methods of instruction do not differ. The null and alternative hypotheses are

$$\text{Hypotheses: } H_0: \mu_1 = \mu_2 = \mu_3$$

$$H_1: \text{The means are not all equal}$$

If the null hypothesis is rejected, the alternative hypothesis that at least two of the means are different from one another is accepted. In this respect, note that the alternative is not that all of the means necessarily are different. Finally, let us specify the level of significance to be used as $\alpha = 0.05$.

After the null and alternative hypotheses are identified and the level of significance specified, five trainees are assigned randomly to each of the three instructional methods. The achievement test scores at the conclusion of the

Table 11-1 Achievement test scores of trainees under three methods of instruction

	Instructional method		
	A_1	A_2	A_3
	86	90	82
	79	76	68
	81	88	73
	70	82	71
	84	89	81
Total	400	425	375
Mean	80	85	75

instructional unit are reported in Table 11-1. The step-by-step analysis of these data now follows.

1. Compute the mean for each sample group and then calculate the standard deviation of the sample means $s_{\bar{X}}$ (standard error of the mean) *based only on the values of the sample means.* For our example, the three sample means are reported in Table 11-1. The standard error of the mean, based on the values of the three sample means, is

$$s_{\bar{X}} = \sqrt{\frac{\Sigma(\bar{X} - \bar{X}_T)^2}{\text{No. means} - 1}} \qquad (11\text{-}1)$$

where $\bar{X}_T$, the overall, or "total," mean of all observations is

$$\bar{X}_T = \frac{\Sigma X}{n_T} = \frac{1,200}{15} = 80 \qquad (11\text{-}2)$$

$$s_{\bar{X}} = \sqrt{\frac{(80 - 80)^2 + (85 - 80)^2 + (75 - 80)^2}{3 - 1}} = \sqrt{\frac{50}{2}} = 5.0$$

Formula (11-1) is a variation of the deviations formula for computing a sample standard deviation, Formula (3-20). In the present application, however, it is the standard deviation of a set of sample *means* rather than a set of sample values.

2. Recall that a necessary assumption in the analysis of variance is that the variances of the several populations are equal. Estimate the value of this variance by reference to the standard error of the mean calculated in step 1. The estimate of the variance can be determined algebraically by solving for s^2 in the general formula for estimating the standard error of the mean based on sample data, [Formula (7-5)]:

$$s_{\bar{X}} = \frac{s}{\sqrt{n}} \qquad s = \sqrt{n}\, s_{\bar{X}}$$

$$s^2 = ns_{\bar{X}}^2 \qquad\qquad (11\text{-}3)$$

This estimate of the population variance is called the *mean square among treatment groups (MSTr)*. This type of value is called a "mean square" in the analysis of variance because the variance is, by definition, the mean of the squared deviations of a set of values with respect to the overall mean of that set. This estimate of the variance is called a "treatment groups" estimate, because it is based solely on the observed differences among the group means. In this respect the standard error of the mean estimated by Formula (11-1) is based only on the treatment group means and the overall mean for all groups combined and not on the variability among individual values within the several groups. Thus, the variance estimate given by Formula (11-3) is defined as the mean square between groups:

$$\text{MSTr} = ns_{\bar{X}}^2 \qquad\qquad (11\text{-}4)$$

One limitation of Formula (11-4) is that equal sample sizes (n) are assumed for the several sample groups. For our example, the mean square between groups is

$$\text{MSTr} = ns_{\bar{X}}^2 = 5(5.0)^2 = 125.0$$

3. Estimate the variance of the population on the basis of determining the sample variances for each of the separate groups and then pooling these several variance estimates. Each sample variance is weighted by $n - 1$ since each variance is calculated with $n - 1$ degrees of freedom. In this respect the procedure is an extension of Formula (8-5) for pooling two sample variances. Of course, if the several samples are equal in size, each sample variance is equally weighted in the pooling procedure. The resulting estimate of the population variance is called the *mean square within groups (MSW)*. Again, any variance is a "mean square." It is a "within-groups" variance estimate, because only the deviations within each sample group serve as the basis for estimating the population variance. The mean square within groups can be defined by

$$\text{MSW} = \hat{\sigma}^2 \qquad\qquad (11\text{-}5)$$

For our example, first we determine the three sample variances using the deviations formula [Formula (3-19)] as follows:

$$s^2 = \frac{\Sigma(X - \bar{X})^2}{n - 1}$$

$$s_1^2 = \frac{(86 - 80)^2 + (79 - 80)^2 + (81 - 80)^2 + (70 - 80)^2 + (84 - 80)^2}{5 - 1}$$

$$= \frac{154}{4} = 38.5$$

$$s_2^2 = \frac{(90 - 85)^2 + (76 - 85)^2 + (88 - 85)^2 + (82 - 85)^2 + (89 - 85)^2}{5 - 1}$$

$$= \frac{140}{4} = 35.0$$

$$s_3^2 = \frac{(82-75)^2 + (68-75)^2 + (73-75)^2 + (71-75)^2 + (81-75)^2}{5-1}$$

$$= \frac{154}{4} = 38.5$$

Then we pool the three sample variances:

$$\hat{\sigma}^2 = \frac{(n_1-1)s_1^2 + (n_2-1)s_2^2 + (n_3-1)s_3^2}{n_1 + n_2 + n_3 - 3}$$

$$= \frac{4(38.5) + 4(35.0) + 4(38.5)}{5+5+5-3} = \frac{448}{12} = 37.3$$

Therefore MSW = 37.3.

4. If the null hypothesis $\mu_1 = \mu_2 = \mu_3 = \cdots = \mu_k$ is true, it follows that the two mean squares obtained in steps 2 and 3 are unbiased and independent estimators of the same population variance σ^2. Therefore these two variance estimators would have the same expected value and would differ only because of sampling variability (sampling error), with either mean square being larger than the other simply by chance. However, if the null hypothesis is false, the expected value of the mean square among treatment groups (MSTr) is larger than the mean square within groups (MSW). *Any difference among the population means will inflate the expected value of MSTr while having no effect on the expected value of MSW.*

Based on the observation above, the F test can be used to test the hypothesis that the two mean squares are estimators of the same population variance, as described in Section 10-9. Because the null hypothesis will be rejected only if MSTr is significantly larger than MSW, a one-tail test is always involved in the analysis of variance. The general form of the F test in the analysis of variance is

$$F_{\mathrm{df_1}, \mathrm{df_2}} = \frac{\mathrm{MSTr}}{\mathrm{MSW}} \tag{11-6}$$

The degrees of freedom associated with the numerator MSTr are $k-1$, where k designates the number of treatment groups (number of means used in the variance estimate), and the degrees of freedom associated with the denominator are $k(n-1)$, or $kn - k$, assuming equal sample sizes for each group. If the computed F ratio exceeds the critical F value at the specified level of significance, the hypothesis that the several sample means came from the same population is rejected. For our example,

$$\text{Critical } F_{2,12,\text{upper } 5\%} = 3.88$$

$$F = \frac{\mathrm{MSTr}}{\mathrm{MSW}} = \frac{125.0}{37.3} = 3.35$$

Since the computed F ratio does not exceed the critical value of 3.88, it is in the region of acceptance of the null hypothesis. Therefore, we cannot reject the null hypothesis that there are no differences among the means of the three populations.

Although the step-by-step procedure is useful for describing and emphasizing the conceptual foundation underlying the analysis of variance, extension of this procedure is cumbersome for designs more complex than the simple comparison of several sample means based on equal sample sizes. For this reason computational formulas and standard summary tables are used, as introduced in Section 11-3. In addition, the symbol system used with these tables is different from the symbol system we used in this step-by-step explanation.

11-3 ONE–FACTOR COMPLETELY RANDOMIZED DESIGN

The *one-factor completely randomized design* of the analysis of variance is concerned with testing the difference among k sample means when the subjects are assigned randomly to each of the k treatment groups. Therefore the example application included in the step-by-step explanation in Section 11-2 is of a one-factor completely randomized design. The "one factor" is the method of instruction, with three treatments, or treatment levels, associated with this factor. The design is "completely randomized," because the 15 trainees were randomly assigned to the three treatments.

As a way of describing and differentiating the various types of experimental designs in the analysis of variance, each type of design can be represented in terms of the linear model that identifies the components influencing the value of the random variable. In the example in the preceding section the random variable is the achievement test score at the conclusion of the instructional unit. The linear equation that represents the one-factor completely randomized design is

$$X_{ik} = \mu + \alpha_k + e_{ik} \tag{11-7}$$

where μ = overall mean of all treatment populations

α_k = effect of the treatment in the particular group k from which the value was sampled

e_{ik} = random error associated with the process of sampling

Table 11-2 is the summary table for the one-factor completely randomized design and includes all required computational formulas. As indicated in Section 11-2, the symbol system in these formulas is different from that used in Section 11-2 because of the need to use a system that can be extended to multiple-factor and other types of complex designs. Thus what we called MSTr in Section 11-2 is now called the *mean square among the A-treatment groups (MSA)*. Similarly, MSW is now called the *mean square error (MSE)*, indicating that this is the variability due to sampling variability alone and does not include any influences associated with the treatments. Finally, note that the definition of the symbols in the context of the analysis of variance is not necessarily consistent with the use of these symbols in other areas of statistical analysis. For example α_k in the linear model in Formula (11-6) identifies the effect on the random variable associated with the treatment and has nothing to do with the definition of α as the level of significance in hypothesis testing. Similarly, N in Table 11-2 designates the total sample size for all treatment groups combined and does not indicate population size.

Table 11-2 Summary table for the one-factor completely randomized design (treatment groups need not be equal)

Source of variation	Sum of squares SS	Degrees of freedom df	Mean square MS	F ratio
Among treatment groups A	$SSA = \sum_{k=1}^{K} \dfrac{T_k^2}{n_k} - \dfrac{T^2}{N}$	$K-1$	$MSA = \dfrac{SSA}{K-1}$	$F = \dfrac{MSA}{MSE}$
Sampling error E	$SSE = SST - SSA$	$N-K$	$MSE = \dfrac{SSE}{N-K}$	$\cdots$
Total T	$SST = \sum_{i=1}^{n} \sum_{k=1}^{K} X^2 - \dfrac{T^2}{N}$	$N-1$	$\cdots$	$\cdots$

The new symbols included in Table 11-2 are T_k, the sum of the values in a given treatment group, and T, the sum of the values in all treatment groups. A new term in this table is "sum of squares," which indicates the sum of the squared deviations from a group mean. Dividing a sum of squares by the associated degrees of freedom yields a mean square, which is an estimator of the population variance.

Instead of the form of the null hypothesis presented in the step-by-step example in Section 11-2, an alternative form of the null hypothesis is used with the linear model. Thus, for the one-factor design the null and alternative hypotheses are

$$\text{Hypotheses: } H_0: \alpha_k = 0 \text{ for all treatments}$$

$$H_1: \alpha_k \neq 0 \text{ for all treatments}$$

If the null hypothesis is true, it follows that $\mu_1 = \mu_2 = \mu_3 = \cdots = \mu_k$, as stated in the null hypothesis in Section 11-2.

As a computational example let us apply the formulas in Table 11-2 to the data reported in Table 11-1, which were previously analyzed by the step-by-step procedure in Section 11-2. The values required in applying the formulas are

$$n_1 = 5 \qquad n_2 = 5 \qquad n_3 = 5 \qquad N = 15$$

$$T_1 = 400 \qquad T_2 = 425 \qquad T_3 = 375 \qquad T = 1,200$$

$$T_1^2 = 160,000 \qquad T_2^2 = 180,625 \qquad T_3^2 = 140,625 \qquad T^2 = 1,440,000$$

$$\sum_{i=1}^{n} \sum_{k=1}^{k} X^2 = 86^2 + 79^2 + \cdots + 81^2 = 96,698$$

The sums of squares (SS) for these data are

$$SST = \sum_{i=1}^{n} \sum_{k=1}^{k} X^2 - \frac{T^2}{N} = 96,698 - 96,000 = 698$$

Table 11-3 ANOVA table for analysis of three methods of instruction for the data in Table 11-1

Source of variation	Sum of squares SS	Degrees of freedom df	Mean square MS	F ratio
Among treatment groups A	250	$3 - 1 = 2$	$\dfrac{250}{2} = 125$	$\dfrac{125}{37.33} = 3.35$
Sampling error E	448	$15 - 3 = 12$	$\dfrac{448}{12} = 37.33$	
Total T	698	$15 - 1 = 14$		

$$\text{SSA} = \sum_{k=1}^{k} \frac{T_k^2}{n_k} - \frac{T^2}{N} = \frac{160,000}{5} + \frac{180,625}{5} + \frac{140,625}{5} - 96,000 = 250$$

$$\text{SSE} = \text{SST} - \text{SSA} = 698 - 250 = 448$$

Table 11-3 is the analysis of variance (ANOVA) table for the data in Table 11-1. As should be the case, the computed F ratio of 3.35 is identical to the ratio computed by the step-by-step procedure in Section 11-2. Again, based on 2 and 12 degrees of freedom for the numerator and denominator, respectively, this computed F is less than the critical F of 3.88 required for significance at the 5 percent level. Thus we conclude that no effects are associated with the treatments (methods of instruction), and thereby we also conclude that the mean achievement scores for the three methods of instruction do not differ.

11-4 FACTORIAL DESIGNS

A *factorial design* in the analysis of variance is a design in which more than one factor is tested for effects. The simplest factorial design is the *two-factor completely randomized design*. For instance, for our example in the preceding sections of this chapter we could have an experiment in which we test not only for the effect of the instructional method but also for the effect associated with different instructors. The data requirements include the necessity that every instructor teach under every method of instruction.

The data for such a two-factor experiment are reported in a two-way table, with the treatments for one factor (e.g., instructional method) being the column headings and the treatments for the other factor (e.g., instructor) being the row headings. Table 11-4 indicates the general form of the data table for the example of three instructional methods and four instructors. The values of the random variable, in our example the achievement test scores, are entered in the cells of this table. As a "completely randomized" design, it is required that the subjects be randomly assigned to the cells, which represent the different combinations of treatments for the two factors. For a complete factorial analysis, it is necessary that every cell have at least two observations; such repetition is referred to as *replication* in the analysis of variance model.

As indicated by the format of Table 11-4, the treatments in the column headings are typically called the *A* treatments while those in the row headings are called *B* treatments. Given that replication is included, the linear equation that represents the two-factor completely randomized design is

$$X_{ijk} = \mu + \beta_j + \alpha_k + \iota_{jk} + e_{ijk} \tag{11-8}$$

where μ = overall mean of all treatment populations

β_j = effect of treatment j in the *B* (row) dimension

α_k = effect of treatment k in the *A* (column) dimension

ι_{jk} = effect of interaction between treatment j (of factor *B*) and treatment k (of factor *A*) (ι is the Greek "iota")

e_{ijk} = random error associated with the process of sampling

Three different null hypotheses are tested when the two-factor completely randomized design is used. These hypotheses are that

1. There are no column effects (the column means are not significantly different)
2. There are no row effects (the row means are not significantly different)
3. There is no interaction between the two factors (the two factors are independent)

Hypotheses: $H_0: \alpha_k = 0$ for all columns

$H_0: \beta_j = 0$ for all rows

$H_0: \iota_{jk} = 0$ for all cells

The test for interaction was not included in the one-factor model in Section 11-3, because such an effect can only be considered in the context of a factorial

Table 11-4 Example of data table for a factorial experiment involving two factors

Instructor	Instructional method		
	A_1	A_2	A_3
B_1			
B_2			
B_3			
B_4			

design. The presence of *interaction* in a two-factor experiment would mean that the treatments are not independent and that the particular effect of the treatment level in one factor differs according to the treatment level of the other factor. For example, if the null hypothesis that there is no interaction were rejected for Table 11-4, this rejection would indicate that the effectiveness of the instructional method varies with the identification of the instructor (and vice versa). We would then conclude that the two factors (instructional method and instructor) are *not independent* but rather that there is a *relationship* between the two factors. When a significant interaction effect exists, the existence of any column and/or row effects may not be meaningful in terms of applying the research results.

The computations required in conjunction with factorial designs are beyond the intended scope of this introductory chapter. However, with the availability of standard computer programs such calculations would seldom be done manually. For factorial designs that include more than two factors all possible interactions among the factors are tested in addition to the main effects. For example, for the three-factor completely randomized design the main effects tested are effects associated with factors A, B, and C. The interactions tested are $A \times B$, $A \times C$, $B \times C$, and $A \times B \times C$. Thus, seven null hypotheses are tested with such a design.

11-5 THE RANDOMIZED–BLOCK DESIGN

Another type of design often used in the analysis of variance, and for which standard computer programs are available, is the *randomized-block design*. Essentially, this design is an extension of the matched-pairs design described in Section 10-3 in which the difference between the means for paired observations was tested. The simplest example of the randomized-block design is one involving just one factor. For instance let us consider the example of testing the effect of different instructional methods on achievement, as presented in Sections 11-2 and 11-3. In the completely randomized design considered in those sections, the fifteen subjects were randomly assigned to the three instructional methods, with five subjects assigned to each treatment. By contrast, in the randomized-block design we would first match groups of three individuals according to some relevant basis, such as ability or previous achievement, and then randomly assign one person from each group to each of the three treatments (methods of instruction). As for the matched-pairs design, for certain types of experiments the same subject could participate under all of the treatment conditions, and for this reason the randomized-block design is sometimes called the treatment $\times$ subject design. But applications in business and economics generally involve matched groups. The word "blocks" refers to the matched groups, the equivalent of the matched pairs in the paired-observations design. Thus, in testing the difference between means, we have the choice of using independent samples or paired observations, as described in Chapter 10. In testing the difference among several means, we have the choice of using the one-factor completely randomized design or the one-factor randomized-block design.

Table 11-5 Example of a data table for the one-factor randomized-block design

Level of ability (block)	Instructional method		
	A_1	A_2	A_3
B_1			
B_2			
B_3			
B_4			
B_5			

Table 11-5 indicates the general form of the data table for the one-factor randomized-block design for the example of three methods of instruction and five levels of ability, as represented by the five blocks. Although this data table appears very similar to Table 11-4 for the two-factor design, there are two important differences: One is that the rows represent the blocks (matched groups) and not treatments or levels of a second factor. A second difference is that there is only one observation in each cell in Table 11-5, instead of the replication required in the factorial design. In terms of data structure the two-factor completely randomized design can be referred to as two-way analysis with replication, while the one-factor randomized-block design can be referred to as two-way analysis without replication. These latter descriptions are used in some textbooks and some computer programs.

The linear equation for the one-factor randomized-block design is

$$X_{jk} = \mu + \beta_j + \alpha_k + e_{jk} \tag{11-9}$$

where μ = overall mean of all treatment populations
  β_j = effect of block j
  α_k = effect of treatment k
  e_{jk} = random error associated with the process of sampling

As with the one-factor completely randomized design described in Section 11-3, the null hypothesis tested is that there is no treatment (column) effect H_0: $\alpha_k = 0$. If this hypothesis is true, it follows that $\mu_1 = \mu_2 = \cdots = \mu_k$. As a matter of convention, however, an F ratio is also calculated for the blocks (row) effect. We would always expect that there would be a significant blocks effect, because the subjects are matched and assigned to blocks on a basis that is supposed to be related to the performance, or effect, being measured. In fact, the absence of a significant blocks effect would indicate that the choice of the blocks was not done on an appropriate basis. Finally, note that the linear model in Formula (11-9) does not include an interaction term. It is not possible to test for interaction in the absence of replication; that is, one cannot test for interaction when there is only one entry per cell in the data table.

11-6 ADDITIONAL CONSIDERATIONS

All models and computational procedures described in this chapter are for *fixed-effects models* of the analysis of variance. In a fixed-effects model all treatment levels of interest are included in the experiment. For instance, in the example in Sections 11-2 and 11-3 we assumed that only three instructional methods were of interest, and all of them are included in the experiment. In contrast a *random-effects model* is one that includes only a random sample of all of the treatments of interest for the factor. For example, of ten instructional methods of interest three might have been randomly chosen for an experiment. A different model and computational procedure are required here, because the null hypothesis is that there are no differences among the various instructional methods in general and not just among the three instructional methods included in the experiment.

Complex designs in the analysis of variance involve not only the consideration of more than one factor but also the combination of different models, such as one factor being a fixed-effects factor while another is a random-effects factor. Also, designs can involve incomplete blocks and other data constraints. Although a number of different null hypotheses can be tested with the same set of data through the use of factorial designs, the extension of such designs can lead to a large number of cells with subsequent small sample sizes within the cells. In turn, the small sample sizes within the cells can result in a large MSE (sampling error) and tests that are less sensitive than with simpler experimental designs.

When the null hypothesis concerning a treatment effect is rejected in the analysis of variance, generally the analyst does not have the basis for final decisions. Typically, we are not only interested in determining whether a treatment effect exists but also in pinpointing the specific differences among the treatments. For example, given that student achievement differs significantly among several instructional methods, we would next want to determine which of the pairs of methods differ from one another. In the context of having several treatment means, it is not appropriate statistically to carry out repeated tests of differences between pairs of means based on the t distribution or the normal distribution. However, a number of types of tests for pairwise comparison following rejection of the null hypothesis in the analysis of variance are available. These tests are described in specialized textbooks on experimental design and are included in standard computer programs. Examples of such tests are the LSD (least-significant-difference) test, Tukey's HSD (honestly significant-difference) test, Scheffe's test, Newman-Keuls test, and Duncan's new multiple-range test.

11-7 SUMMARY

In its simplest form the analysis of variance represents the extension of testing the difference between two means to testing the difference between several means. Two principal assumptions associated with the analysis of variance are that the populations are *normally distributed* and have equal variances (*homogeneity of variance*).

The fundamental idea underlying the analysis of variance is that when there are several treatment groups with random assignment of subjects to the groups, the population variance can be estimated in two independent ways. One estimate is based on the variability among the group means and is the *mean square among treatment groups (MSTr)*. The second estimate of the population variance is based on the variability among the individual values within each group and is called the *mean square within groups (MSW)*. If the null hypothesis that the population means are equal is not true, the MSTr has a higher expected value than MSW. It is on this basis that the F distribution is used for the purpose of a one-tail test in conjunction with the test statistic $F = \text{MSTr}/\text{MSW}$.

The *one-factor completely randomized design* of the analysis of variance is concerned with testing the difference among k sample means when the subjects are assigned randomly to the k treatment groups. In the context of the summary table and notation generally used the mean square associated with the treatments is designated MSA (*mean square among the A-treatment groups*). The mean square error (MSE) indicates the *variability associated with sampling error*. Thus, the test statistic is $F = \text{MSA}/\text{MSE}$.

A *factorial design* in the analysis of variance is a design in which the effects associated with two or more factors are tested. In addition to testing the treatment effects associated with each factor, the factorial design also tests all possible interactions among the factors.

The *randomized-block design* represents an extension of the matched-pairs design to the case of the differences among several means being tested. In this context, the "blocks" are the groups of matched subjects, with one subject from each block randomly assigned to each treatment.

FORMULAS

(11-1) $s_{\bar{X}} = \sqrt{\dfrac{\Sigma(\bar{X} - \bar{X}_T)^2}{\text{No. means} - 1}}$

Standard error of the mean estimated on the basis of the means of the treatment groups.

(11-2) $\bar{X}_T = \dfrac{\Sigma X}{n_T}$

Overall mean of all observations in the analysis of variance.

(11-3) $s^2 = n s_{\bar{X}}^2$

Estimate of the population variance based on a computed standard error of the mean

(11-4) $\text{MSTr} = n s_{\bar{X}}^2$

Mean square among treatment groups, the variance estimate based on variability among the means of the treatment groups. Also designated as MSA.

(11-5) $\text{MSW} = \hat{\sigma}^2$

Mean square within, the variance estimate based on variability of values within each of the treatment groups. Also designated as MSE.

(11-6) $F_{\text{df}_1, \text{df}_2} = \dfrac{\text{MSTr}}{\text{MSW}}$

General form of the F test statistic in the analysis of variance. Also designated as MSA/MSE.

(11-7) $X_{ik} = \mu + \alpha_k + e_{ik}$

Linear equation that represents the one-factor completely randomized design.

(11-8) $X_{ijk} = \mu + \beta_j + \alpha_k + \iota_{jk} + e_{ijk}$

Linear equation that represents the two-factor completely randomized design.

(11-9) $X_{jk} = \mu + \beta_j + \alpha_k + e_{jk}$

Linear equation that represents the one-factor randomized-block design.

EXERCISES

11-1 Since the technique of analysis described in this chapter applies to testing hypotheses concerning the differences among several group *means,* explain why the technique is called analysis of *variance.*

11-2 Four types of advertising displays were set up in twelve retail outlets, with three outlets randomly assigned to each of the displays. The objective of the experiment is to test the null hypothesis that there is no difference in the point-of-sale impact of the four types of displays. Given the data in the table below, test the null hypothesis by applying the step-by-step procedure presented in Section 11-2 and using the 5 percent level of significance.

Product sales according to advertising display used

	Type of display			
	A_1	A_2	A_3	A_4
	40	53	48	48
	44	54	38	61
	43	59	46	47
Total	127	166	132	156
Mean	42.33	55.33	44.00	52.00

11-3 Repeat the analysis of variance for the data in Exercise 11-2 by applying the summary-table procedure presented in Section 11-3 and using the 5 percent level of significance.

11-4 The designs produced by four automobile stylists are evaluated by three different raters, as reported in the table below. Identify the analysis-of-variance model that would be used to test the null hypothesis that the average ratings of the designs do not differ.

Ratings of automobile designs

Rater	Stylist A_1	A_2	A_3	A_4	Total	Mean
B_1	87	79	83	92	341	85.25
B_2	83	73	85	89	330	82.50
B_3	91	85	90	92	358	89.50
Total	261	237	258	273		
Mean	87.0	79.0	86.0	91.0		

11-5 The table below presents the results of an experiment in which eight sales regions were randomly assigned to a total of four experimental marketing conditions: the presence or absence of advertising combined with the presence or absence of discounting. Identify the null hypotheses of interest in such an experimental design and identify the analysis of variance model that would be applicable for the analysis.

Weekly sales with and without advertising and with and without discounting (in $1,000s)

Discounting	Advertising With A_1	Without A_2	Total, $	Mean
With (B_1)	9.8 10.6	6.0 5.3	31.7	7.925
Without (B_2)	6.2 7.1	4.3 3.9	21.5	5.375
Total, $	33.7	19.5		
Mean	8.425	4.875		

11-6 Define the concept of replication in the analysis of variance. Referring to the data tables in Exercises 11-4 and 11-5, identify where replication is used in these designs and the implication in terms of what null hypotheses can be tested.

11-7 As indicated in the heading of Table 11-2, the summary table for the one-factor completely randomized design, the treatment groups need not be equal in size for the computational formulas in this table to be used. The following table reports the average words per minute typed with three different makes of electric typewriters by randomly assigned individuals with no prior experience on these machines and with the same amount of instruction. Using the 5 percent level of significance, test the null hypothesis that the mean words per minute typed on the three machines is not different.

**Average words per minute for
three makes of typewriters,
based on a standard test period**

	Make of typewriter		
	A_1	A_2	A_3
	81	74	79
	48	85	83
	65	72	62
	78	87	51
	55		77
	45		
Total	372	318	352
Mean	62.0	79.5	70.4

11-8 Although the analysis of variance is used when at least three treatment means are to be compared, it can in fact also be applied to test the difference between two means. Given the usual assumptions that the two populations are normally distributed and have equal (but unknown) variances, the F test is directly equivalent to using Student's t distribution to test the null hypothesis that there is no difference between the two population means.

(a) Referring to the table in Exercise 11-7, suppose that data for only the first two makes of typewriters (A_1 and A_2) were obtained. Test the null hypothesis that there is no difference between the two population means at the 5 percent level of significance by using the t distribution.

(b) For the first two makes of typewriters in Exercise 11-7, test the null hypothesis that there is no difference between the two population means at the 5 percent level of significance by using the appropriate analysis of variance model.

(c) Compare the results of your analysis in Exercises 11-8a and 11-8b.

TWELVE

THE CHI–SQUARE TEST

12-1 INTRODUCTION

In this chapter we describe the use of the χ^2 (chi-square) test for the purpose of testing hypotheses concerning *goodness of fit* and concerning the *independence of two variables*. As a general hypothesis-testing procedure, use of the χ^2 test always involves comparison of obtained sample frequencies entered in defined data categories with the expected frequencies for these categories based on the assumption that the null hypothesis is true. As compared with hypotheses concerning the mean, in the present application the data are not on a continuous scale of measurement. Rather the sample data are the *counts* for each category and are thus discrete data, as described in Section 5-1.

The hypothesis-testing situations in which we previously have been concerned with the analysis of counts were in tests dealing with proportions and differences between proportions, as described in Sections 10-4 and 10-6. A sample proportion essentially represents a count because it is the number of "successes" divided by the total number of sample observations. Therefore, the χ^2 test has a basic similarity to tests concerned with proportions and differences between proportions. The difference is that while analysis of proportions involves the assumption that only two data categories–"success" and "failure"–exist, the χ^2 distribution can be used with respect to several data categories. In Section 12-6 of this chapter we identify the forms of the χ^2 test that are comparable to testing a hypothesized proportion and testing the difference between two proportions, and then we describe how the χ^2 test can be used to test the differences among several proportions. Just as the analysis of variance can be viewed as an extension of tests for differences between two means to tests involving several means, so also can the χ^2 test be viewed as an extension of tests for differences between two proportions to tests involving several proportions.

Since use of the χ^2 test always concerns hypothesis testing, the basic steps in hypothesis testing described in Section 9-1 apply in this chapter as well. The χ^2 distribution was described in Section 8-7 on estimating a population variance and Section 10-8 on testing a hypothesized value of the variance. As it happens, the test statistic that concerns the comparison of observed and expected frequencies is distributed as the χ^2 probability distribution, and for this reason the basic procedure described in this chapter is called the χ^2 test.

12-2 GOODNESS–OF–FIT TESTS

The *goodness-of-fit* test is concerned with testing a null hypothesis that the population distribution for a random variable follows a specified form. For instance the null hypothesis could state that within the range of defined categories the distribution is uniform, and therefore the expected frequencies for the data categories are equal; or the null hypothesis could state that the population conforms to such a standard distribution as the binomial, Poisson, or normal probability distribution. On the other hand, the expected frequencies need not be based on a standard distribution but can be based on any specified distribution, such as, for instance, a distribution based on a historical pattern of frequencies.

As an example of a relatively simple situation that would lend itself to a goodness-of-fit test, suppose an insurance company has developed three homeowner policies, coded A_1, A_2, and A_3. The policies were expected to be about equal in popularity, and thus the null hypothesis is that the population distribution of policy sales is a discrete uniform distribution. A random sample of 60 homeowner policies written during the relevant time period is obtained, and the number of each type of homeowner policy sold is $A_1 = 30$, $A_2 = 9$, and $A_3 = 21$. Table 12-1 presents the actual and expected sales, with the latter frequencies based on the hypothesis that the distribution is uniform and therefore that the expected frequencies are equal. In the context of the χ^2 test f_o stands for the observed frequency, and f_e stands for the expected frequency based on the null hypothesis. For this example there are three data categories.

For the sample data to conform perfectly with the null hypothesis, it follows that the observed frequency f_o would have to be exactly equal to the expected frequency f_e for every data category. Of course, this exact conformity is not likely

Table 12-1   Homeowner policy sales according to type of policy

Frequency	A_1	A_2	A_3	Total
		Type of policy		
Actual sales f_O	30	9	21	60
Expected sales f_e	20	20	20	60

to occur, even if the null hypothesis is true. For the null hypothesis to be accepted, the differences between the observed and expected frequencies for the several data categories must be attributable to sampling variability at the designated level of significance. The χ^2 test statistic is based on the sum of the squared differences between the obtained and expected frequencies for each data category, relative to the expected frequency for each data category. The formula for determining the value of the test statistic is

$$\chi^2 = \sum \frac{(f_o - f_e)^2}{f_e} \qquad (12\text{-}1)$$

For the observed and expected frequencies in Table 12-1, the value of the χ^2 test statistic is

$$\chi^2 = \sum \frac{(f_o - f_e)^2}{f_e} = \frac{(30 - 20)^2}{20} + \frac{(9 - 20)^2}{20} + \frac{(21 - 20)^2}{20}$$

$$= \frac{10^2}{20} + \frac{-11^2}{20} + \frac{1^2}{20} = \frac{222}{20} = 11.1$$

If the conformity between the observed and expected frequencies is perfect, the computed χ^2 test statistic is $\chi^2 = 0$. As the difference between the observed and expected frequencies becomes larger, so does the value of the test statistic. Therefore, the χ^2 goodness-of-fit test is always a one-tail test, with the upper tail of the χ^2 distribution representing the region of rejection. The critical value of χ^2 required to reject the null hypothesis depends on the degrees of freedom and the specified level of significance. In goodness-of-fit tests the degrees of freedom df are

$$df = k - m - 1 \qquad (12\text{-}2)$$

where k = number of data categories

m = number of parameter values estimated on the basis of the sample data

For our example, which involves a uniform distribution, no parameter values are required, and therefore $m = 0$. In a later example in Section 12-4, which involves the Poisson distribution, estimation of a parameter will be required. Regardless of any parameter estimation, the 1 has to be subtracted to determine the degrees of freedom. Subtraction of the additional 1 is necessary, because given a designated sample size, once observed frequencies have been entered into $k - 1$

categories of a frequency table, the last cell of that table is in fact not "free" to vary. For instance, given that the first two categories in Table 12-1 have observed frequencies of 30 and 9, respectively, the last category must have a frequency of 21 to cumulate to the designated sample size of $n = 60$. Thus, for the data in Table 12-1

$$\text{df} = k - m - 1 = 3 - 0 - 1 = 2$$

Following is a complete presentation of our example problem, with the critical value of χ^2 based on the 5 percent level of significance:

Hypotheses: H_0: The sale of different homeowner policies follows a uniform distribution.

H_1: The sale of different homeowner policies does not follow a uniform distribution.

Critical χ^2 (df = 2, $\alpha = 0.05$) = 5.99 (from Table B-6)

Computed χ^2 = 11.1 (calculated above)

Because the value of the χ^2 test statistic exceeds the critical value, it is in the region of rejection of the null hypothesis. Therefore at the 5 percent level of significance, we reject the hypothesis that the distribution of frequencies in the population is uniform, and we conclude that the three types of homeowner policies are not equally popular.

Before considering applications of the χ^2 test that are more sophisticated and therefore more interesting from an applications viewpoint, it is necessary to consider the minimum value of an expected frequency for the appropriate use of the χ^2 test and a correction for continuity that is appropriate when df = 1. These matters are considered in the following section, after which we return to an application involving a null hypothesis that a discrete random variable is distributed as the Poisson distribution.

12-3 MINIMUM EXPECTED FREQUENCIES AND THE CORRECTION FOR CONTINUITY

Computed values of the χ^2 test statistic are based on discrete sample data, while the χ^2 distribution is a continuous probability distribution. When the expected frequencies for the cells (categories) of the data table are not small, this factor is not important in terms of the extent to which the distribution of the test statistic is approximated by the χ^2 probability model. But what is the value of f_e that is considered to be "not small"? A frequently used rule is that the expected frequency f_e for every cell, or category, should be at least 5. Cells that do not satisfy this criterion should be combined with adjacent categories so that this requirement is satisfied. An alternative solution to such a problem is to increase the overall sample size used in the analysis and thereby increase the expected frequency for each of the data cells. When adjacent data categories are combined, the reduced number of categories is the basis for the degrees of freedom df used to determine the critical value of the χ^2 test statistic. In Section 12-4 our example includes the necessity of combining adjacent data categories.

Given that the use of the χ^2 probability model is appropriate because the sample is not small, it is still true that the χ^2 test statistic has a systematic positive bias because of the discrete nature of the data. The positive bias in the value of the test statistic is relatively minor when expected frequencies are not small. However, the statistician Yates determined the *correction for continuity* that is appropriate when df = 1. Continuity correction factors for situations in which df > 1 are very complex mathematically. But the systematic error in the χ^2 test statistic is greatest when there are few data categories. Therefore, the availability of a correction factor when df = 1 is particularly convenient because the continuity can be applied when only two data categories (cells) are in the goodness-of-fit test and when such a correction is most needed. The formula for the χ^2 test statistic that includes the correction for continuity and that is applicable when df = 1, is

$$\chi^2 = \sum \frac{(|f_o - f_e| - 0.5)^2}{f_e} \qquad (12\text{-}3)$$

The only difference between Formula (12-3) and the general formula [Formula (12-1)] for the χ^2 test statistic is that in Formula (12-3) the absolute value of the difference between the observed and expected frequencies for each data cell is reduced by 0.5 before being squared. The effect, of course, is to reduce the value of the χ^2 test statistic. Thus failure to use the correction factor when it should be used would result in too-frequent rejection of the null hypothesis. In general the continuity correction should not be used for any data cell where the difference between the observed and expected frequencies is less than 0.5. As a rule of thumb the correction for continuity has little effect and can be omitted when $n \geqslant 50$.

As an example of an application in which use of the correction for continuity is appropriate, suppose that the historical pattern is that 30 percent of the prospects visited by the sales personnel of a firm makes a purchase and 70 percent does not. During a trial period, a salesperson calls on 30 randomly selected prospects and completes four sales. The observed and expected frequencies for this example are entered in Table 12-2. Using the 5 percent level of significance, we test the null hypothesis that the salesperson's pattern of sales does not differ from the historical pattern in the firm as follows:

Hypotheses: H_o: The salesperson's record conforms to the historical pattern of a 30 percent sales rate.

H_e: The salesperson's record is different from the historical pattern.

Critical χ^2 (df = 1, α = 0.05) = 3.84

$$\chi^2 = \sum \frac{(|f_o - f_e| - 0.5)^2}{f_e} = \frac{(|-5| - 0.5)^2}{9} + \frac{(|5| - 0.5)^2}{21}$$

Table 12-2 Observed and expected number of sales

Frequency	Result of call		Total
	Sale	No sale	
Actual sales f_o	4	26	30
Expected sales f_e	9	21	30

$$= \frac{(4.5)^2}{9} + \frac{(4.5)^2}{21} = 2.25 + 0.96 = 3.21$$

Therefore the null hypothesis that this salesperson's performance differs from the historical pattern cannot be rejected at the 5 percent level of significance on the basis of the sample data. Of course the number of sales differs from the expected number, but the difference is within the range of sampling variability for the 5 percent level of significance. Incidentally, if we had not used the correction for continuity, the computed value of the test statistic would have been $\chi^2 = 3.97$, and we would have inappropriately rejected the null hypothesis.

12-4 A FURTHER APPLICATION OF THE GOODNESS–OF–FIT TEST

As a more sophisticated example of applying a goodness-of-fit test, suppose that the null hypothesis is that the number of machine breakdowns per hour in an assembly

Table 12-3 Observed number of machine breakdowns during 40 sampled hours and worksheet for the calculation of the average number of breakdowns per hour

No. of breakdowns X	Observed frequency per hr f_o	$f_o X$
0	0	0
1	6	6
2	8	16
3	11	33
4	7	28
5	4	20
6	3	18
7	1	7
	$n = 40$	$\Sigma f_o X = 128$

plant follows the Poisson distribution, as described in Section 5-4. However, the particular Poisson distribution as defined by the mean λ of the distribution is not specified. Therefore as part of the hypothesis-testing procedure the parameter λ has to be estimated on the basis of the average number of breakdowns per hour for a sample of hours. The number of breakdowns that occur during 40 randomly sampled hours is observed and reported in Table 12-3. This table also serves as the worksheet to calculate the average number of breakdowns per hour in the sample.

The average number of breakdowns per hour for the sampled 40 hours is

$$\bar{X} = \frac{\Sigma f_o X}{n} = \frac{128}{40} = 3.2 \text{ breakdowns per hour} \qquad (12\text{-}4)$$

Therefore the estimated value of λ for the Poisson probability model is $\hat{\lambda} = 3.2$. Now we determine the expected pattern of breakdowns by first determining the probability associated with the occurrence of each number of breakdowns by reference to Table B-3, where $\lambda = 3.2$. Then we determine the expected frequencies for 40 randomly sampled hours by multiplying each of the probability values by 40. Table 12-4 presents these values.

Now that we have determined the expected frequencies based on the null hypothesis that the breakdowns are distributed as the Poisson probability model, we can proceed with the goodness-of-fit test. Table 12-5 presents the observed and expected frequencies and also serves as a worksheet to compute the value of the χ^2 test statistic, which is the sum of the last column of values. Referring to Table 12-5, notice that several categories at each end of the distribution have expected frequencies less than 5. Therefore these categories were combined for the purpose

Table 12-4 Determination of expected frequencies for the machine breakdown example, based on the Poisson distribution with $\lambda = 3.2$ and $n = 40$

No. of breakdowns X	Probability $P(X \mid \lambda = 3.2)$	Expected frequency f_e $(= nP)$
0	0.0408	1.6
1	0.1304	5.2
2	0.2087	8.3
3	0.2226	8.9
4	0.1781	7.1
5	0.1140	4.6
6	0.0608	2.4
7	0.0278	1.1
8	0.0111	0.4
9	0.0040	0.2
10	0.0013	0.1
11	0.0004	0.0
12	0.0001	0.0
13	0.0000	0.0
Total	1.0001	39.9

of analysis, resulting in five categories of data that are finally subjected to the analysis.

When the 5 percent level of significance is used, the complete presentation for this goodness-of-fit test is

Hypotheses: H_0: The distribution of machine breakdowns per hour is a Poisson-distributed variable.

$\qquad$ H_1: The distribution of machine breakdowns per hour is not a Poisson-distributed variable.

$$df = k - m - 1 = 5 - 1 - 1 = 3$$

$$\text{Critical } \chi^2 \ (df = 3, \alpha = 0.05) = 7.81$$

$$\text{Computed } \chi^2 = 0.675 \text{ (from Table 12-5)}$$

The computed χ^2 test statistic clearly is in the region of acceptance of the null hypothesis, and we conclude that the number of machine breakdowns per hour is a Poisson-distributed variable.

In addition to illustrating the necessity of combining several data categories in this example, note that we lost one additional degree of freedom because one parameter value, λ, was estimated on the basis of the sample data. With a different type of hypothesis the additional loss would not occur. For example, suppose that *before observing the sample data,* we formulated the hypothesis that the machine breakdowns follow the Poisson distribution with $\lambda = 3.0$. Then this parameter value would have served as the basis for the probabilities and expected frequencies, and there would be no additional loss in degrees of freedom. On the other hand, suppose that the hypothesis is that a random variable is normally distributed, but

Table 12-5 Observed and expected frequencies for the machine breakdown example and the calculation of the χ^2 test statistic

No. of breakdowns	Observed frequency f_o	Expected frequency f_e	$\dfrac{(f_o - f_e)^2}{f_e}$
0	0 ⎱ 6	1.6 ⎱ 6.8	0.094
1	6 ⎰	5.2 ⎰	
2	8	8.3	0.011
3	11	8.9	0.496
4	7	7.1	0.001
5	4 ⎫	4.6 ⎫	
6	3 ⎪	2.4 ⎪	
7	1 ⎬ 8	1.1 ⎬ 8.8	0.073
8	0 ⎪	0.4 ⎪	
9	0 ⎪	0.2 ⎪	
10	0 ⎭	0.1 ⎭	
			$\chi^2 = 0.675$

the mean and standard deviation are not specified in the hypothesis. Then these *two* parameters would have to be estimated on the basis of the sample, and two additional degrees of freedom would be lost.

12-5 TESTS FOR THE INDEPENDENCE OF TWO VARIABLES (CONTINGENCY–TABLE TESTS)

As contrasted to goodness-of-fit tests, which are concerned with one random variable, tests for independence involve two variables. The null hypothesis tested is that the two variables are statistically independent. Recall the related concepts of independent events and dependent events as explained in Section 4-4. Independence implies that knowledge of the category in which one observation is classified with respect to one variable has no effect on the probability of being in one of the several data categories with respect to the other variable. Or put another way, knowledge of one variable does not help in predicting the other variable. Since two variables are involved, the observed frequencies are entered in a two-way classification table, or *contingency table.* The dimensions of such a table are described by identifying the number of rows r and the number of columns k in the identity $r \times k$. Thus, a 5×3 contingency table is understood to mean a two-way classification table with five rows and three columns.

Extending our example in Section 12-2, suppose that an insurance company has three homeowner policies, A_1, A_2, and A_3, but also has three field offices, B_1, B_2, and B_3, where such policies are written. A random sample of 150 homeowner policies written during the relevant time period is obtained. But instead of now being interested in a goodness-of-fit test, we want to test the null hypothesis that the two variables (type of homeowner policy and field office) are independent variables. Therefore the sample data are entered into the contingency table in Table 12-6. Since each variable has three data categories, this is a 3×3 table.

The procedure in testing for independence is that a table of expected frequencies is determined based on the null hypothesis being true, and then the observed and expected frequencies for each cell location are used to determine the χ^2 test statistic for the data table, through Formula (12-1). Given that the variables are independent, the expected frequency for any given cell in a contingency table is the product of the frequencies observed in that row and that column divided by the overall size of the sample. The formula is

$$f_e = \frac{f_r f_k}{n} \qquad (12\text{-}5)$$

where f_r = sum of the observed frequencies in that row of the contingency table
$\quad$ f_k = sum of the observed frequencies in that column of the contingency table
$\quad$ n = size of the sample

Following is the rationale for Formula (12-5). If the null hypothesis is true, then the two variables A and B are independent, and $P(A \text{ and } B) = P(A) P(B)$ from

Table 12-6 Number of homeowner policies according to type of policy and field office

Type of policy	Field office			Total
	B_1	B_2	B_3	
A_1	25	35	15	75
A_2	5	5	13	23
A_3	30	12	10	52
Total	60	52	38	150

Formula (4-14). Therefore the probability of a random observation being in cell (A_1, B_1), for example, is $P(A_1) P(B_1)$. Since $P(A_1)$ and $P(B_1)$ are unknown, they are estimated from the sample data as $P(A_1) = f_r/n$ and $P(B_1) = f_k/n$, where f_r and f_k are the respective row and column totals associated with cell (A_1, B_1). Then the *expected frequency* of the number of observations in cell (A_1, B_1) is the joint probability multiplied by the overall sample size n. Based on this approach, computational Formula (12-5) is derived as follows:

$$f_e = P(A) P(B) n$$

$$f_e = \frac{f_r}{n} \frac{f_k}{n} n$$

$$f_e = \frac{f_r f_k}{n}$$

The degrees of freedom for a contingency table are the number of rows minus one times the number of columns minus one. Thus

$$df = (r - 1)(k - 1) \tag{12-6}$$

Table 12-7 is the table of expected frequencies for the data in Table 12-6. We construct such a table by first reproducing the dimensions of the data table and copying the row and column totals. Then Formula (12-5) can be used to determine the expected frequency for each cell. For instance, the expected frequency for cell (A_1, B_1) in our example is

$$f_e = \frac{f_r f_k}{n} = \frac{(75)(60)}{150} = 30.0$$

Incidentally, if we choose four cells in Table 12-7 that are not direct arithmetic functions of one another and determine those expected frequencies, the rest of the expected frequencies can be obtained by subtraction with respect to the row and column totals. For example, the four locations can be cells (A_1, B_1), (A_1, B_2), (A_2, B_1), and (A_2, B_2). The other five expected cell frequencies can then all be obtained by subtraction. This outcome directly reflects the fact that there are four degrees of freedom for a 3 X 3 contingency table.

Using the 1 percent level of significance, we now proceed with the complete presentation of the test for independence:

Hypotheses: H_0: Type of policy and field office are independent (not related).

H_1: Type of policy and field office are not independent (the type of policy sold is related to the field office location).

$$df = (r - 1)(k - 1) = (3 - 1)(3 - 1) = 4$$

Critical χ^2 $(df = 4, \alpha = 0.01) = 13.3$

$$\chi^2 = \sum \frac{(f_o - f_e)^2}{f_e}$$

$$= \frac{(25 - 30.0)^2}{30.0} + \frac{(35 - 26.0)^2}{26.0} + \frac{(15 - 19.0)^2}{19.0} + \frac{(5 - 9.2)^2}{9.2} + \frac{(5 - 8.0)^2}{8.0}$$

$$+ \frac{(13 - 5.8)^2}{5.8} + \frac{(30 - 20.8)^2}{20.8} + \frac{(12 - 18.0)^2}{18.0} + \frac{(10 - 13.2)^2}{13.2}$$

$$= 0.83 + 3.12 + 0.84 + 1.92 + 1.12 + 8.94 + 4.07 + 2.00 + 0.78$$

$$= 23.62$$

Because the test statistic exceeds the critical χ^2 value, we reject the null hypothesis that the type of homeowner policy sold and the location of the field office are independent variables. Again, note that a test for independence has nothing to do with whether the sales levels of the three types of policies are equal in the population or whether the numbers of policies sold at three field locations are equal, overall. These two areas of interest could be tested by separate goodness-of-fit tests, and in fact in Section 12-2 based, in that case, on a smaller sample size, we rejected the null hypothesis that the sale of the different types of policies follows a uniform distribution.

Table 12-7 Expected frequencies for the contingency-table data reported in Table 12-6

Type of policy	Field office			Total
	B_1	B_2	B_3	
A_1	30.0	26.0	19.0	75.0
A_2	9.2	8.0	5.8	23.0
A_3	20.8	18.0	13.2	52.0
Total	60.0	52.0	38.0	150.0

The correction for continuity described in Section 12-3 is appropriate for contingency-table tests as well as goodness-of-fit tests. As before, it is the appropriate correction only when df $= 1$ and generally need not be used if $n \geqslant 50$. For contingency tables only the 2 $\times$ 2 table has df $= 1$, and therefore only for the 2 $\times$ 2 table would we consider use of the continuity correction. Also, as for the goodness-of-fit test, the minimum expected frequency for every cell of the contingency table should be 5.0.

12-6 TESTING HYPOTHESES CONCERNING PROPORTIONS

The χ^2 test can be used to test a hypothesis concerning a single population proportion and to test the difference between two proportions. Use of the χ^2 test for these two types of hypotheses is particularly convenient when the sample size is not large enough to warrant use of the normal probability distribution. As explained in Section 10-5, the normal probability distribution can be used to test a difference between proportions when *each* sample size is $n \geqslant 100$. Further, the χ^2 test can also be used to test the differences among *several* proportions and in this respect has a conceptual similarity to the use of the analysis of variance to test the differences among several means. In this section we identify the formats of the χ^2 test used to test (1) a hypothesized proportion, (2) the difference between two proportions, and (3) the differences among several proportions.

When a data situation is such that use of either the normal distribution or χ^2 test is justified, use of the normal distribution generally would be preferred. The probability of type I error (α) can be controlled and set at the same level by the use of either procedure. But because use of the normal distribution results in a test more sensitive to detecting differences that exist, the probability of rejecting a false null hypothesis is enhanced by use of the normal distribution. In this respect greater *power* is associated with use of the normal distribution.

Testing a Hypothesized Proportion

The format of the χ^2 test to test a hypothesis concerning the value of the population proportion involves only two data categories. For convenience we can refer to this format as a 1 $\times$ 2 table. In comparison with hypothesis testing based on use of the normal distribution, as described in Section 10-5, use of the χ^2 test is always the equivalent of the two-tail test of the null hypothesis $H_0: \pi = \pi_H$. Because the χ^2 test involves an analysis of differences between obtained and expected frequencies *regardless of the directions of the differences,* no χ^2 test procedure is the equivalent of a one-tail test concerning the value of a population proportion.

As an example of using the χ^2 test with respect to a hypothesized proportion, suppose it is hypothesized that a proportion of $\pi = 0.30$ of men will react positively to a new disposable razor. A random sample of $n = 20$ men is selected and two of the men have a positive reaction to the new razor and eighteen do not. Table 12-8

**Table 12-8 Reactions of razor blade users
to a new disposable razor**

Frequency	Reaction		Total
	Positive	Not positive	
Observed (f_o):	2	18	20
Expected (f_e):	6	14	20

presents the observed frequencies and the expected frequencies based on the null hypothesis for this example. We test the null hypothesis at the 5 percent level of significance as follows:

Hypotheses:
$$H_0: \pi = 0.30$$
$$H_1: \pi \neq 0.30$$
$$df = k - m - 1 = 20 - 0 - 1 = 1$$
$$\text{Critical } \chi^2 \ (df = 1, \alpha = 0.05) = 3.84$$
$$\chi^2 = \sum \frac{(|f_o - f_e| - 0.5)^2}{f_e}$$

(where use of the continuity correction is appropriate because df $= 1$ and $n < 50$)

$$\chi^2 = \frac{(|2 - 6| - 0.5)^2}{6} + \frac{(|18 - 14| - 0.5)^2}{14}$$
$$= 2.04 + 0.88 = 2.92$$

Because the χ^2 test statistic does not exceed the critical value of 3.84, the null hypothesis that the population proportion is $\pi = 0.30$ cannot be rejected, even though the sample proportion was only $\hat{p} = X/n = 2/20 = 0.10$. Given the relatively small sample, a larger difference is required for significance at the 5 percent level.

Testing the Difference between Two Proportions

The format of the χ^2 test for the hypothesis that two population proportions are equal is the 2 × 2 table. In comparison with hypothesis testing based on use of the normal distribution, as described in Section 10-7, use of the χ^2 test is the equivalent of the two-tail test of the null hypothesis $H_0: \pi_1 = \pi_2$. As is true for testing a single hypothesized proportion, no χ^2 test is equivalent to a one-tail test.

As an example of using a χ^2 test with respect to the hypothesis that two population proportions are not different, suppose that for one brand of disposable razors 2 men of a random sample of $n_1 = 20$ men indicate a positive reaction to the product. For a second brand of disposable razors 9 men of a random sample of $n_2 =$

Table 12-9 Reactions to two brands of disposable razors

Type of reaction	Brand		Total
	1	2	
Positive	2	9	11
Not positive	18	11	29
Total	20	20	40

20 men indicate a positive reaction to the product. Table 12-9 is the 2 × 2 data table for this example, while Table 12-10 is the table of expected frequencies determined by Formula (12-6). We test the null hypothesis at the 5 percent level of significance as follows:

Hypotheses:
$$H_0: \pi_1 = \pi_2$$
$$H_1: \pi_1 \neq \pi_2$$
$$df = (r - 1)(k - 1) = (2 - 1)(2 - 1) = 1$$
$$\text{Critical } \chi^2 \ (df = 1, \alpha = 0.05) = 3.84$$
$$\chi^2 = \sum \frac{(|f_o - f_e| - 0.5)^2}{f_e}$$

(where use of the continuity correction is appropriate because df = 1 and $n < 50$)

$$\chi^2 = \frac{(|2 - 5.5| - 0.5)^2}{5.5} + \frac{(|9 - 5.5| - 0.5)^2}{5.5}$$
$$+ \frac{(|18 - 14.5| - 0.5)^2}{14.5} + \frac{(|11 - 14.5| - 0.5)^2}{14.5}$$
$$= 1.64 + 1.64 + 0.62 + 0.62 = 4.52$$

Because the computed value of the test statistic exceeds the critical χ^2 value of 3.84 based on the 5 percent level of significance, we reject the null hypothesis that the

Table 12-10 Expected frequencies for the data reported in Table 12-9

Reaction	Brand		Total
	1	2	
Positive	5.5	5.5	11
Not positive	14.5	14.5	29
Total	20	20	40

proportion of the men in the population with positive reactions to the two brands of disposable razors is equal, and instead we accept the alternative hypothesis that the proportions are not equal.

Testing the Differences among Several Proportions

The format of the χ^2 test to test the hypothesis that several population proportions are equal is the $2 \times k$ table, where k designates the number of population proportions involved in the test. The null hypothesis is $H_0: \pi_1 = \pi_2 = \cdots = \pi_k$. There is no equivalent test procedure based on use of the normal probability distribution.

As an example of testing the differences among several proportions suppose that we extend our example for the difference between two proportions to a problem involving four brands of disposable razors. The reactions to the four brands by each sample of men is reported in Table 12-11. As indicated in this table, the sample sizes for brands 3 and 4 are larger than those for brands 1 and 2. Table 12-12 indicates the expected frequencies for the cells of this 2×4 table, based on use of Formula (12-6). We test the null hypothesis at the 5 percent level of significance as follows:

Hypotheses: $H_0: \pi_1 = \pi_2 = \pi_3 = \pi_4$

H_1: The population proportions are not all equal.

$$df = (r - 1)(k - 1) = (2 - 1)(4 - 1) = 3$$

$$\text{Critical } \chi^2 \text{ (df = 3, } \alpha = 0.05) = 7.81$$

$$\chi^2 = \sum \frac{(f_o - f_e)^2}{f_e}$$

$$= \frac{(2 - 6.22)^2}{6.22} + \frac{(9 - 6.22)^2}{6.22} + \cdots + \frac{(15 - 17.91)^2}{17.91}$$

$$= 2.86 + 1.24 + 0.29 + 1.05 + 1.29 + 0.56 + 0.13 + 0.47$$

$$= 7.89$$

Table 12-11 Reactions to four brands of disposable razors

	Brand				
Reaction	1	2	3	4	Total
Positive	2	9	6	11	28
Not positive	18	11	18	15	62
Total	20	20	24	26	90

Table 12-12 Expected frequencies for the data reported in Table 12-11

| Reaction | Brand | | | | |
	1	2	3	4	Total
Positive	6.22	6.22	7.47	8.09	28
Not positive	13.78	13.78	16.53	17.91	62
Total	20	20	24	26	90

The computed value of the χ^2 test statistic just exceeds the critical value of 7.81 for the 5 percent level of significance, and therefore we reject the null hypothesis and accept the alternative hypothesis that the population proportions are not all equal to one another.

12-7 SUMMARY

Use of the χ^2 test always involves a comparison between observed frequencies, or counts, and expected frequencies. In this respect the random variable in the analysis is a discrete random variable. The three types of analyses described in this chapter concern testing hypotheses about *goodness of fit, independence of two variables,* and *proportions.*

The hypothesis in a *goodness-of-fit test* is a statement about the form of the distribution of a random variable. The distribution specified can be a standard distribution, such as the uniform distribution (which involves equal probabilities), the binomial distribution, the Poisson distribution, or the normal distribution. On the other hand, the hypothesized distribution can also be based on historical distributions or general managerial expectation or judgment. Whatever its source, the hypothesized distribution serves at the basis for determining the expected frequency for each category, or cell, of the data table. The differences between the *observed frequencies* f_o and the *expected frequencies* f_e serve as the basis for the χ^2 test. A significant χ^2 test statistic is interpreted to mean that the observed distribution, or pattern, of frequencies does not conform to the hypothesized distribution.

Because the χ^2 probability distribution is a continuous distribution while the data analyzed in the χ^2 test are discrete, the χ^2 test statistic follows the form of the χ^2 distribution only approximately. The problem is generally considered to be minor if the expected frequency for every cell of the analysis table is at least 5.0. Further, when $df = 1$, a correction for continuity is available. The use of this correction is generally considered unnecessary if $n \geqslant 50$.

A test for the *independence of two variables* always involves a *contingency table,* which is a two-way classification table for the observed data. The two variables are the factors that serve as the basis for the classifications in the two dimensions of the table. In this respect the variables are similar to the "factors" in the analysis of variance, as described in Chapter 11. A significant χ^2 test statistic is interpreted to mean that the two classification variables are not independent but, rather, are related variables. This test is similar to testing for interaction in the factorial designs of the analysis of variance. Of course in the analysis of variance the data analyzed are measurements that are assumed to be continuous and normally distributed rather than being the discrete counts analyzed by use of the χ^2 test.

The χ^2 test can also be used to test

1. A hypothesized value of a proportion, $H_0: \pi = \pi_H$
2. The hypothesis that two population proportions are equal, $H_0: \pi_1 = \pi_2$
3. The hypothesis that several population proportions are equal, $H_0: \pi_1 = \pi_2 = \cdots = \pi_k$

The χ^2 test generally would be used for the first two types of null hypotheses above only when the data do not permit appropriate use of the methods based on the normal probability model as described in Chapter 10. The reason is that the test procedure based on use of the normal distribution has greater power in that the probability of rejecting a false null hypothesis is greater than it is when the χ^2 test is used at the same level of significance. The format of the χ^2 test to test a *hypothesized proportion* is the 1 × 2 data table. The format to test the *difference between two proportions* is the 2 × 2 data table, and the format to test the *difference among several proportions* is the 2 × k table, where k is the number of population proportions.

FORMULAS

(12-1) $\chi^2 = \sum \dfrac{(f_o - f_e)^2}{f_e}$ χ^2 test statistic.

(12-2) df $= k - m - 1$ Degrees of freedom in a goodness-of-fit test.

(12-3) $\chi^2 = \sum \dfrac{(|f_o - f_e| - 0.5)^2}{f_e}$ χ^2 test statistic that includes the correction for continuity; use of this formula is appropriate when df $= 1$ but generally is considered unnecessary when $n \geqslant 50$.

(12-4) $\bar{X} = \dfrac{\Sigma f_o X}{n}$ Sample mean for observed frequencies, or counts, entered in a classification table.

(12-5) $f_e = \dfrac{f_r f_k}{n}$ Expected frequency for a data cell of a contingency table.

(12-6) df $= (r - 1)(k - 1)$ Degrees of freedom for a contingency table.

EXERCISES

12-1 The table below presents the observed number of people in a consumer panel who prefer the taste of each of four brands of Rhine wine. Using the 1 percent level of significance, test the null hypothesis that the consumer preferences for the four brands are equal.

Consumer panel preferences for four brands of Rhine wine

	Brand			
A	B	C	D	Total
30	20	40	10	100

12-2 Before the results reported in Exercise 12-1 were observed, it was hypothesized that brand *C* is preferred by as many people as the other three brands combined. Test this hypothesis at the 1 percent level of significance.

12-3 In general 20 percent of the people stop to watch a cookingware demonstration in a department store. For a new demonstration format only 3 of 40 people stop to watch the demonstration. Using the 5 percent level of significance, determine whether this result is significantly different from the expected number based on previous experience that in general 20 percent of the people stop to watch such a demonstration.

12-4 A manufacturer of automobile radiators has decided to expand the factory's product line to include automobile air conditioners that are not factory installed. Four models of air conditioners offered for sale by other manufacturers are the economy, standard, deluxe, and custom models. During the past three years, these four models have accounted for 40 percent, 30 percent, 20 percent, and 10 percent of the market, respectively. To determine appropriate production levels for each model of air conditioner, the manufacturer collects data for a random sample of 400 auto air-conditioner installations completed during the past month and finds that 190 were the economy model, 100 were the standard model, 50 were the deluxe model, and 60 were the custom model. Using these data and the 5 percent level of significance, test the null hypothesis that the historical distribution of sales for the four models has not changed.

12-5 An elementary school principal has for some time suspected that the income level of parents is related to their attendance at school programs and activities, but the relationship has not been entirely clear. Accordingly, for a particular month the principal notes such attendance and classifies each family in the categories called "never," "occasionally," and "regular." Available socioeconomic data also make it possible to classify each family in the "low," "middle," and "high" categories in terms of income. The classification of the 420 families is indicated in the table below. Using the 5 percent level of significance, test the null hypothesis that income category is not related to extent of program participation.

Program participation	Income			
	Low	Middle	High	Total
Never	28	48	16	92
Occasional	22	65	14	101
Regular	17	74	3	94
Total	67	187	33	287

12-6 From the data of Exercise 12-5 it is known that 20 percent of the families are in the low-income category, 70 percent are in the middle-income category, and 10 percent are in the high-income category. Using the 5 percent level of significance, determine whether the pattern of families included in the sample differs significantly from this expected distribution. Interpret the result of the test.

12-7 To put a one-year warranty into effect, the buyers of a small appliance are asked to mail a postcard on which several questions relating to the purchase are asked. From a large number of these postcards, a random sample of 100 is selected for analysis. The following frequencies, based on the sample of postcards, describe the purchasers according to place of purchase and source of product knowledge.

Source of knowledge	Place of purchase			Total
	Department store	Discount store	Appliance store	
Friend	10	5	5	20
Newspaper	15	30	5	50
Magazine	5	5	20	30
Total	30	40	30	100

    (*a*) Using the 5 percent level of significance, test the null hypothesis that there is no relationship between place of purchase and source of knowledge.
    (*b*) Would the conclusion in Example 12-7*a* be different if the 1 percent level were used?

12-8 From the data in Exercise 12-7 the management of the company has assumed that the appliance is sold in about equal quantities in the three types of stores. At the 5 percent level of significance test this hypothesis.

12-9 From the data in Exercise 12-7, the management of the company has assumed that 40 percent of the purchases are influenced by friends, 40 percent by newspaper ads, and 20 percent by magazine ads. At the 1 percent level of significance test this hypothesis.

12-10 Before the data for Exercise 12-7 had been collected, it was suggested that newspaper ads are particularly effective for discount store buyers and magazine ads more influential with buyers at appliance stores. Test the null hypothesis that there is no such relationship, using the 1 percent level of significance.

12-11 To compare the quality of rheostats shipped by two subcontractors, a sample of 80 rheostats was taken from recent shipments by each supplier, and in the table below the numbers of defects of any type are noted. The sales representative for supplier *B* suggests that the difference observed is only a chance difference and is not reflective of the general quality of the rheostats supplied by the company.

Inspection result	Supplier		Total
	A	*B*	
Defective	4	12	16
Nondefective	76	68	144
Total	80	80	160

    (*a*) Determine the expected cell frequencies.
    (*b*) At the 5 percent level of significance test the sales representative's claim.

12-12 It has been the experience of a trucking firm that the number of truck arrivals per hour at a loading terminal can be represented as a Poisson process with $\lambda = 3.0$. For 60 sample hours during a particular month, the frequency distribution of the number of arrivals per hour is reported in the table below. Using the 5 percent level, does this distribution differ significantly from the expected distribution based on the Poisson distribution with $\lambda = 3.0$? Briefly discuss the outcome of the test.

No. of truck arrivals per hr	f
0	0
1	4
2	10
3	14
4	12
5	12
6 or more	8
Total	60

12-13 The table below reports the single most important safety feature desired by each of a random sample of $n = 100$ car purchasers. Using the (*a*) 5 percent and (*b*) 1 percent level of significance, test the null hypothesis that the general population of car buyers is uniformly distributed in terms of the primary preference for these safety features.

Identification of most important safety features desired by car buyers

	Safety feature				
Disk brakes	Collapsible steering wheel	Steel-belted radial tires	Automatic door locks	Speed-warning indicator	Total
20	10	30	25	15	100

12-14 As an extension of Exercise 12-13 the opinions of the men and women were tallied separately, as indicated in the table below. Using the 1 percent level of significance, test the null hypothesis that there is no relationship between sex and the safety feature preferred.

Identification of most important safety feature desired by car buyers, according to sex

	Safety feature					
Respondents	Disk brakes	Collapsible steering wheel	Steel-belted radial tires	Automatic door locks	Speed warning indicator	Total
Men	15	5	20	5	5	50
Women	5	5	10	20	10	50
Total	20	10	30	25	15	100

12-15 In a college course in business statistics the historical distribution of the A, B, C, D, and E grades has been 10, 30, 40, 10, and 10 percent, respectively. A particular class taught by a new instructor completes the semester with 8 students earning a grade of A, 17 with B, 20 with C, 3 with D, and 2 with E. Using the 5 percent level of significance, test the null hypothesis that this instructor's grading does not differ from the historical pattern.

12-16 The table below indicates the number of transistors that do not meet a stringent quality requirement in 20 samples of $n = 10$ each. Test the null hypothesis that this distribution is not significantly different from the binomial distribution with $n = 10$ and $p = 0.30$, using the 5 percent level of significance.

Number of defective transistors in 20 samples of size $n = 10$ each

No. defective	0	1	2	3	4	5	6	7	8	9	10
No. samples	0	1	2	4	5	5	2	1	0	0	0

12-17 Sales records for previous periods indicate that dollar sales per customer at a discount department store have averaged $18.00 with a standard deviation of $6.00. Further, the sales amounts have been normally distributed. For a random sample of 200 customers on the day following a change in pricing policy the sales amounts per customer are distributed as indicated in the table below. Using the 5 percent level of significance, test the null hypotheses that the population distribution from which these amounts were sampled is a normal distribution with $\mu = \$18.00$ and $\sigma = \$6.00$.

Sales amount, $	No. of customers
Below 9.00	15
9.00–11.99	15
12.00–14.99	35
15.00–17.99	50
18.00–20.99	40
21.00–23.99	25
24.00–26.99	15
27.00 and above	5

12-18 For Exercises 12-2 and 12-3 each of these problems can be viewed as a test of a hypothesized value of a population proportion. Formulate such null and alternative hypotheses for each of these two exercises.

12-19 The analysis in Exercise 12-11 can be viewed as a test of the null hypothesis that the two population proportions are equal. Viewing the problem from this standpoint, identify the two populations and formulate the null and alternative hypotheses.

12-20 The analysis in Exercise 12-14 can be viewed as a test of the null hypothesis that several population proportions are equal. Viewing the problem from this standpoint, identify the several populations and formulate the null and alternative hypotheses.

THIRTEEN

STATISTICAL DECISION ANALYSIS

13-1 INTRODUCTION

The statistical methods of interval estimation and hypothesis testing described in the last several chapters are considered *classical methods of statistical inference.* These methods are based on the use of sample data and the objective interpretation of probabilities, as described in Section 4-1. In contrast the methods of analysis described in this chapter include managerial judgment as well as sample data as sources of information, incorporate economic consequences in the analysis, and involve the subjective interpretation of probabilities. These latter techniques are collectively called "statistical decision analysis," or "Bayesian statistics," because of a fundamental role that Bayes' theorem, described in Section 4-6, fulfills in these methods of analysis. Of course the classical methods of statistical inference are also concerned with decision analysis. Whether one accepts or rejects a particular null hypothesis, for example, directly affects the choice of managerial action. But in the methods of analysis presented in this chapter the decision alternatives available to a manager are given special prominence.

Techniques of statistical decision analysis have been developed for use with continuous as well as discrete variables. The scope of presentation in this chapter is limited to discrete variables; however, the fundamental concepts developed in this chapter apply as well to continuous variables. We begin any such analysis by identifying the decision alternatives (e.g., amount to be ordered for inventory), the states of nature, or events, that can occur (e.g., level of consumer demand), and the economic consequence, or payoff, associated with every possible combination of decision act and event. The "event," or state of nature, is the variable, and the event leads to different payoffs for a given decision. The information developed is conveniently presented by a two-way table, called a *decision table*, which is described in Section 13-2.

Once we have identified the available decision acts, the possible events, and the economic consequences, the next step is concerned with identifying the one best act for the decision situation. In Section 13-3 we describe the criteria available for determining the best decision act. Although several criteria are described in that section, the *expected-value criterion* is the most complete because it is based on use of probability values as well as economic consequences. In statistical decision analysis, the probability values can be based on historical data and therefore be *objective* in nature; or they can be based on managerial judgment and therefore be *subjective* in nature.

A particular area of flexibility in decision analysis is that after a decision problem is structured, sample information can be collected and used to revise the subjective probability values included in the formulation of the decision problem. It is in this respect that Bayes' theorem is used in statistical decision analysis, as we demonstrate in Section 13-6. Some statisticians restrict use of the term "Bayesian statistics" only to those decision-analysis situations that involve the revision of probabilities by the use of sample data, but the term is often used more broadly, and synonymously with "statistical decision analysis."

13-2 DECISION TABLES

A *decision table,* or *payoff table,* is a table that identifies all possible decision acts, events, and economic consequences for a decision situation. Additionally, such a table may also include the probability value for each event, based either on historical information or managerial judgment.

Table 13-1 portrays the general form of a decision table. In this table the *acts* are the alternative courses of action, or strategies, available to the decision maker. As the result of the analysis, one of these decision acts is chosen as being the best act. At least two alternative acts must be available, as a minimum, so that a choice exists. For example the decision problem concerned with marketing a new product might involve just two alternatives, A_1: Market, A_2: Don't market. On the other hand, a decision concerning the inventory level for an item would involve several alternative inventory levels that can be chosen.

The *events* represented in Table 13-1 are the occurrences outside of the decision maker's control that determine the economic consequence for a decision act.

Table 13-1 General structure of a decision table

| | Event | | |
Decision act	E_1 (P_1)	E_2 (P_2)	E_3 $\cdots E_n$ $(P_3) \cdots (P_n)$
A_1	X_{11}	X_{12}	$X_{13} \cdots X_{1n}$
A_2	X_{21}	X_{22}	$X_{23} \cdots X_{2n}$
A_3	X_{31}	X_{32}	$X_{33} \cdots X_{3n}$
$\vdots$	$\vdots$	$\vdots$	$\vdots$ $\vdots$
A_m	X_{m1}	X_{m2}	$X_{m3} \cdots X_{mn}$

These events are often called "states of nature," or simply *states*. The events are understood to be mutually exclusive, and the identification of the possible events should be exhaustive, in the sense that all possible events should be formally identified and listed in the decision table. For a decision problem to exist, at least two different events must be possible. For example, in a decision problem as to whether a product development project should be funded, the two possible events might be E_1: Successful development and E_2: Development not successful. On the other hand, for a decision problem concerning the inventory level for a product, the events would be the several possible levels of customer demand for the product.

For a complete analysis the *probability* for each event should be included, whether the probability is based on historical information or on managerial judgment. Because the events in the decision table are mutually exclusive and exhaustive, it follows that the sum of the probabilities for all of the possible events must equal 1.0. Of the several criteria for choosing the best act, described in Section 13-3, only the *expected-value criterion* requires that probability values be identified and used in the analysis.

Finally, the cell entries in Table 13-1 are the *economic consequences* that would result from every possible combination of decision act and event. When these values represent revenues or profit figures, they are often called *payoffs* in the literature, and they are conditional in the sense that the economic consequence depends on both the decision act that is chosen and the event that occurs. The economic consequences can also be concerned with comparative costs.

As a specific example of a decision table, suppose an electronics firm has perfected a television receiver with a three-dimensional (3-D) picture based on holography and now faces several alternative choices regarding the scheduling of production and related market-promotion activities for the receiver. Consumer acceptance of the product within the next 10 years is considered certain, but the timing of that acceptance is uncertain, partly because of the necessarily high price of the receiver. Table 13-2 identifies four decision alternatives, ranging from immediate production

Table 13-2 Decision table for the 3-D television receiver problem*

Decision	Event: Consumer acceptance			
	E_1: Immediate $P_1 = 0.30$	E_2: 2 yr $P_2 = 0.40$	E_3: 5 yr $P_3 = 0.20$	E_4: 8 yr $P_4 = 0.10$
A_1: Immediate production and promotion	80	40	−10	−50
A_2: Limited production now	30	40	30	10
A_3: Limited production in 2 yr	20	30	40	15
A_4: Limited production in 5 yr	5	10	30	30

*Economic consequences are expressed in millions of dollars.

and promotion to limited production in five years. Similarly, the possible periods of time before full consumer acceptance are assessed and identified as the events, or states, in Table 13-2. The probability of each event is based on composite managerial judgment, while the economic consequences are based on a financial analysis of the profitability of the product during the 10-year period. In Section 13-3 we use this decision table to illustrate the application of different criteria for identifying the best decision act.

13-3 CRITERIA FOR DETERMINING THE BEST DECISION

In this section we describe four different criteria for identifying the best decision act: the *maximin, maximax, minimax-regret,* and *expected-value criteria.* Which act is identified as the best act depends on the criterion used. Of these four criteria, the expected-value criterion is generally preferred because it is the only criterion that considers the probabilities associated with the possible events. However, we consider the first three criteria for two separate reasons: First, certain concepts related to these criteria are of general importance in decision analysis; second, under certain circumstances one of these criteria might appropriately be used instead of, or at least with, the expected-value criterion. We discuss this point further in the last part of this section, after describing the application of each of the four decision criteria.

A prime consideration in choosing a decision criterion, or rule, for determining the best decision act when the probabilities of the states are unknown and cannot be estimated is the decision maker's general attitude toward the possible losses and gains. The *maximin criterion* identifies the best act as the one for which the minimum (worst) economic consequence is larger than the minimum value associated with any other decision act. Use of this criterion leads to a conservative decision strategy, in that for each decision act the decision maker is entirely concerned with the worst that can happen. Computationally, the minimum value in each row of the decision table is identified, and then the best act is the one for which the minimum value is largest, compared with the other minima. In other words by use of the maximin criterion we *maximize* the *minimum* payoff.

Table 13-3 is an abbreviated version of the decision table presented in Table 13-2 for the problem of production and promotion timing for the new 3-D television receiver. Further, this table also serves as a work table to determine the best decision based on the maximin criterion. The worst economic consequence for each decision is posted in the "minimum result" column. The largest of the four minima is 15, and therefore the best act is A_3, identified in Table 13-2 as "limited production in two years." By making this decision, the manufacturer is assured that at least a 15-million-dollar gain will be made during the 10-year period, a higher value than the minimum economic result that can occur with any other decision.

The *maximax criterion* identifies the best act as the one for which the maximum economic consequence is larger than the maximum value for any other decision act. In a sense the maximax criterion is the opposite of the maximin criterion, because the decision maker is entirely concerned with the best that can happen with respect to each decision act. Computationally, the maximum value in each row of the decision table is identified, and then the best act is the one for which the maximum value is largest compared with the other maxima. In other words by use of the maximax criterion we *maximize* the *maximum* payoff.

Table 13-4 is the work table for determining the best act for our 3-D receiver problem based on the maximax criterion. The best economic result associated with each act is posted in the "Maximum result" column. The largest of these maxima, associated with act A_1, is 80 million dollars. Act A_1, immediate production and

Table 13-3 Identification of the best-decision act for the 3-D receiver problem, based on the maximin criterion*

Decision	Event				Minimum result
	E_1	E_2	E_3	E_4	
A_1	80	40	−10	−50	−50
A_2	30	40	30	10	10
A_3	20	30	40	15	15**
A_4	5	10	30	30	5

*Economic consequences are expressed in millions of dollars.

**Largest of the four minima; therefore decision A_3 is best from the standpoint of the maximin criterion.

promotion, is thus the best act from the standpoint of the maximax criterion. No other act can result in a higher gain. Of course, act A_1 also has the largest possible loss (50 million dollars) associated with it, but loss is not the focus of concern from the standpoint of the maximax criterion.

The *minimax-regret criterion* differs from both the maximin and maximax criteria in that the analysis is based on so-called regret values rather than on conditional economic consequences. A *regret*, or *opportunity loss*, for any given cell of a decision table is the difference between the economic result in that cell and the best result in that column of the decision table. Thus, with reference to each event taken in turn, the opportunity loss is the difference between the economic result for a given decision and the result for the "perfectly matched" decision for that event, or state. The best regret value possible is 0, which indicates the given decision is perfectly matched with the event being considered. Because it is the best decision possible for that event, there is no opportunity loss.

To illustrate the meaning of an opportunity loss, or regret, suppose that we consider the specific event E_3 in Table 13-4, in which the 3-D television receiver wins consumer acceptance in five years. Referring to the economic results in this table, we see that the best economic result for this event is a gain of 40 million dollars, which would occur if act A_3 is chosen (limited production in two years). Therefore the regret value for the cell intersecting at row 3 and column 3 in Table 13-4 is 0. Given E_3, if act A_2 is chosen, the regret is the difference between the 30-million-dollar gain associated with A_2 and the 40-million-dollar gain of the perfectly matched act A_3, or 10 million dollars. Given E_3, if act A_1 is chosen, the regret is the difference between the loss of 10 million dollars associated with A_1 and the alternative gain of 40 million dollars, for a total regret of 50 million dollars. Thus given E_3, if act A_1 is chosen, the opportunity loss of 50 million dollars constitutes two types of regrets: the regret associated with the accounting loss of 10 million dollars

Table 13-4 Identification of the best-decision act for the 3-D receiver problem, based on the maximax criterion*

Decision	Event E_1	E_2	E_3	E_4	Maximum result
A_1	80	40	−10	−50	80**
A_2	30	40	30	10	40
A_3	20	30	40	15	40
A_4	5	10	30	30	30

*Economic consequences are expressed in millions of dollars.

**Largest of the four maxima; therefore decision A_1 is best from the standpoint of the maximax criterion.

Table 13-5 Opportunity-loss table for the 3-D receiver problem and determination of the best act, based on the minimax-regret criterion[*]

Decision	Event				Maximum regret
	E_1	E_2	E_3	E_4	
A_1	0	0	50	80	80
	$(= 80 - 80)$	$(= 40 - 40)$	$[= 40 - (-10)]$	$[= 30 - (-50)]$	
A_2	50	0	10	20	50[**]
	$(= 80 - 30)$	$(= 40 - 40)$	$(= 40 - 30)$	$(= 30 - 10)$	
A_3	60	10	0	15	60
	$(= 80 - 20)$	$(= 40 - 30)$	$(= 40 - 40)$	$(= 30 - 15)$	
A_4	75	30	10	0	75
	$(= 80 - 5)$	$(= 40 - 10)$	$(= 40 - 30)$	$(= 30 - 30)$	

[*]Economic consequences are expressed in millions of dollars.
[**]Smallest of the four maximum regrets; therefore decision A_2 is best from the standpoint of the minimax-regret criterion.

and the further regret of "missing out" on the 40 million dollar gain with the perfectly matched decision.

Table 13-5 is the opportunity-loss table for our 3-D receiver problem. In this table the process by which each regret value was determined is shown in parentheses immediately below that value. Again, note that such a table is constructed by reference to each *column* of economic consequences in the decision table. In each column the highest economic result has a regret of 0, and the other cell locations in that column have regret values that reflect the difference between the economic results in those cells and the best result possible in that column of values.

Once a table of opportunity losses has been constructed, the best decision act from the standpoint of the minimax-regret criterion is that act for which the maximum regret is smallest. In other words, by use of the minimax-regret criterion we *min*imize the *max*imum regret. Referring to Table 13-5, we see that the maximum possible regret of 50 million dollars for act A_2 (limited production now) is lower than the maximum regret resulting from any other decision. Therefore act A_2 is the best act from the standpoint of the minimax-regret criterion. In addition to their use for the minimax-regret criterion, opportunity losses are used to determine the expected value of perfect information (EVPI), as explained in Section 13-5.

The *expected-value* criterion identifies the best act as the one for which the expected economic outcome is the highest. The orientation is not on the consequences of a single decision opportunity but rather the long-run average result over a series of similar decision opportunities. Computationally, each of the possible economic consequences for a given decision act is weighted according to the probability of its occurrence to determine the expected value (expected payoff) for that act. Thus, where X represents each of the possible economic results from a decision act A and $P(X)$ represents the probability of occurrence of each result, the computational process to determine an expected value can be represented by

$$EV(A) = \Sigma XP(X) \qquad\qquad (13\text{-}1)$$

Table 13-6 is the work table for determining the best act for the 3-D television receiver problem, based on the expected-value criterion. For example, the expected value for act A_1 was obtained as follows:

$$EV(A_1) = \Sigma XP(X)$$
$$= 80(0.30) + 40(0.40) + (-10)(0.20) + (-50)(0.10)$$
$$= 33.0 \text{ million}$$

Because this expected value is higher than the expected value associated with any other decision act, act A_1 (immediate production and promotion) is the best act from the standpoint of the expected-value criterion.

As we indicated at the beginning of this section, the expected-value criterion is generally preferred to the maximax, maximin, or minimax-regret criteria because the expected-value criterion considers both probabilities and economic consequences in choosing the best act, whereas the other three criteria consider only the economic consequences. However, when one or more of the possible economic results are unusually desirable or unusually adverse, this factor may limit the appropriateness of using the expected-value criterion. For instance, if a possible result of a decision is a loss so large that it would "put us out of business," we would hesitate to choose that decision even if it is assessed as being the best one from the standpoint of the expected-value criterion. For our television receiver example, in fact, the best decision (immediate production and promotion) includes the possibility that the company will lose 50 million dollars as the result of going into immediate production and promotion. In this example we might want to eliminate this act from consideration and choose act A_2 (limited production now); for act A_2 the expected value is only 1 million dollars less than for act A_1 but act A_2 includes no possibility of a financial loss. In contrast a "second-best" act might be preferred not because of a catastrophic loss possibility of an unusually large gain that represents a breakthrough opportunity for the firm.

Table 13-6 Identification of the best-decision act for the 3-D receiver problem, based on the expected-value criterion[*]

	Event				
Decision	E_1 $(P_1 = 0.30)$	E_2 $(P_2 = 0.40)$	E_3 $(P_3 = 0.20)$	E_4 $(P_4 = 0.10)$	Expected value
A_1	80	40	−10	−50	33.0[**]
A_2	30	40	30	10	32.0
A_3	20	30	40	15	27.5
A_4	5	10	30	30	14.5

[*]Economic consequences are expressed in millions of dollars.
[**]Largest of the four expected values; therefore decision A_1 is best from the standpoint of the expected-value criterion.

To deal with the special meaning of possible large gains or large losses in decision analysis, decision theorists have developed the concept of *utility*. By the utility approach the possible outcomes of each act are converted into utility values, which indicate the true relative values of the various outcomes to the decision maker. Then the best act is the one for which the *expected utility* is maximized. Coverage of utility theory is beyond the scope of this book. Although utility theory appears to clarify the meaning of economic consequences, a difficulty associated with this approach is that utility values are abstractions not represented by any physical measures of value that can be easily interpreted.

13-4 A FURTHER APPLICATION OF THE EXPECTED-VALUE CRITERION

In Section 13-3 we were concerned primarily with defining and differentiating the maximin, maximax, minimax-regret, and expected-value criteria. In this section we present an example in which more attention is given to the construction of the decision table. Because it is the most frequently used basis for identifying the best act, the expected-value criterion is used as the basis for analysis in this example.

Suppose that a rail service has the option of attaching commuter cars to a scheduled Amtrak passenger train. The incremental cost associated with the use of each commuter car is $80, and the revenue for each car "substantially filled" is $200. Based on analysis of commuter-car use in other similar communities, the probability distribution for the number of cars that can be filled on this route has been estimated and is presented in Table 13-7.

Because Table 13-7 indicates that at least one and no more than five commuter cars will be needed, it is obvious that we should consider providing some number between one and five commuter cars as the alternative decision acts. Thus the decision table to be constructed will be a 5×5 decision table. For this decision problem a numerical act (in this example the number of cars provided) corresponds

Table 13-7 States and associated probabilities for the commuter-car problem

No. commuter cars needed	Probability
0	0
1	0.10
2	0.20
3	0.30
4	0.30
5	0.10
Total	1.00

to each possible numerical event (in this example the number of cars needed), resulting in a decision table that has the same number of rows and columns. As a class, decision problems that have a numerical act corresponding to each numerical event are often called *inventory problems.*

We determine the economic result, or payoff, for each cell of the decision table by considering the profit on the commuter cars provided and used minus the cost of any commuter cars provided and not used. For example, if one car is provided and two are needed, we would have a profit only for the one commuter car provided, or $120. If two cars are provided but only one car is needed, we would have a $120 profit on the one car needed minus an $80 loss on the additional car provided but not needed, for a net profit of $40. All the conditional results for the decision table can be determined by this reasoning process. However, it is generally considered to be more convenient to express the economic results by two *linear payoff functions* for such inventory problems. One payoff function applies if the event (number of cars required) is less than or equal to the action (number of cars provided), while the other payoff function applies if the event (number of cars required) is greater than the action (number of cars provided):

$$X_{ij} = 200E_j - 80A_i \qquad\qquad \text{if } E_j \leqslant A_i$$
$$X_{ij} = 200A_i - 80A_i = 120A_i \quad \text{if } E_j > A_i$$

Note that these two equations merely formalize the statements we have already expressed for this problem. The first equation says that when the number of cars needed is less than or equal to the number provided, the net profit is the revenue from the cars needed minus the cost of *all* cars provided (including any unused cars). On the other hand, if the demand exceeds the number of cars provided, we can only have a profit for the number actually provided. Incidentally, for a more complete and realistic analysis of this problem we could also have included a goodwill-loss factor for any cars needed and not provided. This loss would result in an additional subtraction in the second payoff function in the preceding equations, based on the amount by which E_j exceeds A_i.

Table 13-8 is the complete decision table for this commuter-car problem, also including calculation of the expected value for each decision act. You should be able to verify any of the payoff values in this table by use of the appropriate payoff function. For example, if four cars are provided but only two are needed, we have

$$X_{ij} = 200E_j - 80A_i \quad \text{if } E_j \leqslant A_i$$
$$= 200(2) - 80(4) = \$80$$

If two cars are provided but four cars are needed, we have

$$X_{ij} = 120A_i \quad \text{if } E_j > A_i$$
$$= 120(2) = \$240$$

Referring to the expected values in the last column of Table 13-8, we see that the two decision acts of providing three cars and providing four cars have the same

Table 13-8 Decision table for the commuter-car problem*

Decision: No. provided	Event: Number of cars needed					Expected value
	E_1:1 ($P_1 = 0.10$)	E_2:2 ($P_2 = 0.20$)	E_3:3 ($P_3 = 0.30$)	E_4:4 ($P_4 = 0.30$)	E_5:5 ($P_5 = 0.10$)	
A_1:1	120	120	120	120	120	120
A_2:2	40	240	240	240	240	220
A_3:3	−40	160	360	360	360	280**
A_4:4	−120	80	280	480	480	280**
A_5:5	−200	0	200	400	600	220

*Expected-payoff values are expressed in dollars.
**Largest of the five expected values; therefore decisions A_3 and A_4 are best from the standpoint of the expected-value criterion.

maximum expected value of $280. Therefore these two decision alternatives are preferred to the others, and statistically speaking we would be indifferent between providing three commuter cars or providing four cars.

13-5 THE EXPECTED VALUE OF PERFECT INFORMATION (EVPI)

The *expected value of perfect information* is the expected (long-run) value of obtaining information that would remove all uncertainty from the decision situation. Although we often may not be able to obtain such information, the value associated with such information is important, because it provides an upper limit on the value that any sample information can have. Sample information reduces but does not eliminate uncertainty. Therefore the expected value of sample information is always less than the expected value of perfect information.

With perfect information available the decision maker would know which event will occur and make the decision that is best (yields the highest payoff) for that event. For our commuter-car problem in the preceding section, for example, the decision maker would provide exactly the correct number of commuter cars each day and would provide different numbers of cars on different days, according to the demand. Without perfect information, however, the decision maker would provide the same "best" number of cars every day. The expected value of perfect information is the difference between the expected value with perfect information and the expected value of the best act under conditions of uncertainty:

$$\text{EVPI} = \text{EV (with perfect information)} - \text{EV (under uncertainty)} \quad (13\text{-}2)$$

For the commuter-car problem in the preceding section the expected value of the best act under uncertainty is $280, as presented in Table 13-8. With perfect information the probability distribution for the number of cars needed would still be the same as in Table 13-8, but the difference is that the number of cars provided would always match the number needed. That is, the probability distribution is used to indicate the long-run proportion of times that each event (demand level) occurs. On this basis Table 13-9 is the work table to determine the expected value with perfect information for the commuter-car problem. As noted in the table, the long-run expected value (expected payoff) with perfect information is $372. Therefore the expected value of perfect information for the commuter car problem is

$$EVPI = EV \text{ (with perfect information)} - EV \text{ (under uncertainty)}$$

$$= \$372.00 - 280.00 = \$92.00$$

In the above analysis note the distinction between the terms "expected value *with* perfect information" and the "expected value *of* perfect information." The expected value with perfect information is the *total* expected payoff with perfect information, whereas the expected value of perfect information is the difference between that total and the expected payoff of the best act under conditions of uncertainty.

An alternative approach by which EVPI can be determined is by computing the expected opportunity loss (EOL) of the best act as identified by the expected-value criterion. In fact the best act on the basis of the expected-value criterion will always have the lowest expected-opportunity loss, because on the average, less regret is associated with this act than with any other act. Therefore *the act which has the minimum EOL value is also the act that has the maximum expected value EV.* Now, with perfect information there would never be any regret, and the long-run expected opportunity loss would be 0. Thus it logically follows that the expected-opportunity loss for the best act under uncertainty should be the expected value of removing such uncertainty and thus should be the expected value of perfect information.

$$EVPI = EOL \text{ (best act under uncertainty)} \qquad (13\text{-}3)$$

Table 13-10 is the table of opportunity losses for the commuter-car problem, constructed by reference to the decision table in Table 13-8. As indicated in the last column on Table 13-10, the decisions of providing two or three commuter cars both have the same minimum EOL value and thus are the best acts from the standpoint

Table 13-9 Determination of the expected value with perfect information for the commuter-car problem

No. commuter cars needed	Probability (P)	Best act	Conditional value of best act, $ (X)	Expected value, $ XP(X)
1	0.10	A_1:1	120	12
2	0.20	A_2:2	240	48
3	0.30	A_3:3	360	108
4	0.30	A_4:4	480	144
5	0.10	A_5:5	600	60
Total	1.00		Expected value = $\Sigma XP(X) = 372$	

Table 13-10 Opportunity-loss table for the commuter-car problem and determination of expected-opportunity losses*

	Event: number of cars needed					Expected
Decision: No. provided	$E_1:1$ $(P_1 = 0.10)$	$E_2:2$ $(P_2 = 0.29)$	$E_3:3$ $(P_3 = 0.30)$	$E_4:4$ $(P_4 = 0.30)$	$E_5:5$ $(P_5 = 0.10)$	opportunity loss
$A_1:1$	0	120	240	360	480	252
$A_2:2$	80	0	120	240	360	152
$A_3:3$	160	80	0	120	240	92**
$A_4:4$	240	160	80	0	120	92**
$A_5:5$	320	240	160	80	0	152

*Opportunity losses are expressed in dollars.
**Smallest of the expected-opportunity loss values; therefore decisions A_3 and A_4 are best from the standpoint of the expected value criterion.

of the expected-value criterion. This result corresponds with the analysis in the preceding section, in which these same acts were determined as being the best acts by reference to the expected payoffs. Furthermore, the EOL value of \$92 corresponds to the EVPI determined by the first approach presented in this section.

13-6 INCORPORATING SAMPLE INFORMATION

In this section we present the technique by which the probability distribution for the event, or state, is revised based on observed sample information. The methodology is based on use of Bayes' theorem, as covered in Section 4-6. If you have forgotten what this theorem involves, it is very important that you now review Section 4-6 before proceeding any further in this section.

When sample information is incorporated in the decision process, the probability distribution assessed before the collection of any sample information is called the *prior probability distribution.* The *posterior probability distribution* is the probability distribution after sample information has been observed and has been used to revise the prior probability distribution by application of Bayes' theorem. As illustrated in Section 4-6, to apply Bayes' theorem, we must designate the prior probability of the uncertain event, or state, and we must know the conditional probability of the sample result. In Section 4-6 the conditional probabilities in our examples were based on simple rules of probability, since all samples were of size $n = 1$. For larger sample sizes the conditional probabilities typically are determined by reference to a standard probability distribution, such as the binomial distribution, which serves as a model for the sampling situation.

As an example of a decision situation that lends itself to sampling, suppose that we are faced with the choice of accepting a shipment of 1,000 electronic parts from a vendor or performing 100 percent inspection of the shipment. We consider the full decision table for this problem in the next section of this chapter. For now we restrict our attention to the prior probability distribution for the fraction of defective components and the revision of this probability distribution based on sample information. As indicated in Table 13-11, based on historical experience with this vendor, the shipment has four possible fractions defective (proportion of defective items): 0.01, 0.05, 0.10, or 0.20. The prior probability distribution for this random variable is indicated in Table 13-11.

Now suppose that a random sample of $n = 10$ items is taken from the shipment, and one item is found to be defective. The posterior probability associated with each of the possible states could be obtained by applying Bayes' formula four times, as described in Section 4-6. In each application the conditional probability of the sample result is the binomial probability $P(X = 1 | n = 10, p_i)$, where p_i is the fraction defective. However, when more than two possible events, or states, can occur, it is more efficient and easier to use a tabular approach to revise the prior probability values. Table 13-12 is the work table for the revision of the prior probability distribution, given that $X = 1$ defective is observed in a random sample of $n = 10$ items taken from the shipment. We now proceed to explain the computations in this table in some detail and to show the equivalency of this tabular approach to using Bayes' formula.

As identified in Formula (4-18), the general formula for revising a prior probability value with Bayes' theorem is

$$P(A|B) = \frac{P(A \text{ and } B)}{P(B)} \qquad (4\text{-}18)$$

For only two alternative states the computational formula for Bayes' theorem was given in Formula (4-19):

$$P(A|B) = \frac{P(A)\,P(B|A)}{P(A)\,P(B|A) + P(A')P(B|A')} \qquad (4\text{-}19)$$

In the context of revising a prior probability distribution, A in Formulas (4-18) and (4-19) refers to each state in turn (in our example each of the four possible fractions defective) and B is the observed sample result. Thus the posterior

Table 13-11 Prior probability distribution for the fraction defective

Fraction defective P_i	Prior probability P
0.01	0.60
0.05	0.20
0.10	0.10
0.20	0.10
Total	1.00

Table 13-12 Revision of probabilities for the shipment problem

Fraction defective p_i	Prior probability P	Conditional probability of the sample result $P(X = 1 | n = 10, p_i)$	Joint probability	Posterior probability P
0.01	0.60	0.0914	0.05484	$0.29895 \approx 0.30$
0.05	0.20	0.3151	0.06302	$0.34355 \approx 0.34$
0.10	0.10	0.3874	0.03874	$0.21118 \approx 0.21$
0.20	0.10	0.2684	0.02684	$0.14631 \approx 0.15$
Total	1.00		0.18344	1.00

probability $P(A|B)$ is the probability of each state given that a particular sample result has been observed. On the other hand the simple (unconditional) probability value $P(A)$ for each state is the prior probability value.

The "Fraction defective p_i" column Table 13-12 identifies the four possible states A for our fractions-defective example; the "Prior probability distribution P" column identifies the prior probability values $P(A)$ for each state, based on historical experience with this vendor. The third column shows the four conditional probabilities of the four sample results, that is, these conditional probability values are equivalent to $P(B|A)$ and are therefore the second element in the computational formula for Bayes' theorem. The four values in the third column, indicating that we are revising four prior probability values, are based on the binomial probability distribution and obtained from Table B-2. For example the first value is $P(X = 1 | n = 10, \ p = 0.01) = 0.0914$, while the second value in column 3 is $P(X = 1 | n = 10, \ p = 0.05) = 0.3151$. Strictly speaking, the binomial distribution is not applicable when we sample without replacement from a finite population, because the probabilities would not be stationary. However, as we indicated in Section 5-3, use of the binomial distribution is considered to be acceptable when $n \leqslant 0.05N$. In our example the sample of $n = 10$ is less than $0.05(1,000) = 50$.

In statistics the conditional probability of a sample result is referred to as a *likelihood,* and for this example we see that the likelihood of observing one defective item in a sample of $n = 10$ is greatest with the fraction-defective state of 0.10 (the 0.3874 value is the highest one in the third column). *Note that the p_i in the heading of the third column of Table 13-12 refers to each state (in Bayes' formula, A) in turn, not to the prior probability value P(A).*

The "Joint probability" column presents the joint probability of the occurrence of each state with each sample result. Computationally, the value on each line of the second column is multiplied by the value in the third column. *Each value in the "Joint probability" column is in fact the numerator of Bayes' formula.* Referring to the computational version of Bayes' formula, note that each value in the "Joint probability" column is equivalent to $P(A) P(B|A)$.

The four values in the "Joint probability" column include all joint-event probabilities for the occurrence of the sample result. That is, the sample result must occur with one of the four states (fraction defective) by definition, and all four joint probability values are identified in the "Joint probability" column. Therefore the sum of this column is the overall, unconditional, probability of the sample result, or $P(B)$ in Bayes' general theorem. *Therefore the sum of the "Joint probability" column is the denominator of Bayes' formula.*

Finally, we obtain the posterior probability values in the "Posterior probability distribution P" column by dividing each joint probability value (fourth column) by the sum of that column. By reference to Bayes' formula, this represents the arithmetic operation

$$P(A|B) = \frac{P(A \text{ and } B)}{P(B)} \tag{4-18}$$

Referring to the "Posterior probability distribution P" column of Table 13-12, we can observe the general pattern of the change in the posterior probability distribution as compared with the prior probability distribution (in the second column). Given that we have observed one defective item in a sample of $n = 10$, the state for which the probability has been substantially reduced is the 0.01 fraction defective for which the prior probability is 0.60 and the posterior probability is 0.30. The probability values for all of the other states have been increased. The greatest relative increase occurred for the 0.10 state for which the probability more than doubled from 0.10 to 0.21. This result is logical, because the sample result has the highest likelihood value for this state.

The practical implication of determining a posterior probability distribution is that this distribution is then used in place of the prior probability distribution to determine the best decision act, as we demonstrate in the following section of this chapter. In concluding this section, we can also note that the number of samples that we might choose to take is not restricted, except for the usual time and cost constraints. We could, for example, take another sample of size $n = 10$ and use the posterior probability distribution developed above as the new prior distribution and proceed with a second revision of probabilities. Of course the ultimate sample would be a 100 percent sample, or census, in which the posterior probability distribution would be such that one of the four states in our example would have a probability of 1.00 and the other three states would have a probability of 0. But in practical decision-making situations it is usually less expensive and more profitable to base decisions on sample information. The statistical techniques by which the optimum sample size can be determined in Bayesian decision analysis are beyond the scope of this book. Depending on both the cost and the expected value for each sampled item, in certain decision situations no sample may be warranted, while in others a substantial sample may be warranted to optimize the long-run expected return.

13-7 POSTERIOR ANALYSIS AND THE VALUE OF SAMPLE INFORMATION

Posterior analysis refers to the determination of the best act on the basis of a posterior probability distribution, after sample information has been obtained. In this section we determine the best act for the shipment problem presented in the preceding section based first on the prior probability distribution and then based on the posterior probability distribution. We then also estimate the value of the sample information that was obtained based on whether the identification of the best act was changed as the result of incorporating the sample information into the analysis. As compared with the examples of applying the expected value criterion in Sections 13-3 and 13-4, in this section the example involves an analysis of costs. In the previous examples the best act was the one with the *highest expected payoff*. In the example in this section the best act in terms of the expected value criterion is the one with the *lowest expected cost*.

For the vendor shipment in the example introduced in the preceding section of this chapter, 1,000 electronic parts are included in the shipment. The decision is whether to A_1: accept the shipment or A_2: perform 100 percent inspection. The cost of inspecting each item is 40 cents. In the absence of 100 percent inspection the defective electronic parts included in the shipment become part of an assembled component, and the resulting malfunction has to be diagnosed and corrected at a cost of $6.00 for each defective part. Table 13-13 presents the cost table based on this information. For instance, if the true state is a fraction defective of 0.01, there are 0.01 (1,000) = 10 defective parts, and the cost associated with act A_1 in this case is 10 ($6.00) = $60.00. The other conditional costs for the first row of the table are determined in a similar manner. For 100 percent inspection the cost is 1,000 ($0.40) = $400.00, regardless of the fraction defective in the shipment.

The prior probability distribution and the determination of the expected costs for the two decision acts are also included in Table 13-13. The act for which the expected cost is minimized is act A_1: Accept, and therefore this is the best decision from the standpoint of the expected-value criterion. Indeed, were the other act to turn out to be best, it would certainly reflect a lack of confidence in the vendor.

Because it is better to accept the shipment "as is" as compared to taking a 100 percent sample at a cost of $400, it follows that the expected value of perfect information (EVPI) for this problem must be less than $400. Let us verify this by determining the EVPI for this decision problem. We use the second method described in Section 13-5—that of determining the expected opportunity loss (EOL)

Table 13-13 Cost table for the shipment problem and the identification of the best decision, based on the prior probability distribution*

	State: Fraction defective				
Decision	E_1: 0.01 ($P_1 = 0.60$)	E_2: 0.05 ($P_2 = 0.20$)	E_3: 0.10 ($P_3 = 0.10$)	E_4: 0.20 ($P_4 = 0.10$)	Expected cost, $
A_1: Accept	60	300	600	1,200	276**
A_2: 100% inspection	400	400	400	400	400

*Costs of inspection are expressed in dollars.

**Smallest expected cost; therefore decision A_1 is best from the standpoint of the expected-value criterion.

of the best act—so that we can have the practice of constructing an opportunity-loss table from a table of costs. Table 13-14 is the opportunity-loss table for this decision problem. As before, each opportunity-loss value, or regret, is the difference between the value in that cell of the decision table and the best value in that column of the decision table. However, for this example the "best value" is the lowest cost rather than the highest payoff. Thus, for instance, the $340 regret for A_2 given E_1 is the difference between the $400 cost of 100 percent inspection and the cost of just $60 for correcting malfunctioning components when a fraction of only 0.01 of the parts is defective.

As shown in Table 13-14, the expected value of perfect information from Formula (13-3) is

$$\text{EVPI} = \text{EOL (best act under uncertainty)} = \$100$$

As expected, the EVPI of $100 is less than the $400 cost of perfect information in this example.

Suppose now that instead of accepting the shipment outright we take a random sample of 10 parts and inspect them. The revision of the prior probability distribution based on this sample result was accomplished in Section 13-6 (Table 13-12). Table 13-15 is the cost table that includes the posterior probability distribution determined in the preceding section. Incidentally, for the purpose of our illustration we do not make the relatively minor adjustments in the conditional costs resulting from 990 rather than 1,000 items now remaining in the shipment. Based on the expected costs in Table 13-15, after observing one defective item in a sample of $n = 10$ parts, the best decision is to proceed with 100 percent inspection rather than accepting the shipment directly. Thus observing this sample result has caused us to change our decision from what it would have been without the sample result having been observed.

As the final topic in this section we now describe how we estimate the value of sample information (VSI) for a sample that has been obtained. The value of sample information that has been observed is the difference between the posterior expected

Table 13-14 Opportunity-loss table for the shipment problem and determination of expected-opportunity losses*

| Decision | State: Fraction defective | | | | Expected opportunity loss |
	$E_1: 0.01$ ($P_1 = 0.60$)	$E_2: 0.05$ ($P_2 = 0.20$)	$E_3: 0.10$ ($P_3 = 0.10$)	$E_4: 0.20$ ($P_4 = 0.10$)	
A_1: Accept	0	0	200	800	100**
A_2: 100% inspection	340	100	0	0	224

*Opportunity losses are expressed in dollars.

**Smallest expected-opportunity loss; therefore decision A_1 is best from the standpoint of the expected-value criterion.

Table 13-15 Cost table for the shipment problem and the identification of the best act, based on the posterior probability distribution*

Decision	State: Fraction defective				Expected cost
	$E_1: 0.01$ $(P_1 = 0.30)$	$E_2: 0.05$ $(P_2 = 0.34)$	$E_3: 0.10$ $(P_3 = 0.21)$	$E_4: 0.20$ $(P_4 = 0.15)$	
A_1: Accept	60	300	600	1,200	426
A_2: 100% inspection	400	400	400	400	400**

*Costs are expressed in dollars.

**Smallest expected cost; therefore decision A_2 is best from the standpoint of the expected-value criterion.

value of the best posterior act and the posterior expected value of the best prior act. Thus, depending on whether payoffs or costs are involved, we have

$$\text{VSI} = \text{(posterior expected payoff of best posterior act)}$$

$$- \text{(posterior expected payoff of best prior act)} \qquad (13\text{-}4)$$

or $$\text{VSI} = \text{(posterior expected cost of best prior act)}$$

$$- \text{(posterior expected cost of best posterior act)} \qquad (13\text{-}5)$$

Note that in Formulas (13-4) and (13-5) the values subtracted are both *posterior* values; the value of the sample is *not* a "before and after" difference. *A sample can only have value if the sample result causes us to change our decision.* If a posterior expected value is better than a prior expected value but the decision is not changed, the sample had no value, because the higher expected value would have been experienced anyway but without our prior knowledge of this fact. Thus a sample that supports a prior decision may be of psychological value in reinforcing our decision, but it does not have economic value as such. The estimated economic value is based on all information available after the sample and not on any previous expectations. In our example the best decision *was* changed as the result of observing one defective part in the sample of $n = 10$ parts. The estimated value of having observed this sample information is

$$\text{VSI} = \text{(posterior expected cost of the best prior act)}$$

$$- \text{(posterior expected cost of the best posterior act)}$$

$$= \$426.00 - 400.00 = \$26.00$$

13-8 DECISION-TREE ANALYSIS

Use of decision tables is appropriate when one decision has to be selected from several alternative decision acts. However, many decision situations involve the selection of a *series* of decisions in the context of several different, but related, event states. In such a sequential decision process, one decision leads to an outcome that requires a second decision, and so forth, with a final outcome determining the success achieved by the entire series of decisions. In such circumstances, *decision-tree analysis* can be used to portray the overall decision situation and to determine the best decision at each point in the sequence, including the initial decision point. The criterion which serves as the basis for identifying the best acts in decision-tree analysis is the expected-value criterion.

Exhibit 13-1 presents a sequential-decision problem that will be the focal point of analysis in this section. The first step in the analysis is to construct the decision tree. *Tree diagrams,* introduced in Section 4-5, are used to portray a sequence of chance events. In contrast a *decision tree* is used to portray a sequence of decision points and chance events. *Decision points* are the sequential points at which choices of alternative decision acts are required, and each of these points is typically represented by a small square. *Chance events* are the sequential points in the decision tree at which probabilistic events will occur; each of these points is typically represented by a small circle. Figure 13-1 is the complete decision tree for the relatively simple sequential-decision problem presented in Exhibit 13-1. Note how the sequence of required decisions and chance events is represented in the decision tree.

Referring to Figure 13-1, we note that the initial decision point is whether to develop the new product. If the decision alternative "don't develop" is chosen, no further events or decisions are relevant, and the terminal gain is $0. If the decision alternative "develop" is chosen, we will be able to find out if the development effort is successful, which is a chance event. The probability of successful development is 0.70, and the probability of unsuccessful development is 0.30. If development is not successful, this result terminates the sequence with a loss of 2 million dollars. If development is successful, we have to choose between the alternatives of a high manufacturing level or a low manufacturing level. After this choice is made, we can observe the level of demand, which is a chance event. In this example the probability of a high level of demand is 0.40 and the probability of a low level of demand is 0.60, regardless of our choice of manufacturing level in the preceding choice point in the tree diagram. The economic consequences identified at the

Exhibit 13-1 A Sequential Decision Problem

A manufacturer is presented with a proposal for a new product and must decide whether to develop it. The cost of the development project is 2 million dollars with a probability of 0.70 that the project will be successful. If the product is successfully developed, the manufacturer must then decide whether to begin manufacturing the product at a high level or at a low level. If demand is high, the incremental profit given a high level of manufacturing is 7 million dollars and a given low level of manufacturing is 1.5 million dollars. If demand is low, the incremental profit given a high level of manufacturing is 1 million dollars and a given low level of manufacturing is 1.5 million dollars. These incremental profit values are *before* subtraction of the 2-million-dollar development cost, and thus are gross figures. The probability that the market will be high is estimated as $P = 0.40$, that it will be low as $P = 0.60$.

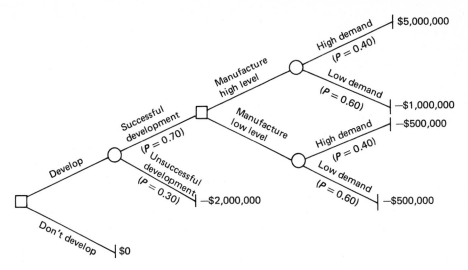

Figure 13-1 Decision tree for the product development problem in Exhibit 13-1.

final four terminal points in Figure 13-1 are based on the information provided in Ex-hibit 13-1 and are net figures. For instance the 5-million-dollar net profit for "high de-mand" following "manufacture high level" is the 7-million-dollar incremental profit minus the 2-million-dollar development cost. Thus the decision tree in Figure 13-1 graphically portrays the sequential problem presented in Exhibit 13-1. The construc-tion of such a diagram serves to make complex sequential decision situations more easily comprehensible than when verbal descriptions alone are presented.

After the decision tree for a sequential decision situation is constructed, the second major step in the analysis is to determine the best decision act at each choice point by determining the expected value associated with each of the decision alternatives. To determine these expected values, it is necessary to work from right to left in the decision tree. For this reason this process of analysis is often called "folding back." Figure 13-2 is the complete decision tree, which includes the expected values and the choices of best acts. We now proceed to explain the process of folding back as applied in this decision tree.

Careful reference to Figure 13-2 on your part is necessary as we describe the process of folding back. Working from right to left, we consider as the first choice point the one concerned with the manufacturing level. The expected value of 1.4 million dollars for "manufacture high level" is determined by calculating the weighted average of the two economic consequences that can follow this decision:

$$\text{EV (mfg. high level)} = \$5,000,000(0.40) + (-\$1,000,000)(0.60)$$

$$= \$1,400,000$$

Similarly, the expected value (loss) of −$500,000 is obtained by calculating the weighted average of −$500,000 and −$500,000, which are equal values in this case.

Comparing the expected values for the two decision alternatives, the best choice clearly is "manufacture high level." Therefore a double bar is entered in the decision tree for the other choice, indicating that it is eliminated from further consideration.

Now we move to the left until we arrive at the next choice point; it is the initial choice point in the diagram. The decision alternatives are "develop" and "don't develop." Again, we determine the expected value for "develop" by calculating the weighted average of the economic consequences that can follow this decision:

$$\text{EV (develop)} = \$1,400,000(0.70) + (-\$2,000,000)(0.30)$$

$$= \$380,000$$

Note that if development is successful ($P = 0.70$), we have an expected gain of 1.4 million dollars for the best act that follows. The $500,000 loss for "manufacture low level" is not relevant because that act was eliminated from further consideration in the preceding step of analysis. Now, comparing the expected value of $380,000 for "develop" with the value of $0 for "don't develop," the best decision act at the initial choice point is "develop," and the other act is eliminated from consideration. This concludes the formal analysis by use of the decision tree. Based on use of the expected-value criterion, we should attempt to develop the product, and then if development is successful, we should manufacture the product at a high level of output.

The construction of a decision tree for sequential-decision situations provides the manager with the opportunity to portray a complex decision situation in a concrete form, thereby making it possible to recognize decision implications that might otherwise not be obvious. For example, even though the expected-value

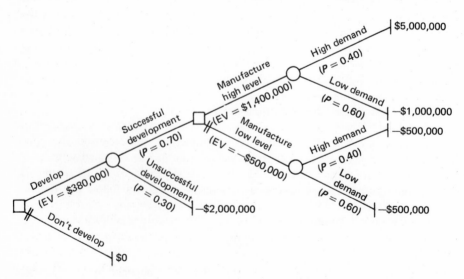

Figure 13-2 Complete decision tree for the product-development problem.

criterion leads to the choice of "develop" at the initial choice point in our example problem, one factor we might want to recognize is that the probabilities do not favor the outcome of a net profit. Of the five terminal economic consequences that can follow the initial decision of "develop" in Figure 13-2, four are net losses. A profit will occur in this product-development example only if the development is successful ($P = 0.70$) *and* if market demand is high ($P = 0.40$). Thus the overall probability of a profit is $0.70 \times 0.40 = 0.28$. Consequently, the probability of a loss is $1.00 - 0.28 = 0.72$. We would certainly want to recognize such implications as we consider our choice of decisions at the first choice point.

13-9 SUMMARY

Whereas classical methods of statistical inference are based on the use of sample information and objective probabilities, statistical decision analysis includes the use of *managerial judgment* as well as sample information, *subjective probabilities,* and special emphasis on *economic consequences.*

A *decision table* is a two-way table that presents the available alternative decision acts, the possible events, or states, and the probability associated with each event when such probabilities are available. In statistical decision analysis such probability values can be based on either historical information or managerial judgment. The cells in this table identify the conditional economic consequences (payoffs) for all possible act/event combinations.

The criteria to determine the best decision act are the maximin, maximax, minimax-regret, and expected-value criteria. The *maximin criterion* gives special attention to the most adverse result for each act, and thus leads to conservative, or defensive, decision choices. The *maximax criterion* gives special attention to the best result for each act and ignores the possibility of adverse results. The *minimax-regret criterion* involves the determination of *opportunity losses.* An opportunity loss is the difference between the economic result for an act given a particular event and the best economic result possible with that event. The *expected-value criterion* is considered the most complete criterion of these four, because it includes consideration of probability values as well as economic consequences.

The *expected value of perfect information* (EVPI) is the long-run expected value of removing all uncertainty from the decision situation. Computationally, this value can be determined by calculating the difference between the expected value with perfect information and the expected value of the best act under conditions of uncertainty. An alternative approach to determining EVPI is to calculate the *expected-opportunity loss* (EOL) for the best act under conditions of uncertainty.

Bayes' theorem plays a key role in decision analysis, because with this theorem a *prior probability distribution* that is assessed before any sample information is obtained can be revised after sample results are observed, resulting in the *posterior probability distribution.* For this reason statistical decision analysis often is also called *Bayesian statistics.* After a posterior probability distribution has been determined, this distribution is the basis for identifying the best act. The particular sample obtained has economic value only if the sample result causes a change in the best decision, as compared with the choice based on the prior probability distribution. The estimated *value of sample information* (VSI) is the difference between the posterior expected value of the best posterior act and the posterior expected value of the best prior act.

Decision-tree analysis is used when the overall decision situation includes a sequence of required decision acts and chance events. The first major step in the analysis is to construct the decision tree for the sequential decision situation. The second major step is to use the process of *folding back* to identify the best decision act at each choice point in the decision tree. The decision tree serves to portray complex, sequential-decision situations in a concrete form, thereby making such situations more comprehensible.

FORMULAS

(13-1) $EV(A) = \Sigma X P(X)$
              Expected value associated with a decision act A.

(13-2) $EVPI = EV$ (with perfect information) $- EV$ (under uncertainty)
              Expected value of perfect information for a decision situation.

(13-3) $EVPI = EOL$ (best act under uncertainty)
              Alternative method for determining the expected value of perfect information for a decision situation.

(13-4) $VSI =$ (posterior expected payoff of best posterior act) $-$ (posterior expected payoff of best prior act)
              Estimated value of sample information when the decision problem involves alternative payoffs, or profits, as the economic consequences.

(13-5) $VSI =$ (posterior expected cost of best prior act) $-$ (posterior expected cost of best posterior act)
              Estimated value of sample information when the decision problem involves alternative costs as the economic consequences.

EXERCISES

13-1 (*a*) What is a "decision criterion"? (*b*) Describe the decision criteria available for the decision-making situation in which the probability values associated with the states are not available.

13-2 In general decision analysts prefer to use the expected-value criterion as the basis for identifying the best decision act. Under what circumstances, however, might the maximin criterion be preferred?

13-3 A small retail store has the choice of ordering 0, 1, 2, or 3 stereo sets from a distributor. The markup on each set is $90 and the amount of loss on any set not sold is $120.

(a) Determine the best decision act from the standpoint of the maximin criterion.

(b) Determine the best decision act from the standpoint of the maximax criterion.

(c) Determine the best decision act from the standpoint of the minimax-regret criterion.

(d) In this stock-ordering situation in which the probabilities associated with the states (levels of demand) are not known, which decision would you make? Why?

13-4 For the stock-ordering situation described in Exercise 13-3 the retailer estimates that the probabilities associated with selling 0, 1, 2, or 3 stereo sets within the relevant period of time are 0.10, 0.40, 0.30, and 0.20, respectively. Determine the best decision act from the standpoint of maximizing the expected value associated with the decision.

13-5 Determine the expected value of perfect information (EVPI) for the decision situation described in Exercises 13-3 and 13-4 by first calculating the expected value with the perfect information.

13-6 The following decision table presents the conditional values (returns) associated with three different investment decisions for a two-year period. Given that the probabilities associated with the states are not available, determine the best decision act from the standpoint of the (a) maximin, (b) maximax, and (c) minimax-regret criteria.

	State of economy during period*		
Investment	E_1: Recession	E_2: Stable	E_3: Expansion
A_1: Savings account	1,000	1,000	1,000
A_2: Common stock	−700	1,000	2,000
A_3: Stock options	10,000	−5,000	12,000

13-7 For the investment decision described in Exercise 13-6 suppose that the investor estimates the probability values associated with the three states as 0.20, 0.50, and 0.30, respectively. Determine the best decision act from the standpoint of maximizing the expected value associated with the decision.

13-8 A retailer buys a certain item for $3.00 per case and sells it for $5.00 per case. The high markup reflects the perishability of the product, since it has no value after five days. Based on experience with similar products, the retailer is confident that the demand for the item will be in the range from 9 to 12 cases, inclusive.

(a) Construct the decision table for this inventory problem, indicating the possible monetary consequences associated with ordering 9, 10, 11, or 12 cases of this perishable item.

(b) Determine the best decision act from the standpoint of the maximin criterion.

(c) Determine the best decision act from the standpoint of the maximax criterion.

(d) Determine the best decision act from the standpoint of the minimax-regret criterion.

13-9 For the decision situation described in Exercise 13-8 suppose the retailer further estimates that the probabilities associated with selling 9 to 12 cases of the item are 0.30, 0.40, 0.20, and 0.10, respectively. Determine the best decision from the standpoint of maximizing the expected payoff.

13-10 Determine the expected value of perfect information (EVPI) for the decision situation described in Exercises 13-8 and 13-9 by calculating the expected opportunity loss (EOL) of the best act.

13-11 An investor is presented with the opportunity of buying common stock in a newly formed electronics company in the amount of $10,000. If the company is successful, the investment will be tripled in value; otherwise the entire investment will be lost. Determine the best decision act ("invest" or "don't invest") from the standpoint of the (a) maximin, (b) maximax, and (c) minimax-regret criteria.

13-12 For the investment decision described in Exercise 13-11 the investor estimates the chance the company will fail as about 40 percent. Taking this information into consideration, what is the best decision? Is this the decision you would make? Why or why not?

13-13 An electronics company is considering the submission of a bid for a government contract. If a bid is submitted, an expenditure of $300,000 will be required to perform the initial research and development activities necessary to define the operational goals to be included with the bid. The estimated profit that can be realized during the time-span of the contract is $500,000, including consideration of the initial expenditure on research and development. If the contract is not awarded to the company, about half of the initial research and development cost is considered a loss with the other half applicable to other company projects. Construct the table of conditional monetary values for this decision-making situation and identify the best decision acts ("bid" or "don't bid") from the standpoint of the (a) maximin, (b) maximax, and (c) minimax-regret criteria.

13-14 For the situation described in Exercise 13-13 management estimates that the chance the company will be awarded the contract as 40 percent. Determine the best decision act based on taking this probability value into consideration.

13-15 When a particular manufacturing process is in control, it produces 1 percent defectives; when it is out of control, it produces 10 percent defectives. At any randomly chosen point in time the probability is just 1 in 20 that the process is out of control. The items are produced in sets of 100 items. The cost of a "100 percent inspection" of each set, including reworking any and all defectives, is $400. In the absence of inspection it costs $200 to replace each defective item entering the assembly process. In terms of the long-run expected cost, would it be better to carry out 100 percent inspection or to put the items into the assembly process without any inspection?

13-16 For the decision problem described in Exercise 13-15 determine the expected value (cost) with perfect information. Compare this value with the expected value (cost) associated with the best act and briefly indicate the reason for the difference.

13-17 Using the expected value calculated in Exercise 13-16 determine the EVPI for the decision situation described in Exercise 13-16 and briefly interpret the meaning of this value.

13-18 For the decision problem described in Exercise 13-15 suppose that a random sample of 10 items taken from a set of 100 items is found to include one defective item. Recompute the expected costs, taking this information into consideration, and indicate whether the remaining 90 items should be subjected to 100 percent inspection or be accepted without further inspection, given that 100 percent inspection of the 90 items would cost $360.

13-19 Estimate the value of the sample information that was obtained in Exercise 13-18. Determine this value only for the 90 items that remain in the set after the 10 items have been sampled.

13-20 Several weeks before an annual "Water Carnival," a college fraternity must decide to order either blankets or beach umbrellas (or neither) for resale at the event. The conditional values associated with the possible decisions depend on the weather conditions on the day of the event and are identified in the table below. Determine the best acts from the standpoint of the (a) maximin, (b) maximax, and (c) minimax-regret criteria.

Item ordered	Weather conditions*	
	Cool	Hot
Blankets	100	−50
Beach umbrellas	−80	150
Neither	0	0

*Expected profits expressed in dollars.

13-21 For the decision problem described in Exercise 13-20 one of the members of the fraternity calls the weather bureau and learns that during the past 10 years the weather has been hot on seven of the ten days on the date when the Water Carnival is to be held. Determine the best decision act by using this information to estimate the probabilities associated with the two states.

13-22 For the college fraternity decision problem described in exercises 13-20 and 13-21

(*a*) Determine the EVPI by the approach based on calculating the expected value with perfect information.

(*b*) Determine the EVPI by the approach based on calculating the EOL of the best act.

(*c*) Compare the results of your two calculations.

13-23 For the fraternity decision problem in the preceding exercises suppose that the fraternity need not commit itself to buying the blankets or beach umbrellas until three days before the event. Therefore the members decide to add the weather bureau's forecast as additional information to the historical data regarding the occurrence of cool versus hot weather on the day of the outing. In general the weather bureau has greater success predicting cool weather than hot weather. Specifically, for a forecast made three days in advance the weather bureau correctly forecasts cool weather 90 percent of the time, and hot weather 70 percent of the time.

(*a*) Construct a tree diagram, using *C* and *H* to designate the historical occurrence of cool and hot weather, respectively, and using *FC* and *FH* to designate the forecast of each type of weather condition.

(*b*) Refer to your tree diagram. What is the probability of the weather bureau being correct in the three-day forecast?

13-24 For the decision situation described in the preceding exercises, suppose that the three-day point has arrived and the weather bureau forecasts cool weather on the day of the outing. Taking this information into consideration, identify the best decision act (order blankets, order beach umbrellas, or order neither).

13-25 Estimate the value of the weather forecast provided in Exercise 13-24.

13-26 An investment analyst estimates that the chance is 50 percent of an "upturn" in the chemical industry during the first quarter of a particular year, with the possibilities of "no change" and a "downturn" being about equal. A client is considering investing $10,000 in a mutual fund specializing in a chemical industry common stocks or investing in corporate AAA-rated bonds yielding 8.0 percent per year. If the chemical industry experiences an upturn during the first quarter, the value of the mutual-fund shares (including dividends) will increase by 15.0 percent during the next 12 months. On the other hand, if the chemical industry experiences no change, the value will increase by 3.0 percent, and if there is a downturn, the value will *decrease* by 10.0 percent. Without considering any commission costs in your analysis,

(*a*) Construct the decision table that identifies the alternative decision acts available to the investor, the possible states, the probabilities of the states, and the conditional economic consequences for this decision situation.

(*b*) Identify the best decision act from the standpoint of maximizing the expected value associated with the decision.

13-27 For the decision problem in Exercise 13-26 determine the expected value with perfect information and the EVPI.

13-28 For the decision problem in Exercise 13-26, by a simplified approach the investment analyst defines "upturn" to mean that (at least) 70 percent of the usual users of chemical products increase their order amounts, "no change" to mean that (about) 50 percent of the users increase their order amounts, and "downturn" to mean that 30 percent (or fewer) of the users increase their order amounts. Contacting a random sample of 20 users of chemical products, the investment analyst finds that 14 of these users are increasing their order amounts compared with previous periods.

(*a*) Revise the prior probability distribution regarding the three possible states of the chemical industry, as given in Exercise 13-26, by taking this sample result into consideration.

(*b*) Using the posterior probability distribution, determine the best-decision act and compare it with your answer in Exercise 13-26*b*.

13-29 Estimate the value of the sample information obtained in Exercise 13-28.

13-30 Using the posterior distribution determined in Exercise 13-28, determine the expected value with perfect information and the EVPI *after* the sample has been taken. Compare your results with those in Exercise 13-27.

13-31 Refer to the commuter car example in Section 13-4. Suppose we estimate a goodwill loss of $50 for each commuter car needed and not provided, based on the loss of passengers for future runs of the train.

(*a*) Revise the linear payoff functions developed in Section 13-4 to take account of this assessment.

(*b*) Construct the new decision table for this decision problem.

(*c*) Determine the best decision act based on the expected value criterion, and compare this decision with the one in Section 13-4 that did not take goodwill loss into consideration.

13-32 With respect to the revision of the probability distribution for the fractions defective in Section 13-6, suppose that a second random sample of $n = 10$ is taken from the shipment and that none of the items is found to be defective.

(*a*) Using the posterior distribution determined in Section 13-6 as the new prior distribution, determine the posterior distribution following this second sample.

(*b*) Combine this second sample with the first sample that was obtained. For the combined sample one defective has been observed in $n = 20$ sampled parts. Now use the original prior probability distribution in Section 13-6 and revise this distribution on the basis of the combined sample results for the two random samples.

(*c*) Compare the posterior probability distributions obtained in Exercise 13-32*a* and 13-32*b* and comment on this comparison.

13-33 An investor is considering placing a deposit of $10,000 to reserve a fast-foods franchise opportunity in a new residential area for one year. There are two areas of uncertainty associated with this sequential-decision situation: whether a prime franchise competitor will decide to locate an outlet in the same area and whether the residential area will develop to be a moderate or large market. Overall, then, the investor must first decide whether to deposit the initial $10,000 as a down payment for the franchise. Then during the one-year period, the decision of the competing franchise system will be revealed, and the investor estimates the chance is 50–50 that the competing franchise system will also develop an outlet. After the decision of the competing system is known, the investor must then decide whether to proceed with constructing the franchise outlet. If the competition is substantial and the market is large, the net gain during the relevant period is estimated at $15,000; if the market is moderate, the net loss will be $10,000. If there is no competition and the market is large, the net gain will be $30,000; if the market is moderate, there will be a net gain of $10,000. All of these net figures include consideration of the franchise deposit fee of $10,000. The investor estimates the chance at 40 percent that the market will be large. Based on this information, construct the decision tree for this situation.

13-34 Referring to your decision tree in Exercise 13-33, determine the best act at the initial decision point ("deposit" or "don't deposit").

13-35 For the sequential decision problem in Exercises 13-33 and 13-34 determine the probability that there will be a profit if the initial deposit is made. Also consider the implications of making the initial deposit in terms of the best acts at the next decision points in your decision tree.

FOURTEEN

REGRESSION AND CORRELATION ANALYSIS

14-1 INTRODUCTION

Regression analysis is the procedure by which an algebraic equation is formulated to estimate the value of a continuous random variable, given the value of another quantitative variable. The variable for which the value is estimated by the regression equation is called the *dependent variable*; the variable used as the basis for the estimate is called the *independent variable*. The methods of analysis in this chapter as well as Chapter 15 are concerned only with *linear* regression analysis. As explained further in Section 14-3, the relationship between the variables can be expressed by a linear algebraic model. This model is by far the most prevalent model used in regression analysis. In this chapter the methods of analysis are concerned with *simple regression analysis*, which means that the value of the dependent variable is estimated on the basis of only *one* independent variable. On the other hand *multiple regression analysis*, covered in Chapter 15, is concerned with estimating the value of the dependent variable on the basis of *two or more* independent variables.

Whereas regression analysis is concerned with estimating the value of a random variable based on knowledge of another quantitative variable, *correlation analysis* is concerned with measuring the degree of relationship between variables. Again, the methods of analysis in this book are predicated on the assumption that the relationship between the variables is *linear*. The coverage in this chapter is restricted to *simple correlation analysis*, which means that there is only one independent variable. *Multiple correlation analysis*, which concerns two or more independent variables, is considered in Chapter 15.

In mathematics a *functional relationship* between two variables indicates that the value of one variable can be determined precisely given the value of the other variable. In contrast the existence of a *statistical relationship* between two variables indicates that there is a general relationship between the variables but that it is not a perfect relationship. In business and economics pairs of variables, such as amount of advertising and level of sales, often have a statistical relationship but not an exact functional relationship. The methods of regression and correlation analysis have been developed specifically to study statistical relationships in data sets.

14-2 ASSUMPTIONS ASSOCIATED WITH SIMPLE LINEAR REGRESSION ANALYSIS

In this section we specify the principal assumptions associated with simple linear regression analysis and briefly consider some implications of these assumptions.

1. The independent and dependent variables have a linear relationship. The linear equation that represents the simple linear regression model is

$$Y_i = \alpha + \beta X_i + e_i \qquad (14\text{-}1)$$

where Y_i = value of the dependent variable in the ith trial, or observation

   α = first parameter of the regression equation, which indicates the value of Y when $X = 0$

   β = second parameter of the regression equation, which indicates the slope of the regression line

   e_i = random error in the ith trial, or observation, associated with the process of sampling

The assumption that the two variables are linearly associated can be investigated by constructing a *scatter diagram* for the sample data, as illustrated in Section 14-2.

2. The dependent variable is a continuous random variable, whereas the independent variable is set at various values and is not random. In this respect the value X in the linear regression model is a designated value, but the observed value of the dependent variable Y must be obtained through the process of sampling.

Thus the value e_i in the linear model is the sampling error associated with the dependent random variable. For example, if we are interested in studying the relationship between advertising and sales, different levels of advertising can be used in different regions, and the associated values of the dependent variable (sales) can be observed in those regions. This type of study, in which the values of the independent variable are designated and controlled, is an example of a *statistical experiment*. On the other hand suppose that we take a random sample of firms from a given industry and observe the level of advertising and the level of sales for each firm. Both variables are random variables, and this study is a *statistical survey*. Strictly speaking, the simple regression model is not appropriate if both variables are random variables. However, if it can be assumed that the value of e_i in the regression model is not related to the value of the independent variable X, which is typically so, the regression model is appropriate. The net result is that regression analysis can generally be used with either experimental data or survey data.

3. The variances of the conditional distributions of the dependent variable, given different values of the independent variable, are equal. This assumption is called *homoscedasticity* in regression analysis. It is similar to the assumption of homogeneity of variance in the analysis of variance. With reference to the linear algebraic model, this means that the variance associated with the sampling error e_i is the same for different values of X_i. This assumption can be investigated by constructing a scatter diagram for the sample data and observing whether the amount of "scatter" is about the same for different values of the independent variable, as illustrated in the following section of this chapter.

4. Successive observed values of the random variable are uncorrelated. More specifically, it is assumed that the amounts of random error e_i in the linear model are uncorrelated for successive observations of the random variable. Given that the process of random sampling is used in either an experiment or a survey, this assumption is generally satisfied. However, the one type of data situation that presents a difficulty is *time-series analysis*, in which values of the dependent variable occur in a series of time periods. In time-series analysis any positive or negative deviation between expected and observed values of the random variable is likely to be related for successive time periods. That is, the values of e_i in the linear model are related for successive time periods. This type of relationship is called *autocorrelation*. Because this problem is particularly troublesome in the context of multiple regression analysis, it is considered further in Section 15-10, while the use of the linear model in time-series analysis is described in Section 16-2. The existence of autocorrelation affects the accuracy of tests of hypotheses or interval estimates in regression analysis, but it does not affect the accuracy of the point estimates.

5. The conditional distributions of the dependent variable, given different values of the independent variable, are all normal distributions. In the linear regression model, this assumption indicates that the distribution of the sampling error e_i is normal. This assumption is required for any tests of hypotheses or interval estimates in regression analysis, but it is not required for point estimation based on the linear regression equation.

14-3 THE SCATTER DIAGRAM

A *scatter diagram* is a graph in which each plotted point represents an observed pair of values for the independent and dependent variables. The value of the independent variable X is plotted in reference to the horizontal axis, and the value of the dependent variable Y is plotted in reference to the vertical axis. As indicated in the preceding section, the construction of a scatter diagram for a set of data pairs is useful, because we can then examine the graph to determine whether the relationship between the variables is approximately linear and whether the points are approximately equally scattered for different values of the independent variable X (assumption of homoscedasticity). Although statistical procedures are available to test these two principal assumptions underlying linear regression analysis, general compliance or noncompliance of the data with these assumptions can usually be observed by constructing a scatter diagram. The statistical methods by which these assumptions can be tested are beyond the scope of this book.

Table 14-1 presents selection test scores and associated performance ratings on the job for a random sample of 20 industrial trainees in a manufacturing firm. The objective is to estimate (predict) job performance on the basis of the selection test score. Therefore it is logical to designate the selection test score as the independent variable and the performance rating as the dependent variable. Although the selection test score is itself a random variable, rather than being set at various values as

Table 14-1 Selection test scores and performance ratings for a sample of industrial trainees

Sampled individual	Selection test score	Performance rating, 20-point scale
1	88	17
2	85	16
3	72	13
4	93	18
5	70	11
6	74	14
7	78	15
8	93	19
9	82	16
10	92	20
11	79	14
12	84	15
13	71	12
14	77	13
15	87	19
16	87	17
17	72	10
18	77	12
19	82	14
20	76	13

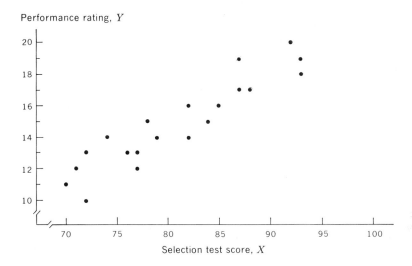

Figure 14-1 Scatter diagram relating selection test scores to performance ratings for a sample of industrial trainees.

required in the linear regression model, it is assumed that the value of the independent variable is not related to the sampling error e_i associated with the dependent variable. Therefore the two variables are considered appropriate for use in regression analysis.

Figure 14-1 is the scatter diagram for the data presented in Table 14-1. There are 20 dots, or points, in this diagram, each one representing a pair of values. For example, in Table 14-1 trainee 5 is identified as having a selection test score of 70 and a performance rating of 11. This pair of values is represented by the dot farthest to the left in Figure 14-1, at the intersection of $X = 70$ and $Y = 11$. From this diagram it appears that the relationship between the variables is essentially linear; that is, a straight line can be drawn through the points on the two-dimensional graph. Further, it appears that the variability in the values of Y, given different values of X, is about the same. That is, the vertical band, or scatter, does not appear much different at the right end of the scatter diagram compared with the left end of the diagram.

If inspection of the scatter diagram indicates that the relationship between the independent variable and dependent variable is essentially linear and that the homoscedasticity assumption is not violated, the linear regression equation for the best-fitting line is determined by the procedures presented in Section 14-4. In addition to providing a basis for checking the assumptions associated with linear regression analysis, the scatter diagram also indicates the nature and extent of relationship between the two variables. A *positive relationship* (also called a direct relationship) exists if the values of Y generally increase as the values of X increase. In a positive relationship the best-fitting line has a positive slope. A *negative relationship* (also called an inverse relationship) exists if the values of Y generally decrease as the values of X increase. In a negative

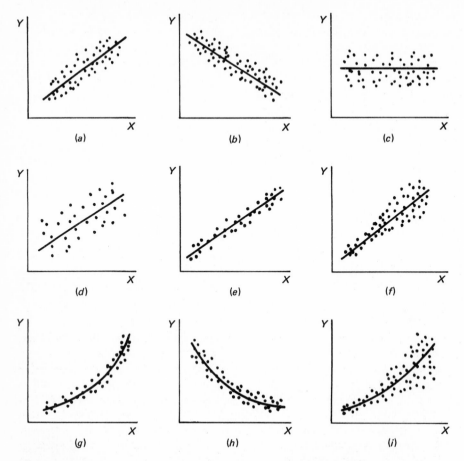

Figure 14-2 Scatter diagrams for several types of data relationships. (*a*) Positive linear relationship. (*b*) Negative linear relationship. (*c*) No relationship. (*d*) Positive linear relationship with lower degree of relationship than in Figure *a*. (*e*) Positive linear relationship with higher degree of relationship than in Figure *a*. (*f*) Positive linear relationship with homoscedasticity assumption violated. (*g*) Positive curvilinear relationship. (*h*) Negative curvilinear relationship. (*i*) Positive curvilinear relationship with homoscedasticity assumption violated.

relationship the best-fitting line has a negative slope. A slope of zero for the best-fitting line indicates a lack of relationship between the variables. Figure 14-2*a–c* illustrate these types of relationships.

The general degree of relationship between the variables is indicated by the extent of scatter with respect to the best-fitting line. This is illustrated by Figure 14-2*d–e*. However, note that how we scale the values on the *Y* axis directly affects the extent of scatter portrayed on a scatter diagram. Differences in extent of scatter indicate different degrees of relationship only if the diagrams being compared have the same dependent variable with the same scale for the *Y* axis.

Figure 14-2*f-i* illustrates various types of violations of the linear regression model. The data in Figure 14-2*i* represent the most extreme violation since neither the assumption of linearity nor the assumption of homoscedasticity is satisfied. Discussion of regression analysis for variables that have a curvilinear relationship is beyond the scope of this book; however, there is a limited discussion of curvilinear trend analysis in Section 16-2. For nonlinear relationships a frequent approach is to investigate methods of transforming the values, particularly the values of the dependent variable, so that the relationship between the transformed variables is linear. Then linear regression analysis is applied to the transformed values, and the estimated values of the dependent variable are then transformed back to the original measurement scale.

14-4 DETERMINING THE LINEAR REGRESSION EQUATION ON THE BASIS OF SAMPLE DATA

The parameters α and β in the linear regression model presented in Formula (14-1) are estimated by the values a and b based on sample data. Thus the linear regression equation to determine the "computed," or estimated, value of the dependent variable, given a value X for the independent variable is

$$Y_c = a + bX \qquad (14\text{-}2)$$

Depending on the mathematical criterion used, different linear equations could be developed as constituting the "best fit" for the data in a particular scatter diagram. The mathematical criterion used most frequently is the *least-squares criterion*. By this criterion the best-fitting regression line is that for which the sum of the squared deviations between the estimated and actual values of the dependent variable is minimized. Graphically, the squared deviations minimized are the vertical deviations from the regression line, as illustrated in Figure 14-3. Recall that from the standpoint of the least-squares criterion the arithmetic mean is the best measure

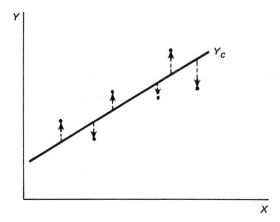

Figure 14-3 Squared deviations for which the sum is minimized by use of the least-squares criterion.

of average, as explained in Section 3-5. There is then a direct correspondence between the arithmetic mean and the linear regression equation based on the least-squares criterion. The regression line relating two variables can be thought of as a "mean line" in that it represents the average relationship between the independent and dependent variables for the relevant range of values of the independent variable.

Based on the least-squares criterion, the computational formulas by which the values of a and b are determined for the linear regression equation are

$$b = \frac{\Sigma XY - n\bar{X}\bar{Y}}{\Sigma X^2 - n\bar{X}^2} \qquad (14\text{-}3)$$

$$a = \bar{Y} - b\bar{X} \qquad (14\text{-}4)$$

Table 14-2 is the worksheet for determining the linear regression equation for the data in Table 14-1. The total of the last column is not required now, but will be used in subsequent calculations. Solving for the point estimators of β and α, we have

$$b = \frac{\Sigma XY - n\bar{X}\bar{Y}}{\Sigma X^2 - n\bar{X}^2}$$

where $\bar{X} = \Sigma X/n = 1{,}619/20 = 80.95$
$\bar{Y} = \Sigma Y/n = 298/20 = 14.90$

Table 14-2 Worksheet for determining the linear regression equation for estimating the performance rating of industrial trainees on the basis of selection test score

Sampled individual	Selection test score X	Performance rating Y	XY	X^2	Y^2
1	88	17	1,496	7,744	289
2	85	16	1,360	7,225	256
3	72	13	936	5,184	169
4	93	18	1,674	8,649	324
5	70	11	720	4,900	121
6	74	14	1,036	5,476	196
7	78	15	1,170	6,084	225
8	93	19	1,767	8,649	361
9	82	16	1,312	6,724	256
10	92	20	1,840	8,464	400
11	79	14	1,106	6,241	196
12	84	15	1,260	7,056	225
13	71	12	852	5,041	144
14	77	13	1,001	5,929	169
15	87	19	1,653	7,569	361
16	87	17	1,479	7,569	289
17	72	10	720	5,184	100
18	77	12	924	5,929	144
19	82	14	1,148	6,724	196
20	76	13	988	5,776	169
Total	1,619	298	24,492	132,117	4,590

$$b = \frac{24{,}492 - 20(80.95)(14.90)}{132{,}117 - 20(80.95)^2} = \frac{24{,}492 - 24{,}123.1}{132{,}117 - 131{,}058.05} = \frac{368.9}{1{,}058.95}$$

$$= 0.3484 \approx 0.35$$

$$a = \bar{Y} - b\bar{X} = 14.90 - 0.35(80.95) = 14.90 - 28.3325 = -13.4325 \approx -13.43$$

Therefore the regression equation for estimating the performance rating on the basis of the selection test score is

$$Y_c = a + bX = -13.43 + 0.35X$$

The value of $b = 0.35$ indicates that the slope of the regression line is 0.35. This means that for each increase of one point in the selection test score there is an increase of 0.35 in the performance rating, on the average. Thus a positive relationship exists between these two variables. The value $a = -13.43$ may appear to be a bit puzzling. Graphically, this is the point of intersection of the regression line with the Y axis, and therefore -13.43 is the value of Y when $X = 0$. But how can there be a negative performance rating when the data in Table 14-2 indicate that only positive ratings are assessed? The answer is that *any regression equation is only meaningful for the range of the values of the independent variable included in the sample.* One cannot legitimately extrapolate the regression line beyond the range of the data in the sample. In this sample the lowest selection test score is 70 and the highest selection test score is 93. Therefore it is not appropriate to use this regression equation to estimate (and in this case to predict) performance for anyone whose selection test score is below 70 or above 93. If such prediction is done, it would be on the basis of the additional assumption that the regression model extends to those additional ranges of values.

Suppose a trainee applicant has a selection test score of 85. This score is within the range of values used to establish the linear regression equation, and we predict performance rating on the job as follows:

$$Y_c = a + bX = -13.43 + 0.35(85) = -13.43 + 29.75 = 16.32 \approx 16$$

If a trainee applicant has a selection test score of 90, the estimated performance rating on the job is

$$Y_c = -13.43 + 0.35(90) = -13.43 + 31.5 = 18.07 \approx 18$$

Of course both of the predictions above are point estimates that will not necessarily be exactly correct. In the next section we present the method by which prediction intervals can be constructed, thereby allowing us to attach probability statements to the estimates.

$a = \bar{Y} - b\bar{X}$

14-5 THE STANDARD ERROR OF ESTIMATE AND PREDICTION INTERVALS

The *standard error of estimate* is the conditional standard deviation of the dependent variable Y given a value of the independent variable X. For population data the standard error of estimate is represented by the symbol $\sigma_{Y.X}$. The deviations formula by which this value is estimated on the basis of sample data is

$$s_{Y.X} = \sqrt{\frac{\Sigma(Y - Y_c)^2}{n - 2}} \qquad (14\text{-}5)$$

To use Formula (14-5), we need to compute a value of Y_c for every observed value of X by repeated application of the regression equation. Therefore the procedure can be quite laborious. The alternative computational formula does not require the determination of the deviation of each observed value of Y from the regression-line value Y_c, and it is therefore more convenient to use

$$s_{Y.X} = \sqrt{\frac{\Sigma Y^2 - a\Sigma Y - b\Sigma XY}{n - 2}} \qquad (14\text{-}6)$$

Figure 14-4 portrays the conditional distributions to which the standard error of estimate applies as a measure of variability. Thus, given that the X and Y variables are related, the amount of scatter in the values of Y *given any particular value of X* will always be less than the total amount of scatter in the values of Y without the given value of X. Also, by reference to Figure 14-4 we can see that the standard error of estimate is meaningful as a constant value given any particular value of X only if the homoscedasticity assumption is satisfied. Otherwise, the conditional standard deviation would have different values, depending on the value of X. Finally, notice that a normal probability distribution is assumed for each of the conditional distributions in Figure 14-4. This assumption does not require that the *sample* values of Y for any given value of X be normally distributed, for rarely would there be many values of Y for a given value of X. Rather, the assumption applies to the *population* from which this sample was taken, and is a necessary assumption for the construction of prediction intervals.

The formula often used to approximate a prediction interval based on sample data is

$$\text{Pred. int.} = Y_c \pm t_{\text{df}} s_{Y.X} \qquad (14\text{-}7)$$

Use of the t distribution is appropriate for constructing such intervals, because the population standard error of estimate is unknown and the random variable is

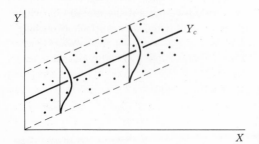

Figure 14-4 Conditional distributions of the dependent variable with respect to the regression line.

assumed to be normally distributed in the population. Section 7-7 contains the summary table that indicates when the t distribution should be used in interval estimation. The degrees of freedom used in constructing a prediction interval is $df = n - 2$, because the two parameters α and β are estimated by the sample statistics a and b, and thus two degrees of freedom are lost.

As indicated in Section 7-5, the normal probability distribution can be used as an approximation of the t distribution when $df \geqslant 29$. Thus the formula to approximate a prediction interval when the sample size is relatively large is

$$\text{Pred. int.} = Y_c \pm z s_{Y.X} \qquad (14\text{-}8)$$

As an example of an approximate prediction interval let us construct the 95 percent prediction interval for the performance rating of an industrial trainee, given a selection test score of 85. In Section 14-4 we determined the point estimate $Y_c = 16.32$ for the performance rating. The prediction interval is

$$95\% \text{ pred. int.} = Y_c \pm t_{df} s_{Y.X}$$

where $Y_c = 16.32$
$t_{18} = 2.101$
$$s_{Y.X} = \sqrt{(\Sigma Y^2 - a\Sigma Y - b\Sigma XY)/(n-2)}$$
$$\sqrt{[4{,}590 - (-13.43)(298) - 0.35(24{,}492)]/(20-2)}$$
$$= \sqrt{(4{,}590 + 4{,}002.14 - 8{,}572.2)/18} = \sqrt{19.92/18} = \sqrt{1.1077} = 1.05$$

$$95\% \text{ pred. int.} = 16.32 \pm 2.101(1.05) = 16.32 \pm 2.21 = 14.11 \text{ to } 18.53$$

Thus, for a trainee applicant whose selection test score is 85, the probability is 0.95 that the trainee's performance rating on the job will be within the limits 14.11 and 18.53.

Two important observations need to be made as we conclude this section. First, the interval estimates are called *prediction intervals* rather than confidence intervals, because the latter term is used when the value of a population *parameter* is estimated. In the present case the individual value of a dependent variable, and not a parameter value, is estimated. Second, note that we indicated that Formulas (14-7) and (14-8) are used to *approximate* a prediction interval rather than to *define* such an interval. Use of these formulas to define a prediction interval would imply that the only uncertainty associated with estimating the conditional value of the dependent variable is represented by the scatter with respect to the regression line. However, because the regression equation is itself based on sample data, we need to recognize that the location of the regression line is also uncertain. The complete prediction interval that takes this additional source of uncertainty into consideration is described in Section 14-6. However, if the sample size n is relatively large ($df \geqslant 29$), the prediction interval defined by Formula (14-8), which is based on use of the normal probability distribution, is considered to be a satisfactory approximation of the complete prediction interval for most situations. If the sample is small but at least $df \geqslant 10$, use of the t distribution with Formula (14-7) is often a satisfactory "rough" estimate of the correct interval.

14-6 INFERENCES CONCERNING THE PARAMETERS IN LINEAR REGRESSION ANALYSIS

We consider three separate but related topics in this section of the chapter:

1. The confidence interval for the conditional mean of the dependent variable
2. The complete prediction interval for the individual value of Y by including consideration of the uncertainty associated with using a regression equation based on sample data
3. Interval estimation and hypothesis testing concerned with the slope β of the linear regression model

Confidence Intervals for the Conditional Mean

The point estimate for the conditional *mean* of a dependent variable, given a specific value of X, is the same value as the point estimate of the individual conditional value. However, note the distinction that we are now concerned with estimating a conditional mean rather than a single conditional value Y_c. Thus, where $\bar{Y}_c$ designates the mean of Y given a particular value of X, we can state this relationship by

$$\bar{Y}_c = Y_c \tag{14-9}$$

or

$$\bar{Y}_c = a + bX \tag{14-10}$$

The estimated standard error of the conditional mean, given a specific value of X and based on sample data, is

$$s_{\bar{Y}.X} = s_{Y.X}\sqrt{\frac{1}{n} + \frac{(X - \bar{X})^2}{\Sigma X^2 - [(\Sigma X)^2/n]}} \tag{14-11}$$

If it were not for the second term under the radical, Formula (14-11) would be identical to Formula (7-5) for the estimated standard error of the mean based on sample data. The second term under the radical is unique to regression analysis. This term increases in magnitude as the given value of X differs from the mean, $\bar{X}$. Thus the standard error of the conditional mean is *not* the same for all values of X; it is at a minimum when $X = \bar{X}$ and is systematically larger as the given X departs in value from $\bar{X}$.

Given the point estimate of the conditional mean and the standard error of the conditional mean, the confidence interval for the conditional mean is defined by

$$\text{Conf. int.} = \bar{Y}_c \pm t_{df}s_{\bar{Y}.X} \tag{14-12}$$

For example let us construct the 95 percent confidence interval for the mean performance rating, given that the selection test score is $X = 85$ for the data in the preceding sections of this chapter. In Section 14-4 we determined that $Y_c = 16.32$, and therefore the conditional mean is

$$\bar{Y}_c = Y_c = 16.32$$

In Section 14-5 we determined that for these data $s_{Y.X} = 1.05$. Using this value and other values based on Table 14-2, the standard error of the conditional mean is

$$s_{\bar{Y}.X} = s_{Y.X} \sqrt{\frac{1}{n} + \frac{(X - \bar{X})^2}{\Sigma X^2 - [(\Sigma X)^2/n]}} = 1.05 \sqrt{\frac{1}{20} + \frac{85 - 80.95}{132{,}117 - [(1{,}619)^2/20]}}$$

$$= 1.05 \sqrt{0.05 + \frac{4.05}{132{,}117 - 131{,}058.05}} = 1.05\sqrt{0.05 + 0.00382}$$

$$= 105(0.232) = 0.244$$

Finally, the 95 percent confidence interval for the conditional mean of the dependent variable, given that $X = 85$, is

$$95\% \text{ conf. int.} = \bar{Y}_c \pm t_{df} s_{\bar{Y}.X}$$

where $\bar{Y}_c = 16.32$
$\quad t_{df} = t_{18} = 2.101$
$\quad s_{\bar{Y}.X} = 0.244$

$\quad 95\% \text{ conf. int.} = 16.32 \pm 2.101(0.244) = 16.32 \pm 0.51 = 15.81 \text{ to } 16.83$

As we would expect, the 95 percent confidence interval for the mean is narrower (more precise) than the 95 percent prediction interval for the individual value of Y, given $X = 85$, as calculated in Section 14-5.

As in constructing a prediction interval (described in Section 14-5), when $df \geqslant 29$, the normal distribution can be used to construct the confidence interval for the conditional mean. Further, the second term in the basic formula for the standard error of the conditional mean can be dropped, leading to the following simplified formula for determining the confidence interval for the conditional mean when the sample is relatively large:

$$\text{Conf. int.} = \bar{Y}_c \pm z \frac{s_{Y.X}}{\sqrt{n}} \tag{14-13}$$

Construction of Complete Prediction Intervals

We now turn to the second major topic covered in this section: the construction of a complete prediction interval for the individual value of the dependent variable by taking into consideration that the regression equation is based on sample data. Essentially, the uncertainty regarding the regression equation is expressed as uncertainty about the correct value of the conditional mean $\bar{Y}_X$. Therefore the complete standard error associated with predicting an individual conditional value of the dependent variable should consider both the amount of variability with respect to the regression line and the uncertainty associated with the conditional mean. This type of complete standard error is called the *standard error of forecast* and is generally designated by $s_{Y(next)}$, in which "next" simply means the next individual value of the dependent variable Y to be estimated. The basic formula for the standard error of forecast is

$$s_{Y(next)} = \sqrt{s_{Y.X}^2 + s_{\bar{Y}.X}^2} \tag{14-14}$$

The computational version of the standard error of forecast is

$$s_{Y(\text{next})} = s_{Y.X} \sqrt{1 + \frac{1}{n} + \frac{(X - \bar{X})^2}{\Sigma X^2 - [(\Sigma X)^2/n]}} \qquad (14\text{-}15)$$

The complete prediction interval for an individual value of the dependent variable, given a specific value of the independent variable X and based on using the standard error of forecast, is

$$\text{Pred. int.} = Y_c \pm t_{\text{df}} s_{Y(\text{next})} \qquad (14\text{-}16)$$

For example, for the data involving selection test score and performance rating let us construct the 95 percent prediction interval for the performance rating Y, given that the selection test score is $X = 85$. In this example we use Formula (14-14) to determine the standard error of forecast because both values required in this formula have been calculated in Sections 14-4 and 14-5:

$$95\% \text{ Pred. int.} = Y_c \pm t_{\text{df}} s_{Y(\text{next})}$$

where $Y_c = 16.32$

$t_{\text{df}} = t_{18} = 2.101$

$s_{Y(\text{next})} = \sqrt{s_{Y.X}{}^2 + s_{\bar{Y}_X}{}^2} = \sqrt{1.05^2 + 0.30^2} = \sqrt{1.1925} = 1.09$

$95\% \text{ pred. int.} = 16.32 \pm 2.101(1.09) = 16.32 \pm 2.29 = 14.03 \text{ to } 18.61$

This 95 percent prediction interval is just slightly wider than the approximate interval of "14.11 to 18.53" constructed in Section 14-5 based solely on the standard error of estimate without considering the uncertainty associated with the value of the conditional mean. As we indicated in the concluding paragraph of Section 14-5, use of the complete standard error of forecast generally is not considered necessary when the sample is relatively large (df $\geqslant$ 29), and even with smaller sample sizes, such as in the present example, the approximation is often acceptable.

Inferences Concerning the Slope

The final topic now covered in this section of the chapter is interval estimation and hypothesis testing concerning the slope β of the linear regression model. The estimated standard error of the sample statistics b, based on sample data, is

$$s_b = \frac{s_{Y.X}}{\sqrt{\Sigma X^2 - n\bar{X}^2}} \qquad (14\text{-}17)$$

Because the standard error of estimate $s_{Y.X}$ in the numerator of Formula (14-17) is based on $n - 2$ degrees of freedom, s_b is also based on $n - 2$ degrees of freedom. The confidence interval for estimating the value of β is

$$\text{Conf. int.} = b \pm t_{\text{df}} s_b \qquad (14\text{-}18)$$

For example the 95 percent confidence interval for estimating the value of β

for the sample data in Table 14-1 using values calculated in previous sections of this chapter is

$$95\% \text{ conf. int.} = b \pm t_{df}s_b$$

where $b = 0.35$

$t_{df} = t_{18} = 2.101$

$s_b = s_{Y.X}/\sqrt{\Sigma X^2 - n\bar{X}^2} = 1.05/\sqrt{132,117 - 20(80.95)^2}$

$= 1.05/\sqrt{132,117 - 131,058.05} = 1.05/\sqrt{1,058.95} = 1.05/32.54 = 0.03$

$95\% \text{ conf. int.} = 0.35 \pm 2.101(0.03) = 0.35 \pm 0.06 = 0.29 \text{ to } 0.41$

A null hypothesis concerning the value of β is tested by computing the test statistic t by

$$t = \frac{b - \beta_0}{s_b} \tag{14-19}$$

The usual null hypothesis tested is that $\beta = 0$, because such a value indicates the absence of any relationship between the independent and dependent variables. Along these lines recall that in Figure 14-2 the absence of any relationship is represented by a horizontal regression line, that is, by a regression line with a slope of 0. The test can be a one-tail or two-tail test, according to the form of the hypothesis. For a one-tail test the alternative hypothesis is not simply that the two variables are related but further that the relationship is of a specified type (positive or negative). For our sample problem we test the null hypothesis that $\beta = 0$ at the 5 percent level of significance as follows:

Hypotheses: $H_0: \beta = 0$

$H_1: \beta \neq 0$

Critical t (df $= 20 - 2 = 18$, $\alpha = 0.05) = \pm 2.101$

$$t = \frac{b - \beta_0}{s_b} = \frac{0.35 - 0}{0.03} = \frac{0.35}{0.03} = 11.67$$

The computed value of the t statistic exceeds the positive critical limit of 2.101. Therefore the null hypothesis that there is no relationship between the selection test scores and ratings of job performance is rejected, and the alternative hypothesis that there is a relationship is accepted.

14-7 ASSUMPTIONS ASSOCIATED WITH CORRELATION ANALYSIS

Whereas regression analysis is concerned with estimating, or predicting, the value of the dependent variable given the value of the independent variable, *correlation analysis* is concerned with measuring and expressing the degree of relationship between the two variables. As was true in our coverage of regression analysis, in this chapter we restrict our coverage of correlation analysis to *simple correlation analysis*, which involves just one independent variable and one dependent variable. *Multiple correlation analysis*, concerned with two or more independent variables and one dependent variable, is considered in Chapter 15.

The principal assumptions associated with simple correlation analysis are similar to the assumptions associated with simple linear regression analysis as described in Section 14-2. Therefore in the following listing we give particular emphasis to the differences between these two sets of assumptions.

1. The independent and dependent variables have a linear relationship. This is the same assumption as for linear regression analysis.

2. Both the independent and the dependent variables are continuous random variables. This assumption differs from the assumption in regression analysis in which the dependent variable is assumed to be a random variable while the independent variable is assumed to be set at various values. The implication of the assumption underlying correlation analysis is that the values of both variables have to be determined by the process of sampling, and neither value can be designated, or controlled, in an experiment.

3. For *each* variable the variances of the conditional distributions of the variable, given various values for the other variable, are equal. That is, the assumption of *homoscedasticity* applies to each variable separately. This assumption differs from the assumption in regression analysis in that in regression analysis only the dependent variable is the random variable and the assumption of homoscedasticity applies only to the conditional distributions for the dependent variable.

4. Successive observed values of the independent variable are uncorrelated and successive observed values of the dependent variable are uncorrelated. This assumption is similar to the assumption in regression analysis, except that, again, the assumption applies to both variables and not just to the dependent variable.

5. For each variable the distributions of the conditional values, given various values for the other variable, are all normal distributions. That is, the distribution for the two variables jointly is a *bivariate normal distribution*.

14-8 THE COEFFICIENTS OF DETERMINATION AND CORRELATION

Suppose that the value of a normally distributed variable Y is to be estimated based only on knowledge of the mean and standard deviation for this population. The population standard deviation σ_Y would serve as the basis for making probability statements about the value of Y. For example the probability is approximately 0.68 that the value will be within plus or minus one standard deviation of the mean. The measure of variability is σ_Y, and statistically we can say that the *measure of uncertainty* in respect to the prediction is the variance σ_Y^2.

Now, in the context of regression analysis, the dependent variable Y is estimated on the basis of a known value of the independent variable X, and the prediction interval is based on use of the standard error of estimate $\sigma_{Y.X}$ for population data. The measure of uncertainty for prediction based on a population regression equation is $\sigma_{Y.X}^2$. Given that a relationship exists between the two variables, $\sigma_{Y.X}^2$ will always be less than σ_Y^2. In fact, if the relationship is perfect, every value of the dependent variable would be equal to the corresponding regression-line value and $\sigma_{Y.X}^2 = 0$. That is, there would be no uncertainty about the predicted value of Y. But the relationship is usually not perfect. The value σ_Y^2 represents the total variance, or uncertainty, with respect to the dependent variable, while $\sigma_{Y.X}^2$ represents the variance, or uncertainty, that remains after the value of the independent variable is considered. Therefore the *proportion of unexplained variance given knowledge of the independent variable* can be defined as

$$\text{Proportion unexplained variance} = \frac{\sigma_{Y.X}^2}{\sigma_Y^2} \tag{14-20}$$

Again, if the relationship is perfect, the numerator in Formula (14-20) would be 0, and the proportion of unexplained variance that remains would be 0. If there is no relationship, $\sigma_{Y.X}^2$ would be equal to σ_Y^2. There would be no reduction in uncertainty associated with knowledge of the independent variable, and the proportion of unexplained variance would be 1.0.

Given that we can determine the proportion of unexplained variance in bivariate analysis (analysis involving two variables), it follows that we can easily determine the proportion of explained variance by subtracting the first proportion from 1.0. The resulting value is called the *coefficient of determination*, and this coefficient indicates the proportion of variance in the dependent variable statistically explained by knowledge of the independent variable. For population data the coefficient of determination is represented by the Greek letter ρ^2 (read: "rho squared") and is defined by

$$\rho^2 = 1 - \frac{\sigma_{Y.X}^2}{\sigma_Y^2} \tag{14-21}$$

Of course, typically we have sample data rather than population data available in bivariate analysis. For sample data the basic formula for estimating the value of the coefficient of determination is

$$r^2 = 1 - \frac{s_{Y.X}^2}{s_Y^2} \tag{14-22}$$

Although Formulas (14-21) and (14-22) present the rationale underlying the coefficient of determination, they are not convenient to use computationally. A computational formula for the sample coefficient of determination is

$$r^2 = \frac{a\Sigma Y + b\Sigma XY - n\bar{Y}^2}{\Sigma Y^2 - n\bar{Y}^2} \tag{14-23}$$

For example the coefficient of determination that indicates the extent of relationship between the selection test scores and the performance ratings for the industrial trainees is calculated as follows [the values substituted in Formula (14-23) were previously determined in Section 14-4]:

$$r^2 = \frac{a\Sigma Y + b\Sigma XY - n\bar{Y}^2}{\Sigma Y^2 - n\bar{Y}^2} = \frac{[(-13.43)(298) + 0.35(24{,}492)] - 20(14.90)^2}{4{,}590 - 20(14.90)^2}$$

$$= \frac{-4{,}002.14 + 8{,}572.2 - 4{,}440.2}{4{,}590 - 4{,}440.2} = \frac{129.86}{149.8} = 0.8669 \approx 0.87$$

Thus we estimate that 87 percent of the variance, or variability, in the performance ratings is statistically explained by knowledge of the selection test scores. Incidentally, because both variables are random variables, we can also say that 87 percent of the variability in the selection test scores is statistically explained by knowledge of the performance rating. But in this example the predictor would certainly be the selection test score.

Although the coefficient of determination r^2 is relatively easy to interpret, it does not lend itself to statistical testing. The square root of the coefficient of determination is called the *coefficient of correlation r*. This sample statistic does make statistical testing possible because the correlation coefficient can be used to define a test statistic distributed as the t distribution when the population correlation ρ equals 0. The arithmetic sign for the coefficient of correlation is the same as the sign of b in the regression equation. A positive correlation coefficient indicates that the relationship is positive, or direct, and a negative correlation coefficient indicates the relationship is negative, or inverse. Thus the coefficient of correlation for sample data, with the sign of the value being the sign of b in the associated linear regression equation, is

$$r = \sqrt{r^2} \tag{14-24}$$

In summary, the sign of the correlation coefficient indicates the *nature* of the relationship between the independent and dependent variables, while the absolute value of the coefficient indicates the *extent* of the relationship. The squared value of the correlation coefficient is the coefficient of determination, which indicates the proportion of the variance in one variable that is statistically explained by knowledge of the other variable. For our example involving selection test score and performance rating, the coefficient of correlation, given that b in the associated regression equation is positive, is

$$r = \sqrt{r^2} = \sqrt{0.8669} = 0.93$$

Incidentally, this is an unusually high correlation value and is not typical of the correlations generally obtained in the prediction of job performance. Figure 14-5 illustrates the general forms of the scatter diagrams associated with several different correlation values.

Finally, Formula (14-25) has been derived as a computational formula to calculate the sample coefficient of correlation. Compared with Formula (14-23), the advantage of Formula (14-25) is that it does not require prior calculation of the values a and b in the linear regression equation, and the sign of the correlation coefficient is determined

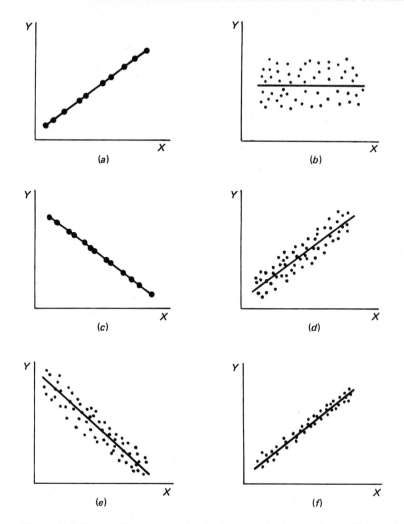

Figure 14-5 Scatter diagrams associated with several values of the coefficient of correlation. (*a*) $r = 1$; (*b*) $r = 0$; (*c*) $r = -1$; (*d*) $r = 0.50$; (*e*) $r = -0.50$; (*f*) $r = 0.90$.

by the formula, without having to observe the direction of slope in the scatter diagram. This formula is generally used when the purpose of analysis is to determine the extent and nature of the relationship between two variables but without an accompanying interest in estimating the values of the dependent variable; the formula is

$$r = \frac{n\Sigma XY - \Sigma X\Sigma Y}{\sqrt{n\Sigma X^2 - (\Sigma X)^2}\sqrt{n\Sigma Y^2 - (\Sigma Y)^2}} \qquad (14\text{-}25)$$

For the data involving selection test scores and performance ratings on the job the correlation coefficient as determined by Formula (14-25) is computed with the values obtained from Table 14-2 as follows:

$$r = \frac{n\Sigma XY - \Sigma X \Sigma Y}{\sqrt{n\Sigma X^2 - (\Sigma X)^2}\sqrt{n\Sigma Y^2 - (\Sigma Y)^2}} = \frac{20(24,492) - 1,619(298)}{\sqrt{20(132,117) - 1,619^2}\sqrt{20(4,590) - 298^2}}$$

$$= \frac{7,378}{\sqrt{21,179}\sqrt{2,996}} = \frac{7,378}{7,965.6941} = 0.93$$

This answer corresponds to the coefficient of correlation computed by Formulas (14-23) and (14-24) for these sample data.

14-9 SIGNIFICANCE OF THE CORRELATION COEFFICIENT

Typically, the null hypothesis of interest is that there is no relationship between the two variables, in other words, that $\rho = 0$. Rejection of this hypothesis results in acceptance of the alternative hypothesis, that there is a relationship between the two variables. The test can also be a one-tail test, according to the form of the null hypothesis. For instance, if the null hypothesis is $H_0 : \rho \leqslant 0$, rejection of this hypothesis means that the alternative hypothesis, that there is a positive relationship, is accepted. Given that the assumptions associated with correlation analysis, as identified in Section 14-7, are satisfied, the following test statistic is distributed as Student's t distribution with $df = n - 2$ when $\rho = 0$:

$$t = \frac{r}{s_r} \tag{14-26}$$

where
$$s_r = \sqrt{\frac{1 - r^2}{n - 2}} \tag{14-27}$$

For our sample problem using the 5 percent level of significance, we test the null hypothesis that $\rho = 0$, as follows:

Hypotheses:
$$H_0 : \rho = 0$$
$$H_1 : \rho \neq 0$$

Critical t (df $= 20 - 2 = 18$, $\alpha = 0.05$) $= \pm 2.101$

$$t = \frac{r}{s_r}$$

where $s_r = \sqrt{(1 - r^2)/(n - 2)} = \sqrt{[1 - (0.93)^2]/(20 - 2)} = \sqrt{0.0075} = 0.087$.

$$t = \frac{0.93}{0.087} = 10.69$$

The computed value of the t statistic exceeds the positive critical value of 2.101. Therefore the null hypothesis that there is no relationship between the selection test scores and the ratings of job performance is rejected, and the alternative hypothesis that there is a relationship is accepted. This conclusion is the same as the conclusion in Section 14-6, in which the equivalent null hypothesis $H_0: \beta = 0$ was tested at the 5 percent level of significance. The computed t statistic is somewhat different because of the rounding of values.

For convenience Table B-8 presents the values of the correlation coefficient required to conclude that the value is different from 0 using the 5 and 1 percent levels of significance. Referring to this table, we see that that required correlation value when df $= 18$ and $\alpha = 0.05$ is 0.4438, as an absolute value. Therefore the sample correlation of $r = 0.93$ is different from 0 at the 5 percent level of significance, which corresponds to the conclusion based on calculating the test statistic in the preceding example.

14-10 PITFALLS AND LIMITATIONS ASSOCIATED WITH REGRESSION AND CORRELATION ANALYSIS

1. If simple regression analysis is used, the assumptions for this technique should be satisfied. The assumptions required to develop the linear regression equation and to estimate the value of the dependent variable by point estimation are that

a. The relationship between the two variables is linear
b. The value of the independent variable is set at various values, while the dependent variable is a random variable
c. The conditional distributions of the dependent variable have equal variances (homoscedasticity)

For assumption b, however, it is usually acceptable if the independent variable is also a random variable. If any interval estimation or hypothesis testing is to be done, additional assumptions required are that

d. Successive observations of the random variable are uncorrelated
e. The conditional distributions of the dependent variable are all normal distributions.

2. The value of the dependent variable cannot be legitimately estimated if the value of the independent variable is outside the range of values in the sample data that served as the basis for determining the linear regression equation. There is no statistical basis to assume that the linear regression model applies outside of the range of the sample data.

3. If the estimate of the dependent variable in fact concerns *prediction*, the historical data used to determine the regression equation may not be appropriate to represent future relationships. Unfortunately, one can only sample past data, not future data.

4. The standard error of estimate is by itself not a complete basis for constructing prediction intervals, because the uncertainty concerning the accuracy of

the regression equation, and specifically of the conditional mean $\bar{Y}_X$, is not considered. The standard error of forecast is the complete measure of variability. However, when the sample is large (df $\geqslant$ 29), use of the standard error of estimate is generally considered acceptable.

5. If correlation analysis is used, all the assumptions for this technique should be satisfied. These assumptions are that

a. The relationship between the two variables is linear
b. Both variables are random variables
c. For each variable the conditional distributions have equal variances (homoscedasticity)
d. For each variable successive observations are uncorrelated
e. The distribution for the two variables jointly is a bivariate normal distribution.

6. A significant correlation does not necessarily indicate causation but rather may indicate a common linkage in a sequence of events. One type of significant-correlation situation is when both variables are influenced by a common cause and therefore are correlated with one another. For example individuals with a higher level of income have both a higher level of savings and a higher level of spending. We might therefore find that there is a positive relationship between level of savings and level of spending, but this does not mean that one of these variable "causes" the other. Another type of situation is one in which two related variables are separated by several steps in a cause–effect chain of events. An interesting example in the medical field is the following sequence of events: warm, humid air → breeding of mosquitoes → existence of mosquitoes in an area → transportation of malaria microorganisms by mosquitoes → incidence of malaria. The existence of warm, humid climatic conditions is not in itself the cause of malaria, but these conditions are several steps removed in the cause–effect sequence. For many years the climate conditions themselves were thought to be the cause, and so this disease was called malaria ("bad air").

7. A "significant" correlation is not necessarily an "important" correlation. There is much confusion regarding the meaning of "significant" in the popular press. It is almost always implied that a relationship that is significant is also thereby important. But from the statistical point of view, a significant correlation simply indicates that a true relationship exists and that the correlation coefficient for the population is different from 0. Significance is necessary to conclude that a relationship exists, but the coefficient of determination r^2 is more useful in judging the importance of the relationship. Given a very large sample, a correlation of, say, $r = 0.10$ can be significantly different from 0 at $\alpha = 0.05$. Yet the coefficient of determination of $r^2 = 0.01$ for this example indicated that only 1 percent of the variance of the dependent variable is statistically explained by knowledge of the independent variable.

8. In a comparison of simple linear regression analysis and correlation analysis, the principal difference in the assumptions is that in regression analysis there is one random variable, while in correlation analysis both variables have to be random. The

sampling design for a study therefore should consider the analysis to be performed. Regression analysis is used when the main objective is to estimate values of the dependent variable, whereas correlation analysis is used when the main objective is to measure and express the degree of relationship between the two variables. When both variables are random variables, either regression analysis or correlation analysis, or both, can usually be applied to the data.

14-11 SUMMARY

Regression analysis is concerned with developing the linear regression equation by which the value of a dependent variable Y can be estimated given a value of an independent variable X. The *principal assumptions* associated with linear regression analysis are

1. The relationship is linear.
2. The dependent variable is a random variable.
3. The assumption of homoscedasticity.

If any interval estimation or hypothesis testing is done, additional required assumptions are

4. Successive observations of the dependent variable are uncorrelated.
5. The conditional distributions of the dependent variable are normal distributions.

The *scatter diagram* is a graph that portrays the relationship between the two variables and can be used to observe whether there is general compliance with the assumptions underlying regression analysis. The mathematical criterion generally used to determine the linear regression equation is the *least-squares criterion* by which the sum of the squared deviations between the estimated and actual values of the dependent variable is minimized. The *standard error of estimate* $s_{Y.X}$ is the measure of variability, or scatter, with respect to the regression line. It is used to establish *prediction intervals* for the dependent variable.

Interval estimation of the conditional *mean* of the dependent variable is based on use of the *standard error of the conditional mean* $s_{\bar{Y}_X}$. The *standard error of forecast* $s_{Y(next)}$ is used to construct a complete prediction interval for an individual value of the dependent variable. By "complete" we mean that the uncertainty regarding the value of the conditional mean is considered in addition to the uncertainty represented by the scatter with respect to the regression line (i.e., by the standard error of estimate $s_{Y.X}$). When the sample is relatively large ($df \geq 29$), approximate prediction intervals based on use of only the standard error of estimate are considered to be acceptable. A final area of inference that we considered was interval estimation and hypothesis testing concerning the slope β of the linear regression model.

Correlation analysis is concerned with measuring and expressing the relationship between two variables. The principal assumptions associated with correlation analysis are

1. The relationship is linear.
2. Both variables are random variables.
3. Homoscedasticity exists for both variables.
4. Successive observations are uncorrelated for both variables.
5. The joint distribution is a bivariate normal distribution.

The most frequently used measure of relationship for sample data is the sample correlation coefficient r. The sign of the correlation coefficient indicates the *nature* (direct or inverse) of the relationship between the two variables, while the absolute value of the correlation coefficient indicates the *extent* of the relationship. The *coefficient of determination* r^2 indicates the proportion of variance in the dependent variable that is explained statistically by knowledge of the independent variable (and vice versa). The null hypothesis most frequently tested in correlation analysis is that the population correlation is zero, represented by $\rho = 0$. Rejection of this hypothesis leads to the conclusion that $\rho \neq 0$ and that the two variables are related.

FORMULAS

(14-1) $Y_i = \alpha + \beta X_i + e_i$
  Mathematical model underlying simple linear regression.

(14-2) $Y_c = a + bX$
  Linear regression equation, based on sample data.

(14-3) $b = \dfrac{\Sigma XY - n\bar{X}\bar{Y}}{\Sigma X^2 - n\bar{X}^2}$
  Value of b for the linear regression equation, based on the least-squares criterion.

(14-4) $a = \bar{Y} - b\bar{X}$
  Value of a for the linear regression equation, based on the least-squares criterion.

(14-5) $s_{Y.X} = \sqrt{\dfrac{\Sigma(Y - Y_c)^2}{n - 2}}$
  Deviations formula for the standard error of estimate, based on sample data.

(14-6) $s_{Y.X} = \sqrt{\dfrac{\Sigma Y^2 - a\Sigma Y - b\Sigma XY}{n - 2}}$
  Computational formula for the standard error of estimate, based on sample data.

(14-7)   Pred. int. $= Y_c \pm t_{df} s_{Y.X}$
  General formula for approximating a prediction interval for the value of a dependent variable.

(14-8) Pred. int. $= Y_c \pm z s_{Y.X}$

Formula to approximate a prediction interval when the sample is relatively large (df $\geqslant 29$).

(14-9) $\bar{Y}_c = Y_c$

Conditional mean of a dependent variable, given a value of the independent variable.

(14-10) $\bar{Y}_c = a + bX$

Conditional mean of a dependent variable, given a value of the independent variable.

(14-11)

$$s_{\bar{Y}.X} = s_{Y.X} \sqrt{\frac{1}{n} + \frac{(X - \bar{X})^2}{\Sigma X^2 - [(\Sigma X)^2/n]}}$$

Standard error of the conditional mean.

(14-12) Conf. int. $= \bar{Y}_c \pm t_{df} s_{\bar{Y}.X}$

Confidence interval for the conditional mean of a dependent variable.

(14-13) Conf. int. $= \bar{Y}_c \pm z \dfrac{s_{Y.X}}{\sqrt{n}}$

Confidence interval for the conditional mean generally considered to be acceptable when the sample is relatively large (df $\geqslant 29$).

(14-14) $s_{Y(\text{next})} = \sqrt{s_{Y.X}^2 + s_{\bar{Y}.X}^2}$

Basic formula for the standard error of forecast.

(14-15)

$$s_{Y(\text{next})} = s_{Y.X} \sqrt{1 + \frac{1}{n} + \frac{(X - \bar{X})^2}{\Sigma X^2 - [(\Sigma X)^2/n]}}$$

Computational formula for the standard error of forecast.

(14-16) Pred. int. $= Y_c \pm t_{df} s_{Y(\text{next})}$

Complete prediction interval for the individual value of a dependent variable, based on use of the standard error of forecast.

(14-17) $s_b = \dfrac{s_{Y.X}}{\sqrt{\Sigma X^2 - n\bar{X}^2}}$

Standard error of the sample statistic b in the linear regression equation.

(14-18) Conf. int. $= b + t_{df} s_b$

Confidence interval for estimating the value of β.

(14-19) $t = \dfrac{b - \beta_0}{s_b}$

The test statistic for testing a hypothesis concerning the value of β.

(14-20) Proportion unexplained variance

$$= \frac{\sigma_{Y.X}^2}{\sigma_Y^2}$$

Ratio representing the proportion of unexplained variance in the dependent variable that remains after consideration of the independent variable.

(14-21) $\rho^2 = 1 - \dfrac{\sigma_{Y.X}{}^2}{\sigma_Y{}^2}$

Coefficient of determination for a population, which indicates the proportion of variance in the dependent variable statistically explained by knowledge of the independent variable.

(14-22) $r^2 = 1 - \dfrac{s_{Y.X}{}^2}{s_Y{}^2}$

Coefficient of determination based on sample data.

(14-23) $r^2 = \dfrac{a\Sigma Y + b\Sigma XY - n\bar{Y}^2}{\Sigma Y^2 - n\bar{Y}^2}$

Computational formula for the coefficient of determination, based on sample data.

(14-24) $r = \sqrt{r^2}$

Sample coefficient of correlation, based on the coefficient of determination having already been calculated.

(14-25)

$r = \dfrac{n\Sigma XY - \Sigma X\Sigma Y}{\sqrt{n\Sigma X^2 - (\Sigma X)^2}\sqrt{n\Sigma Y^2 - (\Sigma Y)^2}}$

Computational formula for the sample coefficient of correlation.

(14-26) $t = \dfrac{r}{s_r}$

Test statistic for testing the null hypothesis $H_0: \rho = 0$.

(14-27) $s_r = \dfrac{1 - r^2}{n - 2}$

Standard error of the sample correlation coefficient when $\rho = 0$.

EXERCISES

14-1 Identify the assumptions underlying simple linear regression analysis.

14-2 Identify the assumptions underlying simple correlation analysis.

14-3 On what basis are the independent variable and the dependent variable differentiated in linear regression analysis?

14-4 On what basis are the independent variable and the dependent variable differentiated in correlation analysis?

14-5 What is the difference between a prediction interval and a confidence interval in regression analysis?

14-6 (a) Under what circumstances is it generally considered acceptable to construct an approximate prediction interval based on use of the standard error of estimate?

(b) Under what circumstances should the standard error of forecast be used?

(c) Differentiate the sources of variability that we measure by these two conditional standard deviation values.

14-7 In regression analysis hypothesis testing is most frequently directed toward the value of β in the linear regression model. Why?

  (a) What is the implication of rejecting the null hypothesis $H_0 : \beta = 0$?

  (b) What is the implication of rejecting the null hypothesis $H_0 : \beta \leqslant 0$?

14-8 The coefficient of correlation and the coefficient of determination are available as measures of association in correlation analysis. Describe the different uses of these two measures of association.

14-9 In correlation analysis, hypothesis testing is concerned with the value of the population coefficient of correlation ρ.

  (a) What is the implication of rejecting the null hypothesis $H_0 : \rho = 0$?

  (b) What is the implication of rejecting the null hypothesis $H_0 : \rho \leqslant 0$?

14-10 Suppose that the sample correlation coefficient for a sample of $n = 27$ is $r = 0.30$. At the 5 percent level of significance, the null hypothesis $H_0 : \rho = 0$ cannot be rejected. That is, Table B-8 indicates that the minimum value needed for significance ($\alpha = 0.05$, df $= 25$) is ± 0.3809.

  (a) How should the coefficient of determination be interpreted with respect to the sample data.

  (b) How should the coefficient of determination be interpreted with respect to the population from which the sample was obtained?

14-11 To investigate the relationship between the level of advertising in local newspapers and the level of sales, the marketing manager of a national firm in the consumer-products field applies different amounts of advertising in 10 randomly selected geographic areas. The following table indicates the level of advertising and the level of sales for the relevant time period in the 10 areas.

Area	Level of advertising, in $100s	Level of sales, in $1,000s
1	10.5	17.3
2	6.0	14.0
3	8.7	19.1
4	9.3	14.5
5	11.8	20.0
6	7.5	16.3
7	15.0	23.8
8	6.3	14.0
9	8.5	17.3
10	5.4	13.3

  (a) Construct a scatter diagram for these data.

  (b) Determine the least-squares regression equation for estimating the level of sales based on the level of advertising. Carry your calculations to one place beyond the decimal point.

  (c) Estimate the level of sales for an area in which $1,000 is spent on advertising, as a point estimate.

  (d) Construct the 95 percent approximate prediction interval for estimating the level of sales, given that $1,000 is spent on advertising, based on using the standard error of estimate.

14-12 For the data in Exercise 14-11

  (a) Construct the 95 percent confidence interval for estimating the mean level of sales, given that $1,000 is spent on advertising.

  (b) Construct the 95 percent complete prediction interval for estimating the level of sales given that $1,000 is spent on advertising, based on use of the standard error of forecast. Compare your answer with the solution to Exercise 14-11d.

(c) Test the hypothesis H_0: $\beta \leqslant 0$ on the basis of the sample data in Exercise 14-11, using the 5 percent level of significance, and interpret the result of your test.

14-13 Refer to the description of the data-collection procedure in Exercise 14-11. In what respect does this procedure not conform to the requirements associated with correlation analysis?

14-14 The table below presents data for a random sample of $n = 8$ students in regard to the hours of study outside of class during a three-week period and the grade earned on an examination at the end of this time period for a class in business statistics.

Sampled student	Hours of study	Examination grade
1	20	64
2	16	61
3	34	84
4	23	70
5	27	88
6	32	92
7	18	72
8	22	77

(a) Plot these data on a scatter diagram.

(b) Determine the regression equation for estimating the examination grade given the hours of study, and enter the regression line on your scatter diagram. Carry your calculations to one place beyond the decimal point.

(c) Use the regression equation to estimate the examination grade for a student who devotes 30 hours to study of the course materials.

(d) Construct the 90 percent approximate prediction interval for estimating the examination grade for a student who devotes 30 hours to study, based on using the standard error of estimate.

14-15 (a) For the data in Exercise 14-14 construct the 90 percent confidence interval for the mean examination grade of all students who devote 30 hours to study of the course materials.

(b) Construct the 90 percent complete prediction interval for estimating the examination grade for a student who devotes 30 hours to study, based on using the standard error of forecast; compare your answer to the solution to Exercise 14-15a, and describe the difference in the meaning of these two intervals; compare your answer with the solution to Exercise 14-14d. Carry your calculations to two places beyond the decimal point.

(c) Using the 1 percent level of significance, test the hypothesis H_0: $\beta \leqslant 0$ on the basis of the sample data in Exercise 14-14, and interpret the result of your test.

14-16 For the data in Exercise 14-14

(a) Compute the values of the coefficient of determination and the coefficient of correlation, taking advantage of the fact that the values of a and b for the regression equation were determined in Exercise 14-14b.

(b) Using the 1 percent level of significance, test the null hypothesis H_0: $\rho = 0$, and interpret the result of your test.

(c) Using the 1 percent level of significance, test the null hypothesis H_0: $\rho \leqslant 0$, and explain why Table B-8 cannot be used in this procedure; compare your answer with the solution to Exercise 14-15c.

14-17 The table below presents data relating the number of weeks of experience in a job involving the wiring of miniature electronic components and the number of components rejected during the past week for 12 randomly selected workers.

Sampled worker	Experience, weeks	No. of rejects
1	7	26
2	9	20
3	6	28
4	14	16
5	8	23
6	12	18
7	10	24
8	4	26
9	2	38
10	11	22
11	1	32
12	8	25

(a) Plot these sample data on a scatter diagram.

(b) Determine the linear regression equation for estimating the number of components rejected given the number of weeks of experience, and enter the regression line on the scatter diagram. Comment on the relationship between the two variables as indicated by the regression equation.

(c) Use the regression equation to estimate the number of components rejected for an employee with three weeks of experience in the job.

(d) Construct the 95 percent approximate prediction interval for estimating the number of components rejected for an employee with three weeks of experience in the job, based on using the standard error of estimate.

14-18 For the data in Exercise 14-17

(a) Construct the 95 percent confidence interval for estimating the mean number of components rejected for all employees with three weeks of work experience.

(b) Construct the 95 percent complete prediction interval for estimating the number of components rejected for an employee with three weeks of experience in the job, based on using the standard error of forecast.

(c) Compare the results in Exercise 14-18b and Exercise 14-17d, and interpret this difference.

14-19 For the data in Exercise 14-17

(a) Construct the 95 percent confidence interval for estimating the value of the population regression coefficient β, and interpret the meaning of this confidence interval.

(b) Using the 5 percent level of significance, test the null hypothesis $H_0: \beta \geqslant 0$, and interpret the result of your test. Why is this null hypothesis appropriate in this study?

14-20 For the sample data in Exercise 14-17

(a) Determine the value of the correlation coefficient by the computational formula that is not based on using the regression equation values of a and b.

(b) Using the 5 percent level of significance, test the null hypothesis $H_0: \rho \geqslant 0$.

    (1) Why cannot Table B-8 be used in this case?

    (2) Why is this an appropriate null hypothesis in this study?

    (3) Compare your solution with the solution to Exercise 14-19b.

(c) Determine the value of the coefficient of determination for the data in Exercise 14-17, and interpret the meaning of this value.

14-21 Suppose that a linear-regression equation has been established between hours of training and job productivity for a sample of employees who had between 10 and 20 hours of training. Explain why one cannot appropriately use this regression equation to estimate the productivity level for an employee with 40 hours of training.

14-22 (*a*) Explain why a "significant" correlation is not necessarily an "important" correlation.

(*b*) Why is it necessary to determine if a sample correlation coefficient is significant before we can consider whether it represents an important relationship between the two variables?

CHAPTER

FIFTEEN

MULTIPLE REGRESSION AND CORRELATION ANALYSIS

15-1 INTRODUCTION

Multiple regression analysis is an extension of simple regression analysis, as described in Chapter 14, to applications in which two or more independent variables serve as the basis for estimating the value of the dependent variable. As was true in our coverage of simple regression analysis in Chapter 14, the methods in this chapter are based on the assumption that the relationship between the independent variables and the dependent variable can be represented by a linear algebraic model.

289

The principal objective associated with multiple regression analysis is to estimate the value of the dependent variable and to determine the extent of statistical error associated with the estimate. To these ends the *multiple regression equation* is determined, based on the method of least squares, and the *standard error of estimate* associated with the use of this equation is calculated. Whereas the regression equation in simple regression analysis can be represented graphically as the best-fitting line in a scatter diagram, in multiple-regression analysis this general concept is extended to *n*-dimensional space. For two independent variables one can conceive of a three-dimensional scatter diagram, as portrayed in Figure 15-1. In Figure 15-1, X_1 and X_2 are the two independent variables, and Y is the dependent variable. The linear regression equation for two independent variables can be represented graphically as a plane in a three-dimensional scatter diagram such as that shown in Figure 15-1. It is the best-fitting plane in the sense that the sum of the squared differences between each value in the scatter diagram and the value on the regression plane is minimized. For cases involving more than two independent variables it is not possible to portray the *n*-dimensional relationships by scatter diagrams, but the same general concepts are applicable.

Multiple correlation analysis is the extension of simple-correlation analysis, as described in Chapter 14, to applications in which we wish to measure the relationship between two or more independent variables taken as a group and the dependent variable. Note that in both multiple regression analysis and multiple correlation analysis there is always only one dependent variable. The word "multiple" describes the number of independent variables. The *coefficient of multiple determination* indicates the proportion of variance in the dependent variable that is statistically accounted for, or explained, by the independent variables we included in the analysis. Whereas the arithmetic sign for a simple

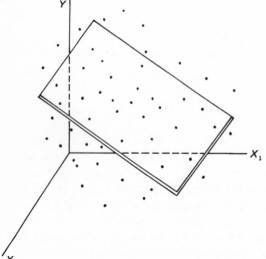

Figure 15-1 A three-dimensional scatter diagram for two independent variables, with the best-fitting plane.

correlation coefficient indicates the direction of the relationship between the two variables, the *coefficient of multiple correlation* is always reported as an absolute value, without an arithmetic sign. The reason the coefficient of multiple correlation never has an arithmetic sign is that for two independent variables, for example, it is possible that one of the variables has a positive relationship with the dependent variable, while the other variable has a negative relationship with the dependent variable. Because of these differences the overall relationship cannot be described as being simply positive or negative.

The techniques associated with multiple correlation analysis also make it possible to express the relationship between any one of the independent variables included in the analysis with the dependent variable, while the other independent variables included in the study are held constant statistically. This measure of relationship is called the *coefficient of partial correlation*, as described in Section 15-9. It differs from a simple correlation coefficient in that in simple-correlation analysis the other variables are ignored rather than being statistically controlled.

15-2 ASSUMPTIONS ASSOCIATED WITH MULTIPLE REGRESSION ANALYSIS

The principal assumptions in multiple regression analysis are similar to the assumptions in simple linear regression analysis, as explained in Section 14-2. These are specified below.

1. The independent variables and the dependent variable have a linear relationship. The linear equation that represents the multiple regression model is

$$Y_i = \alpha + \beta_1 X_{i,1} + \beta_2 X_{i,2} + \cdots + \beta_k X_{i,k} + e_i \tag{15-1}$$

where Y_i = value of the dependent variable in the ith trial, or observation

α = so-called constant in the regression equation, which indicates the value of Y when all $X_k = 0$

$\beta_1 \ldots \beta_k$ = regression coefficients associated with each of the X_k independent variables

$X_{i,j}$ = Value of the jth independent variable in the ith trial, where $j = 1, 2, \ldots, k$

e_i = the random error in the ith trial, or observation, associated with the process of sampling

2. The dependent variable is a continuous random variable, whereas the independent variables are set at various values and are not random. Thus the value e_i in the linear model is the sampling error for the dependent random variable. If it can be assumed that the value of e in the regression model is independent of the values of the independent variables X_k, which typically is so, multiple regression analysis can be used when the independent variables are also random variables.

3. The variances of the conditional distributions of the dependent variable given various combinations of values of the independent variables, are all equal. This is the assumption of homoscedasticity.

4. Successive observed values of the random variable are uncorrelated. Specifically, it is assumed that the amounts of random error e_i in the linear model are uncorrelated for successive observations of the random variable. The existence of such a relationship is called *autocorrelation;* autocorrelation is particularly likely with time-series data in which values of the dependent variable occur and are sampled in a series of time periods. The problem of autocorrelation is considered further in Section 15-10. Autocorrelation affects the accuracy of tests of hypotheses and interval estimates in multiple regression analysis, but it does not affect the accuracy of the point estimates.

5. The conditional distributions of the dependent variable, given various combinations of values of the independent variables, are all normal distributions. That is, the distribution of the sampling error e_i in the multiple linear regression model is normal. This assumption is required for tests of hypotheses and for interval estimates, but it is not required for point estimates based on the regression equation.

15-3 THE MULTIPLE REGRESSION EQUATION

For two independent variables denoted by X_1 and X_2 the multiple regression equation based on sample data is

$$Y_c = a + b_1 X_1 + b_2 X_2 \qquad (15\text{-}2)$$

As before, in Section 14-4, Y_c stands for the "computed," or estimated, value of the dependent variable. In some textbooks and in some computer programs the dependent variable is designated X_1, with the several independent variables then identified sequentially beginning with X_2. However, we continue to designate the dependent variable by Y, as in Chapter 14. Based on using the least-squares criterion, methods of calculus are used to determine the so-called normal equations, which must then be solved to determine the value of a and each of the values of b in the regression equation. For example, for two independent variables the three normal equations that must be solved to determine the values of a, b_1, and b_2 are

$$\Sigma Y = na + b_1 \Sigma X_1 + b_2 \Sigma X_2 \qquad (15\text{-}3a)$$

$$\Sigma X_1 Y = a\Sigma X_1 + b_1 \Sigma X_1^2 + b_2 \Sigma X_1 X_2 \qquad (15\text{-}3b)$$

$$\Sigma X_2 Y = a\Sigma X_2 + b_1 \Sigma X_1 X_2 + b_2 \Sigma X_2^2 \qquad (15\text{-}3c)$$

As the number of independent variables is increased, matrix algebra becomes more useful in representing the systems of equations. However, standard computer programs are widely available for multiple regression analysis. Because this textbook confines its scope to applied statistics, in this chapter we do not present the detailed mathematical calculations for determining normal equations and solving such simultaneous equations. Rather, having already emphasized the assumptions for multiple regression analysis, we will use a standard computer program to obtain the required parameter estimates. A complete example of multiple regression and multiple correlation analysis based on use of a computer program is included in Section 15-11.

The value of a, determined from sample data, is the unbiased estimator of α in the linear regression model in Formula (15-1). Similarly, for two independent variables the values b_1 and b_2 are estimators of β_1 and β_2, respectively, in the multiple regression model. These coefficients are called *partial regression coefficients*, or net regression coefficients, in the context of multiple regression analysis. Each coefficient is a "partial" coefficient in that it is the appropriate coefficient if the other independent variables and their coefficients are included in the regression model. That is, the value of the coefficient b_1, given two independent variables, is not the same as the value of b if the first independent variable were the only independent variable in the analysis. Similarly, if a third independent variable is added to the analysis, the value of b_1 then differs from the value of b_1 when only two independent variables are included in the analysis, even though b_1 is associated with the same variable before and after the addition of the third independent variable. We will have the opportunity to observe such changes in values of the coefficients in our comprehensive example in Section 15-11.

15-4 THE STANDARD ERROR OF ESTIMATE AND PREDICTION INTERVALS

The standard error of estimate in multiple regression analysis is similar in meaning to the standard error for simple regression analysis, as described in Section 14-5. In multiple regression analysis, however, this measure represents the extent of dispersion with respect to a plane (two independent variables) or a hyperplane (more than two independent variables) rather than the dispersion with respect to a line. When two independent variables are included in the analysis, the sample standard error of estimate is represented by the symbol $s_{Y.12}$. This symbol represents the conditional standard deviation of the dependent variable Y, given the values of the two independent variables, coded as subscripts 1 and 2. For two independent variables, this value is estimated on the basis of sample data by the deviations formula

$$s_{Y.12} = \sqrt{\frac{\Sigma(Y - Y_c)^2}{n - 3}} \tag{15-4}$$

The computational formula, which does not require the determination of the deviation of each observed value of Y from the regression-plane value Y_c, is

$$s_{Y.12} = \sqrt{\frac{\Sigma Y^2 - b_1 \Sigma X_1 Y - b_2 \Sigma X_2 Y}{n - 3}} \tag{15-5}$$

Again, we do not present any computational examples at this point, because we will utilize the computer program in Section 15-11 to determine the standard error of estimate for our sample problem.

The prediction interval for estimating the individual value of the dependent variable, given the values of the several independent variables, is defined in the same way as the prediction interval for simple regression analysis was defined in Section 14-5. However, in multiple regression analysis the standard error of estimate is concerned with the several independent variables. For two independent variables the approximate prediction interval is

$$\text{Pred. int.} = Y_c \pm t_{df} s_{Y.12} \qquad (15\text{-}6)$$

Use of the t distribution is appropriate, because the population standard error of estimate is unknown, and the random variable is assumed to be normally distributed. The degrees of freedom used in conjunction with constructing a prediction interval with two independent variables is $df = n - 3$, because the three parameters α, β_1, and β_2 are estimated by the sample statistics a, b_1, and b_2, and thus three degrees of freedom are lost.

As indicated in Section 7-5, the normal probability distribution can be used as an approximation of the t distribution when $df \geqslant 29$. Thus the formula to construct an approximate prediction interval based on two independent variables when the sample size is relatively large is

$$\text{Pred. int.} = Y_c \pm z s_{Y.12} \qquad (15\text{-}7)$$

In Section 14-6 on simple-regression analysis we considered complete prediction intervals that take into consideration the uncertainty associated with using a regression equation based on sample data. Extension of such analyses to multiple regression analysis is quite complex and beyond the scope of this book. However, such adjustments generally are not considered necessary when the sample is relatively large.

15-5 INFERENCES CONCERNING THE PARAMETERS IN MULTIPLE REGRESSION ANALYSIS

To construct a confidence interval for the conditional mean of the dependent variable Y in multiple regression analysis, we must first determine the standard error of the conditional mean. For two independent variables the estimate of the standard error of the conditional mean based on sample data is

$$s_{\bar{Y}.12} = \frac{s_{Y.12}}{\sqrt{n}} \qquad (15\text{-}8)$$

As is true for the approximate prediction intervals in multiple regression analysis, the uncertainty associated with using the values of a and the b coefficients as estimators of α and the β coefficients is not generally included in the analysis. Thus the standard error of the conditional mean is based only on the value of the standard error of estimate. With the z distribution being used in place of the t distribution when $df \geqslant 29$, the approximate confidence interval for the conditional mean of the dependent variable for two independent variables is

$$\text{Conf. int.} = \bar{Y}_c \pm t_{df} s_{\bar{Y}.12} \qquad (15\text{-}9)$$

or

$$\text{Conf. int.} = \bar{Y}_c \pm zs_{\bar{Y}.12} \tag{15-10}$$

As in Section 14-6, $\bar{Y}_c$ always equals Y_c based on the linear regression equation. The degrees of freedom for this confidence interval based on two independent variables is $n - 3$, as it was for the prediction interval for the individual value of Y.

Finally, the determination of the standard error associated with the partial regression coefficients permits us to construct confidence intervals for these coefficients or to test hypotheses concerning the value of such coefficients. These procedures are analogous to the procedures for the simple regression coefficient that were presented in Section 14-6. For two regression coefficients, the estimated standard-error values for the two partial regression coefficients are, respectively,

$$s_{b_1} = \frac{s_{Y.12}}{\sqrt{\Sigma X_1^2 (1 - r_{12}^2)}} \tag{15-11}$$

and

$$s_{b_2} = \frac{s_{Y.12}}{\sqrt{\Sigma X_2^2 (1 - r_{12}^2)}} \tag{15-12}$$

In Formulas (15-11) and (15-12) note that the correlation value r_{12} is the simple correlation coefficient between the two independent variables. If more than two independent variables are included in the analysis, the formulas for the standard error of the partial regression coefficients are considerably more complicated, but these computational procedures have been incorporated in standard computer programs.

As in Section 14-6 for the simple regression coefficient, the confidence interval for estimating the value of the partial regression coefficient for the population is defined by using Student's t distribution, with the degrees of freedom based on the number of parameters we estimated. Again, for two independent variables df $= n - 3$. The general formula for constructing the approximate confidence interval for a partial regression coefficient is

$$\text{Conf. int.} = b_k \pm t_{df} s_{b_k} \tag{15-13}$$

Similarly, a null hypothesis concerning the value of β_k is tested by computing the test statistic t by

$$t = \frac{b_k - \beta_k}{s_{b_k}} \tag{15-14}$$

As with the simple regression coefficient in Section 14-6, the usual null hypothesis tested is that $\beta_k = 0$ because this hypothesis would indicate that when it is used in conjunction with the other independent variables, the independent variable of interest contributes nothing to the estimation of the dependent variable. An alternative procedure to test the significance of the regression effect is based on using the analysis of variance. This approach is described in Section 15-6 and is illustrated in the comprehensive example in Section 15-11.

15-6 ANALYSIS OF VARIANCE IN LINEAR REGRESSION ANALYSIS

Both the analysis of variance and linear regression analysis are based on the use of linear algebraic models. Consider, for example, the similarity between the equations representing the models for one-way and two-way analysis of variance given in Formulas (11-7) and (11-8) and the linear models for simple regression analysis and multiple regression analysis given in Formulas (14-1) and (15-1). In both models a term in the linear equation represents the influence of each independent variable on the value of the dependent variable. Essentially, simple linear regression analysis is the equivalent of the one-factor fixed-effects model of the analysis of variance when the independent variable can be measured along a continuous scale, as described in Section 11-3, while multiple linear regression analysis with two independent variables is equivalent to the two-factor fixed-effects model of the analysis of variance as described in Section 11-4. Higher order models are similarly related. Compared with the analysis of variance, a particular advantage of regression analysis is that it can be used to estimate the value of the dependent variable as well as to test the significance of the effect of each independent variable. On the other hand, the analysis of variance can be used when an independent variable is not quantitative but rather represents qualitative categories (such as instructional method used in relation to the dependent variable of learning effectiveness).

To understand how the analysis of variance is used to test for the significance of the effect of the independent variables in regression analysis, it is useful to return to the simple regression model. All the following observations apply to multiple regression as well, except that the estimated value Y_c would be based on a regression equation for a plane or for a hyperplane rather than for a straight line.

Consider the scatter diagram for simple regression analysis in Figure 15-2. The best-fitting regression line and the line representing the mean value of the dependent variable $\bar{Y}$ are included in this figure. Now, in the absence of regression analysis the best (least-squares) estimate of a randomly selected value of the dependent variable Y is $\bar{Y}$, while in the context of regression analysis the best estimate is Y_c. In general the deviation between Y and Y_c, which we now call the *error deviation,* is less than the deviation between Y and $\bar{Y}$, which we now call the *total deviation.* We can conceive of the total deviation as made up of two parts: the deviation of Y_c from $\bar{Y}$ and the deviation of the sampled value of Y from Y_c. Thus for sample data the total deviation can be partitioned as follows:

$$Y - \bar{Y} = (Y_c - \bar{Y}) + (Y - Y_c) \qquad (15\text{-}15)$$

where $Y - \bar{Y}$ = total deviation
$\quad Y_c - \bar{Y}$ = deviation of estimated value from the mean
$\quad Y - Y_c$ = error deviation (sampling variability)
Although it is not immediately obvious, it can be shown that the sums of the

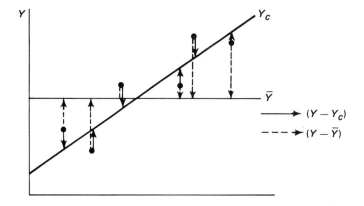

Figure 15-2 A scatter diagram illustrating the error deviations with respect to the regression line and the total deviations with respect to $\bar{Y}$.

squared deviations also have the same kind of arithmetic relationship as the partitioned values in Formula (15-15):

$$\Sigma(Y - \bar{Y})^2 = \Sigma(Y_c - \bar{Y})^2 + \Sigma(Y - Y_c)^2 \qquad (15\text{-}16)$$
$$\text{SST} \quad = \quad \text{SSR} \quad + \quad \text{SSE}$$

where SST = total sum of squared deviations

SSR = sum of squares resulting from the regression

SSE = sum of squares resulting from sampling error

If there is no regression effect, the variance estimate based on SSR will differ only by chance from the variance estimate based on SSE. These respective estimates are the mean square resulting from the regression (MSR) and the mean square resulting from sampling error (MSE). If there is a regression effect, MSR will have an expected value larger than the expected value of MSE. Therefore Table 15-1 presents the standard format of the analysis-of-variance table used to test for the significance of a

Table 15-1 Analysis-of-variance table for testing the significance of the regression effect

Source of variation	Sum of squares SS	Degrees of freedom df	Mean square MS	F ratio
Regression R	SSR	k	$\text{MSR} = \dfrac{\text{SSR}}{k}$	$F = \dfrac{\text{MSR}}{\text{MSE}}$
Sampling error E	SSE	$n - k - 1$	$\text{MSE} = \dfrac{\text{SSE}}{n-k-1}$	
Total T	SST	$n - 1$		

regression effect. In this table k stands for the number of independent variables included in the regression equation, and thus this table is applicable for either simple or multiple regression analysis. For simple regression analysis this test is the equivalent to testing the null hypothesis that $\beta = 0$ by use of Student's t distribution. As indicated in the last column of this table, the significance of the regression effect is tested by computing the sample statistic

$$F = \frac{MSR}{MSE} \tag{15-17}$$

For our coverage we are not concerned with presenting computational formulas for determining SSR and SSE, because these values will be obtained as computer output in the example in Section 15-11.

Many computer programs also provide F tests for each of the partial regression coefficients included in a multiple regression equation. Conceptually, the standard analysis of variance table given in Table 15-1 is expanded so that the SSR is partitioned with respect to each independent variable. Each such test is the equivalent of testing the null hypothesis that $\beta_k = 0$ by use of Student's t distribution, as presented in Section 15-5. Whereas the degrees of freedom associated with the numerator and denominator of Formula (15-17) are k and $n - k - 1$, respectively, as indicated in Table 15-1, the degrees of freedom associated with the test of the null hypothesis that $\beta_k = 0$ are 1 and $n - k - 1$. When the degrees of freedom associated with the numerator of the F ratio is 1, it can be shown that $F = t^2$. This relationship is illustrated in our example in Section 15-11.

15-7 ASSUMPTIONS ASSOCIATED WITH MULTIPLE CORRELATION ANALYSIS

The principal assumptions of multiple correlation analysis are an extension of the assumptions associated with simple correlation analysis, as presented in Section 14-7, and are similar to the assumptions associated with multiple regression analysis, as presented in Section 15-2. These assumptions are outlined below.

1. The independent variables and the dependent variable have a linear relationship.
2. All variables are continuous random variables.
3. For each variable the variances of the conditional distributions of the variable, given various combinations of values for the other variables, are equal. That is, the assumption of homoscedasticity is required with respect to all variables.
4. Successive observed values for each variable are uncorrelated.
5. For each variable the distributions of the conditional values, given various combinations of values for the other variables, are all normal distributions; that is, the distribution of the several variables jointly is a *multivariate normal distribution*.

15-8 THE COEFFICIENTS OF MULTIPLE DETERMINATION AND MULTIPLE CORRELATION

The *coefficient of multiple determination* is designated by $R^2_{Y.12}$ for two independent variables, in which the subscript $Y.12$ indicates that the dependent variable is Y and the independent variables are coded 1 and 2. Similar to the simple coefficient of determination described in Section 14-8, the coefficient of multiple determination indicates the proportion of variance in the dependent variable accounted for statistically by knowledge of the several independent variables. For two independent variables the estimated value of the coefficient of multiple determination based on sample data can be defined by

$$R^2_{Y.12} = 1 - \frac{s^2_{Y.12}}{s_{Y^2}}$$
(15-18)

If the analysis of variance is used with the regression analysis described in Section 15-6, the coefficient of multiple determination for any number of independent variables is defined by

$$R^2 = \frac{\text{SSR}}{\text{SST}}$$
(15-19)

As is true for Formula (15-18), Formula (15-19) also measures the proportion of variance in the dependent variable accounted for statistically by the several independent variables.

The *coefficient of multiple correlation* is designated by $R_{Y.12}$ for two independent variables. Similar to the simple correlation coefficient described in Section 14-8, the coefficient of multiple correlation indicates the extent of the relationship of the several independent variables taken as a group with the dependent variable. As indicated by the general symbol R, the coefficient of multiple correlation is the square root of the coefficient of multiple determination:

$$R = \sqrt{R^2}$$
(15-20)

The multiple coefficient R is always reported as an absolute value without an arithmetic sign. R never has a sign because it is possible for one or more of the independent variables to have a positive relationship with the dependent variable while one or more other independent variables have a negative relationship with the dependent variable. Therefore the multiple correlation cannot necessarily be described as representing simply a "positive" or a "negative" relationship because both types of relationships may be involved.

15-9 PARTIAL CORRELATION ANALYSIS

The *coefficient of partial determination* indicates the proportion of variance in the dependent variable accounted for statistically by *one* designated independent variable of the several independent variables included in the analysis. The coefficient of partial determination differs from the simple coefficient of determination described in Section 14-8 in that for the partial coefficient *the other independent variables are held constant statistically* rather than ignored in the analysis. If two independent variables are included in the analysis, the partial coefficient of determination of the dependent variable with the first independent variable based on sample data is $r_{Y1.2}^2$, while the partial coefficient of determination with the second independent variable is $r_{Y2.1}^2$. Both coefficients indicate the proportion of explained variance in the dependent variable associated with that independent variable, given that the other independent variable is also included in the analysis. Put another way, the coefficient of partial determination measures the marginal contribution of one independent variable when the other independent variables are already included in the regression equation.

The *coefficient of partial correlation* is the square root of the coefficient of partial determination. This coefficient indicates the correlation between one of the independent variables in the multiple correlation analysis and the dependent variable, *with the other independent variables held constant statistically*. The partial correlation with the first of two independent variables, based on sample data, is designated by $r_{Y1.2}$, while the partial correlation with the second of two independent variables is designated by $r_{Y2.1}$. As with simple correlation values, the arithmetic sign associated with a partial correlation coefficient indicates the direction of the relationship. This sign will always be the same as the sign of the associated partial regression coefficient in the multiple regression equation for the same data. The interpretation of the coefficients of partial determination and partial correlation is considered further in the comprehensive example in Section 15-11.

15-10 PITFALLS AND LIMITATIONS ASSOCIATED WITH MULTIPLE REGRESSION AND MULTIPLE CORRELATION ANALYSIS

The general pitfalls for regression and correlation analysis, as described in Section 14-10 on simple regression and correlation analysis, apply to multiple analysis as well. In regard to these pitfalls several areas of concern are particularly important in multiple regression and multiple correlation analysis.

On the general level the assumptions associated with multiple regression and multiple correlation analysis have to be satisfied if the results are to be meaningful. These are described in Section 15-2 and 15-7 and are similar to the assumptions in simple regression and simple correlation analysis. However, in simple analysis involving one variable, several of the assumptions can be roughly checked by constructing the scatter diagram and observing the diagram for such factors as linearity of relationship, homoscedasticity, and approximate normality of scatter with respect to the regression line. Such graphic checks are not possible in the analysis that includes several independent variables, and therefore the risk is greater that a principal assumption is not even approximately satisfied.

A specific area of concern when there are several independent variables is the possible existence of *multicollinearity*. This term describes the situation in which two or more independent variables are highly correlated with one another. Under such conditions, meaning of the partial (or net) regression coefficients in the multiple regression equation are unclear. Similarly, the meaning of the coefficients of partial correlation is questionable. It is possible, for example, that the partial correlation with a given independent variable is highly negative even though the simple correlation is highly positive. The statistical procedures that represent attempts to handle the problem of multicollinearity are described in specialized textbooks in regression and correlation analysis and are beyond the scope of this book. As a practical matter it is sometimes useful simply to eliminate one of two highly correlated independent variables from the analysis, recognizing that the two variables essentially are measuring the same factor. When correlated variables must be included in the analysis, care must be taken in ascribing practical meaning to the partial regression coefficients and to the coefficients of partial correlation.

Another area of specific concern in multiple regression and multiple correlation analysis is the possibility that successive observed values of the dependent variables are correlated rather than uncorrelated. The existence of such a correlation is called *autocorrelation*. The assumption that the successive values of the dependent variable are uncorrelated has already been identified as a principal assumption in simple regression and simple correlation analysis as well as in multiple regression and multiple correlation analysis. However, in simple analysis the existence of such a correlation is easier to observe than in multiple analysis. Typically, autocorrelation occurs when values of the dependent variable are collected as time-series values, that is, when they are collected in a series of time periods. When values of the dependent variable are collected as time-series values, the point estimate of the dependent variable based on the multiple regression equation is not affected. However, the standard error associated with each partial regression coefficient b_k is understated, and the value of the standard error of estimate is understated. The result is that the prediction and confidence intervals are narrower (more precise) than they should be, and null hypotheses concerning the absence of relationship are rejected too frequently. In terms of correlation analysis the coefficients of multiple determination and multiple correlation are both overstated in value.

15-11 A COMPREHENSIVE EXAMPLE

As we indicated at several points in this chapter, generally a standard computer program is used in multiple regression and multiple correlation analysis. In this section we refer to the output of two programs taken from the Statistical Package for the Social Sciences (SPSS),[1] named REGRESSION and PARTIAL CORR.

---

[1] Norman H. Nie, et al., *Statistical Package for the Social Sciences,* 2d ed., McGraw-Hill Book Company, New York, 1975.

Table 15-2 presents the sample data for our analysis. The weekly household income, weekly expenditures for housing, food, and entertainment, and weekly savings are presented for a random sample of 15 hypothetical households. The purpose of this analysis is to estimate weekly savings on the basis of the other variables and to measure the relationship between those variables, individually and as a group, with weekly savings. Incidentally, the sum of the expenditures and savings for each household does not equal the income figure because not all expenditures are included in this analysis. Also we assume, perhaps optimistically, that the weekly savings figure cannot be negative.

Most computer programs for multiple regression and multiple correlation analysis proceed with a solution by adding independent variables in the analysis in a stepwise manner rather than presenting only the final regression equation and associated values. The SPSS program REGRESSION adds a new independent variable at each step in the analysis according to which of the remaining variables will lead to the greatest reduction in the standard error of estimate. In the remainder of this section we discuss the meaning of selected portions of the output from this program and from the program PARTIAL CORR. The portions of the output omitted in our exhibits are not germane to our interests in this chapter.

Exhibit 15-1 includes the relevant portions of the output for our hypothetical sample data from the SPSS program named REGRESSION. The first portion of the output which is presented is a table of simple correlation values. Of course the correlation of any variable with itself is always a perfect correlation, and therefore

Table 15-2 Weekly savings per household as related to weekly income and to several categories of weekly expenditures for a sample of 15 households

Sampled household	Household income X_1, $	Expenditure, $			Weekly savings Y, $
		Housing X_2	Food X_3	Entertainment X_4	
1	250	85	95	25	20
2	190	75	90	10	0
3	420	140	120	40	50
4	340	120	130	0	40
5	280	110	100	30	15
6	310	80	125	25	25
7	520	150	140	55	80
8	440	175	155	45	0
9	360	90	85	20	95
10	385	105	135	35	30
11	205	80	105	0	5
12	265	65	95	15	15
13	195	50	80	10	20
14	250	90	100	25	0
15	480	140	160	45	45

the values along the diagonal of this matrix are all equal to 1.00. We are particularly interested in the correlation of each of the independent variables with the dependent variable. Referring to either the last row or last column of the correlation matrix, we see that X_1 has the highest correlation with the dependent variable. The value $r_{Y1} = 0.61450$ is higher than the correlation of any other independent variable with the dependent variable Y. Therefore it is logical that X_1 should be taken as the independent variable in the first step in developing the multiple regression equation. Before we proceed to this step, note that all of the values in the correlation matrix are positive. This indicates that the several types of expenditures are positively related to income level and to one another and also that the level of expenditure of each type is positively related to level of savings. Of course this does not mean that higher spending leads to higher savings. Rather, a higher income makes it possible to have both a higher level of spending and a higher level of saving.

The next portion of the output indicates the first independent variable entered in the analysis, and as expected on the basis of the simple-correlation values, the variable is X_1. The "multiple R" of 0.61450 is in fact a simple correlation coefficient, because there is only one variable in the analysis. The analysis of variance indicates that the value of the test statistic for the regression effect is

$$F = \frac{\text{MSR}}{\text{MSE}} = \frac{4321.11824}{547.86270} = 7.88723$$

The critical value of F at $\alpha = 0.05$, for $df_1 = 1$ and $df_2 = 13$, is 4.67, by reference to Table B-7, where the subscripts 1 and 2 indicate, respectively, the df for the numerator and denominator values in the table. Therefore the relationship between X_1 (income) and Y (savings) is significant at the 5 percent level of significance. The "Adjusted R square" row in the printout of Exhibit 15-1 includes a correction to the "R square" value so that it is an unbiased parameter estimate. This correction is beyond the scope of this book and is of minor consequence when the sample is relatively large.

The next portion of output for step 1 gives the estimated values of the parameters for the regression equation:

$$Y_c = a + b_1 X_1$$
$$= -24.93032 + 0.16645 X_1$$

The standard error associated with use of this regression equation is $s_{\bar{Y}.1} = 23.40647$. Thus, if the weekly household income is $X_1 = \$300$, we would estimate the amount of savings with a 95 percent approximate prediction interval as

$$\text{Pred. int.} = Y_c \pm t_{df} s_{Y.1}$$

where $Y_c = -24.93032 + 0.16645(300) = 25.00468$
$\quad t_{df} = t_{13} = 2.160$
$\quad s_{Y.1} = 23.40647$

Exhibit 15-1 Selected output of the SPSS program REGRESSION for the data in Table 15-2.

PAGE 3

INCOME AND EXPENDITURE DATA

CORRELATION COEFFICIENTS

A VALUE OF 99.00000 IS PRINTED
IF A COEFFICIENT CANNOT BE COMPUTED.

	X1	X2	X3	X4	Y
X1	1.00000	.86189	.81747	.81658	.61450
X2	.86189	1.00000	.82796	.73542	.27863
X3	.81747	.82796	1.00000	.63664	.14639
X4	.81658	.73542	.63664	1.00000	.33470
Y	.61450	.27863	.14639	.33470	1.00000

PAGE 4

VARIABLE LIST 1
REGRESSION LIST 1

INCOME AND EXPENDITURE DATA

DEPENDENT VARIABLE.. Y

VARIABLE(S) ENTERED ON STEP NUMBER 1.. X1

MULTIPLE R   .61450
R SQUARE   .37761
ADJUSTED R SQUARE   .32973
STANDARD ERROR   23.40647

ANALYSIS OF VARIANCE	DF	SUM OF SQUARES	MEAN SQUARE	F
REGRESSION	1.	4321.11824	4321.11824	7.88723
RESIDUAL	13.	7122.21510	547.86270	

-------- VARIABLES IN THE EQUATION --------

VARIABLE	B	BETA	STD ERROR B	F
X1	.16645	.61450	.05927	7.887
(CONSTANT)	-24.93032			

-------- VARIABLES NOT IN THE EQUATION --------

VARIABLE	BETA IN	PARTIAL	TOLERANCE	F
X2	-.97609	-.62741	.25715	7.700
X3	-1.07294	-.78333	.33175	19.056
X4	-.50145	-.36690	.33320	1.867

VARIABLE(S) ENTERED ON STEP NUMBER 2.. X3

MULTIPLE R   .87150
R SQUARE   .75951
ADJUSTED R SQUARE   .71943
STANDARD ERROR   15.14368

ANALYSIS OF VARIANCE	DF	SUM OF SQUARES	MEAN SQUARE	F
REGRESSION	2.	8691.35996	4345.67998	18.94937
RESIDUAL	12.	2751.97337	229.33111	

-------- VARIABLES IN THE EQUATION --------

VARIABLE	B	BETA	STD ERROR B	F
X1	.40404	1.49159	.06658	36.829
X3	-1.20362	-1.07294	.27572	19.056
(CONSTANT)	35.23142			

-------- VARIABLES NOT IN THE EQUATION --------

VARIABLE	BETA IN	PARTIAL	TOLERANCE	F
X2	-.56144	-.52621	.21125	4.212
X4	-.60613	-.71038	.33032	11.206

INCOME AND EXPENDITURE DATA

DEPENDENT VARIABLE.. Y

VARIABLE(S) ENTERED ON STEP NUMBER 3.. X4

		ANALYSIS OF VARIANCE	DF	SUM OF SQUARES	MEAN SQUARE	F
MULTIPLE R	.93855	REGRESSION	3.	10080.12774	3360.04258	27.11291
R SQUARE	.88087	RESIDUAL	11.	1363.20559	123.92778	
ADJUSTED R SQUARE	.84838					
STANDARD ERROR	11.13229					

-------- VARIABLES IN THE EQUATION -------- ------ VARIABLES NOT IN THE EQUATION ------

VARIABLE	B	BETA	STD ERROR B	F		VARIABLE	BETA IN	PARTIAL	TOLERANCE	F
X1	.55060	2.03268	.06567	70.304		X2	-.44975	-.59089	.20563	5.364
X3	-1.26692	-1.12937	.20356	38.734						
X4	-1.04184	-.60613	.31122	11.206						
(CONSTANT)	21.08153									

* *

VARIABLE(S) ENTERED ON STEP NUMBER 4.. X2

		ANALYSIS OF VARIANCE	DF	SUM OF SQUARES	MEAN SQUARE	F
MULTIPLE R	.96045	REGRESSION	4.	10556.08602	2639.02151	29.74392
R SQUARE	.92247	RESIDUAL	10.	887.24731	88.72473	
ADJUSTED R SQUARE	.89145					
STANDARD ERROR	9.41938					

-------- VARIABLES IN THE EQUATION -------- ------ VARIABLES NOT IN THE EQUATION ------

VARIABLE	B	BETA	STD ERROR B	F		VARIABLE	BETA IN	PARTIAL	TOLERANCE	F
X1	.60437	2.23117	.06022	100.730						
X3	-1.07313	-.95662	.19149	31.406						
X4	-.94097	-.54745	.26691	12.428						
X2	-.36659	-.44975	.15528	5.364						
(CONSTANT)	16.84519									

MAXIMUM STEP REACHED

INCOME AND EXPENDITURE DATA

DEPENDENT VARIABLE.. Y

SUMMARY TABLE

VARIABLE	MULTIPLE R	R SQUARE	RSQ CHANGE	SIMPLE R	B	BETA
X1	.61450	.37761	.37761	.61450	.60437	2.23117
X3	.87150	.75951	.38190	.14639	-1.07313	-.95662
X4	.93855	.88087	.12136	.13370	-.94097	-.54745
X2	.96045	.92247	.04159	.27863	-.36659	-.44975
(CONSTANT)					16.84519	

305

$$\text{Pred. int.} = 25.00468 \pm 2.160(23.40647)$$

$$= 25.00468 \pm 50.557975$$

$$= -\$25.55 \text{ to } \$75.56$$

The prediction interval is so wide it is of little value as an estimation interval, reflecting the effect of the relatively large value of the standard error of estimate. Suppose that we wish to estimate the *mean* savings amounts for a sample of $n = 35$ families, all of whom have a weekly household income of $X_1 = \$300$. The 95 percent approximate confidence interval is

$$\text{Conf. int.} = \bar{Y}_c \pm z s_{\bar{Y}.1}$$

where $\bar{Y}_c = Y_c = 25.00468$
$\quad z = 1.96$
$\quad s_{Y.1} = 23.40647$
$\quad n = 35$
$\quad s_{\bar{Y}.1} = s_{Y.1}/\sqrt{n} = 23,40647/\sqrt{35}$

$$\text{Conf. int.} = 25.00468 \pm 1.96\,\frac{23.40647}{\sqrt{35}}$$

$$= 25.00468 \pm 1.96(3.95642)$$

$$= 25.00468 \pm 7.75458$$

$$= \$17.25 \text{ to } \$32.76$$

As a confidence interval this 95 percent interval is also very wide and lacks precision, once again reflecting the effect of the large standard error of estimate.

The "BETA" in step 1 of the output is not a population regression coefficient, as one might assume. Rather, it is the value of the regression coefficient b_1 when both variables X_1 and Y are transformed to the standard normal variable z. In step 1, in which there is only one independent variable, it is no coincidence that the value of the standardized "BETA" value equals the simple correlation coefficient between X_1 and Y of 0.61450. When there are only two variables, the slope of the regression of the two standardized variables is always equal to the simple correlation coefficient. In fact, it was on the basis of such a regression line that the correlation coefficient was developed. Originally the correlation coefficient was called the "regression coefficient" and thus was designated by the symbol r.

In Section 14-6 we used the t distribution to test the null hypothesis that $\beta = 0$ for the simple regression coefficient. In Exhibit 15-1, however, the hypothesis that each of the regression coefficients is zero is tested by the analysis of variance and use of the F distribution; that is, it is a test of the net regression effect associated with the independent variable being considered. In step 1, of course, only one independent variable is included in the analysis, and therefore the regression coefficient is a simple regression coefficient. As explained in Section 15-6, the degrees of freedom associated with the numerator and denominator of the F ratio for a test of the net regression effect are 1 and $n - k - 1$, respectively. As also covered in Section 15-6, when df $= 1$ for the numerator of an F ratio, $F = t^2$. For example, for step 1 we can test the hypothesis that $\beta = 0$ by computing the t statistic and then square this value and compare it with the F statistic reported on the line of output that gives the value of b and the standard error of b:

$$t = \frac{b - \beta_0}{s_b} = \frac{0.16645 - 0}{0.05927} = 2.8083347$$

$$t^2 = (2.8083347)^2 = 7.887$$

Thus the value of the t statistic corresponds to the value of the F test statistic reported in step 1 for the test of the null hypothesis that $\beta = 0$. For significance at $\alpha = 0.05$ the required value of t for df $= 15 - 2 = 13$ is ± 2.160, as indicated in Table B-5. For significance at $\alpha = 0.05$ the required value of F for $df_1 = 1$ and $df_2 = 13$ is 4.67, as indicated in Table B-7. Thus the critical values of the two test statistics are also consistent with the fact that $t^2 = F$ when $df_1 = 1$. That is, $(2.160)^2 = 4.67$. Similar correspondence can be demonstrated in the remaining steps of the computer output for this program, in which cases the tests are concerned with partial, or net, regression coefficients.

The right portion of the output for step 1 identifies the variables not yet included in the analysis. For our purposes we need consider only the "partial" values, which are partial correlation coefficients of each variable with the dependent variable Y, *given that X_1 is included in the analysis and is therefore held constant statistically*. The highest partial correlation without regard to sign is the partial correlation $r_{Y3.1} = -0.78333$, and therefore adding variable X_3 to the analysis in the next step will lead to the greatest reduction in the standard error of estimate and the greatest increase in the coefficient of multiple correlation. This is in fact the independent variable added to the analysis in step 2.

The "tolerance" reported for each of the variables not yet included in the analysis is not part of the output of most computer programs in multiple regression analysis. In general a tolerance value near 0 indicates severe multicollinearity problems; a value near 1.0 indicates little multicollinearity, because the value indicates the part of the proportion of explained variance that is unique to this variable and that is not explained by the other independent variable(s) already in the regression equation. Finally, the F values reported in the right portion of the output relate to the statistical significance for each partial correlation coefficient and partial regression coefficient. As would be expected, the highest F value, $F = 19.056$, is associated with variable X_3 for which the partial coefficient of correlation is highest.

In step 2 we see that with both X_1 and X_3 included in the analysis $R_{Y.13} = 0.87150$ the standard error of estimate is $s_{Y.13} = 15.14368$, and the F ratio for the test of the overall regression effect is $F = 18.94937$. The multiple regression equation is

$$Y_c = a + b_1 X_1 + b_3 X_3$$

$$= 35.23142 + 0.40404 X_1 - 1.20362 X_3$$

Of the variables not included in the analysis in step 2, the highest partial correlation is represented by $r_{Y4.13} = -0.71038$. Therefore X_4 is the variable added to the analysis in step 3.

In step 3 the coefficient of multiple correlation is now $R^2_{Y.134} = 0.93855$ with an associated F ratio of $F = 27.11291$. The standard error of estimate is now $s_{Y.134} = 11.13229$, and the multiple regression equation is

$$Y_c = a + b_1 X_1 + b_3 X_3 + b_4 X_4$$
$$= 21.08153 + 0.55060 X_1 - 1.26692 X_3 - 1.04184 X_4$$

The last independent variable X_2 is added to the analysis in step 4. The coefficient of multiple correlation is now $R_{Y.1234} = 0.96045$, and the standard error of estimate is $s_{Y.1234} = 9.41938$.

A particular advantage associated with a stepwise procedure in multiple regression and multiple correlation analysis is that a stopping rule can be specified so that not all independent variables, but rather, a limited best combination of independent variables, is included in the final regression equation. For example, we would specify that a new variable should be included only if the *additional* sums of squares attributable to the regression effect are significant at the 5 percent level. In our example all four independent variables make such a contribution. This contribution could be demonstrated by testing the significance of each net regression coefficient in the final multiple regression equation. All the net regression coefficients are in fact significant at the 5 percent level.

Exhibit 15-2 includes selected portions of the SPSS program PARTIAL CORR. As indicated by its assigned name this program determines partial correlation coefficients. The first part of the output, labeled "zero-order partials," is a matrix of simple correlation coefficients and corresponds to the first portion of our output for the REGRESSION program. In the output of Exhibit 15-2, however, additional information includes the degrees of freedom associated with each correlation coefficient and the level of significance at which the null hypothesis that there is no relationship can be rejected. Thus, referring to the first row of the matrix, we see that the only independent variable for which the simple correlation with Y is significant at $\alpha = 0.05$ is X_1, because for the other three variables the reported significance levels are all greater than 0.05.

After the correlation matrix, the next output reports the partial correlation between X_1 and Y with X_2, X_3, and X_4 held constant statistically. Symbolically, we see that $r_{Y1.234} = 0.9538$.

The remaining portions of the output for this program report the partial correlation values for the other three independent variables. That is, we can observe that

$$r_{Y2.134} = -0.5909$$

$$r_{Y3.124} = -0.8709$$

$$r_{Y4.123} = -0.7444$$

Exhibit 15-2 Selected output of the SPSS program **PARTIAL CORR** for the data in Table 15-2.

INCOME AND EXPENDITURE DATA

- - - - - - - - - P A R T I A L   C O R R E L A T I O N   C O E F F I C I E N T S - - - - - - - - -

ZERO ORDER PARTIALS

	Y	X1	X2	X3	X4
Y	1.0000	.6145	.2786	.1464	.3347
	(0)	(13)	(13)	(13)	(13)
	S= .001	S= .015	S= .315	S= .603	S= .223
X1	.6145	1.0000	.8619	.8175	.8166
	(13)	(0)	(13)	(13)	(13)
	S= .015	S= .001	S= .001	S= .001	S= .001
X2	.2786	.8619	1.0000	.8280	.7354
	(13)	(13)	(0)	(13)	(13)
	S= .315	S= .001	S= .001	S= .001	S= .002
X3	.1464	.8175	.8280	1.0000	.6366
	(13)	(13)	(13)	(0)	(13)
	S= .603	S= .001	S= .001	S= .001	S= .011
X4	.3347	.8166	.7354	.6366	1.0000
	(13)	(13)	(13)	(13)	(0)
	S= .223	S= .001	S= .002	S= .011	S= .001

(COEFFICIENT / (D.F.) / SIGNIFICANCE)

(A VALUE OF 99.0000 IS PRINTED IF A COEFFICIENT CANNOT BE COMPUTED)

INCOME AND EXPENDITURE DATA

- - - - - - - - - P A R T I A L   C O R R E L A T I O N   C O E F F I C I E N T S - - - - - - - - -

CONTROLLING FOR.. X1

	X2	X3	X4
Y	.9538		
	(10)		
	S= .001		

(COEFFICIENT / (D.F.) / SIGNIFICANCE)

(A VALUE OF 99.0000 IS PRINTED IF A COEFFICIENT CANNOT BE COMPUTED)

Exhibit 15-2 Selected output of the SPSS program PARTIAL CORR for the data in Table 15-2 (*Continued*).

INCOME AND EXPENDITURE DATA   PAGE   14

- - - - - - - - - P A R T I A L   C O R R E L A T I O N   C O E F F I C I E N T S - - - - - - - - -

CONTROLLING FOR.. X1   X3   X4
                  X2

Y   -.5909
       (10)
       S= .043

(COEFFICIENT / (D.F.) / SIGNIFICANCE)   (A VALUE OF 99.0000 IS PRINTED IF A COEFFICIENT CANNOT BE COMPUTED)

INCOME AND EXPENDITURE DATA   PAGE   18

- - - - - - - - - P A R T I A L   C O R R E L A T I O N   C O E F F I C I E N T S - - - - - - - - -

CONTROLLING FOR.. X1   X2   X4
                  X3

Y   -.8709
       (10)
       S= .001

(COEFFICIENT / (D.F.) / SIGNIFICANCE)   (A VALUE OF 99.0000 IS PRINTED IF A COEFFICIENT CANNOT BE COMPUTED)

INCOME AND EXPENDITURE DATA   PAGE   22

- - - - - - - - - P A R T I A L   C O R R E L A T I O N   C O E F F I C I E N T S - - - - - - - - -

CONTROLLING FOR.. X1   X2   X3
                  X4

Y   -.7444
       (10)
       S= .005

(COEFFICIENT / (D.F.) / SIGNIFICANCE)   (A VALUE OF 99.0000 IS PRINTED IF A COEFFICIENT CANNOT BE COMPUTED)

310

Notice that although all of the simple correlation coefficients between X_2, X_3, X_4, and Y were not significant at the 5 percent level, all of the partial correlation values are significant at this level. This significance indicates that improvement in the multiple correlation is associated with each of these variables being included in the analysis. Also notice that although the simple correlation of each of these types of expenditures (housing, food, and entertainment) with household income was positive, the partial correlations for X_2, X_3, and X_4 with the dependent variable are all negative. Sometimes such reversals of sign in multiple correlation analysis are difficult to explain and are reflective of the problem of multicollinearity described in Section 15-10. In the present case, however, the reversal is understandable. What we are saying is that when the income level and the other categories of expenditure are held constant statistically, the correlation between the level of expenditure in any one category and the level of savings is negative. That is, with income and the other expenses held constant, the relationship between the amount spent and the amount saved is negative.

15-12 SUMMARY

In *multiple regression analysis* the value of the dependent variable is estimated on the basis of known values of two or more independent variables, while the extent of the relationship between the independent variables taken as a group and the dependent variable is measured in *multiple correlation analysis*. For multiple regression analysis the principal assumptions are

1. The relationship can be represented by a linear model.
2. The dependent variable is a continuous random variable.
3. The variances of the conditional distributions of the dependent variable are all equal (homoscedasticity).
4. Successive observed values of the dependent variable are uncorrelated.
5. The conditional distributions of the dependent variable are all normal distributions.

The last two assumptions are not required if the multiple regression analysis is done only for point estimation, but they are required for the construction of estimation intervals or tests of hypotheses. The assumptions for multiple correlation analysis are essentially the same as the five assumptions specified above, except that *all* variables are assumed to be random variables, and therefore the conditional variances for each variable separately are assumed to be equal, and the overall form of the distribution of variables is described as constituting a multivariate normal distribution.

In multiple regression analysis each regression coefficient included in the regression equation is called a *partial regression coefficient,* because the value of the coefficient is determined in the context of the other independent variables also being included in the regression equation. The overall significance of the regression effect can be determined by use of the analysis of variance. The regression effect associated with any one independent variable can also be tested by using the analysis of variance, or the relevant b coefficient can be tested for significance by use of Student's t distribution.

In multiple correlation analysis, in addition to the coefficient of multiple correlation, there is often an interest in partial correlation coefficients. A *coefficient of partial correlation* expresses the relationship between one of the independent variables and the dependent variable, given that the other independent variables are held constant statistically. Thus this coefficient indicates the marginal contribution of the particular independent variable in the multiple correlation model. The technique of partial correlation makes it possible to apply statistical controls to data when such controls were not applied in the experimental design itself. However, in *multicollinearity*, when the independent variables are highly correlated, the meaning of such partial correlation values may be unclear (for example, two correlated variables, such as, for example, age and years of experience in a job, may be two versions of what amounts to the same variable).

Standard computer programs are available for multiple regression and correlation analysis, and in this chapter we used two programs from the Statistical Package for the Social Sciences (SPSS). The availability of such programs has made it easy for the novice to carry out complicated statistical analyses. With increased use of such programs, it is particularly important that you recognize the necessary assumptions about the data being analyzed and the limitations associated with the computer output.

FORMULAS

(15-1) $Y_i = \alpha + \beta_1 X_{i,1} + \beta_2 X_{i,2} + \cdots$
$\quad\quad + \beta_k X_{i,k} + e_i$

Mathematical model underlying multiple regression analysis.

(15-2) $Y_c = a + b_1 X_1 + b_2 X_2$

Multiple regression equation based on sample data for two independent variables.

(15-3a) $\Sigma Y = na + b_1 \Sigma X_1 + b_2 \Sigma X_2$

(15-3b) $\Sigma X_1 Y = a\Sigma X_1 + b_1 \Sigma X_1^2 + b_2 \Sigma X_1 X_2$

(15-3c) $\Sigma X_2 Y = a\Sigma X_2 + b_1 \Sigma X_1 X_2 + b_2 \Sigma X_2^2$

Three so-called normal equations that must be solved as simultaneous equations to determine the values of a, b_1, and b_2, given two independent variables.

(15-4) $s_{Y.12} = \sqrt{\dfrac{\Sigma(Y - Y_c)^2}{n-3}}$

Deviations formula for the standard error of estimate, given two independent variables.

(15-5) $s_{Y.12} = \sqrt{\dfrac{\Sigma Y^2 - b_1 \Sigma X_1 Y - b_2 \Sigma X_2 Y}{n-3}}$

Computational formula for the standard error of estimate, given two independent variables.

(15-6) Pred. int. $= Y_c \pm t_{df}s_{Y.12}$

Approximate prediction interval for estimating an individual value of a dependent variable, given two independent variables.

(15-7) Pred. int. $= Y_c \pm zs_{Y.12}$

Approximate prediction interval for estimating an individual value of a dependent variable, given two independent variables and a relatively large sample (df $\geqslant$ 29).

(15-8) $s_{\bar{Y}.12} = \dfrac{s_{Y.12}}{\sqrt{n}}$

Standard error of the conditional mean, given two independent variables.

(15-9) Conf. int. $= \bar{Y}_c \pm t_{df}s_{\bar{Y}.12}$

Approximate confidence interval for the conditional mean of a dependent variable, given two independent variables.

(15-10) Conf. int. $= \bar{Y}_c \pm zs_{\bar{Y}.12}$

Approximate confidence interval for the conditional mean of a dependent variable, given two independent variables and a relatively large sample (df $\geqslant$ 29).

(15-11) $s_{b_1} = \dfrac{s_{Y.12}}{\sqrt{\Sigma X_1^2\,(1 - r_{12}^2)}}$

Standard error of the partial regression coefficient b_1, given two independent variables.

(15-12) $s_{b_2} = \dfrac{s_{Y.12}}{\sqrt{\Sigma X_2^2\,(1 - r_{12}^2)}}$

Standard error of the partial regression coefficient b_2, given two independent variables.

(15-13) Conf. int. $= b_k \pm t_{df}s_{b_k}$

Approximate confidence interval for estimating the value of the partial regression coefficient b_k.

(15-14) $t = \dfrac{b_k - \beta_k}{s_{b_k}}$

Test statistic for testing a hypothesized value of the partial regression coefficient β_k.

(15-15) $Y - \bar{Y} = (Y_c - \bar{Y}) + (Y - Y_c)$

Total deviation of a randomly selected value Y from the mean $\bar{Y}$ can be partitioned as being the difference between the regression value Y_c and the mean $\bar{Y}$ and the difference between the value Y and the regression value Y_c.

(15-16) $\Sigma(Y - \bar{Y})^2 = \Sigma(Y_c - \bar{Y})^2$
$$+ \Sigma(Y - Y_c)^2$$

Total sum of squares (SST) is equal to the sum of squares associated with the regression (SSR) plus the sum of squares associated with the sampling error (SSE).

(15-17) $F = \dfrac{\text{MSR}}{\text{MSE}}$

Sample statistic used to test the regression effect; that is, it is a test of the null hypothesis that the independent variables taken as a group and the dependent variable are not related.

(15-18) $R_{Y.12}^2 = 1 - \dfrac{s_{Y.12}^2}{s_Y^2}$

Coefficient of multiple determination based on sample data for two independent variables.

(15-19) $R^2 = \dfrac{\text{SSR}}{\text{SST}}$

Coefficient of multiple determination when the analysis of variance is used in multiple regression and multiple correlation analysis.

(15-20) $R = \sqrt{R^2}$

Coefficient of multiple correlation, always reported as an absolute value without an arithmetic sign.

EXERCISES

15-1 Differentiate the meanings of a simple regression coefficient and a partial regression coefficient.

15-2 Differentiate the meanings of a simple correlation coefficient and a partial correlation coefficient.

15-3 Describe the meaning of each of the following symbols verbally:
   (a) $s_{Y.13}$
   (b) r_{Y3}
   (c) $r_{Y3.12}$
   (d) $R_{Y.12}$
   (e) $R_{Y.34}$

15-4 Table 15-3 presents fictional data relating years of experience X_1 and years of post-secondary education X_2 to annual salary Y for a random sample of $n = 12$ systems analysts. Exhibit 15-3 is a selected portion of the output of the SPSS program REGRESSION for these data.

   (a) What is the first variable selected for inclusion in the regression equation?
   (b) What is the regression equation based on just one independent variable being used to estimate the annual salary?
   (c) What is the regression equation based on both independent variables being used to estimate the annual salary?

Exhibit 15-3 Selected output of the SPSS program REGRESSION for the data in Table 15-3.

SALARIES DATA

CORRELATION COEFFICIENTS

A VALUE OF 99.00000 IS PRINTED
IF A COEFFICIENT CANNOT BE COMPUTED.

	X1	X2	Y
X1	1.00000	-1.00057	.55684
X2	-1.00057	1.00000	-.1372
Y	.55684	.51372	1.00000

SALARIES DATA   04 JAN 78   PAGE 4

FILE   NONAME   (CREATION DATE = 04 JAN 78)

* * * * * * * * * * * * * *   M U L T I P L E   R E G R E S S I O N   * * * * * * * * * * * * * *

DEPENDENT VARIABLE..   Y   VARIABLE LIST 1
                                                                              REGRESSION LIST 1
VARIABLE(S) ENTERED ON STEP NUMBER   1..   X1

MULTIPLE R	.55684	ANALYSIS OF VARIANCE	DF	SUM OF SQUARES	MEAN SQUARE	F
R SQUARE	.31008	REGRESSION	1.	39.75372	39.75372	4.49434
ADJUSTED R SQUARE	.24108	RESIDUAL	10.	88.45295	8.84529	
STANDARD ERROR	2.97410					

------------ VARIABLES IN THE EQUATION ------------   ------- VARIABLES NOT IN THE EQUATION -------

VARIABLE	B	BETA	STD ERROR B	F	VARIABLE	BETA IN	PARTIAL	TOLERANCE	F
X1	.72127	.55684	.34022	4.494	X2	.57555	.68940	.98989	8.152
(CONSTANT)	17.68501								

* *

VARIABLE(S) ENTERED ON STEP NUMBER   2..   X2

MULTIPLE R	.79874	ANALYSIS OF VARIANCE	DF	SUM OF SQUARES	MEAN SQUARE	F
R SQUARE	.63798	REGRESSION	2.	81.79328	40.89664	7.93025
ADJUSTED R SQUARE	.55753	RESIDUAL	9.	46.41339	5.15704	
STANDARD ERROR	2.27091					

Exhibit 15-3 Selected output of the SPSS program REGRESSION for the data in Table 15-3 (*Continued*).

		VARIABLES IN THE EQUATION					VARIABLES NOT IN THE EQUATION		
VARIABLE	B	BETA	STD ERROR B	F	VARIABLE	BETA IN	PARTIAL	TOLERANCE	F
X1	.79624	.61473	.26110	9.299					
X2	1.61766	.57555	.56658	8.152					
(CONSTANT)	10.65337								

MAXIMUM STEP REACHED

SALARIES DATA   PAGE 5

* * * * * * * * * * * * * * * * * * M U L T I P L E   R E G R E S S I O N * * * * * * * * * * * * * *

DEPENDENT VARIABLE.. Y   VARIABLE LIST 1
                                                          REGRESSION LIST 1

SUMMARY TABLE

VARIABLE	MULTIPLE R	R SQUARE	RSQ CHANGE	SIMPLE R	B	BETA
X1	.55694	.31008	.31008	.55684	.79624	.61473
X2	.79874	.63798	.32790	.51372	1.61766	.57555
(CONSTANT)					10.65337	

15-5 Continue referring to the data in Table 15-3 and to the computer output in Exhibit 15-3.

(*a*) One difficulty associated with any stepwise procedure in multiple regression analysis is that use of a stopping rule may result in stopping too soon in terms of the addition of variables to the regression equation. Suppose that we had defined the stopping rule that a variable will be added only if the resulting net regression effect is significant at $\alpha = 0.05$. At what point would we have stopped in the construction of the regression equation for estimating the annual salary?

(*b*) Test the null hypothesis that $\beta_k = 0$ for each of the partial regression coefficients in step 2 of the analysis based on use of Student's t distribution and using the 5 percent level of significance.

(*c*) Based on use of the analysis of variance and the 5 percent level of significance, test the net-regression effect associated with each independent variable included in step 2 of the analysis.

15-6 Again, refer to the data in Table 15-3 and to the computer output in Exhibit 15-3.

(*a*) Estimate the annual salary of an individual with 5.0 years of experience and 4.0 years of postsecondary education as a point estimate.

(*b*) Construct the 90 percent approximate prediction interval for estimating the salary of an individual with 5.0 years of experience and 4.0 years of postsecondary education.

(*c*) Construct the 90 percent approximate confidence interval for estimating the mean salary of 25 individuals, all of whom have 5.0 years of experience and 4.0 years of postsecondary education. Differentiate the meaning of this estimation interval compared with the estimation interval in Example 15-6*b*.

15-7 Exhibit 15-4 presents selected output of the SPSS program PARTIAL CORR for the data in Table 15-3.

(*a*) Identify the simple correlation coefficients representing the relationship of each independent variable with the dependent variable. Which of these coefficients is significant at the 5 percent level?

(*b*) Identify the partial correlation coefficients representing the relationship of each independent variable with the dependent variable. Which of these coefficients is significant at the 5 percent level?

(*c*) Compare the results in Exercise 15-7*a* and 15-7*b* and comment upon the implications of these results.

Table 15-3 Annual salaries of a random sample of 12 systems analysts as related to years of experience and years of postsecondary education

Sampled person	Years of experience X_1	Years of postsecondary education X_2	Annual salary, in \$1,000s Y
1	5.5	4.0	19.9
2	9.0	4.0	25.5
3	4.0	5.0	23.9
4	8.0	4.0	24.0
5	9.5	5.0	22.5
6	3.0	4.0	20.5
7	7.0	3.0	21.0
8	1.5	4.5	17.7
9	8.5	5.0	30.0
10	7.5	6.0	25.0
11	9.5	2.0	21.0
12	6.0	2.0	18.6

Exhibit 15-4 Selected output of the SPSS program PARTIAL CORR for the data in Table 15-3.

SALARIES DATA

- - - - - - - - - P A R T I A L   C O R R E L A T I O N   C O E F F I C I E N T S - - - - - - - - - - -

ZERO ORDER PARTIALS

	Y	X1	X2
Y	1.0000 (0) S= .001	.5568 (10) S= .060	.5137 (10) S= .088
X1	.5568 (10) S= .060	1.0000 (0) S= .001	-.1006 (10) S= .756
X2	.5137 (10) S= .088	-.1006 (10) S= .756	1.0000 (0) S= .001

(COEFFICIENT / (D.F.) / SIGNIFICANCE)

(A VALUE OF 99.0000 IS PRINTED IF A COEFFICIENT CANNOT BE COMPUTED)

SALARIES DATA

- - - - - - - - - P A R T I A L   C O R R E L A T I O N   C O E F F I C I E N T S - - - - - - - - - - -

CONTROLLING FOR.. X2

	X1
Y	.7129 (9) S= .014

(COEFFICIENT / (D.F.) / SIGNIFICANCE)

(A VALUE OF 99.0000 IS PRINTED IF A COEFFICIENT CANNOT BE COMPUTED)

SALARIES DATA

- - - - - - - - - P A R T I A L   C O R R E L A T I O N   C O E F F I C I E N T S - - - - - - - - - - -

CONTROLLING FOR.. X1

	X2
Y	.6894 (9) S= .019

(COEFFICIENT / (D.F.) / SIGNIFICANCE)

(A VALUE OF 99.0000 IS PRINTED IF A COEFFICIENT CANNOT BE COMPUTED)

318

15-8 Table 15-4 presents hypothetical data for a situation involving three independent variables and one dependent variable, while Exhibit 15-5 presents selected output of the SPSS program REGRESSION for these data.

(a) What independent variable is added to the analysis in each step of the procedure presented in Exhibit 15-5?

(b) What are the values of the multiple coefficients of correlation when one, two, and then three independent variables are included in the analysis?

(c) Write the final multiple regression equation for estimating the value of the dependent variable.

(d) Estimate the value of the dependent variable as a point estimate for $X_1 = 35$, $X_2 = 20.0$, and $X_3 = 10$.

15-9 From the data in Table 15-4 and the computer output in Exhibit 15-5,

(a) Construct the 95 percent approximate prediction interval for estimating the value of the dependent variable, given that $X_3 = 10$ and that the values of the other independent variables are unknown.

(b) Construct the 95 percent approximate prediction interval for estimating the value of the dependent variable, given that $X_2 = 20.0$ and $X_3 = 10$, with the value of X_1 unknown.

(c) Construct the 95 percent approximate prediction interval for estimating the value of the dependent variable, given that $X_1 = 35$, $X_2 = 20.0$, and $X_3 = 10$.

(d) Compare the prediction intervals obtained in Exercise 15-9a through 15-9c.

15-10 Again, from the data in Table 15-4 and the computer output in Exhibit 15-5,

(a) Based on use of Student's t distribution and the 5 percent level of significance, test the null hypothesis $\beta_k = 0$ for each of the partial regression coefficients in step 3 of the analysis.

(b) Based on use of the analysis of variance and the 5 percent level of significance, test the net regression effect for each independent variable included in step 3 of the analysis.

15-11 From the data in Table 15-4 and the computer output in Exhibit 15-5,

(a) Explain why variable X_2 was added to the regression equation in step 2 of the analysis.

(b) If a stopping rule were used that a variable should be added to the analysis only when the net regression effect associated with the addition of that variable is significant at $\alpha = 0.05$, identify the step in the analysis that addition of variables would have stopped; write the regression equation that would then be used for estimating the value of the dependent variable.

Table 15-4 Hypothetical data for a situation involving three independent variables

Sample no.	X_1	X_2	X_3	Y
1	32	10.0	8	7.6
2	34	14.2	9	14.5
3	35	18.0	14	23.6
4	29	21.0	4	12.2
5	31	29.5	11	27.0
6	42	31.3	20	57.5
7	34	36.5	21	36.9
8	32	20.5	15	32.3
9	41	21.3	17	43.8
10	38	47.5	23	66.3

Exhibit 15-5 Selected output of the SPSS program REGRESSION for the data in Table 15-4.

HYPOTHETICAL DATA

CORRELATION COEFFICIENTS

A VALUE OF 99.00000 IS PRINTED
IF A COEFFICIENT CANNOT BE COMPUTED.

	X1	X2	X3	Y
X1	1.00000	.35266	.72064	.77033
X2	.35266	1.00000	.75826	.82285
X3	.72064	.75826	1.00000	.90526
Y	.77033	.82285	.90526	1.00000

HYPOTHETICAL DATA

* * * * * * * * * * * * M U L T I P L E   R E G R E S S I O N * * * * * * * * * *

DEPENDENT VARIABLE.. Y

VARIABLE(S) ENTERED ON STEP NUMBER 1..   X3

		ANALYSIS OF VARIANCE	DF	SUM OF SQUARES	MEAN SQUARE	F
MULTIPLE R	.90526	REGRESSION	1.	2769.07584	2769.07584	36.32021
R SQUARE	.81950	RESIDUAL	8.	609.92511	76.24064	
ADJUSTED R SQUARE	.79693					
STANDARD ERROR	8.73159					

--------- VARIABLES IN THE EQUATION ---------

VARIABLE	B	BETA	STD ERROR B	F
X3	2.83061	.90526	.46968	36.320
(CONSTANT)	-8.02471			

--------- VARIABLES NOT IN THE EQUATION ---------

VARIABLE	BETA IN	PARTIAL	TOLERANCE	F
X1	.24542	.40048	.48067	1.337
X2	.32096	.49253	.42504	2.242

* *

VARIABLE(S) ENTERED ON STEP NUMBER 2..   X2

		ANALYSIS OF VARIANCE	DF	SUM OF SQUARES	MEAN SQUARE	F
MULTIPLE R	.92913	REGRESSION	2.	2917.03208	1458.51604	22.10022
R SQUARE	.86328	RESIDUAL	7.	461.96886	65.99555	
ADJUSTED R SQUARE	.82428					
STANDARD ERROR	8.12376					

Exhibit 15-5 Selected output of the SPSS program REGRESSION for the data in Table 15-4 (*Continued*).

```
------------ VARIABLES IN THE EQUATION ------------    ------------ VARIABLES NOT IN THE EQUATION ------------

VARIABLE        B        BETA     STD ERROR B    F      VARIABLE    BETA IN    PARTIAL    TOLERANCE    F

X3           2.06962    .66189    .67028      9.534     X1          .45921     .77790      .39213    9.105
X2           -.55282    .32096    .36921      2.242
(CONSTANT)  -11.02809
```

```
HYPOTHETICAL DATA                                      04 JAN 78          PAGE  5

FILE  NONAME  (CREATION DATE = 04 JAN 78)

* * * * * * * * * * * * * * * * * *  M U L T I P L E   R E G R E S S I O N  * * * * * * * * * * * * * * * *    VARIABLE LIST 1
                                                                                                              REGRESSION LIST 1

DEPENDENT VARIABLE..    Y

VARIABLE(S) ENTERED ON STEP NUMBER  3..    X1

MULTIPLE R          .97263        ANALYSIS OF VARIANCE     DF     SUM OF SQUARES    MEAN SQUARE       F
R SQUARE            .94601        REGRESSION               3.       3196.58227      1065.52742    35.04666
ADJUSTED R SQUARE   .91390        RESIDUAL                 6.        182.41867        30.40311
STANDARD ERROR     5.51390
```

```
------------ VARIABLES IN THE EQUATION ------------    ------------ VARIABLES NOT IN THE EQUATION ------------

VARIABLE        B        BETA     STD ERROR B    F      VARIABLE    BETA IN    PARTIAL    TOLERANCE    F

X3            .53849    .17221    .67966       .628
X2            .91341    .53032    .27738     10.844
X1           2.07432    .45921    .68408      9.105
(CONSTANT)  -70.47975
```

MAXIMUM STEP REACHED

(c) One difficulty associated with stepwise procedures in regression analysis is that different procedures can lead to different results. An alternative stepwise procedure to the one we have used is to begin with a complete multiple regression equation and then to eliminate variables that do not represent a significant net contribution to the overall regression effect. Look at the final set of results in step 3 of the output. What variable, if any, would be the first variable eliminated in a "backward" stepwise procedure if we set the rule that the net regression effect of each variable should be significant at the 5 percent level? Compare this with the results obtained in Exercise 15-11b using the "forward" stepwise procedure.

15-12 Table 15-5 presents gasoline mileage data for a random sample of twenty 1977 model automobiles. The independent variables are the size of the engine in cubic inches of displacement (CID), the weight of the automobile, and the length of the automobile. Exhibit 15-6 presents selected portions of the output from the SPSS program REGRESSION for these data.

(a) Refer to the correlation matrix presented in the first portion of the output in Exhibit 15-6. List the correlation values representing the correlation between each pair of independent variables and comment upon these values.

(b) List the correlation values of each independent variable with the dependent variable and comment upon these values.

Table 15-5 Gasoline mileage obtained for a random sample of 20 automobiles *

	Automobile characteristics			
Sampled automobile	Engine size X_1, CID	Weight X_2, lb	Length X_3, in.	Gasoline mileage (city–highway combined) Y
1	302	4,295	220	17
2	140	2,450	169	30
3	440	5,000	231	12
4	351	4,525	224	15
5	350	4,070	220	18
6	305	3,850	212	18
7	85	2,025	159	33
8	305	3,965	210	17
9	130	2,990	193	22
10	232	3,200	170	20
11	318	4,140	218	17
12	85	2,020	163	29
13	85	1,970	157	34
14	400	4,685	227	13
15	250	3,350	197	22
16	225	3,370	201	23
17	91	1,760	150	44
18	250	3,375	198	24
19	97	2,265	165	32
20	111	2,155	171	27

*Data regarding engine size, weight, and length were obtained from *Consumer Reports,* April 1, 1977. Gasoline mileage data were obtained from *1977 Gas Mileage Guide* published by the U.S. Environmental Protection Agency.

Exhibit 15-6 Selected output of the SPSS program REGRESSION for the data in Table 15-5.

AUTOMOBILE MILEAGE DATA

CORRELATION COEFFICIENTS

A VALUE OF 99.00000 IS PRINTED
IF A COEFFICIENT CANNOT BE COMPUTED.

	X1	X2	X3	Y
X1	1.00000	.98001	.94132	-.89388
X2	.98001	1.00000	.97304	-.93483
X3	.94132	.97304	1.00000	-.91755
Y	-.89388	-.93483	-.91755	1.00000

AUTOMOBILE MILEAGE DATA

PAGE 4

* M U L T I P L E   R E G R E S S I O N *

VARIABLE LIST 1
REGRESSION LIST 1

DEPENDENT VARIABLE..   Y

VARIABLE(S) ENTERED ON STEP NUMBER   1..   X2

MULTIPLE R	.93483	ANALYSIS OF VARIANCE	DF	SUM OF SQUARES	MEAN SQUARE	F
R SQUARE	.87391	REGRESSION	1.	1133.06917	1133.06917	124.75618
ADJUSTED R SQUARE	.86691	RESIDUAL	18.	163.48083	9.08227	
STANDARD ERROR	3.01368					

------------ VARIABLES IN THE EQUATION ------------   ------------- VARIABLES NOT IN THE EQUATION -------------

VARIABLE	B	BETA	STD ERROR B	F		VARIABLE	BETA IN	PARTIAL	TOLERANCE	F
X2	-.00754	-.93483	.00067	124.756		X1	.56260	.31520	.03958	1.875
(CONSTANT)	48.91257					X3	-.14893	-.09674	.05320	.161

* *

VARIABLE(S) ENTERED ON STEP NUMBER   2..   X1

MULTIPLE R	.94151	ANALYSIS OF VARIANCE	DF	SUM OF SQUARES	MEAN SQUARE	F
R SQUARE	.88644	REGRESSION	2.	1149.31079	574.65540	66.34878
ADJUSTED R SQUARE	.87308	RESIDUAL	17.	147.23921	8.66113	
STANDARD ERROR	2.94298					

323

Exhibit 15-6 Selected output of the SPSS program REGRESSION for the data in Table 15-5 (*Continued*).

```
------------ VARIABLES IN THE EQUATION: ------------     ------------ VARIABLES NOT IN THE EQUATION: ------------

VARIABLE        B        BETA     STD ERROR B      F         VARIABLE     BETA IN    PARTIAL    TOLERANCE      F

X2          -.01198   -1.48619      .00331      13.086       X3           -.02069    -.01365     .04940      .003
X1           .03978     .56260      .02905       1.875
(CONSTANT)  53.50345
```

F-LEVEL OR TOLERANCE-LEVEL INSUFFICIENT FOR FURTHER COMPUTATION

AUTOMOBILE MILEAGE DATA   PAGE   5


```
* * * * * * * * * * * * * * * * * * * * *   M U L T I P L E   R E G R E S S I O N   * * * * * * * * * * * * * * * * * * * * *

DEPENDENT VARIABLE..   Y                                                           VARIABLE LIST   1
                                                                                  REGRESSION LIST 1

                                  SUMMARY TABLE

VARIABLE       MULTIPLE R   R SQUARE   RSQ CHANGE   SIMPLE R        B          BETA

X2              .93483      .87391      .87391      -.93483     -.01198     -1.48619
X1              .94151      .88644      .01253      -.89388      .03978       .56260
(CONSTANT)                                                      53.50345
```

Exhibit 15-7 Selected output of the SPSS program PARTIAL CORR for the data in Table 15-5.

AUTOMOBILE MILEAGE DATA

- - - - - - - - - - - P A R T I A L   C O R R E L A T I O N   C O E F F I C I E N T S - - - - - - - - - -   PAGE   11

CONTROLLING FOR..   X2   X3
                     X1

Y   .3017
         (16)
      S= .224

(COEFFICIENT / (D.F.) / SIGNIFICANCE)   (A VALUE OF 99.0000 IS PRINTED IF A COEFFICIENT CANNOT BE COMPUTED)

AUTOMOBILE MILEAGE DATA

- - - - - - - - - - - P A R T I A L   C O R R E L A T I O N   C O E F F I C I E N T S - - - - - - - - - -   PAGE   17

CONTROLLING FOR..   X1   X3
                     X2

Y   -.4936
         (16)
      S= .037

(COEFFICIENT / (D.F.) / SIGNIFICANCE)   (A VALUE OF 99.0000 IS PRINTED IF A COEFFICIENT CANNOT BE COMPUTED)

AUTOMOBILE MILEAGE DATA

- - - - - - - - - - - P A R T I A L   C O R R E L A T I O N   C O E F F I C I E N T S - - - - - - - - - -   PAGE   23

CONTROLLING FOR..   X1   X2
                     X3

Y   -.0136
         (16)
      S= .957

(COEFFICIENT / (D.F.) / SIGNIFICANCE)   (A VALUE OF 99.0000 IS PRINTED IF A COEFFICIENT CANNOT BE COMPUTED)

325

15-13 Again, refer to the data in Table 15-5 and to the computer output in Exhibit 15-6.

(*a*) The addition of variables stopped at step 2 because the addition of the last variable X_3 would have led to an increase in the value of the standard error of estimate. Make reference to the formula for the standard error of estimate and explain how this kind of result is possible (*Hint:* Consider the change in the denominator of this formula as variables are added to the analysis.)

(*b*) If a stopping rule were used that a variable should be added to the analysis only when the net regression effect associated with the addition of that variable is significant at $\alpha = 0.05$, at what point in the analysis would the addition of variables have stopped? Write the regression equation that would be used to estimate the value of the dependent variable.

(*c*) Using the regression equation in Exercise 15-13*b*, construct the 95 percent approximate prediction interval for the gasoline mileage for an automobile that weighs 3,500 pounds.

15-14 From Exhibit 15-7, which presents selected output of the SPSS program PARTIAL CORR for the data in Table 15-5,

(*a*) Compare the partial correlation coefficients reported in Exhibit 15-7 with the respective simple correlation coefficients reported in the first portion of Exhibit 15-6.

(*b*) From the comparisons in Exercise 15-14*a* explain the meaning of any reversals of arithmetic sign with respect to the simple correlation of each independent variable with the dependent variable and the associated partial correlation value. What special type of problem, or area of concern, is illustrated by any difficulties in interpreting such values?

(*c*) Which of the partial correlation coefficients are significant at $\alpha = 0.05$? How do these results compare with the results reported in Exhibit 15-6?

TIME–SERIES ANALYSIS AND FORECASTING

16-1 THE CLASSICAL TIME–SERIES MODEL

A *time series* is a set of observed values, such as production or sales data, for a sequentially ordered series of time periods. Examples of time series are a listing of a company's total annual sales for a series of years and a record of the monthly sales of a particular product for a series of months. Thus time-series values may pertain to a group of products or to just one specific product, and the time periods may be yearly periods, or they may be portions of a year, such as quarters, months, or weeks.

The data that constitute a time series can be listed in a table or can be portrayed by a line graph with the time periods represented on the horizontal axis and the amounts represented on the vertical axis. Table 16-1 presents the factory sales of domestic passenger cars in the United States, in millions of units, for the period 1950–1976. These data will be used as the basis for the computational examples in this chapter. The line graph for this time series is presented in Figure 16-1.

Refer to Figure 16-1. A *peak* in a time series is a value that represents a new high compared with the amounts in preceding time periods and that is followed by lower values in the immediately succeeding periods. Such peaks in factory sales of automobiles to dealers can be observed as occurring in 1955, 1965, and 1973. A *trough* in a time series is a value which represents the culmination of a series of declining values, followed by higher amounts in the immediately succeeding periods. Such troughs in the factory car sales can be observed as occurring in 1952, 1958, 1970, and 1975 in Figure 16-1.

One particular point that should be noted regarding time-series values is that such values are not random-sample data. Rather, the values represent population data from the statistical point of view. When time-series values are used as a basis for forecasting, the methods of statistical inference are not applicable, because the historical values collected cannot be considered a random sample of future events. Therefore such methods as interval-estimation and hypothesis testing are not applicable in time-series analysis.

Table 16-1 Factory sales of domestic passenger cars from plants in the United States, 1950–1976

Year	Factory sales, in millions of units
1950	6.513
1951	5.090
1952	4.154
1953	5.954
1954	5.352
1955	7.666
1956	5.623
1957	5.953
1958	4.132
1959	5.474
1960	6.530
1961	5.402
1962	6.754
1963	7.444
1964	7.554
1965	9.101
1966	8.337
1967	7.070
1968	8.407
1969	7.807
1970	6.187
1971	8.122
1972	8.353
1973	9.079
1974	6.721
1975	6.073
1976	7.838

(Source: U.S. Department of Commerce, Survey of Current Business.)

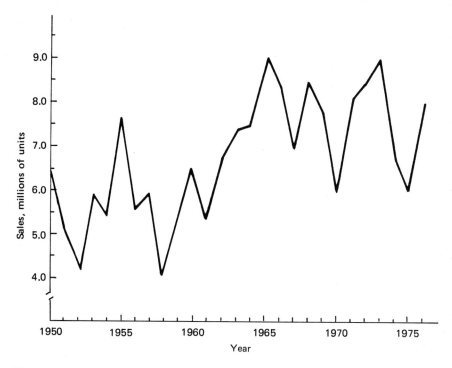

Figure 16-1 Factory sales of domestic passenger cars from plants in the United States, 1950–1976. (Data from Table 16-1.)

The basic idea underlying time-series analysis is that systematic influences that are associated with time affect time-series values. The objective of the analysis is to identify and measure the influences of the different time-related factors. Once the separate factors, or components, have been identified, such an understanding can be used both to aid in interpreting historical time-series values and to forecast future time-series values. The classical approach to time-series analysis identifies four such influences, or components:

1. *Secular trend* (*T*). The general long-term movement in the time-series values (*Y*) over an extended period of years.
2. *Cyclical fluctuations* (*C*). The recurrent up-and-down wavelike variations from secular trend that have a duration of several years.
3. *Seasonal variations* (*S*). The up-and-down variations from secular trend that occur within a year and that recur annually. Such variations typically are identified with monthly or quarterly data.
4. *Irregular variations* (*I*). The erratic variations from secular trend that cannot be ascribed to the cyclical or seasonal influences.

Figure 16-2 portrays a hypothetical time series for which monthly values are plotted on the line graph for a 12-year period. The time-series values are represented

Level (e.g., production, sales, etc.), Y

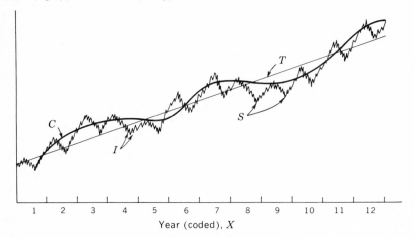

Year (coded), X

Figure 16-2 The components of a monthly time series.

by the jagged line. The secular trend associated with this series is represented as the straight line with the positive slope, labeled T. We can also observe wavelike fluctuations occurring over a period of years, and the wavy line superimposed on the time series to represent this cyclical component is labeled C. By close inspection of the time-series values within each year in Figure 16-2, we can see that in every year values decline between about March and August, followed by increasing values during the last few months of each year. This seasonal trend is easiest seen by comparing the monthly movements within year 1 with those in year 2, and such within-year systematic variations are indicative of the influence of the seasonal S component of the time series. Finally, there are many month-to-month minor variations in Figure 16-2, and these are labeled I to indicate the influence of the irregular component of the time series.

The model underlying classical time-series analysis is based on the assumption that the time-series amount for any designated period is determined by the joint influences of the secular-trend, cyclical, seasonal, and irregular components. Further, the components in the model are assumed to have a multiplicative relationship. Where Y represents the time-series value, the classical time-series model is

$$Y = TCSI \tag{16-1}$$

On the one hand the model represented by Formula (16-1) can be used as the basis for identifying the apparent influence of each component of the time-series on a historical value, or amount, On the other hand one can forecast a future time-series value by multiplying the trend, cyclical, and seasonal components as they apply to the designated period (of course, the irregular component cannot be forecast). The model is simple enough; however, the identification of the influences associated with the several components of the time series is not so simple, and most of the remainder of this chapter is devoted to the methods by which these influences are identified.

16-2 TREND ANALYSIS

Identification of the trend component of a time series generally is done using annual data, because the influence of secular trend concerns the long-term direction of movement of the time series. At least 15 to 20 years of data should be used as the basis for this analysis to ensure that cyclical movements involving several years' duration are not assumed to be indicative of the overall trend of the time series.

Several different methods can be used to fit a trend line to a time series, including the possibility of fitting such a line on a time-series graph by the freehand method. But the method most frequently used is that of determining the equation for the line by the method of least squares, as explained in Section 14-3 on regression analysis. We should note, however, that an equation for the trend line is not a regression equation from the standpoint of the requirements associated with regression analysis. The time-series values Y are not random-sample data but rather are accumulated historical values. Also, there is only one such value for each time period and not a distribution of values for any given period. Finally, and perhaps most seriously, the series of values clearly are dependent rather than independent. The value in one period does affect the magnitude of the value in a succeeding time period principally because of common cyclical influences. This correlation within the series is called *autocorrelation*, as explained in Section 15-10. The existence of autocorrelation does not affect the use of the least-squares trend equation, but it does preclude use of either statistical estimation or hypothesis testing with such data.

When the long-term increase or decrease appears to follow a linear trend based on graphic inspection of the time series, the equation for the trend line is

$$Y_T = a + bX \tag{16-2}$$

where X is the designated year of the time series.

In this form of the equation for a straight line, the a represents the point of intersection of the line with the vertical (Y) axis, while the b represents the slope of the line. Thus a positive slope would indicate that the long-term trend in the values is upward, while a negative slope would indicate that the long-term trend in the values is downward. Where X is each year (usually as a coded value) and Y is the time series value for each year, the formulas for determining the values of a and b for the linear trend equation are

$$b = \frac{\Sigma XY - n\bar{X}\bar{Y}}{\Sigma X^2 - n\bar{X}^2} \tag{16-3}$$

$$a = \bar{Y} - b\bar{X} \tag{16-4}$$

For the data in Table 16-1, concerning the factory sales of automobiles, the time-series graph in Figure 16-1 includes a number of cyclical fluctuations but appears to reflect a general linear trend with a positive slope. Table 16-2 is the worksheet to calculate the values required for determining the linear trend equation. The values of b and a for the linear trend equation are determined as follows:

$$\bar{X} = \frac{\Sigma X}{n} = \frac{351}{27} = 13.0 \qquad \bar{Y} = \frac{\Sigma Y}{n} = \frac{182.690}{27} = 6.766$$

$$b = \frac{\Sigma XY - n\bar{X}\bar{Y}}{\Sigma X^2 - n\bar{X}^2} = \frac{2,550.585 - 27(13.0)(6.766)}{6,201 - 27(169.0)} = \frac{175.719}{1,638.0} = 0.107$$

$$a = \bar{Y} - b\bar{X} = 6.766 - 0.107(13.0) = 5.375$$

Therefore the linear trend equation for the annual factory sales of domestic

Table 16-2 Factory sales of domestic passenger cars from plants in the United States, 1950–1976, and calculations for determining the linear trend equation

Year	Coded year X	Factory sales Y, millions of units	XY	X^2
1950	0	6.513	0	0
1951	1	5.090	5.090	1
1952	2	4.154	8.308	4
1953	3	5.954	17.862	9
1954	4	5.352	21.408	16
1955	5	7.666	38.330	25
1956	6	5.623	33.738	36
1957	7	5.953	41.671	49
1958	8	4.132	33.056	64
1959	9	5.474	49.266	81
1960	10	6.530	65.300	100
1961	11	5.402	59.422	121
1962	12	6.754	81.048	144
1963	13	7.444	96.772	169
1964	14	7.554	105.756	196
1965	15	9.101	136.515	225
1966	16	8.337	133.392	256
1967	17	7.070	120.190	289
1968	18	8.407	151.326	324
1969	19	7.807	148.333	361
1970	20	6.187	123.740	400
1971	21	8.122	170.562	441
1972	22	8.353	183.766	484
1973	23	9.079	208.817	529
1974	24	6.721	161.304	576
1975	25	6.073	151.825	625
1976	26	7.838	203.788	676
Totals	351	182.690	2,550.585	6,201

U.S. automobiles during the 27-year period 1950–1976, with the years sequentially coded beginning with 1950 = 0, is

$$Y_T = a + bX = 5.375 + 0.107X$$

The positive value of the slope of 0.107 for this equation indicates that the trend in the factory sales of automobiles during this time period was positive. Further, the value of this slope indicates that the average increase in factory car sales per year during this period was 0.107 in millions of units, or about 107,000 units annually. Of course the linear equation for trend would be different if a different time period were used, such as, for instance, the 22-year period 1955–1976. In this type of example the judgment of the analyst is the determining factor. As indicated previously, we always want a sufficient number of years so that several cyclical movements are included, thereby making it possible to differentiate the trend component from the cyclical component of the time series. Further, the analyst would want to avoid beginning the series at either a cyclical trough or a cyclical peak, for beginning at either point would provide an unrealistic basis for the analysis. From this standpoint it happens that 1955 was a cyclical peak, and the factory car sales for that year were not exceeded until 1965. Therefore beginning the series at 1955 would be a poor choice. Factory car sales in 1950 were neither at a trough nor a peak, based on pre-1950 car sales. Further, this year was sufficiently post–World War II that the postwar bulge in car sales had been completed. (No new cars were made available for sale to the general public during World War II.)

Having established the linear trend equation for these annual data, we can use this equation for historical analysis to determine the influence of the cyclical component of the time series. This application is presented in Section 16-3, "Analysis of Cyclical Fluctuations." The trend equation can also be used as part of the basis for forecasting future time-series values. The application of the linear trend equation for the purpose of forecasting is illustrated in Section 16-6.

For nonlinear trend a number of different types of equations can be formulated. Such analysis is included in specialized textbooks in time-series analysis. One type of trend curve often used is the *exponential trend curve*. A typical application of the exponential trend curve is for a time series which reflects a constant rate (percent) of growth during the series of years, such as might apply to the sale of electronic calculators during the 1960s and 1970s. Figure 16-3 portrays the general form of the exponential trend curve. The exponential curve has been so named because the value X of the independent variable is the exponent of b in the general equation for such a curve:

$$Y_T = ab^X \qquad (16-5)$$

The exponential equation for a curve can be transformed to a linear equation by taking the logarithm of both sides of the equation, as follows:

$$\log Y_T = \log a + X \log b \qquad (16-6)$$

The advantage of transformation into logarithms is that the linear equation for trend analysis can be applied to the logs of the time-series valus when such values

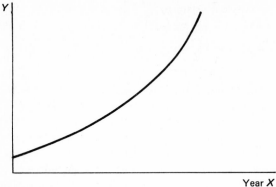

Figure 16-3 A typical exponential trend curve.

follow an exponential form. The computed trend values Y_T can then be reconverted to the original measurement units by taking the antilog of such values. Again, such applications are included in specialized books in time-series analysis.

16-3 ANALYSIS OF CYCLICAL FLUCTUATIONS

Annual time-series values reflect only the effects of the trend and cyclical components of the series, because the seasonal and irregular components are defined as short-run influences that occur within the course of each year. Thus for annual data the components of the time series can be represented by the model

$$Y = TC \tag{16-7}$$

Given that the influence of the trend component for a historical year of the time series has been determined, the cyclical component for that year can be determined by solving Formula (16-7) for C:

$$C = \frac{Y}{T} = \frac{Y}{Y_T} \tag{16-8}$$

The ratio determined by Formula (16-8) is multiplied by 100 and is called a *cyclical relative*. Thus a cyclical relative of 100 would indicate the absence of any cyclical influence on the particular time-series value.

Table 16-3 reports the factory sales of domestic passenger cars from 1950 through 1976 and the expected sales based on the trend equation developed in Section 16-2. The last column of Table 16-3 reports the cyclical relative for each year of this time series. For example, for 1970, which is the coded year 20, the expected-sales level based on the trend equation is

$$Y_T = a + bX = 5.375 + 0.107(20) = 7.515 \text{ million units}$$

The actual level of factory car sales in 1970 was 6.187 million units, resulting in a cyclical relative of 82.3. This value indicates that the level of sales in 1970 was 82.3 percent of the estimated value based on the trend component of the time series and thus that the cyclical influence resulted in a reduction of the factory sales level with respect to the long-run trend. Recall from Section 16-1 that 1970 is in fact one of the trough years in this time series.

To enhance the historical analysis of the effects of the cyclical component on the time series values, a *cycle chart* that presents the cyclical relatives according to year is often prepared. Figure 16-4 is the cycle chart for the data in Table 16-3. The peaks and troughs associated with the cyclical component of the time series are particularly highlighted by such a chart. In Figure 16-4, for example, the peaks in factory automobile sales at the years 1955, 1965, and 1973 are quite prominent.

Although the cycle chart is useful for historical analysis, its value in forecasting the cyclical influence is very limited. Instead, a number of business indicators are used to forecast cyclical turning points, as described in Section 16-7.

Table 16-3 Determination of cyclical relatives for annual factory sales of domestic passenger cars from plants in the United States, 1970–1976

Year	Coded year X	Sales, millions of units		Cyclical relative $100Y/Y_T$
		Actual, Y	Expected, Y_T	
1950	0	6.513	5.375	121.2
1951	1	5.090	5.482	92.8
1952	2	4.154	5.589	74.3
1953	3	5.954	5.696	104.5
1954	4	5.352	5.803	92.3
1955	5	7.666	5.910	129.7
1956	6	5.623	6.017	93.5
1957	7	5.953	6.124	97.2
1958	8	4.132	6.231	66.3
1959	9	5.474	6.338	86.4
1960	10	6.530	6.445	101.3
1961	11	5.402	6.552	82.4
1962	12	6.754	6.659	101.4
1963	13	7.444	6.766	110.0
1964	14	7.554	6.873	109.9
1965	15	9.101	6.980	130.4
1966	16	8.337	7.087	117.6
1967	17	7.070	7.194	98.3
1968	18	8.407	7.301	115.1
1969	19	7.807	7.408	105.4
1970	20	6.187	7.515	82.3
1971	21	8.122	7.622	106.6
1972	22	8.353	7.729	108.1
1973	23	9.079	7.836	115.9
1974	24	6.721	7.943	84.6
1975	25	6.073	8.050	75.4
1976	26	7.838	8.157	96.1

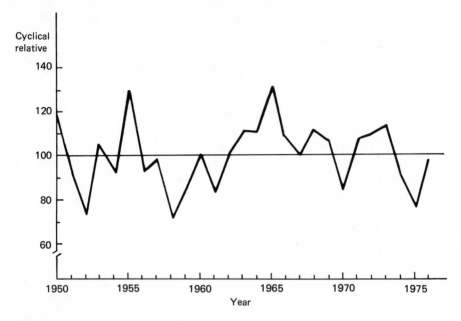

Figure 16-4 Cycle chart for annual factory sales of domestic passenger cars from plants in the United States. (Data from last column of Table 16-3.)

16-4 MEASUREMENT OF SEASONAL VARIATIONS

The influence of the seasonal component on time-series values is identified by determining the seasonal index number for each month, or each quarter, of the year. Thus monthly or quarterly data are required for the determination of seasonal influences.

The procedure most frequently used to determine the seasonal index number for each month or quarter is the *ratio-to-moving-average method*. By this method the first step is to determine a moving average for each month (or quarter) for four to six years of a time series, with each month at the center of the one-year period used as the basis for the average. Conceptually, such a moving average results in both the seasonal and irregular components of the time series being "averaged out." Thus we can say that a moving average based on inclusion of 12 months (or four quarters) of time-series data reflects the influence of only the long-term time-series components:

$$\text{Moving average} = TC \qquad (16\text{-}9)$$

The next step in the ratio-to-moving-average method is to divide each monthly (or quarterly) time-series value by the moving average centered at that month. The result of this division is that the effects of the trend and cyclical components of the time series are removed, leaving the effects of the short-term seasonal and irregular components:

$$\frac{Y}{\text{Moving average}} = \frac{TCSI}{TC} = SI \qquad (16\text{-}10)$$

The final step in the ratio-to-moving-average method is to average the effects of the irregular component from the monthly or quarterly ratios determined by Formula (16-10), thereby determining the seasonal index numbers. As illustrated in the example that follows, this averaging is done by listing the several ratios applicable to the same month (or quarter) for the several years, eliminating the highest and lowest ratios, and then computing the mean of the remaining ratios.

Table 16-4 presents the monthly factory sales of domestic passenger cars in the United States for January 1972 to December 1976 and is the worksheet for the determination of the ratios to moving average. Certain calculations in this worksheet appear to be slightly inaccurate because the computer analysis carried more digits than are reported in the table. The reason 24-month moving totals are determined before 12-month averages are calculated is that a "regular" 12-month moving total and moving average is centered between two months, rather than at a particular month. For example the January through December moving total of 8,352.5 reported in Table 16-4 is centered between June and July 1972. Because the figure of 8,352.5 represents the total sales for the 12 months January through December, this total is listed at the midpoint for this time period (between the lines for June 1972 and July 1972). Now, if we add this moving total to the next 12-month moving total of 8,546.3 for February 1972 through January 1973, the result is the 24-month moving total of 16,898.8, centered at July 1972. Division of the total by 24 results in the 12-month *centered* moving average of 704.12 in Table 16-4. In fact this average is based on the sales figures for 13 months, with the first month (January 1972) and the last month (January 1973) included once in the 24-month total and all other months in between these two included twice in the total. The final column in Table 16-4 reports the ratio of each monthly sales amount to the 12-month centered moving average, as a percent. As explained previously, this ratio reflects the monthly influences of the seasonal and irregular components of the time series.

Table 16-5 lists the several ratios to moving average by month. To average the influence of the irregular component of the time series on these two ratios, we eliminate the highest and lowest ratio from consideration and then calculate a mean for the remaining ratios (in this example, the remaining two ratios). Thus, in this context the label "modified mean" signifies that the highest and lowest values are eliminated. As in Table 16-4, some of the calculations may appear to be off slightly because the computer analysis carried more digits than reported in the table.

Because the sum of the 12 monthly seasonal indexes should be 1,200, as the final step in the analysis the modified means have to be adjusted to determine the monthly index numbers. For quarterly data the required total of the four index

Table 16-4 Factory sales of domestic passenger cars from plants in the United States and worksheet for determination of the ratios to the moving average

Year	Month	Factory sales, millions of units	12-month moving total	24-month centered moving total	12-month centered moving average	Ratio to moving average, %
1972	January	666.0				
	February	716.1				
	March	765.2				
	April	736.9				
	May	798.0				
	June	761.6	8,352.5			
	July	393.6	8,546.3	16,898.8	704.12	55.90
	August	371.0	8,645.7	17,192.0	716.33	51.80
	September	808.8	8,763.3	17,409.0	725.37	111.51
	October	841.7	8,813.0	17,576.3	732.35	114.94
	November	827.4	8,895.1	17,708.1	737.84	112.14
	December	666.2	9,006.8	17,901.9	745.91	89.32
1973	January	859.8	9,290.7	18,297.5	762.40	112.78
	February	815.5	9,335.4	18,626.1	776.09	105.08
	March	882.8	9,192.7	18,528.1	772.00	114.36
	April	786.6	9,238.2	18,430.9	767.95	102.43
	May	880.1	9,237.9	18,476.1	769.84	114.33
	June	873.3	9,078.8	18,316.7	763.20	114.43
	July	677.5	8,771.1	17,849.9	743.75	91.10
	August	415.7	8,457.1	17,228.2	717.84	57.91
	September	666.1	8,131.4	16,588.5	691.19	96.38
	October	887.2	7,962.2	16,093.6	670.57	132.31
	November	827.1	7,761.1	15,723.3	655.14	126.25
	December	507.1	7,506.0	15,267.1	636.13	79.72
1974	January	552.1	7,343.7	14,849.7	618.74	89.24
	February	501.5	7,343.8	14,687.5	611.98	81.95
	March	557.1	7,286.5	14,630.3	609.60	91.39
	April	617.4	7,161.9	14,448.4	602.02	102.56
	May	679.0	6,834.4	13,996.3	583.18	116.44
	June	618.2	6,721.3	13,555.7	564.82	109.46
	July	515.2	6,532.0	13,253.3	552.22	93.30
	August	415.8	6,387.8	12,919.8	538.32	77.24
	September	608.8	6,267.5	12,655.3	527.30	115.46
	October	762.6	6,180.0	12,447.5	518.65	147.04
	November	499.6	6,056.2	12,236.2	509.84	98.00
	December	394.0	6,009.3	12,065.5	502.73	78.38
1975	January	362.8	5,960.6	11,969.9	498.75	72.75
	February	357.3	5,992.7	11,953.3	498.05	71.74
	March	436.8	5,989.6	11,982.3	499.26	87.49
	April	529.9	5,900.4	11,890.0	495.42	106.97
	May	555.2	5,939.2	11,839.6	493.32	112.55
	June	571.3	6,073.4	12,012.6	500.52	114.15
	July	466.5	6,316.7	12,390.1	516.25	90.37
	August	447.9	6,589.5	12,906.2	537.76	83.30
	September	605.7	6,920.6	13,510.1	562.92	107.60
	October	673.4		14,035.7	584.82	115.15

Table 16-4 Factory sales of domestic passenger cars from plants in the United States and worksheet for determination of the ratios to the moving average (*Continued*)

Year	Month	Factory sales, millions of units	12-month moving total	24-month centered moving total	12-month centered moving average	Ratio to moving average, %
	November	538.4	7,115.1	14,386.0	599.42	89.83
	December	528.2	7,270.9	14,756.9	614.87	85.91
1976	January	606.1	7,486.0	15,029.9	626.25	96.79
	February	630.1	7,543.9	15,123.0	630.12	100.00
	March	767.9	7,579.1	15,147.7	631.15	121.67
	April	724.4	7,568.6	15,092.4	628.85	115.20
	May	711.0	7,523.8	15,210.7	633.78	112.18
	June	786.4	7,686.9	15,524.7	646.86	121.58
	July	524.4	7,837.8			
	August	483.1				
	September	595.2				
	October	628.6				
	November	701.5				
	December	679.1				

(Source: U.S. Department of Commerce, Survey of Current Business.)

numbers is of course 400. Depending on whether monthly or quarterly data are involved, the adjustment factor is determined by

$$\text{Adjustment factor} = \frac{1,200}{\text{sum of modified means}} \qquad (16\text{-}11)$$

or
$$\text{Adjustment factor} = \frac{400}{\text{sum of modified means}} \qquad (16\text{-}12)$$

For the monthly data in Table 16-5 the sum of the modified means is 1,198.85. Therefore the adjustment factor by which each modified mean is to be multiplied to determine the seasonal index for that month is

$$\text{Adjustment factor} = \frac{1,200}{1,198.85} = 1.0010$$

The last column of Table 16-5 reports the seasonal index number for each month, based on analysis of the monthly data for 1972–1976. The lowest index, 67.65, is associated with August. In other words factory car sales in August averaged 67.65 percent of the sales in a typical month, a *negative* influence of 32.35 percent by the seasonal component for that month. On the other hand the highest seasonal index number, 123.86, is reported for October. This means that on the average there is a *positive* seasonal influence of 23.86 percent for October. A review of the 12 seasonal indexes in Table 16-5 indicates a positive seasonal influence for factory car sales during the spring months of March through June,

Table 16-5 Calculation of the seasonal index numbers from the 12-month moving averages

Month	12-month moving averages, % 1972	1973	1974	1975	1976	Modified mean	Seasonal index (mean × 1.0010)
January		112.78	89.24	72.75	96.79	93.01	93.11
February		105.08	81.95	71.74	100.00	90.98	91.07
March		114.36	91.39	87.49	121.67	102.88	102.98
April		102.43	102.56	106.97	115.20	104.76	104.87
May		114.33	116.44	112.55	112.19	113.44	113.55
June		114.43	109.46	114.15	121.58	114.29	114.40
July	55.90	91.10	93.30	90.37		90.73	90.83
August	51.80	57.91	77.24	83.30		67.58	67.65
September	111.51	96.38	115.46	107.60		109.56	109.67
October	114.94	132.31	147.04	115.15		123.73	123.86
November	112.14	126.25	98.00	89.83		105.07	105.18
December	89.32	79.72	78.38	85.91		82.82	82.90
Total						1,198.85	1,200.06

traditional months for new-car purchases in much of the country, and positive seasonal influences during September through November when the first runs of the new-model automobiles are produced and shipped to dealers.

16-5 APPLYING SEASONAL ADJUSTMENTS

When monthly data are reported for a historical time series, it is desirable to eliminate the influence of the seasonal component, generally so that effects of the trend and cyclical components can be detected. One way of eliminating the seasonal component is to compare the result for a month "this year" with the result for the same month "last year." For instance in Table 16-4 we can see that the factory car sales for December 1976 were 150,900 units higher than in December 1975 (679.1 compared with 528.2, in thousands of units). One important limitation for such "year-ago" comparisons is that adjoining months cannot be easily compared because of different seasonal influences. A more sophisticated approach is to eliminate the influence of the seasonal component from the time series by dividing each monthly (or quarterly) time-series value by the seasonal index number and then multiplying by 100 so that the units of measurement are the same as those in the original time series. No doubt, you have read and heard comparisons that have been made using such "seasonally adjusted values." The formula for determining the seasonally adjusted values is

$$\text{Seasonally adjusted value} = \frac{Y}{S} \times 100 \qquad (16\text{-}13)$$

where Y = monthly (or quarterly) time-series value

S = monthly (or quarterly) seasonal index number

Conceptually, we can observe that application of Formula (16-13) to all of the values in a monthly or quarterly times series eliminates the influence of the seasonal component, leaving the influences of the trend, cyclical, and irregular components:

$$\frac{Y}{S} = \frac{TCSI}{S} = TCI \qquad (16\text{-}14)$$

Table 16-6 reports the seasonally adjusted factory car sales based on the monthly sales reported in Table 16-4 and adjusted for the seasonal indexes determined in Table 16-5. Because the units reported are adjusted totals and not actual units of sales, it is most meaningful to make comparisons between such adjusted data in terms of percentage differences rather than differences in units as such. Thus by reference to Table 16-6 we can observe that on a seasonally adjusted basis factory sales in December 1976 increased compared with November 1976 by 22.8 percent $[(819.17/666.97) \times 100 = 122.8]$. Referring to Table 16-4, the change in factory car sales for the unadjusted data for these two months was a *decrease* of 3.2 percent $[(679.1/701.5) \times 100 = 96.8]$. How can the adjusted monthly data indicate an increase when there was actually a decrease? The fact is that there was a decrease in factory car sales in December 1976 compared with the preceding month but not nearly the decrease that would be expected based on the seasonal indexes for these two months. Note in Table 16-5 that the seasonal index for November is 105.18 and for December it is 82.90. Thus on a seasonally adjusted basis factory car sales increased in December 1976, indicating the existence of other positive influences for that month. Since the trend component is minor in month-to-month differences, the positive influences reflect primarily the effects of the cyclical and irregular components.

Table 16-6 Seasonally adjusted factory sales of domestic passenger cars from plants in the United States

Month	Factory sales, in millions of units				
	1972	1973	1974	1975	1976
January	715.31	923.46	592.97	389.66	650.97
February	786.32	895.47	550.68	392.34	691.89
March	743.06	857.26	540.98	424.16	745.68
April	702.68	750.08	588.73	505.29	690.76
May	702.75	775.05	597.96	488.93	626.14
June	665.71	763.35	540.36	499.37	687.39
July	433.36	745.93	567.24	513.62	577.37
August	548.41	614.48	614.63	662.08	714.11
September	737.51	607.39	555.14	552.31	542.74
October	679.58	716.31	615.71	543.69	507.52
November	786.68	786.39	475.01	511.90	666.97
December	803.61	611.70	475.27	637.15	819.17

16-6 FORECASTING BASED ON TREND AND SEASONAL FACTORS

Most of our attention in this chapter has been devoted to the analysis and identification of the historical influences on time-series values. Once the trend, cyclical, and seasonal components are identified, it would appear logical that this analysis should serve as the basis for forecasting future time-series values. Whereas the trend component can be represented by a least-squares equation and the seasonal component by a set of index numbers, no standard representation for the cyclical component serves as the basis for forecasting the influence of this component in future time-series values. However, use of business indicators of cyclical turning points, as described in the following section of this chapter, is the principal way by which the anticipated effects of the cyclical factor can be incorporated in a forecast.

Even though a forecast based only on the trend and seasonal components of a time series is decidedly incomplete, such a projected value is at least a beginning point in the forecasting process. In addition to adjusting such a forecast for anticipated cyclical effects, the analyst would also need to consider the unique market factors likely to influence production or sales during the period of concern.

While the trend equation is based on annual data, forecasts generally need to be made for particular months or quarters of a given year. Therefore the first step in using the trend equation for such a forecast is to "step down" the equation so that it is expressed in months (or quarters). The trend equation based on annual data has the base point at the middle of the first year of the time series. In the example in Table 16-2 the base year is 1950 and it is coded $X = 0$. To step down such an annual equation so that projected monthly values are obtained and so that the base point is at January 15 of the base year rather than at the midpoint in the year, we need to determine the following transformed equation:

$$Y_T(\text{monthly}) = \frac{a}{12} - 5.5\left(\frac{b}{144}\right) + \frac{b}{144}X \qquad (16\text{-}15)$$

In Formula (16-15) the values of a and b are obtained from the trend equation for the annual data. Similarly, a trend equation transformed to obtain projected quarterly trend values, and with the base point placed at the midpoint of the first quarter of the base year, is

$$Y_T(\text{quarterly}) = \frac{a}{4} - 1.5\left(\frac{b}{16}\right) + \frac{b}{16}X \qquad (16\text{-}16)$$

For example suppose that we wish to determine the projected monthly trend values for factory car sales of domestic passenger cars for January, February, and March of 1980. In Section 16-2 the annual trend equation was found to be

$$Y_T = a + bX = 5.375 + 0.107X$$

with the base year for this analysis being 1950 and with this year coded as $X = 0$.

This trend equation is transformed to a monthly equation with $X = 0$ at January 15 of 1950 as follows:

$$Y_T(\text{monthly}) = \frac{a}{12} - 5.5\left(\frac{b}{144}\right) + \frac{b}{144}X = \frac{5.375}{12} - 5.5\left(\frac{0.107}{144}\right) + \frac{0.107}{144}X$$

$$= 0.44792 - 0.00409 + 0.00074X = 0.44383 + 0.00074X$$

For monthly projection it is more convenient to express car sales in thousands of units instead of millions of units. Therefore we multiply the above equation by 1,000 so that the projected values are in thousands of units:

$$Y_T(\text{monthly}) = 1,000(0.44383 + 0.00074X) = 443.83 + 0.74X$$

Based on this transformed trend equation, the projected monthly trend values in thousands of units for January, February, and March of 1980, with $X = 0$ at January 1950, are, respectively,

$$Y_T = 443.83 + 0.74(360) = 710.23 \approx 710,230 \text{ units}$$

$$Y_T = 443.83 + 0.74(361) = 710.97 \approx 710,970 \text{ units}$$

$$Y_T = 443.83 + 0.74(362) = 711.71 \approx 711,710 \text{ units}$$

After the projected monthly trend values have been determined, each value is then multiplied by the seasonal index for that month (and divided by 100 to preserve the decimal location) to establish the projected value based on the historical analysis of both the trend and seasonal components of the series. The seasonal indexes for the factory sales of domestic passenger cars were determined in Table 16-5. The projected values for January, February, and March of 1980, based on the trend and seasonal components of the time series, are, respectively,

$$Y_{TS} = 710,230\left(\frac{93.11}{100}\right) = 661,295 \approx 661,000 \text{ units}$$

$$Y_{TS} = 710,970\left(\frac{91.07}{100}\right) = 647,480 \approx 647,000 \text{ units}$$

$$Y_{TS} = 711,710\left(\frac{102.98}{100}\right) = 732,919 \approx 733,000 \text{ units}$$

16-7 CYCLICAL FORECASTING AND BUSINESS INDICATORS

For short-term forecasting the effect of the cyclical component is often assumed to be the same as for the most recent period. Indeed, one approach to forecasting a value in the next period is simply to take the result for the last period and adjust it for the seasonal factor. However, when forecasts are concerned with results several months or quarters in the future or for even shorter periods during economic instability, the identification of *cyclical turning points* for the national economy is important. Of course the cyclical variations associated with a particular product may or may not coincide with the general business cycles.

The National Bureau of Economic Research (NBER) of the U.S. Department of Commerce has identified a number of economic time series that have historically tended to lead, coincide with, or lag behind the broad movements in aggregate economic activity. The groups of indexes described in this section are based on the 1975 revision to these indexes, which followed several years of review of the cyclical indicators previously used.

One group of indicators, called the *leading indicators*, have usually reached cyclical turning points before the corresponding change in general economic activity. Because of their importance in forecasting, these 12 series are listed in Table 16-7. The indexes are combined to form one composite index that can be used to forecast a cyclical turning point. Thus an analyst can refer to the leading indicators to incorporate the cyclical factor in his forecast. However, the indexes that are considered to be leading indicators of cyclical turning points are by no means completely consistent with one another. Also, incorrect signals of coming changes have occurred, and the length of time between correct signals and the actual cyclical turning point has varied historically. Therefore the forecaster has the ultimate responsibility for making judgments about future economic activity and cannot simply rely mechanistically on the leading indicators.

Two other groups of indexes identified by NBER are the *coincident indicators* and the *lagging indicators*. The coincident indicators are time series that have generally had turning points coinciding with the general business cycle. This composite index of four coincident indicators includes:

(41) Employees on nonagricultural payrolls
(47) Industrial production
(51) Personal income less transfer payments, in 1972 dollars
(57) Manufacturing and trade sales, in 1972 dollars

The lagging indicators are those time series for which the peaks and troughs usually lag behind those of the general business cycle. The composite index of six lagging indicators includes:

(62) Labor cost per unit of output, manufacturing
(70) Manufacturing and trade inventories, total, in 1972 dollars
(72) Commercial and industrial loans outstanding, weekly reporting of large commercial banks
(91) Average duration of unemployment (inverted)
(95) Ratio, consumer installment debt to personal income
(109) Average prime rate charged by banks

In addition to considering the effect of cyclical fluctuations and attempting to forecast cyclical turning points, as part of a total forecasting effort we also need to

Table 16-7 Composite index of 12 leading indicators (with individual index numbers)

Index no.	Indicator
1	Average work week of production workers, manufacturing
3	Layoff rate, manufacturing (inverted)
8	New orders, consumer goods and materials, 1972 dollars
12	Net business formation
19	Stock prices, 500 common stocks
20	Contracts and orders, plant and equipment, 1972 dollars
29	New building permits, private housing
32	Vendor performance
36	Change in inventories on hand and on order, 1972 dollars (smoothed)
92	Change in sensitive prices (smoothed)
104	Change in total liquid assets (M7) (smoothed)
105	Money supply (M1), 1972 dollars

(Source: U.S. Department of Commerce, Business Conditions Digest, September, 1977, p. 59.)

study specific causative factors that have influenced the time-series values in the past. For example such relationships as the effect of pricing strategy on sales volume can be studied by the application of regression and correlation analysis, as described in Chapters 14 and 15. Beyond historical analysis the possible effects associated with new products and with changing marketing environments also have to be considered. In the final analysis we are not only interested in forecasting the future but in exerting some control over future results.

16-8 EXPONENTIAL SMOOTHING AS A FORECASTING METHOD

A forecasting method widely used with time-series data, but not based directly on the use of the historical time-series components as such, is *exponential smoothing.* Essentially, it is a method by which the forecast is a kind of moving average, with the greatest weight given to the most recent results. It is not our purpose here to consider the mathematical foundation of exponential smoothing. In fact there are several types of exponential-smoothing models, and the method we present in this section is *single exponential smoothing*, which is the simplest of the several models available. Although it is not obvious by the way such smoothed values are calculated, the projected value is a weighted value of all past values, with the weight assigned to each value decreasing exponentially as that period is further removed historically from the forecast period.

The formula for determining the forecasted value for the next period in a time series by single exponential smoothing is

$$\hat{Y}_{t+1} = \hat{Y}_t + \alpha(Y_t - \hat{Y}_t) \qquad (16\text{-}17)$$

where $\hat{Y}_{t+1}$ = forecast for the next period

$\quad\quad\quad \hat{Y}_t$ = forecast for the last period

$\quad\quad\quad \alpha$ = smoothing constant with $(0 \leqslant \alpha \leqslant 1)$

$\quad\quad\quad Y_t$ = actual value for the last period

Because the actual value for the last period (which precedes the forecast period) has to be available to determine a forecast by exponential smoothing, it follows that such a forecast can only be made for the next period in the time series, not for several periods into the future. As indicated by Formula (16-17), the basis for the forecast for the next period is the forecast for the last (preceding) period plus the forecast error $Y_t - \hat{Y}_t$ multiplied by the smoothing constant α. When the value of α is set close to zero, previous forecasting errors are given a low weight, and the forecast tends toward a smooth moving average. When the value of α is set close to one, the forecast is more heavily weighted by the most recent results. If period-to-period forecast errors are largely a result of the irregular component of the time series, α should be set at a low value. On the other hand, if the forecast errors generally reflect trend or cyclical influences, α should be set at a high value so that the forecast will be responsive to such changes.

As an example of using single exponential smoothing, let us apply this technique to develop year-by-year forecasts for factory sales of domestic passenger cars for the years 1967 to 1977. Further, to demonstrate the effect on the forecast of using different α values, we determine two sets of forecasts with one based on $\alpha = 0.10$ and the other on $\alpha = 0.90$.

Table 16-8 reports the factory sales data as included originally in Table 16-1. Note that to begin the exponential-smoothing process a forecast *not* based on exponential smoothing has to be entered for the first year of the series. In Table 16-8 we begin simply by taking the actual sales amount of 8.337 million units for

Table 16-8 Single exponential forecasts for factory sales of domestic passenger cars in the United States

Year t	Factory sales, in millions of units* Y_t	$\alpha = 0.10$		$\alpha = 0.90$	
		Forecast $\hat{Y}_t$	Forecast error $(Y_t - \hat{Y}_t)$	Forecast $\hat{Y}_t$	Forecast error $(Y_t - \hat{Y}_t)$
1967	7.070	8.337	−1.267	8.337	−1.267
1968	8.407	8.210	0.197	7.197	1.210
1969	7.807	8.230	−0.423	8.286	−0.479
1970	6.187	8.188	−2.001	7.855	−1.668
1971	8.122	7.988	0.134	6.354	1.768
1972	8.353	8.001	0.352	7.945	0.408
1973	9.979	8.036	1.043	8.312	0.767
1974	6.721	8.140	−1.419	9.002	−2.281
1975	6.073	7.998	−1.925	6.949	−0.876
1976	7.838	7.806	0.032	6.161	1.677
1977		7.809		7.670	

*Source of data: Table 16-1.

1966 (from Table 16-1) as the forecast for 1967 for both sets of calculations. This "seed" forecast could also have been the forecasted trend value for that year or an average based on several preceding years. The forecast for 1968 with $\alpha = 0.10$ was determined as follows:

$$\hat{Y}_{t+1} = \hat{Y}_t + \alpha(Y_t - \hat{Y}_t)$$

$$\hat{Y}_{1968} = \hat{Y}_{1967} + \alpha(Y_{1967} - \hat{Y}_{1967})$$

$$\hat{Y}_{1968} = 8.337 + 0.10(-1.267) = 8.337 - 0.1267 = 8.2103 \approx 8.210$$

Similarly, the forecast for 1968 with $\alpha = 0.90$ was determined as follows:

$$\hat{Y}_{1968} = 8.337 + 0.90(-1.267) = 8.337 - 1.1403 = 7.1967 \approx 7.197$$

The year-by-year forecasts for the years following 1968 were similarly calculated. As compared with the forecasts based on $\alpha = 0.10$, the forecasts based on $\alpha = 0.90$ are more responsive to the yearly variations in the factory car sales, and for these data the absolute values of the forecast error based on $\alpha = 0.10$ are lower. Of course it may be that some other value of α would yield still a better exponential moving average, and historical analysis could be directed toward such a search.

In general, single exponential smoothing is most effective as a forecasting method when cyclical and irregular components comprise the main effects on the time-series values. When there is a definite linear trend effect, double exponential smoothing yields a better forecast. Triple exponential smoothing is appropriate when the trend equation is not linear, and other methods are available that incorporate the effect of the seasonal component. These more advanced models in exponential smoothing are covered in specialized textbooks on forecasting.

16-9 SUMMARY

Classical time-series analysis is concerned with the analysis of historical time-series data to determine the time-related influences of the *trend* (*T*), *cyclical* (*C*), *seasonal* (*S*), and *irregular* (*I*) components of the time series. The model underlying the analysis is based on the assumption that these components have a multiplicative relationship. Where Y represents the time-series value, the classical time-series model is $Y = TCSI$. This model serves as the basis for analyzing the influence of each component on historical time-series data and as a possible basis for forecasting future time-series values.

The *trend component* of the time series is defined algebraically by identifying the least-squares equation for the long-term trend in the time-series values. Because the historical time-series values are not random-sample data and because autocorrelation typically exists with such data, it is not appropriate statistically to construct prediction intervals for forecasted trend values.

For historical data the influence of the *cyclical component* of the time series can be determined by dividing annual data by the respective trend values, thus identifying the cyclical relative for each year. These cyclical relatives can then be graphed to form a cycle chart. However, such cyclical relatives do not constitute a basis for forecasting. Instead, the *leading indicators* as identified by the National Bureau of Economic Research (NBER) are useful in the attempt to forecast *cyclical turning points.* The NBER has also identified time series that are useful as *coincident indicators* and *lagging indicators* of broad movements in aggregate economic activity.

Seasonal variations occur within each year of a time series, and the effect of this component is represented by a set of monthly (or quarterly) seasonal index numbers. The procedure most frequently used to determine such seasonal indexes is the *ratio-to-moving-average method.* After the seasonal indexes have been determined, historical data can be *deseasonalized* so that month-to-month comparisons can be made with the seasonal influence removed. Such deseasonalized values are also called *seasonally adjusted values.*

The trend and historical components of the time series can be used as a basic-beginning point for forecasting. When the forecasts are to be made for monthly (or quarterly) results, it is necessary to *step down* the annual trend equation so that it is directed toward monthly (or quarterly) results. The projected trend value is then adjusted by use of the seasonal index. The business indicators can then be referenced to make judgments about the likely effect of the cyclical component in the forecast period. Beyond this, specific product plans and specific market conditions need to be considered.

Another forecasting method widely used with time-series data is *exponential smoothing.* Of several methods available, the technique of *single exponential smoothing* was described in this chapter. The name of this technique is derived from the fact that the historical values of the time series are assigned weights that decrease exponentially as the period is further removed from the forecast period, and this weighted, or smoothed, average serves as the basis for the forecast. However, the computational method used in the method of exponential smoothing does not make it necessary to determine the weights as such.

FORMULAS

(16-1) $Y = TCSI$ Classical time-series model.

(16-2) $Y_T = a + bX$ Linear trend equation.

(16-3) $b = \dfrac{\Sigma XY - n\bar{X}\bar{Y}}{\Sigma X^2 - n\bar{X}^2}$ Value of b for the linear trend equation, which is the slope of the trend line.

(16-4) $a = \bar{Y} - b\bar{X}$ The value of a for the linear trend equation.

(16-5) $Y_T = ab^X$ Exponential trend equation.

(16-6) $\log Y_T = \log a + X \log b$ Transformation of the exponential trend equation into a linear equation by taking the logarithm of both sides of the exponential equation.

(16-7) $Y = TC$

Components of the time series for annual data.

(16-8) $C = \dfrac{Y}{T} = \dfrac{Y}{Y_T}$

Determining the effect of the cyclical component for historical time-series data.

(16-9) Moving average $= TC$

Twelve-month or four-quarter moving average, which reflects the influence of the trend and cyclical components of the time series.

(16-10) $\dfrac{Y}{\text{Moving average}} = \dfrac{TCSI}{TC} = SI$

Dividing a monthly (or quarterly) time-series value by a twelve-month (or four-quarter) moving average leaves the effects associated with the seasonal and irregular components of the time series.

(16-11) Adjustment factor

$$= \dfrac{1{,}200}{\text{sum of modified means}}$$

Adjustment factor used in the final step of the ratio-to-moving-average method for determining monthly seasonal index numbers.

(16-12) Adjustment factor

$$= \dfrac{400}{\text{sum of modified means}}$$

Adjustment factor used in the final step of the ratio-to-moving-average method for determining quarterly seasonal index numbers.

(16-13) Seasonally adjusted values

$$= \dfrac{Y}{S} \times 100$$

Determination of seasonally adjusted, or deseasonalized, values.

(16-14) $\dfrac{Y}{S} = \dfrac{TCSI}{S} = TCI$

Dividing monthly (or quarterly) time-series values by the seasonal index leaves the influence of the trend, cyclical, and irregular components in the deseasonalized data.

(16-15) $Y_T(\text{monthly}) = \dfrac{a}{12} - 5.5\left(\dfrac{b}{144}\right)$

$$+ \dfrac{b}{144}X$$

Stepping down of an annual trend equation so that it is applicable for projecting monthly trend values.

(16-16) $\quad Y_T(\text{quarterly}) = \dfrac{a}{4} - 1.5\left(\dfrac{b}{16}\right)$

$$+ \dfrac{b}{16}X$$

Stepping down of an annual trend equation so that it is applicable for projecting quarterly trend values.

(16-17) $\quad \hat{Y}_{t+1} = \hat{Y}_t + \alpha(Y_t - \hat{Y}_t)$

Determining the forecasted time-series value for the next period by single exponential smoothing.

EXERCISES

16-1 Indicate the component of the time series with which each of the following events would be associated by posting a T for trend, S for seasonal, C for cyclical, and I for irregular:

_____(a) An upturn in business activity

_____(b) Inclement weather resulting in the postponement of consumer purchases

_____(c) A fire at the subcontractor's plant resulting in a delay in parts deliveries

_____(d) The annual January white sale in a department store

_____(e) General increase in the demand for videotape recorders

16-2 The following data represent the annual sales of the Acme Tool Company (fictional), which began operations in 1970.

(a) Construct a line chart to portray these data graphically.

(b) Determine the linear trend equation for these data by the least-squares method, coding 1970 as 0 and carrying all values to two places beyond the decimal point.

(c) Enter the trend line on the graph constructed in Exercise 16-2a.

Year	Sales, in $millions
1970	0.2
1971	0.4
1972	0.5
1973	0.9
1974	1.1
1975	1.5
1976	1.3
1977	1.1
1978	1.7
1979	1.9
1980	2.3

16-3 Construct a cycle chart for the data in Exercise 16-2, utilizing the linear trend equation determined in Exercise 16-2b.

16-4 The following data are the quarterly sales for the Acme Tool Company (fictional) for the years 1975–1980.

(a) Compute the four-quarter moving averages and the moving totals for these data.

(b) Compute the centered moving average.

(c) Determine the quarterly seasonal indexes for these data by the ratio-to-moving-average method. Calculate the percents of moving average and the seasonal index numbers to the first position beyond the decimal point.

(d) Interpret the meaning of the indexes determined in Exercise 16-4c.

	Annual sales, in $1,000s					
Quarter	1975	1976	1977	1978	1979	1980
1	500	450	350	550	550	750
2	350	350	200	350	400	500
3	250	200	150	250	350	400
4	400	300	400	550	600	650

16-5 For the data in Exercise 16-4

(*a*) Compute the seasonally adjusted value for each quarter, rounding the value to whole thousand dollar amounts.

(*b*) Compare the results in the third and fourth quarters of 1980 based on (1) the reported level of sales and (2) the seasonally adjusted values.

16-6 Step down the trend equation determined in Exercise 16-2*b* so that it is expressed in terms of quarters instead of years. Also adjust the equation so that the trend values are in thousands of dollars instead of millions of dollars. Carry the final values to the first place beyond the decimal point.

16-7 Based on the quarterly trend and seasonal components of the time series in Exercise 16-4, as determined in Exercises 16-6 and 16-4, respectively, forecast the level of quarterly sales for each quarter of 1981.

16-8 Refer to the data in Exercise 16-2. Using the actual level of sales for 1974 (1.1 million dollars) as the forecast for 1975, determine the forecast for each annual sales amount for the years 1976–1981 by the method of single exponential smoothing. Apply a smoothing constant of $\alpha = 0.20$, and round your forecast to one place beyond the decimal point.

16-9 With respect to Exercise 16-8 apply a smoothing constant of $\alpha = 0.80$ to determine the forecast amounts. Compare your results with those obtained in Exercise 16-8.

16-10 The following data represent the monthly sales volume, in thousands of dollars, of a fictional toy-manufacturing firm incorporated July 1, 1977.

(*a*) Construct a line chart to portray graphically the annual sales totals, using the fiscal year of July 1 to June 30, rather than the calendar year, as the basis for the totals.

(*b*) Determine the linear trend equation for these data by the least-squares method, coding the 1977–1978 fiscal year as 0. Carry all calculated values to the second position beyond the decimal point.

(*c*) Enter the trend line on the graph constructed in Exercise 16-10*a*.

	Year				
Month	1977	1978	1979	1980	1981
January	. . .	2.7	2.9	4.3	4.8
February	. . .	2.8	3.6	4.2	5.4
March	. . .	3.4	4.1	4.8	6.0
April	. . .	3.6	4.5	5.7	6.7
May	. . .	3.8	4.9	6.1	7.0
June	. . .	4.0	5.0	6.2	6.9
July	3.5	4.3	5.2	6.6	. . .
August	3.4	4.5	5.1	6.8	. . .
September	4.5	5.7	6.0	8.5	. . .
October	5.5	7.0	8.2	10.1	. . .
November	6.0	6.9	7.9	10.3	. . .
December	4.8	5.0	6.0	7.4	. . .

16-11 From the data in Exercise 16-10

(a) Determine the seasonal indexes for the sales values; because percents of moving average for only three years will be available at that step of your calculations, determine the monthly indexes by calculating the means of these ratios, instead of calculating modified means. Calculate the percents of moving average and the seasonal index numbers to the first position beyond the decimal point.

(b) For which month is the seasonal index highest?

(c) For which month is the seasonal index lowest?

16-12 From Exercise 16-10

(a) Compute the seasonally adjusted values for the monthly data using the indexes determined in Exercise 16-11.

(b) Compare the actual monthly sales for this company for the months of November and December 1980. Then compare the seasonally adjusted values for November and December 1980. Explain the difference in the two comparisons.

16-13 Step down the linear trend equation determined in Exercise 16-10 so that it is expressed in months instead of years, with $X = 0$ at July 1977 for these fiscal year data. Round the values in the final equation to the third place beyond the decimal.

16-14 Based on the monthly trend and seasonal components of the time series in Exercise 16-10, as determined in Exercises 16-13 and 16-11, respectively, forecast the level of monthly sales for the 1981–1982 fiscal year, which begins at July 1, 1981. Round the forecasts to the first place beyond the decimal point (expressed in thousands of dollars).

16-15 Refer to the data in Exercise 16-10.

(a) Using the annual sales total of 48.0 thousand dollars for the 1977–1978 fiscal year as the forecast ("seed") for the 1978–1979 fiscal year, use the method of single exponential smoothing to forecast the sales amounts for the 1979–1980, 1980–1981, and 1981–1982 fiscal years. Use a smoothing constant of $\alpha = 0.80$.

(b) Compare the forecast for the 1981–1982 fiscal year based on exponential smoothing with the forecast that would be made using the linear trend equation determined in Exercise 16-10b.

16-16 The following table indicates new plant and equipment expenditures for manufacturing industries in the United States for the 20-year period 1957–1976. Determine the linear-trend equation for these data, designating 1957 as the base ($X = 0$ at 1957). Carry your calculations to the second place beyond the decimal point.

Year	Expenditures, in $billions	Year	Expenditures, in $billions
1957	15.96	1967	28.51
1958	11.44	1968	28.37
1959	12.08	1969	31.68
1960	14.48	1970	31.95
1961	13.68	1971	29.99
1962	14.68	1972	31.35
1963	15.69	1973	38.01
1964	18.58	1974	46.01
1965	22.45	1975	47.95
1966	26.99	1976	52.48

(Source: U.S. Department of Commerce, Survey of Current Business.)

16-17 Construct a line chart for the data in Exercise 16-16, and enter the trend line on this chart.

16-18 For the data reported in Exercise 16-16

    (*a*) Determine the cyclical relatives for the annual time-series.

    (*b*) Prepare a cycle chart.

16-19 The following table presents quarterly data for new plant and equipment expenditures for manufacturing industries in the United States for the five-year period 1972–1976, in billions of dollars. Determine the seasonal indexes for these expenditures by the ratio-to-moving-average method. Calculate the percents of moving average to two places beyond the decimal point and the seasonal index numbers to the first place beyond the decimal point.

Quarter	Annual plant and equipment expenditures, in $billions				
	1972	1973	1974	1975	1976
I	6.61	7.80	9.49	10.84	10.96
II	7.63	9.16	11.27	12.15	12.66
III	7.74	9.62	11.62	11.67	13.48
IV	9.38	11.43	13.63	13.30	15.38

(Source: U.S. Department of Commerce, Survey of Current Business.)

16-20 (*a*) Determine the seasonally adjusted values for the quarterly plant and equipment expenditures presented in Exercise 16-19, using the seasonal indexes determined in that exercise.

    (*b*) Compare the actual expenditures for plant and equipment in the third and fourth quarters of 1976; similarly, compare the seasonally adjusted values for these two quarters, and explain the difference between these two comparisons.

16-21 Step down the trend equation determined in Exercise 16-16 so that it is expressed in quarters, with the base quarter being the first quarter of 1972. Round your final equation to the third place beyond the decimal.

16-22 Based on the quarterly trend and seasonal components of the time series presented in Exercise 16-16, as determined in Exercises 16-21 and 16-19, respectively, forecast the quarterly level of plant and equipment expenditures for the four quarters of 1977.

16-23 Refer to the data in Exercise 16-16.

    (*a*) Using the 1970 expenditures amount of 31.95 billion dollars as the forecast for 1971, determine the year-by-year forecasts for 1972–1977 by the method of single exponential smoothing; use a smoothing constant of $\alpha = 0.80$.

    (*b*) Determine the forecast for 1977 based on the linear trend equation determined in Exercise 16-16, and compare this forecast with the forecast for 1977 determined in Exercise 16-23*a*.

16-24 Identify the types of business indicators published by the National Bureau of Economic Research (NBER) and describe their use in cyclical forecasting.

SEVENTEEN

INDEX NUMBERS

17-1 INTRODUCTION

An *index number* is a percentage ratio of prices, quantities, or values for two time periods or two points in time. The time period that serves as the basis for the comparison and for which the measure is in the denominator of the ratio is called the *base period*. The period that is compared with the base period and for which the measure is in the numerator of the ratio is called the *given period*.

Measurements compared by an index number can be concerned with quantity, price, or value. An index number that represents a percentage comparison of the number of automobiles sold in a given month as compared with that of a base month is an example of a *quantity index*. An index number of 110 would mean that automobile sales in the given month were 10 percent higher than in the base month. A quantity index of 90 would indicate that the number of automobiles sold in the given month was 90 percent of the quantity sold in the base month, or a reduction of 10 percent in quantity sold. A *price index* represents a comparison of prices between two time periods. For example a price index of 108 for a designated make of automobile would indicate that the price in the given period was 8 percent higher than the price in the base period. Finally, a *value index* is one that represents a comparison of the total value of production or sales in two time periods without regard to whether the observed difference is a result of differences in quantity, price, or both. Thus an index number that compares the level of retail sales in two time periods in terms of dollars is an example of a value index.

Index numbers are also differentiated according to the number of commodities or products included in the comparison. A *simple index number* is a percentage ratio that represents a comparison for a *single* product or commodity. Thus a price index for the per-gallon price of lead-free gasoline in January 1980 compared with January 1978 would be a simple price index. An *aggregate index number*, or *composite index number*, is one that represents a comparison for a group of products or commodities. The Consumer Price Index (CPI), which represents a price comparison for a group of commodities rather than for a single commodity, is an example of a composite price index. Two problems inherent in the determination of composite indexes are which commodities should be included in the comparison and how the respective prices (or quantities) should be weighted. That is, if we were simply to aggregate the price per unit of each commodity, such as one-half gallon of milk and one dozen eggs, the resulting composite might not be meaningful because it would not reflect the importance of each of the commodities to consumers. Various approaches to applying statistical weights to the prices of individual commodities are described in Section 17-3 on the construction of aggregate price indexes.

17-2 CONSTRUCTION OF SIMPLE INDEXES

Where p_n designates the price of a single commodity in the given period and p_0 indicates the price of the commodity in the base period, the general formula for calculating the *simple price index*, or *price relative*, is

$$I_p = \frac{p_n}{p_0} \times 100 \qquad (17\text{-}1)$$

Table 17-1 reports the average price and the monthly per-capita consumption for three commodities in 1975 and in 1980, with 1975 taken as the base year for

Table 17-1 Price and consumption data for three commodities in a particular metropolitan area, 1975 and 1980

Commodity	Unit quotation	Average price, $		Per-capita consumption, mo	
		1975, p_0	1980, p_n	1975, q_0	1980, q_n
Milk, homogenized	$\frac{1}{2}$ gal	0.69	0.84	12.0	15.5
Bread, white	1-lb loaf	0.50	0.59	3.9	3.8
Coffee, regular grind	1-lb can	1.78	3.10	1.1	0.7

the comparison (data are fictional). The simple price index for milk, based on these data, is

$$I_p = \frac{p_n}{p_0} \times 100 = \frac{0.84}{0.69} \times 100 = 121.7$$

This price index of 121.7 indicates that the price of one-half gallon of milk was 21.7 percent higher in 1980 compared with 1975. The student may wish to verify that the simple price indexes for bread and coffee are 118.0 and 174.2, respectively.

Where q_n designates the quantity of an item produced or sold in the given period and q_0 indicates the quantity produced or sold in the base period, the general formula for calculating the *simple quantity index*, or *quantity relative*, is

$$I_q = \frac{q_n}{q_0} \times 100 \qquad (17\text{-}2)$$

Refer to Table 17-1. The simple quantity index comparing the consumption of coffee during 1980 with 1975 is

$$I_q = \frac{q_n}{q_0} \times 100 = \frac{0.7}{1.1} \times 100 = 63.6$$

This quantity index of 63.6 indicates that consumption of coffee in 1980 was 63.6 percent of the consumption in 1975, or a reduction of 36.4 percent. Based on the data in Table 17-1, the simple quantity indexes for milk and bread are 129.2 and 97.4, respectively.

Finally, the *value* of a commodity in a particular time period is equal to the price of the commodity multiplied by the quantity produced (or sold). Therefore $p_n q_n$ designates the value of a commodity in the given period and $p_0 q_0$ designates the value of the commodity in the base period. The general formula for the *simple value index*, or *value relative*, is

$$I_v = \frac{p_n q_n}{p_0 q_0} \times 100 \qquad (17\text{-}3)$$

Based on the data in Table 17-1, the simple value index for milk is

$$I_v = \frac{p_n q_n}{p_0 q_0} \times 100 = \frac{0.84(15.5)}{0.69(12.0)} \times 100 = 157.2$$

Thus the per-capita value of the milk consumed in 1980 was 57.2 percent higher in 1980 than in 1975 in this metropolitan area. The student may wish to verify that the value relatives for bread and coffee are 115.0 and 110.8, respectively.

17-3 CONSTRUCTION OF AGGREGATE PRICE INDEXES

Typically, the objective of constructing an aggregate price index is to provide the basis for comparing the general price levels for a large group of commodities. For example the Consumer Price Index is often used as an indicator of the cost of living. For such an index the universe of commodities to be described must first be defined. The number of commodities typically is large, and therefore a sample of commodities must usually be chosen for use in calculating the aggregate price index. Because of the necessity of using a sample of items that includes the most important commodities and that is considered representative of the total group of commodities, the sample is chosen based on historical analysis and judgment. Furthermore, to have comparability from period to period, the same commodities are often included in the sample for each period. Thus the sampling method used in constructing such an aggregate price index is a judgment sample rather than a random sample, and the methods of statistical inference, such as interval estimation and hypothesis testing, cannot be used in conjunction with such a sample. The Consumer Price Index, however, is an aggregate price index that incorporates probability sampling.

Having chosen the commodities to be used as the sample items for an aggregate price index, the analyst must then decide how to weight the price of each item in the composite index. One possible approach would be simply to accumulate the unit prices of the several commodities included in the index. Such an index, called a *simple aggregate price index*, is determined by the following formula:

$$I_p(\text{simple aggregate}) = \frac{\Sigma p_n}{\Sigma p_0} \times 100 \qquad (17\text{-}4)$$

Usually, a simple aggregate price index is not meaningful and is not representative of broader price changes or even of the expenditures for the particular commodities included in the index. The reason it is not representative is that the weight of each item in the index is based on the unit of quotation rather than on the importance of the commodity in terms of the amount purchased by the typical consumer. For the data given in Table 17-1 the simple aggregate price relative is

$$I_p(\text{simple aggregate}) = \frac{\Sigma p_n}{\Sigma p_0} \times 100 = \frac{0.84 + 0.59 + 3.10}{0.69 + 0.50 + 1.78} \times 100 = \frac{4.53}{2.97} \times 100$$

$$= 152.5$$

Although this index indicates a composite price rise of 52.5 percent, it does not recognize that the commodity with the largest price rise (coffee) has a lower level of per-capita consumption per month in terms of its unit of quotation compared with the other commodities. For example in the base year 1975, 12.0 half-gallons of milk were consumed per month while only 1.1 pounds of coffee were consumed each month. To weight these two commodities arbitrarily according to unit of quotation results in a misleading aggregate price index. In the remainder of this section we describe several basic approaches used to assign weights to the prices of the commodities in an aggregate price index. All of these methods are based on using quantities as weights but differ in whether base-period or given-period quantities are used, and how these quantity weights are used.

The *Laspeyres price index*, named after the statistician who first suggested the use of this index, is an aggregate price index in which the price of each commodity is weighted by the quantity of consumption in the *base period*. The formula for calculating this index is

$$I_p(\text{L}) = \frac{\Sigma p_n q_0}{\Sigma p_0 q_0} \times 100 \qquad (17\text{-}5)$$

Table 17-2 is the worktable for determining the Laspeyres price index for the data in Table 17-1. The Laspeyres aggregate price index for these data is

$$I_p(\text{L}) = \frac{\Sigma p_n q_0}{\Sigma p_0 q_0} \times 100 = \frac{15.79}{12.19} \times 100 = 129.5$$

This price index of 129.5 indicates that this market basket of goods cost 29.5 percent more in 1980 than in 1975, using the quantities (consumption) of the base period as the basis for the weights. One criticism of the Laspeyres index is associated with the fact that important price changes often cause patterns of consumption to change, with consumption increasing for commodities with decreasing prices and consumption decreasing for items with relatively large increases in price. However, because the Laspeyres index uses base-period weights, it does not recognize such shifts in consumption and therefore tends to result in a positive bias in the value of the composite price index. In our example we can observe that the price of coffee increased from \$1.78 to \$3.10 per pound between 1975 and 1980, while per-capita consumption decreased from 1.1 to 0.7 pound per month, perhaps partly in response to this price rise. Because the Laspeyres index utilizes base-period quantities as weights, this decline in consumption is not reflected in the composite price index.

The *Paasche price index* is an aggregate price index in which the price of each commodity is weighted by the quantity of consumption in the *given period*. The formula for calculating this index is

$$I_p(\text{P}) = \frac{\Sigma p_n q_n}{\Sigma p_0 q_n} \times 100 \qquad (17\text{-}6)$$

Table 17-3 is the worktable for determining the Paasche index for the data in Table 17-1. The Paasche aggregate price index for these data is

$$I_p(\text{P}) = \frac{\Sigma p_n q_n}{\Sigma p_0 q_n} \times 100 = \frac{17.43}{13.85} \times 100 = 125.8$$

Table 17-2 Worktable for calculating Laspeyres aggregate price index

Commodity	$p_0 q_0$	$p_n q_0$
Milk, homogenized	8.28	10.08
Bread, white	1.95	2.30
Coffee, regular grind	1.96	3.41
	$\Sigma p_0 q_0 = 12.19$	$\Sigma p_n q_0 = 15.79$

Table 17-3 Worktable for calculating the Paasche aggregate price index

Commodity	$p_0 q_n$	$p_n q_n$
Milk, homogenized	10.70	13.02
Bread, white	1.90	2.24
Coffee, regular grind	1.25	2.17
	$\Sigma p_0 q_n = 13.85$	$\Sigma p_n q_n = 17.43$

Thus this Paasche price index of 125.8 is somewhat lower than the Laspeyres price index of 129.5. Although the Paasche index recognizes shifts in consumption by using given-period quantities as weights, to the extent that consumers are forced to curtail certain purchases and lower their standard of living, the Paasche index tends to understate the price increase in the market basket of goods. Another difficulty associated with using the Paasche price index is that the weights, or quantities, must be obtained for every period for which price indexes are to be computed, thereby adding considerably to the cost of data collection.

The *Fisher ideal price index* represents an attempt to correct the positive bias inherent in the Laspeyres index and the negative bias inherent in the Paasche index by defining the composite price index as the geometric mean of the other two indexes. The computational formula for the Fisher ideal price index is

$$I_p(F) = \sqrt{\frac{\Sigma p_n q_0}{\Sigma p_0 q_0} \frac{\Sigma p_n q_n}{\Sigma p_0 q_n}} \times 100 \tag{17-7}$$

or

$$I_p(F) = \sqrt{I_p(L) \, I_p(P)} \tag{17-8}$$

Based on the calculations in Table 17-2 and 17-3, the Fisher ideal index for the data in Table 17-1 is

$$I_p(F) = \sqrt{\frac{\Sigma p_n q_0}{\Sigma p_0 q_0} \frac{\Sigma p_n q_n}{\Sigma p_0 q_n}} \times 100 = \sqrt{\frac{15.79}{12.19} \frac{17.43}{13.85}} \times 100 = \sqrt{1.295(1.258)} \times 100$$

$$= 127.6$$

Thus the Fisher ideal index of 127.6 indicates that there was a 27.6 percent increase in the price of the market basket of goods represented by the commodities in Table 17-1. As was true for the Paasche index, the Fisher ideal index also requires determination of quantity weights for every period for which a price index is to be determined, and thus it is also a relatively expensive method to use.

The Laspeyres, Paasche, and Fisher methods of constructing aggregate price indexes can be described as following the *weighted-aggregate-of-prices approach*. An alternative is the *weighted-average-of-price-relatives approach*. By this method the simple price index for each commodity in the market basket is weighted by a value figure *pq*. The values used may be either the base-period values $p_0 q_0$ or the given-period values $p_n q_n$. Of these two possibilities the base-period values are more frequently used because of the greater cost associated with determining given-period values for every period for which a price index is to be determined. With base-period values used as weights, the formula for the weighted average of price relatives is

$$I_p(W) = \frac{\Sigma(p_0 q_0)[(p_n/p_0) \times 100]}{\Sigma p_0 q_0} \qquad (17\text{-}9)$$

Table 17-4 is the worktable for determining the weighted average of price relatives for the data in Table 17-1. The aggregate price index is

$$I_p(W) = \frac{\Sigma(p_0 q_0)[(p_n/p_0) \times 100]}{\Sigma p_0 q_0} = \frac{1,579.21}{12.19} = 129.5$$

The fact that this price index is equal to the Laspeyres price index for our example is not a coincidence. Algebraically, the weighted average of price relatives is equivalent to the Laspeyres index when base-period values are used as the weights. The weighted-average-of-price-relatives is frequently used. The reason for the popularity of this method is that by this procedure the simple price indexes are computed first, and these simple indexes typically are desired for purposes of comparison in addition to the aggregate price indexes. Although the base-period values often are used as the weights in determining such a price index, after an index series has been calculated for a number of years, the base-year consumption patterns are not very representative of consumption patterns in the later years of the series. For this reason some intermediate year in the series is then generally designated as the year for which the value weights are used, although the prices are still the base-year prices. For instance in September 1978 the consumer price index was calculated with 1967 as the base year but with the 1972-1973 period providing the value weights.

In this section we have been concerned only with the determination of aggregate price indexes. When *aggregate quantity indexes* are determined, the same problems of sampling the commodities and of weighting the quantities of the individual commodities are encountered. While the quantities, or levels of consumption, are used as the basis for attaching weights to the individual prices in an aggregate price index, the prices of the commodities are used as the basis for the weights when an aggregate quantity index is calculated. Again, we have the alternatives of whether the prices in the base period, the given period, or some intermediate period should be used.

Table 17-4 Worktable for calculating the weighted average of price relatives

Commodity	Price relative $(p_n/p_0) \times 100$	Value weight $p_0 q_0$	Price relative $\times$ value weight
Milk, homogenized	121.7	8.28	1,007.68
Bread, white	118.0	1.95	230.10
Coffee, regular grind	174.2	1.96	341.43
		$\Sigma p_0 q_0 = 12.19$	$\Sigma = 1,579.21$

17-4 SPLICING TWO SERIES OF INDEX NUMBERS

An aggregate index number may undergo substantial change by the addition or deletion of items or products or by changes in the weights used to calculate the index. The year in which such a major change is made often is defined as the *base year* for a new series of index numbers. But for the purposes of historical comparison it may be desirable to have a unified series of index numbers that includes the time periods before the change in items or products (denoted by "old") as well as after the change (denoted by "new"). The process by which two series of index numbers based on different products and/or different weights are combined is called *splicing*. Splicing two such time series of index numbers to form one continuous series requires that the two series have one year of overlap such that both types of index numbers have been calculated for that year (or period). The index numbers then revised in the process of splicing are the index numbers of the old series, with the overlap year serving as the base for the combined series. As indicated above, this year typically is also the year in which the changes in products and/or weights was made.

For an aggregate price index, suppose that the old index number for the overlap year in the combined time series is designated $I_p(\text{old})$. The first step in the process of splicing is to determine the quotient obtained by dividing the new index number for this overlap year by the old index for this year. Because this overlap year typically is the new base year, $I_p(\text{new}) = 100$, and the quotient is determined by

$$Q = \frac{I_p(\text{new})}{I_p(\text{old})} = \frac{100}{I_p(\text{old})} \qquad (17\text{-}10)$$

The second step in the process of splicing is to multiply each of the index numbers in the old time series by the quotient determined by Formula (17-10) to calculate the new index numbers:

$$I_p(\text{new}) = I_p(\text{old})Q \qquad (17\text{-}11)$$

As an example of splicing two series of index numbers, Table 17-5 presents two fictional series of aggregate price indexes: one computed for a group of commodities for the years 1970–1975 with the base year being 1970, and the other beginning in 1975 for a revised group of commodities. Thus 1975 is the overlap year for which both types of indexes were determined. The index quotient for 1975 as the overlap year is

$$Q = \frac{100}{I_p(\text{old})} = \frac{100}{134.4} = 0.7446$$

Multiplication of each of the old index numbers in the first column of Table 17-5 by this quotient yields the revised index numbers for 1970–1975 posted in the last column of the table.

Table 17-5 Splicing two series of aggregate price indexes

Year	Old price-index series (1970 = 100)	New price-index series (1975 = 100)	Spliced price-index series (1975 = 100)
1970	100.0		74.5
1971	103.1		76.8
1972	109.7		81.7
1973	118.2		88.0
1974	126.6		94.3
1975	134.3	100.0	100.0
1976		105.9	105.9
1977		111.4	111.4
1978		116.2	116.2
1979		121.1	121.1
1980		125.0	125.0

Although splicing makes it possible to achieve a form of numerical comparability between two series of indexes, use of this method does not solve the basic problem of changing consumption patterns and the associated changes that have to be made in the products that serve as the sample for the aggregate index and the weights attached to their prices. For example refer to the last column of Table 17-5. It is correct to compare any of the indexes before 1975 with the 1975 index, because the old 1975 index was based on the same market basket of items as the indexes for the earlier years. Similarly, the new indexes after 1975 can be compared with the 1975 index because the index of 100 for 1975 is based on the new market basket. (Recall that as the overlap year, two indexes were determined for 1975, one for the old market basket and one for the new market basket.) But any of the indexes for the years after 1975 cannot be compared directly with the indexes for the years before 1975, because they are based on a different market basket of items. Because of this problem, it is desirable that the market basket that serves as the basis for an aggregate price index be changed only infrequently so that direct numerical comparability can be maintained. Yet, changing consumption patterns require that the market basket be periodically modified so that it is reflective of the prices for products important in the current time period.

17-5 THE CONSUMER PRICE INDEX (CPI)

The *Consumer Price Index* (CPI) is the most widely known of the published indexes because of its use as an indicator of the cost of living. There is some controversy among statisticians as to whether the objective of measuring the cost of living is in fact achieved. It is published monthly by the Bureau of Labor Statistics of the United States Department of Labor.

The CPI has its origins in the development of the so-called cost-of-living index by the Bureau of Labor Statistics for use in determining "fair" wage scales in the shipbuilding industry during World War I. In February 1921 regular, periodic publication of the National Consumer Price Index in roughly its present form was established, with the base period being 1917-1919. Quarterly indexes were initiated in 1935, and monthly indexes were initiated in 1940. Although many changes in scope, coverage, frequency, and publication format have occurred over the years, the consistent objective of the index has been to measure changes in the retail price of a fixed market basket of goods and services.

Several major revisions of the Consumer Price Index have been made. The first major revision was completed in 1940, in which emphasis was placed on food-expenditure patterns in cities rather than regions, new commodities were added, and the base period was shifted to 1935-1939. During World War II, the weights to calculate the index were adjusted to reflect the realities of wartime shortages and rationing, and in 1946 prewar weight patterns were restored, and improvements in price-survey techniques were instituted. Another comprehensive revision was begun in 1949 and completed in 1953 for which the 1947-1949 period then served as the base period. In 1964 a new and expanded sample of metropolitan areas and small urban places was introduced based on the 1960 census. For the first time probability-sampling techniques were used to select items for pricing, and the base period was changed to 1957-1959.

The lastest revision of the CPI was begun in 1970 and completed in 1978. As with previous revisions, underlying objectives included the updating of weights, sample items, and the sample of retail stores surveyed. In addition the use of sophisticated methods of probability sampling was expanded. However, a broader objective was associated with the interpretation, or meaning, given to the CPI. Up to the 1978 revision the Consumer Price Index measured the movement of goods and services purchased specifically by urban wage earners and clerical workers. Yet, it came to be used as a general indicator of cost of living. For this reason in addition to revising the original CPI for urban wage and clerical workers, now called CPI-W, the Department of Labor established a new and broader index, known as CPI-U, for all urban consumers. The CPI-U represents price changes for 80 percent of the population, as compared with roughly half of the population represented by CPI-W. For both of these indexes the weights are based on 1972-1973 survey data, but the base period for price comparison was established as 1967.

Compared with the standard aggregate price indexes described in this chapter, the CPI-U and CPI-W indexes essentially are weighted averages of price relatives, because the simple price index for each sampled item is weighted to calculate the aggregate price index. However, as indicated above, the value weights are associated with 1972-1973 consumption patterns, while the base period is 1967. Table 17-6 indicates the percent distribution of the CPI market basket associated with the several revisions of this index. Although the CPI-U is likely to be increasingly considered as "the" consumer price index, the CPI-W continues to be of some importance because it is more directly comparable with the CPI indexes published before 1978 and, particularly, because many cost-of-living provisions in labor contracts are still tied to the CPI-W index.

The Consumer Price Index is calculated and published both monthly and annually. Table 17-7 lists the values of the CPI for the years 1967-1977. Referring

Table 17-6 Percent distribution of the Consumer Price Index market basket by major expenditure group, benchmark years

Major group	Wage earners and clerical workers				All urban consumers, 1972-1973§
	1935–1939*	1952**	1963†	1972-1973§	
Food and alcoholic beverages	35.4	32.2	25.2	20.4	18.8
Housing	33.7	33.5	34.9	39.8	42.9
Apparel	11.0	9.4	10.6	7.0	7.0
Transportation	8.1	11.3	14.0	19.8	17.7
Medical care	4.1	4.8	5.7	4.2	4.6
Entertainment	2.8	4.0	3.9	4.3	4.5
Personal care	2.5	2.1	2.8	1.8	1.7
Other goods and services	2.4	2.7	2.9	2.7	2.8

(Source: U.S. Department of Labor, Bureau of Labor Statistics, 1977, Report 517, The Consumer Price Index: Concepts and Content Over the Years.)

*Relative importance for the survey period 1934–1936 (updated for price change).

**Relative importance for the survey period 1947–1949 (updated for price change).

†Relative importance for the survey period 1960–1961 (updated for price change).

§Relative importance for the survey period 1972–1973.

to Table 17-7, we can observe that since 1967 is the base year for this index, the index of 181.5 for 1977 indicates that the prices of the market basket of commodities and services for urban and clerical workers increased by 81.5 percent between 1967 and 1977. Or interpreting the CPI for 1977 differently, we can observe that the market basket of commodities and services that cost $10.00 in 1967 cost $18.15 in 1977. If we wish to compare the prices in a given year with

Table 17-7 Consumer Price Indexes, 1967–1977

Year	CPI
1967	100.0
1968	104.2
1969	109.8
1970	116.3
1971	121.3
1972	125.3
1973	133.1
1974	147.7
1975	161.2
1976	170.5
1977	181.5

(Source: U.S. Department of Commerce, Survey of Current Business.)

some year other than the base year, we simply calculate the ratio of the CPI values for these two years (and multiply by 100 to preserve the decimal point locations). The year for which the CPI value is in the denominator of the ratio serves as the base year for the comparison. For example suppose that we are interested in the percentage increase in the CPI between 1970 and 1975. We first calculate the ratio of these two indexes, with the CPI for the earlier year being in the denominator of this ratio:

$$\frac{\text{CPI (1975)}}{\text{CPI (1970)}} \times 100 = \frac{161.2}{116.3} \times 100 = 138.6$$

This index for 1975, with 1970 used as the base year for comparison, indicates that the Consumer Price Index increased 38.6 percent during the five-year period from 1970 to 1975. Also, we can say that the market basket of commodities and services that cost $10.00 in 1970 had a cost of $13.86 in 1975.

17-6 PURCHASING POWER AND THE DEFLATION OF TIME-SERIES VALUES

Two closely related concepts and procedures are those concerned with determining the purchasing power of the dollar and correcting historical time-series values for the effects of inflation or deflation.

The *purchasing power* of the dollar represents the value of a dollar in a given year compared with a base year. Computationally, this value is determined by taking the reciprocal of the price index for the given year and multiplying by 100 to preserve correct decimal placement. The price index most frequently used to determine the purchasing power of the dollar is the Consumer Price Index (CPI), as described in Section 17-5. However, for some purposes the Producer Price Indexes, described in the following section, might be more appropriate. Based on use of the CPI, the computational formula for determining the purchasing power of the dollar with respect to 1967 dollars is

$$\text{Purchasing power} = \frac{1}{\text{CPI}} \times 100 \qquad (17\text{-}12)$$

For example in June 1978 the CPI-U was 195.3 on the 1967 base. The purchasing power of the dollar during that month in terms of 1967 dollars was

$$\text{Purchasing power} = \frac{1}{\text{CPI-U}} \times 100 = \frac{1}{195.3} \times 100 = 0.5120 \approx \$0.51$$

Thus in comparison with the purchasing power of the dollar for urban consumers in 1967 the value of the dollar in June 1978 was $0.51.

When historical time-series values are stated in current dollars, one difficulty in interpreting such values is that the dollar amounts do not represent the same purchasing power. *Deflation of a time series* is the process by which such current-year values are converted to constant-dollar values. When the time series is

Table 17-8 Average wage rates paid to workers in a particular firm, 1970-1977

Year	Wage rate, $	CPI (1967 = 100)	Deflated wage rate, $
1970	3.89	116.3	3.34
1971	4.27	121.3	3.52
1972	4.49	125.3	3.58
1973	4.67	133.1	3.51
1974	5.14	147.7	3.48
1975	5.41	161.2	3.36
1976	5.91	170.5	3.47
1977	6.21	181.5	3.42

concerned with such dollar values as retail sales amounts or wage rates, the price index most frequently used to achieve deflation of such a series is the Consumer Price Index. The procedure used is to divide each annual (or monthly) value in the time series by the CPI for that period and then multiply by 100 to preserve the decimal location. Thus the process of deflation can be represented by

$$\text{Deflated amount} = \frac{\text{reported amount}}{\text{CPI}} \times 100 \qquad (17\text{-}13)$$

For example consider the average hourly wage paid in a firm between the years 1970-1977, as reported in the first column of Table 17-8. The increase in the hourly rate from \$3.89 in 1970 to \$6.21 in 1977 certainly appears substantial. The deflated wage rates in the last column of Table 17-8 were determined by the application of Formula (17-13) for each wage rate. For instance the deflated wage rate for 1977 is

$$\text{Deflated amount} = \frac{\text{reported amount}}{\text{CPI}} \times 100 = \frac{\$6.21}{181.5} \times 100 = \$3.42$$

Referring to the deflated wage rates in the last column of Table 17-8, we can observe the changes in the wage rates when they are expressed in constant dollars. In this example some of the wage increase amounted to wage-rate reductions in terms of the purchasing power represented by the new wage rate. That these deflated wage rates are stated in 1967 dollars is not as relevant as that they are all stated in constant dollars and thus can be compared directly with one another. Of course, the accuracy of these comparisons is based on the assumption that the CPI does in fact correctly gauge changes in the cost of living.

17-7 OTHER PUBLISHED INDEXES

Two extensively used sets of indexes published by the federal government are the Producer Price Indexes and the Index of Industrial Production.

The Producer Price Indexes replaced the Wholesale Price Index in 1978. Before August 1977 the prices reflected by the Wholesale Price Index were those involving the *first* commercial transaction for commodities sold in primary markets. Therefore the word "wholesale" in the name of the index was somewhat misleading. Starting with the August 1977 report, however, the Bureau of Labor Statistics changed the format of the Wholesale Price Index. The new index focused on prices of finished goods, such as automobiles, furniture, farm equipment, and food sold to supermarkets, rather than focusing on commodity prices in primary markets. Because the commercial transactions studied were those just preceding the retail transactions, this revised index was more correctly a "wholesale" price index. In 1978 the Bureau of Labor Statistics added price indexes for *crude materials* and *intermediate materials*, as well as *finished goods*, and the set of three indexes is called the Producer Price Indexes. It is possible that the finished goods component of this group of indexes will continue to be identified as the "wholesale price index" in the popular press. Further, changes in the price index for finished goods are used as leading indicators of changes in the Consumer Price Index.

The *Index of Industrial Production* is compiled and published monthly by the Federal Reserve Board. This index is an aggregate quantity index that measures the output of the nation's factories, mines, and electric and gas utilities. The fabrication of materials into final products is covered directly, but the distribution of products and their use in construction is only indirectly covered. Separate indexes are published for a number of industry groupings and for a number of market groupings. The base year for this index is $1967 = 100$, and the value weights used to weight the individual quantity relatives are also based on 1967 data. Thus this aggregate quantity index can be described as being a weighted average of quantity relatives. This index is used as a measure of current business conditions and is included among the "coincident indicators" of the business cycle, as described in Section 16-7.

17-8 SUMMARY

For any index number, the *base period* is the time period that serves as the basis for the comparison, while the *given period* is the period for which the measure is compared to the base period. The measurements compared can be concerned with *price, quantity,* or *value.* A *simple index number* is concerned with a comparison for only a single product or commodity, while an *aggregate index number*, or *composite index number*, is one that represents a comparison for a group of products or commodities.

When an aggregate price index is to be constructed, the universe of products or commodities must first be defined, and then the sample of items to be included in the index is determined. Finally, the basis to be used for weighting the prices of the items included in the index is established. A *simple aggregate price index* is one in which the unit prices of the items are accumulated without the use of weights as such. The units of measure are the implicit basis for the weights, and such an index seldom is representative of general price changes. The *Laspeyres price index* is an aggregate price index in which base-period quantities serve as the weights, while the *Paasche price index* is an aggregate price index in which the given-period quantities serve as the weights. The *Fisher ideal price index* is the geometric mean of these two indexes, and represents an attempt to correct the positive bias inherent in the Laspeyres index and the negative bias inherent in the Paasche index. All three of these indexes can be described as following the *weighted-average-of-prices* approach. In the *weighted-average-of-price-relatives approach*, value weights are used in conjunction with the simple price relatives for the items in the index. When base-period values are used as the weights, this index is algebraically equivalent to the Laspeyres index.

When the commodities or weights that serve as the basis for an index number are changed substantially, the usual effect is that a new index series with a new base period is established. By the process of *splicing*, the old index series can be combined with the new series, with the requirement being that there be one year (which is usually the new base year) for which indexes with respect to both the old series and the new series have been determined. Although splicing makes it possible to form one combined series of index numbers, index numbers based on different commodities or weights cannot be compared meaningfully.

The *Consumer Price Index* (CPI) is the most widely known of the indexes published by the federal government because of its use as an indicator of the cost of living. There are, in fact, two versions of this index: one for urban wage and clerical workers (CPI-W) and one for urban consumers in general (CPI-U). Each of these two indexes is a weighted average of price relatives, with the base year being 1967 and the value weights based on patterns of consumption in 1972-1973. The reciprocal of the Consumer Price Index for a given period often is used to indicate the *purchasing power* of the dollar in that period as compared with the base year 1967. When a historical time series is stated in current dollars, the Consumer Price Index can also be used to *deflate* the time-series values by dividing the dollar value for each period by the CPI for that period. By this procedure all values in the time series are converted into constant dollars, with the effects of inflation (or deflation) removed.

The *Producer Price Indexes* include price indexes for crude materials, intermediate materials, and finished goods. The price index for finished goods is used as an indicator of changes in wholesale prices. The *Index of Industrial Production* is a weighted average of quantity relatives that measures changes in the output of the nation's factories, mines, and electric and gas utilities.

FORMULAS

(17-1) $I_p = \dfrac{p_n}{p_0} \times 100$

Simple price index, or price relative.

(17-2) $I_q = \dfrac{q_n}{q_0} \times 100$

Simple quantity index, or quantity relative.

(17-3) $I_v = \dfrac{p_n q_n}{p_0 q_0} \times 100$ Simple value index, or value relative.

(17-4) $I_p(\text{simple aggregate}) = \dfrac{\Sigma p_n}{\Sigma p_0} \times 100$ Simple aggregate price index.

(17-5) $I_p(\text{L}) = \dfrac{\Sigma p_n q_0}{\Sigma p_0 q_0} \times 100$ Laspeyres aggregate price index.

(17-6) $I_p(\text{P}) = \dfrac{\Sigma p_n q_n}{\Sigma p_0 q_n} \times 100$ Paasche aggregate price index.

(17-7) $I_p(\text{F}) = \sqrt{\dfrac{\Sigma p_n q_0}{\Sigma p_0 q_0} \dfrac{\Sigma p_n q_n}{\Sigma p_0 q_n}} \times 100$ Fisher ideal aggregate price index.

(17-8) $I_p(\text{F}) = \sqrt{I_p(\text{L}) I_p(\text{P})}$ Alternative formula for the Fisher ideal price index when the Laspeyres and Paasche price indexes have already been calculated.

(17-9) $I_p(\text{W}) = \dfrac{\Sigma(p_0 q_0)[(p_n/p_0) \times 100]}{\Sigma p_0 q_0}$ Weighted average of price relatives using base-period values as weights.

(17-10) $Q = \dfrac{I_p(\text{new})}{I_p(\text{old})} = \dfrac{100}{I_p(\text{old})}$ Index quotient used for splicing two series of index numbers.

(17-11) $I_p(\text{new}) = I_p(\text{old})Q$ Conversion of an old index number into a new index number to combine the two time series through splicing.

(17-12) Purchasing power $= \dfrac{1}{\text{CPI}} \times 100$ Purchasing power of the dollar in terms of base-year dollars of the Consumer Price Index.

(17-13) Deflated amount

$= \dfrac{\text{reported amount}}{\text{CPI}} \times 100$ Deflation of a time-series amount by use of the Consumer Price Index, so that such amounts are expressed in constant-dollar terms (with the effect of inflation removed).

EXERCISES

17-1 The following data reporting yearly production of butter and American cheese and average wholesale prices for these commodities are taken from the U.S. Department of Commerce, *Survey of Current Business.*

    (*a*) Compute the simple price indexes for butter for these four years using 1974 as the base.

    (*b*) Compute the price indexes for cheese for these four years, also using 1974 as the base.

	1974	1975	1976	1977
Factory butter production, millions of lb	961.7	983.8	978.6	1,093.6
Wholesale price, per lb, $	0.674	0.818	0.944	1.015
Factory cheese production (American),				
millions of lb	1,858.6	1,654.5	2,062.4	2,035.7
Wholesale price, per lb, $	0.973	1.044	1.161	1.187

17-2 (*a*) For the data of Exercise 17-1 what are the percentage changes in the wholesale prices of butter and cheese between 1974 and 1977, taken as a whole?

(*b*) Compute the simple quantity indexes for both butter and cheese for 1977, using 1974 as the base, and interpret in terms of percentage change.

17-3 (*a*) Compute the total dollar value of butter and cheese production in 1974 and 1977 using the data in Exercise 17-1.

(*b*) From the results of Exercise 17-3*a*, compute the simple value indexes for butter and cheese for 1977, using 1974 as the base; interpret these indexes.

17-4 The following simplified data represent average prices and monthly quantities of some of the supplies used in a business office.

(*a*) Compute the simple price and quantity relatives for the bond paper, using 1970 as the base.

(*b*) Compute the simple value relatives for the bond and onionskin paper and compare them.

Item	Unit quotation	Average price, $		Monthly consumption	
		1970, p_0	1978, p_n	1970, q_0	1978, q_n
Paper, white bond	Ream	2.50	4.00	2.2	2.8
Paper, onionskin	Ream	2.00	4.25	5.0	2.5
Paper clips	Pkg. of 100	0.15	0.20	2.0	2.0
Typewriter ribbon	Each	1.00	1.50	4.0	5.0

17-5 (*a*) For the data of Exercise 17-4 compute the Laspeyres price index and interpret its meaning.

(*b*) Compute the Paasche price index and interpret its meaning.

(*c*) Compute the Fisher ideal price index for the above data.

(*d*) Compute the weighted average of price relatives and compare its value with that of the Laspeyres and Paasche indexes.

17-6 The following indexes are taken from the *Survey of Current Business.*

(*a*) What kind of indexes are reported in the table?

(*b*) What was the percentage change in prices between 1967 and 1977?

(*c*) What was the percentage change in prices between 1974 and 1977?

	Average wholesale prices (1967 = 100)			
	1974	1975	1976	1977
Home electronic equipment	93.1	93.5	91.3	87.7

17-7 Refer to the data of Exercise 17-6.

(a) Given that the average wholesale price of a radio receiver during 1967 was $24, estimate its price in 1977.

(b) Given a radio receiver with a 1974 wholesale price of $24, estimate its price in 1977.

17-8 The following wholesale prices are taken from the *Survey of Current Business*, published by the Department of Commerce.

(a) What was the percentage increase in the wholesale price of household appliances between 1973 and 1977?

(b) What was the percentage increase in wholesale furniture prices during the same time period?

	Average wholesale prices (1967 = 100)				
	1973	1974	1975	1976	1977
Household appliances	108.5	117.9	132.3	139.2	144.9
Household furniture	123.0	136.6	146.3	153.6	162.2

17-9 (a) For the data of Exercise 17-8, if the average wholesale price of an appliance was $150 in 1973, what is the estimate of its average wholesale price in 1977?

(b) If the average wholesale price of an item of furniture was $400 in 1977, what is the estimate of its average wholesale price in 1973?

17-10 Identify two important errors in the statement: "The figures given in Exercise 17-9 indicate that in 1977 the average consumer spent 17.3 percent more dollars on household furniture than on household appliances."

17-11 Given the following simplified data regarding average retail price and the weekly patterns of consumption for a selected family of four, compute the simple price and quantity indexes for the two commodities, using 1970 as the base.

Commodity	Quantity	Average price, $		Weekly consumption	
		1970, p_0	1978, p_n	1970, q_0	1978, q_n
Bread	$1\frac{1}{2}$-lb loaf	0.40	0.60	4.5	4.5
Milk	$\frac{1}{2}$ gal	0.60	0.80	4.0	6.0

17-12 (a) Compute the Laspeyres price index for the data of Exercise 17-11.

(b) Compute the Paasche price index for the data in Exercise 17-11.

(c) Compute the Fisher ideal price index for the data in Exercise 17-11.

17-13 Compute the weighted average of price relatives for the data in Exercise 17-11, using the price relatives determined in that exercise. Compare this index with the aggregate price indexes calculated in Exercise 17-12.

17-14 The following data are taken from the 1977 *Annual Report* of Texaco, Inc. Compute index numbers for total net income, using 1972 as the base.

Year	Total net income, in $millions
1972	820.0
1973	1,243.0
1974	1,544.7
1975	830.6
1976	830.6
1977	930.8

17-15 The table below presents Consumer Price Indexes for 1967 through 1977, with the base year being 1967. Determine the purchasing power of the dollar for each of these years in terms of the value of the dollar in 1967.

Year	Consumer Price Index
1967	100.0
1968	104.2
1969	109.8
1970	116.3
1971	121.3
1972	125.3
1973	133.1
1974	147.7
1975	161.2
1976	170.5
1977	181.5

(Source: U.S. Department of Commerce, Survey of Current Business.)

17-16 (*a*) Referring to Exercise 17-15, determine the purchasing power of the dollar in 1977, based on 1970 dollars.

(*b*) Referring to Exercise 17-15, determine the purchasing power of the dollar in 1970, based on 1977 dollars.

17-17 The following table reports the Consumer Price Index for the years 1960–1967, using the base period 1957–1959, and the revised Consumer Price Index for the years 1967–1977, using the base year 1967. Splice these two series of index numbers, using a common base year of 1967.

Year	Old CPI (1957–1959 = 100)	New CPI (1967 = 100)
1960	103.1	
1961	104.2	
1962	105.4	
1963	106.7	
1964	108.1	
1965	109.9	
1966	113.1	
1967	116.3	100.0
1968		104.2
1969		109.8
1970		116.3
1971		121.3
1972		125.3
1973		133.1
1974		147.7
1975		161.2
1976		170.5
1977		181.5

(Source: U.S. Department of Commerce, Survey of Current Business.)

17-18 The following table indicates the annual salary amounts of an accountant who began employment with a business firm in 1972.

(*a*) Deflate these salary amounts so that they are all expressed in terms of 1967 dollars.

(*b*) What percentage increase in real salary did this individual experience between 1972 and 1977?

Year	Salary, $
1972	9,900
1973	10,600
1974	11,700
1975	13,300
1976	14,500
1977	16,000

EIGHTEEN

NONPARAMETRIC STATISTICS

18-1 SCALES OF MEASUREMENT

Before we consider how nonparametric statistical methods differ from the parametric methods that constitute most of this book, it is useful to consider first the four types of measurement scales in terms of the level of precision represented by the values assigned to the random variable. In the order of increasing precision these scales are the nominal, ordinal, interval, and ratio scales of measurement.

The *nominal scale* involves the use of numbers only to identify categories. For example, if we have four sales regions, these regions might be sequentially numbered 1, 2, 3, and 4. Similarly, for the qualitative variable of sex male might be coded as 1 and female as 2. The numeric values in the nominal scale of measurement do not indicate any amount or quantity as such. Rather, as is implied by the word "nominal," the numbers simply serve as names for categories.

The *ordinal scale* of measurement involves the use of numbers as ranks. Thus, if an investment analyst ranks five stocks from highest to lowest in terms of appreciation potential, the stock issue ranked 1 is considered to be a better investment than the one ranked 2, and so forth. When numbers are used as ranks, they indicate relative magnitude, but the differences between the ranks are not assumed to be equal. Thus the difference in the appreciation potential between the two stocks ranked 1 and 2 generally would not be the same as the difference in the appreciation potential between the two stocks ranked 2 and 3.

The *interval scale* considers the difference between measurements as well as their ordering. When the interval scale is used, equal differences between values indicate equal amounts of difference in the variable being measured. However, the zero point of an interval scale is arbitrary and defined as a matter of convenience. For instance both the Farenheit and Celsius temperature scales are interval scales of measurement. Although for the Farenheit scale $32°$ is defined as the freezing point of water and for the Celsius scale $0°$ is defined as the freezing point of water, for either temperature scale we can say that $30°$ is $10°$ warmer than $20°$, and that $40°$ is $10°$ warmer than $30°$. Other examples of interval scales are test scores and time scales. In both examples the zero point (or beginning point) is arbitrary.

The highest level of measurement sophistication is represented by the *ratio scale*. In the ratio scale the measurement units are equal, and a true zero point has been defined. The implication of this definition is that the measurements of the random variable can be compared in the form of ratios. For example we can say that an inventory value of \$1,200 is twice as great as that of \$600 and that 400 feet is half the distance of 800 feet. In both of these examples the value of 0 would indicate a complete absence of any quantity of the variable being measured. By contrast we cannot say that $40°$ is twice as warm as $20°$ on either the Farenheit or Celsius temperature scales. Similarly, we cannot say that a score of 80 on an examination is twice as good as a score of 40.

18-2 PARAMETRIC VERSUS NONPARAMETRIC STATISTICAL METHODS

The principal methods of statistical inference thus far described in this book are called *parametric methods*, because the focal point of the analysis is some particular population *parameter* for which a hypothesized value is assumed or estimated by a sample statistic. Inherent in this procedure are two additional considerations: One is that some assumption concerning the *distribution* of the population is required so that we have a basis for statistical inference. As we have indicated throughout the book, such an assumption is particularly important with small samples, because the central-limit theorem frequently permits use of the normal distribution when a large sample has been obtained even though the population of concern is decidedly nonnormal. The second additional consideration underlying the use of parametric statistical methods is that the measurements to be analyzed be at least at the *interval* scale of measurement. Thus any measurements at the nominal or ordinal scales do not fulfill the requirement associated with the principal methods we have described thus far, such as testing a hypothesis concerning the difference between two means.

The *nonparametric methods* of statistical analysis are methods that can be used when one or more of the assumptions required for the use of parametric methods are not satisfied. Again, the three principal assumptions are concerned with

1. A population parameter and its value
2. The form of the population distribution
3. Measurement at the interval or ratio scale of measurement

Therefore, even though the word "nonparametric" is particularly associated with the first of these assumptions, this term has come to be used to describe the methods considered appropriate when any of the three assumptions is not satisfied. An alternative term sometimes used to describe some of the techniques is *distribution-free methods*, which is particularly associated with the second assumption required with parametric methods, that the form of the population distribution be known.

The development of nonparametric statistical methods has broadened the data situations in which statistical analysis can be applied. However, if a data situation satisfies the assumptions associated with the parametric methods, we would prefer to use such methods rather than the nonparametric methods. In hypothesis testing, for example, we would generally prefer to use the normal distribution or Student's t distribution rather than the Mann-Whitney U test for testing the difference between the means of two independent samples; the Mann-Whitney U test, the equivalent nonparametric procedure, is described in the next section of this chapter. The reason for preferring the normal distribution or Student's t distribution is that if we use the same level of significance for both tests, the power associated with a nonparametric test will always be less than the power associated with the equivalent parametric test. (Recall from Section 9-3 that the power of a statistical test is the probability of rejecting the null hypothesis when it is in fact false.) Of course the particular advantage of nonparametric methods is that we can use such techniques when one or more of the assumptions of the parametric methods are not satisfied, and therefore the fact that nonparametric tests are less powerful than parametric tests is not a relevant issue for data situations in which parametric methods should not be applied. The existence of the nonparametric methods provides the opportunity for data analysis that otherwise would not be possible.

Entire textbooks are devoted to the presentation of nonparametric methods, and therefore the methods described in this chapter constitute only an introduction to such techniques. Most nonparametric methods are concerned with statistical testing rather than interval estimation, and therefore the methods described in this chapter are all concerned with hypothesis testing. As indicated by the section titles, the next several sections describe the nonparametric tests that are equivalent to testing the difference between two means based on independent samples, the difference between two means based on paired observations, and the differences among several means based on independent samples (which is equivalent to the analysis of variance as a parametric method). Then the Spearman rank correlation coefficient is described as the nonparametric equivalent of the parametric correlation coefficient. Finally, one special-purpose test is described: the *runs test* for testing the randomness of a sample.

Of the statistical methods already described in this book, two applications are categorized as nonparametric methods. First, the use of Chebyshev's inequality to construct a confidence interval for the population mean (Section 7-6) or to test a hypothesis concerning the population mean (Section 9-6) represents a nonparametric procedure. In these applications a specific parameter is involved, and the level of measurement is at least at the interval scale, as required for the parametric methods. However, no assumption is required concerning the population distribution, thus constituting a nonparametric procedure. The second category of methods considered to be nonparametric methods are the uses of the chi-square (χ^2) test, as described in Chapter 12. This testing procedure is used for goodness-of-fit tests and for testing the independence of two variables. Recall that the use of the χ^2 test is appropriate for data entered into a designated number of categories, with each category having a numeric or alphabetic name assigned to it. Therefore, because the data are at the nominal scale of measurement, the χ^2 test is considered to be nonparametric. We devoted a separate chapter to this test because of the extent and variety of applications it has had in applied statistics.

18-3 THE MANN–WHITNEY *U* TEST FOR TWO INDEPENDENT SAMPLES

Purpose

The Mann-Whitney *U* test has been developed to test the null hypothesis that two independent random samples have been drawn from the same population or from two populations with the same distribution. If it is assumed that two samples are obtained from populations with the same form and dispersion, any difference would result only from the difference in the location of the two distributions. That is, the Mann-Whitney *U* test is then the nonparametric equivalent to the normal distribution or Student's *t* distribution (described in Sections 10-1 and 10-2) for testing the difference between the means of two independent samples.

Assumptions

Two random samples are independent samples (not matched pairs) for which measurements are at least at the ordinal scale. The samples need not be equal in size.

Procedure

Two samples are combined into one ordered array, with each sample value identified according to the original sample group. The values are then ranked from lowest to highest, with the rank of 1 assigned to the lowest observed sample value. For equal values the mean rank is assigned to the tied, or equal, values. If the null hypothesis is true, the average of the ranks for each sample group should be approximately equal. The statistic calculated to carry out this test is designated *U*, and it can be based on the sum of the ranks in either of the two random samples, as follows:

$$U_1 = n_1 n_2 + \frac{n_1(n_1 + 1)}{2} - R_1 \qquad (18\text{-}1)$$

or

$$U_2 = n_1 n_2 + \frac{n_2(n_2 + 1)}{2} - R_2 \qquad (18\text{-}2)$$

where n_1 = size of the first sample
n_2 = size of the second sample
R_1 = sum of the ranks in the first sample
R_2 = sum of the ranks in the second sample

Given that $n_1 > 10$, $n_2 > 10$, and the null hypothesis is true, the sampling distribution of U is approximately normal, with the following parameters:

$$\mu_U = \frac{n_1 n_2}{2} \qquad (18\text{-}3)$$

$$\sigma_U = \sqrt{\frac{n_1 n_2 (n_1 + n_2 + 1)}{12}} \qquad (18\text{-}4)$$

Therefore the test statistic for testing the null hypothesis that the two independent samples came from the same population or from two populations with the same distribution is

$$z = \frac{U - \mu_U}{\sigma_U} \qquad (18\text{-}5)$$

where U equals U_1 or U_2.

For data situations in which $n_1 < 10$, $n_2 < 10$ or both n_1 and $n_2 < 10$, the normal probability distribution cannot be used for this test. However, special tables for the U statistic are available for such small samples in specialized textbooks on nonparametric statistics.

Example To evaluate and compare two methods of instruction for industrial apprentices, a training director assigns 15 randomly selected trainees to each of the two methods. Because of normal attrition not related to either of the training methods, 14 apprentices complete the course taught by method 1 and 12 apprentices complete the course taught by method 2. The same achievement test is then given to both trainee groups to determine the level of knowledge and skill after course completion. Table 18-1 reports these examination scores for the two groups of apprentices.

Table 18-2 lists the achievement test scores in one array, ranked from lowest to highest score. The ranks are presented in the second column of Table 18-2. Notice the way the rankings are assigned to the tied scores: For the three test scores of 82, for example, the scores are at the rank positions 12, 13, and 14 in the second column of the table. Therefore the mean of these three ranks, 13, is assigned to these three test scores. Then note that the next rank assigned is 15, not 14, because

Table 18-1 Achievement test scores of apprentice trainees taught by two methods of instruction

Method 1	Method 2
70	86
90	78
82	90
64	82
86	65
77	87
84	80
79	88
82	95
89	85
73	76
81	94
83	
66	

the assignment of the mean rank of 13 to the three scores of 82 has brought the 83 score to the 15th position in the array. Similarly, there are two scores of 86; the ranks for these two positions are 18 and 19, and therefore the mean rank of 18.5 is assigned to each of these scores. The next score in the array, 87, is assigned the rank 20. The last two columns in Table 18-2 list the ranks according to the sample, which represents the teaching method used, and the sums of these two columns of ranks are the two values R_1 and R_2, respectively.

Applying Formula (18-1), we determine the value of U_1 as follows:

$$U_1 = n_1 n_2 + \frac{n_1(n_1 + 1)}{2} - R_1 = 14(12) + \frac{14(14 + 1)}{2} - 161$$

$$= 168 + \frac{210}{2} - 161 = 112$$

Because $n_1 > 10$ and $n_2 > 10$, the normal probability distribution can be used to test the null hypothesis that the value of μ_U is the same for both samples. The test is to be carried out with the 5 percent level of significance. Based on Formula (18-3), the value of μ_U is

$$\mu_U = \frac{n_1 n_2}{2} = \frac{14(12)}{2} = 84$$

Thus the hypotheses are

$$H_0 : \mu_U = 84$$

$$H_1 : \mu_U \neq 84$$

Table 18-2 Combined array of the achievement test scores with associated ranks

Score*	Rank	Method 1 ranks	Method 2 ranks
64	1	1	
65	2		2
66	3	3	
70	4	4	
73	5	5	
76	6		6
77	7	7	
78	8		8
79	9	9	
80	10		10
81	11	11	
82	13	13	
82	13	13	
82	13		13
83	15	15	
84	16	16	
85	17		17
86	18.5	18.5	
86	18.5		18.5
87	20		20
88	21		21
89	22	22	
90	23.5	23.5	
90	23.5		23.5
94	25		25
95	26		26
Totals		$R_1 = 161.0$	$R_2 = 190.0$

*Scores for method 1 are underscored.

Based on Formula (18-4), the standard error of U is

$$\sigma_U = \sqrt{\frac{n_1 n_2 (n_1 + n_2 + 1)}{12}} = \sqrt{\frac{14(12)(14 + 12 + 1)}{12}} = \sqrt{\frac{4,536}{12}} = 19.4$$

Applying Formula (18-5), we determine the value of the z test statistic as follows:

$$z = \frac{U_1 - \mu_0}{\sigma_U} = \frac{112 - 84}{19.4} = 1.44$$

Because the critical values of z for a test at the 5 percent level of significance are $z = \pm 1.96$, the null hypothesis that there is no difference between the two distributions of achievement test scores cannot be rejected.

18-4 THE SIGN TEST FOR PAIRED OBSERVATIONS

Purpose

The sign test is used to test the null hypothesis that the values in two populations are not different in level, or magnitude, where the values for the two samples have been collected as paired observations. Therefore it is a nonparametric equivalent to using Student's t distribution to test the difference between two means based on paired observations, as described in Section 10-3. Because this test is based only on the direction of the differences between the paired values and not on the magnitude of the differences, it is not as sensitive a test as the Wilcoxon test described in Section 18-5.

Assumptions

The two random samples have been obtained as paired observations, as described in Section 10-3, and the measurements are at least at the ordinal scale. No assumptions are required about the forms of the two distributions.

Procedure

A plus $(+)$ sign is assigned for each pair of values for which the measurement in the first sample is greater than the measurement in the second sample, and a minus $(-)$ sign is assigned when the opposite condition is true. If a pair of measurements have the same value, these tied values are dropped from the analysis, with the sample size thereby being reduced. If the hypothesis that the two populations are at the same level of magnitude is true, the number of plus signs should approximately equal the number of minus signs. Therefore, the null hypothesis tested is H_0: $\pi = 0.50$, where π is the population proportion of the plus (or the minus) signs. If the number of sample pairs is small $(n < 30)$, the binomial distribution is used to carry out this test, as described in Section 10-4. If the sample is large $(n \geqslant 30)$, the normal distribution can be used, as described in Section 10-5. Note that although two samples have been collected, the test is applied to the one set of plus and minus signs that results from the comparison of the pairs of measurements.

Example   A consumer panel that includes 14 individuals is asked to rate two brands of teabags according to a point-evaluation system based on several criteria, including the taste characteristics of both hot tea and iced tea for the two brands. Table 18-3 reports the points assigned to each brand of tea bags by each of the 14 panel members. Further, the last column of Table 18-3 indicates the sign of the difference for each pair of ratings by a given panel member.

Assuming that this test panel is a random sample of consumers, suppose we wish to test the null hypothesis that there is no difference in the consumer preference for the two brands of teabags, using the 5 percent level of significance. The specific hypotheses in terms of the proportion of plus signs are

Table 18-3 Ratings assigned to two brands of teabags by a consumer panel

Panel member	Point rating assigned to each brand		Sign of difference
	Brand 1	Brand 2	
1	20	16	+
2	24	26	−
3	28	18	+
4	24	17	+
5	20	20	0
6	29	21	+
7	19	23	−
8	27	22	+
9	20	23	−
10	30	20	+
11	18	18	0
12	28	21	+
13	26	17	+
14	24	26	−

Hypotheses:
$$H_0: \pi = 0.50$$
$$H_1: \pi \neq 0.50$$

Referring again to Table 18-3, we see that two of the consumers rated the two brands of teabags as equal, and therefore these two panel members are omitted from the following analysis, resulting in an effective sample size of $n = 12$. Of the twelve signs eight are plus signs.

Because the sample size is $n < 30$, the binomial distribution is the appropriate basis for this test. The method used is exactly the same as explained in Section 10-4 in which we tested the hypothesis that a coin was fair by observing the results on five tosses of the coin. The only difference is that in this case $n = 12$ instead of $n = 5$. Referring to Table B-2, we observe the binomial probability distribution for $n = 12$ and $p = 0.50$. For a two-tail test at the 5 percent level of significance the region of rejection at each tail should not exceed a probability of 0.025. At the lower tail this means that the number of plus signs would have to be either 0, 1, or 2 for rejection of the null hypothesis. The sum of the three probability values associated with 0, 1, or 2 plus signs is $P = 0.0002 + 0.0029 + 0.0161 = 0.0192$, which is less than 0.025. However, the addition of the category "4 plus signs" to the lower-tail region of rejection would result in a value larger than 0.025. Similarly, rejection of the null hypothesis at the upper tail would mean that the number of plus signs would have to be 10, 11, or 12.

In summary, based on the binomial distribution, we can reject the null hypothesis at the 5 percent level of significance if the number of plus signs is fewer than four or greater than nine. In fact we observed eight plus signs. Therefore, the null hypothesis that the two brands of teabags have equal consumer preference cannot be rejected.

Now, suppose that a larger consumer panel had been used. Let us assume that the effective sample size was $n = 36$ instead of $n = 12$ and that the number of plus signs was 24 (thus resulting in the same sample proportion as for our small sample). Again, the hypotheses in terms of the population proportion of plus signs are

Hypotheses: $H_0: \pi = 0.50$

$H_1 : \pi \neq 0.50$

As explained in Section 10-5, use of the normal probability distribution to test a hypothesized value of the proportion is appropriate when $n \geqslant 30$, $n\pi_0 \geqslant 5$, and $n(1 - \pi_0) \geqslant 5$. These assumptions are all satisfied in the present example, with $n = 36$, $n\pi_0 = 36(0.50) = 18$, and $n(1 - \pi_0) = 36(1 - 0.50) = 18$. Therefore we calculate the sample proportion of plus signs and the standard error of the proportion as follows:

$$\hat{p} = \frac{X}{n} = \frac{24}{36} = 0.667$$

$$\sigma_{\hat{p}} = \sqrt{\frac{\pi_0(1 - \pi_0)}{n}} = \sqrt{\frac{0.50(0.50)}{36}} = 0.083$$

Finally, we calculate the value of the test statistic z:

$$z = \frac{\hat{p} - \pi_0}{\sigma_{\hat{p}}} = \frac{0.667 - 0.50}{0.083} = \frac{0.167}{0.083} = 2.01$$

Because the critical values of the test statistic are $z = \pm 1.96$ for a two-tail test at the 5 percent level of significance, based on the sample of sizes $n = 36$, we reject the null hypothesis that the two brands of teabags have equal consumer preference.

18-5 THE WILCOXON TEST FOR PAIRED OBSERVATIONS

Purpose

Just as for the sign test, the Wilcoxon rank-sum test is used to test the null hypothesis that the values in two populations are not different in level, or magnitude, where the values for the two samples are collected as paired observations. However, the Wilcoxon test considers the magnitude of the difference between each matched pair and not just the direction, or sign, of the difference. As is true for the sign test, the Wilcoxon test is a nonparametric equivalent to using Student's t distribution to test the difference between two means based on paired observations, as described in Section 10-3. Because the Wilcoxon rank-sum test considers the magnitude of the differences between the matched pairs, it is a more powerful test than the sign test.

Assumptions

The two random samples have been obtained as paired observations, as described in Section 10-3, and the measurements are at least at the interval scale. The interval-scale assumption is required because the difference between each pair of measurements is determined as part of the test procedure. No assumptions are required about the forms of the two distributions.

Procedure

The difference between each pair of values is determined, and this difference, with the associated arithmetic sign, is designated by d. If any difference is equal to zero, this pair of observations is dropped from the analysis, thus reducing the effective sample size. Then the absolute values of the differences are ranked from lowest to highest, with the rank of 1 assigned to the smallest absolute difference. When absolute differences are equal, the mean rank is assigned to the tied values. Finally, the sum of the ranks is obtained separately for the positive and negative differences. The smaller of these two sums is the Wilcoxon T statistic, which is used as the test statistic. Table B-9 identifies the critical values of T according to sample size and level of significance.

When $n \geqslant 25$ and the null hypothesis is true, the T statistic is approximately normally distributed. The mean and the standard error associated with this sampling distribution are, respectively,

$$\mu_T = \frac{n(n + 1)}{4} \tag{18-6}$$

$$\sigma_T = \sqrt{\frac{n(n + 1)(2n + 1)}{24}} \tag{18-7}$$

Therefore the test can be carried out by using the normal probability distribution and computing the z test statistic as follows:

$$z = \frac{T - \mu_T}{\sigma_T} \tag{18-8}$$

Example As indicated in this section, both the sign test and the Wilcoxon test can be used with paired observations. Therefore let us apply the Wilcoxon test to the consumer-panel data in Table 18-3, in which 14 panel members rated two brands of teabags. The null hypothesis to be tested is that the ratings assigned to the two brands of teabags by the population of consumers are not different, using the 5 percent level of significance. We repeat these ratings in Table 18-4, determine the values of d, rank the absolute values of d, and finally, we determine the sum of the plus and minus rankings.

Table 18-4 Ratings assigned to two brands of teabags by a consumer panel and the determination of signed ranks

Panel member	Brand 1, X_1	Brand 2, X_2	Difference $d = X_1 - X_2$	Rank of $\|d\|$	Signed rank (+)	Signed rank (−)
1	20	16	4	4.5	4.5	
2	24	26	−2	1.5		1.5
3	28	18	10	11.5	11.5	
4	24	17	7	7.5	7.5	
5	20	20	0			
6	29	21	8	9	9	
7	19	23	−4	4.5		4.5
8	27	22	5	6	6	
9	20	23	−3	3		3
10	30	20	10	11.5	11.5	
11	18	18	0			
12	28	21	7	7.5	7.5	
13	26	17	9	10	10	
14	24	26	−2	1.5		1.5
Total					67.5	$T = 10.5$

Referring to Table 18-4, note that the two panel members who rated the two brands of teabags equally are dropped from the analysis, because the difference $d = 0$ is not assigned a rank. Therefore the effective sample size is $n = 12$. Of the 12 absolute values of d several tied pairs result in the assignment of mean ranks. For instance there are two absolute differences tied for the positions of rank 1 and rank 2; therefore each of these absolute differences is assigned the mean rank 1.5. The next rank assigned is then rank 3. Because the sum of the ranks for the negative differences is smaller than the sum for the positive differences, this smaller sum is labeled T in Table 18-4.

Table B-9 indicates that for $n = 12$ (the effective sample size) the critical value of the Wilcoxon T statistic for a two-tail test at the 5 percent level of significance is $T = 14$. Because T is the smaller sum of the signed ranks, the critical value of T is always the lower tail critical value, regardless of whether a one-tail or two-tail test is involved in the particular application. That is, the obtained value of the T statistic must be equal to or less than the critical value of T for the null hypothesis to be rejected. In this example the obtained value $T = 10.5$ is less than the critical value of $T = 14$, and therefore the null hypothesis that there is no difference in the ratings for the two brands of teabags is rejected.

Note that the null hypothesis of no difference could not be rejected at the 5 percent level when the sign test was applied to these same data in Section 18-4. Because the Wilcoxon test considers the magnitude of the difference between each matched pair and not just the sign of the difference, the Wilcoxon test for paired observations is a more powerful test than the sign test.

18-6 THE KRUSKAL–WALLIS TEST FOR SEVERAL INDEPENDENT SAMPLES

Purpose

The Kruskal-Wallis test can be viewed as an extension of the Mann-Whitney U test, as described in Section 18-3, when there are more than two populations. It is the nonparametric equivalent of the one-factor completely randomized design of the analysis of variance, as described in Section 11-3. For this reason the Kruskal-Wallis test for several independent samples is sometimes called the one-factor analysis of variance by ranks. The null hypothesis tested is that the several populations have the same distribution, with the alternative hypothesis being that at least one population is different. If the assumption is made that the several populations have the same form and dispersion, rejection of the null hypothesis indicates the populations are different in level.

Assumptions

The several samples are mutually independent (not matched) for which measurements are at least at the ordinal scale. No assumptions are required about the forms or variances of the distributions, for such differences as well as differences in level can constitute the basis for rejecting the null hypothesis. The samples need not be equal in size.

Procedure

The several samples are first viewed as one array of values, and each value in this combined group is ranked from lowest to highest. For equal values the mean rank is assigned to the tied values. If the null hypothesis is true, the average of the ranks for each sample group should be about equal. The test statistic calculated is designated H and is based on the sum of the ranks in each of the several random samples, as follows:

$$H = \frac{12}{N(N+1)} \sum \frac{R_j^2}{n_j} - 3(N+1) \qquad (18\text{-}9)$$

where N = combined sample size of the several samples (note that N does not designate population size in this case)

R_j = sum of the ranks for the jth sample

n_j = number of observations in the jth sample

Given that the size of each treatment group is at least $n_j \geqslant 5$ and the null hypothesis is true, the sampling distribution of H is approximately distributed as the χ^2 distribution with df $= K - 1$, where K is the number of treatment, or sample, groups. The χ^2 value that approximates the critical value of the test statistic is always the upper tail value. This test procedure is analogous to the upper tail of the F distribution being used in the analysis of variance.

For tied ranks the test statistic H should be corrected. The corrected value of the test statistic is designated H_c and is computed as follows:

$$H_c = \frac{H}{1 - [\Sigma(t_j^3 - t_j)/(N^3 - N)]} \tag{18-10}$$

where t_j represents the number of tied scores in the jth sample.

The effect of this correction is to increase the value of the calculated H statistic. Therefore, if the uncorrected value of H leads to the rejection of the null hypothesis, there is no need to correct this value for the effect of tied ranks.

Example In Sections 11-2 and 11-3 on the one-factor completely randomized design of the analysis of variance we presented achievement test scores for a random sample of $n = 5$ trainees randomly assigned to each of three instructional methods. In those sections the null hypothesis was that the mean levels of achievement for the three different levels of instruction do not differ, and it was necessary to assume that the three populations are normally distributed and have equal variances. If we cannot make these assumptions, the Kruskal-Wallis test can be used to test the null hypothesis that the several populations have the same distribution. Table 18-5 repeats the data from Table 11-1 and also includes the ranks having the achievement scores viewed as one combined group. We will test the null hypothesis using the 5 percent level of significance.

With reference to Table 18-5 we compute the value of the test statistic as follows:

$$H = \frac{12}{N(N+1)} \sum \frac{R_j^2}{n_j} - 3(N+1)$$

$$= \frac{12}{15(15+1)} \left[\frac{(38.5)^2}{5} + \frac{(56.5)^2}{5} + \frac{(25.0)^2}{5} \right] - 3(15+1)$$

$$= \frac{12}{240} \left(\frac{5,299.5}{5} \right) - 48 = \frac{63,594}{1,200} - 48 = 52.995 - 48 = 4.995$$

Table 18-5 Achievement test scores of trainees under three methods of instruction

Method A_1		Method A_2		Method A_3	
Score	Rank	Score	Rank	Score	Rank
86	12	90	15	82	9.5
79	6	76	5	68	1
81	7.5	88	13	73	4
70	2	82	9.5	71	3
84	11	89	14	81	7.5
Total	$R_1 = 38.5$		$R_2 = 56.5$		$R_3 = 25.0$

Because these were some ties in the achievement test scores, it is appropriate to correct the value of the test statistic:

$$H_c = \frac{H}{1 - [\Sigma(t_j^3 - t_j)/(N^3 - N)]}$$

$$= \frac{4.995}{1 - \{[(1^3 - 1) + (1^3 - 1) + (2^3 - 2)]/(15^3 - 15)\}}$$

$$= \frac{4.995}{1 - [(0 + 0 + 6)/(3,375 - 15)]} = \frac{4.995}{1 - (6/3,360)}$$

$$= \frac{4.995}{1 - 0.00179} = \frac{4.995}{0.99821} = 5.004$$

Thus the corrected value $H_c = 5.004$ is only slightly larger than the uncorrected value of $H = 4.995$, and the ties have a negligible effect on the value of the test statistic. With $df = K - 1 = 3 - 1 = 2$ Table B-6 indicates that the critical value of the test statistic is $\chi^2 = 5.99$. Because the observed value of the test statistic is less than this critical value, the null hypothesis that the three sample groups were obtained from populations that have the same distributions cannot be rejected at the 5 percent level of significance. This conclusion is consistent with the conclusion in Sections 11-2 and 11-3 in which the analysis of variance was applied to these data.

18-7 THE SPEARMAN RANK CORRELATION COEFFICIENT

Purpose

The Spearman rank correlation coefficient is the nonparametric equivalent of the parametric correlation coefficient described in Section 14-6. As is true for the value of the parametric correlation coefficient r, the value of the rank correlation coefficient can range from $r_r = -1$ to $r_r = 1$. The sign of the coefficient indicates the nature of relationship, while the absolute value of the coefficient expresses the extent of relationship. A value of $r_r = -1$ indicates a perfect negative (inverse) relationship, a value of $r_r = 0$ indicates a lack of relationship, and a value or $r_r = 1$ indicates a perfect positive (direct) relationship between two variables. In addition to the descriptive use of this measure of relationship, the null hypothesis that can be tested is that the two variables, designated by X and Y, are uncorrelated. Rejection of this hypothesis results in the conclusion that there is a relationship between the two variables.

Assumptions

The pairs of observations are at least at the ordinal scale of measurement and have been randomly sampled from a bivariate population of continuous random variables. No assumptions are required regarding the forms of the two distributions.

Procedure

A random sample of pairs of measurements, which generally are obtained as ranks, is collected. If the measurements are on the interval or ratio scales, the values are converted to ranks, with the ranks assigned separately for each variable, X and Y—not by considering the two sets of values as one group. The mean of the ranks is assigned to any values that are equal. In assigning ranks, the rank of 1 generally is assigned to the lowest value. However, the rank of 1 can be assigned to the highest value, as long as the same order of ranking is followed for both groups. After the set of paired ranks is listed, the next step is to calculate the difference d between each pair of ranks. The Spearman rank correlation is then computed by the following formula, which can be derived from the formula for the parametric correlation coefficient by using ranks as the values of X and Y:

$$r_r = 1 - \frac{6\Sigma d^2}{n(n^2 - 1)} \tag{18-11}$$

where $d = X - Y$ for each pair of ranks
$\quad n$ = number of paired observations
Given that $n \geqslant 10$, the null hypothesis that the population correlation ρ ("rho") is zero and thus that there is no relationship between the two variables can be tested in the same way as for the Pearson coefficient of correlation. That is, the test statistic is based on Student's t distribution with df $= n - 2$, and the test statistic is

$$t = \frac{r_r}{\sqrt{(1 - r_r^2)/(n - 2)}} \tag{18-12}$$

Where the sample size is smaller than $n = 10$, tables are available in specialized textbooks in nonparametric statistics for determining the significance of the rank correlation coefficient.

Example A random sample of 10 supervisors is selected in a large manufacturing firm, and the performance rating obtained by each supervisor at the last annual review is noted together with the average of the ratings the supervisor assigned to subordinates. These ratings are reported in Table 18-6. This table also indicates the rank assigned within each group of values, from lowest to highest. For the ratings of the supervisors two ratings were tied at 89. Because these two ratings are at the ranks of 6 and 7 for this group of values, each of these two ratings was assigned the mean rank of 6.5.

The final two columns of Table 18-6 present the values of d and of d^2, based on the set of paired ranks listed in the preceding two columns. As indicated, the sum of the squared differences between the pairs of ranks is $\Sigma d^2 = 38.5$. Based on this sum, the rank correlation coefficient is calculated as follows:

$$r_r = 1 - \frac{6\Sigma d^2}{n(n^2 - 1)} = 1 - \frac{6(38.5)}{10(100 - 1)} = 1 - \frac{231}{990} = 1 - 0.23 = 0.77$$

Table 18-6 Performance ratings obtained and average performance ratings assigned by 10 supervisors

Supervisor	Rating of supervisor	Average rating of subordinates	Rank of supervisor rating, X	Rank of subordinate rating, Y	d	d^2
A	80	77.5	3	3	0	0
B	82	82.7	4	6	−2	4
C	89	87.4	6.5	8	−1.5	2.25
D	97	91.1	10	9	1	1
E	77	71.5	2	1	1	1
F	73	73.6	1	2	−1	1
G	84	79.6	5	5	0	0
H	89	83.4	6.5	7	−0.5	0.25
I	94	78.7	9	4	5	25
J	90	92.3	8	10	−2	4
						$\Sigma d^2 = 38.5$

Thus there appears to be a positive relationship between the ranks of the ratings assigned to the supervisors and the ranks of the average ratings assigned by them to their subordinates. Suppose that before the sample data were collected, we believed that a positive relationship exists between these variables. Using the 5 percent level of significance, we test the significance of this correlation value as a one-tail test, *not* giving the benefit of the doubt to our assumption, by testing the null hypothesis that the population correlation is $\rho \leqslant 0$, as follows:

Hypotheses: $$H_0: \rho \leqslant 0$$

$$H_1: \rho > 0$$

$$\text{Critical } t \ (\text{df} = n - 2 = 8, \ \alpha = 0.05) = 1.860$$

$$t = \frac{r_r}{\sqrt{(1 - r_r^2)/(n - 2)}} = \frac{0.77}{\sqrt{(1 - 0.5929)/(10 - 2)}} = \frac{0.77}{\sqrt{0.0509}} = \frac{0.77}{0.23} = 3.35$$

Because the obtained value of the t test statistic is greater than the critical value for this one-tail test, we reject the null hypothesis, and we conclude that there is a significant positive relationship between the ratings of the supervisors and the average ratings they assign to their subordinates.

18-8 THE RUNS TEST FOR RANDOMNESS

Purpose

An important assumption underlying the application of the methods of statistical inference is that the sample constitutes a group of randomly selected observations. This general assumption is required for both parametric and nonparametric methods.

The runs test is used to test the randomness of a set of observations when each observation can be assigned to one of two categories. The test is based on observing the number of runs that occur in the sequence of the two types of sampled items, where a *run* is a series of like items. For instance suppose that a sample of 12 individuals taken from a population in which the numbers of men (M) and women (W) are about equal includes five men and seven women observed in the sequence: W, W, W, W, W, W, W, M, M, M, M, M. Now, while the proportion of men and women appears to correspond to the population, there are only two runs of like items in this sample: one run of Ws and one run of Ms. Therefore we might very well question whether such a series represents a random series of observations. On the other hand suppose that the 12 individuals are observed in the following order: W, M, W, M, W, M, W, M, W, M, W, W. In this case there are 11 runs, and we might very well question whether such a large number of runs is likely to occur in a random sample.

Although we can most easily apply the runs test when the data involve an obvious dichotomy, by employing a number of classification schemes, we can apply it to numerically sequential data. One common approach is to determine the median of all the observations and then to classify each numeric observation as being either above or below the median. Whatever the basis used for classifying the observations, the purpose of the runs test is to test the null hypothesis that the sampling process used to select the items is a random process. The alternative hypothesis is that the process is not random. That is, that there is some dependency among the items that were selected.

Assumptions

The sample observations are listed in the order that they were obtained, with each sampled item assigned to one of two data categories on a predetermined basis.

Procedure

The number of runs of like items is determined for the sample data, with the symbol R used to designate the number of observed runs. Where n_1 equals the number of sampled items of one type and n_2 equals the number of sampled items of the second type, the mean and the standard error associated with the sampling distribution of the R test statistic when the sequence is random are

$$\mu_R = \frac{2n_1 n_2}{n_1 + n_2} + 1 \tag{18-13}$$

$$\sigma_R = \sqrt{\frac{2n_1 n_2 (2n_1 n_2 - n_1 - n_2)}{(n_1 + n_2)^2 (n_1 + n_2 - 1)}} \tag{18-14}$$

If either $n_1 > 20$ or $n_2 > 20$, the sampling distribution of r approximates the normal distribution. Therefore under such circumstances the R statistic can be converted to the z test statistic as follows:

$$z = \frac{R - \mu_R}{\sigma_R} \qquad (18\text{-}15)$$

Where both $n_1 \leqslant 20$ and $n_2 \leqslant 20$, tables of critical values for the R test statistic are available in specialized textbooks in nonparametric statistics.

Example A sample of 36 individuals were interviewed in a market-research survey, with 22 women (W) and 14 men (M) included in the sample. The sampled individuals were obtained in the following order: M̲, W̲, W, W, W, M̲, M, M, W̲, M̲, W̲, W, W, M̲, M, W̲, W, W, W, M̲, W̲, W, W, M̲, M, W̲, W, W, M̲, W̲, M̲, M, W̲, W, W, M̲. The number of runs in this sample is $R = 17$, as indicated by the underscores above. Where n_1 = the number of women and n_2 = the number of men, we can use the normal distribution to test the null hypothesis that the sampling process was random, because $n_1 > 20$. We compute the mean and the standard error of the sampling distribution of R as follows:

$$\mu_R = \frac{2 n_1 n_2}{n_1 + n_2} + 1 = \frac{2(22)(14)}{22 + 14} + 1 = \frac{616}{36} + 1 = 18.1$$

$$\sigma_R = \sqrt{\frac{2 n_1 n_2 (2 n_1 n_2 - n_1 - n_2)}{(n_1 + n_2)^2 (n_1 + n_2 - 1)}} = \sqrt{\frac{2(22)(14)[2(22)(14) - 22 - 14]}{(22 + 14)^2 (22 + 14 - 1)}}$$

$$= \sqrt{\frac{616(616 - 36)}{36^2 (35)}} = \sqrt{\frac{357{,}280}{45{,}360}} = \sqrt{7.8765} = 2.81$$

When the 5 percent level of significance is used, the critical values of the z statistic are $z = \pm 1.96$. The value of the z test statistic for these data is

$$z = \frac{R - \mu_R}{\sigma_R} = \frac{17 - 18.1}{2.81} = \frac{-1.1}{2.81} = -0.39$$

Therefore, using the 5 percent level of significance, we cannot reject the null hypothesis that the sequence of women and men occurred randomly. Note that this test is not concerned with the proportion of women (or men) that was observed. Such a hypothesis would be tested with the binomial distribution, as described in Section 10-4, or by the use of the normal distribution, as described in Section 10-5. Given the number of sample observations in the two categories, the runs test is only concerned with the randomness of the occurrence of the two types of outcomes.

18-9 SUMMARY

Nonparametric statistical methods can be used when one or more of the three principal assumptions associated with the use of parametric methods are not satisfied. These assumptions are concerned with (1) a population parameter and its value, (2) the form of the population distribution, and (3) measurement at the interval or ratio scale. Although nonparametric statistical tests are less powerful than the equivalent parametric tests, they are the only methods applicable in many data situations.

Two categories of statistical methods described in the earlier chapters of this book are in fact nonparametric procedures: *Chebyshev's inequality*, used to construct confidence intervals and to test hypotheses regarding the mean when the form of the distribution cannot be specified (Sections 7-6 and 9-6), is a nonparametric procedure. The χ^2 test for goodness of fit and for testing the independence of two variables, which was covered in Chapter 12 and which involves the analysis of nominal data, is also a nonparametric procedure.

Of the methods covered in this chapter the *Mann-Whitney* U *test* is used to test the null hypothesis that two independent random samples have been obtained from the same population. In contrast both the *sign test* and the *Wilcoxon test* for paired observations are used to test the null hypothesis that two matched samples were obtained from the same population. Because the Wilcoxon test takes into consideration the magnitude of the difference between each matched pair rather than just the sign of the difference, it is more powerful than the sign test. The other test for the null hypothesis that samples have been obtained from the same population is the *Kruskal-Wallis test* for several independent samples, which is the nonparametric equivalent of the one-factor completely randomized design of the analysis of variance.

The *Spearman rank correlation coefficient* can be used to measure the relationship between two variables that were measured at least at the ordinal scale. The coefficient obtained is interpreted similarly to the parametric Pearson product-moment correlation coefficient. Finally, the *runs test* is useful in a variety of data situations as a test of randomness.

FORMULAS

(18-1) $\quad U_1 = n_1 n_2 + \dfrac{n_1(n_1 + 1)}{2} - R_1$

Test statistic for the Mann-Whitney U test for two independent samples.

(18-2) $\quad U_2 = n_1 n_2 + \dfrac{n_2(n_2 + 1)}{2} - R_2$

Alternative test statistic for the Mann-Whitney U test.

(18-3) $\quad \mu_U = \dfrac{n_1 n_2}{2}$

Mean of the sampling distribution of U.

(18-4) $\quad \sigma_U = \sqrt{\dfrac{n_1 n_2 (n_1 + n_2 + 1)}{12}}$

Standard error of the sampling distribution of U.

(18-5) $z = \dfrac{U - \mu_U}{\sigma_U}$

Use of the z test statistic in conjunction with the Mann-Whitney U test for two independent samples; appropriate when both $n_1 > 10$ and $n_2 > 10$.

(18-6) $\mu_T = \dfrac{n(n+1)}{4}$

Mean of the sampling distribution for the Wilcoxon T statistic for paired observations, in which T is the smaller sum of the signed differences between the ranks of the paired observations.

(18-7) $\sigma_T = \sqrt{\dfrac{n(n+1)(2n+1)}{24}}$

Standard error of the sampling distribution of the Wilcoxon T statistic.

(18-8) $z = \dfrac{T - \mu_T}{\sigma_T}$

Use of the z test statistic in conjunction with the Wilcoxon test for paired observations; appropriate when $n \geqslant 25$.

(18-9) $H = \dfrac{12}{N(N+1)} \sum \dfrac{R_j^2}{n_j} - 3(N+1)$

Test statistic in the Kruskal-Wallis test for several independent samples.

(18-10) $H_c = \dfrac{H}{1 - [\Sigma(t_j^3 - t_j)/(N^3 - N)]}$

Corrected value of the H test statistic in the case of tied ranks.

(18-11) $r_r = 1 - \dfrac{6\Sigma d^2}{n(n^2 - 1)}$

Spearman rank correlation coefficient.

(18-12) $t = \dfrac{r_r}{\sqrt{(1 - r_r^2)/(n - 2)}}$

Use of Student's t distribution to test the null hypothesis of no relationship; appropriate when $n \geqslant 10$.

(18-13) $\mu_R = \dfrac{2n_1 n_2}{n_1 + n_2} + 1$

Mean of the sampling distribution of R in the runs test for randomness, in which R = number of observed runs.

(18-14) $\sigma_R = \sqrt{\dfrac{2n_1 n_2 (2n_1 n_2 - n_1 - n_2)}{(n_1 + n_2)^2 (n_1 + n_2 - 1)}}$

Standard error of the sampling distribution of the R test statistic.

$$(18\text{-}15) \quad z = \frac{R - \mu_R}{\sigma_R}$$

Use of the z test statistic in conjunction with the runs test for randomness; appropriate when either $n_1 > 20$ or $n_2 > 20$, where these are the number of observations assigned to each of the two data categories that serve to define a run.

EXERCISES

18-1 A quality control department wishes to compare the time required for two alternative systems to diagnose equipment failure. A sample of 30 equipment failures are randomly assigned for diagnosis to the two systems with 14 failures assigned for diagnosis to the first system and 16 assigned for diagnosis to the second system. The table below reports the total time, in minutes, required to diagnose each failure. No assumption can be made concerning the distribution of the total time required to diagnose such failures. Using the 10 percent level of significance, test the null hypothesis that the two samples have been obtained from the same population of values.

System 1	System 2
25	18
29	37
42	40
16	56
31	49
14	28
33	20
45	34
26	39
34	47
30	31
43	65
28	38
19	32
	24
	49

18-2 In addition to the data obtained in Exercise 18-1 suppose that a third system for diagnosing equipment failure is also evaluated by randomly assigning 12 failures to this system and observing the time required in minutes to diagnose each failure. The required time periods are 21, 36, 34, 19, 46, 25, 38, 31, 20, 26, 30, and 18. Using the 10 percent level of significance, test the null hypothesis that the three samples were obtained from the same population.

18-3 Instead of the experimental design used in Exercise 18-1, the same random sample of 10 equipment failures is diagnosed by the two systems. Thus each of the 10 pieces of equipment is subjected to diagnosis twice, and the time required in minutes to diagnose the failure by each system is noted. The table below indicates the number of minutes required for each diagnosis. Using the 10 percent level of significance, test the null hypothesis that the two samples came from populations that are not different in level. That is, the null hypothesis is that there is no difference in the amount of time required to diagnose equipment failures by the two methods. Use the sign test for this analysis.

Sampled equipment	System 1	System 2
1	23	21
2	40	48
3	35	45
4	24	22
5	17	19
6	32	37
7	27	29
8	32	38
9	25	24
10	30	36

18-4 At the 10 percent level of significance apply the Wilcoxon test for matched pairs to the data in Exercise 18-3, again testing the null hypothesis that there is no difference in the amount of time required by the two methods. Compare your results with those obtained in Exercise 18-3.

18-5 For the data reported in Exercise 18-3 we would expect a positive correlation between the times required to diagnose equipment failure by the two systems. Given that we cannot make any assumption about the forms of the two population distributions calculate a coefficient of correlation for the time required by the two systems. Using the 1 percent level of significance, test the null hypothesis $\rho \leq 0$. Of course rejection of this hypothesis would permit us to conclude that a positive relationship exists in the time required by the two systems of diagnosis.

18-6 The following two-digit values have been obtained from a table of random numbers by starting at an arbitrary point in the table and copying the numbers that follow that point as two-digit values, with a total of 45 two-digit values being obtained in the following sequence:

35, 58, 79, 33, 10, 48, 89, 74, 84, 93, 39, 80, 80, 05, 49,
33, 18, 50, 48, 05, 05, 43, 19, 45, 98, 97, 65, 41, 62, 32,
64, 05, 18, 34, 52, 01, 19, 78, 69, 35, 28, 02, 16, 15, 70.

(a) Test the randomness of this sequence by classifying each two-digit value as being an odd or an even value, using the 5 percent level of significance for the test.

(b) Test the randomness of this sequence by classifying each two-digit value as being above or below the value 49.5, which is the long-run expected value of the median for a population of random two-digit numbers ranging in value from 00 to 99. Again, use the 5 percent level of significance for the test.

18-7 A training and development department sends self-instructional course material on budgeting to four regional sales offices. After completion of the course the participating personnel at the four locations took a standardized test, for which the achievement scores are reported in the table below. Using the 5 percent level of significance, test the null hypothesis that the four groups of sample results were obtained from the same population distribution of scores. No assumptions can be made about the form of the population distribution.

	Location		
A	B	C	D
78	60	92	82
89	88	83	70
73	93	87	95
82	54	84	69
91	68	86	78
	93	90	74
	85		

18-8 The table below lists the ranks assigned by two securities analysts to 12 stock issues in terms of the amount of risk involved, with rank 1 = highest risk.

Stock issue	Rank by analyst 1	Rank by analyst 2
A	7	6
B	8	4
C	2	1
D	1	3
E	9	11
F	3	2
G	12	12
H	11	10
I	4	5
J	10	9
K	6	7
L	5	8

(*a*) Determine the correlation between the ranks assigned by the two analysts.

(*b*) Considering these stock issues to be a random sample, determine whether the correlation between the sets of ranks for the two analysts is significant at the 5 percent level.

18-9 A random sample of 15 people attend a public information session on the commercial potential of solar energy. The table below indicates the score of each individual on a 20-point attitude survey regarding solar energy before and after participation in the program. No assumption can be made about the form of the distribution of such attitude scores in the population. Using the 5 percent level of significance and using the most powerful nonparametric test available, test the null hypothesis that the two sets of attitude scores were obtained from populations of attitudes that are not different in level. The alternative hypothesis is that the level of attitude scores after the information session is higher than the level before the session. Of course failure to reject the null hypothesis would indicate that the public information session was not effective in increasing positive attitudes toward solar energy.

Individual	Before	After
A	12	18
B	9	8
C	11	16
D	20	20
E	16	19
F	6	4
G	10	14
H	14	16
I	8	4
J	10	16
K	15	18
L	14	18
M	5	5
N	7	2
O	12	17

18-10 Test the null hypothesis in Exercise 18-9 by a one-tail test using the less-powerful nonparametric procedure that can be used with such data.

18-11 The table below indicates the net rate of return, including capital gains or losses, for ten randomly selected common stock issues during a recession year and during a year of economic expansion. No assumptions can be made about the forms of the population distributions.

Stock issue	Return in year of recession, %	Return in year of expansion, %
1	4.0	5.0
2	−10.6	12.5
3	2.5	8.3
4	−6.3	18.7
5	−3.3	9.0
6	−18.4	22.1
7	−26.9	15.6
8	5.1	6.8
9	2.1	7.8
10	−8.0	9.4

(*a*) Determine the correlation between the performance of the stock issues during these two periods, and interpret the value of the correlation coefficient.

(*b*) Using the 5 percent level of significance, test the null hypothesis that there is no relationship between the performance of the stock issues during the two time periods.

18-12 As part of a test-marketing study, a product is packaged in two different types of containers for retail sale in discount department stores. Package A is sent to 12 randomly selected stores and package B is sent to 12 other randomly selected stores. The unit sales of the product during one week are reported in the table below. Based on experiences with similar products, we have reason to believe that the form and dispersion of the population sales amounts are the same for the two types of packages but that the level of sales may differ because of the packaging. Using the nonparametric procedure applicable to two independent samples and using the 5 percent level of significance, test the null hypothesis that the level of sales for the two types of product packaging is not different.

Package A	Package B
42	46
51	39
38	54
32	59
27	33
35	48
43	29
56	47
40	57
33	53
47	42
44	46

18-13 Suppose that we are able to assume that the population of sales amounts for each type of package in Exercise 18-12 is approximately normally distributed. Using the 5 percent level of significance, test the null hypothesis $H_0: \mu_1 = \mu_2$ by the appropriate parametric procedure and compare your results with those obtained in Exercise 18-12.

18-14 The following data relate the number of weeks of experience in a job involving the wiring of miniature electronic components and the number of components rejected during the past week for a random sample of 12 workers. (In Exercise 14-20 these data were used to calculate the parametric coefficient of correlation.)

Sampled worker	Weeks of experience	Number of rejects
1	7	26
2	9	20
3	6	28
4	14	16
5	8	23
6	12	18
7	10	24
8	4	26
9	2	38
10	11	22
11	1	32
12	8	25

(a) Suppose that we cannot assume a normal distribution for either the weeks of experience or number of rejects. Determine the value of the appropriate correlation coefficient for these data and compare the results with the correlation value determined in Exercise 14-20.

(b) Before any data were observed, it was claimed that there is a negative correlation between weeks of experience and number of rejects. To avoid giving this claim the benefit of the doubt, the appropriate null hypothesis is $H_0: \rho \geqslant 0$. Test this null hypothesis at $\alpha = 0.05$.

USE OF COMPUTERS
IN STATISTICAL ANALYSIS

A-1 GENERAL CONCEPTS

For analyzing statistical data, the large majority of computer system users make use of the *library programs*, or "canned" programs, already stored in the system rather than developing and writing their own computer programs. A computer center typically has a listing of such programs available, with descriptions of program output and the required form of input. A *computer program* is a set of coded statements that directs the computer to perform a series of computational or data-processing tasks in a specific, sequential manner.

Two principal types of languages in which a computer program can be written are *machine language* and *procedure-oriented language.* A machine language is unique to each make and model of computer, and therefore it is not practical for typical computer-system users. On the other hand procedure-oriented languages are similar to the structure of general mathematical statements and the English language. This factor plus the fact that such languages can be used with all computer systems has made the use of such languages widespread. Examples of procedure-oriented languages are BASIC, FORTRAN IV, PL/1, ALGOL, COBOL, and APL. The reason that such languages can be used with various computer systems is that manufacturers have provided special computer programs, called *compilers*, that translate procedure-oriented languages into the appropriate machine-processable language.

For the computer user involved with using a library program rather than writing a program, the principal concern is what input is required to use a stored program. Figure A-1 shows a typical input deck associated with the use of a library program

401

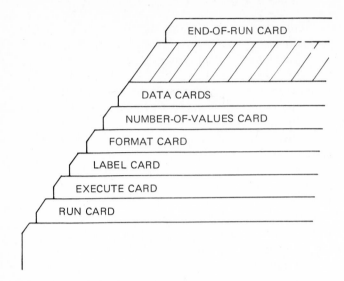

Figure A-1 Typical input deck associated with the use of a library program.

in a batch-processing system, where the form of input is on punched cards and output is on a high-speed printer.

The *run card*, or job card, identifies the user by account number and may include other required information, according to computer-center policies. The *execute card*, or search card, includes the coded name of the library program to be used. In essence this card takes the place of an entire computer program being input. The *label card*, or header card, includes the information to be used as the label or heading on the computer output. Typically, the user would include name and a title for the analysis being performed.

After the label card the *format card* in Figure A-1 identifies the specific form of the input values on the data cards. If the library program instructions specify data placement according to particular card-column locations, the format card is not required. When it is required, the user indicates that the values are all discrete integers by the code "I" (for integers) or indicates that they are values measured on a continuous scale by the code "F" (for *floating-point*). The integers are usually referred to as *fixed-point* values. Following the I or F on the format card, the user also indicates the maximum number of digits for each input value and the placement of the decimal point for the floating-point values. Thus I8 indicates that on the data cards eight card columns are reserved for each input value and that each value is an integer. F8.2 also indicates that eight card columns have been reserved for each input value but, further, that in the input the last two digits are to the right of the decimal point. Finally, the number preceding the I or F indicates the number of such fields, or groups of columns, included in each input card. Since each card includes 80 columns, no greater number than 80 can be designated by the format specification. Thus "10I8" or 10F8.2" designates that there are 10 fields of eight columns each, resulting in use of all 80 columns of the card.

Following the format card, another card that may be required is the *number-of-values card*. When such a card is not required, the computer simply reads the values included in the data deck until the first blank field is encountered.

The *data cards* in Figure A-1 contain the data to be analyzed. Of course entry of the values on these cards must be consistent with program-input specifications or with the format identified on the format card, if such a card was required in the input deck. Thus, if the format specification is 10F8.2, each value must be included within one of the eight-column fields. No decimal point should ever be punched for integer, or fixed-point, values. For floating-point values, however, the user can choose either to punch the decimal point or to omit it. If it is punched, of course only seven digits can be included in an eight-column field, for example. If the decimal point is not punched, a full eight numeric digits can be included in an eight-column field and the decimal point is automatically located by the computer by reference to the format statement. For input data in general it is at least desirable and often necessary to right-justify all values. That is, any blanks within a field should be to the left of the numeric input.

The final card in Figure A-1 is the *end-of-run card*, which signals the end of the entire input deck. The specific card layout varies according to computer center.

When time-sharing terminals are used for data analysis, the procedure from the user's point of view differs from the above description, which is concerned with batch-processing systems. However, the basic concepts associated with the use of library programs in time-sharing systems and the required format of input data are essentially the same as for batch-processing systems.

A-2 KEYPUNCH OPERATING INSTRUCTIONS

The following operating instructions are concerned with the IBM 29 Keypunch, a keypunch machine used to prepare punched cards for the batch processing of data. You should be seated at the keypunch machine as you read these instructions.

1. Make sure the power switch is on; it is located at your right knee when you are seated at the keypunch machine. Turn on the PRINT toggle switch; it is located just above the keyboard. Make sure that the feed hopper has an adequate number of cards.
2. Press the FEED key to feed a card from the feed hopper.
3. Press the REG (register) key to position the card under the punching station.
4. Punch alphabetic information by pressing appropriate keys. Keys are labeled. To determine the column ready to be punched next, observe the indicator inside the glass cover located to the left of the feed hopper. Punch numeric information by holding the NUM (numeric) key down. Keys are labeled. Space by means of the long space bar.
5. To remove a card from the punching station, press the REL (release) key (in some keypunches the label is EJECT instead of REL). If you want to punch another card, go to reference point 2 above and repeat the cycle. If you have

finished, press REL, then REG, then REL. The card will move to the output stacker in the upper left of the keypunch.

6. To duplicate a card that has just been punched, press the REL key to advance the card to the reading station. Press FEED, then REG to position a blank card under the punching station. Depress the DUP (duplicate) key. Holding the DUP key down causes duplication at the rate of 10 columns per second. Tapping the DUP key advances the card one column at a time.

7. To duplicate portions of a card or to punch corrections or additions, place the original card in the reading station. Press FEED, then REG. To duplicate a number of columns, press the DUP key. To punch in some columns, punch as usual.

8. To backspace, depress the backspace key located directly below the reading station of the punch.

9. For more efficient punching turn on AUTO FEED toggle switch. Then depress FEED twice. After that, every time you depress REL, a new card is fed and registered automatically, thus eliminating the need to depress FEED and REG every time. However, when making duplications or corrections, turn off the AUTO FEED switch.

TABLES

Table B-1 Table of random numbers

10097	85017	84532	13618	23157	86952	02438	76520
37542	16719	82789	69041	05545	44109	05403	64894
08422	65842	27672	82186	14871	22115	86529	19645
99019	76875	20684	39187	38976	94324	43204	09376
12807	93640	39160	41453	97312	41548	93137	80157
66065	99478	70086	71265	11742	18226	29004	34072
31060	65119	26486	47353	43361	99436	42753	45571
85269	70322	21592	48233	93806	32584	21828	02051
63573	58133	41278	11697	49540	61777	67954	05325
73796	44655	81255	31133	36768	60452	38537	03529
98520	02295	13487	98662	07092	44673	61303	14905
11805	85035	54881	35587	43310	48897	48493	39808
83452	01197	86935	28021	61570	23350	65710	06288
88685	97907	19078	40646	31352	48625	44369	86507
99594	63268	96905	28797	57048	46359	74294	87517
65481	52841	59684	67411	09243	56092	84369	17468
80124	53722	71399	10916	07959	21225	13018	17727
74350	11434	51908	62171	93732	26958	02400	77402
69916	62375	99292	21177	72721	66995	07289	66252
09893	28337	20923	87929	61020	62841	31374	14225
91499	38631	79430	62421	97959	67422	69992	68479
80336	49172	16332	44670	35089	17691	89246	26940
44104	89232	57327	34679	62235	79655	81336	85157
12550	02844	15026	32439	58537	48274	81330	11100
63606	40387	65406	37920	08709	60623	2237	16505
61196	80240	44177	51171	08723	39323	05798	26457
15474	44910	99321	72173	56239	04595	10836	95270
94557	33663	86347	00926	44915	34823	51770	67897
42481	86430	19102	37420	41976	76559	24358	97344
23523	31379	68588	81675	15694	43438	36879	73208
04493	98086	32533	17767	14523	52494	24826	75246
00549	33185	04805	05431	94598	97654	16232	64051
35963	80951	68953	99634	81949	15307	00406	26898
59808	79752	02529	40200	73742	08391	49140	45427
46058	18633	99970	67348	49329	95236	32537	01390
32179	74029	74717	17674	90446	00597	45240	87379
69234	54178	10805	35635	45266	61406	41941	20117
19565	11664	77602	99817	28573	41430	96382	01758
45155	48324	32135	26803	16213	14938	71961	19476
94864	69074	45753	20505	78317	31994	98145	36168

Table B-2 Binomial probabilities*

n	x	.01	.05	.10	.15	.20	.25	p .30	.35	.40	.45	.50
1	0	.9900	.9500	.9000	.8500	.8000	.7500	.7000	.6500	.6000	.5500	.5000
	1	.0100	.0500	.1000	.1500	.2000	.2500	.3000	.3500	.4000	.4500	.5000
2	0	.9801	.9025	.8100	.7225	.6400	.5625	.4900	.4225	.3600	.3025	.2500
	1	.0198	.0950	.1800	.2550	.3200	.3750	.4200	.4550	.4800	.4950	.5000
	2	.0001	.0025	.0100	.0225	.0400	.0625	.0900	.1225	.1600	.2025	.2500
3	0	.9703	.8574	.7290	.6141	.5120	.4219	.3430	.2746	.2160	.1664	.1250
	1	.0294	.1354	.2430	.3251	.3840	.4219	.4410	.4436	.4320	.4084	.3750
	2	.0003	.0071	.0270	.0574	.0960	.1406	.1890	.2389	.2880	.3341	.3750
	3	.0000	.0001	.0010	.0034	.0080	.0156	.0270	.0429	.0640	.0911	.1250
4	0	.9606	.8145	.6561	.5220	.4096	.3164	.2401	.1785	.1296	.0915	.0625
	1	.0388	.1715	.2916	.3685	.4096	.4219	.4116	.3845	.3456	.2995	.2500
	2	.0006	.0135	.0486	.0975	.1536	.2109	.2646	.3105	.3456	.3675	.3750
	3	.0000	.0005	.0036	.0115	.0256	.0469	.0756	.1115	.1536	.2005	.2500
	4	.0000	.0000	.0001	.0005	.0016	.0039	.0081	.0150	.0256	.0410	.0625
5	0	.9510	.7738	.5905	.4437	.3277	.2373	.1681	.1160	.0778	.0503	.0312
	1	.0480	.2036	.3280	.3915	.4096	.3955	.3602	.3124	.2592	.2059	.1562
	2	.0010	.0214	.0729	.1382	.2048	.2637	.3087	.3364	.3456	.3369	.3125
	3	.0000	.0011	.0081	.0244	.0512	.0879	.1323	.1811	.2304	.2757	.3125
	4	.0000	.0000	.0004	.0022	.0064	.0146	.0284	.0488	.0768	.1128	.1562
	5	.0000	.0000	.0000	.0001	.0003	.0010	.0024	.0053	.0102	.0185	.0312
6	0	.9415	.7351	.5314	.3771	.2621	.1780	.1176	.0754	.0467	.0277	.0156
	1	.0571	.2321	.3543	.3993	.3932	.3560	.3025	.2437	.1866	.1359	.0938
	2	.0014	.0305	.0984	.1762	.2458	.2966	.3241	.3280	.3110	.2780	.2344
	3	.0000	.0021	.0146	.0415	.0819	.1318	.1852	.2355	.2765	.3032	.3125
	4	.0000	.0001	.0012	.0055	.0154	.0330	.0595	.0951	.1382	.1861	.2344
	5	.0000	.0000	.0001	.0004	.0015	.0044	.0102	.0205	.0369	.0609	.0938
	6	.0000	.0000	.0000	.0000	.0001	.0002	.0007	.0018	.0041	.0083	.0156
7	0	.9321	.6983	.4783	.3206	.2097	.1335	.0824	.0490	.0280	.0152	.0078
	1	.0659	.2573	.3720	.3960	.3670	.3115	.2471	.1848	.1306	.0872	.0547
	2	.0020	.0406	.1240	.2097	.2753	.3115	.3177	.2985	.2613	.2140	.1641
	3	.0000	.0036	.0230	.0617	.1147	.1730	.2269	.2679	.2903	.2918	.2734
	4	.0000	.0002	.0026	.0109	.0287	.0577	.0972	.1442	.1935	.2388	.2734
	5	.0000	.0000	.0002	.0012	.0043	.0115	.0250	.0466	.0774	.1172	.1641
	6	.0000	.0000	.0000	.0001	.0004	.0013	.0036	.0084	.0172	.0320	.0547
	7	.0000	.0000	.0000	.0000	.0000	.0001	.0002	.0006	.0016	.0037	.0078
8	0	.9227	.6634	.4305	.2725	.1678	.1002	.0576	.0319	.0168	.0084	.0039
	1	.0746	.2793	.3826	.3847	.3355	.2670	.1977	.1373	.0896	.0548	.0312
	2	.0026	.0515	.1488	.2376	.2936	.3115	.2965	.2587	.2090	.1569	.1094
	3	.0001	.0054	.0331	.0839	.1468	.2076	.2541	.2786	.2787	.2568	.2188
	4	.0000	.0004	.0046	.0185	.0459	.0865	.1361	.1875	.2322	.2627	.2734

*Example: $P(X = 3 \mid n = 5, p = 0.30) = 0.1323$.

407

Table B-2 Binomial probabilities (*Continued*)

n	x	.01	.05	.10	.15	.20	.25	.30	.35	.40	.45	.50
8	5	.0000	.0000	.0004	.0026	.0092	.0231	.0467	.0808	.1239	.1719	.2188
	6	.0000	.0000	.0000	.0002	.0011	.0038	.0100	.0217	.0413	.0403	.1094
	7	.0000	.0000	.0000	.0000	.0001	.0004	.0012	.0033	.0079	.0164	.0312
	8	.0000	.0000	.0000	.0000	.0000	.0000	.0001	.0002	.0007	.0017	.0039
9	0	.9135	.6302	.3874	.2316	.1342	.0751	.0404	.0207	.0101	.0046	.0020
	1	.0830	.2985	.3874	.3679	.3020	.2253	.1556	.1004	.0605	.0339	.0176
	2	.0034	.0629	.1722	.2597	.3020	.3003	.2668	.2162	.1612	.1110	.0703
	3	.0001	.0077	.0446	.1069	.1762	.2336	.2668	.2716	.2508	.2119	.1641
	4	.0000	.0006	.0074	.0283	.0661	.1168	.1715	.2194	.2508	.2600	.2461
	5	.0000	.0000	.0008	.0050	.0165	.0389	.0735	.1181	.1672	.2128	.2461
	6	.0000	.0000	.0001	.0006	.0028	.0087	.0210	.0424	.0743	.1160	.1641
	7	.0000	.0000	.0000	.0000	.0003	.0012	.0039	.0098	.0212	.0407	.0703
	8	.0000	.0000	.0000	.0000	.0000	.0001	.0004	.0013	.0035	.0083	.0176
	9	.0000	.0000	.0000	.0000	.0000	.0000	.0000	.0001	.0003	.0008	.0020
10	0	.9044	.5987	.3487	.1969	.1074	.0563	.0282	.0135	.0060	.0025	.0010
	1	.0914	.3151	.3874	.3474	.2684	.1877	.1211	.0725	.0403	.0207	.0098
	2	.0042	.0746	.1937	.2759	.3020	.2816	.2335	.1757	.1209	.0763	.0439
	3	.0001	.0105	.0574	.1298	.2013	.2503	.2668	.2522	.2150	.1665	.1172
	4	.0000	.0010	.0112	.0401	.0881	.1460	.2001	.2377	.2508	.2384	.2051
	5	.0000	.0001	.0015	.0085	.0264	.0584	.1029	.1536	.2007	.2340	.2461
	6	.0000	.0000	.0001	.0012	.0055	.0162	.0368	.0689	.1115	.1596	.2051
	7	.0000	.0000	.0000	.0001	.0008	.0031	.0090	.0212	.0425	.0746	.1172
	8	.0000	.0000	.0000	.0000	.0001	.0004	.0014	.0043	.0106	.0229	.0439
	9	.0000	.0000	.0000	.0000	.0000	.0000	.0001	.0005	.0016	.0042	.0098
	10	.0000	.0000	.0000	.0000	.0000	.0000	.0000	.0000	.0001	.0003	.0010
11	0	.8953	.5688	.3138	.1673	.0859	.0422	.0198	.0088	.0036	.0014	.0005
	1	.0995	.3293	.3835	.3248	.2362	.1549	.0932	.0518	.0266	.0125	.0054
	2	.0050	.0867	.2131	.2866	.2953	.2581	.1998	.1395	.0887	.0513	.0269
	3	.0002	.0137	.0710	.1517	.2215	.2581	.2568	.2254	.1774	.1259	.0806
	4	.0000	.0014	.0158	.0536	.1107	.1721	.2201	.2428	.2365	.2060	.1611
	5	.0000	.0001	.0025	.0132	.0388	.0803	.1321	.1830	.2207	.2360	.2256
	6	.0000	.0000	.0003	.0023	.0097	.0268	.0566	.0985	.1471	.1931	.2256
	7	.0000	.0000	.0000	.0003	.0017	.0064	.0173	.0379	.0701	.1128	.1611
	8	.0000	.0000	.0000	.0000	.0002	.0011	.0037	.0102	.0234	.0462	.0806
	9	.0000	.0000	.0000	.0000	.0000	.0001	.0005	.0018	.0052	.0126	.0269
	10	.0000	.0000	.0000	.0000	.0000	.0000	.0000	.0002	.0007	.0021	.0054
	11	.0000	.0000	.0000	.0000	.0000	.0000	.0000	.0000	.0000	.0002	.0005
12	0	.8864	.5404	.2824	.1422	.0687	.0317	.0138	.0057	.0022	.0008	.0002
	1	.1074	.3413	.3766	.3012	.2062	.1267	.0712	.0368	.0174	.0075	.0029
	2	.0060	.0988	.2301	.2924	.2835	.2323	.1678	.1088	.0639	.0339	.0161
	3	.0002	.0173	.0852	.1720	.2362	.2581	.2397	.1954	.1419	.0923	.0537
	4	.0000	.0021	.0213	.0683	.1329	.1936	.2311	.2367	.2128	.1700	.1208
	5	.0000	.0002	.0038	.0193	.0532	.1032	.1585	.2039	.2270	.2225	.1934
	6	.0000	.0000	.0005	.0040	.0155	.0401	.0792	.1281	.1766	.2124	.2256

Table B-2 Binomial probabilities (*Continued*)

n	x	.01	.05	.10	.15	.20	.25	p .30	.35	.40	.45	.50
12	7	.0000	.0000	.0000	.0006	.0033	.0115	.0291	.0591	.1009	.1489	.1934
	8	.0000	.0000	.0000	.0001	.0005	.0024	.0078	.0199	.0420	.0762	.1208
	9	.0000	.0000	.0000	.0000	.0001	.0004	.0015	.0048	.0125	.0277	.0537
	10	.0000	.0000	.0000	.0000	.0000	.0000	.0002	.0008	.0025	.0068	.0161
	11	.0000	.0000	.0000	.0000	.0000	.0000	.0000	.0001	.0003	.0010	.0029
	12	.0000	.0000	.0000	.0000	.0000	.0000	.0000	.0000	.0000	.0001	.0002
13	0	.8775	.5133	.2542	.1209	.0550	.0238	.0097	.0037	.0013	.0004	.0001
	1	.1152	.3512	.3672	.2774	.1787	.1029	.0540	.0259	.0113	.0045	.0016
	2	.0070	.1109	.2448	.2937	.2680	.2059	.1388	.0836	.0453	.0220	.0095
	3	.0003	.0214	.0997	.1900	.2457	.2517	.2181	.1651	.1107	.0660	.0349
	4	.0000	.0028	.0277	.0838	.1535	.2097	.2337	.2222	.1845	.1350	.0873
	5	.0000	.0003	.0055	.0266	.0691	.1258	.1803	.2154	.2214	.1989	.1571
	6	.0000	.0000	.0008	.0063	.0230	.0559	.1030	.1546	.1968	.2169	.2095
	7	.0000	.0000	.0001	.0011	.0058	.0186	.0442	.0833	.1312	.1775	.2095
	8	.0000	.0000	.0001	.0001	.0011	.0047	.0142	.0336	.0656	.1089	.1571
	9	.0000	.0000	.0000	.0000	.0001	.0009	.0034	.0101	.0243	.0495	.0873
	10	.0000	.0000	.0000	.0000	.0000	.0001	.0006	.0022	.0065	.0162	.0349
	11	.0000	.0000	.0000	.0000	.0000	.0000	.0001	.0003	.0012	.0036	.0095
	12	.0000	.0000	.0000	.0000	.0000	.0000	.0000	.0000	.0001	.0005	.0016
	13	.0000	.0000	.0000	.0000	.0000	.0000	.0000	.0000	.0000	.0000	.0001
14	0	.8687	.4877	.2288	.1028	.0440	.0178	.0068	.0024	.0008	.0002	.0001
	1	.1229	.3593	.3559	.2539	.1539	.0832	.0407	.0181	.0073	.0027	.0009
	2	.0081	.1229	.2570	.2912	.2501	.1802	.1134	.0634	.0317	.0141	.0056
	3	.0003	.0259	.1142	.2056	.2501	.2402	.1943	.1366	.0845	.0462	.0222
	4	.0000	.0037	.0349	.0998	.1720	.2202	.2290	.2022	.1549	.1040	.0611
	5	.0000	.0004	.0078	.0352	.0860	.1468	.1963	.2178	.2066	.1701	.1222
	6	.0000	.0000	.0013	.0093	.0322	.0734	.1262	.1759	.2066	.2088	.1833
	7	.0000	.0000	.0002	.0019	.0092	.0280	.0618	.1082	.1574	.1952	.2095
	8	.0000	.0000	.0000	.0003	.0020	.0082	.0232	.0510	.0918	.1398	.1833
	9	.0000	.0000	.0000	.0000	.0003	.0018	.0066	.0183	.0408	.0762	.1222
	10	.0000	.0000	.0000	.0000	.0000	.0003	.0014	.0049	.0136	.0312	.0611
	11	.0000	.0000	.0000	.0000	.0000	.0000	.0002	.0010	.0033	.0093	.0222
	12	.0000	.0000	.0000	.0000	.0000	.0000	.0000	.0001	.0005	.0019	.0056
	13	.0000	.0000	.0000	.0000	.0000	.0000	.0000	.0000	.0001	.0002	.0009
	14	.0000	.0000	.0000	.0000	.0000	.0000	.0000	.0000	.0000	.0000	.0001
15	0	.8601	.4633	.2059	.0874	.0352	.0134	.0047	.0016	.0005	.0001	.0000
	1	.1303	.3658	.3432	.2312	.1319	.0668	.0305	.0126	.0047	.0016	.0005
	2	.0092	.1348	.2669	.2856	.2309	.1559	.0916	.0476	.0219	.0090	.0032
	3	.0004	.0307	.1285	.2184	.2501	.2252	.1700	.1110	.0634	.0318	.0139
	4	.0000	.0049	.0428	.1156	.1876	.2252	.2186	.1792	.1268	.0780	.0417

409

Table B-2 Binomial probabilities (*Continued*)

n	x	.01	.05	.10	.15	.20	.25	*p* .30	.35	.40	.45	.50
15	5	.0000	.0006	.0105	.0449	.1032	.1651	.2061	.2123	.1859	.1404	.0916
	6	.0000	.0000	.0019	.0132	.0430	.0917	.1472	.1906	.2066	.1914	.1527
	7	.0000	.0000	.0003	.0030	.0138	.0393	.0811	.1319	.1771	.2013	.1964
	8	.0000	.0000	.0000	.0005	.0035	.0131	.0348	.0710	.1181	.1647	.1964
	9	.0000	.0000	.0000	.0001	.0007	.0034	.0116	.0298	.0612	.1048	.1527
	10	.0000	.0000	.0000	.0000	.0001	.0007	.0030	.0096	.0245	.0515	.0916
	11	.0000	.0000	.0000	.0000	.0000	.0001	.0006	.0024	.0074	.0191	.0417
	12	.0000	.0000	.0000	.0000	.0000	.0000	.0001	.0004	.0016	.0052	.0139
	13	.0000	.0000	.0000	.0000	.0000	.0000	.0000	.0001	.0003	.0010	.0032
	14	.0000	.0000	.0000	.0000	.0000	.0000	.0000	.0000	.0000	.0001	.0005
	15	.0000	.0000	.0000	.0000	.0000	.0000	.0000	.0000	.0000	.0000	.0000
16	0	.8515	.4401	.1853	.0743	.0281	.0100	.0033	.0010	.0003	.0001	.0000
	1	.1376	.3706	.3294	.2097	.1126	.0535	.0228	.0087	.0030	.0009	.0002
	2	.0104	.1463	.2745	.2775	.2111	.1336	.0732	.0353	.0150	.0056	.0018
	3	.0005	.0359	.1423	.2285	.2463	.2079	.1465	.0888	.0468	.0215	.0085
	4	.0000	.0061	.0514	.1311	.2001	.2252	.2040	.1553	.1014	.0572	.0278
	5	.0000	.0008	.0137	.0555	.1201	.1802	.2099	.2008	.1623	.1123	.0667
	6	.0000	.0001	.0028	.0180	.0550	.1101	.1649	.1982	.1983	.1684	.1222
	7	.0000	.0000	.0004	.0045	.0197	.0524	.1010	.1524	.1889	.1969	.1746
	8	.0000	.0000	.0001	.0009	.0055	.0197	.0487	.0923	.1417	.1812	.1964
	9	.0000	.0000	.0000	.0001	.0012	.0058	.0185	.0442	.0840	.1318	.1746
	10	.0000	.0000	.0000	.0000	.0002	.0014	.0056	.0167	.0392	.0755	.1222
	11	.0000	.0000	.0000	.0000	.0000	.0002	.0013	.0049	.0142	.0337	.0667
	12	.0000	.0000	.0000	.0000	.0000	.0000	.0002	.0011	.0040	.0115	.0278
	13	.0000	.0000	.0000	.0000	.0000	.0000	.0000	.0002	.0008	.0029	.0085
	14	.0000	.0000	.0000	.0000	.0000	.0000	.0000	.0000	.0001	.0005	.0018
	15	.0000	.0000	.0000	.0000	.0000	.0000	.0000	.0000	.0000	.0001	.0002
	16	.0000	.0000	.0000	.0000	.0000	.0000	.0000	.0000	.0000	.0000	.0000
17	0	.8429	.4181	.1668	.0631	.0225	.0075	.0023	.0007	.0002	.0000	.0000
	1	.1447	.3741	.3150	.1893	.0957	.0426	.0169	.0060	.0019	.0005	.0001
	2	.0117	.1575	.2800	.2673	.1914	.1136	.0581	.0260	.0102	.0035	.0010
	3	.0006	.0415	.1556	.2359	.2393	.1893	.1245	.0701	.0341	.0144	.0052
	4	.0000	.0076	.0605	.1457	.2093	.2209	.1868	.1320	.0796	.0411	.0182
	5	.0000	.0010	.0175	.0668	.1361	.1914	.2081	.1849	.1379	.0875	.0472
	6	.0000	.0001	.0039	.0236	.0680	.1276	.1784	.1991	.1839	.1432	.0944
	7	.0000	.0000	.0007	.0065	.0267	.0668	.1201	.1685	.1927	.1841	.1484
	8	.0000	.0000	.0001	.0014	.0084	.0279	.0644	.1134	.1606	.1883	.1855
	9	.0000	.0000	.0000	.0003	.0021	.0093	.0276	.0611	.1070	.1540	.1855
	10	.0000	.0000	.0000	.0000	.0004	.0025	.0095	.0263	.0571	.1008	.1484
	11	.0000	.0000	.0000	.0000	.0001	.0005	.0026	.0090	.0242	.0525	.0944
	12	.0000	.0000	.0000	.0000	.0000	.0001	.0006	.0024	.0081	.0215	.0472
	13	.0000	.0000	.0000	.0000	.0000	.0000	.0001	.0005	.0021	.0068	.0182
	14	.0000	.0000	.0000	.0000	.0000	.0000	.0000	.0001	.0004	.0016	.0052

Table B-2 Binomial probabilities (*Continued*)

n	x	.01	.05	.10	.15	.20	.25	p .30	.35	.40	.45	.50
17	15	.0000	.0000	.0000	.0000	.0000	.0000	.0000	.0000	.0001	.0003	.0010
	16	.0000	.0000	.0000	.0000	.0000	.0000	.0000	.0000	.0000	.0000	.0001
	17	.0000	.0000	.0000	.0000	.0000	.0000	.0000	.0000	.0000	.0000	.0000
18	0	.8345	.3972	.1501	.0536	.0180	.0056	.0016	.0004	.0001	.0000	.0000
	1	.1517	.3763	.3002	.1704	.0811	.0338	.0126	.0042	.0012	.0003	.0001
	2	.0130	.1683	.2835	.2556	.1723	.0958	.0458	.0190	.0069	.0022	.0006
	3	.0007	.0473	.1680	.2406	.2297	.1704	.1046	.0547	.0246	.0095	.0031
	4	.0000	.0093	.0700	.1592	.2153	.2130	.1681	.1104	.0614	.0291	.0117
	5	.0000	.0014	.0218	.0787	.1507	.1988	.2017	.1664	.1146	.0666	.0327
	6	.0000	.0002	.0052	.0301	.0816	.1436	.1873	.1941	.1655	.1181	.0708
	7	.0000	.0000	.0010	.0091	.0350	.0820	.1376	.1792	.1892	.1657	.1214
	8	.0000	.0000	.0002	.0022	.0120	.0376	.0811	.1327	.1734	.1864	.1669
	9	.0000	.0000	.0000	.0004	.0033	.0139	.0386	.0794	.1284	.1694	.1855
	10	.0000	.0000	.0000	.0001	.0008	.0042	.0149	.0385	.0771	.1248	.1669
	11	.0000	.0000	.0000	.0000	.0001	.0010	.0046	.0151	.0374	.0742	.1214
	12	.0000	.0000	.0000	.0000	.0000	.0002	.0012	.0047	.0145	.0354	.0708
	13	.0000	.0000	.0000	.0000	.0000	.0000	.0002	.0012	.0045	.0134	.0327
	14	.0000	.0000	.0000	.0000	.0000	.0000	.0000	.0002	.0011	.0039	.0117
	15	.0000	.0000	.0000	.0000	.0000	.0000	.0000	.0000	.0002	.0009	.0031
	16	.0000	.0000	.0000	.0000	.0000	.0000	.0000	.0000	.0000	.0001	.0006
	17	.0000	.0000	.0000	.0000	.0000	.0000	.0000	.0000	.0000	.0000	.0001
	18	.0000	.0000	.0000	.0000	.0000	.0000	.0000	.0000	.0000	.0000	.0000
19	0	.8262	.3774	.1351	.0456	.0144	.0042	.0011	.0003	.0001	.0000	.0000
	1	.1586	.3774	.2852	.1529	.0685	.0268	.0093	.0029	.0008	.0002	.0000
	2	.0144	.1787	.2852	.2428	.1540	.0803	.0358	.0138	.0046	.0013	.0003
	3	.0008	.0533	.1796	.2428	.2182	.1517	.0869	.0422	.0175	.0062	.0018
	4	.0000	.0112	.0798	.1714	.2182	.2023	.1491	.0909	.0467	.0203	.0074
	5	.0000	.0018	.0266	.0907	.1636	.2023	.1916	.1468	.0933	.0497	.0222
	6	.0000	.0002	.0069	.0374	.0955	.1574	.1916	.1844	.1451	.0949	.0518
	7	.0000	.0000	.0014	.0122	.0443	.0974	.1525	.1844	.1797	.1443	.0961
	8	.0000	.0000	.0002	.0032	.0166	.0487	.0981	.1489	.1797	.1771	.1442
	9	.0000	.0000	.0000	.0007	.0051	.0198	.0514	.0980	.1464	.1771	.1762
	10	.0000	.0000	.0000	.0001	.0013	.0066	.0220	.0528	.0976	.1449	.1762
	11	.0000	.0000	.0000	.0000	.0003	.0018	.0077	.0233	.0532	.0970	.1442
	12	.0000	.0000	.0000	.0000	.0000	.0004	.0022	.0083	.0237	.0529	.0961
	13	.0000	.0000	.0000	.0000	.0000	.0001	.0005	.0024	.0085	.0233	.0518
	14	.0000	.0000	.0000	.0000	.0000	.0000	.0001	.0006	.0024	.0082	.0222
	15	.0000	.0000	.0000	.0000	.0000	.0000	.0000	.0001	.0005	.0022	.0074
	16	.0000	.0000	.0000	.0000	.0000	.0000	.0000	.0000	.0001	.0005	.0018
	17	.0000	.0000	.0000	.0000	.0000	.0000	.0000	.0000	.0000	.0001	.0003

Table B-2 Binomial probabilities (*Continued*)

n	x	.01	.05	.10	.15	.20	.25	p .30	.35	.40	.45	.50
	18	.0000	.0000	.0000	.0000	.0000	.0000	.0000	.0000	.0000	.0000	.0000
	19	.0000	.0000	.0000	.0000	.0000	.0000	.0000	.0000	.0000	.0000	.0000
20	0	.8179	.3585	.1216	.0388	.0115	.0032	.0008	.0002	.0000	.0000	.0000
	1	.1652	.3774	.2702	.1368	.0576	.0211	.0068	.0020	.0005	.0001	.0000
	2	.0159	.1887	.2852	.2293	.1369	.0669	.0278	.0100	.0031	.0008	.0002
	3	.0010	.0596	.1901	.2428	.2054	.1339	.0716	.0323	.0123	.0040	.0011
	4	.0000	.0133	.0898	.1821	.2182	.1897	.1304	.0738	.0350	.0139	.0046
	5	.0000	.0022	.0319	.1028	.1746	.2023	.1789	.1272	.0746	.0365	.0148
	6	.0000	.0003	.0089	.0454	.1091	.1686	.1916	.1712	.1244	.0746	.0370
	7	.0000	.0000	.0020	.0160	.0545	.1124	.1643	.1844	.1659	.1221	.0739
	8	.0000	.0000	.0004	.0046	.0222	.0609	.1144	.1614	.1797	.1623	.1201
	9	.0000	.0000	.0001	.0011	.0074	.0271	.0654	.1158	.1597	.1771	.1602
	10	.0000	.0000	.0000	.0002	.0020	.0099	.0308	.0686	.1171	.1593	.1762
	11	.0000	.0000	.0000	.0000	.0005	.0030	.0120	.0336	.0710	.1185	.1602
	12	.0000	.0000	.0000	.0000	.0001	.0008	.0039	.0136	.0355	.0727	.1201
	13	.0000	.0000	.0000	.0000	.0000	.0002	.0010	.0045	.0146	.0366	.0739
	14	.0000	.0000	.0000	.0000	.0000	.0000	.0002	.0012	.0049	.0150	.0370
	15	.0000	.0000	.0000	.0000	.0000	.0000	.0000	.0003	.0013	.0049	.0148
	16	.0000	.0000	.0000	.0000	.0000	.0000	.0000	.0000	.0003	.0013	.0046
	17	.0000	.0000	.0000	.0000	.0000	.0000	.0000	.0000	.0000	.0002	.0011
	18	.0000	.0000	.0000	.0000	.0000	.0000	.0000	.0000	.0000	.0000	.0002
	19	.0000	.0000	.0000	.0000	.0000	.0000	.0000	.0000	.0000	.0000	.0000
	20	.0000	.0000	.0000	.0000	.0000	.0000	.0000	.0000	.0000	.0000	.0000
25	0	.7778	.2774	.0718	.0172	.0038	.0008	.0001	.0000	.0000	.0000	.0000
	1	.1964	.3650	.1994	.0759	.0236	.0063	.0014	.0003	.0000	.0000	.0000
	2	.0238	.2305	.2659	.1607	.0708	.0251	.0074	.0018	.0004	.0001	.0000
	3	.0018	.0930	.2265	.2174	.1358	.0641	.0243	.0076	.0019	.0004	.0001
	4	.0001	.0269	.1384	.2110	.1867	.1175	.0572	.0224	.0071	.0018	.0004
	5	.0000	.0060	.0646	.1564	.1960	.1645	.1030	.0506	.0199	.0063	.0016
	6	.0000	.0010	.0239	.0920	.1633	.1828	.1472	.0908	.0442	.0172	.0053
	7	.0000	.0001	.0072	.0441	.1108	.1654	.1712	.1327	.0800	.0381	.0143
	8	.0000	.0000	.0018	.0175	.0623	.1241	.1651	.1607	.1200	.0701	.0322
	9	.0000	.0000	.0004	.0058	.0294	.0781	.1336	.1635	.1511	.1084	.0609
	10	.0000	.0000	.0000	.0016	.0118	.0417	.0916	.1409	.1612	.1419	.0974
	11	.0000	.0000	.0000	.0004	.0040	.0189	.0536	.1034	.1465	.1583	.1328
	12	.0000	.0000	.0000	.0000	.0012	.0074	.0268	.0650	.1140	.1511	.1550
	13	.0000	.0000	.0000	.0000	.0003	.0025	.0115	.0350	.0760	.1236	.1550
	14	.0000	.0000	.0000	.0000	.0000	.0007	.0042	.0161	.0434	.0867	.1328
	15	.0000	.0000	.0000	.0000	.0000	.0002	.0013	.0064	.0212	.0520	.0974
	16	.0000	.0000	.0000	.0000	.0000	.0000	.0004	.0021	.0088	.0266	.0609
	17	.0000	.0000	.0000	.0000	.0000	.0000	.0001	.0006	.0031	.0115	.0322
	18	.0000	.0000	.0000	.0000	.0000	.0000	.0000	.0001	.0009	.0042	.0143
	19	.0000	.0000	.0000	.0000	.0000	.0000	.0000	.0000	.0002	.0013	.0053

Table B-2 Binomial probabilities (*Continued*)

n	x	.01	.05	.10	.15	.20	.25	p .30	.35	.40	.45	.50
25	20	.0000	.0000	.0000	.0000	.0000	.0000	.0000	.0000	.0000	.0001	.0016
	21	.0000	.0000	.0000	.0000	.0000	.0000	.0000	.0000	.0000	.0000	.0004
	22	.0000	.0000	.0000	.0000	.0000	.0000	.0000	.0000	.0000	.0000	.0001
30	0	.7397	.2146	.0424	.0076	.0012	.0002	.0000	.0000	.0000	.0000	.0000
	1	.2242	.3389	.1413	.0404	.0093	.0018	.0003	.0000	.0000	.0000	.0000
	2	.0328	.2586	.2277	.1034	.0337	.0086	.0018	.0003	.0000	.0000	.0000
	3	.0031	.1270	.2361	.1703	.0785	.0269	.0072	.0015	.0003	.0000	.0000
	4	.0002	.0451	.1771	.2028	.1325	.0604	.0208	.0056	.0012	.0002	.0000
	5	.0000	.0124	.1023	.1861	.1723	.1047	.0464	.0157	.0041	.0008	.0001
	6	.0000	.0027	.0474	.1368	.1795	.1455	.0829	.0353	.0115	.0029	.0006
	7	.0000	.0005	.0180	.0828	.1538	.1662	.1219	.0652	.0263	.0081	.0019
	8	.0000	.0001	.0058	.0420	.1106	.1593	.1501	.1009	.0505	.0191	.0055
	9	.0000	.0000	.0016	.0181	.0676	.1298	.1573	.1328	.0823	.0382	.0133
	10	.0000	.0000	.0004	.0067	.0355	.0909	.1416	.1502	.1152	.0656	.0280
	11	.0000	.0000	.0001	.0022	.0161	.0551	.1103	.1471	.1396	.0976	.0509
	12	.0000	.0000	.0000	.0006	.0064	.0291	.0749	.1254	.1474	.1265	.0806
	13	.0000	.0000	.0000	.0001	.0022	.0134	.0444	.0935	.1360	.1433	.1115
	14	.0000	.0000	.0000	.0000	.0007	.0054	.0231	.0611	.1101	.1424	.1354
	15	.0000	.0000	.0000	.0000	.0002	.0019	.0106	.0351	.0783	.1242	.1445
	16	.0000	.0000	.0000	.0000	.0000	.0006	.0042	.0177	.0489	.0953	.1354
	17	.0000	.0000	.0000	.0000	.0000	.0002	.0015	.0079	.0269	.0642	.1115
	18	.0000	.0000	.0000	.0000	.0000	.0000	.0005	.0031	.0129	.0379	.0806
	19	.0000	.0000	.0000	.0000	.0000	.0000	.0001	.0010	.0054	.0196	.0509
	20	.0000	.0000	.0000	.0000	.0000	.0000	.0000	.0003	.0020	.0088	.0280
	21	.0000	.0000	.0000	.0000	.0000	.0000	.0000	.0001	.0006	.0034	.0133
	22	.0000	.0000	.0000	.0000	.0000	.0000	.0000	.0000	.0002	.0012	.0055
	23	.0000	.0000	.0000	.0000	.0000	.0000	.0000	.0000	.0000	.0003	.0019
	24	.0000	.0000	.0000	.0000	.0000	.0000	.0000	.0000	.0000	.0001	.0006
	25	.0000	.0000	.0000	.0000	.0000	.0000	.0000	.0000	.0000	.0000	.0001

Table B-3 Poisson probabilities*

X	0.1	0.2	0.3	0.4	λ 0.5	0.6	0.7	0.8	0.9	1.0
0	.9048	.8187	.7408	.6703	.6065	.5488	.4966	.4493	.4066	.3679
1	.0905	.1637	.2222	.2681	.3033	.3293	.3476	.3595	.3659	.3679
2	.0045	.0164	.0333	.0536	.0758	.0988	.1217	.1438	.1647	.1839
3	.0002	.0011	.0033	.0072	.0126	.0198	.0284	.0383	.0494	.0613
4	.0000	.0001	.0002	.0007	.0016	.0030	.0050	.0077	.0111	.0153
5	.0000	.0000	.0000	.0001	.0002	.0004	.0007	.0012	.0020	.0031
6	.0000	.0000	.0000	.0000	.0000	.0000	.0001	.0002	.0003	.0005
7	.0000	.0000	.0000	.0000	.0000	.0000	.0000	.0000	.0000	.0001

X	1.1	1.2	1.3	1.4	λ 1.5	1.6	1.7	1.8	1.9	2.0
0	.3329	.3012	.2725	.2466	.2231	.2019	.1827	.1653	.1496	.1353
1	.3662	.3614	.3543	.3452	.3347	.3230	.3106	.2975	.2842	.2707
2	.2014	.2169	.2303	.2417	.2510	.2584	.2640	.2678	.2700	.2707
3	.0738	.0867	.0998	.1128	.1255	.1378	.1496	.1607	.1710	.1804
4	.0203	.0260	.0324	.0395	.0471	.0551	.0636	.0723	.0812	.0902
5	.0045	.0062	.0084	.0111	.0141	.0176	.0216	.0260	.0309	.0361
6	.0008	.0012	.0018	.0026	.0035	.0047	.0061	.0078	.0098	.0120
7	.0001	.0002	.0003	.0005	.0008	.0011	.0015	.0020	.0027	.0034
8	.0000	.0000	.0001	.0001	.0001	.0002	.0003	.0005	.0006	.0009
9	.0000	.0000	.0000	.0000	.0000	.0000	.0001	.0001	.0001	.0002

X	2.1	2.2	2.3	2.4	λ 2.5	2.6	2.7	2.8	2.9	3.0
0	.1225	.1108	.1003	.0907	.0821	.0743	.0672	.0608	.0550	.0498
1	.2572	.2438	.2306	.2177	.2052	.1931	.1815	.1703	.1396	.1494
2	.2700	.2681	.2652	.2613	.2565	.2510	.2450	.2384	.2314	.2240
3	.1890	.1966	.2033	.2090	.2138	.2176	.2205	.2225	.2237	.2240
4	.0992	.1082	.1169	.1254	.1336	.1414	.1488	.1557	.1622	.1680
5	.0417	.0476	.0538	.0602	.0668	.0735	.0804	.0872	.0940	.1008
6	.0146	.0174	.0206	.0241	.0278	.0319	.0362	.0407	.0455	.0504
7	.0044	.0055	.0068	.0083	.0099	.0118	.0139	.0163	.0188	.0216
8	.0011	.0015	.0019	.0025	.0031	.0038	.0047	.0057	.0068	.0081
9	.0003	.0004	.0005	.0007	.0009	.0011	.0014	.0018	.0022	.0027
10	.0001	.0001	.0001	.0002	.0002	.0003	.0004	.0005	.0006	.0008
11	.0000	.0000	.0000	.0000	.0000	.0001	.0001	.0001	.0002	.0002
12	.0000	.0000	.0000	.0000	.0000	.0000	.0000	.0000	.0000	.0001

(Source: From R. S. Burington and D. C. May, Jr., Handbook of Probability and Statistics with Tables, 1970, McGraw-Hill Book Co., New York. Reproduced with permission.)

*Example: $P(X = 5 | \lambda = 2.5) = 0.0668$.

Table B-3 Poisson probabilities (*Continued*)

X	λ 3.1	3.2	3.3	3.4	3.5	3.6	3.7	3.8	3.9	4.0
0	.0450	.0408	.0369	.0334	.0302	.0273	.0247	.0224	.0202	.0183
1	.1397	.1304	.1217	.1135	.1057	.0984	.0915	.0850	.0789	.0733
2	.2165	.2087	.2008	.1929	.1850	.1771	.1692	.1615	.1539	.1465
3	.2237	.2226	.2209	.2186	.2158	.2125	.2087	.2046	.2001	.1954
4	.1734	.1781	.1823	.1858	.1888	.1912	.1931	.1944	.1951	.1954
5	.1075	.1140	.1203	.1264	.1322	.1377	.1429	.1477	.1522	.1563
6	.0555	.0608	.0662	.0716	.0771	.0826	.0881	.0936	.0989	.1042
7	.0246	.0278	.0312	.0348	.0385	.0425	.0466	.0508	.0551	.0595
8	.0095	.0111	.0129	.0148	.0169	.0191	.0215	.0241	.0269	.0298
9	.0033	.0040	.0047	.0056	.0066	.0076	.0089	.0102	.0116	.0132
10	.0010	.0013	.0016	.0019	.0023	.0028	.0033	.0039	.0045	.0053
11	.0003	.0004	.0005	.0006	.0007	.0009	.0011	.0013	.0016	.0019
12	.0001	.0001	.0001	.0002	.0002	.0003	.0003	.0004	.0005	.0006
13	.0000	.0000	.0000	.0000	.0001	.0001	.0001	.0001	.0002	.0002
14	.0000	.0000	.0000	.0000	.0000	.0000	.0000	.0000	.0000	.0001

X	λ 4.1	4.2	4.3	4.4	4.5	4.6	4.7	4.8	4.9	5.0
0	.0166	.0150	.0136	.0123	.0111	.0101	.0091	.0082	.0074	.0067
1	.0679	.0630	.0583	.0540	.0500	.0462	.0427	.0395	.0365	.0337
2	.1393	.1323	.1254	.1188	.1125	.1063	.1005	.0948	.0894	.0842
3	.1904	.1852	.1798	.1743	.1687	.1631	.1574	.1517	.1460	.1404
4	.1951	.1944	.1933	.1917	.1898	.1875	.1849	.1820	.1789	.1755
5	.1600	.1633	.1662	.1687	.1708	.1725	.1738	.1747	.1753	.1755
6	.1093	.1143	.1191	.1237	.1281	.1323	.1362	.1398	.1432	.1462
7	.0640	.0686	.0732	.0778	.0824	.0869	.0914	.0959	.1002	.1044
8	.0328	.0360	.0393	.0428	.0463	.0500	.0537	.0575	.0614	.0653
9	.0150	.0168	.0188	.0209	.0232	.0255	.0280	.0307	.0334	.0363
10	.0061	.0071	.0081	.0092	.0104	.0118	.0132	.0147	.0164	.0181
11	.0023	.0027	.0032	.0037	.0043	.0049	.0056	.0064	.0073	.0082
12	.0008	.0009	.0011	.0014	.0016	.0019	.0022	.0026	.0030	.0034
13	.0002	.0003	.0004	.0005	.0006	.0007	.0008	.0009	.0011	.0013
14	.0001	.0001	.0001	.0001	.0002	.0002	.0003	.0003	.0004	.0005
15	.0000	.0000	.0000	.0000	.0001	.0001	.0001	.0001	.0001	.0002

X	λ 5.1	5.2	5.3	5.4	5.5	5.6	5.7	5.8	5.9	6.0
0	.0061	.0055	.0050	.0045	.0041	.0037	.0033	.0030	.0027	.0025
1	.0311	.0287	.0265	.0244	.0225	.0207	.0191	.0176	.0162	.0149
2	.0793	.0746	.0701	.0659	.0618	.0580	.0544	.0509	.0477	.0446
3	.1348	.1293	.1239	.1185	.1133	.1082	.1033	.0985	.0938	.0892
4	.1719	.1681	.1641	.1600	.1558	.1515	.1472	.1428	.1383	.1339

Table B-3 Poisson probabilities (*Continued*)

X	5.1	5.2	5.3	5.4	λ 5.5	5.6	5.7	5.8	5.9	6.0
5	.1753	.1748	.1740	.1728	.1714	.1697	.1678	.1656	.1632	.1606
6	.1490	.1515	.1537	.1555	.1571	.1584	.1594	.1601	.1605	.1606
7	.1086	.1125	.1163	.1200	.1234	.1267	.1298	.1326	.1353	.1377
8	.0692	.0731	.0771	.0810	.0849	.0887	.0925	.0962	.0998	.1033
9	.0392	.0423	.0454	.0486	.0519	.0552	.0586	.0620	.0654	.0688
10	.0200	.0220	.0241	.0262	.0285	.0309	.0334	.0359	.0386	.0413
11	.0093	.0104	.0116	.0129	.0143	.0157	.0173	.0190	.0207	.0225
12	.0039	.0045	.0051	.0058	.0065	.0073	.0082	.0092	.0102	.0113
13	.0015	.0018	.0021	.0024	.0028	.0032	.0036	.0041	.0046	.0052
14	.0006	.0007	.0008	.0009	.0011	.0013	.0015	.0017	.0019	.0022
15	.0002	.0002	.0003	.0003	.0004	.0005	.0006	.0007	.0008	.0009
16	.0001	.0001	.0001	.0001	.0001	.0002	.0002	.0002	.0003	.0003
17	.0000	.0000	.0000	.0000	.0000	.0001	.0001	.0001	.0001	.0001

X	6.1	6.2	6.3	6.4	λ 6.5	6.6	6.7	6.8	6.9	7.0
0	.0022	.0020	.0018	.0017	.0015	.0014	.0012	.0011	.0010	.0009
1	.0137	.0126	.0116	.0106	.0098	.0090	.0082	.0076	.0070	.0064
2	.0417	.0390	.0364	.0340	.0318	.0296	.0276	.0258	.0240	.0223
3	.0848	.0806	.0765	.0726	.0688	.0652	.0617	.0584	.0552	.0521
4	.1294	.1249	.1205	.1162	.1118	.1076	.1034	.0992	.0952	.0912
5	.1579	.1549	.1519	.1487	.1454	.1420	.1385	.1349	.1314	.1277
6	.1605	.1601	.1595	.1586	.1575	.1562	.1546	.1529	.1511	.1490
7	.1399	.1418	.1435	.1450	.1462	.1472	.1480	.1486	.1489	.1490
8	.1066	.1099	.1130	.1160	.1188	.1215	.1240	.1263	.1284	.1304
9	.0723	.0757	.0791	.0825	.0858	.0891	.0923	.0954	.0985	.1014
10	.0441	.0469	.0498	.0528	.0558	.0558	.0618	.0649	.0679	.0710
11	.0245	.0265	.0285	.0307	.0330	.0353	.0377	.0401	.0426	.0452
12	.0124	.0137	.0150	.0164	.0179	.0194	.0210	.0227	.0245	.0264
13	.0058	.0065	.0073	.0081	.0089	.0098	.0108	.0119	.0130	.0142
14	.0025	.0029	.0033	.0037	.0041	.0046	.0052	.0058	.0064	.0071
15	.0010	.0012	.0014	.0016	.0018	.0020	.0023	.0026	.0029	.0033
16	.0004	.0005	.0005	.0006	.0007	.0008	.0010	.0011	.0013	.0014
17	.0001	.0002	.0002	.0002	.0003	.0003	.0004	.0004	.0005	.0006
18	.0000	.0001	.0001	.0001	.0001	.0001	.0001	.0002	.0002	.0002
19	.0000	.0000	.0000	.0000	.0000	.0000	.0000	.0001	.0001	.0001

X	7.1	7.2	7.3	7.4	λ 7.5	7.6	7.7	7.8	7.9	8.0
0	.0008	.0007	.0007	.0006	.0006	.0005	.0005	.0004	.0004	.0003
1	.0059	.0054	.0049	.0045	.0041	.0038	.0035	.0032	.0029	.0027
2	.0208	.0194	.0180	.0167	.0156	.0145	.0134	.0125	.0116	.0107
3	.0492	.0464	.0438	.0413	.0389	.0366	.0345	.0324	.0305	.0286
4	.0874	.0836	.0799	.0764	.0729	.0696	.0663	.0632	.0602	.0573

Table B-3 Poisson probabilities (*Continued*)

X	7.1	7.2	7.3	7.4	λ 7.5	7.6	7.7	7.8	7.9	8.0
5	.1241	.1204	.1167	.1130	.1094	.1057	.1021	.0986	.0951	.0916
6	.1468	.1445	.1420	.1394	.1367	.1339	.1311	.1282	.1252	.1221
7	.1489	.1486	.1481	.1474	.1465	.1454	.1442	.1428	.1413	.1396
8	.1321	.1337	.1351	.1363	.1373	.1382	.1388	.1392	.1395	.1396
9	.1042	.1070	.1096	.1121	.1144	.1167	.1187	.1207	.1224	.1241
10	.0740	.0770	.0800	.0829	.0858	.0887	.0914	.0941	.0967	.0993
11	.0478	.0504	.0531	.0558	.0585	.0613	.0640	.0667	.0695	.0722
12	.0283	.0303	.0323	.0344	.0366	.0388	.0411	.0434	.0457	.0481
13	.0154	.0168	.0181	.0196	.0211	.0227	.0243	.0260	.0278	.0296
14	.0078	.0086	.0095	.0104	.0113	.0123	.0134	.0145	.0157	.0169
15	.0037	.0041	.0046	.0051	.0057	.0062	.0069	.0075	.0083	.0090
16	.0016	.0019	.0021	.0024	.0026	.0030	.0033	.0037	.0041	.0045
17	.0007	.0008	.0009	.0010	.0012	.0013	.0015	.0017	.0019	.0021
18	.0003	.0003	.0004	.0004	.0005	.0006	.0006	.0007	.0008	.0009
19	.0001	.0001	.0001	.0002	.0002	.0002	.0003	.0003	.0003	.0004
20	.0000	.0000	.0001	.0001	.0001	.0001	.0001	.0001	.0001	.0002
21	.0000	.0000	.0000	.0000	.0000	.0000	.0000	.0000	.0001	.0001

X	8.1	8.2	8.3	8.4	λ 8.5	8.6	8.7	8.8	8.9	9.0
0	.0003	.0003	.0002	.0002	.0002	.0002	.0002	.0002	.0001	.0001
1	.0025	.0023	.0021	.0019	.0017	.0016	.0014	.0013	.0012	.0011
2	.0100	.0092	.0086	.0079	.0074	.0068	.0063	.0058	.0054	.0050
3	.0269	.0252	.0237	.0222	.0208	.0195	.0183	.0171	.0160	.0150
4	.0544	.0517	.0491	.0466	.0443	.0420	.0398	.0377	.0357	.0337
5	.0882	.0849	.0816	.0784	.0752	.0722	.0692	.0663	.0635	.0607
6	.1191	.1160	.1128	.1097	.1066	.1034	.1003	.0972	.0941	.0911
7	.1378	.1358	.1338	.1317	.1294	.1271	.1247	.1222	.1197	.1171
8	.1395	.1392	.1388	.1382	.1375	.1366	.1356	.1344	.1332	.1318
9	.1256	.1269	.1280	.1290	.1299	.1306	.1311	.1315	.1317	.1318
10	.1017	.1040	.1063	.1084	.1104	.1123	.1140	.1157	.1172	.1186
11	.0749	.0776	.0802	.0828	.0853	.0878	.0902	.0925	.0948	.0970
12	.0505	.0530	.0555	.0579	.0604	.0629	.0654	.0679	.0703	.0728
13	.0315	.0334	.0354	.0374	.0395	.0416	.0438	.0459	.0481	.0504
14	.0182	.0196	.0210	.0225	.0240	.0256	.0272	.0289	.0306	.0324
15	.0098	.0107	.0116	.0126	.0136	.0147	.0158	.0169	.0182	.0194
16	.0050	.0055	.0060	.0066	.0072	.0079	.0086	.0093	.0101	.0109
17	.0024	.0026	.0029	.0033	.0036	.0040	.0044	.0048	.0053	.0058
18	.0011	.0012	.0014	.0015	.0017	.0019	.0021	.0024	.0026	.0029
19	.0005	.0005	.0006	.0007	.0008	.0009	.0010	.0011	.0012	.0014
20	.0002	.0002	.0002	.0003	.0003	.0004	.0004	.0005	.0005	.0006

Table B-3 Poisson probabilities (*Continued*)

X	8.1	8.2	8.3	8.4	λ 8.5	8.6	8.7	8.8	8.9	9.0
21	.0001	.0001	.0001	.0001	.0001	.0002	.0002	.0002	.0002	.0003
22	.0000	.0000	.0000	.0000	.0001	.0001	.0001	.0001	.0001	.0001

X	9.1	9.2	9.3	9.4	λ 9.5	9.6	9.7	9.8	9.9	10.0
0	.0001	.0001	.0001	.0001	.0001	.0001	.0001	.0001	.0001	.0000
1	.0010	.0009	.0009	.0008	.0007	.0007	.0006	.0005	.0005	.0005
2	.0046	.0043	.0040	.0037	.0034	.0031	.0029	.0027	.0025	.0023
3	.0140	.0131	.0123	.0115	.0107	.0100	.0093	.0087	.0081	.0076
4	.0319	.0302	.0285	.0269	.0254	.0240	.0226	.0213	.0201	.0189
5	.0581	.0555	.0530	.0506	.0483	.0460	.0439	.0418	.0398	.0378
6	.0881	.0851	.0822	.0793	.0764	.0736	.0709	.0682	.0656	.0631
7	.1145	.1118	.1091	.1064	.1037	.1010	.0982	.0955	.0928	.0901
8	.1302	.1286	.1269	.1251	.1232	.1212	.1191	.1170	.1148	.1126
9	.1317	.1315	.1311	.1306	.1300	.1293	.1284	.1274	.1263	.1251
10	.1198	.1210	.1219	.1228	.1235	.1241	.1245	.1249	.1250	.1251
11	.0991	.1012	.1031	.1049	.1067	.1083	.1098	.1112	.1125	.1137
12	.0752	.0776	.0779	.0822	.0844	.0866	.0888	.0908	.0928	.0948
13	.0526	.0549	.0572	.0594	.0617	.0640	.0662	.0685	.0707	.0729
14	.0342	.0361	.0380	.0399	.0419	.0439	.0459	.0479	.0500	.0521
15	.0208	.0221	.0235	.0250	.0265	.0281	.0297	.0313	.0330	.0347
16	.0118	.0127	.0137	.0147	.0157	.0168	.0180	.0192	.0204	.0217
17	.0063	.0069	.0075	.0081	.0088	.0095	.0103	.0111	.0119	.0128
18	.0032	.0035	.0039	.0042	.0046	.0051	.0055	.0060	.0065	.0071
19	.0015	.0017	.0019	.0021	.0023	.0026	.0028	.0031	.0034	.0037
20	.0007	.0008	.0009	.0010	.0011	.0012	.0014	.0015	.0017	.0019
21	.0003	.0003	.0004	.0004	.0005	.0006	.0006	.0007	.0008	.0009
22	.0001	.0001	.0002	.0002	.0002	.0002	.0003	.0003	.0004	.0004
23	.0000	.0001	.0001	.0001	.0001	.0001	.0001	.0001	.0002	.0002
24	.0000	.0000	.0000	.0000	.0000	.0000	.0000	.0001	.0001	.0001

Table B-4 Areas for the standard normal distribution*

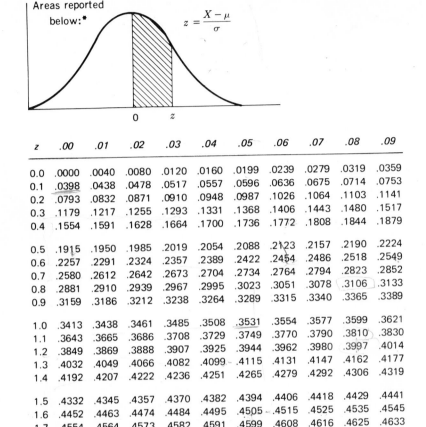

Areas reported below:*

$$z = \frac{X - \mu}{\sigma}$$

z	.00	.01	.02	.03	.04	.05	.06	.07	.08	.09
0.0	.0000	.0040	.0080	.0120	.0160	.0199	.0239	.0279	.0319	.0359
0.1	.0398	.0438	.0478	.0517	.0557	.0596	.0636	.0675	.0714	.0753
0.2	.0793	.0832	.0871	.0910	.0948	.0987	.1026	.1064	.1103	.1141
0.3	.1179	.1217	.1255	.1293	.1331	.1368	.1406	.1443	.1480	.1517
0.4	.1554	.1591	.1628	.1664	.1700	.1736	.1772	.1808	.1844	.1879
0.5	.1915	.1950	.1985	.2019	.2054	.2088	.2123	.2157	.2190	.2224
0.6	.2257	.2291	.2324	.2357	.2389	.2422	.2454	.2486	.2518	.2549
0.7	.2580	.2612	.2642	.2673	.2704	.2734	.2764	.2794	.2823	.2852
0.8	.2881	.2910	.2939	.2967	.2995	.3023	.3051	.3078	.3106	.3133
0.9	.3159	.3186	.3212	.3238	.3264	.3289	.3315	.3340	.3365	.3389
1.0	.3413	.3438	.3461	.3485	.3508	.3531	.3554	.3577	.3599	.3621
1.1	.3643	.3665	.3686	.3708	.3729	.3749	.3770	.3790	.3810	.3830
1.2	.3849	.3869	.3888	.3907	.3925	.3944	.3962	.3980	.3997	.4014
1.3	.4032	.4049	.4066	.4082	.4099	.4115	.4131	.4147	.4162	.4177
1.4	.4192	.4207	.4222	.4236	.4251	.4265	.4279	.4292	.4306	.4319
1.5	.4332	.4345	.4357	.4370	.4382	.4394	.4406	.4418	.4429	.4441
1.6	.4452	.4463	.4474	.4484	.4495	.4505	.4515	.4525	.4535	.4545
1.7	.4554	.4564	.4573	.4582	.4591	.4599	.4608	.4616	.4625	.4633
1.8	.4641	.4649	.4656	.4664	.4671	.4678	.4686	.4693	.4699	.4706
1.9	.4713	.4719	.4726	.4732	.4738	.4744	.4750	.4756	.4761	.4767
2.0	.4772	.4778	.4783	.4788	.4793	.4798	.4803	.4808	.4812	.4817
2.1	.4821	.4826	.4830	.4834	.4838	.4842	.4846	.4850	.4854	.4857
2.2	.4861	.4864	.4868	.4871	.4875	.4878	.4881	.4884	.4887	.4890
2.3	.4893	.4896	.4898	.4901	.4904	.4906	.4909	.4911	.4913	.4916
2.4	.4918	.4920	.4922	.4925	.4927	.4929	.4931	.4932	.4934	.4936
2.5	.4938	.4940	.4941	.4943	.4945	.4946	.4948	.4949	.4951	.4952
2.6	.4953	.4955	.4956	.4957	.4959	.4960	.4961	.4962	.4963	.4964
2.7	.4965	.4966	.4967	.4968	.4969	.4970	.4971	.4972	.4973	.4974
2.8	.4974	.4975	.4976	.4977	.4977	.4978	.4979	.4979	.4980	.4981
2.9	.4981	.4982	.4983	.4983	.4984	.4984	.4985	.4985	.4986	.4986
3.0	.4987									
3.5	.4997									
4.0	.4999									

*Example: For $z = 1.96$, shaded area is 0.4750 out of the total area of 1.0000.

419

Table B-5 Areas for Student's t distribution

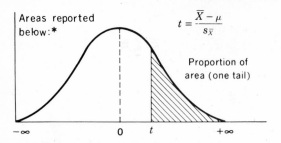

Areas reported below:*

$$t = \frac{\overline{X} - \mu}{s_{\overline{X}}}$$

Proportion of area (one tail)

$-\infty$ 0 t $+\infty$

df	0.10	0.05	0.025	0.01	0.005	df	0.10	0.05	0.025	0.01	0.005
1	3.078	6.314	12.706	31.821	63.657	21	1.323	1.721	2.080	2.518	2.831
2	1.886	2.920	4.303	6.965	9.925	22	1.321	1.717	2.074	2.508	2.819
3	1.638	2.353	3.182	4.541	5.841	23	1.319	1.714	2.069	2.500	2.807
4	1.533	2.132	2.776	3.747	4.604	24	1.318	1.711	2.064	2.492	2.797
5	1.476	2.015	2.571	3.365	4.032	25	1.316	1.708	2.060	2.485	2.787
6	1.440	1.943	2.447	3.143	3.707	26	1.315	1.706	2.056	2.479	2.779
7	1.415	1.895	2.365	2.998	3.499	27	1.314	1.703	2.052	2.473	2.771
8	1.397	1.860	2.306	2.896	3.355	28	1.313	1.701	2.048	2.467	2.763
9	1.383	1.833	2.262	2.821	3.250	29	1.311	1.699	2.045	2.462	2.756
10	1.372	1.812	2.228	2.764	3.169	30	1.310	1.697	2.042	2.457	2.750
11	1.363	1.796	2.201	2.718	3.106	40	1.303	1.684	2.021	2.423	2.704
12	1.356	1.782	2.179	2.681	3.055	60	1.296	1.671	2.000	2.390	2.660
13	1.350	1.771	2.160	2.650	3.012	120	1.289	1.658	1.980	2.358	2.617
14	1.345	1.761	2.145	2.624	2.977	∞	1.282	1.645	1.960	2.326	2.576
15	1.341	1.753	2.131	2.602	2.947						
16	1.337	1.746	2.120	2.583	2.921						
17	1.333	1.740	2.110	2.567	2.898						
18	1.330	1.734	2.101	2.552	2.878						
19	1.328	1.729	2.093	2.539	2.861						
20	1.325	1.725	2.086	2.528	2.845						

[Source: Reprinted with permission of the authors and publishers from Fisher and Yates, Statistical Tables for Biological, Agricultural, and Medical Research (Table III), 6th ed., 1974, published by Longman Group Ltd., London (previously published by Oliver & Boyd, Edinburgh).]

*Example: For shaded area to represent 0.05 of the total area of 1.0, value of t with 10 degrees of freedom is 1.812.

Table B-6 Areas for the χ^2 distribution

Areas reported below.*

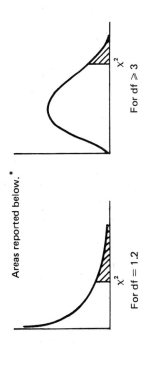

For df = 1.2

For df ≥ 3

$\frac{x-0.}{.052?} = 1.35$

Proportion of area

df	0.995	0.990	0.975	0.950	0.900	0.500	0.100	0.050	0.025	0.010	0.005
1	0.00004	0.00016	0.00098	0.00393	0.0158	0.455	2.71	3.84	5.02	6.63	7.88
2	0.0100	0.0201	0.0506	0.103	0.211	1.386	4.61	5.99	7.38	9.21	10.60
3	0.072	0.115	0.216	0.352	0.584	2.366	6.25	7.81	9.35	11.34	12.84
4	0.207	0.297	0.484	0.711	1.064	3.357	7.78	9.49	11.14	13.28	14.86
5	0.412	0.554	0.831	1.145	1.61	4.251	9.24	11.07	12.83	15.09	16.75
6	0.676	0.872	1.24	1.64	2.20	5.35	10.64	12.59	14.45	16.81	18.55
7	0.989	1.24	1.69	2.17	2.83	6.35	12.02	14.07	16.01	18.48	20.28
8	1.34	1.65	2.18	2.73	3.49	7.34	13.36	15.51	17.53	20.09	21.96
9	1.73	2.09	2.70	3.33	4.17	8.34	14.68	16.92	19.02	21.67	23.59
10	2.16	2.56	3.25	3.94	4.87	9.34	15.99	18.31	20.48	23.21	25.19
11	2.60	3.05	3.82	4.57	5.58	10.34	17.28	19.68	21.92	24.73	26.76
12	3.07	3.57	4.40	5.23	6.30	11.34	18.55	21.03	23.34	26.22	28.30
13	3.57	4.11	5.01	5.89	7.04	12.34	19.81	22.36	24.74	27.69	29.82
14	4.07	4.66	5.63	6.57	7.79	13.34	21.06	23.68	26.12	29.14	31.32
15	4.60	5.23	6.26	7.26	8.55	14.34	22.31	25.00	27.49	30.58	32.80

Table B-6 Areas for the χ^2 distribution (*Continued*)

					Proportion of area						
df	0.995	0.990	0.975	0.950	0.900	0.500	0.100	0.050	0.025	0.010	0.005
16	5.14	5.81	6.91	7.96	9.31	15.34	23.54	26.30	28.85	32.00	34.27
17	5.70	6.41	7.56	8.67	10.09	16.34	24.77	27.59	30.19	33.41	35.72
18	6.26	7.01	8.23	9.39	10.86	17.34	25.99	28.87	31.53	34.81	37.16
19	6.84	7.63	8.91	10.12	11.65	18.34	27.20	30.14	32.85	36.19	38.58
20	7.43	8.26	9.59	10.85	12.44	19.34	28.41	31.41	34.17	37.57	40.00
21	8.03	8.90	10.28	11.59	13.24	20.34	29.62	32.67	35.48	38.93	41.40
22	8.64	9.54	10.98	12.34	14.04	21.34	30.81	33.92	36.78	40.29	42.80
23	9.26	10.20	11.69	13.09	14.85	22.34	32.01	35.17	38.08	41.64	44.18
24	9.89	10.86	12.40	13.85	15.66	23.34	33.20	36.42	39.36	42.98	45.56
25	10.52	11.52	13.12	14.61	16.47	24.34	34.38	37.65	40.65	44.31	46.93
26	11.16	12.20	13.84	15.38	17.29	25.34	35.56	38.89	41.92	45.64	48.29
27	11.81	12.83	14.57	16.15	18.11	26.34	36.74	40.11	43.19	46.96	49.64
28	12.46	13.56	15.31	16.93	18.94	27.34	37.92	41.34	44.46	48.28	50.99
29	13.12	14.26	16.05	17.71	19.77	28.34	39.09	42.56	45.72	49.59	52.34
30	13.79	14.95	16.79	18.49	20.60	29.34	40.26	43.77	46.98	50.89	53.67
40	20.71	22.16	24.43	26.51	29.05	39.34	51.81	55.76	59.34	63.69	66.77
50	27.99	29.71	32.36	34.76	37.69	49.33	63.17	67.50	71.42	76.15	79.49
60	35.53	37.43	40.48	43.19	46.46	59.33	74.40	79.08	83.30	88.38	91.95
70	43.28	45.44	48.76	51.74	55.33	69.33	85.53	90.53	95.02	100.4	104.2
80	51.17	53.54	51.17	60.39	64.28	79.33	98.58	101.9	106.6	112.3	116.3
90	59.20	61.75	65.65	69.13	73.29	89.33	107.6	113.1	118.1	124.1	128.3
100	67.33	70.06	74.22	77.93	82.36	99.33	118.5	124.3	129.6	135.8	140.2

[*Source: From Table IV of Fisher and Yates, Statistical Tables for Biological, Agricultural and Medical Research, 6th ed., 1974, published by Longman Group Ltd., London (previously published by Oliver & Boyd, Edinburgh), by permission of the authors and publishers.*]

*Example: For the shaded area to represent 0.05 of the total area of 1.0 under the density function, the value of χ^2 is 18.31 when df = 10.

Table B-7 Values of F exceeded with probabilities of 5 and 1 percent

Each cell shows the 5 percent value (top) and 1 percent value (bottom).

df (denominator)	1	2	3	4	5	6	7	8	(9)	10	11	12	14	16	20	24	30	40	50	75	100	200	500	∞
1	161 / 4,052	200 / 4,999	216 / 5,403	225 / 5,625	230 / 5,764	234 / 5,859	237 / 5,928	239 / 5,981	241 / 6,022	242 / 6,056	243 / 6,082	244 / 6,106	245 / 6,142	246 / 6,169	248 / 6,208	249 / 6,234	250 / 6,261	251 / 6,286	252 / 6,302	253 / 6,323	253 / 6,334	254 / 6,352	254 / 6,361	254 / 6,366
2	18.51 / 98.49	19.00 / 99.00	19.16 / 99.17	19.25 / 99.25	19.30 / 99.30	19.33 / 99.33	19.36 / 99.36	19.37 / 99.37	19.38 / 99.39	19.39 / 99.40	19.40 / 99.41	19.41 / 99.42	19.42 / 99.43	19.43 / 99.44	19.44 / 99.45	19.45 / 99.46	19.46 / 99.47	19.47 / 99.48	19.47 / 99.48	19.48 / 99.49	19.49 / 99.49	19.49 / 99.49	19.50 / 99.50	19.50 / 99.50
3	10.13 / 34.12	9.55 / 30.82	9.28 / 29.46	9.12 / 28.71	9.01 / 28.24	8.94 / 27.91	8.88 / 27.67	8.84 / 27.49	8.81 / 27.34	8.78 / 27.23	8.76 / 27.13	8.74 / 27.05	8.71 / 26.92	8.69 / 26.83	8.66 / 26.69	8.64 / 26.60	8.62 / 26.50	8.60 / 26.41	8.58 / 26.35	8.57 / 26.27	8.56 / 26.23	8.54 / 26.18	8.54 / 26.14	8.53 / 26.12
4	7.71 / 21.20	6.94 / 18.00	6.59 / 16.69	6.39 / 15.98	6.26 / 15.52	6.16 / 15.21	6.09 / 14.98	6.04 / 14.80	6.00 / 14.66	5.96 / 14.54	5.93 / 14.45	5.91 / 14.37	5.87 / 14.24	5.84 / 14.15	5.80 / 14.02	5.77 / 13.93	5.74 / 13.83	5.71 / 13.74	5.70 / 13.69	5.68 / 13.61	5.66 / 13.57	5.65 / 13.52	5.64 / 13.48	5.63 / 13.46
5	6.61 / 16.26	5.79 / 13.27	5.41 / 12.06	5.19 / 11.39	5.05 / 10.97	4.95 / 10.67	4.88 / 10.45	4.82 / 10.29	4.78 / 10.15	4.74 / 10.05	4.70 / 9.96	4.68 / 9.89	4.64 / 9.77	4.60 / 9.68	4.56 / 9.55	4.53 / 9.47	4.50 / 9.38	4.46 / 9.29	4.44 / 9.24	4.42 / 9.17	4.40 / 9.13	4.38 / 9.07	4.37 / 9.04	4.36 / 9.02
6	5.99 / 13.74	5.14 / 10.92	4.76 / 9.78	4.53 / 9.15	4.39 / 8.75	4.28 / 8.47	4.21 / 8.26	4.15 / 8.10	4.10 / 7.98	4.06 / 7.87	4.03 / 7.79	4.00 / 7.72	3.96 / 7.60	3.92 / 7.52	3.87 / 7.39	3.84 / 7.31	3.81 / 7.23	3.77 / 7.14	3.75 / 7.09	3.72 / 7.02	3.71 / 6.99	3.69 / 6.94	3.68 / 6.90	3.67 / 6.88
7	5.59 / 12.25	4.74 / 9.55	4.34 / 8.45	4.12 / 7.85	3.97 / 7.46	3.87 / 7.19	3.79 / 7.00	3.73 / 6.84	3.68 / 6.71	3.63 / 6.62	3.60 / 6.54	3.57 / 6.47	3.52 / 6.35	3.49 / 6.27	3.44 / 6.15	3.41 / 6.07	3.38 / 5.98	3.34 / 5.90	3.32 / 5.85	3.29 / 5.78	3.28 / 5.75	3.25 / 5.70	3.24 / 5.67	3.23 / 5.65
8	5.32 / 11.26	4.46 / 8.65	4.07 / 7.59	3.84 / 7.01	3.69 / 6.63	3.58 / 6.37	3.50 / 6.19	3.44 / 6.03	3.39 / 5.91	3.34 / 5.82	3.31 / 5.74	3.28 / 5.67	3.23 / 5.56	3.20 / 5.48	3.15 / 5.36	3.12 / 5.28	3.08 / 5.20	3.05 / 5.11	3.03 / 5.06	3.00 / 5.00	2.98 / 4.96	2.96 / 4.91	2.94 / 4.88	2.93 / 4.86
9	5.12 / 10.56	4.26 / 8.02	3.86 / 6.99	3.63 / 6.42	3.48 / 6.06	3.37 / 5.80	3.29 / 5.62	3.23 / 5.47	3.18 / 5.35	3.13 / 5.26	3.10 / 5.18	3.07 / 5.11	3.02 / 5.00	2.98 / 4.92	2.93 / 4.80	2.90 / 4.73	2.86 / 4.64	2.82 / 4.56	2.80 / 4.51	2.77 / 4.45	2.76 / 4.41	2.73 / 4.36	2.72 / 4.33	2.71 / 4.31
10	4.96 / 10.04	4.10 / 7.56	3.71 / 6.55	3.48 / 5.99	3.33 / 5.64	3.22 / 5.39	3.14 / 5.21	3.07 / 5.06	3.02 / 4.95	2.97 / 4.85	2.94 / 4.78	2.91 / 4.71	2.86 / 4.60	2.82 / 4.52	2.77 / 4.41	2.74 / 4.33	2.70 / 4.25	2.67 / 4.17	2.64 / 4.12	2.61 / 4.05	2.59 / 4.01	2.56 / 3.96	2.55 / 3.93	2.54 / 3.91
11	4.84 / 9.65	3.98 / 7.20	3.59 / 6.22	3.36 / 5.67	3.20 / 5.32	3.09 / 5.07	3.01 / 4.88	2.95 / 4.74	2.90 / 4.63	2.86 / 4.54	2.82 / 4.46	2.79 / 4.40	2.74 / 4.29	2.70 / 4.21	2.65 / 4.10	2.61 / 4.02	2.57 / 3.94	2.53 / 3.86	2.50 / 3.80	2.47 / 3.74	2.45 / 3.70	2.42 / 3.66	2.41 / 3.62	2.40 / 3.60
12	4.75 / 9.33	3.88 / 6.93	3.49 / 5.95	3.26 / 5.41	3.11 / 5.06	3.00 / 4.82	2.92 / 4.65	2.85 / 4.50	2.80 / 4.39	2.76 / 4.30	2.72 / 4.22	2.69 / 4.16	2.64 / 4.05	2.60 / 3.98	2.54 / 3.86	2.50 / 3.78	2.46 / 3.70	2.42 / 3.61	2.40 / 3.56	2.36 / 3.49	2.35 / 3.46	2.32 / 3.41	2.31 / 3.38	2.30 / 3.36
13	4.67 / 9.07	3.80 / 6.70	3.41 / 5.74	3.18 / 5.20	3.02 / 4.86	2.92 / 4.62	2.84 / 4.44	2.77 / 4.30	2.72 / 4.19	2.67 / 4.10	2.63 / 4.02	2.60 / 3.96	2.55 / 3.85	2.51 / 3.78	2.46 / 3.67	2.42 / 3.59	2.38 / 3.51	2.34 / 3.42	2.32 / 3.37	2.28 / 3.30	2.26 / 3.27	2.24 / 3.21	2.22 / 3.18	2.21 / 3.16
14	4.60 / 8.86	3.74 / 6.51	3.34 / 5.56	3.11 / 5.03	2.96 / 4.69	2.85 / 4.46	2.77 / 4.28	2.70 / 4.14	2.65 / 4.03	2.60 / 3.94	2.56 / 3.86	2.53 / 3.80	2.48 / 3.70	2.44 / 3.62	2.39 / 3.51	2.35 / 3.43	2.31 / 3.34	2.27 / 3.26	2.24 / 3.21	2.21 / 3.14	2.19 / 3.11	2.16 / 3.06	2.14 / 3.02	2.13 / 3.00
15	4.54 / 8.68	3.68 / 6.36	3.29 / 5.42	3.06 / 4.89	2.90 / 4.56	2.79 / 4.32	2.70 / 4.14	2.64 / 4.00	2.59 / 3.89	2.55 / 3.80	2.51 / 3.73	2.48 / 3.67	2.43 / 3.56	2.39 / 3.48	2.33 / 3.36	2.29 / 3.29	2.25 / 3.20	2.21 / 3.12	2.18 / 3.07	2.15 / 3.00	2.12 / 2.97	2.10 / 2.92	2.08 / 2.89	2.07 / 2.87
16	4.49 / 8.53	3.63 / 6.23	3.24 / 5.29	3.01 / 4.77	2.85 / 4.44	2.74 / 4.20	2.66 / 4.03	2.59 / 3.89	2.54 / 3.78	2.49 / 3.69	2.45 / 3.61	2.42 / 3.55	2.37 / 3.45	2.33 / 3.37	2.28 / 3.25	2.24 / 3.18	2.20 / 3.10	2.16 / 3.01	2.13 / 2.96	2.09 / 2.98	2.07 / 2.86	2.04 / 2.80	2.02 / 2.77	2.01 / 2.75

df (numerator)

Table B-7 Values of F exceeded with probabilities of 5 and 1 percent (*Continued*)

df (denominator)	1	2	3	4	5	6	7	8	9	10	11	12	14	16	20	24	30	40	50	75	100	200	500	∞
17	4.45	3.59	3.20	2.96	2.81	2.70	2.62	2.55	2.50	2.45	2.41	2.38	2.33	2.29	2.23	2.19	2.15	2.11	2.08	2.04	2.02	1.99	1.97	1.96
	8.40	6.11	5.18	4.67	4.34	4.10	3.93	3.79	3.68	3.59	3.52	3.45	3.35	3.27	3.16	3.08	3.00	2.92	2.86	2.79	2.76	2.70	2.67	2.65
18	4.41	3.55	3.16	2.93	2.77	2.66	2.58	2.51	2.46	2.41	2.37	2.34	2.29	2.25	2.19	2.15	2.11	2.07	2.04	2.00	1.98	1.95	1.93	1.92
	8.28	6.01	5.09	4.58	4.25	4.01	3.85	3.71	3.60	3.51	3.44	3.37	3.27	3.19	3.07	3.00	2.91	2.83	2.78	2.71	2.68	2.62	2.59	2.57
19	4.38	3.52	3.13	2.90	2.74	2.63	2.55	2.48	2.43	2.38	2.34	2.31	2.26	2.21	2.15	2.11	2.07	2.02	2.00	1.96	1.94	1.91	1.90	1.88
	8.18	5.93	5.01	4.50	4.17	3.94	3.77	3.63	3.52	3.43	3.36	3.30	3.19	3.12	3.00	2.92	2.84	2.76	2.70	2.63	2.60	2.54	2.51	2.49
20	4.35	3.49	3.10	2.87	2.71	2.60	2.52	2.45	2.40	2.35	2.31	2.28	2.23	2.18	2.12	2.08	2.04	1.99	1.96	1.92	1.90	1.87	1.85	1.84
	8.10	5.85	4.94	4.43	4.10	3.87	3.71	3.56	3.45	3.37	3.30	3.23	3.13	3.05	2.94	2.86	2.77	2.69	2.63	2.56	2.53	2.47	2.44	2.42
21	4.32	3.47	3.07	2.84	2.68	2.57	2.49	2.42	2.37	2.32	2.28	2.25	2.20	2.15	2.09	2.05	2.00	1.96	1.93	1.89	1.87	1.84	1.82	1.81
	8.02	5.78	4.87	4.37	4.04	3.81	3.65	3.51	3.40	3.31	3.24	3.17	3.07	2.99	2.88	2.80	2.72	2.63	2.58	2.51	2.47	2.42	2.38	2.36
22	4.30	3.44	3.05	2.82	2.66	2.55	2.47	2.40	2.35	2.30	2.26	2.23	2.18	2.13	2.07	2.03	1.98	1.93	1.91	1.87	1.84	1.81	1.80	1.78
	7.94	5.72	4.82	4.31	3.99	3.76	3.59	3.45	3.35	3.26	3.18	3.12	3.02	2.94	2.83	2.75	2.67	2.58	2.53	2.46	2.42	2.37	2.33	2.31
23	4.28	3.42	3.03	2.80	2.64	2.53	2.45	2.38	2.32	2.28	2.24	2.20	2.14	2.10	2.04	2.00	1.96	1.91	1.88	1.84	1.82	1.79	1.77	1.76
	7.88	5.66	4.76	4.26	3.94	3.71	3.54	3.41	3.30	3.21	3.14	3.07	2.97	2.89	2.78	2.70	2.62	2.53	2.48	2.41	2.37	2.32	2.28	2.26
24	4.26	3.40	3.01	2.78	2.62	2.51	2.43	2.36	2.30	2.26	2.22	2.18	2.13	2.09	2.02	1.98	1.94	1.89	1.86	1.82	1.80	1.76	1.74	1.73
	7.82	5.61	4.72	4.22	3.90	3.67	3.50	3.36	3.25	3.17	3.09	3.03	2.93	2.85	2.74	2.66	2.58	2.49	2.44	2.36	2.33	2.27	2.23	2.21
25	4.24	3.38	2.99	2.76	2.60	2.49	2.41	2.34	2.28	2.24	2.20	2.16	2.11	2.06	2.00	1.96	1.92	1.87	1.84	1.80	1.77	1.74	1.72	1.71
	7.77	5.57	4.68	4.18	3.86	3.63	3.46	3.32	3.21	3.13	3.05	2.99	2.89	2.81	2.70	2.62	2.54	2.45	2.40	2.32	2.29	2.23	2.19	2.17
26	4.22	3.37	2.98	2.74	2.59	2.47	2.39	2.32	2.27	2.22	2.18	2.15	2.10	2.05	1.99	1.95	1.90	1.85	1.82	1.78	1.76	1.72	1.70	1.69
	7.72	5.53	4.64	4.14	3.82	3.59	3.42	3.29	3.17	3.09	3.02	2.96	2.86	2.77	2.66	2.58	2.50	2.41	2.36	2.28	2.25	2.19	2.15	2.13
27	4.21	3.35	2.96	2.73	2.57	2.46	2.37	2.30	2.25	2.20	2.16	2.13	2.08	2.03	1.97	1.93	1.88	1.84	1.80	1.76	1.74	1.71	1.68	1.67
	7.68	5.49	4.60	4.11	3.79	3.56	3.39	3.26	3.14	3.06	2.98	2.93	2.83	2.74	2.63	2.55	2.47	2.38	2.33	2.25	2.21	2.16	2.12	2.10
28	4.20	3.34	2.95	2.71	2.56	2.44	2.36	2.29	2.24	2.19	2.15	2.12	2.06	2.02	1.96	1.91	1.87	1.81	1.78	1.75	1.72	1.69	1.67	1.65
	7.64	5.45	4.57	4.07	3.76	3.53	3.36	3.23	3.11	3.03	2.95	2.90	2.80	2.71	2.60	2.52	2.44	2.35	2.30	2.22	2.18	2.13	2.09	2.06
29	4.18	3.33	2.93	2.70	2.54	2.43	2.35	2.28	2.22	2.18	2.14	2.10	2.05	2.00	1.94	1.90	1.85	1.80	1.77	1.73	1.71	1.68	1.65	1.64
	7.60	5.42	4.54	4.04	3.73	3.50	3.33	3.20	3.08	3.00	2.92	2.87	2.77	2.68	2.57	2.49	2.41	2.32	2.27	2.19	2.15	2.10	2.06	2.03
30	4.17	3.32	2.92	2.69	2.53	2.42	2.34	2.27	2.21	2.16	2.12	2.09	2.04	1.99	1.93	1.89	1.84	1.79	1.76	1.72	1.69	1.66	1.64	1.62
	7.56	5.39	4.51	4.02	3.70	3.47	3.30	3.17	3.06	2.98	2.90	2.84	2.74	2.66	2.55	2.47	2.38	2.29	2.24	2.16	2.13	2.07	2.03	2.01
32	4.15	3.30	2.90	2.67	2.51	2.40	2.32	2.25	2.19	2.14	2.10	2.07	2.02	1.97	1.91	1.86	1.82	1.76	1.74	1.69	1.67	1.64	1.61	1.59
	7.50	5.34	4.46	3.97	3.66	3.42	3.25	3.12	3.01	2.94	2.86	2.80	2.70	2.62	2.51	2.42	2.34	2.25	2.20	2.12	2.08	2.02	1.98	1.96

df																								
34	1.57	1.59	1.61	1.64	1.67	1.71	1.74	1.80	1.84	1.89	1.95	2.00	2.05	2.08	2.12	2.17	2.23	2.30	2.38	2.49	2.65	2.88	3.28	4.13
	1.91	1.94	1.98	2.04	2.08	2.15	2.21	2.30	2.38	2.47	2.58	2.66	2.76	2.82	2.89	2.97	3.08	3.21	3.38	3.61	3.93	4.42	5.29	7.44
36	1.55	1.56	1.59	1.62	1.65	1.69	1.72	1.78	1.82	1.87	1.93	1.98	2.03	2.06	2.10	2.15	2.21	2.28	2.36	2.48	2.63	2.86	3.26	4.11
	1.87	1.90	1.94	2.00	2.04	2.12	2.17	2.26	2.35	2.43	2.54	2.62	2.72	2.78	2.86	2.94	3.04	3.18	3.35	3.58	3.89	4.38	5.25	7.39
38	1.53	1.54	1.57	1.60	1.63	1.67	1.71	1.76	1.80	1.85	1.92	1.96	2.02	2.05	2.09	2.14	2.19	2.26	2.35	2.46	2.62	2.85	3.25	4.10
	1.84	1.86	1.90	1.97	2.00	2.08	2.14	2.22	2.32	2.40	2.51	2.59	2.69	2.75	2.82	2.91	3.02	3.15	3.32	3.54	3.86	4.34	5.21	7.35
40	1.51	1.53	1.55	1.59	1.61	1.66	1.69	1.74	1.79	1.84	1.90	1.95	2.00	2.04	2.07	2.12	2.18	2.25	2.34	2.45	2.61	2.84	3.23	4.07
	1.81	1.84	1.88	1.94	1.97	2.05	2.11	2.20	2.29	2.37	2.49	2.56	2.66	2.73	2.80	2.88	2.99	3.12	3.29	3.51	3.83	4.31	5.18	7.31
42	1.49	1.51	1.54	1.57	1.60	1.64	1.68	1.73	1.78	1.82	1.89	1.94	1.99	2.02	2.06	2.11	2.17	2.24	2.32	2.44	2.59	2.83	3.22	4.07
	1.78	1.80	1.85	1.91	1.94	2.02	2.08	2.17	2.26	2.35	2.46	2.54	2.64	2.70	2.77	2.86	2.96	3.10	3.26	3.49	3.80	4.29	5.15	7.27
44	1.48	1.50	1.52	1.56	1.58	1.63	1.66	1.72	1.76	1.81	1.88	1.92	1.98	2.01	2.05	2.10	2.16	2.23	2.31	2.43	2.58	2.82	3.21	4.06
	1.75	1.78	1.82	1.88	1.92	2.00	2.06	2.15	2.24	2.32	2.44	2.52	2.62	2.68	2.75	2.84	2.94	3.07	3.24	3.46	3.78	4.26	5.12	7.24
46	1.46	1.48	1.51	1.54	1.57	1.62	1.65	1.71	1.75	1.80	1.87	1.91	1.97	2.00	2.04	2.09	2.14	2.22	2.30	2.42	2.57	2.81	3.20	4.05
	1.72	1.76	1.80	1.86	1.90	1.98	2.04	2.13	2.22	2.30	2.42	2.50	2.60	2.66	2.73	2.82	2.92	3.05	3.22	3.44	3.76	4.24	5.10	7.21
48	1.45	1.47	1.50	1.53	1.56	1.61	1.64	1.70	1.74	1.79	1.86	1.90	1.96	1.99	2.03	2.08	2.14	2.21	2.30	2.41	2.56	2.80	3.19	4.04
	1.70	1.73	1.78	1.84	1.88	1.96	2.02	2.11	2.20	2.28	2.40	2.48	2.58	2.64	2.71	2.80	2.90	3.04	3.20	3.42	3.74	4.22	5.08	7.19
50	1.44	1.46	1.48	1.52	1.55	1.60	1.63	1.69	1.74	1.78	1.85	1.90	1.95	1.98	2.02	2.07	2.13	2.20	2.29	2.40	2.56	2.79	3.18	4.03
	1.68	1.71	1.76	1.82	1.86	1.94	2.00	2.10	2.18	2.26	2.39	2.46	2.56	2.62	2.70	2.78	2.88	3.02	3.18	3.41	3.72	4.20	5.06	7.17
55	1.41	1.43	1.46	1.50	1.52	1.58	1.61	1.67	1.72	1.76	1.83	1.88	1.93	1.97	2.00	2.05	2.11	2.18	2.27	2.38	2.54	2.78	3.17	4.02
	1.64	1.66	1.71	1.78	1.82	1.90	1.96	2.06	2.15	2.23	2.35	2.43	2.53	2.59	2.66	2.75	2.85	2.98	3.15	3.37	3.68	4.16	5.01	7.12
60	1.39	1.41	1.44	1.48	1.50	1.56	1.59	1.65	1.70	1.75	1.81	1.86	1.92	1.95	1.98	2.04	2.10	2.17	2.25	2.37	2.52	2.76	3.15	4.00
	1.60	1.63	1.68	1.74	1.79	1.87	1.93	2.03	2.12	2.20	2.32	2.40	2.50	2.56	2.63	2.72	2.82	2.95	3.12	3.34	3.65	4.13	4.98	7.08
65	1.37	1.39	1.42	1.46	1.49	1.54	1.57	1.63	1.68	1.73	1.80	1.85	1.90	1.94	1.98	2.02	2.08	2.15	2.24	2.36	2.51	2.75	3.14	3.99
	1.56	1.60	1.64	1.71	1.76	1.84	1.90	2.00	2.09	2.18	2.30	2.37	2.47	2.54	2.61	2.70	2.79	2.93	3.09	3.31	3.62	4.10	4.95	7.04
70	1.35	1.37	1.40	1.45	1.47	1.53	1.56	1.62	1.67	1.72	1.79	1.84	1.89	1.93	1.97	2.01	2.07	2.14	2.23	2.35	2.50	2.74	3.13	3.98
	1.53	1.56	1.62	1.69	1.74	1.82	1.88	1.98	2.07	2.15	2.28	2.35	2.45	2.51	2.59	2.67	2.77	2.91	3.07	3.29	3.60	4.08	4.92	7.01
80	1.32	1.35	1.38	1.42	1.45	1.51	1.54	1.60	1.65	1.70	1.77	1.82	1.88	1.91	1.95	1.99	2.05	2.12	2.21	2.33	2.48	2.72	3.11	3.96
	1.49	1.52	1.57	1.65	1.70	1.78	1.84	1.94	2.03	2.11	2.24	2.32	2.41	2.48	2.55	2.64	2.74	2.87	3.04	3.25	3.56	4.04	4.88	6.96
100	1.28	1.30	1.34	1.39	1.42	1.48	1.51	1.57	1.63	1.68	1.75	1.79	1.85	1.88	1.92	1.97	2.03	2.10	2.19	2.30	2.46	2.70	3.09	3.94
	1.43	1.46	1.51	1.59	1.64	1.73	1.79	1.89	1.98	2.06	2.19	2.26	2.36	2.43	2.51	2.59	2.69	2.82	2.99	3.20	3.51	3.98	4.82	6.90
125	1.25	1.27	1.31	1.36	1.39	1.45	1.49	1.55	1.60	1.65	1.72	1.77	1.83	1.86	1.90	1.95	2.01	2.08	2.17	2.29	2.44	2.68	3.07	3.92
	1.37	1.40	1.46	1.54	1.59	1.68	1.75	1.85	1.94	2.03	2.15	2.23	2.33	2.40	2.47	2.56	2.65	2.79	2.95	3.17	3.47	3.94	4.78	6.84
150	1.22	1.25	1.29	1.34	1.37	1.44	1.47	1.54	1.59	1.64	1.71	1.76	1.82	1.85	1.89	1.94	2.00	2.07	2.16	2.27	2.43	2.67	3.06	3.91
	1.33	1.37	1.43	1.51	1.56	1.66	1.72	1.83	1.91	2.00	2.12	2.20	2.30	2.37	2.44	2.53	2.62	2.76	2.92	3.14	3.44	3.91	4.75	6.81
200	1.19	1.22	1.26	1.32	1.35	1.42	1.45	1.52	1.57	1.62	1.69	1.74	1.80	1.83	1.87	1.92	1.98	2.05	2.14	2.26	2.41	2.65	3.04	3.89
	1.28	1.33	1.39	1.48	1.53	1.62	1.69	1.79	1.88	1.97	2.09	2.17	2.28	2.34	2.41	2.50	2.60	2.73	2.90	3.11	3.41	3.88	4.71	6.76

Table B-7 Values of F exceeded with probabilities of 5 and 1 percent (*Continued*)

df (denominator)	\ 1	2	3	4	5	6	7	8	9	10	11	12	14	16	20	24	30	40	50	75	100	200	500	∞
400	3.86	3.02	2.62	2.39	2.23	2.12	2.03	1.96	1.90	1.85	1.91	1.78	1.72	1.67	1.60	1.54	1.49	1.42	1.38	1.32	1.28	1.22	1.16	1.13
	6.70	4.66	3.83	3.36	3.06	2.85	2.69	2.55	2.46	2.37	2.29	2.23	2.12	2.04	1.92	1.84	1.74	1.64	1.57	1.47	1.42	1.32	1.24	1.19
1,000	3.85	3.00	2.61	2.38	2.22	2.10	2.02	1.95	1.89	1.84	1.80	1.76	1.70	1.65	1.58	1.53	1.47	1.41	1.36	1.30	1.26	1.19	1.13	1.08
	6.66	4.62	3.80	3.34	3.04	2.82	2.66	2.53	2.43	2.34	2.26	2.20	2.09	2.01	1.89	1.81	1.71	1.61	1.54	1.44	1.38	1.28	1.19	1.11
∞	3.84	2.99	2.60	2.37	2.21	2.09	2.01	1.94	1.88	1.83	1.79	1.75	1.69	1.64	1.57	1.52	1.46	1.40	1.35	1.28	1.24	1.17	1.11	1.00
	6.64	4.60	3.78	3.32	3.02	2.80	2.64	2.51	2.41	2.32	2.24	2.18	2.07	1.99	1.87	1.79	1.69	1.59	1.52	1.41	1.36	1.25	1.15	1.00

df (numerator)

(*Source:* Reprinted by permission from George W. Snedecor and William G. Cochran, *Statistical Methods*, 6th ed., 1967. © 1967, Iowa State University Press, Ames, Iowa.)

Table B-8 Absolute values of the simple correlation coefficient needed for significance[*]

df, (n−2)	0.05	0.01	df, (n−2)	0.05	0.01
1	.996917	.9998766	25	.3809	.4869
2	.95000	.990000	30	.3494	.4487
3	.8783	.95873	35	.3246	.4182
4	.8114	.91720	40	.3044	.3932
5	.7545	.8745	45	.2875	.3721
6	.7067	.8343	50	.2732	.3541
7	.6664	.7977	60	.2500	.3248
8	.6319	.7646	70	.2319	.3017
9	.6021	.7348	80	.2172	.2830
10	.5760	.7079	90	.2050	.2673
			100	.1946	.2540
11	.5529	.6835			
12	.5324	.6614			
13	.5139	.6411			
14	.4973	.6226			
15	.4821	.6055			
16	.4683	.5897			
17	.4555	.5751			
18	.4438	.5614			
19	.4329	.5487			
20	.4227	.5368			

[Source: Reprinted with permission of the authors and publishers from Fisher and Yates, Statistical Tables for Biological, Agricultural, and Medical Research (Table VI), 6th ed., 1974, published by Longman Group Ltd., London (previously published by Oliver & Boyd, Edinburgh).]
[*]Example: With 20 degrees of freedom, a correlation coefficient of 0.4227 is needed for significance at the 0.05 level.

Table B-9 Critical values of T in the Wilcoxon matched-pairs signed-ranks test

1-sided	2-sided	n = 5	n = 6	n = 7	n = 8	n = 9	n = 10
P = 0.05	P = 0.10	1	2	4	6	8	11
P = 0.025	P = 0.05		1	2	4	6	8
P = 0.01	P = 0.02			0	2	3	5
P = 0.005	P = 0.01				0	2	3

1-sided	2-sided	n = 11	n = 12	n = 13	n = 14	n = 15	n = 16
P = 0.05	P = 0.10	14	17	21	26	30	36
P = 0.025	P = 0.05	11	14	17	21	25	30
P = 0.01	P = 0.02	7	10	13	16	20	24
P = 0.005	P = 0.01	5	7	10	13	16	19

1-sided	2-sided	n = 17	n = 18	n = 19	n = 20	n = 21	n = 22
P = 0.05	P = 0.10	41	47	54	60	68	75
P = 0.025	P = 0.05	35	40	46	52	59	66
P = 0.01	P = 0.02	28	33	38	43	49	56
P = 0.005	P = 0.01	23	28	32	37	43	49

1-sided	2-sided	n = 23	n = 24	n = 25	n = 26	n = 27	n = 28
P = 0.05	P = 0.10	83	92	101	110	120	130
P = 0.025	P = 0.05	73	81	90	98	107	117
P = 0.01	P = 0.02	62	69	77	85	93	102
P = 0.005	P = 0.01	55	68	68	76	84	92

1-sided	2-sided	n = 29	n = 30	n = 31	n = 32	n = 33	n = 34
P = 0.05	P = 0.10	141	152	163	175	188	201
P = 0.025	P = 0.05	127	137	148	159	171	183
P = 0.01	P = 0.02	111	120	130	141	151	162
P = 0.005	P = 0.01	100	109	118	128	138	149

1-sided	2-sided	n = 35	n = 36	n = 37	n = 38	n = 39	
P = 0.05	P = 0.10	214	228	242	256	271	
P = 0.025	P = 0.05	195	208	222	235	250	
P = 0.01	P = 0.02	174	186	198	211	224	
P = 0.005	P = 0.01	160	171	183	195	208	

1-sided	2-sided	n = 40	n = 41	n = 42	n = 43	n = 44	n = 45
P = 0.05	P = 0.10	287	303	319	336	353	371
P = 0.025	P = 0.05	264	279	295	311	327	344
P = 0.01	P = 0.02	238	252	267	281	297	313
P = 0.005	P = 0.01	221	234	248	262	277	292

1-sided	2-sided	n = 46	n = 47	n = 48	n = 49	n = 50	
P = 0.05	P = 0.10	389	408	427	446	466	
P = 0.025	P = 0.05	361	379	397	415	434	
P = 0.01	P = 0.02	329	345	362	380	398	
P = 0.005	P = 0.01	307	323	339	356	373	

(Source: From F. Wilcoxon and R. A. Wilcox, Some Rapid Approximate Statistical Procedures, 1964, Reproduced with permission of R. A. Wilxcox and the American Cyanamid Company.)

Table B-10 Squares and square roots

N	N^2	$\sqrt{N}$	$\sqrt{10N}$	N	N^2	$\sqrt{N}$	$\sqrt{10N}$
				50	2 500	7.071 068	22.36068
1	1	1.000 000	3.162 278	51	2 601	7.141 428	22.58318
2	4	1.414 214	4.472 136	52	2 704	7.211 103	22.80351
3	9	1.732 051	5.477 226	53	2 809	7.280 110	23.02173
4	16	2.000 000	6.324 555	54	2 916	7.348 469	23.23790
5	25	2.236 068	7.071 068	55	3 025	7.416 198	23.45208
6	36	2.449 490	7.745 967	56	3 136	7.483 315	23.66432
7	49	2.645 751	8.366 600	57	3 249	7.549 834	23.87467
8	64	2.828 427	8.944 272	58	3 364	7.615 773	24.08319
9	81	3.000 000	9.486 833	59	3 481	7.681 146	24.28992
10	100	3.162 278	10.00000	60	3 600	7.745 967	24.49490
11	121	3.316 625	10.48809	61	3 721	7.810 250	24.69818
12	144	3.464 102	10.95445	62	3 844	7.874 008	24.89980
13	169	3.605 551	11.40175	63	3 969	7.937 254	25.09980
14	196	3.741 657	11.83216	64	4 096	8.000 000	25.29822
15	225	3.872 983	12.24745	65	4 225	8.062 258	25.49510
16	256	4.000 000	12.64911	66	4 356	8.124 038	25.69047
17	289	4.123 106	13.03840	67	4 489	8.185 353	25.88436
18	324	4.242 641	13.41641	68	4 624	8.246 211	26.07681
19	361	4.358 899	13.78405	69	4 761	8.306 824	26.26785
20	400	4.472 136	14.14214	70	4 900	8.366 600	26.45751
21	441	4.582 576	14.49138	71	5 041	8.426 150	26.64583
22	484	4.690 416	14.83240	72	5 184	8.485 281	26.83282
23	529	4.795 832	15.16575	73	5 329	8.544 004	27.01851
24	576	4.898 979	15.49193	74	5 476	8.602 325	27.20294
25	625	5.000 000	15.81139	75	5 625	8.660 254	27.38613
26	676	5.099 020	16.12452	76	5 776	8.717 798	27.56810
27	729	5.196 152	16.43168	77	5 929	8.774 964	27.74887
28	784	5.291 503	16.73320	78	6 084	8.831 761	27.92848
29	841	5.385 165	17.02939	79	6 241	8.888 194	28.10694
30	900	5.477 226	17.32051	80	6 400	8.944 272	28.28427
31	961	5.567 764	17.60682	81	6 561	9.000 000	28.46050
32	1 024	5.656 854	17.88854	82	6 724	9.055 385	28.63564
33	1 089	5.744 563	18.16590	83	6 889	9.110 434	28.80972
34	1 156	5.830 952	18.43909	84	7 056	9.165 151	28.98275
35	1 225	5.916 080	18.70829	85	7 225	9.219 544	29.15476
36	1 296	6.000 000	18.97367	86	7 396	9.273 618	29.32576
37	1 369	6.082 763	19.23538	87	7 569	9.327 379	29.49576
38	1 444	6.164 414	19.49359	88	7 744	9.380 832	29.66479
39	1 521	6.244 998	19.74842	89	7 921	9.433 981	29.83287
40	1 600	6.324 555	20.00000	90	8 100	9.486 833	30.00000
41	1 681	6.403 124	20.24846	91	8 281	9.539 392	30.16621
42	1 764	6.480 741	20.49390	92	8 464	9.591 663	30.33150
43	1 849	6.557 439	20.73644	93	8 649	9.643 651	30.49590
44	1 936	6.633 250	20.97618	94	8 836	9.695 360	30.65942
45	2 025	6.708 204	21.21320	95	9 025	9.746 794	30.82207
46	2 116	6.782 330	21.44761	96	9 216	9.797 959	30.98387
47	2 209	6.855 655	21.67948	97	9 409	9.848 858	31.14482
48	2 304	6.928 203	21.90890	98	9 604	9.899 495	31.30495
49	2 401	7.000 000	22.13594	99	9 801	9.949 874	31.46427
50	2 500	7.071 068	22.36068	100	10 000	10.00000	31.62278

Table B-10 Squares and square roots (*Continued*)

N	N²	√N	√10N	N	N²	√N	√10N
100	10 000	10.00000	31.62278	150	22 500	12.24745	38.72983
101	10 201	10.04988	31.78050	151	22 801	12.28821	38.85872
102	10 404	10.09950	31.93744	152	23 104	12.32883	39.98718
103	10 609	10.14889	32.09361	153	23 409	12.36932	39.11521
104	10 816	10.19804	32.24903	154	23 716	12.40967	39.24283
105	11 025	10.24695	32.40370	155	24 025	12.44990	39.37004
106	11 236	10.29563	32.55764	156	24 336	12.40000	39.49684
107	11 449	10.34408	32.71085	157	24 649	12.52996	39.62323
108	11 664	10.39230	32.86335	158	24 964	12.56981	39.74921
109	11 881	10.44031	33.01515	159	25 281	12.60952	39.87480
110	12 100	10.48809	33.16625	160	25 600	12.64911	40.00000
111	12 321	10.53565	33.31666	161	25 921	12.68858	40.12481
112	12 544	10.58301	33.46640	162	26 244	12.72792	40.24922
113	12 769	10.63015	33.61547	163	26 569	12.76715	40.37326
114	12 996	10.67708	33.76389	164	26 896	12.80625	40.49691
115	13 225	10.72381	33.91165	165	27 225	12.84523	40.62019
116	13 456	10.77033	34.05877	166	27 556	12.88410	40.74310
117	13 689	10.81665	34.20526	167	27 889	12.92285	40.86563
118	13 924	10.86278	34.35113	168	28 224	12.96148	40.98780
119	14 161	10.90871	34.49638	169	28 561	13.00000	41.10961
120	14 400	10.95445	34.64102	170	28 900	13.03840	41.23106
121	14 641	11.00000	34.78505	171	29 241	13.07670	41.35215
122	14 884	11.04536	34.92850	172	29 584	13.11488	41.47288
123	15 129	11.09054	35.07136	173	29 929	13.15295	41.59327
124	15 376	11.13553	35.21363	174	30 276	13.19091	41.71331
125	15 625	11.18034	35.35534	175	30 625	13.22876	41.83300
126	15 876	11.22497	35.49648	176	30 976	13.26650	41.95235
127	16 129	11.26943	35.63706	177	31 329	13.30413	42.07137
128	16 384	11.31371	35.77709	178	31 684	13.34166	42.19005
129	16 641	11.35782	35.91657	179	32 041	13.37909	42.30839
130	16 900	11.40175	36.05551	180	32 400	13.41641	42.42641
131	17 161	11.44552	36.19392	181	32 761	13.45362	42.54409
132	17 424	11.48913	36.33180	182	33 124	13.49074	42.66146
133	17 689	11.53256	36.46917	183	33 489	13.52775	42.77850
134	17 956	11.57584	36.60601	184	33 856	13.56466	42.89522
135	18 225	11.61895	36.74235	185	34 225	13.60147	43.01163
136	18 496	11.66190	36.87818	186	34 596	13.63818	43.12772
137	18 769	11.70470	37.01351	187	34 969	13.67479	43.24350
138	19 044	11.74734	37.14835	188	35 344	13.71131	43.35897
139	19 321	11.78983	37.28270	189	35 721	13.74773	43.47413
140	19 600	11.83216	37.41657	190	36 100	13.78405	43.58899
141	19 881	11.87434	37.54997	191	36 481	13.82027	43.70355
142	20 164	11.91638	37.68289	192	36 864	13.85641	43.81780
143	20 449	11.95826	37.81534	193	37 249	13.89244	43.93177
144	20 736	12.00000	37.94733	194	37 636	13.92839	44.04543
145	21 025	12.04159	38.07887	195	38 025	13.96424	44.15880
146	21 316	12.08305	38.20995	196	38 416	14.00000	44.27189
147	21 609	12.12436	38.34058	197	38 809	14.03567	44.38468
148	21 904	12.16553	38.47077	198	39 204	14.07125	44.49719
149	22 201	12.20656	38.60052	199	39 601	14.10674	44.60942
150	22 500	12.24745	38.72983	200	40 000	14.14214	44.72136

Table B-10 Squares and square roots (*Continued*)

N	N²	$\sqrt{N}$	$\sqrt{10N}$	N	N²	$\sqrt{N}$	$\sqrt{10N}$
200	40 000	14.14214	44.72136	250	62 500	15.81139	50.00000
201	40 401	14.17745	44.83302	251	63 001	15.84298	50.09990
202	40 804	14.21267	44.94441	252	63 504	15.87451	50.19960
203	41 209	14.24781	45.05552	253	64 009	15.90597	50.29911
204	41 616	14.28296	45.16636	254	64 516	15.93738	50.39841
205	42 025	14.31782	45.27693	255	65 025	15.96872	50.49752
206	42 436	14.35270	45.38722	256	65 536	16.00000	50.59644
207	42 849	14.38749	45.49725	257	66 049	16.03122	50.69517
208	43 264	14.42221	45.60702	258	66 564	16.06238	50.79370
209	43 681	14.45683	45.71652	259	67 081	16.09348	50.89204
210	44 100	14.49138	45.82576	260	67 600	16.12452	50.99020
211	44 521	14.52584	45.93474	261	68 121	16.15549	51.08816
212	44 944	14.56022	46.04346	262	68 644	16.18641	51.18594
213	45 369	14.59452	46.15192	263	69 169	16.21727	51.28353
214	45 796	14.62874	46.26013	264	69 696	16.24808	51.38093
215	46 225	14.66288	46.36809	265	70 225	16.27882	51.47815
216	46 656	14.69694	46.47580	266	70 756	16.30951	51.57519
217	47 089	14.73092	46.58326	267	71 289	16.34013	51.67204
218	47 524	14.76482	46.69047	268	71 824	16.37071	51.76872
219	47 961	14.79865	46.79744	269	72 361	16.40122	51.86521
220	48 400	14.83240	46.90415	270	72 900	16.43168	51.96152
221	48 841	14.86607	47.01064	271	73 441	16.46208	52.05766
222	49 284	14.89966	47.11688	272	73 984	16.49242	52.15362
223	49 729	14.93318	47.22288	273	74 529	16.52271	52.24940
224	50 176	14.96663	47.32864	274	75 076	16.55295	52.34501
225	50 625	15.00000	47.43416	275	75 625	16.58312	52.44044
226	51 076	15.03330	47.53946	276	76 176	16.61325	52.53570
227	51 529	15.06652	47.64452	277	76 729	16.64332	52.63079
228	51 984	15.09967	47.74935	278	77 284	16.67333	52.72571
229	52 441	15.13275	47.85394	279	77 841	16.70329	52.82045
230	52 900	15.16575	47.95832	280	78 400	16.73320	52.91503
231	53 361	15.19868	48.06246	281	78 961	16.76305	53.00943
232	53 824	15.23155	48.16638	282	79 524	16.79286	53.10367
233	54 289	15.26434	48.27007	283	80 089	16.82260	53.19774
234	54 756	15.29706	48.37355	284	80 656	16.85230	53.29165
235	55 225	15.32971	48.47680	285	81 225	16.88194	53.38539
236	55 696	15.36229	48.57983	286	81 796	16.91153	53.47897
237	56 169	15.39480	46.68265	287	82 369	16.94107	53.57238
238	56 644	15.42725	48.78524	288	82 944	16.97056	53.66563
239	57 121	15.45962	48.88763	289	83 521	17.00000	53.75872
240	57 600	15.49193	48.98979	290	84 100	17.02939	53.85165
241	58 081	15.52417	49.09175	291	84 681	17.05872	53.94442
242	58 564	15.55635	49.19350	292	85 264	17.08801	54.03702
243	59 049	15.58846	49.29503	293	85 849	17.11724	54.12947
244	59 536	15.52050	49.39636	294	86 436	17.14643	54.22177
245	60 025	15.65248	49.49747	295	87 025	17.17556	54.31390
246	60 516	15.68439	49.59839	296	87 616	17.20465	54.40588
247	61 009	15.71623	49.69909	297	88 209	17.23369	54.49771
248	61 504	15.74802	49.79960	298	88 804	17.26268	54.58938
249	62 001	15.77973	49.89990	299	89 401	17.29162	54.68089
250	62 500	15.81139	50.00000	300	90 000	17.32051	54.77226

Table B-10 Squares and square roots (*Continued*)

N	N²	√N	√10N	N	N²	√N	√10N
300	90 000	17.32051	54.77226	350	122 500	18.70829	59.16080
301	90 601	17.34935	54.86347	351	123 201	18.73499	59.24525
302	91 204	17.37815	54.95453	352	123 904	18.76166	59.32959
303	91 809	17.40690	55.04544	353	124 609	18.78829	59.41380
304	92 416	17.43560	55.13620	354	125 316	18.81489	59.49790
305	93 025	17.46425	55.22681	355	126 025	18.84144	59.58188
306	93 636	17.49288	55.31727	356	126 736	18.86796	59.66574
307	94 249	17.52142	55.40758	357	127 449	18.89444	59.74948
308	94 864	17.54993	55.49775	358	128 164	18.92089	59.83310
309	95 481	17.57840	55.58777	359	128 881	18.94730	59.91661
310	96 100	17.60682	55.67764	360	129 600	18.97367	60.00000
311	96 721	17.63519	55.76737	361	130 321	19.00000	60.08328
312	97 344	17.66352	55.85696	362	131 044	19.02630	60.16644
313	97 969	17.69181	55.94640	363	131 769	19.05256	60.24948
314	98 596	17.72005	56.03670	364	132 496	19.07878	60.33241
315	99 225	17.74824	56.12486	365	133 225	19.10497	60.41523
316	99 856	17.77639	56.21388	366	133 956	19.13113	60.49793
317	100 489	17.80449	56.30275	367	134 689	19.15724	60.58052
318	101 124	17.83255	56.39149	368	135 424	19.18333	60.66300
319	101 761	17.86057	56.48008	369	136 161	19.20937	60.74537
320	102 400	17.88854	56.56854	370	136 900	19.23538	60.82763
321	103 041	17.91647	56.65686	371	137 641	19.26136	60.90977
322	103 684	17.94436	56.74504	372	138 384	19.28730	60.99180
323	104 329	17.97220	56.83309	373	139 129	19.31321	61.07373
324	104 976	18.00000	56.92100	374	139 876	19.33908	61.15554
325	105 625	18.02776	57.00877	375	140 625	19.36492	61.23724
326	106 276	18.05547	57.09641	376	141 376	19.39072	61.31884
327	106 929	18.08314	57.18391	377	142 129	19.41649	61.40033
328	107 584	18.11077	57.27128	378	142 884	19.44222	61.48170
329	108 241	18.13836	57.35852	379	143 641	19.46792	61.56298
330	108 900	18.16590	57.44563	380	144 000	19.49359	61.64414
331	109 561	18.19341	57.53260	381	145 161	19.51922	61.72520
332	110 224	18.22087	57.61944	382	145 924	19.54483	61.80615
333	110 889	18.24829	57.70615	383	146 689	19.57039	61.88699
334	111 556	18.27567	57.79273	384	147 456	19.59592	61.96773
335	112 225	18.30301	57.87918	385	148 225	19.62142	62.04837
336	112 896	18.33030	57.96551	386	148 996	19.64688	62.12890
337	113 569	18.35756	58.05170	387	149 769	19.67232	62.20932
338	114 224	18.38478	57.13777	388	150 544	19.69772	62.28965
339	114 921	18.41195	58.22371	389	151 321	19.72308	62.36986
340	115 600	18.43909	58.30952	390	152 100	19.74842	62.44998
341	116 281	18.46619	58.39521	391	152 881	19.77372	62.52999
342	116 694	18.49324	58.48077	392	153 664	19.79899	62.60990
343	117 649	18.52026	58.56620	393	154 449	19.82423	62.68971
344	118 336	18.54724	58.65151	394	155 236	19.84943	62.76942
345							
345	119 025	18.57418	58.73670	395	156 025	19.87461	62.84903
346	119 716	18.60108	58.82176	396	156 816	19.89975	62.92853
347	120 409	18.62794	58.90671	397	157 609	19.92486	63.00794
348	121 104	18.65476	58.99152	398	158 404	19.94994	63.08724
349	121 801	18.68154	59.07622	399	159 201	19.97498	63.16645
350	122 500	18.70829	59.16080	400	160 000	20.00000	63.24555

Table B-10 Squares and square roots (*Continued*)

N	N^2	$\sqrt{N}$	$\sqrt{10N}$	N	N^2	$\sqrt{N}$	$\sqrt{10N}$
400	160 000	20.00000	63.24555	450	202 500	21.21320	67.08204
401	160 801	20.02498	63.32456	451	203 401	21.23676	67.15653
402	161 604	20.04994	63.40347	452	204 304	21.26029	67.23095
403	162 409	20.07486	63.48228	453	205 209	21.28380	67.30527
404	163 216	20.09975	63.56099	454	206 116	21.30728	67.37952
405	164 025	20.12461	63.63961	455	207 025	21.33073	67.45369
406	164 836	20.14944	63.71813	456	207 936	21.35416	67.52777
407	165 649	20.17424	63.79655	457	208 849	21.37756	67.60178
408	166 464	20.19901	63.87488	458	209 764	21.40093	67.67570
409	167 281	20.22375	63.95311	459	210 681	21.42429	67.74954
410	168 100	20.24846	64.03124	460	211 600	21.44761	67.82330
411	168 921	20.27313	64.10928	461	212 521	21.47091	67.89698
412	169 744	20.29778	64.18723	462	213 444	21.49419	67.97058
413	170 569	20.32240	64.26508	463	214 369	21.51743	68.04410
414	171 396	20.34699	64.34283	464	215 296	21.54066	68.11755
415	172 225	20.37155	64.42049	465	216 225	21.56386	68.19091
416	173 056	20.39608	64.49806	466	217 156	21.58703	68.26419
417	173 889	20.42058	64.57554	467	218 089	21.61018	68.33740
418	174 724	20.44505	64.65292	468	219 024	21.63331	68.41053
419	175 561	20.46949	64.73021	469	219 961	21.65641	68.48357
420	176 400	20.49390	64.80741	470	220 900	21.67948	68.55655
421	177 241	20.51828	64.88451	471	221 841	21.70253	68.62944
422	178 084	20.54264	64.96153	472	222 784	21.72556	68.70226
423	178 929	20.56696	65.03845	473	223 729	21.74856	68.77500
424	179 776	20.59126	65.11528	474	224 676	21.77154	68.84706
425	180 625	20.61553	65.19202	475	225 625	21.79449	68.92024
426	181 476	20.63977	65.26808	476	226 576	21.81742	68.99275
427	182 329	20.66398	65.34524	477	227 529	21.84033	69.06519
428	183 184	20.68816	65.42171	478	228 484	21.86321	69.13754
429	184 041	20.71232	65.49809	479	229 441	21.88607	69.20983
430	184 900	20.73644	65.57439	480	230 400	21.90800	69.28203
431	185 761	20.76054	65.65059	481	231 361	21.93171	69.35416
432	186 624	20.78461	65.72671	482	232 324	21.95450	69.42622
433	187 489	20.80865	65.80274	483	233 280	21.97726	69.40820
434	188 356	20.83267	65.87868	484	234 256	22.00000	69.57011
435	189 225	20.85665	65.95453	485	235 225	22.02272	69.64194
436	190 096	20.88061	66.03030	486	236 196	22.04541	69.71370
437	190 969	20.90454	66.10598	487	237 169	22.06808	69.78530
438	191 844	20.92845	66.18157	488	238 144	22.09072	69.85700
439	192 721	20.95233	66.25708	489	239 121	22.11334	69.92853
440	193 600	20.97618	66.33250	490	240 100	22.13594	70.00000
441	194 481	21.00000	66.40783	491	241 081	22.15852	70.07139
442	195 364	21.02380	66.48308	492	242 064	22.18107	70.14271
443	196 249	21.04757	66.55825	493	243 049	22.20360	70.21396
444	197 136	21.07131	66.63332	494	244 036	22.22611	70.28513
445	198 025	21.09502	66.70832	495	245 025	22.24860	70.35624
446	198 916	21.11871	66.78323	496	246 016	22.27106	70.42727
447	199 809	21.14237	66.85806	497	247 009	22.29350	70.49823
448	200 704	21.16601	66.93280	498	248 004	22.31519	70.56912
449	201 601	21.18962	67.00746	499	249 001	22.33831	70.63993
450	202 500	21.21320	67.08204	500	250 000	22.36068	70.71068

Table B-10 Squares and square roots (*Continued*)

N	N²	√N	√10N	N	N²	√N	√10N
500	250 000	22.36068	70.71068	550	302 500	23.45208	74.16198
501	251 001	22.38303	70.78135	551	303 601	23.47339	74.22937
502	252 004	22.40536	70.85196	552	304 704	23.49468	74.29670
503	253 009	22.42766	70.92249	553	305 809	23.51595	74.36397
504	254 016	22.44994	70.99296	554	306 916	23.53720	74.43118
505	255 025	22.47221	71.06335	555	308 025	23.55844	74.49832
506	256 036	22.49444	71.13368	556	309 136	23.57965	74.56541
507	257 049	22.51666	71.20393	557	310 249	23.60085	74.63243
508	258 064	22.53886	71.27412	558	311 364	23.62202	74.69940
509	259 081	22.56103	71.34424	559	312 481	23.64318	74.76630
510	260 100	22.58318	71.41428	560	313 600	23.66432	74.83315
511	261 121	22.60531	71.48426	561	314 721	23.68544	74.89993
512	262 144	22.62742	71.55418	562	315 844	23.70654	74.96666
513	263 169	22.64950	71.62402	563	316 969	23.72762	75.03333
514	264 196	22.67157	71.69379	564	318 096	23.74868	75.09993
515	265 225	22.69361	71.76350	565	319 225	23.76973	75.16648
516	266 256	22.71563	71.83314	566	320 356	23.79075	75.23297
517	267 289	22.73763	71.90271	567	321 489	23.81176	75.29940
518	268 324	22.75961	71.97222	568	322 624	23.83275	75.36577
519	269 361	22.78157	72.04165	569	323 761	23.85372	75.43209
520	270 400	22.80351	72.11103	570	324 900	23.87467	75.49834
521	271 441	22.82542	72.18033	571	326 041	23.89561	75.56454
522	272 484	22.84732	72.24957	572	327 184	23.91652	75.63068
523	273 529	22.86919	72.31874	573	328 329	23.93742	75.69676
524	274 576	22.89105	72.38784	574	329 476	23.95830	75.76279
525	275 625	22.91288	72.45688	575	330 625	23.97916	75.82875
526	276 676	22.93469	72.52586	576	331 776	24.00000	75.89466
527	277 729	22.95648	72.59477	577	332 929	24.02082	75.96052
528	278 784	22.97825	72.66361	578	334 084	24.04163	76.02631
529	279 841	23.00000	72.73239	579	335 241	24.06242	76.09205
530	280 900	23.02173	72.80110	580	336 400	24.08319	76.15773
531	281 961	23.04344	72.86975	581	337 561	24.10394	76.22336
532	283 024	23.06513	72.93833	582	338 724	24.12468	76.28892
533	284 089	23.08679	73.00685	583	339 889	24.14539	76.35444
534	285 156	23.10844	73.07530	584	341 056	24.16609	76.41989
535	286 225	23.13007	73.14369	585	342 225	24.18677	76.48529
536	287 296	23.15167	73.21202	586	343 396	24.20744	76.55064
537	288 369	23.17326	73.28028	587	344 569	24.22808	76.61593
538	289 444	23.19483	73.34848	588	345 744	24.24871	76.68116
539	290 521	23.21637	73.41662	589	346 921	24.26932	76.74634
540	291 600	23.23790	73.48469	590	348 100	24.28992	76.81146
541	292 681	23.25941	73.55270	591	349 281	24.31049	76.87652
542	293 764	23.28089	73.62065	592	350 464	24.33105	76.94154
543	294 849	23.30236	73.68853	593	351 649	24.35159	77.00649
544	295 936	23.32381	73.75636	594	352 836	24.37212	77.07140
545	297 025	23.34524	73.82412	595	354 025	24.39262	77.13624
546	298 116	23.36664	73.89181	596	355 216	24.41311	77.20104
547	299 209	23.38803	73.95945	597	356 409	24.43358	77.26578
548	300 304	23.40940	74.02702	598	357 604	24.45404	77.33046
549	301 401	23.43075	74.09453	599	358 801	24.47448	77.39509
550	302 500	23.45208	74.16198	600	360 000	24.49490	77.45967

Table B-10 Squares and square roots (*Continued*)

N	N²	√N	√10N	N	N²	√N	√10N
600	360 000	24.49490	77.45967	650	422 500	25.49510	80.62258
601	361 201	24.51530	77.52419	651	423 801	25.51470	80.68457
602	362 404	24.53569	77.58868	652	425 409	25.55386	80.80842
603	363 609	24.55606	77.65307	653	426 409	25.55386	80.80842
604	364 816	24.57641	77.71744	654	427 716	25.57342	80.87027
605	366 025	24.59675	77.78175	655	429 025	25.59297	80.93207
606	367 236	24.61707	77.84600	656	430 336	25.61250	80.99383
607	368 449	24.63737	77.91020	657	431 649	25.63201	81.05554
608	369 664	24.65766	77.97435	658	432 964	25.65151	81.11720
609	370 881	24.67793	78.03845	659	434 281	25.67100	81.17881
610	372 100	24.69818	78.10250	660	435 600	25.69047	81.24038
611	373 321	24.71841	78.16649	661	436 921	25.70992	81.30191
612	374 544	24.73863	78.23043	662	438 244	25.72936	81.36338
613	375 769	24.75884	78.29432	663	439 569	25.74879	81.42481
614	376 996	24.77902	78.35815	664	440 896	25.76820	81.48620
615	378 225	24.79919	78.42194	665	442 225	25.78759	81.54753
616	379 456	24.81935	78.48567	666	443 556	25.80698	81.60882
617	380 689	24.83948	78.54935	667	444 889	25.82634	81.67007
618	381 924	24.85961	78.61298	668	446 224	25.84570	81.73127
619	383 161	24.87971	78.67655	669	447 561	25.86503	81.79242
620	384 400	24.89980	78.74008	670	448 900	25.88436	81.85353
621	385 641	24.91987	78.80355	671	450 241	25.90367	81.91459
622	386 884	24.93993	78.86698	672	451 584	25.92296	81.97561
623	288 129	24.95997	78.93035	673	452 929	25.94224	82.03658
624	389 376	24.97999	78.99367	674	454 276	25.96151	82.09750
625	390 625	25.00000	79.05694	675	455 625	25.98076	82.15838
626	391 876	25.01999	79.12016	676	456 976	26.00000	82.21922
627	393 129	25.03997	79.18333	677	458 329	26.01922	82.28001
628	394 384	25.05993	79.24645	678	459 684	26.03843	82.34076
629	395 641	25.07987	79.30952	679	461 041	26.05763	82.40146
630	396 900	25.09980	79.37254	680	462 400	26.07681	82.46211
631	398 161	25.11971	79.43551	681	463 761	26.09598	82.42272
632	399 424	25.13961	79.49843	682	465 124	26.11513	82.58329
633	400 689	25.15949	79.56130	683	466 489	26.13427	82.64381
634	401 956	25.17936	79.62412	684	467 856	26.15339	82.70429
635	403 225	25.19921	79.68689	685	469 225	26.17250	82.76473
636	404 496	25.21904	79.74961	686	470 596	26.19160	82.82512
637	405 769	25.23886	79.81228	687	471 969	26.21068	82.88546
638	407 044	25.25866	79.87490	688	473 344	26.22975	82.94577
639	408 321	25.27845	79.93748	689	474 721	26.24881	83.00602
640	409 600	25.29822	80.00000	690	476 100	26.26785	83.06624
641	410 881	25.31798	80.06248	691	477 481	26.28688	83.12641
642	412 164	25.33772	80.12490	692	478 864	26.30589	83.18654
643	413 449	25.35744	80.18728	693	480 249	26.32489	83.24662
644	414 736	25.37716	80.24961	694	481 636	26.34388	83.30666
645	416 025	25.39685	80.31189	695	483 025	26.36285	83.36666
646	417 316	25.41653	80.37413	696	484 416	26.38181	83.42661
647	418 609	25.43619	80.43631	697	485 809	26.40076	83.48653
648	419 904	25.45584	80.49845	698	487 204	26.41969	83.54639
649	421 201	25.47548	80.56054	699	488 601	26.43861	83.60622
650	422 500	25.49510	80.62258	700	490 000	26.45751	83.66600

Table B-10 Squares and square roots (*Continued*)

N	N²	√N	√10N	N	N²	√N	√10N
700	490 000	26.45751	83.66600	750	562 500	27.38613	86.60254
701	491 401	26.47640	83.72574	751	564 001	27.40438	86.66026
702	492 804	26.49528	83.78544	752	565 504	27.42262	86.71793
703	494 209	26.51415	83.84510	753	567 009	27.44085	86.77557
704	495 616	26.53300	83.90471	754	568 516	27.45906	86.83317
705	497 025	26.55184	83.96428	755	570 025	27.47726	86.89074
706	498 436	26.57066	84.02381	756	571 536	27.49545	86.94826
707	499 849	26.58947	84.08329	757	573 049	27.51363	87.00575
708	501 264	26.60827	84.14274	758	574 564	27.53180	87.06320
709	502 681	26.62705	84.20214	759	576 081	27.54995	87.12061
710	504 100	26.64583	84.26150	760	577 600	27.56810	87.17798
711	505 521	26.66458	84.32082	761	579 121	27.58623	87.23531
712	506 944	26.68333	84.38009	762	580 644	27.60435	87.29261
713	508 369	26.70206	84.43933	763	582 169	27.62245	87.34987
714	509 796	26.72078	84.49852	764	583 696	27.64055	87.40709
715	511 225	26.73948	84.55767	765	585 225	27.65863	87.46428
716	512 656	26.75818	84.61578	766	586 756	27.67671	87.52143
717	514 089	26.77686	84.67585	767	588 289	27.69476	87.57854
718	515 524	26.79552	84.73488	768	589 824	27.71281	87.63561
719	516 961	26.81418	84.79387	769	591 361	27.73085	87.69265
720	518 400	26.83282	84.85281	770	592 900	27.74887	87.74964
721	519 841	26.85144	84.91172	771	594 441	27.76689	87.80661
722	521 284	26.87006	84.97058	772	595 984	27.78489	87.86353
723	522 729	26.88866	85.02941	773	597 529	27.80288	87.92042
724	524 176	26.90725	85.08819	774	599 076	27.82086	87.97727
725	525 625	26.92582	85.14693	775	600 625	27.83882	88.03408
726	527 076	26.94439	85.20563	776	602 176	27.85678	88.09086
727	528 529	26.96294	85.26429	777	603 729	27.87472	88.14760
728	529 984	26.98148	85.32292	778	605 284	27.89265	88.20431
729	531 411	27.00000	85.38150	779	606 841	27.91057	88.26098
730	532 900	27.01851	85.44004	780	608 400	27.92848	88.31761
731	534 361	27.03701	85.49854	781	609 961	27.94638	88.37420
732	535 824	27.05550	85.55700	782	611 524	27.96426	88.43076
733	537 289	27.07397	85.61542	783	613 089	27.98214	88.48729
734	538 756	27.09243	85.67380	784	614 656	28.00000	88.54377
735	540 225	27.11088	85.73214	785	616 225	28.01785	88.60023
736	541 696	27.12932	85.79044	786	617 796	28.03569	88.65664
737	543 169	27.14774	85.84870	787	619 369	28.05352	88.71302
738	544 644	27.16616	85.90693	788	620 944	28.07134	88.76936
739	546 121	27.18455	85.96511	789	622 521	28.08914	88.82567
740	547 600	27.20294	86.02325	790	624 100	28.10694	88.88194
741	549 081	27.22132	86.08136	791	625 681	28.12472	88.93818
742	550 564	27.23968	86.13942	792	627 264	28.14249	88.99438
743	552 049	27.25803	86.10745	793	628 849	28.16026	89.05055
744	553 536	27.27636	86.25543	794	630 436	28.17801	89.10668
745	555 025	27.29469	86.31338	795	632 025	28.19574	89.16277
746	556 516	27.31300	86.37129	796	633 616	28.21347	89.21883
747	558 009	27.33130	86.42916	797	635 209	28.23119	89.27486
748	559 504	27.34959	86.48609	798	636 804	28.24889	89.33085
749	561 001	27.36786	86.54479	799	638 401	28.26659	89.38680
750	562 500	27.38613	86.60254	800	640 000	28.28427	89.44272

Table B-10 Squares and square roots (*Continued*)

N	N²	√N	√10N	N	N²	√N	√10N
800	640 000	28.28427	89.44272	850	722 500	29.15476	92.19544
801	641 601	28.30194	89.49860	851	724 201	29.17190	92.24966
802	643 204	28.31960	89.55445	852	725 904	29.18904	92.30385
803	644 809	28.33725	89.61027	853	727 609	29.20616	92.35800
804	646 416	28.35489	89.66605	854	729 316	29.22328	92.41212
805	648 025	28.37252	89.72179	855	731 025	29.24038	92.46621
806	649 636	28.39014	89.77750	856	732 736	29.25748	92.52027
807	651 249	28.40775	89.83318	857	734 449	29.27456	92.57429
808	652 864	28.42534	89.88882	858	736 164	29.29164	92.62829
809	654 481	28.44293	89.94443	859	737 881	29.30870	92.68225
810	656 100	28.46050	90.00000	860	739 600	29.32576	92.73618
811	657 721	28.47806	90.05554	861	741 321	29.34280	92.79009
812	659 344	28.49561	90.11104	862	743 044	29.35984	92.84396
813	660 969	28.51315	90.16651	863	744 769	29.37686	92.89779
814	662 596	28.53069	90.22195	864	746 496	29.39388	92.95160
815	664 225	28.54820	90.27735	865	748 225	29.41088	93.00538
816	665 856	28.56571	90.33272	866	749 956	29.42788	93.05912
817	667 489	28.58321	90.38805	867	751 689	29.44486	93.11283
818	669 124	28.60070	90.44335	868	753 424	29.46184	93.16652
819	670 761	28.61818	90.49862	869	755 161	29.47881	93.22017
820	672 400	28.63564	90.55385	870	756 900	29.49576	93.27379
821	674 041	28.65310	90.60905	871	758 641	29.51271	93.32738
822	675 684	28.67054	90.66422	872	760 384	29.52965	93.38094
823	677 329	28.68798	90.71935	873	762 129	29.54657	93.43447
824	678 976	28.70540	90.77445	874	763 876	29.56349	93.48797
825	680 625	28.72281	90.82951	875	765 625	29.58040	93.54143
826	682 276	28.74022	90.88454	876	767 376	29.59730	93.59487
827	683 929	28.75761	90.93954	877	769 129	29.61419	93.64828
828	685 584	28.77499	90.99451	878	770 884	29.63106	93.70165
829	687 241	28.79236	91.04944	879	772 641	29.64793	93.75500
830	688 900	28.80972	91.10434	880	774 400	29.66479	93.80832
831	690 561	28.82707	91.15920	881	776 161	29.68164	93.86160
832	692 224	28.84441	91.21403	882	777 924	29.69848	93.91486
833	693 889	28.86174	91.26883	883	779 689	29.71532	93.96808
834	695 556	28.87906	91.32360	884	781 456	29.73214	94.02027
835	697 225	28.89637	91.37833	885	783 225	29.74895	94.07444
836	698 896	28.91366	91.43304	886	784 996	29.76575	94.12757
837	700 569	28.93095	91.48770	887	786 769	29.78255	94.18068
838	702 244	28.94823	91.54234	888	788 544	29.79933	94.23375
839	703 921	28.96550	91.59694	889	790 321	29.81610	94.28680
840	705 600	28.98275	91.65151	890	792 100	29.83287	94.33981
841	707 281	29.00000	91.70605	891	793 881	29.84962	94.39280
842	708 964	29.01724	91.76056	892	795 664	29.86637	94.44575
843	710 649	29.03446	91.81503	893	797 449	29.88311	94.49868
844	712 336	29.05168	91.86947	894	799 236	29.89983	94.55157
845	714 025	29.06888	91.92388	895	801 025	29.91655	94.60444
846	715 716	29.08608	91.97826	896	802 816	29.93326	94.65728
847	717 409	29.10326	92.03260	897	804 609	29.94996	94.71008
848	719 104	29.12044	92.08692	898	806 404	29.96665	94.76286
849	720 801	29.13760	92.14120	899	808 201	29.98333	94.81561
850	722 500	29.15476	92.19544	900	810 000	30.00000	94.86833

Table B-10 Squares and square roots (*Continued*)

N	N²	√N	√10N	N	N²	√N	√10N
900	810 000	30.00000	94.86833	950	902 500	30.82207	97.46794
901	811 801	30.01666	94.92102	951	904 401	30.83829	97.51923
902	813 604	30.03331	94.97368	952	906 304	30.85450	97.57049
903	815 409	30.04996	95.02631	953	908 209	30.87070	97.62172
904	817 216	30.06659	95.07891	954	910.116	30.88689	97.67292
905	819 025	30.08322	95.13149	955	912 025	30.90307	97.72410
906	820 836	30.09983	95.18403	956	913 936	30.91925	97.77525
907	822 649	30.11644	95.23655	957	915 849	30.93542	97.82638
908	824 464	30.13304	95.28903	958	917 764	30.95158	97.87747
909	826 281	30.14963	95.34149	959	919 681	30.96773	97.92855
910	828 100	30.16621	95.39392	960	921 600	30.98387	97.97959
911	829 921	30.18278	95.44632	961	928 521	31.00000	98.03061
912	831 744	30.19934	95.49869	962	925 444	31.01612	98.08160
913	833 569	30.21589	95.55103	963	927 369	31.03224	98.13256
914	835 396	30.23243	95.60335	964	929 296	31.04835	98.18350
915	837 225	30.24897	95.65563	965	931 225	31.06445	98.23441
916	839 056	30.26549	95.70789	966	933 156	31.08054	98.28530
917	840 889	30.28201	95.76012	967	935 089	31.09662	98.33616
918	842 724	30.29851	95.81232	968	937 024	31.11270	98.38699
919	844 561	30.31501	95.86449	969	938 961	31.12876	98.43780
920	846 400	30.33150	95.91663	970	940 900	31.14482	98.48858
921	848 241	30.34798	95.96874	971	942 841	31.16087	98.53933
922	850 084	30.36445	96.02083	972	944 784	31.17691	98.59006
923	851 929	30.38092	96.07289	973	946 729	31.19295	98.64076
924	853 776	30.39735	96.12492	974	948 676	31.20897	98.69144
925	855 625	30.41381	96.17692	975	950 625	31.22499	98.74209
926	857 476	30.43025	96.22889	976	952 576	31.24100	98.79271
927	859 329	30.44667	96.28084	977	954 529	31.25700	98.84331
928	861 184	30.46309	96.33276	978	956 484	31.27299	98.89388
929	863 041	30.47950	96.28465	979	958 441	31.28898	98.94443
930	864 900	30.49590	96.43651	980	960 400	31.30495	98.99495
931	866 761	30.51229	96.48834	981	962 361	31.32092	99.04544
932	868 624	30.52868	96.54015	982	964 324	31.33688	99.09591
933	870 489	30.54505	96.59193	983	966 144	31.43247	99.44848
934	872 356	30.56141	96.64368	984	968 256	31.36877	99.19677
935	874 225	30.57777	96.69540	985	970 225	31.38471	99.24717
936	876 096	30.59412	96.74709	986	972 196	31.40064	99.29753
937	877 969	30.61046	96.79876	987	974 169	31.41656	99.34787
938	879 844	30.62679	96.85040	988	976 144	31.43247	99.39819
939	881 721	30.64311	96.90201	989	978 121	31.44837	99.44848
940	883 600	30.65942	96.95360	990	980 100	31.46427	99.49874
941	885 481	30.67572	97.00515	991	982 081	31.48015	99.54898
942	887 364	30.69202	97.05668	992	984 064	31.49603	99.59920
943	889 249	30.70831	97.10819	993	986 049	31.51190	99.64939
944	891 136	30.72458	97.15966	994	988 036	31.52777	99.69955
945	893 025	30.74085	97.21111	995	990 025	31.54362	99.74969
946	894 916	30.75711	97.26253	996	992 016	31.55947	99.79980
947	896 809	30.77337	97.31393	997	994 009	31.57531	99.84989
948	898 704	30.78961	97.36529	998	996 004	31.59114	99.89995
949	900 601	30.80584	97.41663	999	998 001	31.60696	99.94999
950	902 500	30.82207	97.46794	1000	1 000 000	31.62278	100.00000

ANSWERS TO SELECTED EXERCISES

CHAPTER 1

1-1 (a) P (b) S (c) P (d) P (e) S (f) S (g) P (h) S

CHAPTER 2

2-1 Class boundaries: 2.5–5.5; 5.5–8.5; 8.5–11.5; 11.5–14.5; 14.5–17.5. The class interval $i = B_U - B_L = 5.5 - 2.5 = 3.0$ (same interval size for all classes).

2-4 The frequency curve for the data is negatively skewed (skewed to the left).

2-6 (a) seventy-fifth percentile point (b) 13

2-11 $400

2-15 The frequency curve is positively skewed.

2-17 (a) ninetieth percentile point (b) $670

2-18 (a) 30 (b) 32 (c) 30.0 (d) 32.0 (e) 31.0

2-20 Class boundaries: 0–5.0; 5.0–18.0; 18.0–45.0; 45.0–65.0; 65.0–(open end).

2-21 The class interval i corresponding to each of the first four classes in Exercise 2-20 is 5.0; 13.0; 27.0; 20.0.

CHAPTER 3

3-1 (a) $\mu = 3.0$ (b) Median $= 2.0$ (c) Mode $= 2.0$

3-3 (a) $Q_1 = 1.25$ (b) $Q_2 = 2.0$ (c) $Q_3 = 4.5$

3-4 (a) $R = 9.0$ (b) Middle 90% $R = 8.55$

3-5 $\sigma = \sqrt{5.7915} \approx 2.4$

3-6 $\sigma = \sqrt{5.7917} \approx 2.4$

3-7 (a) $\mu = 7.1$ (b) Median = 7.0   (c) Mode = 7.0

3-8 (a) $Q_1 = 6.0$ (b) $Q_3 = 8.0$

3-9 (a) $R = 3.0$ (b) Middle 50% $R = 2.0$

3-10 $\sigma = \sqrt{0.98} = 0.94$

3-11 (a) 7.53%   (b) 5.87%

3-12 (a) $\mu = 9.6$ (b) Median = 10.0   (c) Mode = 10.0

3-14 (a) $Q_1 = 7.0$ (b) $P_{30} = 8.5$

3-15 (a) $R = 13.0$ (b) Middle 80% $R = 11.5$

3-16 $\sigma = \sqrt{15.64} \approx 4.0$

3-17 (a) $\bar{X} = 19.1$ ounces   (b) Median = 17.5 ounces   (c) There is no mode.

3-18 (a) $Q_3 = 25.0$ ounces   (b) $P_{70} = 23.0$ ounces

3-19 (a) $R = 20.0$ ounces   (b) Middle 50% $R = 11.0$ ounces

3-20 $s = \sqrt{45.655} \approx 6.8$

3-21 (a) $\mu = 76.7$ (b) Median = 80.0   (c) Mode = 84.0

3-22 The distribution is negatively skewed.

3-23 (a) $Q_2 = 80.0$ (b) $P_{50} = 80.0$

3-24 (a) $R = 58.0$ (b) Middle 90% $R = 54.5$

3-25 (a) $\sigma = \sqrt{233.91} \approx 15.3$ (b) $\sigma = \sqrt{233.91} \approx 15.3$

3-26 (a) 4.70%   (b) 5.49%

3-29 (a) $\mu = 2.50$ (b) Median = 2.55   (c) Mode = 2.63

3-31 (a) $Q_1 = 2.06$ (b) $Q_3 = 2.92$

3-32 $P_{60} = 2.70$

3-33 (a) $R = 3.00$ (b) Middle 90% $R = 2.42$

3-34 $\sigma = \sqrt{0.4457} = 0.67$

3-35 $\sigma = \sqrt{0.4457} = 0.67$

3-36 (a) $\mu = \$749.50$ (b) Median = \$713.80   (c) Mode = \$624.50

3-37 (a) $Q_1 = \$374.50$ (b) $Q_3 = \$1,062.00$

3-38 $P_{90} = \$1,399.50$

3-39 (a) $R = \$2,000.00$ (b) Middle 80% $R = \$1,250.00$

3-40 $\sigma = \sqrt{194,444.44} = \$440.96$

3-41 (a) $\bar{X} = \$1,109.50$ (b) Median = \$954.05   (c) Mode = \$646.17

3-42 The distribution is positively skewed

3-43 (a) $Q_2 = \$954.05$ (b) $P_{95} = \$2,299.50$

3-44 (a) $R = \$2,800.00$ (b) Middle 50% $R = \$892.31$

3-45 $s = \sqrt{393,743.58} = \$627.49$

CHAPTER 4

4-1 (a) $1/25 = 0.04$
4-2 (a) $1/6 = 0.17$
4-3 (a) $2/3 = 0.67$
4-4 (a) $2/3 = 0.67$ (b) $1:4$ (c) $3/4 = 0.75$ (d) $1:2$
4-5 (a) $2:1$ (b) $9:1$ (c) $1/3 = 0.33$ (d) $5/6 = 0.83$
4-6 (a) $P = 0.60$ (b) $P = 0.70$
4-8 (a) $P\,(D \text{ or } W) = 0.80$ (b) $P\,(D' \text{ and } W') = 0.20$
4-10 (a) $P = 1/27$ (b) $P = 19/27$
4-12 $P = 0.56$
4-13 $P = 0.03$
4-15 (a) $P = 0.80$ (b) $P = 0.20$
4-16 $P\,(S \text{ or } B) = 0.80$
4-17 The events are independent.
4-19 (a) $P = 0.01$ (b) $P = 0.18$
4-21 (a) $P = 5/14$ (b) $P = 9/14$
4-22 $P = 0.62$
4-24 (a) $P = 0.07$ (b) $P = 0.47$ (c) $P = 0.93$
4-25 (b) $P = 1/2 = 0.50$ (c) $P = 1/3 = 0.33$ (d) $P = 1.0$
4-26 (a) $P = 2/3$ (b) $P = 1/2$
4-27 (a) $P = 1.0$ (b) $P = 4/5$
4-28 (b) $P = 0.80$
4-29 (a) $P = 0.40$ (b) $P = 0.70$
4-30 $P = 0.52$

CHAPTER 5

5-4 (a) 0.0264 (b) 0.9445 (c) 0.0000 (d) 0.0348 (e) 0.6778
5-5 $P = 0.1276$
5-9 (a) 0.2401 (b) 0.2646 (c) 0.0837
5-10 (a) 0.2401 (b) 0.2646 (c) 0.0837
5-11 (a) 0.2401 (b) 0.2646 (c) 0.0837
5-13 Nine machines should be installed as a minimum.
5-14 (a) 0.0576 (b) 0.1115 (c) 1.0000 (d) 0.5443 (e) 0.9872
5-15 (a) 0.0746 (b) 0.3020
5-16 0.0672
5-17 (a) 0.1755 (b) 0.1106 (c) 0.0419 (d) 0.4232 (e) 0.1620
5-18 (a) 0.0136 (b) 0.0067

5-19 (*a*) 0.3679 (*b*) 0.0361 (*c*) 0.0185 (*d*) 0.0213 (*e*) 0.0404

5-20 (*a*) 0.1606 (*b*) 0.2851 (*c*) 0.3679 (*d*) 0.6065

5-21 (*a*) 0.8008 (*b*) 0.9596 (*c*) 0.9048

5-22 (*a*) 0.1333 (*b*) 0.0680

5-23 (*a*) 0.9044

5-24 0.1428.

5-25 0.6634

5-26 0.2381

CHAPTER 6

6-1 (*a*) 0.2486 (*b*) 0.0918 (*c*) 0.0228 (*d*) 0.6568 (*e*) 0.0456

6-2 (*a*) 0.3707 (*b*) 0.2206

6-3 0.0107

6-4 (*a*) 0.0475 (*b*) 0.1587

6-5 0.050941 ≈ 0.05

6-6 (*a*) 0.8413 (*b*) 0.0099

6-7 (*a*) 121 tires (*b*) 126 tires

6-8 (*a*) 0.0625 (*b*) 0.50096 ≈ 0.50

6-9 (*a*) 86.64% (*b*) 228

6-10 628

6-11 (*a*) 0.2514 (*b*) 0.4536

6-12 (*a*) 92.2 ≈ 92 seconds (*b*) 204.25 ≈ 204 seconds

6-13 0.2061

6-14 57,042

6-15 (*a*) 0.5987 (*b*) 0.0116

6-16 (*a*) 0.5636 (*b*) 0.0721

6-17 0.1847

6-18 0.1401

6-19 0.4305

6-20 (*a*) 0.0026 (*b*) 0.0951

6-21 0.0839

6-22 0.1894

CHAPTER 7

7-1 (*a*) $\sigma_{\bar{X}} = 50.00$

7-2 (*a*) Est. $\mu = \bar{X} = 9,800$ (*b*) $s_{\bar{X}} = 53.3$

7-3 (*a*) $3.00 (*b*) $0.095

7-4 (*a*) \$3.00   (*b*) \$0.10

7-5 $\sigma_{\bar{X}} = \$3.00$

7-6 $\sigma_{\bar{X}} = \$2.82$

7-7 (*a*) 1.5 ounces   (*b*) 0.014 ounce

7-8 (*a*) 1.5 ounces   (*b*) 0.011 ounce

7-9 $\sigma_{\bar{X}} = \$40.00$

7-10 (*a*) $\sigma_{\bar{X}} = \$34.80$

7-11 (*a*) \$27.00   (*b*) \$8.00   (*c*) \$13,500.00   (*d*) 350

7-12 (*a*) \$49.70 to \$56.30   (*b*) \$49.08 to \$56.92   (*c*) \$47.84 to \$58.16

7-13 (*a*) \$149,000 to \$168,900   (*b*) \$147,240 to \$170,760   (*c*) \$143,520 to \$174,480

7-14 (*a*) \$25.59 to \$28.41   (*b*) \$12,794.40 to \$14,205.60

7-15 (*a*) 72.8 to 82.2   (*b*) 72.0 to 83.0   (*c*) 70.2 to 84.8

7-16 86,400 to 99,600 employees

7-17 2.338 to 2.362 centimeters

7-18 41.96 to 42.54 kilograms

7-19 (*a*) 650 hours   (*b*) 7.14   (*c*) 641 to 659 hours

7-20 (*b*) \$19,667 to \$20,333

7-21 \$4.66 to \$4.84

7-22 \$4.55 to \$4.95

7-23 10.8 to 11.2 ounces

7-24 10.6 to 11.4 ounces

7-25 \$8.18 to \$8.82

7-26 \$8.16 to \$8.84

7-27 \$7.94 to \$9.06

7-28 $n = 16$

7-29 $n = 30$

7-30 $n = 44$

CHAPTER 8

8-1 −\$16.74 to −\$2.58

8-2 2.3 to 53.5

8-3 −5.8 to 61.6

8-4 \$0.02 to \$0.88

8-5 0 to 0.4

8-6 \$8.28 to \$341.72

8-7 \$64.19 to \$285.81

8-8 (*a*) 52 to 68%   (*b*) 50 to 70%   (*c*) 47 to 73%

8-9 $n = 151$

8-10 2,740 to 3,836

8-11 (a) 0.501 to 0.669 (b) 3,256 to 4,385

8-12 (a) 32.2 to 47.8% (b) 388 to 572

8-13 −0.31 to −0.09

8-14 0.04 to 0.12

8-15 $n = 139$

8-16 0 to 0.20

8-17 $n = 683$

8-18 $n = 100$

8-19 (a) $21,277 \leqslant \sigma^2 \leqslant 108,108$ (b) $145.9 \leqslant \sigma \leqslant 328.8$

8-20 (a) $0.0426 \leqslant \sigma^2 \leqslant 0.3000$ (b) $0.21 \leqslant \sigma \leqslant 0.55$

8-21 (a) $0.0587 \leqslant \sigma^2 \leqslant 0.1705$ (b) $0.24 \leqslant \sigma \leqslant 0.41$

CHAPTER 9

9-3 $H_0: \mu = 2,500$; critical z ($\alpha = 0.05$) $= \pm 1.96$; $z = -1.75$; the null hypothesis (claim) cannot be rejected.

9-4 $H_0: \mu \geqslant 2,500$; critical z ($\alpha = 0.05$) $= -1.65$; $z = -1.75$; the null hypothesis is rejected.

9-5 $H_0: \mu \geqslant 32.0$; critical z ($\alpha = 0.05$) $= -1.65$; $z = -1.52$; the null hypothesis cannot be rejected.

9-6 $H_0: \mu \leqslant 32.0$; critical z ($\alpha = 0.05$) $= 1.65$; $z = -1.52$; the null hypothesis cannot be rejected.

9-7 (a) 0.0823 (b) 0.9177

9-9 $H_0: \mu \geqslant 35.0$; critical z ($\alpha = 0.01$) $= -2.33$; $z = -2.41$; the null hypothesis is rejected.

9-10 $n = 44$

9-11 $H_0: \mu \leqslant 408.0$; critical z ($\alpha = 0.05$) $= 1.65$; $z = 1.69$; the null hypothesis is rejected.

9-12 $H_0: \mu \leqslant 408.0$; critical z ($\alpha = 0.05$) $= 1.65$; $z = 1.57$; the null hypothesis is not rejected.

9-13 $H_0: \mu \leqslant 60.0$; critical z ($\alpha = 0.01$) $= 2.33$; $z = 3.30$; the null hypothesis is rejected.

9-14 (a) 0.01 (b) 0.0192

9-15 $H_0: \mu \geqslant 3.0$; critical z ($\alpha = 0.05$) $= -1.65$; $z = -2.22$; the null hypothesis is rejected.

9-16 $n = 9$ minutes

9-17 $H_0: \mu \leqslant 3.0$; critical z ($\alpha = 0.05$) $= 1.65$; $z = 1.11$; the null hypothesis is accepted.

9-19 (a) $\bar{X} = 11.90$ (b) $s = 0.1414$ (c) $s_{\bar{X}} = 0.045$
 (d) $H_0: \mu \geqslant 12.0$; critical t (df $= 9$, $\alpha = 0.05$) $= -1.833$; $t = -2.22$; the null hypothesis is rejected.

9-20 $H_0: \mu \geqslant \$6.85$; critical t (df $= 24$, $\alpha = 0.05$) $= -1.711$; $t = -2.273$; the null hypothesis is rejected.

9-21 $H_0: \mu \geqslant 11.2$; critical t (df $= 9$, $\alpha = 0.05$) $= -1.833$; $t = -2.105$; the null hypothesis is rejected.

9-22 $H_0: \mu \leqslant 200.0$; critical t (df $= 19$, $\alpha = 0.05$) $= 1.729$; $t = 1.267$; the null hypothesis cannot be rejected.

9-23 $H_0: \mu \leqslant 200.0$; critical z ($\alpha = 0.05$) $= 1.65$; $z = 2.00$; the null hypothesis is rejected.

9-24 $H_0: \mu = 4.00$; critical t (df $= 9$, $\alpha = 0.05$) $= \pm 2.262$; $t = 1.562$; the null hypothesis cannot be rejected.

9-25 $n = 14$

9-26 $H_0: \mu = 100.0$; critical t (df $= 9$, $\alpha = 0.10$) $= 1.833$; $t = -3.319$; the null hypothesis is rejected.

9-27 $H_0: \mu \geqslant \$10.00$; critical t (df $= 19$, $\alpha = 0.05$) $= -1.729$; $t = -1.395$; the null hypothesis cannot be rejected.

9-28 (a) $H_0: \mu = 4.00$; critical k ($\alpha = 0.05$) $= \pm 4.472$; $k = 1.562$; the null hypothesis cannot be rejected.
     (b) $H_0: \mu = 4.00$; critical k ($\alpha = 0.10$) $= \pm 3.162$; $k = 1.562$; the null hypothesis cannot be rejected.

9-29 (a) $H_0: \mu = 100.0$; critical k ($\alpha = 0.05$) $= \pm 4.472$; $k = -3.319$; the null hypothesis cannot be rejected.
     (b) $H_0: \mu = 100.0$; critical k ($\alpha = 0.10$) $= \pm 3.162$; $k = -3.319$; the null hypothesis is rejected.

9-30 (a) $H_0: \mu \leqslant 120$ minutes; critical z ($\alpha = 0.05$) $= 1.65$; $z = 2.58$; the null hypothesis is rejected.
     (b) No standard testing procedure is available for such a one-tail test.

CHAPTER 10

10-1 $H_0: \mu_1 = \mu_2$; critical z ($\alpha = 0.05$) $= \pm 1.96$; $z = -1.79$; the null hypothesis cannot be rejected.

10-2 $H_0: \mu_1 \leqslant \mu_2$; critical z ($\alpha = 0.05$) $= 1.65$; $z = -1.79$; the null hypothesis cannot be rejected; in fact, the sample result represents positive support for the null hypothesis.

10-3 (a) $H_0: \mu_1 = \mu_2$; critical z ($\alpha = 0.05$) $= \pm 1.96$; $z = -0.77$; the null hypothesis cannot be rejected.
     (b) $H_0: \mu_1 \geqslant \mu_2$; critical z ($\alpha = 0.05$) $= -1.65$; $z = -0.77$; the null hypothesis cannot be rejected.

10-4 $H_0: \mu_1 = \mu_2$; critical z ($\alpha = 0.05$) $= \pm 1.96$; $z = 1.73$; the null hypothesis cannot be rejected.

10-5 $H_0: \mu_1 \leqslant \mu_2$; critical z ($\alpha = 0.05$) $= 1.65$; $z = 1.73$; the null hypothesis is rejected.

10-6 $H_0: \mu_1 = \mu_2$; critical t (df $= 18$, $\alpha = 0.05$) $= \pm 2.101$; $t = 1.754$; the null hypothesis cannot be rejected; required assumptions are that the populations are normally distributed and that the variances of the two populations are equal.

10-7 $H_0: \mu_1 \leqslant \mu_2$; critical t (df $= 18$, $\alpha = 0.05$) $= 1.734$; $t = 1.754$; the null hypothesis is rejected.

10-8 $H_0: \mu_1 = \mu_2$; critical t (df $= 20$, $\alpha = 0.01$) $= \pm 2.845$; $t = 2.190$; the null hypothesis cannot be rejected.

10-9 $H_0: \mu_1 = \mu_2$; critical z ($\alpha = 0.01$) $= \pm 2.58$; $z = 3.10$; the null hypothesis is rejected.

10-10 $H_0: \mu_1 = \mu_2$; critical t (df $= 22$, $\alpha = 0.05$) $= \pm 2.074$; $t = 0.826$; the null hypothesis cannot be rejected.

10-11 $H_0: \mu_1 = \mu_2$; critical t (df $= 9$, $\alpha = 0.05$) $= \pm 2.262$; $t = -2.423$ (the paired-observations design is used); the null hypothesis is rejected.

10-12 $H_0: \pi \geqslant 0.30$; the salesperson's claim cannot be rejected [use of binomial distribution: $P (X \leqslant 1)|(n = 10, \pi_0 = 0.30) = 0.1493$].

10-13 (a) $H_0: \pi \geqslant 0.30$; critical z ($\alpha = 0.05$) $= -1.65$; $z = -2.17$; the null hypothesis is rejected.
     (b) $H_0: \pi \geqslant 0.30$; critical z ($\alpha = 0.01$) $= -2.33$; $z = -2.17$; the null hypothesis cannot be rejected.

10-14 H_0: $\pi \leqslant 0.20$; critical z ($\alpha = 0.05$) = 1.65; $z = 1.92$; the null hypothesis is rejected, and therefore the special issue should be published.

10-15 (a) $n = 884$ (b) $n = 455$

10-16 H_0: $\pi \geqslant 0.40$; the null hypothesis cannot be rejected [use of binomial probability distribution: $P(X < 6)|(n = 20, \pi_0 = 0.40) = 0.2499$].

10-17 H_0: $\pi \geqslant 0.40$; critical z ($\alpha = 0.10$) = -1.28; $z = -2.04$; the null hypothesis is rejected.

10-18 $n = 245$

10-19 H_0: $\pi_1 = \pi_2$; critical z ($\alpha = 0.05$) = ±1.96; $z = -1.43$; the null hypothesis cannot be rejected.

10-20 (a) H_0: $\sigma^2 \leqslant 225$; critical χ^2 (df = 14, $\alpha = 0.05$) = 23.68; $\chi^2 = 24.83$; the null hypothesis is rejected.
    (b) H_0: $\sigma^2 \leqslant 225$; critical χ^2 (df = 14, $\alpha = 0.01$) = 29.14; $\chi^2 = 24.83$; the null hypothesis cannot be rejected.

10-21 (a) H_0: $\sigma^2 \leqslant 250{,}000$; critical χ^2 (df = 19, $\alpha = 0.05$) = 30.14; $\chi^2 = 22.24$; the null hypothesis cannot be rejected.
    (b) H_0: $\sigma^2 \leqslant 250{,}000$; critical χ^2 (df = 19, $\alpha = 0.01$) = 36.19; $\chi^2 = 22.24$; the null hypothesis cannot be rejected.

10-22 H_0: $\sigma_1^2 = \sigma_2^2$; critical F (9, 9, upper 0.05) = 3.18; $F = 2.25$; the null hypothesis cannot be rejected.

10-23 H_0: $\sigma_1^2 = \sigma_2^2$; critical F (9, 11, upper 0.01) = 4.63; $F = 1.31$; the null hypothesis cannot be rejected.

CHAPTER 11

11-2 Critical F (3, 8, 0.05) = 4.07; $F = 4.52$; the null hypothesis is rejected.

11-3 Critical F (3, 8, 0.05) = 4.07; $F = 4.53$; the null hypothesis is rejected.

11-7 Critical F (2, 12, 0.05) = 3.88; $F = 2.16$; the null hypothesis cannot be rejected.

11-8 (a) H_0: $\mu_1 = \mu_2$; critical t (df = 8, $\alpha = 0.05$) = ±2.306; $t = -2.100$; the null hypothesis cannot be rejected.
    (b) H_0: $\alpha_k = 0$; critical F (1, 8, 0.05) = 5.32; $F = 4.41$; the null hypothesis cannot be rejected.

CHAPTER 12

12-1 Critical χ^2 (df = 3, $\alpha = 0.01$) = 11.34; $\chi^2 = 20.00$; the null hypothesis is rejected.

12-2 Critical χ^2 (df = 1, $\alpha = 0.01$) = 6.63; $\chi^2 = 3.61$; the null hypothesis cannot be rejected.

12-3 Critical χ^2 (df = 1, $\alpha = 0.05$) = 3.84; $\chi^2 = 3.16$; the null hypothesis cannot be rejected.

12-4 Critical χ^2 (df = 3, $\alpha = 0.05$) = 7.81; $\chi^2 = 30.21$; the null hypothesis is rejected.

12-5 Critical χ^2 (df = 4, $\alpha = 0.05$) = 9.49; $\chi^2 = 17.11$; the null hypothesis is rejected.

12-6 Critical χ^2 (df = 2, $\alpha = 0.05$) = 5.99; $\chi^2 = 3.21$; the null hypothesis cannot be rejected.

12-7 (a) Critical χ^2 (df = 4, $\alpha = 0.05$) = 9.49; $\chi^2 = 34.93$; the null hypothesis is rejected.
    (b) Critical χ^2 (df = 4, $\alpha = 0.01$) = 13.28; $\chi^2 = 34.93$; the null hypothesis is rejected.

12-8 Critical χ^2 (df = 2, $\alpha = 0.05$) = 5.99; $\chi^2 = 2.01$; the null hypothesis cannot be rejected.

12-9 Critical χ^2 (df = 2, $\alpha = 0.01$) = 9.21; $\chi^2 = 17.5$; the null hypothesis is rejected.

12-10 Critical χ^2 (df $= 1$, $\alpha = 0.01$) $= 6.63$; $\chi^2 = 23.365$; the null hypothesis is rejected.

12-11 (b) Critical χ^2 (df $= 1$, $\alpha = 0.05$) $= 3.84$; $\chi^2 = 3.40$; the null hypothesis (the salesperson's claim) cannot be rejected.

12-12 Critical χ^2 (df $= 5$, $\alpha = 0.05$) $= 11.07$; $\chi^2 = 14.17$; the null hypothesis is rejected.

12-13 (a) Critical χ^2 (df $= 4$, $\alpha = 0.05$) $= 9.49$; $\chi^2 = 12.50$; the null hypothesis is rejected at the 5 percent level of significance. .

     (b) Critical χ^2 (df $= 4$, $\alpha = 0.01$) $= 13.28$; $\chi^2 = 12.50$; the null hypothesis cannot be rejected at the 1 percent level of significance.

12-14 Critical χ^2 (df $= 4$, $\alpha = 0.01$) $= 13.28$; $\chi^2 = 19.00$; the null hypothesis is rejected.

12-15 Critical χ^2 (df $= 4$, $\alpha = 0.05$) $= 9.49$; $\chi^2 = 4.67$; the null hypothesis cannot be rejected.

12-16 Critical χ^2 (df $= 2$, $\alpha = 0.05$) $= 5.99$; $\chi^2 = 8.29$; the null hypothesis is rejected.

12-17 Critical χ^2 (df $= 7$, $\alpha = 0.05$) $= 14.07$; $\chi^2 = 11.97$; the null hypothesis cannot be rejected.

CHAPTER 13

13-3 (a) A_1 : stock 0 sets   (b) A_4 : stock 3 sets   (c) A_2 : stock 1 set

13-4 A_2 : stock 1 set (EV $= \$69$)

13-5 EVPI $= \$75$

13-6 (a) A_1 : savings account   (b) A_3 : stock options   (c) A_2 : common stocks

13-7 A_1 : savings account (EV $= \$1,000$)

13-8 (b) A_1 : order 9 cases   (c) A_4 : order 12 cases   (d) A_2 : order 10 cases

13-9 A_2 : order 10 cases (EV $= \$18.50$)

13-10 EVPI $= \$1.70$

13-11 (a) A_2 : don't invest   (b) A_1 : invest   (c) A_1 : invest

13-12 A_1 : invest (EV $= \$8,000$)

13-13 (a) A_2 : don't bid   (b) A_1 : bid   (c) A_1 : bid

13-14 A_1 : bid (EV $= \$110,000$)

13-15 No inspection (exp. cost $= \$290.00$)

13-16 $\$210.00$

13-17 EVPI $= \$80.00$

13-18 100% inspection (exp. cost $= \$360.00$)

13-19 VSI $= \$111.60$

13-20 (a) A_3 : order neither   (b) A_2 : order beach umbrellas   (c) A_3 : order neither

13-21 A_2 : order beach umbrellas (EV $= \$40.50$)

13-22 (a) EVPI $= \$27.00$ (b) EVPI $= \$27.00$

13-23 (b) P (correct forecast) $= 0.76$

13-24 A_1 : order blankets (EV $= \$17.00$)

13-25 VSI $= \$6.40$

13-26 (b) A_2 : AAA bonds (EV $= \$800.00$)

13-27 EVPI $= \$350.00$

13-28 (b) A_1: mutual fund (EV = $1,392.00)

13-29 VSI = $592.00

13-30 EVPI = $45.00

13-31 (a) $X_{ij} = 200E_j - 80A_i$ if $E_j \leqslant A_i$; $X_{ij} = 120A_i - 50(E_j - A_i)$ if $E_j > A_i$.
   (c) A_4: provide four commuter cars (EV = $275).

13-32 (c) The same final posterior probability distribution is obtained by either approach.

13-34 Make the deposit (EV = $9,000)

13-35 P (profit) = 0.70

CHAPTER 14

14-11 (b) $Y_c = 8.1 + 1.0X$ (c) $Y_c = 18.1 = $18,100$ (d) 15.29 to 20.91 ≈ $15,290 to $20,910

14-12 (a) 17.14 to 19.06 ≈ $17,140 to $19,060
   (b) 15.13 to 21.07 ≈ $15,130 to $21,070
   (c) H_0: $\beta \leqslant 0$; critical t (df = 8, $\alpha = 0.05$) = ±2.306; $t = 7.246$; the null hypothesis is rejected.

14-14 (b) $Y_c = 40 + 1.5X$ (c) $Y_c = 85$ (d) 73.07 to 96.93 ≈ 73 to 97

14-15 (a) 79.03 to 90.97 ≈ 79 to 91
   (b) 71.63 to 98.37 ≈ 72 to 98
   (c) H_0: $\beta \leqslant 0$; critical t (df = 6, $\alpha = 0.01$) = 3.143; $t = 4.167$; the null hypothesis is rejected.

14-16 (a) $r = 0.86$
   (b) H_0: $\rho = 0$; critical t (df = 6, $\alpha = 0.01$) = ±3.707; $t = 4.128$; the null hypothesis is rejected.
   (c) H_0: $\rho \leqslant 0$; critical t (df = 6, $\alpha = 0.01$) = 3.143; $t = 4.128$; the null hypothesis is rejected.

14-17 (b) $Y_c = 35.57 - 1.40X$ (c) $Y_c = 31.37 ≈ 31$ (d) 25.67 to 37.07 ≈ 26 to 37 rejects

14-18 (a) 28.74 to 34.00 ≈ 29 to 34 rejects   (b) 25.09 to 37.65 ≈ 25 to 38 rejects

14-19 (a) −1.85 to −0.95
   (b) H_0: $\beta \geqslant 0$; critical t (df = 10, $\alpha = 0.05$) = −1.812; $t = -7.000$; the null hypothesis is rejected.

14-20 (a) $r = -0.91$
   (b) H_0: $\rho \geqslant 0$; critical t (df = 10, $\alpha = 0.05$) = −1.812; $t = -6.878$; the null hypothesis is rejected.
   (c) $r^2 = (-0.908)^2 = 0.8245 ≈ 0.82$

CHAPTER 15

15-4 (a) X_1: years of experience   (b) $Y_c = 17.68501 + 0.72127X_1$ (c) $Y_c = 10.65337 + 0.79624X_1 + 1.61766X_2$

15-5 (b) H_0: $\beta_1 = 0$; critical t (df = 9, $\alpha = 0.05 = ±2.262$; $t = 3.050$; reject the null hypothesis; H_0: $\beta_2 = 0$; critical t (df = 9, $\alpha = 0.05$) = ±2.262; $t = 2.855$; reject the null hypothesis.
   (c) H_0: $\beta_1 = 0$; critical F (1, 9, $\alpha = 0.05$) = 5.12; $F = 9.299$; reject the null hypothesis; H_0: $\beta_2 = 0$; critical F (1, 9, $\alpha = 0.05$) = 5.12; $F = 8.152$; reject the null hypothesis.

15-6 (a) $Y_c = 21.10521 ≈ $21,100$ (b) Pred. int. = 16.94263 to 25.26779 ≈ $16,900 to $25,300   (c) Conf. int. = 19.90357 to 22.30685 ≈ $19,900 to $22,300

15-7 (a) $r_{Y1} = 0.5568$; $r_{Y2} = 0.5137$ (b) $r_{Y1.2} = 0.7129$; $r_{Y2.1} = 0.6894$

15-8 (a) Step 1: X_3; Step 2: X_2; Step 3: X_1
(b) $R_{Y.3} = 0.90526$; $R_{Y.23} = 0.92913$; $R_{Y.123} = 0.97263$
(c) $Y_c = -70.47975 + 2.07432X_1 + 0.91341X_2 + 0.53849X_3$
(d) $Y_c = 25.77455 \approx 25.8$

15-9 (a) Pred. int. = 0.146344 to $40.41636 \approx 0.1$ to 40.4 (b) Pred. int. = 1.511818 to $39.937202 \approx 1.5$ to 39.9 (c) Pred. int. = 12.282037 to $39.267063 \approx 12.3$ to 39.3

15-10 (a) H_0: $\beta_1 = 0$; critical t (df = 6, $\alpha = 0.05$) = ±2.447; $t = 3.032$; the null hypothesis is rejected; H_0: $\beta_2 = 0$; critical t (df = 6, $\alpha = 0.05$) = ±2.447; $t = 3.293$; the null hypothesis is rejected; H_0: $\beta_3 = 0$; critical t (df = 6, $\alpha = 0.05$) = ±2.447; $t = 0.792$; the null hypothesis cannot be rejected.
(b) H_0: $\beta_1 = 0$; critical F (1, 6, $\alpha = 0.05$) = 5.99; $F = 9.195$; the null hypothesis is rejected; H_0: $\beta_2 = 0$; critical F (1, 6, $\alpha = 0.05$) = 5.99; $F = 10.844$; the null hypothesis is rejected; H_0: $\beta_3 = 0$; critical F (1, 6, $\alpha = 0.05$) = 5.99; $F = 0.628$; the null hypothesis cannot be rejected.

15-11 (b) $Y_c = -8.02471 + 2.83061X_3$ (c) X_3 would be the first variable eliminated in a "backward" stepwise procedure.

15-12 (a) $r_{12} = 0.98001$; $r_{13} = 0.94132$; $r_{23} = 0.97304$ (b) $r_{Y1} = -0.89388$; $r_{Y2} = -0.93483$; $r_{Y3} = -0.91755$

15-13 (b) $Y_c = 48.01257 - 0.00754X_2$ (c) Pred. int. = 15.3 to 27.5 miles per gallon

15-14 (c) Only $r_{Y2.13} = -0.4936$ is significant at $\alpha = 0.05$.

CHAPTER 16

16-1 (a) C (b) I (c) I (d) S (e) T

16-2 (b) $Y_T = 0.22 + 0.19X$

16-6 $Y_{T(\text{quarterly})} = 37.2 + 11.9X$ (in thousands of dollars, with $X = 0$ at the first quarter of 1970)

16-7 The forecasts for the four quarters are 752.0, 501.1, 375.3, and 680.6.

16-10 (b) $Y_T = 47.63 + 12.68X$ (with $X = 0$ at the 1977–1978 fiscal year)

16-11 (b) Highest index is for October = 147.8; lowest index is for January = 66.8.

16-13 $Y_{T(\text{monthly})} = 3.402 + 0.88X$

16-15 (a) $Y_{1981-1982} = 82.6$ (b) $Y_{T(1981-1982)} = 97.35 \approx 97.4$

16-16 $Y_T = 7.62 + 2.00X$

16-19 The seasonal indexes are QI = 89.1; QII = 99.9; QIII = 98.3; QIV = 112.6.

16-21 $Y_{T(\text{quarterly})} = 1.717 + 0.125X$ (with $X = 0$ at the first quarter of 1957)

16-22 The forecasted values, in billions, are QI = $10.44, QII = $11.83, QIII = $11.76, QIV = $13.62.

16-23 (a) $\hat{Y}_{1977} = 51.42$ billion dollars (b) $Y_{T(1977)} = 47.62$ billion dollars

CHAPTER 17

17-1 (a) 100.0; 121.4; 140.1; 150.6 (b) 100.0; 107.3; 119.3; 122.0

17-2 (a) Butter: 50.6% increase; cheese: 22.0% increase
(b) Butter: $I_q = 113.7$; Cheese: $I_q = 109.5$

17-3 (b) Butter: $I_v = 171.2$; Cheese: $I_v = 133.6$

17-4 (a) $I_p = 160.0$; $I_q = 127.3$ (b) Bond paper: $I_v = 203.6$; Onionskin: $I_v = 106.2$

17-5 (a) $I_p(L) = 184.1$ (b) $I_p(P) = 171.8$ (c) $I_p(F) = 177.9$ (d) $I_p(W) = 184.1$

17-6 (a) Simple price relatives   (b) 12.3% decline   (c) 5.8% decline

17-7 (a) $21.05   (b) $22.61

17-8 (a) 33.5%   (b) 31.9%

17-9 (a) $200.32   (b) $303.33

17-11 Bread: $I_p = 150.0, I_q = 100.0$; Milk: $I_p = 133.3, I_q = 150.0$

17-12 (a) $I_p(L) = 140.5$ (b) $I_p(P) = 138.9$ (c) $I_p(F) = 139.7$

17-13 $I_p(W) = 140.5$

17-16 (a) $0.64   (b) $1.56

17-18 (b) 11.6%

CHAPTER 18

18-1 The Mann-Whitney U test is used. H_0: $\mu_U = 112$; $\sigma_U = 23.27$; critical z ($\alpha = 0.10$) $= \pm 1.65$; $z = 1.87$; the null hypothesis is rejected.

18-2 The Kruskal-Wallis test is used. Critical χ^2 (df $= 2$, $\alpha = 0.10$) $= 4.61$; $H = 5.12$; the null hypothesis is rejected.

18-3 H_0: $\pi = 0.50$; the null hypothesis cannot be rejected when the sign test is used.

18-4 Critical T ($n = 10$, $\alpha = 0.10$) $= 11$; $T = 8.0$; the null hypothesis is rejected by use of the Wilcoxon test.

18-5 $r_r = 0.997$; H_0: $\rho \leqslant 0$; critical t (df $= 8$, $\alpha = 0.01$) $= 2.896$; $t = 36.926$; the null hypothesis is rejected.

18-6 (a) Critical z ($\alpha = 0.05$) $= \pm 1.96$; $\mu_R = 23.49$; $\sigma_R = 3.31$; $z = -0.45$; the null hypothesis cannot be rejected.
   (b) Critical z ($\alpha = 0.05$) $= \pm 1.96$; $\mu_R = 22.60$; $\sigma_R = 3.18$; $z = -0.82$; the null hypothesis cannot be rejected.

18-7 The Kruskal-Wallis test is used. Critical χ^2 (df $= 3$, $\alpha = 0.05$) $= 7.81$; $H = 2.39476$; $H_c = 2.40$; the null hypothesis cannot be rejected.

18-8 (a) $r_r = 0.86$
   (b) H_0: $\rho = 0$; critical t (df $= 10$, $\alpha = 0.05$) $= \pm 2.228$; $t = 5.342$; the null hypothesis is rejected.

18-9 The Wilcoxon test for matched pairs is used. Critical T ($n = 13$, $\alpha = 0.05$) $= 21$; $T = 20.5$; the null hypothesis is rejected.

18-10 H_0: $\pi \geqslant 0.50$; the null hypothesis cannot be rejected when the sign test is used.

18-11 (a) $r_r = -0.88$
   (b) H_0: $\rho = 0$; critical t (df $= 8$, $\alpha = 0.05$) $= \pm 2.306$; $t = -5.238$; the null hypothesis is rejected.

18-12 The Mann-Whitney U test is used. H_0: $\mu_u = 72.0$; critical z ($\alpha = 0.05$) $= \pm 1.96$; $U_1 = 98.5$; $\mu_U = 72.0$; $\sigma_U = 17.32$; $z = 1.53$; the null hypothesis cannot be rejected.

18-13 H_0: $\mu_1 = \mu_2$; critical t (df $= 22$, $\alpha = 0.05$) $= \pm 2.074$; $\bar{X}_1 = 40.67$; $\bar{X}_2 = 46.08$; $s_1 = 8.32$; $s_2 = 9.20$; $\hat{\sigma}^2 = 76.89$; $\hat{\sigma}_{\bar{X}_1 - \bar{X}_2} = 3.58$; $t = -1.51$; the null hypothesis cannot be rejected.

18-14 (a) $r_r = -0.93$
   (b) H_0: $\rho \geqslant 0$; critical t (df $= 10$, $\alpha = 0.05$) $= -1.812$; $t = -8.02$; the null hypothesis is rejected.

INDEX